Here are your

2005 Year Book Cross-Reference Tabs

For insertion in your WORLD BOOK set

Put these Tabs in the appropriate volumes of your **World Book Encyclopedia** now. Then, when you later look up some topic in **World Book** and find a Tab near the article, you will know that one of your **Year Books** has newer or more detailed information about that topic.

How to use these Tabs

First, remove this page from the **YEAR BOOK**.

Begin with the first Tab, **ARISTIDE, JEAN-BERTRAND.** Take the A volume of your **World Book** set and find the **ARISTIDE, JEAN-BERTRAND,** article in it. Moisten the **ARISTIDE, JEAN-BERTRAND,** Tab and affix it to that page.

Glue all the other Tabs in the appropriate **World Book** volume.

The 2005 World Book

YEAR BOOK

A REVIEW OF THE EVENTS OF 2004

The Annual
Supplement to
The World Book
Encyclopedia

World Book, Inc.
a Scott Fetzer company
Chicago

www.worldbook.com

World Book, Inc.
233 N. Michigan Ave.
Chicago, IL 60601

ISBN: 0-7166-0459-0
ISSN: 0084-1439
Library of Congress Control Number: 62004818

Printed in the United States of America.

STAFF

EDITORIAL

Managing Editor, Annuals and General Publishing
Maureen Mostyn Liebenson

Managing Editor, The Year Book
Scott Thomas

Senior Editors
Timothy D. Frystak
Kristina A. Vaicikonis

Staff Editors
Heather McShane
S. Thomas Richardson

Contributing Editors
Dan Blunk
Robert Knight
Barbara A. Mayes
Alfred J. Smuskiewicz

Editorial Assistant
Ethel Matthews

Cartographic Services
H. George Stoll, Head
Wayne K. Pichler, Manager, Digital Cartography
John M. Rejba, Staff Cartographer

Indexing Services
David Pofelski, Head
Aamir Burki, Staff Indexer

Permissions Editor
Janet Peterson

ART

Manager, Graphics and Design
Sandra M. Dyrlund

Senior Designer, The Year Book
Brenda B. Tropinski

Senior Designers
Don Di Sante
Isaiah W. Sheppard

Designer
Kim Saar

Contributing Designer
Lucy Lesiak

Photographs Editors
Tom Evans
Sylvia Ohlrich

Production and Administrative Support
John Whitney

RESEARCH SERVICES

Manager, Research Services
Loranne K. Shields

Researchers
Madolynn H. Cronk
Lynn Durbin
Cheryl Graham
Karen A. McCormack

Library Services
Jon Fjortoft, Head

PRODUCTION

Director, Manufacturing and Pre-Press
Carma Fazio

Manufacturing Manager
Barbara Podczerwinski

Senior Production Manager
Madelyn S. Underwood

Production Manager
Anne Fritzinger

Proofreading
Anne Dillon, Head

Text Processing
Curley Hunter
Gwendolyn Johnson

MARKETING

Director, Direct Marketing
Mark R. Willy

Marketing Analyst
Zofia Kulik

Editor in Chief
Dale W. Jacobs

General Managing Editor
Paul A. Kobasa

CONTRIBUTORS

Contributors not listed on these pages are members of the editorial staff.

ANDREWS, PETER J., B.A., M.S.; free-lance writer. **[Chemistry]**

BARNHART, BILL, B.A., M.S.T., M.B.A.; financial markets columnist, *Chicago Tribune*. **[Stocks and bonds]**

BARRETT, NORMAN, M.A.; free-lance writer. **[Soccer]**

BAYNHAM, SIMON, B.A., M.A., Ph.D.; Senior Research Associate, Centre for Defence & International Security Studies, University of Lancaster, U.K. **[Africa and African country articles]**

BERGER, ERIC R., B.A, M.A.; science writer, *Houston Chronicle*. **[Houston]**

BOULDREY, BRIAN, B.A., M.F.A.; Assistant Professor of English, Northwestern University. **[Literature, American; Literature, World; Poetry; Prison; Pulitzer Prizes]**

BOYD, JOHN D., B.S.; Managing News Editor, *Transport Topics*. **[Economics; International trade; Manufacturing]**

BRADSHER, HENRY S., A.B., B.J.; foreign affairs analyst. **[Asia and Asian country articles]**

BRETT, CARLTON E., B.A., M.S., Ph.D.; Professor of Geology, University of Cincinnati. **[Paleontology]**

BUERKLE, TOM, B.A.; European Editor, *Institutional Investor*. **[Europe and Western European country articles]**

CAMPBELL, GEOFFREY A., B.J.; free-lance writer. **[U.S. government articles]**

CARDINALE, DIANE P., B.A.; Research Associate, Toy Industry Association, Incorporated. **[Toys and games]**

CARLSON, ROB, B.A., M.S.; Deputy Executive Director, Library and Information Technology Association, American Library Association. **[Library]**

CASEY, MIKE, B.S., M.A.; Assistant Editor, *Kansas City Star*. **[Automobile]**

DEEB, MARIUS K., B.A., Ph.D.; Professor, School of Advanced International Studies, Johns Hopkins University. **[Middle East and Middle Eastern country articles; North African country articles]**

DEEB, MARY-JANE, B.A., Ph.D.; Arab World Area Specialist, Library of Congress. **[Middle East and Middle Eastern country articles; North African country articles]**

DeFRANK, THOMAS M., B.A., M.A.; Washington Bureau Chief, *New York Daily News*. **[Armed forces]**

DILLON, DAVID, B.A., M.A., Ph.D.; architecture and design editor, *The Dallas Morning News*. **[Architecture]**

ELLIS, GAVIN, Editor in Chief, *The New Zealand Herald & Weekend Herald*. **[New Zealand]**

FARR, DAVID M. L., D.Phil., LL.D.; Professor Emeritus of History, Carleton University. **[Canada; Canada, Prime Minister of; Canadian provinces; Canadian territories]**

FERRELL, KEITH, free-lance writer. **[Computer; Electronics]**

FISHER, ROBERT W., B.A., M.A.; free-lance writer. **[Labor and employment]**

FITZGERALD, MARK, B.A.; editor at large, *Editor & Publisher* magazine. **[Magazine; Newspaper]**

FOX, THOMAS C., B.A., M.A.; Publisher, *The National Catholic Reporter*. **[Roman Catholic Church]**

FRIEDMAN, EMILY, B.A.; health policy and ethics analyst. **[Health care issues]**

GADOMSKI, FRED, B.S., M.S.; Meteorologist, Pennsylvania State University. **[Weather]**

GATTY, ROBERT C., free-lance writer, *Gatty Edits*. **[Food]**

GOLDEN, JONATHAN J., B.A., M.J.Ed.; Chair, History Department at the Gann Academy, New Jewish High School of Great Boston. **[Judaism]**

GOLDNER, NANCY, B.A.; free-lance dance critic. **[Dance]**

HARAKAS, STANLEY SAMUEL, B.A., B.Th., Th.D.; Archbishop Iakovos Professor (Emeritus) of Orthodox Theology, Holy Cross Greek Orthodox School of Theology. **[Eastern Orthodox Churches]**

HAVERSTOCK, NATHAN A., A.B.; affiliate scholar, Oberlin College. **[Latin America Special Report: Haiti: In Search of Higher Ground; Latin America and Latin American country articles]**

HELMS, CHRISTINE MOSS, B.A., PH.D.; Writer and Middle East analyst. **[Middle East Special Report: A Quest for Political Identity in a Second Year of War]**

HENDERSON, HAROLD, B.A.; staff writer, *Chicago Reader*. **[Chicago]**

HOFFMAN, ANDREW J., B.S., M.S., Ph.D.; Holcim Professor of Enterprise, University of Michigan. **[Environmental pollution]**

JOHANSON, DONALD C., B.S., M.A., Ph.D.; Director and Professor, Institute of Human Origins, Arizona State University. **[Anthropology]**

JOHNSON, CHRISTINA S., B.A., M.S.; free-lance science writer. **[Ocean]**

JOHNSON, JULIET, A.B., M.A., Ph.D.; Associate Professor of Political Science, McGill University. **[Russia and other former Soviet republic articles]**

KATES, MICHAEL, B.S.J.; Associate Sports Editor, *Chicago Tribune*. **[Sports articles]**

KENNEDY, BRIAN, M.A.; free-lance writer. **[Australia; Australia, Prime Minister of; Australian rules football]**

KILGORE, MARGARET, B.A., M.B.A.; free-lance writer, Kilgore and Associates. **[Los Angeles]**

KING, MIKE, reporter, *The* (Montreal) *Gazette*. **[Montreal]**

KLINTBERG, PATRICIA PEAK, B.A.; Director of Constituent Affairs, Office of Communications, U.S. Department of Agriculture. **[Agriculture]**

KRONHOLZ, JUNE, B.S.J.; staff reporter, *The Wall Street Journal.* **[Education** Special Report: **Broken Promises: The Crisis in Higher Education; Education]**

LAWRENCE, ALBERT, B.A., M.A., M.Ed.; Executive Director, World Chess Hall of Fame. **[Chess]**

LEWIS, DAVID C., M.D.; Professor of Medicine and Community Health, Brown University. **[Drug abuse]**

LIEBENSON, DONALD, B.A.; free-lance writer. **[Popular music; various Portraits; Television]**

LYE, KEITH, B.A., F.R.G.S.; free-lance writer and editor. **[Cricket]**

MARCH, ROBERT H., A.B., M.S., Ph.D.; Professor Emeritus of Physics and Liberal studies, University of Wisconsin at Madison. **[Physics]**

MARSCHALL, LAURENCE A., B.S., Ph.D.; W.K.T. Sahm Professor of Physics, Gettysburg College. **[Astronomy]**

MARTY, MARTIN E., Ph.D.; Fairfax M. Cone Distinguished Service Professor Emeritus, University of Chicago. **[Protestantism]**

MAUGH, THOMAS H., II, Ph.D.; science/medical writer, *Los Angeles Times.* **[Biology]**

MAY, SALLY RUTH, B.A., M.A.; free-lance art writer. **[Art]**

McDONALD, ELAINE STUART, B.A.; free-lance public policy writer and editor. **[State government]**

McWILLIAM, ROHAN, B.A., M.A., D.Phil; Senior Lecturer in History, Anglia Polytechnic University, Cambridge, U.K. **[Ireland; Northern Ireland; United Kingdom; United Kingdom, Prime Minister of]**

MINER, TODD J., B.S., M.S.; Meteorologist, Pennsylvania State University. **[Weather]**

MORITZ, OWEN, B.A.; urban affairs editor, *New York Daily News.* **[New York City]**

MORRING, FRANK, Jr., B.A.; Senior Space Technology editor, *Aviation Week & Space Technology* magazine. **[Space exploration]**

MORRIS, BERNADINE, B.A., M.A.; free-lance fashion writer. **[Fashion]**

MULLINS, HENRY T., B.S., M.S., Ph.D.; Professor of Geology, Syracuse University. **[Geology]**

NGUYEN, J. TUYET, M.A.; United Nations correspondent, Deutsche Presse-Agentur. **[Population; United Nations]**

OGAN, EUGENE, B.A., Ph.D.; Professor Emeritus of Anthropology, University of Minnesota. **[Pacific Islands]**

PAETH, GREGORY, B.A.; business writer, *The Cincinnati Post.* **[Radio]**

POKORNY, KYM, B.A.; Garden writer, *The Oregonian.* **[Gardening]**

REINHART, A. KEVIN, B.A., M.A., Ph.D.; Associate Professor of Religious Studies, Dartmouth College. **[Islam]**

RICCIUTI, EDWARD, B.A.; free-lance writer. **[Conservation; Zoos]**

ROSE, MARK J., B.A., M.A., Ph.D.; Executive Editor, *Archaeology* magazine. **[Archaeology]**

RUBENSTEIN, RICHARD E., B.A., M.A., J.D.; Professor of Conflict Resolution and Public Affairs, George Mason University. **[Terrorism]**

RUSSELL, MARY HARRIS, B.A., M.A, Ph.D.; Professor of English, Indiana University. **[Literature for children]**

SARNA, JONATHAN D., Ph.D.; Joseph H. & Belle R. Braun Professor of American Jewish History, Brandeis University. **[Judaism]**

SAVAGE, IAN, B.A., Ph.D.; Associate Professor of Economics and Transportation, Northwestern University. **[Aviation; Transportation]**

SHAPIRO, HOWARD, B.S.; staff writer and travel columnist, *The Philadelphia Inquirer.* **[Philadelphia; Washington, D.C.]**

STEIN, DAVID LEWIS, B.A., M.S.; former urban affairs columnist, *The Toronto Star.* **[Toronto]**

TANNER, JAMES C., B.J.; former news editor—energy, *The Wall Street Journal.* **[Energy supply]**

TATUM, HENRY K., B.A.; Retired Associate Editor, *The Dallas Morning News.* **[Dallas]**

THOMAS, PAULETTE, B.A.; free-lance writer. **[Bank]**

VAN, JON, B.A., M.A.; technology writer, *Chicago Tribune.* **[Telecommunications]**

von RHEIN, JOHN, B.A.; classical music critic, *Chicago Tribune.* **[Classical music]**

WILSON, DAVE, B.A.; Producer, Cable News Network. **[Computer** Special Report: **Search Engines: Driving the Information Age; Internet]**

WOLCHIK, SHARON L., B.A., M.A., Ph.D.; Professor of Political Science and International Affairs, George Washington University. **[Eastern European country articles]**

WRIGHT, ANDREW G., B.A.; Managing Senior Editor, *Engineering News-Record* magazine. **[Building and construction]**

WUNTCH, PHILIP, B.A.; film critic, *The Dallas Morning News.* **[Motion pictures]**

YEZZI, DAVID, B.F.A., M.F.A.; Director, Unterbeerg Poetry Center. **[Museums** Special Report: **Museum Blockbusters; Theater]**

CONTENTS

From the U.S. presidential campaign and election to the continuing conflict in Iraq, 2004 was a year of extraordinary events. On these three pages are stories the editors picked as some of the most important of the year, along with details on where to find more information about them in this volume.

The Editors

2004

BOSTON RED SOX WIN THE WORLD SERIES

In October, the Boston Red Sox sweep the St. Louis Cardinals in four games to capture the Sox's first World Series since 1918. The victory breaks the fabled "Curse of the Bambino," which many fans claim had kept their beloved Red Sox from winning the World Series for 86 years. See **Baseball,** page 76; **Sports,** page 364.

PRESIDENTIAL ELECTION

ABU GHRAIB PRISON SCANDAL

Photographs of Iraqi prisoners being abused and humiliated by U.S. military guards at the Abu Ghraib Prison outside Baghdad, initially broadcast on a television program in April, trigger an international scandal. See **Armed forces,** page 51; **Human rights,** page 216; **Islam,** page 242; **United States, Government of the,** page 398.

THE WAR IN IRAQ CONTINUES

The conflict in Iraq continues through 2004 with both Shiah Muslims in the south and Sunni Muslims, joined by foreign militants, in central Iraq launching insurgencies. See **Year in brief**, pages 13–35; **Islam**, page 242; **Iraq: A Special Report**, page 228; **Middle East**, page 273.

President George W. Bush defeats Massachusetts Senator John Kerry on November 2 after one of the most contentious and far reaching of election campaigns. See **Democratic Party**, page 149; **Elections**, page 175; **Literature, American**, page 261; **Motion pictures**, page 278; **People in the news**, page 324; **Protestantism**, page 342; **Republican Party**, page 346; **Roman Catholicism**, page 347; **United States, President of the**, page 403.

INTERNATIONAL TERRORISM

The scourge of terrorism touched the lives of millions of people worldwide in 2004. See **Europe**, page 183; **Indonesia**, page 224; **Nepal**, page 296; **Netherlands**, page 297; **Pakistan**, page 322; **Philippines**, page 334; **Russia**, page 349; **Spain**, page 363; **Terrorism**, page 383.

EUROPEAN UNION EXPANDS

In May, 10 Eastern European nations—Cyprus, Czech Republic, Estonia, Hungary, Latvia, Lithuania, Malta, Poland, Slovakia, and Slovenia—join the European Union (EU), an organization that promotes cooperation among member nations. See **Europe**, page 183 and the individual nations.

OLYMPIC DREAMS

The greatest athletes in the world gather in Athens, Greece, in August to compete in the Summer Games of the XXVIII Olympiad of the modern era. See **Greece**, page 201; **Olympics, A Special Report**, page 308; **People in the news**, page 324.

9

continued

HURRICANES IN FLORIDA

Four hurricanes hit Florida and parts of the southeastern United States in August and September, wreaking havoc with heavy rains and winds of more than 100 miles (160 kilometers) per hour. See **Weather**, page 412.

DISASTER IN SOUTH ASIA

The world's strongest earthquake in 40 years triggers tsunamis that leave tens of thousands of people dead across south Asia. See **Year in brief**, page 35; **Asia**, page 56; **Disasters**, page 152; **Geology**, page 196; **India**, page 219; **Indonesia**, page 224; **Ocean**, page 307; **Sri Lanka**, page 367; **Thailand**, page 384.

ROVERS ON MARS

The National Aeronautics and Space Administration lands two rovers on Mars in January. Spirit and Opportunity explore the barren landscape for evidence that liquid water once existed on Mars and send home unprecedented, detailed views of the red planet. See **Year in brief**, pages 13–14; **Astronomy**, page 60; **Space exploration**, page 359.

2004

YEAR IN BRIEF

A month-by-month listing of the most significant world events that occurred during 2004.

2 The government of North Korea agrees to allow U.S. government officials and nuclear weapons experts to inspect its Yongbyon nuclear plant.

British Airways cancels a flight to Washington, D.C., for the second day in a row, amid fears of a terrorist attack.

4 Voters in the Republic of Georgia elect Mikhail Saakashvili president. Saakashvili led the peaceful revolt that ousted former President Eduard Shevardnadze in late 2003.

Delegates to a national meeting in Kabul ratify a constitution, making Afghanistan, for the first time in its history, a democracy. The constitution guarantees men and women equal rights before the law.

5 A powerful antenna connected to a robotic probe named Spirit, which landed on Mars on January 3, is activated and begins to beam a three-dimensional panorama to Earth.

6 India and Pakistan, which were at the brink of war in 2002 over the disputed territory of Jammu and Kashmir, agree to restart peace talks.

8 Thousands of plant and animal species may become extinct over the next 50 years if global warming continues, warn British scientists. Conservation biologist Chris Thomas of the University of Leeds notes that biological groups are already rapidly responding to climate warming.

8 All nine U.S. Army personnel aboard a military helicopter are killed when their UH-60 Black Hawk is shot down near Al Fallujah, a stronghold of the insurgency in Iraq. On January 2, rebels in Al Fallujah brought down a OH-58 Kiowa Warrior helicopter.

11 Former Secretary of the U.S. Treasury Paul O'Neill tells a television interviewer that the administration of President George W. Bush began planning the war in Iraq shortly after taking office in January 2001. O'Neill, who was a member of Bush's National Security team before being dismissed from the Cabinet in 2002, claims that he never saw evidence that Iraq possessed weapons of mass destruction.

14 Andrew Fastow, the former chief financial officer of Enron Corp., the Houston-based energy trading company that failed in 2001, pleads guilty to federal conspiracy charges involving one of the largest corporate frauds in history. In the weeks before the collapse, Fastow and other executives sold at least $1 billion in Enron stock and gave themselves $100 million in bonuses. The bankruptcy ruined the retirement accounts of many of Enron's 20,000 employees who were barred from selling their shares even as the value plummeted.

An image showing a panoramic landscape of a mountain range on Mars is transmitted to Earth by NASA's robotic probe Spirit in January 2004. Spirit landed on Mars on January 3.

15 The U.S. robotic probe Spirit rolls off its lander onto the surface of Mars and successfully completes a 78-second trip onto the planet's red soil.

17 Three U.S. soldiers on patrol north of Baghdad are killed in a roadside bombing. Their deaths bring to 500 the number of U.S. soldiers killed in Iraq since the war began in March 2003.

18 A suicide bomber detonates a powerful device inside a pickup truck just outside the main gate of the U.S. occupation headquarters in Baghdad, killing more than 30 people.

19 Senator John Kerry of Massachusetts comes from behind to win the Iowa caucuses for the Democratic presidential nomination.

20 Thousands of Iraqis, primarily Shiah Muslims, march in Baghdad, Al Basrah, An Najaf, and Karbala demanding direct elections as a first step toward self-rule.

24 NASA's second Mars rover, Opportunity, successfully lands on Mars and begins transmitting images.

26 The U.S. Food and Drug Administration issues new rules designed to prevent the spread of mad cow disease. The rules include a ban on feeding cow blood and chicken wastes to cattle and using dead or disabled cows in products for people.

27 Senator John Kerry of Massachusetts wins the New Hampshire Democratic primary, the first primary election of the 2004 U.S. presidential campaign.

27 Logging in California's Sierra Nevada Mountains is to be increased by 400 percent, announce officials with the U.S. Department of Agriculture's Forest Service. The service plans to permit logging of 700,000 acres (283,280 hectares) over the next 20 years in what officials describe as an "effort to curb wildfires." Various environmental groups, and some California state officials, have condemned the plan as a "giveaway to the timber industry" that shows "disregard for the environment."

29 A Palestinian suicide bomber detonates an explosive device on a crowded city bus outside the Jerusalem residence of Israeli Prime Minister Ariel Sharon. The explosion leaves at least 10 passengers dead and 50 others wounded.

An explosion at a weapons cache near the Afghan city of Ghazni, 60 miles (95 kilometers) southwest of Kabul, the capital, kills seven U.S. soldiers and wounds three other soldiers.

31 A car bomb explodes outside a police station in the northern Iraqi city of Mosul, killing nine people. A bombing near Kirkuk, another city north of Baghdad, the capital, leaves three U.S. soldiers dead. Five Iraqi civilians are killed in a mortar attack in a residential neighborhood in Baghdad.

FEBRUARY

2004

1 Simultaneous suicide bombings in Arbil at the headquarters of Iraq's two leading Kurdish parties leave at least 100 people dead, including senior Kurdish political figures.

More than 120 members of Iran's 290-seat parliament resign to protest the Guardian Council's sweeping disqualification of some 3,000 candidates from running in parliamentary elections. The council is Iran's hardline Islamic religious authority.

The New England Patriots beat the Carolina Panthers 32 to 29 to win Super Bowl XXXVIII in Houston.

2 Israeli Prime Minister Ariel Sharon orders the evacuation of all Jewish settlers from Gaza. The order covers approximately 7,500 people living in 17 settlements.

Halliburton Co., a Houston-based corporation providing logistical support to the U.S. military in Iraq, allegedly overcharged the Army by more than $16 million for meals during the first seven months of 2003, disclose auditors with the U.S. Department of Defense. According to the Defense Department, Halliburton charged for an average of 42,000 meals a day at one base, but served only 14,053 meals.

3 Senator John Kerry of Massachusetts sweeps five of the day's seven primaries and caucuses for the Democratic nomination for president of the United States. The Massachusetts senator confirms his front runner status with victories in Arizona, Delaware, Missouri, New Mexico, and North Dakota.

4 Mad cow disease is now "indigenous in North America," an international panel informs the U.S. Department of Agriculture (USDA). Agricultural experts from New Zealand, Switzerland, the United Kingdom, and the United States recommend that the USDA test many more cattle than the current 40,000 out of some 30 million slaughtered annually.

5 The director of the Central Intelligence Agency (CIA), George Tenet, announces that U.S. intelligence analysts never claimed Iraq posed an imminent threat to the United States. Tenet states that CIA analysts held varying opinions on Iraq's biological, chemical, and nuclear weapons programs and those differences were presented to President George W. Bush in October 2002.

5 A powerful explosion aboard a crowded Moscow subway train leaves at least 39 people dead and more than 120 others injured. Russian President Vladimir Putin blames the explosion on Chechen rebels.

10 More than 50 Iraqis are killed and at least 50 others wounded when a car bomb explodes outside a police station in Iskandariya, a largely Shiah Muslim town south of Baghdad. The bombing occurs one day after U.S. officials revealed the existence of documents, found in Baghdad, that outline an al-Qa'ida plan to incite civil war by targeting Shiah Muslims.

The Mars rover Spirit travels almost 70 feet (21 meters), crossing the Gusev Crater toward a crater nicknamed "Bonneville," about 800 feet (240 meters) from where the rover landed.

11 A suicide bomber plows into a crowd of Iraqi army recruits in Baghdad, killing at least 47 people.

12 Scientists from Seoul National University in South Korea reveal that they have cloned 30 human embryos. The scientists emphasize that their goal is not to clone humans, but to obtain stem cells that they hope to use for treating disease.

Following a directive by Mayor Gavin Newsom, San Francisco authorities perform at least 15 same-sex marriages in direct violation of a measure passed by California voters in 2000 that defines marriage as a union between a man and a woman.

14 The presidential campaign of Senator John F. Kerry of Massachusetts continues to pick up momentum as Kerry wins Democratic primary elections in Nevada and Washington, D.C. Kerry has won 14 of 16 Democratic primaries and caucuses.

15 Dale Earnhardt, Jr., wins NASCAR's Daytona 500 before 180,000 fans in Daytona Beach, Florida. The victory comes three years after his father, Dale Earnhardt, was killed in the same race.

16 Major League Baseball Commissioner Bud Selig approves the trade of Texas Rangers shortstop Alex Rodriquez to

Haitians loot shipping containers on the wharves of Port-au-Prince, the capital, on February 27. Civil authority broke down as the government of Jean-Bertrand Aristide crumbled in the face of a rebellion that forced Aristide to flee Haiti on February 29.

the New York Yankees. The Yankees paid $67 million—the most cash in a trade in major league history—and exchanged second baseman Alfonso Soriano.

18 Former Vermont Governor Howard Dean ends his campaign for the Democratic nomination for the U.S. presidency. Political experts note that while Dean failed to win a single primary election, his antiwar campaign energized the party while demonstrating the potency of the Internet in grass-roots fund-raising.

23 The United States sends 50 Marines to Port-au-Prince, Haiti, to defend the U.S. embassy from a possible rebel attack. Seeking to overthrow President Jean-Bertrand Aristide, rebels overran Cap-Haitien on February 22.

25 The president of Turkmenistan, Saparmurat Niyazov, announces on state television that men can no longer wear their hair long and that young men are not allowed to grow beards. Niyazov also forbids listening to car radios or smoking in the street. Opera and ballet performances are banned as "unnecessary."

26 The president of Macedonia, Boris Trajkovski, is killed in a plane crash over Bosnia-Herzegovina.

28 An Islamic extremist group in the Philippines, Abu Sayyaf, claims responsibility for bombing a ferry on February 27 that killed more than 180 people. An Abu Sayyaf spokesperson claims the bombing was set in reprisal for the victimization of Muslim women in southern Mindanao.

29 Jean-Bertrand Aristide resigns as president of Haiti and flees Port-au-Prince, the capital, for the Central African Republic. The chief justice of Haiti's supreme court, Bonifice Alexandre, is sworn in as interim president as chaos engulfs Port-au-Prince.

MARCH

2004

1 Iraq's Governing Council agrees to a temporary constitution that is to serve as a framework for a civilian government and a bill of rights protecting freedom of speech, religious expression, and equal treatment under the law regardless of gender or ethnicity.

2 Parts of Mars were once soaked with water, announces the National Aeronautics and Space Administration. Instruments aboard the Mars rover Opportunity have beamed to Earth compelling evidence that water once existed on Mars.

More than 140 Iraqis are killed in a series of bomb blasts during religious ceremonies in Baghdad and Karbala, a Shiah holy city southwest of the capital. In Karbala, five simultaneous explosions occur in the center of hundreds of thousands of pilgrims praying on the holiest of Shiah holidays. In Baghdad, crowds respond to the insurgent violence by hurling stones at American soldiers.

3 An early morning explosion, apparently detonated by a suicide bomber, disables Baghdad's main phone exchange, cutting service to hundreds of thousands of Iraqis. The telecommunications center went into service less than one week ago.

9 The Hubble Space Telescope has captured an image of space so deep as to be close to the Big Bang itself, announce astronomers at the Space Telescope Science Institute in Baltimore. The image, named the Hubble Ultra Deep Field (HUDF), shows the first galaxies that emerged from the end of the so-called "dark ages," when the first stars reheated the cold, dark universe after the Big Bang.

11 A coordinated series of powerful bombs explode aboard crowded commuter trains in Madrid. The explosions leave 191 people dead and more than 1,800 others injured.

12 Two million Spaniards march through Madrid, demonstrating against the March 11 bombings—Europe's deadliest terrorist attacks since the 1988 Lockerbie, Scotland, airliner bombing.

Cyclone Gafilo struck Madagascar in the Indian Ocean twice during the week of March 7, killing some 170 people, reports the Madagascar state radio. Most of the victims were passengers on a ferry capsized by waves described as "mountainous" during a trip between the island of Anjouan and Madagascar's port of Mahajanga.

14 Spanish voters oust the ruling Popular Party in favor of the Socialists in parliamentary elections. In a stunning upset, the opposition takes 42.6 percent of the vote, compared with the Popular Party's 37.7 percent. Just hours before the polls opened, the government announced that a videotape had been found on which the al-Qa'ida terrorist network claimed responsibility for the March 11 bombings that killed 191 people.

Russian president Vladimir Putin is re-elected to a second term in a landslide. Putin receives 71 percent of the vote, compared with his closest competitor, Nikolai M. Kharitonov, who polled under 14 percent.

15 Spain's prime minister-elect, Jose Luis Rodriguez Zapatero, calls the war in Iraq "a disaster" and pledges to break with his predecessor's policy of support of the U.S.-led war.

The discovery of what scientists describe as the farthest known object in the solar system is announced by an astronomer at the California Institute of Technology. Mike Brown, leader of the team that found the object, describes it as a "planetoid" of rock and ice that is between 800 miles (1,285 kilometers) and 1,100 miles (1,770 kilometers) in diameter—too small to be classified as a planet. Its orbit around the sun, some 8 billion miles (12.8 billion kilometers) from Earth, is highly elliptical and takes 10,500 years to complete.

16 Pakistani troops engage in a "ferocious gun battle" with tribesmen close to Pakistan's border with Afghanistan. The offensive is aimed at rounding up members of the Taliban and al-Qa'ida terrorist network.

Massachusetts Senator John Kerry wins the Illinois primary, giving him the delegates necessary to secure the Democratic nomination for president.

17 U.S. Secretary of State Colin L. Powell, on an official visit to India, assures Indian leaders that the Bush administration will not try to halt the outsourcing of high-technology jobs

Demonstrators rally in Madrid's Colon Square in a protest against terrorism on March 12, one day after the bombing of four commuter trains in the Spanish capital killed 191 people and injured more than 1,800 others. Investigators eventually uncovered evidence suggesting that the bombings had been carried out by the al-Qa'ida terrorist network to punish Spain for its participation in the Iraq War.

to India. Powell notes: "Outsourcing is a natural effect of the global economic system and the rise of the Internet... but, at the same time, when you outsource jobs it becomes a political issue in anybody's country."

22 Sheik Ahmed Yassin, founder of the Palestinian militant group Hamas, is killed by a missile fired from an Israeli helicopter gunship. The attack is made as Yassin, a quadriplegic in a wheelchair, was returning home from morning prayers at a mosque in Gaza City.

Growth of the world population is slowing, reports the U.S. Census Bureau. Women, particularly in the United States and Europe, are having fewer children, and people are dying from AIDS in ever increasing numbers.

24 A former U.S. counterterrorism official, Richard Clark, testifies before the National Commission on Terrorist Attacks that the administration of President George W. Bush failed to heed his warnings about the threat of terrorist attacks. Clark asserts that the administration considered antiterrorism efforts important but not "urgent" before Sept. 11, 2001, despite warnings that such attacks could be imminent.

29 U.S. President George W. Bush formally welcomes seven new members—Bulgaria, Estonia, Latvia, Lithuania, Romania, Slovakia, and Slovenia—to the North Atlantic Treaty Organization (NATO).

31 A series of particularly violent attacks leaves at least 10 Americans dead in and around the Iraqi city of Al Fallujah.

A U.S. serviceman prepares to unload coffins from Iraq, where at least 135 American soldiers died in April, the second deadliest single month since the war began.

1 The Dow Jones industrial average of 30 major U.S. corporations drops AT&T Corp., Eastman Kodak Co., and International Paper as component companies. They are to be replaced by drugmaker Pfizer Inc.; Verizon Communications Inc., a telecommunications company; and AIG, Inc., an insurance company.

2 The U.S. economy generated 308,000 new jobs in March, compared with 46,000 new jobs in February, announces a spokesperson from the U.S. Department of Labor. The increase is the largest in nearly four years.

4 A Shiah cleric in Iraq unleashes an uprising against the U.S.-led occupation in Baghdad and in cities to the south. In Sadr City, Baghdad's largest Shiite neighborhood, members of the "Al-Mahdi Army," a militia loyal to a young, militant cleric—Moqtada al-Sadr—attack U.S. forces with a wide array of weapons, and eight Americans are killed. Tension between al-Sadr and the U.S.-led occupation escalated when L. Paul Bremer III, the top U.S. civilian in Iraq, closed Sadr City's newspaper on the grounds that it incited violence.

5 U.S. Marines seal off the city of Al Fallujah, west of Baghdad, in an operation designed to crush the insurrection in the so-called Sunni Triangle. In Baghdad, U.S. tanks patrol the Sadr City neighborhood as followers of militant Shiah cleric Moqtada al-Sadr barricade the main street with cars, tires, and chunks of concrete. In An Najaf, a Shiah holy city, gunmen force Iraqi police out of their stations and launch mortar attacks on the bases of the Spanish forces in control of the area.

The University of Connecticut men's basketball team wins the NCAA national championship, defeating Georgia Tech 82 to 73.

6 The Lithuanian parliament impeaches and dismisses from office President Rolandas Paksas. In a narrow vote, the legislature finds Paksas guilty of leaking classified material and extending Lithuanian citizenship to a Russian businessman in exchange for money.

Shiite insurgents take control of An Najaf as their leader, Moqtada al-Sadr, a militant Shiah cleric, takes up residence in one of the city's many mosques.

The University of Connecticut women's basketball team triumphs over the University of Tennessee, 70 to 61, to take its third straight NCAA national women's championship. The victory makes Connecticut the first school in college basketball history to win both the men's and women's NCAA tournaments in a single year.

8 National Security Adviser Condoleezza Rice publicly testifies before the commission investigating the 2001 terrorist attacks on the United States. She acknowledges that the preparations made by the Bush and previous administrations proved insufficient in the face of the attacks on Sept. 11, 2001. Under questioning, Rice testifies that President Bush was told during a special security briefing on Aug. 6, 2001, that al-Qa'ida leader Osama bin Laden was "determined to attack inside the United States." Rice notes, however, that that information was based on "old reporting—there was no new threat."

U.S. military officials report that 40 U.S. troops died in combat in Iraq in the first seven days of April.

11 An Iraqi battalion of several hundred soldiers refused to participate in the U.S. offensive against Sunni insurgents in Al Fallujah, confirms U.S. Army spokesman Brigadier General Mark Kimmitt.

13 Members on the independent commission investigating the terrorist attacks on the United States on Sept. 11, 2001, sharply condemn the Federal Bureau of Investigation (FBI) for its counterterrorism measures prior to the attacks.

San Francisco Giants slugger Barry Bonds slams the 661st homerun of his career. The run, on a 1-2 pitch off Ben Ford of the Milwaukee Brewers, surpasses Willie Mays's record of 660, putting Bonds in third place—behind Hank Aaron and Babe Ruth—for baseball's career homerun record.

14 Consumer prices in the United States rose by 0.5 percent in March, announce officials at the U.S. Department of Labor. According to the Labor Department, the increase, which followed a 0.3 percent jump in February, was fueled by rising oil prices.

18 Spain's new prime minister, Jose Luis Rodriguez Zapatero, announces that he has ordered all Spanish troops out of Iraq.

19 The Iraqi Governing Council, local officials in Al Fallujah, and the U.S-led coalition forces in Iraq agree to a truce in the standoff between insurgents and U.S. Marines in Al Fallujah.

The president of Honduras, Ricardo Maduro, announces that he has ordered all Honduran troops out of Iraq. Honduras's 370 troops are serving under Spanish command in An Najaf.

20 The U.S. Department of Labor announces new rules that extend overtime protection to white-collar employees who earn up to $100,000 a year and to workers making less than $23,660. Current federal law guarantees overtime pay but makes exceptions for three types of employees—administrators, executives, and professionals.

21 A series of nearly simultaneous suicide car bombings outside police stations in Al Basrah in southern Iraq leave more than 70 people dead and some 200 others wounded. Several of the victims are children killed as their school bus passes one of the exploding cars.

Sunni militants in Al Fallujah, west of Baghdad, break the cease-fire with U.S. forces surrounding the city with attacks on U.S. Marines.

The explosion of a suicide car bomb outside the national police headquarters in Riyadh, Saudi Arabia, kills 4 people and wounds nearly 150 others.

22 Railroad cars carrying ammonium nitrate fertilizer and fuel tankers filled with oil and gasoline touch live overhead power lines while being sidelined in a rail station in Ryongchon, North Korea. The subsequent explosion kills as many as 160 people and leaves more than 1,300 others injured; 500 people are blinded by flying debris. Nearly half of the victims are children, killed when their school is obliterated.

29 U.S. military officials in Iraq agree to withdraw American forces from Al Fallujah in an arrangement with local leaders to end a three-week-old standoff. U.S. Marines have encircled and battled insurgents in Al Fallujah, a hotbed of Sunni resistance, since April 5 in an attempt to stabilize the city.

MAY

2004

1 The European Union (EU) expands to 25 nations with the addition of 10 new members—Cyprus, the Czech Republic, Estonia, Hungary, Latvia, Lithuania, Malta, Poland, Slovakia, and Slovenia. With a population of 455 million, the EU is now the world's largest trading bloc.

2 The Israeli military launches a helicopter missile strike at Gaza City radio stations affiliated with Hamas and Yasir Arafat's Fatah organization. The strike is made after Palestinian gunmen killed a Jewish settler and her four children in Gaza.

5 President George W. Bush denounces as "abhorrent" the mistreatment of Iraqi prisoners of war by U.S. soldiers in Iraq. In interviews on Arab television networks, the president declares that the abuse, exposed on U.S. television on April 28, is not indicative of the American people as a whole.

President George W. Bush asks Congress for an additional $25 billion to fund military operations in Iraq for the fiscal year that begins in October.

The government of Prime Minister Silvio Berlusconi, which has served for 1,060 days, becomes Italy's longest-serving administration since the country became a republic in 1946.

Pablo Picasso's 1905 painting *Boy with a Pipe* sells at auction in New York City for $104 million, the highest price ever paid for a work of art.

6 President George W. Bush, making a public apology for the treatment of Iraqi prisoners at the Abu Ghraib prison in Iraq, rejects calls for the resignation of Secretary of Defense Donald H. Rumsfeld.

7 Donald H. Rumsfeld apologizes to the Iraqi prisoners mistreated by U.S. guards in the Abu Ghraib prison in 2003, noting that as secretary of defense he is ultimately accountable for the abuse.

The price of a barrel of oil hits $40, close to the all-time high of $41.15, reached in October 1990 after Iraq invaded Kuwait.

8 Vladimir Putin is inaugurated for his second term as president of Russia.

China issues a warning to members of the Hong Kong legislature to stop criticizing the central government for failing to grant the former British colony full democracy.

9 The president of the Republic of Chechnya, Akhmad Kadyrov, is killed by the explosion of a remotely controlled bomb planted in a stadium in the capital, Groznyy. Political experts suggest that the assassination is a severe blow to Russian President Vladimir Putin, who maneuvered Kadyrov's election in an effort to end the Chechen rebellion.

10 U.S. forces in Iraq level the Baghdad office of the militant Shiah cleric Moqtada al-Sadr after a series of running gun battles with his followers in the Sadr City district.

11 A videotape showing an Islamic militant beheading an American man surfaces on the Internet. Before being murdered, the victim identified himself as Nick Berg, a U.S. civilian in Iraq. The murderer declares that he is carrying out the execution in retaliation for the abuse of Iraqi prisoners.

13 Indian Prime Minister Atal Bihari Vajpayee resigns with the defeat of his governing Bharatiya Janata Party (BJP) in general elections.

14 In An Najaf, south of Baghdad, U.S. forces are engaged in fierce fighting with the Al Mahdi Army in a huge cemetery near the Imam Ali Shrine, the most revered of Shiah holy places.

South Korea's Constitutional Court rejects charges of incompetence and mismanagement against Roh Moo Hyun and restores the impeached president to power.

16 Militia fighters loyal to the militant Shiah cleric Moqtada al-Sadr drive Italian forces out of the southern city of An Nasiriyah and attack coalition headquarters in the city with grenade and mortar fire.

17 The head of the Iraqi Governing Council, Ezzedine Salim, is assassinated outside coalition headquarters in Baghdad.

More than 3,500 U.S. soldiers are being transferred from duty in South Korea to Iraq, announces the U.S. Department of Defense.

Gay couples exchange marriage vows in Massachusetts, where the state

Images of the physical abuse and humiliation of Iraqi prisoners at Abu Ghraib Prison outside Baghdad—broadcast by the CBS News program "60 Minutes" in late April— sparked an international scandal, prompting U.S. President George W. Bush to publicly denounce such treatment as "abhorrent" on May 5 and 6.

supreme court granted same-sex couples the right to marry.

19 India's president asks Manmohan Singh to form a new government. Singh was nominated by Sonia Gandhi, who leads India's Congress Party, but refused to accept the premiership.

20 U.S. soldiers and Iraqi police raid the Baghdad offices and residence of Ahmed Chalabi, an Iraqi Governing Council member whom U.S. Defense Department officials once had slated to run postwar Iraq. Authorities with the U.S.-led occupation disclose that judges have issued arrest warrants for Chalabi. According to the General Accounting Office, the U.S. government has paid Chalabi at least $33 million since 2001.

21 The U.S.-led coalition in Iraq suspends military operations in An Najaf against the militia loyal to militant Shiah cleric Moqtada al-Sadr. In a truce brokered by moderate Shiah clerics, al-Sadr agrees to pull his militia off the streets of the city.

29 The national memorial to the 16 million Americans who served in uniform in World War II is dedicated in Washington, D.C., by President George W. Bush. The memorial stands between the Lincoln Memorial and the Washington Monument west of the Mall.

31 At least 10 people are killed over the Memorial Day weekend in a massive chain of thunderstorms across the South, Midwest, and East. The storms spawn dozens of tornadoes in a line stretching from Louisiana to New England.

Iraq's interim prime minister, Ayad Allawi (third from left), and the top U.S. administrator in Iraq, L. Paul Bremer III (third from right), review the document formally transfering sovereignty to the interim government at a secret ceremony in Baghdad, the capital, on June 28.

3 George J. Tenet, director of the Central Intelligence Agency (CIA), has resigned, announces President George W. Bush, who denies that Tenet was dismissed. Tenet was the target of widespread criticism for intelligence failures related to the war in Iraq and terrorist attacks on the United States in 2001.

4 U.S. commanders and Shiite militia leaders withdraw from the holy cities of An Najaf and Al Kufah, ending the two-month standoff with militia fighters loyal to the militant Shiah cleric Moqtada al-Sadr.

The U.S. economy generated 248,000 new jobs in May and nearly 1 million new jobs in the second quarter of 2004, reports the U.S. Department of Labor. However, unemployment held steady at 5.6 percent.

5 Ronald Reagan, the 40th president of the United States, dies at the age of 93 at his residence in Los Angeles.

6 The Israeli Cabinet tentatively backs Prime Minister Ariel Sharon's revised plan to pull out of the Gaza Strip.

The United States informs South Korea that the U.S. Department of Defense plans to withdraw one-third of the 37,000 U.S. troops stationed in South Korea by 2005.

10 Current and past world leaders gather at the National Cathedral in Washing-

last at least 10 days, costing $60 million a day in revenue.

16 The independent commission investigating the terrorist attacks on the United States on Sept. 11, 2001, reports that "no credible evidence" has been uncovered to support claims that Saddam Hussein's government collaborated with the al-Qa'ida terrorist network.

17 A car bomb attack on the main Iraqi Army recruitment center in Baghdad kills 35 Iraqis. A bombing at the same recruiting center in February killed 47 people.

24 Coordinated insurgent attacks in Baghdad and four Iraqi cities north and west of the capital leave at least 95 people dead, including 3 U.S. soldiers.

The U.S. Supreme Court refuses to order the administration of President George W. Bush to reveal details of Vice President Dick Cheney's energy task force.

25 Fighting between U.S. Marines and Iraqi insurgents continues for a second day in Al Fallujah, a stronghold of resistance to the U.S.-led occupation.

28 The United States hands over sovereignty in Iraq to the Iraqi interim government two days ahead of schedule. In a secret ceremony in Baghdad, the U.S. civilian administrator in Iraq, L. Paul Bremer III, formally transfers power to Iraq's interim prime minister, Iyad Allawi.

The Supreme Court of the United States rejects the claim made by the administration of President George W. Bush that suspected terrorists or "enemy combatants" can be held without recourse to legal action. In an 8-to-1 decision, the court declares that U.S. citizens detained as enemy combatants retain legal rights, even in times of war.

Canadian Prime Minister Paul Martin and his Liberal Party retain power in national parliamentary elections in the face of a strong challenge by the Conservatives. However, the Liberals lose their absolute majority in the House of Commons.

29 As many as 5,600 U.S. reserve soldiers from the rarely tapped Individual Ready Reserve are being called up for service.

30 The Federal Reserve, the nation's central bank, raises a key short-term interest rate by one quarter of a percent. The increase in the federal funds rate to 1.25 percent is the first in four years.

ton, D.C., for the state funeral of Ronald Reagan, 40th president of the United States.

14 Documents confirming that Enron Corp., the failed Houston-based energy company, manipulated the energy market during the 2000–2001 energy crisis are released by Washington state's Snohomish Public Utility District. Enron's manipulation of the market from January 2000 to June 2001 cost West Coast electricity customers at least $1.1 billion. In one transaction, Enron made $222,678 in three hours by moving power from California to Oregon, then selling it back to California at a highly inflated price.

16 Bomb attacks on an oil pipeline shut down Iraq's key southern terminals in Al Basrah and Khor al-Amaya, which handle nearly all oil exports. Officials expect the shutdown to

JULY

2004

1 Lieutenant General Ricardo Sanchez hands over command of the U.S.-led multinational force in Iraq to General George Casey in a ceremony in Baghdad. Insurgent attacks during and after the ceremony kill eight people.

3 Maria Sharapova upsets Serena Williams 6-1, 6-4 to win her first women's singles tennis championship at Wimbledon. She is the first Russian woman to win the Wimbledon title.

4 Roger Federer of Switzerland takes his second straight men's singles tennis championship at Wimbledon with a 4-6, 7-5, 7-6 (3), 6-4 victory over Andy Roddick of the United States.

Greece, an underdog team that experts predicted would be eliminated in the first wave, beats Portugal 1-0 to win the European soccer championship in a final that sports writers variously describe as "bizarre, unlikely, and wonderful."

5 Saboteurs blast a pipeline running from northern to southern Iraq, disrupting the flow of crude oil. The attack comes less than 24 hours after a similar breach to another pipeline and two weeks after sabotage shut down all oil exports for approximately 10 days.

6 More than 38 million people worldwide are infected with HIV, the virus that causes AIDS, reports UNAIDS, the Joint United Nations Program on HIV/AIDS. The authors of the report warn that Asian governments need to focus attention on the disease in order to prevent "a full-blown AIDS catastrophe" in an area that is home to 60 percent of the world's population.

8 The U.S. Department of Justice charges Kenneth Lay, the former chairman and chief operating officer of Enron Corp., with 11 criminal charges, including bank fraud, share trading fraud, and making false statements. Lay sold $184 million in Enron stock before Enron's bankruptcy in December 2001. The collapse put more than 20,000 Enron employees out of work and cost investors—which included many employees—billions of dollars.

11 The governments of Iraq and Syria agree to take steps to seal their border in an attempt to stop Islamic militants from crossing into Iraq to carry out terrorist attacks.

13 Federal rules that kept nearly 60 million acres (2.4 billion hectares) of national forest off-limits to road-building and, therefore, to logging, are to be abandoned by the administration of President George W. Bush. Secretary of the U.S. Department of Agriculture Ann Veneman announces that under a new federal policy those 60 million acres of forests will be open to road building and logging unless governors of the affected states petition the federal government to keep certain areas roadless. The secretary notes, however, the federal government is not legally bound to honor such a petition.

Zimbabwe introduces ox-drawn ambulances for rural areas around the capital, Harare, as well as more remote regions, where motorized transport no longer functions.

14 The Philippine government begins withdrawing peacekeeping troops from Iraq. The government orders the withdrawal in response to the threat made by Iraqi insurgents that they would behead a Filipino they hold captive if Philippine forces were not withdrawn by July 20.

An effort to pass a constitutional amendment barring same-sex couples from marrying fails to rally the necessary support in a procedural vote in the U.S. Senate.

16 Domestic diva Martha Stewart is sentenced to five months in prison and fined $30,000 in a federal court in New York City for lying to federal officials about a stock transaction.

21 Work will continue on the West Bank security barrier despite its condemnation by the United Nations (UN) General Assembly and a UN world court. A spokesperson for Israeli Prime Minister Ariel Sharon confirms that Sharon's government intends to complete the barrier designed

Senators John Kerry and John Edwards acknowledge delegate support at the Democratic National Convention in Boston on July 29 after Kerry accepted the nomination as the party's candidate for president of the United States. Kerry chose Edwards as his running mate prior to the convention.

to separate Israel from Palestinian communities in the West Bank.

22 The commission investigating the terrorist attacks on the United States on Sept. 11, 2001, delivers its conclusions on the attacks and its recommendations on the various U.S. agencies that gather and disseminate intelligence. The commission recommends that the current position of director of the Central Intelligence Agency be replaced with a national intelligence director who would oversee and control the budget of the 15 intelligence agencies that currently function within various government departments. Committee Chairman Thomas H. Kean of New Jersey notes that "an attack of even greater magnitude is now possible and even probable—we do not have the luxury of time."

The number of U.S. citizens under the control of the criminal justice system climbed to nearly 6.9 million people in 2003, up by more than 130,700 in 2002, announces a spokesperson from the U.S. Department of Justice. The total accounts for approximately 3.2 percent of the entire adult population of the United States.

28 Delegates at the Democratic convention in Boston officially nominate Senator John Kerry of Massachusetts as the party's nominee for president of the United States.

29 The overall income of U.S. citizens shrank by 9.2 percent from 2000 through 2002, reports the Internal Revenue Service. Total adjusted gross income on tax returns fell by 5.1 percent in 2002, and average income declined by 5.7 percent in the same year. The reduction in total national income was the first since the modern tax system was introduced during World War II.

25

AUGUST

2004

Stefano Baldini of Italy rounds the Panathinaiko Stadium in Athens to win the men's marathon, the final event at the 2004 Summer Olympic Games, which closed on August 29. The United States, Russia, China, Australia, and Germany led in the winning of medals.

1 A heightened terrorist alert status is announced by the U.S. Department of Homeland Security. According to terrorism experts, the code orange, or "high risk," alert is based on detailed information about specific targets.

2 Reversing an ealier position, President George W. Bush endorses the creation of a national intelligence office and counterterrorism center—key recommendations of the commission investigating the terrorist attacks on the United States on Sept. 11, 2001.

3 Bangladesh appeals to the United Nations for disaster aid. With 60 percent of the country underwater, most crops have been lost. At least 30 mil-lion people have been displaced, and damage to infrastructure is estimated at $7 billion.

4 The director of the Federal Aviation Administration tells airline executives, meeting in Washington, D.C., that if U.S. airlines do not voluntarily reduce the number of scheduled flights at Chicago's O'Hare International Airport, the government will do it for them. Transportation Secretary Norman Mineta notes that congestion at O'Hare, considered the world's busiest airport, is choking the entire U.S. air transportation system.

5 Radical Shiah cleric Moqtada al-Sadr calls on all Iraqis to join in a "revolution" against U.S.-led forces in Iraq. The call to arms signals the collapse of a two-month truce between al-Sadr's militia, the Mahdi Army, and the U.S. military.

6 Fierce fighting continues between U.S.-led forces and members of a Shiite militia in Iraq. For a second day, U.S. troops and Iraqi security guards battle the Mahdi Army in the Shiah holy city of An Najaf.

10 President George W. Bush nominates Representative Porter Goss (R., Florida) as the director of the Central Intelligence Agency.

12 U.S.-led forces surround the center of An Najaf and engage in fierce fighting with an estimated 1,000 members of the Mahdi Army. Approximately 1,800 Iraqi soldiers, backed by 2,000 U.S. marines and warplanes, battle insurgents in the city's vast Valley of Peace cemetery.

13 Hurricane Charley, driving a surge of sea water 13 to 15 feet- (3 to 4 meters-) high, smashes into Florida's West Coast with winds of up to 145 miles (233 kilometers) per hour. The category 4 hurricane makes landfall at Captiva and Sanibel islands, off Fort Myers, and barrels into Punta Gorda and Port Charlotte.

The Summer Olympic Games open in Athens, with a spectacular ceremony tracing the journey from Greece's mythical past to its emergence as a modern European nation and host of the 2004 Games.

16 Iraqi police in An Najaf order all journalists out of the city on the grounds that their safety can no longer be assured. A truce to negotiate a cease-fire in An Najaf collapsed on August 14, and U.S.-led forces subsequently renewed their shelling of the city's vast cemetery, where members of the Mahdi Army remain holed up.

18 Oil prices hit a record high of $47.20 a barrel on world markets.

19 A mortar attack on an An Najaf police station leaves at least seven Iraqi policemen dead and more than 20 others wounded. Fierce fighting also takes place in Sadr City, the vast Baghdad slum that is largely inhabited by members of the Shiah branch of Islam.

22 Thieves armed with rifles burst into a museum in Oslo, Norway, and pull two Edvard Munch paintings, *The Scream* and *Madonna*, off the walls and flee with them to a waiting getaway car. Critics consider *The Scream*, painted in 1893, to be one of the iconic images of modern art with a likely value of $100 million.

26 Grand Ayatollah Ali al-Sistani, Iraq's most powerful Shiah cleric, arrives in An Najaf, leading an enormous convoy of followers. His entourage, traveling in some 30 vehicles, was joined by at least 1,000 cars as it progressed through towns between Al Basrah, in far southern Iraq, and An Najaf. He asks that all foreign forces withdraw from An Najaf and that the responsibility for security be returned to Iraqi police.

The number of low income people in the United States grew in 2003 for the third straight year, reports the U.S. Census Bureau. The poverty rate rose from 12.1 percent in 2002 to 12.5 percent of the population in 2003. The Census Bureau defined a family of two adults and two children as "poor" if the family had an income of less than $18,660 in 2003.

27 Thousands of Shiah Muslim pilgrims throng the Imam Ali Mosque in An Najaf as Shiite rebels withdraw and U.S.-led forces pull back from the Shiah holy city. The leader of the rebellion, militant Shiah cleric Moqtada al-Sadr, reportedly surrendered the keys to the mosque to Grand Ayatollah Ali al-Sistani. The cease-fire and withdrawal was mediated by al-Sistani, who is one of Iraq's most respected Shiah leaders.

29 More than 100,000 protestors march through midtown Manhattan in one of the largest demonstrations ever staged against the war in Iraq. The protest takes place on the eve of the Republican National Convention, which opens on August 30 at New York City's Madison Square Garden.

The 2004 Summer Olympic Games close in an elaborate ceremony in Athens.

30 A spate of insurgent attacks on oil pipelines brings Iraq's oil exports to a complete halt.

31 Nearly simultaneous explosions aboard two buses in the Israeli city of Beersheba kill 15 people and injure more than 80 others. The Palestinian militant group Hamas claims responsibility.

A suicide bomber detonates an explosive device outside the entrance to a subway station in Moscow, killing herself and 10 other people. The attack comes one week after suicide bombers caused the crashes of two Russian airliners.

The Cleveland Indians rout the New York Yankees 22 to 0 in the biggest Yankee loss in the 101-year history of the team.

1 Chechen rebels storm a school in Beslan in southern Russia and take more than 1,000 people, including many students, hostage. The rebels demand the withdrawal of Russian troops from Chechnya.

2 President George W. Bush officially accepts the Republican Party's nomination to run for re-election in a speech closing the Republican National Convention. Bush vows to continue the war on terror, pledging "a safer world and a more hopeful America."

3 The standoff between Russian troops and Chechen rebels occupying a school in Beslan, a town in southern Russia, ends with the troops storming the school amid explosions and intense gunfire. More than 330 hostages are killed, including some 155 children.

5 Hurricane Frances, a category 1 hurricane with winds of 105 miles (169 kilometers) per hour, makes landfall on the east coast of Florida. The storm leaves approximately 2 million residences without power.

6 Former U.S. President Bill Clinton undergoes quadruple heart bypass surgery for arterial blockage.

7 Intense fighting between U.S. forces and Shiah insurgents in Baghdad leave at least 34 people dead. A total of 13 Americans die in action in Iraq in the last 24 hours.

Typhoon Songda slams into Japan with winds of 145 miles (230 kilometers) per hour. The typhoon is the seventh to hit Japan in 2004. The Pacific Ocean has incubated 19 typhoons so far in 2004—35 percent more than usual.

8 The number of deaths of U.S. military personnel in Iraq has surpassed the 1,000 mark, report officials with the U.S. Department of Defense.

9 The cost of health insurance for workers in the United States increased by an average of 11.2 percent in the last 12 months, five times faster than wages, announces the Kaiser Family Foundation.

10 U.S. jets pound rebel strongholds in Al Fallujah for a fourth day in an attempt to loosen insurgent control of the city. After ending a three-week siege in April, U.S. marines turned the city over to a U.S.-sanctioned Iraqi security force that dissipated in the face of rebel attacks.

11 President George W. Bush of the United States has received intelligence reports that suggest that North Korea may be preparing to conduct its first test explosion of a nuclear weapon, confirms the Bush administration.

12 A surge of rebel violence in Baghdad and in the Sunni Triangle region north and west of the Iraqi capital leaves 78 people dead.

14 A suicide bomber detonates an explosive device packed with artillery shells in a car outside a Baghdad police station, killing 47 people, many of whom are young men waiting to apply for jobs.

14 The administration of President George W. Bush shifts $3.46 billion from Iraqi reconstruction projects to fund efforts to improve security and increase oil output in Iraq.

16 Hurricane Ivan makes landfall at Gulf Shores, Alabama, blasting nearby Mobile with winds of 130 miles (209 kilometers) per hour. More than 20 people are killed by the storm, which pounds a 370-mile (595-kilometer) stretch of the Gulf Coast, from Florida to Louisiana, with hurricane-force winds and waves of up to 25 feet (7.5 meters) in height.

17 Barry Bonds hits his 700th career homerun with a 392-foot (120-meter) shot to left-center field in a San Francisco Giants home game.

18 Insurgents in Iraq carry out another string of car bombings, killing at least 20 Iraqis and 2 U.S. soldiers, bringing to more than 300 the number of people killed in Iraq since September 12.

More than 2,000 people are killed in Haiti in flooding and mudslides triggered by heavy rains from Tropical Storm Jeanne.

19 Chinese leader Jiang Zemin turns over his final important position, chief of China's enormous military, to President Hu Jintao, in the first orderly transfer of power in the history of China's Communist Party.

President George W. Bush and First Lady Laura Bush (left) are joined by Vice President Dick Cheney and his wife, Lynne Cheney, on the podium after the president accepted his party's nomination for president at the Republican National Convention in New York City on September 2.

19 Iraqi interim Prime Minister Ayad Allawi, on a visit to London, tells British Prime Minister Tony Blair that terrorists are flooding into Iraq from across the Muslim world.

24 Iraqi Prime Minister Ayad Allawi, speaking before a joint session of the U.S. Congress, insists that the interim Iraqi government is succeeding in establishing freedom and democracy in Iraq.

26 Hurricane Jeanne makes landfall at Hutchinson Island off Florida's east coast, with winds of 120 miles (193 kilometers) per hour. Jeanne is Florida's fourth hurricane in six weeks.

26 The Federal National Mortgage Association—a private corporation, usually referred to as Fannie Mae, chartered by the United States government to help assure that enough money is available for home mortgages—agrees to demands by federal regulators to increase the company's capital reserve by $5 billion over the next nine months, pushing up its total reserve to about $9.4 billion.

28 The price of U.S. light crude oil climbs to $50 a barrel on world markets.

29 Insurgents launched more than 2,350 attacks on military and civilian targets in Iraq between August 29 and September 28, announces a private security company that compiles and analyzes data in Iraq for the U.S. military. While more than 40 percent of the assaults took place in Baghdad, the capital, attacks were made in nearly every major population center, with the exception of the Kurdish north.

OCTOBER

2004

1 The U.S. military in Iraq launches a major assault on Samarra, a rebel stronghold in the Sunni Triangle.

4 More than 25 people are killed and dozens wounded in a series of suicide car bombings in Iraq.

General Susilo Bambang Yudhoyono is declared the winner over the incumbent, President Megawati Sukarnoputri, in Indonesia's September 20 presidential election.

SpaceShipOne climbs 70 miles (113 kilometers) into space for the second time in one week to claim the $10-million Ansari X Prize.

5 Ten Iraqi policemen are killed in two separate attacks on a 15-mile (24-kilometer) stretch of highway south of Baghdad, which is regarded as one of the most dangerous in Iraq. According to a survivor, the assailants took off with $1 million that the police had in their possession.

6 The U.S. House of Representatives ethics committee admonishes Tom DeLay (R., Texas), the House majority leader, for the second time in a week. The latest admonishment is for appearing to connect legislative action to political donations and for involving Federal Aviation Administration officials in a redistricting fight among state legislators in Texas. DeLay maintains that the accusations against him are politically motivated.

7 Bombings at three Egyptian resorts kill at least 33 people, many of whom were Israeli tourists. In the most violent of the attacks, two suicide bombings cause 10 floors of a luxury hotel in Taba to collapse, killing at least 31 people. Car bombings at campgrounds outside Nuwaybi and Ras al-Sultan—Red Sea resorts popular with Israeli backpackers—kill two others.

9 Australian voters re-elect a majority of Prime Minister John Howard's Liberals, a center-right party, to Parliament, giving the prime minister a fourth term.

14 Insurgents penetrate Baghdad's Green Zone, headquarters of the U.S. embassy, and detonate two bombs that kill five people, including four Americans. Suicide bombers apparently hand-carried the explosives into the area in what military officials describe as a "major security breach."

15 For the first time, a vaccine against malaria has been proven to be at least partially effective, announces the Malaria Vaccine Initiative.

20 Typhoon Tokage slams into western Japan with winds of nearly 80 miles (126 kilometers) per hour. The typhoon is the second to hit Japan in less than two weeks and a record tenth so far in 2004.

The Boston Red Sox win the American League pennant by defeating the New York Yankees 10-3 at Yankee Stadium. The Red Sox is the first team in modern Major League Baseball history to overcome a 3-0 series deficit.

Hundreds of British soldiers are to be deployed from southern to central Iraq, confirms British Defense Secretary Geoff Hoon. Hoon informs the House of Commons that the deployment of the Black Watch regiment is to last "weeks rather than months."

22 Russia's lower house of parliament, the Duma, votes 334 to 73 to ratify the Kyoto Protocol, the international treaty to cut greenhouse gas emissions. The treaty, backed by 126 nations, must be ratified by Russia before it can go into effect.

24 The bodies of 49 Iraqi army recruits are found near the Iranian border in northeastern Iraq. According to Iraqi officials, all of the soldiers appear to have been executed. The terrorist group led by Jordanian militant Abu Mussab al-Zarqawi claims responsibility for the massacre.

Hamid Karzai's chief opponent in presidential elections in Afghanistan concedes that Karzai has won the simple majority needed to avoid a run off. Yunus Qanuni announces his concession with 94 percent of the votes counted from the October 9 election.

25 Nearly 380 tons (345 metric tons) of conventional, but highly powerful, explosives are missing from Iraq, announces the International Atomic Energy Agency (IAEA). The IAEA informs the United Nations Security Council that the explosives apparently

European leaders meet on October 29 at the Michelangelo-designed Campidoglio in Rome to sign the European Union (EU) Constitution. Six European leaders met in the same room in 1957 to sign the original treaty that founded the EU, which in 2004 grew to include 25 member nations.

were looted from al-Qaqaa, a chemical and explosive munitions facility outside Baghdad, in April or May 2003.

26 The Israeli Knesset votes to remove Israeli settlements and soldiers from the Gaza Strip. International affairs experts consider the vote a major victory for Prime Minister Ariel Sharon.

27 The Boston Red Sox win the World Series for the first time since 1918 in a four-game sweep of the St. Louis Cardinals. The Red Sox top the Cardinals 3-0 in game 4 in St. Louis, Missouri.

29 European leaders, meeting in Rome, sign the European Union (EU) Constitution. The document, which includes a charter of fundamental rights, is signed at the Michelangelo-designed Campidoglio, where in 1957 Belgium, France, Germany, Italy, Luxembourg, and the Netherlands signed the treaty that founded the EU.

29 The U.S. economy grew at a rate of 3.7 percent in the third quarter of 2004, reports the Department of Commerce.

Norodom Sihamoni is crowned king of Cambodia in Phnom Penh, the capital. Sihamoni is the son of King Norodom Sihanouk, who retired from the throne.

30 A suicide bomber rams a car packed with explosives into a U.S. convoy near Al Fallujah, in Iraq's restive Sunni Triangle area, killing nine U.S. marines.

NOVEMBER

2004

President George W. Bush and First Lady Laura Bush wave as they depart a November 3 event in Washington, D.C., celebrating his re-election as president on November 2.

2 Some 60 percent of eligible voters, the highest since 1968, turn out for the presidential election, which is too close to call on election night.

In congressional elections, Republicans enlarge their majority in both the United States Senate and House of Representatives.

The U.S. Department of Defense extends the tours of duty of 6,500 U.S. troops in Iraq.

3 George W. Bush wins re-election as president of the United States with 51 percent of the popular vote. His opponent, Senator John F. Kerry of Massachusetts, concedes in a telephone call to the president.

4 The international aid agency Doctors Without Borders pulls out of Iraq. An agency spokesperson notes that Iraq has become too dangerous "to guarantee an acceptable level of security for our staff."

The government of Cote d'Ivoire launches airstrikes in Bouake and Korhogo, rebel strongholds in the north.

6 A series of suicide car bombings and motor and rocket attacks across central Iraq leave at least 33 people dead and more than 60 others wounded, including 24 U.S. soldiers.

8 U.S. forces backed by newly trained Iraqi troops are engaged in a major assault on Al Fallujah, with thousands of marines and members of the Army's 1st Infantry Division driving tanks and armored carriers into what is considered the center of the Iraqi insurgency.

10 France begins evacuating French nationals from Cote d'Ivoire in the face of four days of attacks on French residents and widespread looting. Anti-French demonstrations in Abidjan, the main port, have left at least 1,000 people injured. The disturbances were triggered by France's destruction of the Ivorian air force after an Ivorian airstrike on rebel-held territory resulted in the deaths of nine French soldiers on November 6.

U.S. marines are in control of about 70 percent of Al Fallujah. Nevertheless, a fierce battle continues in the city center.

11 Yasir Arafat, head of the Palestine Liberation Organization (PLO), dies at age 75 in a hospital in Paris. Former Palestinian Prime Minister Mahmoud Abbas is to assume command of the PLO.

Insurgent violence escalates dramatically in the northern Iraqi city of Mosul and in Baghdad in what military experts suggest is a guerrilla campaign to divert troops from the fighting in Al Fallujah. Masked gunmen roam the streets of Mosul, setting fire to police cars and looting weapons and ammunition from police stations. In Baghdad, a car bomb explodes in the center of a crowded street, killing 17 people. A similar bombing killed 10 people in the capital on November 10, one of several insurgent attacks outside Al Fallujah that left 28 people dead in a single day.

12 Violence escalates across Iraq, with insurgents carrying out ambushes, bombings, and mortar attacks in Ar Ramadi, Baghdad, Baqubah, Hawijah, Kirkuk, Mosul, Samarra, and Tikrit.

14 Iran agrees to suspend its nuclear programs in exchange for guarantees made by France, Germany, and the United Kingdom that Iran will not face United Nations Security Council sanctions as long as the agreement remains in effect.

16 U.S. President George W. Bush nominates Condoleezza Rice, currently the president's national security adviser, to replace Colin L. Powell as secretary of state.

Democrats in the U.S. Senate elect Harry Reid of Nevada as their minority leader. Senator Richard Durbin of Illinois is elected the Democratic whip.

17 Sears, Roebuck and Co., the giant Chicago area-based retail company, and Kmart, the discount retail chain based in Troy, Michigan, are to merge, announce the two corporations. The new company, to be called Sears Holding Corporation, will be the third largest U.S. retailer with approximately 3,450 stores.

Republicans in the House of Representatives abandon an 11-year-old rule that required party leaders to step aside temporarily if indicted on criminal charges. According to House Democrats, the rule is rescinded to protect Majority Leader Tom DeLay of Texas, who may be prosecuted in Texas on charges that he used corporate funds to help Republicans win state legislative races in 2002.

18 The U.S. dollar falls to a record $1.3059 against the euro in London markets.

19 Persistent U.S. trade deficits pose a risk to the economy, warns Federal Reserve Chairman Alan Greenspan. In the second quarter of 2004, the trade deficit soared to $166.2 billion.

Sudan's vice president, Ali Osman Taha, and main rebel leader, John Garang, sign an accord to complete peace talks to end Sudan's civil war—21 years of conflict that cost the lives of 2 million people.

22 More than 200,000 Ukrainians rally outside the parliament in Kiev, the capital, to protest the results of the presidential election on November 21. Prime Minister Viktor Yanukovych has been declared the winner, though exit polls indicate that his challenger, Viktor Yushchenko, should have won by a large margin.

23 The U.S. dollar slides to another new low against the euro, which climbs to $1.31 in trading on European markets.

27 Ukraine's parliament, meeting in an emergency session in Kiev, declares the November 21 presidential election invalid and passes a vote of no-confidence in Ukraine's Central Elections Commission.

30 At least 136 U.S. soldiers were killed in Iraq in November, the highest death toll of any month since the war began in March 2003, announces the Associated Press, based on the news agency's unofficial tally.

1 U.S. military commanders announce that the number of troops in Iraq is to be increased to 150,000.

3 Ukraine's supreme court rules that the results of the highly disputed runoff presidential election, which took place on November 21, are invalid, and the election must be repeated.

4 The Philippine government suspends all logging in the wake of a series of violent storms that triggered flooding and mudslides that killed at least 1,000 people in the last two weeks.

5 A wave of insurgent violence in Iraq leaves more than 80 people dead in the last three days. In the latest attacks, rebels outside Tikrit surround a bus and gun down 17 passengers. Insurgent attacks on two Baghdad police stations on December 3 left 24 people dead, including 16 officers. On December 4, eight policemen died in a suicide bomb attack on a third Baghdad station. In Mosul, on December 4, a suicide car bomber detonated a powerful explosive device alongside a bus carrying Kurdish militiamen; 18 Kurds were killed 3 others wounded. A variety of other attacks, primarily in the so-called Sunni Triangle region, killed at least 14 other people, including 4 U.S. and 4 Iraqi soldiers.

8 The U.S. Senate, in a 89 to 2 vote, passes legislation to restructure the 15 agencies that gather intelligence for the federal government. The legislation is based on the recommendations of the independent commission that investigated the terrorist attacks on the United States on Sept. 11, 2001. The bill, which was passed in the House of Representatives by a vote of 336 to 75 on December 7, enacts most of the commission's major recommendations.

11 Taiwan's Nationalist Party takes 114 of 225 parliamentary seats in parliamentary elections, leaving the coalition government of President Chen Shui-bian without a majority. Political experts suggest that the Taiwanese electorate has voted for a parliament that will act as a brake on Chen's controversial plans, which include constitutional changes and an $18-billion purchase of arms from the United States.

12 Eight U.S. marines are killed in three separate insurgent attacks on military convoys in Iraq's Anbar province west of Baghdad.

14 The world's highest road bridge, the Millau bridge over the River Tarn in the Massif Central Mountains in France, is officially opened by French President Jacques Chirac. The highest of the bridge's seven piers is 1,125 feet (343 meters)—75 feet (23 meters) higher than the Eiffel Tower in Paris.

16 Assassins gun down a top official of the Iraqi interim government in Baghdad. Kassim Imhawi, the director-general of the ministry of communication, is shot and killed while being driven to his office.

17 Leaders of Israel's ruling Likud Party and opposition Labour Party agree to form a new coalition government. Labour is to have eight ministerial posts and its leader, Shimon Peres, is be deputy prime minister. Political experts note that the agreement should help Prime Minister Arial Sharon implement his plan to withdraw all Jewish settlers from Gaza.

Turkey's prime minister, Recep Tayyip Erdogan, signs a protocol with European Union (EU) leaders that schedules negotiations for Turkey to enter the EU to begin in October 2005.

A storm with hurricane-force winds hits Paris without warning, leaving thousands of households without power. At least six people are killed as winds of 80 miles (130 kilometers) per hour topple trees and blow roof tiles onto city streets.

18 Syria, under pressure from the United Nations Security Council, withdraws some of its 14,000 troops from Lebanon.

19 More than 60 Iraqis are killed in suicide car bombings in An Najaf and Karbala. A leading Shiah cleric describes the attacks, which take place near mosques in two of Shiah Islam's holiest cities, as an attempt to provoke violence between Iraq's Shiah and Sunni populations.

Secondary waves crash over the terrace of a resort on Penang, already flooded by enormous tsunamis that hit the Malaysian island on December 26. Triggered by a 9.0-magnitude earthquake off the Indonesian island of Sumatra, the tsunamis devastated coastal communities in 11 Asian and African nations. At least 125,000 people had been confirmed dead on December 31.

21 A suicide bombing in a huge mess tent on a U.S. military base in the northern Iraqi city of Mosul kills 22 people, including 14 U.S. soldiers, 4 American contract workers, and 4 Iraqi soldiers. At least 70 other people are injured, many seriously, in one of the deadliest attacks on U.S. forces in Iraq since the war began in March 2003.

Franklin Raines, chairman and chief executive of the Federal National Mortgage Association, commonly known as Fannie Mae, resigns days after the company was found to have violated accounting rules. The Office of Federal Housing Enterprise Oversight demanded significant changes in senior management after disclosing that Fannie Mae had failed significantly to meet its capital requirements.

23 The U.S. dollar falls to a new record low—$1.3505—against the euro.

26 The world's strongest earthquake in 40 years occurs off the Indonesian island of Sumatra and triggers tsunamis that devastate southern Asia. At least 125,000 people are killed by walls of water some 40 feet (12 meters) high that raced across thousands of miles of ocean from the earthquake's epicenter, off the northern tip of Sumatra, to Thailand, Sri Lanka, India, and even Somalia in Africa. The quake, which registered 9.0, was so strong that it reportedly disturbed the rotation of the Earth.

27 Viktor Yushchenko takes Ukraine's December 26 presidential rematch with a clear margin of victory. With 98 percent of the vote counted, election officials declare Yushchenko the winner with 52.3 percent of the vote, compared with Prime Minister Viktor Yanukovych's 43.9 percent. Yushchenko, a former prime minister, urges closer relations with the West and political reform. Yanukovych advocated tightening ties with Russia.

2004 UPDATE

The major events of 2004 are summarized in more than 250 alphabetically arranged articles, from "Afghanistan" to "Zoos." Included are Special Reports that offer an in-depth look at subjects ranging from the Olympics to the Iraq War. The Special Reports are found on the following pages.

Afghanistan. Hamid Karzai, head of Afghanistan's interim government since 2001, was elected to a five-year term as president on Oct. 9, 2004. Karzai, Afghanistan's first popularly elected leader, was sworn in on December 7.

Election. Karzai won 55 percent of the roughly 8 million votes cast in the election. The result highlighted the country's troublesome ethnic split. Karzai, a member of the largest ethnic group, the Pashtuns, won most of his votes in Pashtun areas. The runner-up, Yunis Qanooni, won 16 percent of the votes, mostly in Tajik ethnic areas, while third-place Abdul Rashid Dostum took 10 percent, primarily in his Uzbek ethnic area.

Two vice presidents elected on Karzai's ticket, Karim Khalili and Ahmed Zia Massoud, were members of the Hazara and Tajik ethnic groups, respectively. Massoud was the brother of Ahmed Shah Massoud, a legendary guerrilla leader in Afghanistan during its 1979-1989 war against the Soviet Union. Ahmed Zia Massoud and Khalili failed to win many Tajik or Hazara votes for Karzai's ticket.

The election highlighted a split between Karzai's technocrats, who ran the interim government, and warlords, such as Dostum, who emerged as a power after a quarter century of conflict. Despite efforts to disband their private armies, warlords continued to dominate many regions of the country in 2004. Karzai said in July that warlords were the main threat to national progress. The United Nations (UN) said warlords intimidated voters.

The election, which had been postponed twice because of organizational problems, sparked controversy. While a commission of UN and Afghan officials certified the results, some of the 17 presidential candidates running against Karzai accused him of large-scale fraud.

Violence. The election campaign was marked by violence, which was blamed on remnants of the Taliban. The extremist Islamic group had controlled most of Afghanistan until 2001 and sheltered Osama bin Laden, leader of the al-Qa'ida terrorist organization. American-led military action in 2001 ended Taliban control, and bin Laden became a hunted fugitive.

Guerrilla attacks and ambushes in 2004 had left more than 950 people dead in Afghanistan by the time of the October election. Some 30 of the 10,500 United States soldiers in Afghanistan died in the first 10 months of 2004. Most of the soldiers hunted for terrorists, while others worked at pacifying and rebuilding the war-ravaged country. On May 27, a spokesperson for the European Union said the blurring of lines between military and aid activities put the lives of humanitarian relief workers at risk.

Attacks, usually in the Pashtun-inhabited east and south of Afghanistan, targeted workers registering people to vote; those who had gotten registration cards; and foreign aid workers. A single terrorist attack in Kabul, the capital, on August 29 killed nine employees of a firm training Afghan police and providing security for Karzai.

Herat, the primary city in western Afghanistan, was torn by conflict during 2004. On March 21, Mirwais Sadiq, the minister of aviation in Karzai's Cabinet, was killed in fighting. Sadiq was a son of Herat's warlord, Ismail Khan. In August, Khan's forces fought those of Amanullah Khan, another area warlord, until Karzai's government, with help from the U.S. ambassador, Zalmay Khalilzad, restored order. In September, Karzai replaced Khan as governor in Herat, which led to renewed fighting. Offices of the UN and aid agencies in Herat were looted and burned. Some of the 2,300 humanitarian organizations and 337 international aid agencies that worked in Afghanistan after 2001 were driven out by terrorist attacks in 2003 and 2004.

After Taliban attempts to disrupt the election campaign, including attacks aimed at Karzai, the actual voting went off peacefully. No significant attacks were made on polling stations. A U.S. military spokesman said intelligence reports indicated the failure to disrupt the election led to serious disagreements among the Taliban leaders.

Progress. Karzai informed the UN on September 21 that almost 3.5 million refugees had returned to Afghanistan since 2001; that schools had reopened; and that economic conditions were improving. However, aid was desperately needed. Health officials said 45 to 50 percent of the population suffered chronic malnutrition, and one-quarter of all children died before the age of 5.

An international conference held in Berlin in March 2004 ended with pledges of approximately $4.2 billion in aid for Afghanistan over the course of the 2005 fiscal year and a total of $8.2 billion in aid by 2007. Foreign aid made up 94 percent of the budget of Karzai's government.

The conference also coordinated plans to try to limit the growth of opium poppies in Afghanistan. The United Nations reported in 2004 that more than three-quarters of the world's opium supply originated in Afghanistan. In early April, a report by the World Bank, a UN affiliate, declared that many warlords depended upon the opium trade and that the trade accounted for one-third of the country's total economic activity. This limited the government's ability to raise tax revenues and establish a firm financial base upon which to run the country. In November, a UN report warned that Afghanistan was on the verge of becoming a "narco-state," noting that opium production increased 66 percent in 2004.   ■ Henry S. Bradsher

See also **Asia; Terrorism.**

AFRICA

The nations of Africa moved toward greater continental unity on March 18, 2004, with the inauguration of a Pan-African Parliament in Ethiopia's capital, Addis Ababa. The parliament was created as an organ of the African Union (AU), a political and economic association of 53 countries formed in July 2002. The body was to eventually wield wide legislative powers, but during its first five years, the chamber was to exercise an advisory role.

On May 25, 2004, the AU inaugurated its Peace and Security Council, a body functioning much like the United Nations (UN) Security Council, that AU founders hoped would provide stability. Officials said the new council would have the authority to resolve conflicts and to intervene in cases of *genocide* (the systematic extermination of a cultural or racial group) and other crimes against humanity.

AU leaders also endorsed plans to develop a standby, rapid deployment corps to enforce council decisions. The corps was to be brought to full 15,000-member strength by 2010. Political analysts contrasted the emergent AU with its predecessor, the Organization of African Unity (OAU). The OAU, which lacked a security council and member forces, had proved ineffectual in its efforts at crisis intervention.

Censure. Breaking with a longstanding tradition of solidarity among African leaders, the AU executive council on July 4, 2004, adopted a report condemning President Robert Mugabe's government in Zimbabwe for the arbitrary detention and torture of journalists, opposition politicians, and human rights advocates. Mugabe and his ruling party, the Zimbabwe African National Union-Patriotic Front (ZANU-PF), have come under intense international criticism for a variety of alleged human rights abuses.

AU intervention in Darfur. In mid-August, the AU dispatched a small contingent of troops to the Darfur region of western Sudan to protect observers overseeing a shaky cease-fire between the Sudanese government and Darfur rebels. Further dispatches of AU troops brought the total to more than 1,100 by the end of 2004, with plans for total deployment of 3,500 troops by mid-2005.

A conflict between rebel groups and ethnic militias armed and encouraged by Sudan's central government created a humanitarian crisis in Darfur in 2004. According to human rights groups, the fighting left at least 70,000 civilians dead and displaced as many as 1.5 million people who sought shelter in makeshift refugee camps.

AU-sponsored peace talks between representatives of the Darfur rebel groups and the Sudanese government took place during August and October in Abuja, Nigeria. Nigerian President Olusegun Obasanjo, serving as AU chairman, hosted the meetings.

NEPAD. At a February summit meeting in Kigali, Rwanda, nine African heads of state decided that four African nations would undergo "peer reviews" of their governments' performances. The leaders were acting under the provisions of the New Partnership for Africa's Development (NEPAD), a compact in which African countries promise to promote human rights and the rule of law in return for financial assistance from wealthy countries. The leaders at the Kigali summit chose Ghana, Kenya, Mauritius, and Rwanda for peer review. Ghana, the first, underwent its inspection in mid-2004.

Despite the ambitious NEPAD review schedule, officials of some donor countries sharply criticized

A Mauritanian youth surveys a landscape swarming with locusts in August. According to the United Nations Food and Agriculture Organization, Mauritania and other parts of northern Africa and the Middle East were infested with as many as 200,000 locusts per acre in late 2004. The infestation was caused by unusually heavy rains in the normally dry region, UN experts concluded.

the NEPAD initiative in 2004. They charged that NEPAD, with its mission to promote human rights, was not effectively addressing the human rights crisis in Zimbabwe, where they alleged the Mugabe regime was violating NEPAD principles.

The AIDS crisis in Africa continued unabated in 2004. Of the world's 38 million HIV-positive people, 25 million lived in sub-Saharan Africa, the Joint United Nations Program on HIV/AIDS (UNAIDS) reported in July. HIV is the virus that causes AIDS. UNAIDS officials also noted that nearly three-quarters of worldwide AIDS-related deaths occurred in Africa—amounting to the loss of 2.2 million Africans in 2003. Adult infection rates in 2004 varied from less than 1 percent in Mauritania to nearly 40 percent in Botswana.

Inadequate resources continued to hamper organized efforts to combat HIV transmission and to treat infected people, international AIDS experts asserted. UNAIDS officials predicted that, to combat the AIDS crisis effectively, agencies would need four times the current level of international donor funding, which amounted to

$5 billion in 2003. In a speech at the 15th International AIDS Conference in Bangkok, Thailand, in July 2004, UNAIDS head administrator Peter Piot recommended that the international community forgive $15 billion of foreign debt held by African nations and encourage those countries to use the money to fund AIDS programs.

Tsunamis. A magnitude-9.0 earthquake off the northern coast of the Indonesian island of Sumatra on December 26 caused tsunamis that crashed into a number of Asian and African countries. The giant waves left some 100 dead and thousands of others homeless in Somalia. Waves also struck Kenya, the Seychelles, and Tanzania.

Southern Africa. In April, the international community applauded 10 years of democracy and stability in South Africa, where President Thabo Mbeki's ruling African National Congress (ANC) won a second consecutive victory since it first took power in 1994. Prior to 1994, a white-dominated government in South Africa had enforced the policy of *apartheid,* which denied basic civil rights to nonwhites.

Country	Population	Government	Monetary unit*	Foreign trade (million U.S.$)	
				Exports[†]	Imports[†]
Algeria	32,480,000	President Abdelaziz Bouteflika; Prime Minister Ahmed Ouyahia	dinar (72.65 = $1)	24,960	12,420
Angola	14,777,000	President Jose Eduardo dos Santos	readj. kwanza (86.82 = $1)	9,669	4,080
Benin	7,007,000	President Mathieu Kerekou	CFA franc (528.54 = $1)	485	726
Botswana	1,575,000	President Festus Mogae	pula (4.74 = $1)	2,544	1,753
Burkina Faso	12,988,000	President Blaise Compaore	CFA franc (528.54 = $1)	293	634
Burundi	7,154,000	President Domitien Ndayizeye	franc (1,075.20 = $1)	40	128
Cameroon	16,191,000	President Paul Biya	CFA franc (528.54 = $1)	1,873	1,959
Cape Verde	473,000	President Pedro Pires; Prime Minister Jose Maria Pereira Neves	escudo (89.35 = $1)	51	316
Central African Republic	3,967,000	President Francois Bozize	CFA franc (528.54 = $1)	172	136
Chad	8,899,000	President Idriss Deby	CFA franc (528.54 = $1)	365	760
Comoros	631,000	President of the Union Assoumani Azali	franc (403.00 = $1)	28	88
Congo (Brazzaville)	3,401,000	President Denis Sassou-Nguesso	CFA franc (528.54 = $1)	2,293	667
Congo (Kinshasa)	58,103,000	President Joseph Kabila	CFA franc (528.54 = $1)	1,417	933
Cote d'Ivoire (Ivory Coast)	17,381,000	President Laurent Gbagbo	CFA franc (528.54 = $1)	5,299	2,781
Djibouti	658,000	President Ismail Omar Guelleh; Prime Minister Mohamed Dileita Dileita	franc (169.75 = $1)	155	665
Egypt	72,534,000	President Hosni Mubarak; Prime Minister Ahmed Mohamed Nazif	pound (6.24 = $1)	8,759	14,750
Equatorial Guinea	511,000	President Teodoro Obiang Nguema Mbasogo; Prime Minister Miguel Abia Biteo Borico	CFA franc (528.54 = $1)	2,100	1,371
Eritrea	4,037,000	President Isaias Afworki	nafka (13.79 = $1)	56	600
Ethiopia	69,195,000	President Girma Woldegiorgis; Prime Minister Meles Zenawi	birr (8.63 = $1)	537	1,964
Gabon	1,357,000	President El Hadj Omar Bongo; Prime Minister Jean-Francois Ntoutoume-Emane	CFA franc (528.54 = $1)	2,891	1,079
Gambia	1,432,000	Head of State Yahya Jammeh	dalasi (29.50 = $1)	156	271
Ghana	20,087,000	President John Agyekum Kufuor	cedi (9,010.00 = $1)	2,642	3,240
Guinea	8,648,000	President Lansana Conte	franc (2,615.00 = $1)	726	646
Guinea-Bissau	1,319,000	President Henrique Rosa	CFA franc (528.54 = $1)	54	104
Kenya	31,524,000	President Mwai Kibaki	shilling (80.90 = $1)	2,514	3,705
Lesotho	2,297,000	King Letsie III; Prime Minister Pakalitha Mosisili	maloti (6.44 = $1)	450	661

*Exchange rates as of Oct. 1, 2004, or latest available data.   [†]Latest available data.

Country	Population	Government	Monetary unit*	Foreign trade (million U.S.$)	
				Exports[†]	Imports[†]
Liberia	3,415,000	Chairman Gyude Bryant	dollar (1 = $1)	1,079	5,051
Libya	5,771,000	Leader Muammar Muhammad al-Qadhafi; General People's Committee Secretary (Prime Minister) Shukri Muhammad Ghanim	dinar (1.32 = $1)	14,320	6,282
Madagascar	17,856,000	President Marc Ravalomanana	franc (10,372.00 = $1)	700	920
Malawi	11,293,000	President Bingu wa Mutharika	kwacha (108.75 = $1)	455	505
Mali	12,731,000	President Amadou Toumani Toure; Prime Minister Ousmane Issoufi Maiga	CFA franc (528.54 = $1)	915	927
Mauritania	2,995,000	President Maaouya Ould Sid Ahmed Taya	ouguiya (253.60 = $1)	541	860
Mauritius	1,199,000	President Sir Anerood Jugnauth; Prime Minister Paul Berenger	rupee (28.53 = $1)	1,965	2,136
Morocco	32,063,000	King Mohamed VI; Prime Minister Driss Jettou	dirham (8.88 = $1)	8,466	12,750
Mozambique	19,614,000	President Joaquim Alberto Chissano; Prime Minister Luisa Diogo	metical (20,950.00 = $1)	795	1,142
Namibia	1,844,000	President Sam Nujoma; Prime Minister Theo-Ben Gurirab	dollar (6.46 = $1)	1,090	1,371
Niger	12,493,000	President Mamadou Tandja; Prime Minister Hama Amadou	CFA franc (528.54 = $1)	280	400
Nigeria	136,769,000	President Olusegun Obasanjo	naira (132.25 = $1)	21,800	14,540
Rwanda	8,272,000	President Paul Kagame	franc (561.85 = $1)	73	246
Sao Tome and Príncipe	160,000	President Fradique de Menezes	dobra (8,875.00 = $1)	6	30
Senegal	10,403,000	President Abdoulaye Wade; Prime Minister Idrissa Seck	CFA franc (528.54 = $1)	1,230	1,753
Seychelles	84,000	President James Alix Michel	rupee (5.42 = $1)	250	384
Sierra Leone	5,261,000	President Ahmad Tejan Kabbah	leone (2,455.00 = $1)	49	264
Somalia	10,352,000	President Abdullahi Yusuf Ahmed	shilling (2,782.00 = $1)	79	344
South Africa	44,552,000	President Thabo Mvuyelwa Mbeki	rand (6.46 = $1)	36,770	33,890
Sudan	34,056,000	President Umar Hasan Ahmad al-Bashir	dinar (258.64 = $1) pound (2,586.40 = $1)	2,450	2,383
Swaziland	1,030,000	King Mswati III; Prime Minister Absalom Themba Dlamini	lilangeni (6.46 = $1)	906	1,088
Tanzania	38,493,000	President Benjamin William Mkapa; Prime Minister Frederick Sumaye	shilling (1,057.50 = $1)	978	1,674
Togo	5,007,000	President Gnassingbe Eyadema	CFA franc (528.54 = $1)	398	501
Tunisia	9,898,000	President Zine El Abidine Ben Ali; Prime Minister Mohamed Ghannouchi	dinar (1.26 = $1)	8,035	10,300
Uganda	26,418,000	President Yoweri Kaguta Museveni; Prime Minister Apollo Nsibambi	shilling (1,740.00 = $1)	495	1,179
Zambia	11,320,000	President Levy Mwanawasa	kwacha (4,840.00 = $1)	1,039	1,128
Zimbabwe	13,524,000	President Robert Mugabe	dollar (5,300.00 = $1)	1,261	1,691

Zambia's President Levy Mwanawasa stated in June 2004 that he would pardon his predecessor, Frederick Chiluba, of corruption charges if Chiluba were to return at least 70 percent of some $30 million that Chiluba allegedly stole from state coffers while in office. The offer created legal complications in the former president's ongoing trial on charges of corruption in Lusaka, the capital, legal experts said. As the trial continued through 2004, prosecutors were unable to produce witnesses who could definitely link Chiluba with the disappearance of state funds.

On August 9, Zambian Local Government Minister Sylvia Masebo announced that local elections scheduled for November would be postponed until 2006. Noting that "democracy is very expensive," Masebo claimed that Zambia could not afford the $85 million required to mount the elections in 2004. Opposition leaders charged that the government was afraid of losing the elections.

On November 15 and November 16, the Namibian lands minister, Hifikepunye Pohamba, won election by a wide margin to become Namibia's president, and his party, the South West Africa People's Organization (SWAPO), swept three-quarters of the seats in the country's parliament. Pohamba was to replace retiring President Sam Nujoma, the SWAPO leader who ruled Namibia since the country won independence in 1990.

Analysts anticipated that Pohamba, as president, would speed up Namibia's land reform program. The program is designed to buy up lands from white farmers and redistribute them to poor black farmers. In 2004, whites accounted for 6 percent of Namibia's population but owned over half of the country's arable farmland. Some white farmers in mid-2004 alleged that they were being pressured by the government to sell their farms at prices below market value.

Botswana's High Court began hearing a landmark case on July 12 regarding the forceful eviction of the San from the Central Kalahari Game Reserve in the late 1990's and early 2000's. The San sued the Botswana government to regain the right to return to their ancestral lands. The San, sub-Saharan Africa's last nomadic people, have lived as hunter-gatherers in the Kalahari dessert for as long as 20,000 years. In 2004, only about 160 San still lived in the Central Kalahari.

Botswana's President Festus Mogae claimed that the government's forced removal of 2,000 San to 65 resettlement camps between 1997 and 2002 had been altruistically motivated. However, Survival International, a London-based organization that campaigns for indigenous peoples, alleged that the resettlements were conducted to make way for diamond exploration.

West Africa. In Cote d'Ivoire, a French-brokered peace deal, accepted in January 2003 by President Laurent Gbagbo's government in the southern part of the country and rebels in the north, suffered serious setbacks in 2004. Even the presence in Cote d'Ivoire of thousands of French troops, West African peacekeepers, and UN peacekeepers authorized by the Security Council on February 27, failed to deter fighting.

In early November, as a cease-fire renegotiated in July broke down, government jets bombed rebel targets in the north. One of the airstrikes killed at least nine French peacekeepers—apparently by mistake—near the town of Bouake. French forces promptly destroyed two Ivorian jets and several helicopters. As the crisis deepened, the UN Security Council voted on November 15 to impose an arms embargo on Cote d'Ivoire and threatened imposition of sanctions on specific leaders if the factions did not soon re-establish a cease-fire.

On February 6, international donors at a UN conference in New York City pledged $520 million toward reconstruction of Liberia, where a violent, 14-year civil war came to an end in 2003. In April 2004, UN peacekeepers in Liberia began the task of disarming some 40,000 former combatants. Meanwhile, Gyude Bryant, head of the country's interim government, promised democratic elections for 2005.

On July 14, 2004, Nigeria and Cameroon exchanged villages along their contested border as part of a plan to resolve a longstanding dispute. However, the agreement broke down on September 15, when Nigeria failed to transfer the oil-rich Bakassi peninsula to Cameroon as previously mandated in arbitration by the World Court in The Hague, Netherlands. The Nigerian government refused to explain its failure to vacate the peninsula, and the joint Cameroon-Nigeria border commission overseeing the border settlement appealed to UN General Secretary Kofi Annan to mediate.

Central Africa. In Burundi on August 13, some 160 Tutsi men, women, and children were massacred in a refugee camp near the country's border with the Democratic Republic of Congo (DRC), also known as Congo (Kinshasa). Burundian Hutu extremists who opposed a 2001 power-sharing pact between Burundi's Hutu majority and Tutsi minority claimed responsibility.

In neighboring Rwanda, President Paul Kagame, from the minority Tutsi tribe, claimed that Rwandan Hutu insurgents were raiding his country in 2004 from bases in the DRC. Both Burundi and Rwanda threatened to invade DRC territory to hunt down the killers. The chain of events threatened to destabilize the whole central African region, which had been disrupted during the 1998 to 2003 by a civil war in the DRC that cost some 3 million lives.

In 1994, Hutu-Tutsi tensions erupted in a brutal killing spree by Hutu extremists that led to the genocide of up to 1 million Tutsis and moderate Hutus in Rwanda. On April 7, 2004, Rwanda's people observed three minutes of silence in remembrance of the dead. Meanwhile, prosecutors at a special UN tribunal in Arusha, Tanzania, continued proceedings against former Rwandan officials accused of participation in the 1994 genocide. As 2004 progressed, more defendants were convicted and sentenced.

On July 9, the Kimberley Process expelled Congo (Brazzaville) from the multibillion-dollar world diamond trade. The Kimberley Process is a UN-backed body set up to prevent diamond revenues from being used to fund wars and terrorism in Africa. Without a license issued by the Kimberley Process, a country is unable to engage in legal diamond trade. According to Kimberley officials, Congo's license was revoked because the country had been exporting vastly more diamonds than it produced, raising suspicions that it was funneling "blood diamonds"—diamonds mined to fund rebel movements.

Eastern Africa and the Horn. In October, UN officials voiced fresh concerns over the deadlocked boundary dispute between Eritrea and Ethiopia following reports that the Ethiopian government was settling Ethiopians in the border town of Badme. An independent international border commission in April 2002 had awarded the town to Eritrea. From 1998 to 2000, Ethiopia and Eritrea had fought a war at the cost of 100,000 lives. Throughout 2004, a force of 4,200 UN peacekeepers continued to patrol a buffer zone between the two countries.

On October 10, a 275-member transitional parliament of factional Somali leaders meeting in Nairobi, Kenya, elected Abdullahi Yusuf Ahmed as Somalia's president, the country's first national leader in 13 years. Since a warlord-instigated civil war broke out in Somalia in 1991, the country has effectively been without a functioning central government. Plans called for the parliament to be moved to Mogadishu, Somalia's capital, when the security situation there permitted.

Nobel award. The Nobel Prize Committee announced on Oct. 8, 2004, that Wangari Maathai was the winner of the Nobel Peace Prize for 2004. Maathai, a Kenyan environmentalist, led a movement to prevent soil erosion by planting millions of trees in Kenya. She was the first African woman to win the Nobel peace award.

■ Simon Baynham

See also **AIDS; Nobel Prizes; People in the news** (Wangari Maathai); **United Nations;** and the various African country articles.

Agriculture. Generally favorable global weather boosted world production of grains and cotton to record levels in 2004. In the United States, harvests of corn, soybeans, cotton, and rice set new records. Trade in U.S. and Canadian beef was suspended for much of the year. In each country, the discovery of a single case of bovine spongiform encephalopathy (BSE)—mad cow disease—in 2003 had shut down beef exports.

World crop production. According to a U.S. Department of Agriculture (USDA) report released in November 2004, the world's wheat producers harvested a record 618 million metric tons in 2004, a 12-percent increase over the 2003 harvest. Ukraine, Russia, and Kazakhstan together harvested 70 million metric tons of wheat, 42 percent above the drought-reduced crop of 2003. The 2004 wheat harvest in the 25 member countries of the European Union (EU-25) came in at 135 million metric tons, 24 percent above the 2003 crop. Among major wheat producers, only Australia and the United States produced smaller wheat crops in 2004 than in 2003.

Production of small grains—corn, barley, sorghum, and oats—amounted to a record-setting 990 million metric tons, up 9 percent from 2003. The United States, Argentina, the EU-25, Southeast Asia, and China all scored production gains in 2004.

Oilseed production, including soybeans, sunflower seeds, cottonseed, rapeseed, and peanuts, totaled 390 million metric tons. The big producers—the United States, Argentina, Brazil, and China—all brought in harvests well above 2003 levels. In the EU-25, rapeseed production in 2004 reached 14.5 million metric tons, an increase of 3.5 million over 2003 levels.

Large rice crops in the United States and China boosted the global rice harvest in 2004 to 398 million metric tons. China's production increased by 12 million to 126 million metric tons, accounting for one-third of the world rice crop. Japan, a country the size of California, harvested 8 million metric tons of rice in 2004, compared with the U.S. harvest of 7 million metric tons.

World cotton production in 2004 hit 114 million bales, up 20 percent from the 2003 record crop. One bale is equivalent to 480 pounds (217 kilograms) of cotton. The 2004 increase was largely due to record crops in the United States, India, Pakistan, and Turkey. China, with a 2004 harvest of 30 million bales, held on to its distinction as the world's largest cotton producer.

U.S. crop production. Farmers in the United States produced a record 11.7-billion-bushel corn crop in 2004, 15 percent above the 2003 harvest. The U.S. soybean crop also set a record in 2004, coming in at 3.11 billion bushels, 27 percent above the 2003 harvest. U.S. cotton growers produced 23 million bales, an increase of 18 percent over the 2003 crop.

Soybean fungus. On Nov. 10, 2004, USDA officials announced the discovery of the soybean rust fungus (*Phakospora pachyrhizi*) in Louisiana. Soon afterward, the fungus was detected in other states in the lower Mississippi Valley. The fungus attacks leaves of the soybean plant, weakening them and reducing crop yield, but it does not taint the beans themselves. Dispersed by wind, the fungus began spreading from its native Australian habitat more than 30 years ago. USDA officials recommended spraying affected soybean fields with fungicides.

GM crops. Farmers in the United States continued to embrace genetically modified (GM) crops of corn, soybeans, and cotton. GM crops are designed to resist herbicides or insects—or both. U.S. plantings of GM crops in 2004 accounted for 46 percent of the nation's corn acreage, up 6 percent from 2003; 86 percent of soybean acreage, up 5 percent from 2003; and 76 percent of cotton acreage, up 3 percent from 2003. United States farmers in 2004 planted a total of 147 million acres in GM crops.

In January, the International Society for the Acquisition of Agri-Biotech Applications—an organization that promotes agricultural biotechnologies in developing countries—reported that farmers in 18 countries planted GM crops on 167 million acres (75.6 million hectares) in 2003. That acreage marked a 15-percent increase over 2002.

In May 2004, the Food and Agricultural Organization of the United Nations endorsed the role of biotechnology in feeding the world's growing population. The organization advocated research to develop GM varieties for cassava, millet, sorghum, and other crops commonly used as food staples in developing countries.

GM wheat shelved. Officials of Monsanto Corporation of St. Louis, Missouri, announced in May 2004 that the company was suspending plans to market a GM variety of wheat that researchers had developed to be herbicide-resistant. The Monsanto officials cited consumer resistance and adverse market forces as reasons for their decision. According to analysts, international consumers were much more resistant to acceptance of GM wheat, which is used primarily in human food products, than to crops used primarily in animal feed or for other purposes.

BSE. In December 2003, USDA officials learned that a 7-year-old Holstein dairy cow slaughtered in Washington state was infected with BSE, a degenerative disease of the nervous system. Further investigation determined that the cow was born and infected in Alberta, Canada.

Customers of U.S. exports in Japan, South Korea, Mexico, and other countries immediately stopped buying U.S. beef. Export sales of U.S. beef and beef products, which had totaled $3.86 billion in 2003, dropped by 80 percent in 2004.

To restore confidence in the nation's beef industry, Secretary Ann M. Veneman of the Department of Agirculture announced on Dec. 30, 2003, an expanded BSE testing program on U.S. cattle. The USDA extended BSE testing on high-risk, older animals from 20,000 head per year to 260,000 head. As of late 2004, no more animals in U.S. cattle herds had tested positive for BSE.

In March, Mexico reopened its market to some U.S. beef products, including boneless beef. In October, officials of Japan and the United States signed a framework agreement that was to pave the way for resumption of U.S. beef exports to Japan, probably some time in 2005. According to the agreement, the USDA was to help U.S. beef producers implement a Beef Export Verification (BEV) system, in which all beef products for export would be verifiable as coming from animals no more than 20 months in age.

Canadian beef producers continued to experience hardship in 2004 due to BSE-inspired export bans. In June, Statistics Canada reported that Canada's 2003 farm income was at its lowest level in 25 years due to the bans on beef exports and several years of drought in major agricultural regions.

Trade. On July 31, 2004, members of the World Trade Organization (WTO) agreed to move forward on improving market access and lowering agricultural subsidies worldwide. The WTO oversees global trade agreements and arbitrates disputes among member countries. According to some economists, farm subsidies in highly developed economies, such as those of the United States and Western Europe, render agricultural producers in many developing countries unable to compete in world markets.

The WTO ruled on September 8 that U.S. government payments to cotton growers exceeded limits to which the United States had previously agreed. U.S. trade officials said they planned to appeal the ruling, which if upheld, would require changes in U.S. farm support programs. A decision on the appeal was expected in 2005.

On Nov. 22, 2004, the USDA projected that agricultural exports would reach $62 billion in 2004, surpassing the 1996 record of $59.8 billion. China was the largest market for U.S. farm products in 2004, accounting for $6 billion in sales of soybeans, cotton, wheat, hides, and skins.

Food aid. The United States donated 3.72 million metric tons of food to countries around the world in 2004. The donations were valued at $1.1 billion.   ■ Patricia Peak Klintberg

See also **Canada; Food; International Trade.**

AIDS. Record numbers of people worldwide are contracting HIV, the virus that causes AIDS, and dying of this disease, despite international efforts to halt the spread of the HIV/AIDS epidemic, according to a July 2004 report by the Joint United Nations Programme on HIV/AIDS (UNAIDS). In its latest report, issued every two years, UNAIDS said that it had recorded 4.8 million new cases of HIV infection and 2.9 million deaths from AIDS in 2003. In addition, 37.8 million people were living with the virus, the highest number ever recorded.

UNAIDS reported that infection rates had risen in all areas of the world, with countries in eastern Europe and East Asia experiencing the fastest growth. The report also charted the rise in the proportion of women infected with HIV—nearly 50 percent of all those living with the virus in 2004, compared with 41 percent in 1997.

According to the report, only 7 percent of HIV-positive people in low- and middle-income countries were receiving the drugs they needed. Fewer than one in five people at risk of contracting the virus had access to prevention services.

U.S. rates. The number of people living with HIV in the United States continued to climb, UNAIDS reported, from 900,000 in 2001 to 950,000 in 2003. African Americans accounted for half of all new U.S. infections, the report revealed.

Effective anti-HIV "cocktail." Health officials in 2004 heralded findings from the first studies comparing the effectiveness of various combinations of anti-HIV drugs used to treat people who have become newly infected with the virus. Two separate studies found that a combination of zidovudine (also known as AZT), lamivudine (3TC), and efavirenz (EFV) worked more quickly and for longer periods to keep the virus from multiplying than did other anti-HIV "cocktails."

The first study was reported in 2003 by a team of U.S. and Italian researchers. The second study, which appeared in April 2004, was led by Roy M. Gulick, director of the Cornell HIV Clinical Trials Unit at Weill Medical College in New York City.

Even before the publication of the studies' results, the AZT-3TC-EFV cocktail ranked as one of the most prescribed anti-HIV treatment regimens in the United States. In 2002, the World Health Organization, a UN agency, recommended the combined use of the three drugs as part of a plan to simplify the treatment of HIV-infected people in poor countries. ■ Barbara A. Mayes

See also **Africa; Drugs; Public health and safety; South Africa.**

Air pollution. See Environmental pollution.

Alabama. See State government.

Alaska. See State government.

Albania. In July 2004, Albania's ruling Socialist Party and the country's chief opposition, the Democratic Party, agreed to reform Albania's electoral law. Changes in the law were advocated by the European Union (EU) and the Organization for Security and Cooperation in Europe (OSCE), an association of more than 50 Eastern and Western nations that works for international security. In October 2003, OSCE election monitors reported numerous irregularities in local elections in Albania. The country was scheduled to hold parliamentary elections in mid-2005.

In September 2004, Albanian and EU officials signed a framework agreement. The agreement provided a legal basis for Albania to participate as a nonmember in various EU programs.

Economists reported that Albania's gross domestic product (GDP)—the value of all goods and services produced in a country in one year—grew by 6 percent in 2004, about the same rate of growth as in 2003. However, the Food and Agriculture Organization (FAO), a United Nations agency that works to defeat hunger, reported in October 2004 that more than half of Albania's population lived on $2 a day and that one in four Albanians survived on less than $1 a day. Albanian leaders disputed the FAO findings.

■ Sharon L. Wolchik

See also **Europe.**

Algeria. In January 2004, Algeria was elected one of the nonpermanent members of the United Nations (UN) Security Council. The Security Council consists of 5 permanent and 10 nonpermanent members.

Abdallah Baali, the Algerian Permanent Representative on the Security Council, supported a UN resolution in August that called for a more active role for the international community in dealing with the growing humanitarian and political crisis in Sudan. In September, Baali abstained from voting on a resolution calling for the withdrawal of Syrian troops from Lebanon and for noninterference by Syria in the Lebanese presidential election. The resolution, however, passed.

President Bouteflika re-elected. President Abdelaziz Bouteflika, of the National Democratic Assembly, was re-elected to a five-year term in April. Bouteflika won with 85 percent of the vote in his victory over five other candidates. Former Prime Minister Ali Benflis, of the National Liberation Front, finished second, with 6.4 percent of the vote.

Benflis claimed there was massive fraud in the election. However, this claim was denied by Bruce George, the designated monitor of the election on behalf of the Organization for Security and Cooperation in Europe, an international associa-

Algerian President Abdelaziz Bouteflika speaks at an election rally in the capital, Algiers, in April. Later in the month, Bouteflika was re-elected, with 85 percent of the vote, to a five-year term.

tion of European countries dedicated to improving regional security. George was 1 of more than 120 foreign observers monitoring the election. He declared that Bouteflika's election had been fair and free, noting that it was "one of the best-conducted elections, not just in Algeria, but in Africa and much of the Arab world."

Mixed economic news. Algeria's economy benefited from high oil and natural gas revenues in 2004. Economists expected that Algeria's *gross domestic product* (GDP, the value of all goods and services produced in a country in a given year) would grow by 6.4 percent in 2004. Algeria's foreign reserves were expected to rise much higher in 2004 than the $30-billion mark achieved in late 2003, and the nation's external debt in 2004 fell to its lowest level in a decade.

Despite positive economic figures, unemployment remained high in 2004—at least as high as the official figure of 30 percent—and a large black market continued to thrive. Intense social and political unrest continued to plague the Kabylie region, east of the capital, Algiers. Unemployment was especially high in this region.

■ Mary-Jane Deeb

See also **Africa; Lebanon; Sudan; United Nations.**

Angola. See Africa.
Animal. See Biology; Conservation; Zoos.

Anthropology. Scientists reported in October 2004 that they had excavated skeletons of eight individuals—each about only 3.5 feet (1.1 meters) tall—in a cave on the Indonesian island of Flores. Paleoanthropologist Peter Brown of the University of New England in Australia and his colleagues described the dwarf-sized individuals as a previously unknown species of human, which they called *Homo floresiensis.* They said this species lived from before 30,000 years ago until at least 18,000 years ago. The scientists suggested that *H. floresiensis* evolved from a population of *Homo erectus* that became isolated on Flores.

Brown's group noted that the skeletons were the first evidence of dwarfism in *hominids* (humans, human ancestors, and their relatives). In dwarfism, an isolated species becomes smaller over time as competition for a limited food supply favors individuals with diminished energy requirements.

The Flores hominids had brains that were approximately the size of chimpanzee brains. However, the investigators discovered charred bones of dwarf elephants and other animals with the hominid skeletons, as well as a variety of such stone tools as blades, points, and scrapers. This finding led the scientists to conclude that *H. floresiensis* possessed the intelligence to selectively hunt and cook its prey.

Some scientists expressed doubts that the new find was a member of the hominid genus *Homo;* others said it might be just a deformed *H. sapiens.* Scientists hoped further research would clarify the nature of the Flores specimens.

Beginning of bipedalism. Researchers reported in September that *bipedalism* (walking on two legs) among hominids may have begun as early as 6 million years ago. Mechanical engineer Karol Galik of Allegheny General Hospital in Pittsburgh, Pennsylvania, described his teams' study of a fossilized *femur* (thigh bone) that French investigators had discovered in 2000 in the Tugen Hills of northern Kenya. The bone belonged to the species *Orrorin tugenensis.*

Galik and his colleagues made *computed tomography* (CT) scans of the head and neck of the 6-million-year-old femur. CT is an X-ray system used to produce detailed three-dimensional images of bones and organs inside the body. The images and measurements of the femur's head and neck revealed that the structure of the bone was much more similar to that of bipeds than that of apes, which amble about on four limbs.

The Pittsburgh researchers said that the *O. tugenensis* fossil might represent the oldest evidence of hominid bipedalism. They noted, however, that the teeth and jaws of this species were rather primitive. This suggested to them that bipedalism, rather than skull or facial features, may have been the earliest characteristic that distinguished human ancestors from their apelike relatives.

Roots of the human family. Six fossilized teeth, dated to between 5.6 million and 5.8 million years ago, may represent one of the earliest species in the human family tree, according to a report in March 2004. An international team led by anthropologist Yohannes Haile-Selassie of the Cleveland Museum of Natural History in Ohio described the teeth, which had been uncovered in geological deposits in Ethiopia in 2002.

The teeth, noted Haile-Selassie, show unique features in the interlocking nature of the canines and premolars. He said these features were intermediate in development between apes and humans. In apes, this dental region is dominated by a "cutting" complex in which the back edge of the upper canine becomes sharpened as it rubs against the lower premolar. In humans, by contrast, these teeth lack such a self-sharpening mechanism.

Haile-Selassie assigned the teeth to the species *Ardipithecus kadabba.* He proposed that *A. kadabba* lived very close in time to the proposed common ancestor of the African ape lineage and the human lineage.

■ Donald C. Johanson

See also **Archaeology.**

Archaeology. A brewery more than 1,000 years old was discovered at Cerro Baul, a mountaintop site of the Wari empire in southern Peru, in July 2004. The Wari ruled over most of what is now Peru from about A.D. 600 to 1000. Archaeologists and anthropologists from the University of Florida in Gainesville and The Field Museum in Chicago said they excavated *sherds* (pottery fragments) of at least 20 large ceramic vats, which each had been capable of holding 10 to 15 gallons (38 to 57 liters). The investigators also found seeds from the molle pepper plant at the site. They said berries from this plant were used to make chicha, a spicy alcoholic drink similar to beer.

The team described how the Wari destroyed the brewery in a ceremonial "closing rite." After setting the building on fire, the Wari threw their drinking mugs into the flames. In addition, the Wari placed several necklaces of semiprecious stones on the burning embers. The researchers noted that these items were preserved among the collapsed walls of the ancient brewery.

Thracian gold mask. In August 2004, an archaeologist excavating a tomb near the town of Stara Zagora in southern Bulgaria uncovered a pure gold mask from the 300's B.C. Georgi Kitov of the Institute of Archaeology and Museum in Sofia, the capital of Bulgaria, discovered the mask in a burial mound known as Goljamata Kosmatka. According to Kitov, the bearded and mustached man depicted on the mask is King Seutus III, ruler of the Thracians.

The Thracians lived on the fringes of the ancient Greek and Roman civilizations, in what is today Bulgaria and parts of Romania, Turkey, Macedonia, and Greece. Seutus is most famous for leading the Thracian tribes and their allies in a successful revolt against their Macedonian overlords.

Along with the mask, Kitov excavated more than 70 other artifacts. These finds included a bronze head, silver and bronze vessels, and a golden ring, believed to portray a rower from the ancient Olympic Games.

Viking cemetery. A metal-detector enthusiast's discovery of two elaborate copper brooches in March 2004 led archaeologists to an ancient Viking cemetery in northwestern England. The cemetery was reported in September by the Museums, Libraries and Archives Council, a national history and preservation agency headquartered in London. Excavators also uncovered weapons, spurs, a bridle, a bracelet, and various other artifacts.

The burials, of four men and two women, date from the A.D. 900's, when Vikings were beginning to integrate themselves into English life. The bodies were interred in an east-west

A bearded mummy from an ancient cemetery in Siberia lies in a laboratory at the Russian Academy of Sciences in the Urals. Archaeologists reported the discovery of this and several other 1,000-year-old mummies in January. The mummies, which had been naturally preserved in *permafrost* (frozen soil), were wrapped in the skins of reindeer, bear, and other animals. Some of the mummies also had copper masks or plates on them.

orientation, apparently following an early Christian tradition. However, some of the goods buried with the men, including swords, spears, and knives, reflected the Viking concept of a warrior's afterlife. The mixture of religious practices is not surprising, noted the archaeologists, because the burials date close to the time of King Olaf I of Norway, who converted to Christianity in about A.D. 995.

The finely crafted brooches and other items indicated that the people interred in the graves were from the upper levels of society. The archaeologists said the burials provide a window on a pivotal time in the transition of Vikings from raiders to settlers.

Human sacrifice in Egypt. The first firm evidence of human sacrificial burials in ancient Egypt was reported in March 2004 by a team of archaeologists led by David O'Connor of New York University in New York City. The archaeologists excavated five of six tombs next to a wall surrounding the funeral chapel of King Aha, the first ruler of the First Dynasty, which many Egyptologists date from 2950 to 2775 B.C.

The tombs had been plundered in antiquity, but the remaining artifacts included seals with Aha's name, finely crafted wooden coffins, and jewelry made from such imported materials as lapis lazuli and ivory. These artifacts, as well as the closeness of the tombs to the king's funeral complex, suggested to the investigators that the dead were courtiers or other important officials at the king's court. The archaeologists said the evidence indicated that the individuals were all killed at the same time to accompany the king into the afterlife.

50,000-year-old Americans? Excavations along the Savannah River in South Carolina suggest that humans may have lived in North America tens of thousands of years earlier than generally believed. Archaeologist Albert Goodyear of the University of South Carolina reported in November 2004 that he had dated sediment containing possible stone tools at the so-called Topper site to at least 50,000 years ago. Goodyear excavated the sediment from beneath a level in which he had previously found stone tools from the 11,000-year-old Clovis culture—the oldest widely accepted culture in North America.

The 50,000-year-old date of the sediment had not yet been confirmed by other researchers at the end of 2004. Furthermore, some researchers believed that the stone items in the sediment might have been formed by natural processes, rather than human hands.

Rancher Waldo Wilcox became an instant archaeological hero in June, when it was reported that he had sold his family's ranch in eastern Utah to a public trust, which then turned the title over to the state of Utah. The vast ranch includes hundreds of immaculately preserved sites associated with the Fremont people, whose culture peaked between about A.D. 1000 and 1250. ■ Mark Rose

See also **Anthropology.**

Architecture.
The largest public design competition in American history—with more than 5,000 submissions—ended in January 2004. A 13-member jury selected Michael Arad, an architect with the New York City Housing Authority, and landscape architect Peter Walker to design the World Trade Center Memorial in New York City. The memorial will commemorate the 2,749 victims of the terrorist attacks on the twin towers on Sept. 11, 2001.

The winning design, called "Reflecting Absence," features a paved stone field surrounding two large reflecting pools, which mark the footprints of the towers. From this field, visitors descend to a meditative space framed by curtains of water and a ribbon of names of the dead. "I hope I will be able to create a place where we may all grieve and find meaning," said Arad.

Museum of Modern Art renovation. The $424-million renovation and expansion of the Museum of Modern Art in New York City was unveiled on Nov. 21, 2004. Japanese architect Yoshio Taniguchi wove elements of the previous 1939 and 1956 buildings into an intricate new composition that doubles the size of the original museum and expands Philip Johnson's popular outdoor sculpture garden. From the galleries and concourses, visitors see new and surprising views of adjacent buildings and the Manhattan skyline.

Although most critics generally praised this new openness and transparency, many felt that the new galleries were too large and stark.

The National Museum of the American Indian, which cost $220 million and was 12 years in the making, opened in September on the Mall in Washington, D.C. Architect Douglas Cardinal, a Blackfoot Indian, created a bold Kosota limestone building with no straight lines, as though it had been sculpted by wind and water instead of humans. A large rotunda serves as a kind of observatory for tracking the movements of the sun and stars. Beyond are galleries, meeting rooms, spaces for traditional story-telling and dancing, and a restaurant serving Native American food. The entire structure is surrounded by a creek and wetland that evoke the original site.

The William J. Clinton Presidential Center in Little Rock, Arkansas, designed by Polshek Partnership Architects of New York City, is the most architecturally ambitious presidential library since John F. Kennedy's 40 years ago. Dedicated in November, the museum portion manages to be delicate and weighty, elegant and inviting, picking up the beefy industrial details of nearby bridges, yet wrapping them with a glass gallery that offers stunning views of the city and the Arkansas River. An attached wing contains the archives, including 80 million pages of presidential paper and 2 million photographs.

The Oklahoma City Federal Building, the replacement for the Alfred P. Murrah Building destroyed in a 1995 terrorist attack, opened in December 2004. The building projects security and permanence without putting off employees and the public. Architect Carol Ross Barney designed a U-shaped, three-story building with a no-nonsense facade that opens to a landscaped courtyard and garden. Many offices have uninterrupted views of the memorial to the bombing victims, a risky but ultimately popular decision. The employees who initially wanted no part of the new building have moved in, a powerful statement of commitment and resolve in the face of horrific tragedy.

The Seattle Central Library, designed by Dutch architect Rem Koolhaas and the Office for Metropolitan Architecture, was billed as "the first great library of the 21st century" upon its opening in May. True or not, the planners certainly reinvented and reinterpreted many basic library functions. The main reference room has become a gigantic information trading floor—likened to "a stock exchange of ideas"—while the book stacks are reconfigured as a zigzagging ramp that rises through the building's center. The library's gyrating steel-and-glass form adds a dramatic punctuation mark to Seattle's staid skyline.

Frank Gehry's Stata Center. For sheer

Architect Yoshio Taniguchi's renovation of New York City's Museum of Modern Art, which opened in November, weaves elements of previous buildings into an intricate new composition that offers views of the museum's famed sculpture garden framed by the Manhattan skyline.

bravura, nothing tops Frank Gehry's Ray and Maria Stata Center at the Massachusetts Institute of Technology (MIT). The Center, which opened in May, is the latest addition to the school's $1-billion architectural makeover. A stunning collage of swooping forms and tipping towers, the $300-million building houses MIT's computer science and artificial intelligence departments. The interior spaces are open, accessible, and decorated with intertwined bridges and staircases that, according to the school's dean, "enable new intersections of thought and ideas to happen."

Awards. The 2004 Pritzker Prize, the "Nobel Prize" of architecture, was presented to Iraqi-born architect Zaha Hadid, whose radical geometries and bold use of materials have produced both passionate admirers and loud dissenters. The Rosenthal Center for Contemporary Art in Cincinnati, Ohio, is her most important building in the United States to date.

The 2004 American Institute of Architects Gold Medal, the most prestigious U.S. architectural award, went to the late Samuel Mockbee. Mockbee's most enduring achievement is the Auburn University Rural Studio in Hale County, Alabama, where students learn to design utilitarian structures out of ordinary materials for the poor and dispossessed.　■ David Dillon

See also **Art; Building and construction; Indian, American; News bytes.**

Argentina. In August 2004, Argentine President Nestor Kirchner and International Monetary Fund (IMF) Managing Director Rodrigo de Rato reached agreement on a process for restructuring Argentina's foreign debt. The IMF, a United Nations affiliate that assists nations experiencing financial difficulties, agreed to allow Argentina to set aside debt repayments until the Kirchner administration developed a fair formula for compensating foreign bondholders. President Kirchner insisted that the IMF stay out of negotiations with these bondholders, who held more than $100 billion in defaulted Argentine debt.

Anti-IMF protests. Argentines took to the streets repeatedly in 2004 to support President Kirchner in his hard-line approach with the IMF. During the August talks between Kirchner and de Rato, hundreds of people burned tires in front of the presidential palace and economy ministry in Buenos Aires, the capital, to show their disapproval of the IMF's initial demands for full repayments to bondholders.

IMF admits mistakes. In July, the IMF released a report critical of its own inaction during the period leading up to the Argentine economic collapse of 2001. By failing to help Argentina at that crucial moment, the report noted, the IMF had forced the country to default on its public debt repayments; abandon the linkage of its currency to the United States dollar; and impose draconian limits on withdrawals from personal bank accounts. Argentine officials blamed these measures for pushing millions of Argentines into poverty in 2001 and 2002, as the country's economy suffered through the worst depression in its history.

Economic recovery. As the Argentine economy recovered in 2004, government economists predicted that exports would increase by 14 percent during the year, reaching a record value of $33.5 billion. They credited much of this growth to high prices for oil and record harvests for soybeans; harvests had increased in size because of the widespread use of genetically modified seed in Argentina.

The corporation Swift Armour S.A. Argentina, the nation's largest meat products company, led the boost in Argentina's exports. In 2004, Swift Armour expected to export beef products worth more than $200 million to 70 countries.

With the economy showing signs of recovery and a resolution of the national debt problem in sight, a growing number of foreign investors returned to Argentina in 2004. Such prestigious banks as Citigroup Inc. and JP Morgan Chase & Co., both of New York City, competed to underwrite new bond issues. Such bonds helped Argentine companies, including the communications giant Telecom Argentina S.A., restructure their debts.

War on corruption. A federal judge ordered a freeze on the personal assets of former President Carlos Saul Menem in February. The move, which was part of an ongoing aggressive war on government corruption, followed the discovery that Menem failed to declare at least $500,000 in a Swiss bank account.

Acquittals in bombing. The trial of four former Argentine police officers and a car thief accused of complicity in the 1994 bombing of a Jewish community center in Buenos Aires ended in acquittals in September 2004. The anti-Semitic attack had left 85 people dead and more than 300 others wounded.

The acquittals meant that the case remained unsolved—despite the longest and most complex trial in Argentine history. The proceedings had lasted three years and involved testimony by more than 1,000 witnesses.

Museum of torture. In March, President Kirchner announced that a "museum of memory" would be established at the site of the former Navy Mechanics School in Buenos Aires. Thousands of Argentines had been tortured at the school during the country's 1976 to 1983 military dictatorship. ■ Nathan A. Haverstock

See also **Latin America.**

Arizona. See **State government.**

Arkansas. See **State government.**

Armed forces. United States military affairs in 2004 were dominated by the Iraq War and efforts by the administration of U.S. President George W. Bush to restore stability to Iraq and install a democratic government. One year after the military phase of the war to topple Saddam Hussein was declared over in 2003, more than 150,000 U.S. troops remained stationed in Iraq and engaged in battling an expanding insurgency.

Casualties mount. Although large areas of Iraq remained peaceful during 2004, the guerrilla insurgency against the U.S. armed forces and the interim Iraqi government intensified in Baghdad, the capital, and several other population centers, causing a steady increase in U.S. casualties. On September 7, the U.S. death toll reached 1,000. Many of the deaths were the result of ambushes using "improvised explosive devices," bombs buried along convoy routes taken by U.S. troops.

The war forced the Department of Defense to call thousands of members of Army Reserve and National Guard units to active duty and to deploy active units from other trouble spots to Iraq. On May 18, the Defense Department announced that a brigade from the Army's 2nd Infantry Division in South Korea would be sent to Iraq.

After an upsurge of fighting in Al Fallujah and other cities in early April, Secretary of Defense Donald H. Rumsfeld announced that approximately 21,000 troops scheduled to return to the United States after their one-year tours of duty would remain in Iraq until July. The decision affected nearly 12,000 troops from the First Armored Division, 3,200 troops from an armored cavalry regiment, and 6,000 National Guard and reserve members from 20 states. The Army also began recalling to active duty approximately 5,600 soldiers from the Individual Ready Reserve to fill shortages in Iraq, including in military police and civil affairs positions. Members of the Individual Ready Reserve had military training, had served previously in the reserves, and had some period of a military obligation remaining.

On April 21, General Richard Myers, chairman of the Joint Chiefs of Staff, cautioned members of the U.S. Congress that the high monetary cost of the war in Iraq and combat operations in Afghanistan was rapidly depleting the $87 billion appropriated in 2003 to pay for the war. Defense Department officials said that they would request another $50 billion in funding for Iraq and Afghanistan in 2005.

While regular forces bore the brunt of the Iraq fatalities, the mounting deaths of reserve personnel had a significant impact on recruiting. On Sept. 23, 2004, Defense Department officials confirmed that the National Guard would fall short of its 56,000 person annual recruiting goal by approximately 5,000 soldiers.

With some 135,000 U.S. troops scheduled to remain in Iraq at least until the end of 2005, critics of the war argued that a return to the military draft was inevitable. President Bush ruled out a draft, saying that the military had enough troops to win in Iraq and Afghanistan and keep the peace in Europe, South Korea, and other nations.

By the end of 2004, the Defense Department had 150,000 troops stationed in Iraq and another 20,000 troops stationed in Afghanistan. More than 1,300 Americans soldiers had died in Iraq, and more than 8,000 others had been wounded in action. Casualties in Afghanistan totaled 150 dead since 2001 and approximately 400 others wounded.

Al Fallujah. On Nov. 8, 2004, U.S. forces and Iraqi troops launched an assault against several thousand insurgents occupying the Sunni Muslim stronghold of Al Fallujah, a city west of Baghdad, the capital. The offensive was the largest since the occupation in Iraq began in 2003.

After a week of heavy door-to-door combat, U.S. military commanders declared that Al Fallujah had been cleared. More than 50 U.S. soldiers and Marines died in the Al Fallujah fighting, and an estimated 1,200 insurgents were killed.

In the days following the first assault on Al Fallujah, a counteroffensive erupted in the northern Iraqi city of Mosul, Baghdad, and various cities in the Sunni Triangle north and west of Baghdad. Iraqi and U.S. soldiers countered by conducting a series of defensive strikes on suspected rebel targets.

Iraq prison scandal. Abuse of Iraqi prisoners at the Abu Ghraib prison near Baghdad came to public attention on April 28, 2004, when a national television network aired shocking photographs of prisoners being physically abused and humiliated by military guards.

On August 24, a Defense Department review panel released a report citing "a failure of military leadership and discipline" at all levels of the military and civilian chain of command. The report faulted Secretary of Defense Rumsfeld for pressuring the military to use tougher interrogation techniques but recommended that Rumsfeld should not be dismissed.

Another report by three senior U.S. Army generals, released on August 25, faulted several senior officers for failing to adequately supervise the situation. Lieutenant General Ricardo S. Sanchez, the military commander in Iraq at the time, was criticized for failing to take aggressive corrective measures after he became aware of the extent of the abuses in November 2003. The report also implicated senior military intelligence officials in charge of the prison for allegedly condoning the abuses.

More than 900 pairs of combat boots dot the lawn of the Vermont Statehouse in Montpelier in August. The boots represented each soldier killed in Iraq between March 2003 and August 2004. A tag with the name, rank, and hometown of a soldier was attached to each pair.

Seven enlisted members of a reserve military police company from Maryland were court-martialed in 2004 and charged with conspiracy, dereliction of duty, assault, cruelty toward prisoners, and indecent acts in connection with the scandal. Attorneys for the accused soldiers claimed that they were following orders from military intelligence officers in charge of the prison. The first defendant was found guilty in October.

Troop redeployment. President Bush announced a sweeping repositioning of overseas U.S. military forces on August 16. The realignment primarily affects soldiers and their families in Europe. Under the plan, approximately 70,000 of the 230,000 troops stationed overseas are to return to the United States by 2014. About 100,000 military families and civilian defense employees are also to return to the United States. Hundreds of U.S. military installations in Western Europe are to close and be replaced by smaller bases and training camps in such Eastern European countries as Bulgaria, Hungary, Poland, and Romania. A significant number of the 38,000 American troops in South Korea also are to be redeployed.

Weapons systems. The Army canceled its $39-billion Comanche attack helicopter program on Feb. 23, 2004, after spending $8 billion on the project. The project had been in development since 1983. The first helicopters were scheduled to be delivered to the Army in 2009. Defense Department officials said the sophisticated system was too expensive for a defense budget stretched to the limit because of the Iraq War. The cost of the Comanche had skyrocketed from an estimated $8 million per helicopter to more than $50 million.

On June 15, 2004, the Navy awarded a $23-billion contract to Chicago-based Boeing Company to upgrade its aging antisubmarine fleet. Naval officials said its P-3 Orion submarine-hunting turboprop planes, in use since the 1970's,

needed to be replaced by modern jet aircraft.

The Navy awarded a $1.6-billion contract to Northrop Grumman Corporation on May 21, 2004, to begin preparatory work on CVN-21, the next generation of nuclear aircraft carriers. The first new carrier is expected to join the fleet in 2008.

Air Force tanker controversy. In October 2004, the U.S. Congress cancelled a controversial $23-billion plan to lease aerial refueling tankers for the Air Force after a scandal involving the program was uncovered by defense investigators. The Air Force had wanted to lease 100 Boeing 767 jumbo jets, convert them into aerial refueling aircraft, and purchase the airplanes at the end of the leasing contracts. Congressional critics charged that the arrangement would cost far more than simply buying the planes outright. On October 1, a former senior Air Force procurement official was sentenced to nine months in prison after admitting that she had inflated the cost of the tanker contract as a "parting gift" to Boeing officials before retiring from her job to accept a position with the defense contractor. On October 16, Congress authorized the Air Force to purchase

100 aircraft to begin replacing its refueling fleet.

Halliburton investigation. In October, the Federal Bureau of Investigation (FBI) launched an inquiry into whether Defense officials unlawfully awarded contracts to Halliburton, a Houston-based oil services corporation formerly headed by Vice President Dick Cheney. An officer in the U.S. Army Corps of Engineers had accused the Army of unfairly awarding no-bid contracts worth billions of dollars to a Halliburton subsidiary for work in Iraq. The FBI in 2004 also was investigating whether Halliburton overcharged the military by as much as $60 billion for fuel in Iraq.

Defense budget. On February 2, Defense Department officials proposed spending $401.7 billion for the U.S. military for fiscal year 2005 (Oct. 1, 2004, to Sept. 30, 2005). The request of more than $1.1 billion a day reflected a 7-percent increase from fiscal year 2004 (Oct. 1, 2003, to Sept. 30, 2004) and did not include tens of billions of dollars needed to fund combat operations in Iraq and Afghanistan.

The Defense Department request included $10.2 billion for strategic missile defense; $4.7

billion for 24 F-22 Raptor jet fighters; $4.6 billion for the Joint Strike Fighter; $3.1 billion for 42 F/A-18 Hornet fighter jets; $2.6 billion for a Virginia-class nuclear attack submarine; $2.6 billion for Army helicopters; $2 billion for 17 unmanned aerial vehicles; $1.8 billion for 11 V-22 Osprey tilt-wing aircraft; $979 million for the CVN-21 class aircraft carrier; and $877 million for 5 Trident II submarine-launched nuclear ballistic missiles.

On Aug. 5, 2004, President Bush signed a $417-billion defense bill that included funds for all the administration's major weapons programs.

Command changes. General George W. Casey, Jr., the U.S. Army vice chief of staff, became the commander of U.S. forces in Iraq on July 1, 2004, replacing Lieutenant General Ricardo S. Sanchez. On March 11, Secretary of the Air Force James P. Roche asked that his nomination as Secretary of the Army be withdrawn. Roche was nominated for the Army's top civilian position in 2003, but the Senate Armed Services Committee never scheduled a vote. On Nov. 16, 2004, Roche resigned as air force secretary. Also on November 16, the U.S. Senate approved Francis J. Harvey as Secretary of the Army.

■ Thomas M. DeFrank

See also **Congress of the United States; Human rights; Iraq: A Special Report; United States, Government of the.**

Art. Thieves stole one of the most famous paintings in the world, Norwegian modern master Edvard Munch's *The Scream,* from the Munch Museum in Oslo in broad daylight on Aug. 22, 2004. The armed and hooded men also took Munch's *Madonna,* another priceless work. Both paintings are considered early examples of the Expressionist art movement. Although the thieves' images had been captured on video surveillance cameras, the police reported that they were of such poor quality that they would be of no help in the investigation.

Vermeer authenticated. Experts in 2004 confirmed that a painting whose authenticity had long been questioned was, indeed, the work of the 1600's Dutch master Jan Vermeer. The discovery brought the number of definitive Vermeers to 36. The picture, entitled *Young Woman Seated at the Virginal,* is a delicately lit scene of a young woman playing a *virginal,* a keyboard instrument. The work dates from about 1670 and measures 10 by 8 inches (25 by 20 centimeters).

The painting was thought to have once belonged to Pieter van Ruijven, Vermeer's most important patron. It then passed through the hands of various collectors until the late Belgian art dealer Baron Frederic von Rolin purchased it in 1960. Von Rolin brought the painting to

A visitor studies the newly restored *David* by Michelangelo at the Galleria dell'Accademia in Florence, Italy. Restoration of the Renaissance masterpiece was completed in May 2004, in time for celebrations marking the 500th anniversary of the statue's placement in its original location, the Piazza della Signoria, in September 1504.

experts at Sotheby's auction house in London, where, after a decade of extensive research and a cleaning, scholars were convinced that the picture was truly a Vermeer. Von Rolin's heirs sold the work through Sotheby's in July 2004, making it the first Vermeer to be on the market in more than 80 years. The painting sold for $30 million.

David. Restoration of the Renaissance masterpiece *David* by Michelangelo was completed in Florence, Italy, in May 2004. The cleaning of the sculpture was done in preparation for celebrations marking the 500th anniversary of its placement in the Piazza della Signoria in September 1504. In 1873, the 14-foot (4.2-meter) statue was moved indoors to the Galleria dell'Accademia to protect it from the elements.

The $500,000 restoration was not without controversy. Some experts feared that the choice of a wet-cleaning method would damage the statue's marble. The method involves using compresses of distilled water applied with layers of rice paper. However, in September 2003, restorer Cinzia Parnigoni began using the technique to remove grime and stains. In some areas, she used mineral spirits, a solvent, to dissolve beeswax that had been applied during the 1800's to protect the statue. Parnigoni also restored a previous repair to the sculpture's left arm, which had been broken during a riot in the piazza in 1527, and repaired a toe that had been smashed by a hammer-wielding visitor in 1991.

Restored *Demoiselles* in renovated MoMA. *Les Demoiselles d'Avignon* by the Spanish master Pablo Picasso underwent major restoration in 2004 in preparation for the November opening of the renovated Museum of Modern Art (MoMA) in New York City. The 1907 painting shows five severely distorted naked women. The picture's lack of naturalism and its geometric treatment of form heralded the birth of the revolutionary movement of Cubism. Conservator Michael Duffy removed dirt and varnish from the 8-foot- (2.4-meter-) tall painting and retouched areas where paint had been lost. The picture emerged fresher and brighter, with Picasso's vigorous brushstrokes visible once again.

MoMA's $858-million renovation, undertaken to showcase the world's largest collection of modern and contemporary art and to celebrate the museum's 75th anniversary, more than doubled the facility's size. Japanese architect Yoshio Taniguchi's design resulted in 630,000 square feet (58,500 square meters) of new and renovated space on six floors. The museum's famous sculpture garden, which had been reduced in previous renovations, was restored to its original size.

Refurbished Brooklyn Museum. In April 2004, the Brooklyn Museum in New York City unveiled its completed two-year, $63-million ren-ovation. A sweeping new entrance pavilion includes a semicircular, glass-topped entrance with a stepped glass roof that cascades down to a newly landscaped plaza. Rows of seating along the left side of the pavilion form an amphitheater for outdoor performances as well as for providing a place to enjoy a striking new fountain. Many galleries were also redesigned.

London fire. In May, a fire in a London warehouse owned by Momart, a leading art storage and handling company, destroyed millions of dollars' worth of work by leading contemporary British artists. Those who lost works included Damien Hirst, Chris Ofili, Tracey Emin, and the Chapman brothers, Jake and Dinos. All of the artists belonged to the influential Young British Artist movement championed by advertising mogul and art collector Charles Saatchi, who also lost dozens of works in the fire. The fire, whose cause was under investigation, destroyed many important paintings by the late Patrick Heron, a leading British abstract painter of the 1900's.

Byzantine art at the Met. "Byzantium: Faith and Power (1261-1557)" at the Metropolitan Museum of Art in New York City from March 23 to July 5, 2004, explored the last centuries of Byzantium, the East Roman Empire based in Constantinople. The exhibition included painted icons, illuminated manuscripts, tiny mosaics, and gilded metalwork from some 30 nations. The exhibit was the culmination of three Met shows over almost 30 years exploring early Christian and Byzantine art from the 300's to the 1500's.

Art from Spanish-speaking Americas. "Courtly Art of the Ancient Maya" opened at the National Gallery of Art in Washington, D.C., on April 4, 2004. The show examined the sophisticated jade, limestone, and ceramic sculptures produced by the Maya culture, a civilization that flourished from A.D. 250 to about 900 in southern Mexico and Central America. The exhibit traveled to San Francisco in July 2004.

The Denver Art Museum exhibited "Painting a New World: Mexican Art and Life, 1521–1821" from April to July 2004. The Spanish colonial art ranged from Christian religious icons of the 1500's decorated with iridescent bird feathers by Indian craftsmen to pictures of European-style madonnas and saints adorned in native fabrics in Mexican settings.

Modigliani retrospective. From May 21 to Sept. 19, 2004, crowds in New York City lined up outside the Jewish Museum to see the first major retrospective in more than 50 years of the modern Italian artist Amedeo Modigliani. "Modigliani: Beyond the Myth" featured some 100 of the artist's delicately abstracted sculptures, drawings, and paintings. ■ Sally Ruth May

See also **Architecture; Museum: A Special Report.**

ASIA

Across the sweep of Asia, a continent long known for dictatorships and other forms of authoritarian government, more than half a billion people voted in 2004 in democratic elections. Economically, Asia also was the most dynamic region of the world in 2004.

Elections. Parliamentary elections were held across Asia in 2004, from the world's most populous democracy, India, where almost 380 million people voted, to one of the least populous, Mongolia. In both nations, previous governments were ousted. New parliaments also were chosen in Indonesia, Malaysia, South Korea, Sri Lanka, and Taiwan. Parliamentary balances of power remained intact in Japan and Malaysia. In a second election in Indonesia, voters rejected the standing president in favor of a new one. In Afghanistan, the Philippines, and Taiwan, presidents remained in office. In 2004, China, Myanmar, North Korea, and Vietnam remained dictatorships.

Diseases cast a cloud over Asia during 2004. According to a study by the Asian Development Bank, a United Nations affiliate, more than 7 million people were living with AIDS or HIV, the virus that causes AIDS, in Asia in 2004, and some 500,000 people died every year from the disease.

Some countries, such as Thailand, funded programs in an attempt to limit the AIDS problem. Other countries did little. India, with 600,000 people suffering from AIDS and more than 4.5 million with HIV infections, spent little on public health in general, including on AIDS. China's public health system had fallen into neglect by 2004, and critics accused the Chinese government of failing to face the AIDS problem.

In 2004, the World Health Organization (a United Nations [UN] affiliate) and other medical specialists expressed concern about avian influenza, or bird flu, in Asia. Bird flu had spread through poultry flocks in 10 Asian nations by early 2004. The viral disease had by then killed 13 people who apparently had had contact with sick birds in Vietnam and Thailand. By late 2004, 32 of 44 people infected with bird flu in Southeast Asia had died. Health officials' concerns grew in September after the death of a Thai woman who had not been in contact with birds but had cared for a fatally infected child. Possible human transmission of this highly lethal flu raised fears of a worldwide epidemic. The discovery of bird flu in hogs in China also heightened concern because pigs regularly pass various diseases to humans.

Economy. Asia's economic output grew by more than 6 percent during 2004, while some countries, such as Myanmar and Nepal, remained mired in economic stagnation and guerrilla wars. Agriculture and industry prospered in most Asian nations, raising living standards for many people across the continent.

Two possible problems loomed ahead for 2005. On January 1, a global system of quotas on textiles and clothing was set to end. The quotas limited Asian exports to Europe, the United States, and other markets, in order to protect domestic producers. An agreement reached in 1995 by the World Trade Organization, a UN affiliate, scheduled an end to the 30-year-old quota system for 2005. Economists were concerned that lifting the ban would allow big, low-cost producers in countries such as China and India to flood Western markets with cheap goods. Finally, on Dec. 12, 2004, China's Commerce Ministry caved in to pressures and announced that it would impose tariffs on textile exports.

Small producers, such as Bangladesh, faced losing much of their foreign trade, which formed the backbone of their economy. In Bangladesh, three-quarters of such earnings came from the manufacture of garments, an industry that employed half of its industrial work force. Mongolia worried that the cashmere industry, its second largest export earner, would lose out to larger and more efficient Chinese factories.

China's growing demand for coal, oil, and other basic resources posed a second problem with even wider implications. As China's boom economy moved toward becoming the second largest in the world after the United States, China needed more and more raw materials, which helped to drive up worldwide prices for oil, copper, and some other commodities. The increased tonnage of imports for China, Japan, South Korea, and Taiwan also raised shipping prices worldwide.

Terrorism plagued Asia in 2004. The deadliest

Afghan citizens wait to receive their voter identity cards at a mosque in Kabul on July 20, 2004. Although terrorist attacks were feared, Afghanistan's first democratic election went smoothly, and interim President Hamid Karzai was elected to a five-year term as president.

attack occurred in the Philippines on February 27. Abu Sayyaf, a Filipino group believed to have ties with the al-Qa'ida terrorist organization, planted a bomb on a ferry in Manila Bay, killing 116 people. On September 9, a bombing outside the Australian embassy in Jakarta, Indonesia, killed 11 people and wounded more than 180 others.

In Pakistan, terrorism was directed against Americans, Chinese, and other foreigners. The most deadly attacks, however, were made on mosques and gatherings of Sunnis and Shiites in fanatical fights between these two main divisions of Pakistani Muslims. Such clashes left more than 160 people dead in 2004.

Earthquake and tsunamis. A 9.0-magnitude, undersea earthquake off the Indonesian island of Sumatra on December 26 caused widespread destruction in Indonesia, where 80,000 people were confirmed dead by December 31. The quake triggered tsunamis that swept across the Bay of Bengal at speeds approaching 500 miles (800 kilometers) per hour. Walls of water as high as 40 feet (12 meters) crashed onto coastlines in Bangladesh, Myanmar, India, Indonesia, the Maldives, Malaysia, Sri Lanka, and Thailand, causing enormous destruction. By December 31, more than 125,000 people in Asia had been confirmed killed by the earthquake and tsunamis.

Bad weather ravaged Asia during 2004. Farmers in central and southern India, who had benefited from good monsoon rains in

Country	Population	Government	Monetary unit*	Foreign trade (million U.S.$)	
				Exports[†]	Imports[†]
Afghanistan	25,150,000	President Hamid Karzai	afghani (50.00 = $1)	98	1,007
Armenia	3,465,000	President Robert Kocharian	dram (503.00 = $1)	735	1,180
Azerbaijan	8,232,000	President Ilham Aliyev	manat (4,908.50 = $1)	2,605	2,498
Bangladesh	131,035,000	President Iajuddin Ahmed; Prime Minister Khaleda Zia	taka (59.35 = $1)	6,713	9,459
Bhutan	2,312,000	King Jigme Singye Wangchuck	ngultrum (45.94 = $1)	154	196
Brunei	352,000	Sultan Sir Hassanal Bolkiah	dollar (1.69 = $1)	3,439	1,630
Cambodia (Kampuchea)	13,210,000	King Norodom Sihamoni; Prime Minister Hun Sen	riel (3,850.00 = $1)	1,616	2,124
China	1,319,377,000	Communist Party General Secretary Hu Jintao; Premier Wen Jiabao	yuan (8.28 = $1)	436,100	397,400
East Timor	828,000	President Jose Alexander Gusmao; Prime Minister Mari Bin Amude Alkatiri	dollar (1 = $1)	8	237
Georgia	5,151,000	President Mikhail Saakashvili	lari (2.15 = $1)	615	1,250
India	1,075,516,000	President Abdul Kalam; Prime Minister Manmohan Singh	rupee (45.85 = $1)	57,240	74,150
Indonesia	213,483,000	President Susilo Bambang Yudhoyono; Vice President Muhammad Yusuf Kalla	rupiah (9,158.00 = $1)	63,890	40,220
Iran	74,293,000	Supreme Leader Ayatollah Ali Hoseini-Khamenei; President Mohammad Khatami-Ardakani	rial (8,759.00 = $1)	29,880	25,260
Japan	127,638,000	Emperor Akihito; Prime Minister Junichiro Koizumi	yen (110.44 = $1)	447,100	346,600
Kazakhstan	14,879,000	President Nursultan Nazarbayev	tenge (134.27 = $1)	12,720	8,621
Korea, North	22,880,000	Korean Workers' Party General Secretary Kim Chong-il	won (2.20 = $1)	1,044	2,042
Korea, South	47,986,000	President Roh Moo-hyun; Prime Minister Lee Hae-chan	won (1,148.50 = $1)	201,300	175,600
Kyrgyzstan	5,153,000	President Askar Akayev	som (43.65 = $1)	548	601
Laos	5,782,000	President Khamtai Siphandon; Prime Minister Boungnang Volachit	kip (7,841.00 = $1)	332	492

2003, lost crops due to insufficient rain in 2004. Across northern India and adjacent parts of Bangladesh, Nepal, and Pakistan, unusually heavy rainfall swept down deforested hillsides to bury villages in water and silt. By October, more than 2,300 people had been killed by floods and flood-related diseases, and millions of others were left homeless. When 5,000 flood victims gathered to demand food and medicine in Patna, India, on August 14, police responded to rock throwing with gunfire, killing a 14-year-old boy.

China reported more than 1,000 deaths from flooding and mudslides in 2004. The southwestern provinces of Yunnan and Sichuan were hit hard-est. In eastern China, typhoon Rananim, the most powerful typhoon to hit China in 50 years, killed at least 164 people in August. Japan was swept by 10 typhoons in 2004, the highest number in more than 50 years.

East Timor. The UN, which supervised East Timor from 1999 until its independence in 2002, agreed on Nov. 16, 2004, to continue support for a final six months, until May 20, 2005. East Timor had rebuilt much of the infrastructure that had been destroyed during the 1999 withdrawal of Indonesia, which had occupied East Timor since 1975. However, East Timor was far from being self-sufficient.

Country	Population	Government	Monetary unit*	Foreign trade (million U.S.$)	
				Exports[†]	Imports[†]
Malaysia	23,786,000	Paramount Ruler Tuanku Syed Sirajuddin ibni Almarhum Tuanku Syed Putra Jamalullail; Prime Minister Abdullah Ahmad Badawi	ringgit (3.80 = $1)	98,400	74,400
Maldives	303,000	President Maumoon Abdul Gayoom	rufiyaa (12.80 = $1)	90	392
Mongolia	2,484,000	President Natsagiyn Bagabandi; Prime Minister Tsakhiagiyn Elbedorj	tugrik (1,202.00 = $1)	524	691
Myanmar (Burma)	50,003,000	State Peace and Development Council Chairman Than Shwe; Prime Minister Khin Nyunt	kyat (6.42 = $1)	2,434	2,071
Nepal	25,257,000	King Gyanendra Bir Bikram Shah Dev; Prime Minister Sher Bahadur Deuba	rupee (72.00 = $1)	568	1,419
Pakistan	156,164,000	President Pervez Musharraf	rupee (59.24 = $1)	11,700	12,510
Philippines	82,351,000	President Gloria Macapagal-Arroyo	peso (56.34 = $1)	34,560	35,970
Russia	141,802,000	President Vladimir Putin	ruble (29.21 = $1)	134,400	74,800
Singapore	4,305,000	President Sellapan Rama Nathan; Prime Minister Lee Hsien Loong	dollar (1.68 = $1)	142,400	121,600
Sri Lanka	19,646,000	President Chandrika Kumaratunga; Prime Minister Mahinda Rajapaksa	rupee (103.50 = $1)	5,269	6,626
Taiwan	22,912,000	President Chen Shui-bian; Vice President Lu Annette	dollar (33.97 = $1)	143,000	119,600
Tajikistan	6,298,000	President Emomali Rahmonov; National Assembly Chairman Makhmadsaid Ubaydulloyev	somoni (3.06 = $1)	750	890
Thailand	63,418,000	King Phumiphon Adunyadet; Prime Minister Thaksin Shinawatra	baht (41.36 = $1)	75,990	65,300
Turkmenistan	5,103,000	President Saparmurat Niyazov	manat (5,200.00 = $1)	3,355	2,472
Uzbekistan	26,293,000	President Islam Karimov	som (115.90 = $1)	2,830	2,310
Vietnam	82,280,000	Communist Party General Secretary Nong Duc Manh; President Tran Duc Luong; Prime Minister Phan Van Khai	dong (15,750.00 = $1)	19,880	22,500

*Exchange rates as of Oct. 1, 2004, or latest available data.
[†]Latest available data.

In September 2004, the country continued talks with Australia begun in 2003 on a boundary dispute, though no agreement was reached. East Timor sought a larger share of revenue from a seabed natural gas project than Australia offered. When Indonesia controlled East Timor, Indonesia had agreed upon a boundary that gave Australia control of what were later found to be rich undersea oil and gas beds. East Timor argued for a boundary halfway between their shores, while Australia tried to retain rights closer to East Timor.

Brunei. Sultan Hassanal Bolkiah on Sept. 29, 2004, signed constitutional amendments that consolidated his absolute powers while allowing elections to a legislative council. The council had been abolished in 1984, when Brunei gained independence from the United Kingdom. The sultan convened a new council with 21 appointed members on Sept. 25, 2004. The council then passed amendments that the sultan said would "widen the opportunities of the public to engage and contribute to national progress."

Mongolia held parliamentary elections on June 27, 2004. In 2000, the Mongolian People's Revolutionary Party (MPRP), the former Communist party that controlled Mongolia as a satellite of the former Soviet Union for 70 years, had won 72 out of 76 seats in the Great Hural, or parliament.

However, after years of poor economic performance and high unemployment, the MPRP won only 36 seats in the 2004 elections. In an upset, the Motherland Democratic Coalition, which advocated faster economic reforms, also won 36 seats. After long talks, the coalition's Tsakhilganiin Elbegdorj became prime minister on August 20 in a power-sharing agreement with the MPRP.

Good weather and foreign investment greatly aided Mongolia's economy in 2004. The foreign investment resulted from the need for raw materials for neighboring China's booming industries, especially for the mining of copper and other minerals.

Maldives. On August 13, approximately 3,000 people demonstrated in Male, the capital, for political reform. Police responded with a violent putdown, and the government of President Maumoon Abdul Gayoom declared a state of emergency. After the European Union threatened to block its aid package to Maldives and called for the release of political prisoners, the government lifted the state of emergency on October 10.

The tsunamis triggered by the December 26 earthquake off Sumatra swamped the Maldives, which are only about 3 feet (1 meter) above sea level. Huge waves left dozens of people dead and large areas of Male flooded and destroyed.

■ Henry S. Bradsher

See also **Disasters; Geology; Ocean; Terrorism;** various Asian country articles.

Astronomy. The National Aeronautics and Space Administration (NASA) landed two roving spacecraft on Mars in 2004, and another spacecraft began sending back spectacular images of Saturn and its moons. A probe studying the sun suffered a serious mishap, and astronomers discovered a mysterious object at the edge of the solar system and a new class of planets.

Mars rovers. NASA landed two geological rovers—one named Spirit and the other named Opportunity—on opposite hemispheres of Mars in January. Each rover crawled slowly across the surface of the red planet while taking photographs and measurements of the soil and rocks. The rovers used tools to scrape away at the ground for a close look at geological samples. Although the rovers were designed for just 90 days of exploration, they continued to operate for the remainder of 2004.

Spirit, which landed in a crater named Gusev, spent its first 160 days exploring the volcanic rocks of the crater. It then moved to a nearby

The Hubble Ultra-Deep Field, an image released in March by the Space Telescope Science Institute in Baltimore, Maryland, shows more than 10,000 of the most distant galaxies ever viewed. Astronomers produced the Hubble Ultra-Deep Field by combining numerous images taken by cameras on the Hubble Space Telescope during 400 orbits.

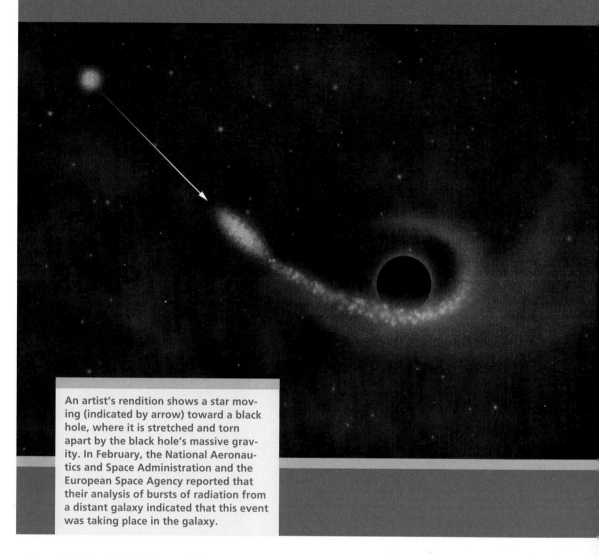

An artist's rendition shows a star moving (indicated by arrow) toward a black hole, where it is stretched and torn apart by the black hole's massive gravity. In February, the National Aeronautics and Space Administration and the European Space Agency reported that their analysis of bursts of radiation from a distant galaxy indicated that this event was taking place in the galaxy.

region called Columbia Hills to search for geologic evidence of water. Opportunity landed at a spot called Meridiani Planum and investigated several nearby craters. At one crater, called Endurance, it found clear evidence that rock strata had been laid down by water. Along the way, Opportunity discovered deposits of crystals produced by the evaporation of water, as well as a mineral called hematite, which is often produced in watery conditions.

The evidence gathered by Spirit and Opportunity was the strongest to date that Mars, which is now a dry and inhospitable planet, had large bodies of water on its surface at some point in the past.

Cassini explores Saturn. The Cassini space probe, the first mission to Saturn in two decades, arrived at the ringed planet in June. Cassini began a mission that was scheduled to include at least 76 orbits of Saturn.

Images returned to Earth by Cassini indicated that Saturn's largest moon, Titan, has strange light and dark patches on a crater-free surface. Other images revealed fine details on the pockmarked surfaces of two smaller moons, Phoebe and Iapetus. Cassini's views of the thousands of complex rings surrounding Saturn were much sharper than any obtained previously. In August, Cassini's cameras discovered two previously unknown Saturnian moons, each barely 2 miles (3 kilometers) in diameter. Cassini discovered a faint new outer ring around the planet in September.

In December, Cassini released the Huygens probe, which was scheduled to land on Titan's surface in January 2005. Huygens was designed to gather data on the composition of Titan's atmosphere and take images of Titan's surface.

Crash landing for Genesis. The Genesis space probe crash-landed in the Utah desert on Sept. 8, 2004, following a three-year mission to study the sun. The probe's parachutes failed to deploy after it re-entered the atmosphere.

Genesis was carrying samples of the *solar wind,* the stream of electrically charged particles that boils off of the sun's surface. Scientists reported that much of the sample material survived the crash. They planned to examine the particles for clues to the composition of the material out of which the sun and planets formed some 5 billion years ago.

Mysterious Sedna. In March, astronomers using a telescope on Palomar Mountain in California discovered a faint object orbiting the sun at a distance of 8 billion miles (13 billion kilometers)—twice the distance of Pluto. The scientists, from the California Institute of Technology in Pasadena; the Gemini Observatory in Hilo, Hawaii; and Yale University in New Haven, Connecticut, named the object Sedna, after the Inuit goddess of the sea. Sedna, which is about 1,000 miles (1,600 kilometers) in diameter, was the furthest object yet discovered in the solar system.

Astronomers speculated that Sedna might be an object that escaped from the Oort cloud, a cluster of cometlike bodies 10 times more distant from the sun than Sedna. However, they were not sure how one of these objects happened to stray close enough to be detected.

New class of planets. Two teams of astronomers reported the discovery of three of the smallest known planets outside our solar system in August.

Two of the new planets were described by a team that included Geoff Marcy of the University of California at Berkeley; Paul Butler of the Carnegie Institution of Washington, D.C.; and Barbara McArthur of the University of Texas at Austin. These planets—one orbiting the sunlike star 55 Cancri, the other orbiting the smaller, cooler star Gliese 436—are approximately 20 times as massive as Earth, making the planets about the size of Neptune or Uranus. Previously, most extrasolar planets discovered were giants at least as large as Jupiter.

An even smaller planet, estimated to be only 14 times the mass of Earth, was discovered by European astronomers at the European Southern Observatory in Chile. *Spectroscopic analysis,* in which an object's light is analyzed for clues to its chemical composition, indicated that this planet might have a rocky surface, similar to Earth. The planet orbits a sunlike star named mu Arae.

Planet-hunting technology in 2004 was not yet capable of detecting planets as small as Earth. However, astronomers expected that improved technology would allow them to find Earth-sized planets in the future.

■ Laurence A. Marschall

See also **Space exploration.**

Prime Minister John Howard and his conservative coalition government won a historic fourth term on Oct. 9, 2004. Howard's Liberal Party won 74 seats in the 150-seat House of Representatives (the lower house of Parliament), and its coalition partner, the National Party, won 12 seats. The rival Australian Labor Party won 60 seats. The election also delivered the coalition control of the 76-member Senate, Parliament's upper house, for the first time since 1981.

Political experts credited Prime Minister Howard's victory to the healthy state of the econ-

AUSTRALIA

omy, as well as to coalition advertising that claimed there would be an increase in interest rates if Labor won power. Various local issues, such as the coalition's support for continued logging in Tasmania, also played a part in its victory, according to election analysts. Most commentators maintained that Howard's strong support for the United States-led war in Iraq had little effect on the outcome of the election.

The Australian Green Party received more than 7 percent of the vote, increasing its Senate seats from two to four. These wins positioned the Greens to replace the Democrats as the third

strongest political force in Australia. A new religious party, Family First, debuted in the election and won one seat in the Senate.

State leaders. In state elections held on Feb. 7, 2004, Peter Beattie, the leader of the Labor Party in Queensland, was returned as premier. On February 23, Jim Bacon, the Labor leader in Tasmania, announced he was retiring as state premier because he had inoperable lung cancer. He was succeeded by his friend Paul Lennon. Bacon died on June 20.

Richard Butler, Tasmania's state governor, resigned on August 9. Butler stated that he was stepping down because a "malicious campaign" against him was damaging the reputation of Tasmania. Although the governor position involves acting as the state representative of Queen Elizabeth II, Butler had been an outspoken opponent of the continuation of Australia as a monarchy.

The economy. The Australian economy saw its 14th consecutive year of growth in

Police confront a group of Aboriginal demonstrators during a nine-hour riot in the Sydney suburb of Redfern on the night of February 15. More than 40 officers were injured in the violence, which began after local leaders accused the police of causing the death of an Aborginal teen-ager. Police arrested several of the rioters.

2004. The country's *gross domestic product,* the value of all goods and services produced in a country in a given time, increased more than 4 percent. Interest rates remained stable at 5.25 percent, and inflation stayed around 2 percent, while the unemployment rate dropped below 6 percent. The Australian dollar soared to U.S. 80 cents in February, but by May, it had settled back to approximately U.S. 70 cents, where it remained for most of the rest of 2004.

The Australian stock exchange reached record highs in 2004. Natural resource companies, such as the mining giants Rio Tinto and BHP Billiton, led the way, largely because China continued to demand Australian mining products.

In April, Rupert Murdoch, the executive chairman and leading shareholder of The News Corporation, announced that he planned to relocate the headquarters of the international media organization from South Australia to Delaware. Murdoch said the corporation would benefit by the move to the United States, where it conducted most of its business. The change meant the removal of The News Corporation from its domestic listing on the Australian stock exchange, where it made up more than 7 percent of the total value of stocks. Shareholders voted to approve the move in October.

Iraq and terrorism. More than 800 members of the Australian defense forces continued to serve in Iraq during 2004. The troops were engaged in a variety of tasks, including instructing Iraqis in air traffic control at the airport in Baghdad, the Iraqi capital.

An inquiry into Australia's intelligence services headed by Philip Flood, a former diplomat, released its report in July. The inquiry found that, contrary to some critics of the Howard administration, the federal government had not applied pressure on spy services to help make the case for going to war with Iraq in 2003. Nevertheless, the report concluded that the intelligence provided before the war was "thin, ambiguous, and incomplete."

Flood's report also criticized Australia's intelligence services for failing to recognize the threat posed by the Islamic terrorist group Jemaah Islamiyah before the bombings in Bali that killed more than 200 people, including 88 Australians, in 2002. The report recommended that the budget of the Office of National Assessments, a body that advises the government on international affairs, should be doubled to $25 million and its staff increased to 145. (All amounts are in Australian dollars.) Prime Minister Howard supported these recommendations.

Terrorist attacks and trials. A car bomb exploded outside the Australian embassy in Jakarta, the capital of Indonesia, in September 2004. The explosion killed 11 people outside the embassy.

In October, Abu Bakar Bashir, the alleged leader of Jemaah Islamiyah, went on trial in Jakarta. He was charged with having approved the bombings in Bali, in addition to a bombing at the Jakarta Marriott Hotel in 2003 that killed 12 people.

In May 2004, Perth's District Court convicted Jack Roche, an Australian recruited by Jemaah Islamiyah, of conspiring to bomb the Israeli embassy in Canberra, Australia's capital. Roche was the first Australian to be convicted of a terrorist-related offense.

Bilal Khazal, a former baggage handler at Sydney's airport who was charged with terrorist activities, was released from prison on bail in June. Many Australians were outraged by the release. In response, Parliament passed legislation preventing bail for terror suspects, except under special circumstances.

Free trade agreement. In February, the governments of the United States and Australia finalized the details of the Australia-United States Free Trade Agreement (AUSFTA) after 11 months of negotiations. Under the terms of the agreement, 97 percent of U.S. tariffs on Australia's nonagricultural exports were to become duty free by January 2005. The remaining nonagricultural exports were to be lifted by 2015. Prime Minister Howard outlined a number of industries in the manufacturing, mining, and agricultural sectors that stood to benefit from AUSFTA. However, the Labor Party attacked the agreement as likely to be harmful to Australia's pharmaceutical, motion picture, and television industries. The Parliament passed a revised agreement, addressing some of Labor's concerns, in August 2004.

Tourism initiative. In May, Federal Tourism Minister Joe Hockey launched Australia's most aggressive effort ever to attract tourists. Spearheading the $300-million campaign were international advertisements featuring Australian celebrities, including pop singer Delta Goodrem, cricket legend Richie Benaud, and renowned poet Les Murray.

New energy strategy. Prime Minister Howard unveiled a new national energy strategy in June. The initiatives included $700 million in incentives to reduce emissions of *greenhouse gases.* Scientists blame these gases, which are produced in large amounts by the burning of fossil fuels, for a gradual warming of Earth's surface and lower atmosphere. The energy strategy included a novel scheme to pump carbon dioxide, the main greenhouse gas, deep underground, where it would be *sequestered,* or removed from environmental circulation. Howard's plan also provided money to develop technologies in renewable energy, such as solar power and *geothermal energy,* energy produced by underground steam or hot water.

Conservation groups criticized the plan for its continued heavy reliance on coal and other fossil fuels. These groups also attacked the government for failing to sign the Kyoto Protocol, an international agreement to decrease the rate at which carbon dioxide and other greenhouse gases are released into the atmosphere. Prime

MEMBERS OF THE AUSTRALIAN HOUSE OF REPRESENTATIVES

The House of Representatives of the 41st Parliament first met Nov. 16, 2004. As of November 24, 2004, the House of Representatives consisted of the following members: 74 Liberal Party of Australia, 60 Australian Labor Party, 12 National Party of Australia, 3 independents, and 1 Northern Territory Country Liberal Party. This table shows each legislator and party affiliation. An asterisk (*) denotes those who served in the 40th Parliament.

Australian Capital Territory
Annette Ellis, A.L.P.*
Bob McMullan, A.L.P.*

New South Wales
Tony Abbott, L.P.*
Anthony Albanese, A.L.P.*
John Anderson, N.P.*
Peter Andren, Ind.*
Bruce Baird, L.P.*
Bob Baldwin, L.P.*
Kerry Bartlett, L.P.*
Sharon Bird, A.L.P.
Bronwyn Bishop, L.P.*
Chris Bowen, A.L.P.
Tony Burke, A.L.P.
Alan Cadman, L.P.*
Ian Causley, N.P.*
John Cobb, N.P.*
Justine Elliot, A.L.P.
Pat Farmer, L.P.*
Laurie Ferguson, A.L.P.*
Joel Fitzgibbon, A.L.P.*
Peter Garrett, A.L.P.
Joanna Gash, L.P.*
Jennie George, A.L.P.*
Sharon Grierson, A.L.P.*
Jill Hall, A.L.P.*
Luke Hartsuyker, N.P.*
Michael Hatton, A.L.P.*
Kelly Hoare, A.L.P.*
Joe Hockey, L.P.*
John Howard, L.P.*
Kay Hull, N.P.*
Julia Irwin, A.L.P.*
Jackie Kelly, L.P.*
Mark Latham, A.L.P.*
Sussan Ley, L.P.*
Jim Lloyd, L.P.*
Louise Markus, L.P.
Robert McClelland, A.L.P.*
Daryl Melham, A.L.P.*
John Murphy, A.L.P.*
Gary Nairn, L.P.*
Brendan Nelson, L.P.*
Julie Owens, A.L.P.
Tanya Plibersek, A.L.P.*
Roger Price, A.L.P.*
Philip Ruddock, L.P.*
Alby Schultz, L.P.*
Ken Ticehurst, L.P.*
Malcolm Turnbull, L.P.
Mark Vaile, N.P.*
Danna Vale, L.P.*
Tony Windsor, Ind.*

Northern Territory
Warren Snowdon, A.L.P.*
David Tollner, C.L.P.*

Queensland
Arch Bevis, A.L.P.*
Mal Brough, L.P.*
Steven Ciobo, L.P.*
Peter Dutton, L.P.*
Kay Elson, L.P.*
Craig Emerson, A.L.P.*
Warren Entsch, L.P.*
Teresa Gambaro, L.P.*
Gary Hardgrave, L.P.*
Michael Johnson, L.P.*
David Jull, L.P.*
Robert Katter, Ind.*
De-Anne Kelly, N.P.*
Andrew Laming, L.P.
Peter Lindsay, L.P.*
Kirsten Livermore, A.L.P.*
Ian Macfarlane, L.P.*
Margaret May, L.P.*
Paul Neville, N.P.*
Bernie Ripoll, A.L.P.*
Kevin Rudd, A.L.P.*
Bruce Scott, N.P.*
Peter Slipper, L.P.*
Alexander Somlyay, L.P.*
Wayne Swan, A.L.P.*
Cameron Thompson, L.P.*
Warren Truss, N.P.*
Ross Vasta, L.P.

South Australia
Alexander Downer, L.P.*
Trish Draper, L.P.*
Kate Ellis, A.L.P.
David Fawcett, L.P.
Steve Georganas, A.L.P.
Christopher Pyne, L.P.*
Kym Richardson, L.P.
Rodney Sawford, A.L.P.*
Patrick Secker, L.P.*
Andrew Southcott, L.P.*
Barry Wakelin, L.P.*

Tasmania
Dick Adams, A.L.P.*
Mark Baker, L.P.
Michael Ferguson, L.P.
Duncan Kerr, A.L.P.*
Harry Quick, A.L.P.*

Victoria
Kevin Andrews, L.P.*
Fran Bailey, L.P.*
Phillip Barresi, L.P.*
Bruce Billson, L.P.*
Russell Broadbent, L.P.
Anna Burke, A.L.P.*
Anthony Byrne, A.L.P.*
Ann Corcoran, A.L.P.*
Peter Costello, L.P.*
Simon Crean, A.L.P.*
Michael Danby, A.L.P.*
Martin Ferguson, A.L.P.*
John Forrest, N.P.*
Petro Georgiou, L.P.*
Steve Gibbons, A.L.P.*
Julia Gillard, A.L.P.*
Alan Griffin, A.L.P.*
David Hawker, L.P.*
Greg Hunt, L.P.*
Harry Jenkins, A.L.P.*
Catherine King, A.L.P.*
Jenny Macklin, A.L.P.*
Stewart McArthur, L.P.*
Peter McGauran, N.P.*
Brendan O'Connor, A.L.P.*
Gavan O'Connor, A.L.P.*
Sophie Panopoulos, L.P.*
Chris Pearce, L.P.*
Andrew Robb, L.P.
Nicola Roxon, A.L.P.*
Bob Sercombe, A.L.P.*
Tony Smith, L.P.*
Sharman Stone, L.P.*
Lindsay Tanner, A.L.P.*
Kelvin Thomson, A.L.P.*
Maria Vamvakinou, A.L.P.*
Jason Wood, L.P.

Western Australia
Kim Beazley, A.L.P.*
Julie Bishop, L.P.*
Graham Edwards, A.L.P.*
Barry Haase, L.P.*
Stuart Henry, L.P.
Dennis Jensen, L.P.
Michael Keenan, L.P.
Carmen Lawrence, A.L.P.*
Judi Moylan, L.P.*
Geoffrey Prosser, L.P.*
Don Randall, L.P.*
Stephen Smith, A.L.P.*
Wilson Tuckey, L.P.*
Mal Washer, L.P.*
Kim Wilkie, A.L.P.*

Minister Howard countered that Australia was already well on the way to meeting most of the targets recommended by the protocol.

Water resources. The federal government and all states except Western Australia and Tasmania signed the first national water initiative in June. The agreement granted farmers the right to legally own water and to trade water rights—rather than just possess rights of access to water resources. The initiative also provided $500 million to help the states return water from overirrigated inland areas to the Murray-Darling river system, Australia's longest and most important waterway. Critics maintained that the agreement failed to ensure the long-term health of the river system, which faced such ecological problems as water depletion and excess saltiness.

Because of a long-term drought in southern and eastern Australia, restrictions on water use in these areas continued throughout 2004. By the middle of the year, the reservoir of the Warragamba Dam—Sydney's main source of water—had dropped to a record low of approximately 40 percent of capacity. The New South Wales government announced plans in 2004 to pump water from the Shoalhaven district to the Sydney catchment area.

Western Australia also made plans to cope with water shortages in 2004. These plans included the recycling of water and *desalinization,* the removal of salt from seawater to make it usable.

Transportation. The newly completed section of railroad between Alice Springs and Darwin, in the Northern Territory, opened in January. In February, Mike Rann, the premier of South Australia, and Clare Martin, the chief minister of the Northern Territory, were among 400 passengers who boarded the *Ghan* train as it began its first 47-hour journey from Adelaide to Darwin.

The federal government unveiled AusLink, its new land transport plan, in June. The plan provided nearly $12 billion to upgrade the two-lane Hume Highway between Sydney and Melbourne as a four-lane road by 2012. Similar work on the Pacific Highway between Sydney and Brisbane was to be completed by 2016.

Aboriginal unrest. The Sydney suburb of Redfern erupted in nine hours of riots on the night of Feb. 15, 2004. More than 40 police officers were injured in the violence. Authorities said the incident was sparked by the death of Thomas Hickey, an Aboriginal teen-ager who died after his bicycle crashed into a fence. Local Aboriginal leaders blamed police for the death, claiming that officers were chasing Hickey when the accident occurred. An official inquiry, however, later cleared police of any wrongdoing.

In July, a group of Aboriginal activists set up a camp that they called a "tent embassy" in Victoria Park, near Redfern. The activists demanded that the government recognize Aboriginal *sovereignty* (freedom from outside control) at the local, state, and national levels. The group removed the tents in August, after the Sydney city government agreed to work with Aboriginal representatives to develop a "memorandum of understanding." In October, the New

South Wales state government announced a 10-year plan to rejuvenate the Redfern area.

Visual and literary arts. In March, the Archibald Prize—Australia's most prestigious award for painting—was won by Sydney artist Craig Ruddy for his charcoal-based drawing of Aboriginal actor David Gulpilil. A week later, Tony Johansen, another Sydney artist, took legal action against the Art Gallery of New South Wales, which awarded the prize. Johansen claimed that Ruddy's entry was not valid because it was a drawing, rather than a painting. By mid-year, the case was before the Supreme Court of New South Wales, where the art gallery defended the award.

In June 2004, *The Great Fire,* author Shirley Hazzard's first novel in more than 20 years, won Australia's leading book prize, the Miles Franklin Literary Award. The award is bestowed annually for a work portraying various aspects of Australian life.

In July, Malcolm Knox, a journalist at the *Sydney Morning Herald,* uncovered a literary hoax that shocked readers of Norma Khouri's international bestseller, *Forbidden Love.* The book purports to tell the true story of how the father of Khouri's friend Dalia, in the Islamic kingdom of Jordan, murdered Dalia after she fell in love with a Christian. Khouri described how she fled from Jordan to Australia after the murder. Knox, however, revealed that Khouri had actually left Jordan at the age of three and had spent most of her adult life in the United States. Following this report, the publishers of *Forbidden Love* withdrew the book from sale.

Stage and screen. Australian actor Hugh Jackman won a Tony Award in June for his portrayal on the New York City stage of Australian entertainer Peter Allen in the musical, *The Boy from Oz.* Another Australian-born actor, Geoffrey Rush, received high praise in Australia and overseas in 2004 for his performance in the leading role of the motion picture, *The Life and Death of Peter Sellers.* The movie depicts the life of the late English actor, best known for portraying Inspector Clouseau in several *Pink Panther* films.

In October, the drama *Somersault,* starring actress Abbie Cornish, scored a record 13 awards at the annual Australian Film Industry Awards presentation in Melbourne.

Olympic Games. At the Olympic Games in Athens in August, Australian athletes won a total of 49 medals, including a record 17 gold medals. The tally placed Australia in fourth place, behind the United States, China, and Russia.

■ Brian Kennedy

See also **Art; Australia, Prime Minister of; Economics; Indonesia; Iraq: A Special Report; Olympics: A Special Report; Terrorism.**

Australia, Prime Minister of. In

May 2004, John Howard, leader of the Liberal Party, celebrated 30 years in politics and announced that he intended to retain the leadership as long as the party wanted him. Despite findings that Iraq had no weapons of mass destruction, Howard defended the decision to support the United States-led invasion of Iraq in 2003 on the grounds that it was based on the best advice available at the time. He said that he did not regret that Saddam Hussein was no longer leader of Iraq.

Domestic issues rather than the Iraq war dominated public discussion before the Oct. 9, 2004, elections. Howard's Liberal-National Party coalition government won a fourth term. On December 22, Howard became the second longest serving prime minister in Australia's history.

On April 25, Howard joined Australian troops serving in Iraq at a dawn service in Baghdad to observe Anzac Day, which marks the landing of Australian and New Zealand troops at Gallipoli, Turkey, in 1915. Howard visited France in June 2004 to commemorate the 60th anniversary of the D-Day landings during World War II (1939–1945). In October 2004, he flew to Jakarta for the inauguration of Susilo Bambang Yudhoyono as president of Indonesia. ■ Brian Kennedy

See also **Australia; Iraq: A Special Report.**

Australian rules football. South

Australia's Port Adelaide defeated the Queensland team, the Brisbane Lions, by 40 points to win the 2004 Australian Football League (AFL) premiership in Melbourne, Australia, on September 25. Brisbane, which had won three successive premierships, led by a goal midway through the third quarter. However, Port Adelaide kicked nine goals to Brisbane's one in the rest of the match. In the end, Port Adelaide defeated Brisbane 17 goals 11 behinds (113 points) to 10 goals 13 behinds (73 points).

Port Adelaide's Byron Pickett won the Norm Smith medal for the best player on the ground in the grand final match. West Coast's Chris Judd received the Charles Brownlow medal for the best and fairest player.

Regionals. In the Football Victoria grand final, the Calder Cannons defeated the Eastern Ranges 19.20 (134) to 9.10 (64). In Tasmania's Southern Football League, Clarence beat New Norfolk 17.12 (114) to 12.9 (81). In the Western Australian Football League, Subiaco outclassed Claremont 15.9 (99) to 7.9 (51). In the South Australian National Football League, Central District crushed the Eagles 23.15 (153) to 4.4 (28). In the AFL Queensland grand final, the Morningside Panthers defeated the Southport Sharks 12.18 (90) to 12.11 (83). ■ Brian Kennedy

Austria. Voters elected Heinz Fischer to the largely ceremonial post of Austria's presidency on April 25, 2004. Fischer, a veteran member of parliament from the opposition Social Democratic Party, defeated Foreign Minister Benita Ferrero-Waldner, the candidate of the conservative People's Party, by 52.4 percent to 47.6 percent. The result suggested voter dissatisfaction with the People's Party of Chancellor Wolfgang Schuessel, which has governed Austria since 2000. Fischer, who took office in July 2004, was the first Social Democrat to hold the presidency since 1986.

Fischer had emphasized traditional Social Democratic positions during the campaign, including continued support for Austria's military neutrality and social welfare programs. Ferrero-Waldner resigned in October 2004 to become Austria's new European Union (EU) commissioner. She was replaced as foreign minister by Ursula Plassnik, Schuessel's chief of staff.

The retiring president, Thomas Klestil, died of heart failure on July 6, two days before Fischer's swearing-in ceremony. Klestil, who was 71 and a former career diplomat, had served two six-year terms. He was best remembered for restoring respect for the office and repairing the damage to Austria's image that was caused by the revelations that his predecessor, Kurt Waldheim, had served in a German army unit that committed war crimes during World War II (1939-1945).

Ski train verdict. An Austrian court in February 2004 found 16 people not guilty of criminal liability for a fire on a *funicular train* (a train pulled up the side of a mountain by a moving cable) that killed 155 people in November 2000. The defendants included the operator of the train, equipment suppliers, and inspectors. Prosecutors said a defective heater on the train started the fire. Separate civil court cases were underway in the United States and Germany, where many of the victims lived.

Economy. The government approved tax cuts in May 2004 that were intended to promote economic growth. The package included a cut in the corporate income tax rate from 34 percent to 25 percent. The reduction was designed to make Austria competitive with neighboring countries in Central and Eastern Europe, which have used low tax rates to attract investment and jobs from the West. The package also increased the income level at which individuals begin to pay tax and increased tax credits for families. The measures were to take effect in January 2005.

Austria experienced a modest acceleration of growth in 2004 as part of the general European recovery. EU economists forecast that economic output would increase by 1.6 percent while unemployment remained stable at around 4.5 percent, one of the lowest rates in the 25-nation European Union. ■ Tom Buerkle

See also **Europe.**

Postage stamps released in Austria in August 2004 bear the image of California Governor Arnold Schwarzenegger. Schwarzenegger, a former bodybuilder, was born in Austria. He emigrated to the United States in 1968.

Automobile. Sales of light trucks and cars in the United States rebounded in 2004 after remaining sluggish in 2003. Sales totaled 12.8 million units through September 2004, a 1.2-percent increase over the same period in 2003, according to industry analysts. Analysts expected sales to reach approximately 17 million units by the end of 2004, compared with 16.7 million sold by the end of 2003. However, automakers were forced to offer no-interest loans and thousands of dollars in incentives on a number of vehicles to stimulate sales.

In September 2004, the average manufacturer incentive was approximately $3,100 per vehicle sold—20 percent higher than the average manufacturer incentive in September 2003, according to industry analysts. The traditional Big Three domestic automakers—General Motors (GM) Corporation of Detroit; Ford Motor Company of Dearborn, Michigan; and the U.S. division of DaimlerChrysler AG of Germany—offered buyers the highest incentives. The Big Three had average incentives of $4,279 per vehicle in September 2004. Japanese automakers spent the least on incentives at an average of $911 per vehicle. Korean carmakers spent $2,207 per unit, and European automakers averaged $2,497 per vehicle.

Despite such incentives, GM, Ford, and Chrysler saw their combined market share decline to 60.5 percent through September, compared with 61.6 percent for the same period in 2003. Asian manufacturers recorded the greatest increase, garnering 34.4 percent of the market for the first nine months of 2004. Through September, European companies took 5.1 percent of the U.S. market, compared with 5.4 percent for the first nine months of 2003.

Top sellers. Ford remained the top seller of light trucks during the 2004 model year with the F-series pickup truck. The F-series dominated the market, selling more than 916,000 units. The Toyota Camry was the number-one selling car, with 418,000 units of the 2004 model year sold. Both the F-series pickup truck and the Toyota Camry were the top sellers during the 2003 model year as well.

The Big Three. GM boosted its U.S. sales during the first nine months of 2004. Sales totaled 3.6 million units through September, 0.9 percent ahead of the same period in 2003. GM's market share fell to 28 percent, a small drop compared with 28.1 percent in the previous nine months. Through September, GM recorded a net income of $3.1 billion, compared with $2.8 billion for the first nine months of 2003.

Officials at the number-one automaker adopted different strategies in their worldwide operations in efforts to improve profits during 2004. In October, GM announced that the company would reduce its European workforce by up to 12,000 employees as part of a plan to save $600 million by 2006. In June 2004, GM said it planned to invest at least $3 billion by 2007 in China and with its joint ventures introduce 20 new or improved models in the fast-growing market. In the United States, GM planned to boost its 2005 sales with a new Chevrolet Corvette. The company also planned to roll out the new Chevrolet Cobalt to replace the discontinued Chevrolet Cavalier.

Ford's U.S. sales fell to 2.5 million units in the first nine months of 2004, a 5.2-percent decline from the first nine months of 2003. Ford's market share dropped to 19.4 percent through September 2004, compared with 20.7 percent for the same period in 2003. Nevertheless, the second largest automaker in the United States improved profits during 2004. Analysts credited the increases in part to cost-cutting measures the company started in 2002. Ford earned $3.4 billion in the first nine months of 2004, compared with $1.3 billion for the same period in 2003. Among its most widely publicized vehicles in 2004, Ford introduced the Escape Hybrid, the first hybrid sport-utility vehicle. The Escape Hybrid runs on a four-cylinder engine and electric traction motor. For 2005, Ford looked to increase corporate profits through better sales from its remodeled Mustang and a new 500-series sedan.

In April 2004, Ford and GM announced a joint venture in which the companies planned to invest $720 million in three existing plants to construct a fuel-saving, 6-speed automatic transmission. The transmission for front-wheel drive vehicles will be built at Ford's Sterling Heights, Michigan, and Sharonville, Ohio, plants and GM's Warren, Michigan, facility.

The Chrysler Group of DaimlerChrysler AG was the only domestic company to see its sales and market share increase for the first nine months of 2004. The Chrysler Group's sales rose 3.2 percent to 1.7 million units sold through September. Chrysler's market share also increased to 13.1 percent the first nine months of 2004, compared with 12.8 percent for the first nine months of 2003. Through September 2004, the Chrysler Group had an operating profit of $1.7 billion, compared with a loss of $806 million for the same period in 2003. The company credited sales of the Crossfire sports car and 300-series sedan in part for its increased profitability.

In 2004, DaimlerChrysler AG took two important steps in its relationship with Asian automakers. In April, DaimlerChrysler officials decided not to pump additional money into the struggling Japanese automaker Mitsubishi, reducing its ownership in Mitsubishi from 37

The 2006 Pontiac Solstice's convertible top is designed to fold flat behind a clamshell cover on the rear deck so that the top is hidden from view. The roadster features a 2.4-liter, 170 horsepower engine.

Chrysler's 2005 Crossfire Roadster features a fabric top that automatically folds down into the rear deck. The two-seat roadster, which offers motorists a 3.2-liter V-6 215 horsepower engine, proved to be popular following its debut in fall 2004.

Convertible models returned to the spotlight—and sunshine—as new car designs in 2004.

Chrysler's 2005 PT Cruiser Convertible combined practical usage with stylish design. Drivers raise or lower the top with the push of a button. The PT Cruiser comes equipped with a 2.4-liter, 180 horsepower engine.

percent to less than 25 percent. In August, DaimlerChrysler AG sold its 10.5-percent stake in South Korean automaker Hyundai.

Asian automakers. Toyota Motor Corporation, the largest automobile manufacturer in Japan, improved its sales and market share in 2004, compared with 2003. For the first nine months of 2004, Toyota's sales rose to 1.5 million units, an increase of 9.4 percent more units than in 2003, in part due to increased sales of the Toyota Camry. Toyota's market share increased to 12.1 percent in September 2004 from 11.2 percent in September 2003. In September 2004, Toyota officials announced plans to spend $250 million to expand a plant in Huntsville, Alabama. The plant, which manufactures 8-cylinder engines, should add 300 jobs to the area.

Honda sales in 2004 totaled 1 million units in the first nine months, equaling the number sold in 2003. Honda held approximately 8.2 percent of the U.S. market.

Nissan also reported an increase in sales in 2004, posting 726,961 units sold through September, a 22-percent increase compared with 2003. Nissan's market share increased to 5.7 percent, compared with 4.7 percent for the same period in 2003. Nissan also launched its 2005 Frontier pickup truck at its Smyrna, Tennessee, plant in October 2004.　■ Mike Casey

Automobile racing.
German Formula One driver Michael Schumacher dominated his circuit in historic fashion in 2004, winning 12 of the first 13 races of the 18-race season. He finished with 13 wins and clinched his record seventh overall world title at the Belgian Grand Prix in Spa-Francorchamps in August.

In January, NASCAR adopted a new scoring system to counter criticism stemming from the fact that the 2003 champion, Matt Kenseth, won only one race. NASCAR got its wish, with five drivers in a position to win until the final race.

Indianapolis 500. Buddy Rice won the Indy 500 on May 30, 2004. The race was shortened by rain for the first time since 1976. Near the end of the event, the lead changed hands as teams were forced to make pit stops. However, Rice retook the lead when the rain began to fall. The race was stopped after 180 laps. Rice became the first *polesitter* (racer with the fastest qualifying times) to win since Arie Luyendyk of Holland in 1997.

Formula One. Schumacher took his unprecedented seventh title with his second-place finish in the Belgian Grand Prix in Spa-Francorchamps, on Aug. 29, 2004. Schumacher showed his dominance by claiming the title with four races remaining in the 18-race schedule.

NASCAR. Kurt Busch captured the Nextel Cup championship with his fifth-place finish at the Ford 500 in Homestead, Florida, on Nov. 21, 2004.

NASCAR introduced a new scoring system in January in an effort to boost interest and television ratings. Under the new format, the top 10 drivers and any others within 400 points of the leader after 26 races earn a berth in the "Chase for the Championship." Those drivers will begin the final 10 races with adjusted points totals. The leader receives 5,050 points, the second-place driver receives 5,045 points, and so on, with each additional driver starting with five fewer points. Busch finished with 6,506 points, eight more than the second-place finisher, Jimmie Johnson, who took second in the final race of the season.

The circuit also introduced new rules in July after a spate of caution-flag finishes, in which the order of racers was frozen until the end of the race, preventing racers from moving up in the order. To prevent this, NASCAR adopted a "green-white-checkered" format in which a race could not end under a yellow, or caution, flag. In the event of such an occurrence, racers would restart under a green flag and then take a white flag, which signals the last lap of the race, on the first pass, before taking the checkered flag at the finish.

IRL. Michael Andretti's Green Racing team captured 6 of the first 9 races of the 16-race Indy Racing League (IRL) schedule, with Tony Kanaan of Brazil surging to the points lead with three of those victories. Kanaan clinched the points title on October 3 with his second-place finish at the Toyota Indy 400 at the California Speedway in Fontana. Kanaan also became the first open-wheel driver in history to finish every lap of every race in a season.

Champ Car. Sebastien Bourdais won 4 of the first 6 races in the Champ Car World Series, the 14-race circuit previously known as Championship Auto Racing Teams (CART). Bourdais captured the points title on November 7 by winning the final race of the season in Mexico City.

Endurance. Tom Kristensen of Denmark won a record-tying sixth championship at the 24 Hours of Le Mans on June 13 in Le Mans, France. (Jacky Ickx of Belgium also had won the race six times.) Kristensen, driving with Seiji Ara of Japan and Rinaldo Capello of Italy, completed a record 379 laps, breaking the previous mark of 377 laps set by Kristensen, Capello, and Guy Smith in 2003.

Christian Fittipaldi, Terry Borcheller, Andy Pilgrim, and Forest Barber won the Rolex 24-hour race on Feb. 1, 2004, in Daytona Beach, Florida.

Dragsters. Tony Schumacher won the 2004 National Hot Rod Association (NHRA) top fuel division championship; John Force won the funny car division; and Greg Anderson won the pro stock division.　■ Michael Kates

See also **Sports.**

Aviation. Many major airlines suffered financial difficulties in 2004 despite a recovering global economy that boosted demand for business and leisure travel. The price of jet fuel was one factor. Increased worldwide demand for oil and continuing conflict in the Middle East pushed fuel prices up by 50 percent in 2004. Fuel typically represents about one-sixth of an airline's operating cost.

United Airlines, the second largest airline in the United States, remained in bankruptcy protection through the end of 2004. In June, the Elk Grove Village, Illinois-based airline was unsuccessful in its third and final attempt to obtain more than $1 billion in loan guarantees from the Air Transportation Stabilization Board (ATSB). The ATSB was created after terrorists attacked the United States in 2001. The board provides guarantees for commercial loans sought by airlines in financial difficulty.

United attempted to return to solvency in February 2004 by launching low-fare flights marketed under the name Ted. The move was designed to prevent loss of market share to low-fare airlines.

United also attempted to reduce costs by renegotiating labor contracts. However, it suffered a setback in July when unions objected to the airline's announcement that it would not be paying $500 million to the company pension plan during the final months of 2004.

Bankruptcy. US Airways Inc. of Arlington, Virginia, filed for bankruptcy on September 12. The airline had filed for bankruptcy in 2002 but rebounded in 2003 after negotiating reduced wages and benefits from its employees. However, airline officials said the company was unsuccessful in obtaining $800 million in cost cuts from union members necessary to reduce costs.

ATA Holdings Corp. of Indianapolis filed for bankruptcy on Oct. 26, 2004. ATA officials said that the increased cost of jet fuel and lower fare prices had placed the airline in financial peril.

Security concerns continued at airports in 2004 following ongoing fears of terrorist hijackings of commercial flights. Several flights from Europe to the United States were canceled during 2004 after authorities intercepted suspicious communications from suspected terrorists.

In July, Tom Ridge, secretary of the U.S. Department of Homeland Security, said that the federal government had scrapped plans for the proposed Computer Assisted Passenger Pre-screening System (CAPPS II). CAPPS II would have collected personal information on airline passengers to try to identify who was a security risk. Opponents claimed that the system invaded passengers' privacy. Other opponents argued that the system could be ineffective if terrorists used false identities.

The Transportation Security Administration (TSA), an agency of the U.S. Department of Homeland Security, announced plans in August to test a passenger-screening system designed to keep suspicious passengers from boarding domestic flights. Secure Flight compares airline passengers' names with a Homeland Security Department terrorist watch list.

Testing on another system began in June at several airports. Under the Registered Traveler program, frequent travelers provided personal data, fingerprints, and an iris scan for identity authentication. Travelers not posing a security risk would join a shorter line at checkpoints, though they and their luggage would still be screened.

Travel delays resulted in major changes at Chicago's O'Hare International Airport in 2004. On August 18, representatives of the two largest airlines announced plans to cut flights at O'Hare to ease some of the congestion that delayed flights across the country.

Officials at American Airlines of Dallas-Fort Worth, Texas, along with officials at United Airlines agreed to cut or move 37 flights scheduled to arrive during peak afternoon and evening travel periods at the airport. Under the agreement, American, which has 550 arrivals at O'Hare each day, canceled or rescheduled 17 flights. United, which has 650 daily flights at the airport, canceled or rescheduled 20 flights. The restrictions took effect on November 1 and were scheduled to expire in April 2005. U.S. Secretary of Transportation Norman Mineta

said that he had contacted executives at both airlines and asked them to agree to the temporary flight-reduction agreement.

New aircraft. Representatives of the Boeing Company, headquartered in Chicago, announced in April 2004 that the company had received the first orders for its new mid-sized jet aircraft to be known as the 7E7 Dreamliner. The new aircraft is designed to seat between 200 and 300 passengers and fly between 3,500 and 8,500 miles (6,500 and 16,000 kilometers) before refueling. All Nippon Airways (ANA) of Tokyo, Japan, agreed to purchase 50 aircraft. The 7E7 airplanes were scheduled to be delivered in 2008.

Speed record. The X-43A, an experimental unpiloted aircraft, reached a record speed of 6,600 miles (10,621 kilometers) per hour on Nov. 16, 2004. The National Aeronautics and Space Administration owns the 12-foot (3.7-meter) long X-43A. An aircraft carried the X-43A from the runway at the Dryden Flight Research Center at Edwards Air Force Base, California. Once released from the aircraft the X-43A fired a booster rocket, which carried the aircraft to an altitude of about 40,000 feet (13,000 meters). It then separated from the booster and reached an altitude of about 110,000 feet (36,000 meters) under its own power. The experimental aircraft flew freely for a few minutes before gliding back to earth. ■ Ian Savage

Azerbaijan. Seven prominent Azerbaijani political opposition leaders were sentenced on Oct. 22, 2004, to prison terms of 2½ to 5 years for their roles in violent protests following the controversial presidential election of Oct. 15, 2003. Although then-Prime Minister Ilham Aliyev won the election decisively, international observers condemned the process as severely flawed.

The clashes between protestors and police in Baku, the capital, following the election resulted in hundreds of detentions and more than 120 criminal convictions. The Baku office of the Organization for Security and Cooperation in Europe (OSCE) stated that it was "deeply concerned by the severity of the sentences."

President Aliyev, the son of the previous president, Heydar Aliyev, systematically strengthened his control over Azerbaijani politics in 2004. While international pressures encouraged the regime to release some political prisoners, Aliyev's repression of alternative parties and newspapers has effectively neutralized the Azerbaijani political opposition.

■ Juliet Johnson

See also **Asia.**

Bahamas. See West Indies.

Bahrain. See Middle East.

Ballet. See Dance.

A section of wing of the giant Airbus A380 is transported from a manufacturing plant in Broughton, Wales, to an assembly facility in Toulouse, France, in April 2004. Airbus, the European manufacturer of passenger jets, has scheduled the first flights of the 555-passenger superjumbo jet for 2006.

Baltic states. Estonia, Latvia, and Lithuania joined the North Atlantic Treaty Organization (NATO) and the European Union (EU) in 2004, completing a formal reintegration with Western Europe that began when the then-Soviet republics declared their independence from the Soviet Union in 1990. The Soviet Union had annexed the Baltic states in 1940 after Russia signed a nonaggression pact with Germany in August 1939 that placed the Baltics in the Soviet sphere of influence.

Joining Europe. On April 2, 2004, the Baltic states joined NATO as the security alliance's membership expanded to incorporate seven formerly Communist countries. Russia grudgingly accepted this development, with the Duma (the lower legislative house) adopting a nonbinding resolution labeling NATO an "offensive" bloc. On May 1, the Baltic states and seven other countries joined the EU. On June 27, Estonia and Lithuania fixed their currencies against the euro in preparation for eventual entry into the European monetary union. All three Baltic states hoped to switch to the euro by 2007.

Russian relations. Tensions over NATO and EU expansion, the rights of ethnic Russian minorities, and compensation for the Soviet occupation dominated Baltic-Russian relations in 2004. The Latvian parliament passed a bill on September 30 that prohibited Latvians who have dual citizenship with Russia from holding national office. In May, Estonia announced that it would sue Russia for financial compensation for damages caused during the Soviet occupation. Latvia and Lithuania later announced that they, too, would seek compensation.

Political shakeups rocked the Baltic nations in 2004. On February 5, Latvian Prime Minister Einars Repse's minority government resigned due to lack of support. Latvian President Vaira Vike-Freiberga invited Green Party leader Indulis Emsis to form a new coalition government. Emsis and his Cabinet survived no-confidence measures in June and September but were forced to resign on October 28 when the Latvian parliament voted down their draft budget bill. On December 2, the parliament voted to approve a four-party coalition government led by Prime Minister Aigars Kalvitis.

The Lithuanian parliament impeached President Rolandas Paksas on April 6. Opponents had accused Paksas of granting citizenship and passing state secrets to Russian arms dealer Yuri Borisov, among other charges. Former President Valdas Adamkus won the June presidential election to replace Paksas. Following inconclusive parliamentary elections on October 4, Lithuania's ruling coalition of Social Democrats and Social Liberals agreed to form a new government in November with the populist, pro-Russian Labor Party. Prime Minister Algirdas Brazauskas retained his post.   ■ Juliet Johnson

See also **Europe; Russia.**

Flood victims stand in line for food in Bangladesh's capital, Dhaka, in August. Unusually heavy summer monsoons left two-thirds of Bangladesh underwater for weeks, forcing the government to appeal to other nations for food aid for 20 million starving people.

Bangladesh. The people of Bangladesh suffered through severe weather and its effects in 2004. In July, the most severe flooding in 15 years inundated large parts of the capital, Dhaka. Two-thirds of the country, located in the delta of three major Asian rivers, was submerged for weeks.

More than 600 people were killed and thousands of others were sickened by polluted drinking water and spoiled food. The government appealed for food aid for 20 million people after flooding destroyed crops. Dhaka was hit again in September by the heaviest rainfall in 50 years. Between September 11 and 13, the city received almost 20 inches (50.8 centimeters) of rain.

Explosions shook rallies staged by the opposition Awami League on August 7, killing one person in the northern city of Sylhet. League leader Sheikh Hasina Wajed blamed the bombings on the Bangladesh Nationalist Party led by Prime Minister Khaleda Zia. Wajed and Zia have been fierce political rivals for many years, with control of Bangladesh switching back and forth between them since the 1990's. When some 20,000 people rallied in Dhaka on Aug. 21, 2004, to hear Wajed condemn the violence, hand grenades were thrown into the crowd, killing 21 people. The League responded with nationwide strikes, which led to more violence.   ■ Henry S. Bradsher

See also **Asia; Disasters.**

Consumer Reports magazine, sent petitions to banking regulators asking for safeguards, such as suspending fees on bounced checks for the first two months of the law. Bank officials, however, countered that the new law eases electronic processing of checks.

JP Morgan Chase & Co. announced plans on January 14 to acquire Bank One Corp. for about $58 billion in stock. The acquisition created the second largest bank in the United States, with assets of about $1.1 trillion. The new bank, which retained the JP Morgan Chase & Co. name, was slightly smaller than Citigroup Inc. of New York City, which had loans and assets of about $1.2 trillion. The headquarters of the combined JP Morgan Chase remained in New York City. The consumer services businesses remained in Chicago, where Bank One was headquartered.

Economists noted that the merger was an example of a new strategy by the nation's biggest bankers. In 2004, larger institutions were less focused on corporate underwriting—helping corporations issue stocks and bonds to raise money—and more interested in small borrowers and credit card users.

Industry earnings. The banking industry continued to report record-breaking profits for most of 2004. In the first quarter, the industry reported combined earnings of $31.8 billion. In the second quarter, the industry reported net income of $31.2 billion, the second highest total in history. Although still very strong, the second quarter marked the first time in six consecutive financial quarters that earnings failed to set a new profit record.

In the 2004 third quarter, the industry reported net income of $32.5 billion, a quarterly record. Increased lending to consumers and businesses fueled the profits. The banks also reported higher gains from the sales of securities and other assets. Meanwhile, the industry's holdings of *noncurrent loans,* which are 90 or more days past due, continued to decline. In the third quarter, the industry reported that the collective total of noncurrent loans had fallen for the eighth consecutive quarter.

Citigroup. The nation's largest bank faced significant challenges in 2004. On May 10, Citigroup agreed to pay $2.58 billion to settle a lawsuit brought by investors of the former WorldCom Inc. of Clinton, Mississippi. The group of investors lost billions of dollars when WorldCom, a telecommunications giant, filed for bankruptcy in 2002 after a massive accounting scandal. The securities class action settlement was the second largest in history.

On May 27, 2004, the Fed ordered a subsidiary of Citigroup to pay $70 million for abuses in personal and mortgage loans to low-income and

Bank. The Federal Reserve System (the Fed), the central bank of the United States, raised short-term interest rates five times in 2004 and suggested that it would continue to raise rates through 2005. The Fed sets short-term interest rates on overnight loans between banks. It raises interest rates at times of economic strength in order to stem inflation, and it lowers rates when the economy is weak, by making it cheaper to borrow money.

The final short-term interest rate increase of 2004 was announced on December 14, when the Fed raised rates by one-quarter point to 2.25 percent. It had also raised rates by one-quarter percent on November 10, September 21, August 10, and June 30.

Check 21. A new law took effect on October 28 that allowed banks to decrease the amount of time between when a check is deposited and when the amount of that check is debited from an account. However, Check 21—officially known as the Check Clearing for the 21st Century Act—did not shorten the amount of time that banks can hold checks deposited by customers.

Many consumer groups opposed the new law, saying that it creates a "mismatch" in timing that may cause consumers to unwittingly write checks on accounts with insufficient funds. Consumers Union, a consumer watchdog and publisher of

high-risk borrowers. The penalty was the largest ever imposed by the Fed for consumer-lending violations. The Citigroup unit, CitiFinancial Credit Co., was fined because it converted personal loans into home equity loans without adequately assessing the ability of borrowers to repay. In these loans, the borrower's residence was the bank's "security" and could be repossessed if the consumer did not pay on the loan.

In September, the government of Japan ordered Citigroup to close its private banking unit in Japan for failing to guard against money laundering. Money laundering occurs when criminals use bank accounts to make illegally obtained funds appear legitimate. On October 25, Citigroup's Chief Executive Charles Prince apologized for the failings and bowed before Japanese officials. Citigroup also discharged several top executives involved in the incident.

Citigroup announced in January that it took a $242-million *charge* (write-off) for losses connected to the collapse of Italy's giant dairy company, Parmalat. Citigroup was one of Parmalat's biggest lenders, and authorities were investigating how much Citigroup executives knew about Parmalat's troubles prior to its insolvency.

Bank of America. On April 1, 2004, another banking giant, Bank of America Corp., based in Charlotte, North Carolina, completed its acquisition of FleetBoston Financial. The acquisition took place just days after Bank of America agreed to pay $675 million in fines, penalties, and fee reductions as a result of a Securities and Exchange Commission (SEC) investigation into the bank's mutual fund trading. The SEC alleged that the bank experienced a breakdown in internal controls in its broker-dealer and clearing operations, which are used to process trades. SEC officials believed that some of the bank's employees had used market timing to benefit some of its clients and shortchange other parties. As part of the settlement, Bank of America agreed to divest itself of its broker-dealer unit and to settle the $10-million charge that it delayed the investigation by failing to produce documents promptly.

Riggs Bank. The U.S. Department of Justice announced in July 2004 that it was launching a criminal investigation into Riggs Bank of Washington, D.C. Several news organizations had alleged that Riggs Bank had money-laundering ties to overseas terrorists. Additionally, a report by the U.S. Senate Permanent Subcommittee on Investigations alleged that Riggs Bank employees helped former Chilean Dictator Augusto Pinochet hide millions of illegally obtained dollars.

The bank agreed to be acquired in July by PNL Financial Services Group of Pittsburgh, Pennsylvania, for $779 million.   ■ Paulette Thomas
See also **Economics; Stocks and bonds.**

Baseball. The Boston Red Sox in 2004 captured the team's first World Series title in 86 years in historic fashion, sweeping the St. Louis Cardinals in four games without ever trailing. Earlier in the post-season, the Red Sox became the first team in the history of Major League Baseball (MLB) to come back after losing the first three games of a series, storming through to stun the New York Yankees 4 games to 3 in the American League Championship Series (ALCS).

By sweeping St. Louis, the Red Sox became the first team to win eight consecutive post-season games in one year and broke the "Curse of the Bambino," which many fans blamed for the team's long World Series drought. The curse, many believed, stemmed from Boston's decision to trade legendary slugger Babe Ruth to the rival New York Yankees in 1920.

No action was taken by MLB officials in 2004 to institute a tougher ban on steroid use by players, despite the fact that several star players testified before a federal grand jury investigating the Bay Area Laboratory Co-Operative (BALCO). The case involved high-level BALCO executives being investigated for allegedly distributing illegal steroids to several high-profile athletes. San Francisco Giants slugger Barry Bonds, who testified before the grand jury, faced questions early in the season because his personal trainer, Greg Anderson, was indicted by the grand jury for allegedly conspiring to distribute human growth hormone, which some athletes use to improve their performance.

World Series. The Red Sox, who had won the American League wild-card to gain the play-offs, became just the fourth team in history to never trail in a World Series game, joining the 1989 Oakland Athletics, the 1966 Baltimore Orioles, and the 1963 Los Angeles Dodgers.

Boston captured Game 1 in Boston on Oct. 23, 2004, jumping out to a 4-0 lead in the first inning. St. Louis rallied to tie the game at 7 in the sixth inning, but Mark Bellhorn's two-run homer in the bottom of the eighth secured the victory.

In Game 2, the next night, Boston pitching ace Curt Schilling underwent an experimental procedure for the second time in the play-offs to be able to pitch. Physicians sutured his dislocated tendon into place to prevent it from sliding. Schilling led Boston to a 6-2 victory. Boston won Game 3 in St. Louis, Missouri, on October 26 by a score of 4-1 behind terrific pitching by Pedro Martinez. Boston completed the sweep of the Cardinals with a 3-0 win on October 27.

Play-offs. In the American League Division Series, Boston swept the Anaheim Angels 3 games to none while the Yankees beat the Minnesota Twins 3 games to 1. In the ALCS, the Yankees took an easy 3-0 series lead, including a 19-8 drubbing of Boston on October 16 in Boston's Fenway Park.

Boston faced being swept from the play-offs in Game 4, trailing 4 to 3 with three outs to go. However, Boston did the seemingly impossible and tied the game against Yankees closer Mariano Rivera, considered to be one of the best closing pitchers of all time. The Red Sox won in the 12th inning on David Ortiz's two-run walk-off home run. (A walk-off home run is when the home team hits a home run to win the game, after which the teams walk off the field.)

The next night, still facing elimination, Boston was losing 4 to 2 in the eighth inning when they again rallied with two runs to force extra innings. And again Ortiz answered the call, dropping a bloop single into center field in the 14th inning to drive in the winning run. The game, which lasted 5 hours, 49 minutes, was the longest in post-season history.

In Game 6, Schilling, who was ineffective in Game 1 because of his ankle injury, underwent the

FINAL STANDINGS IN MAJOR LEAGUE BASEBALL

AMERICAN LEAGUE

American League champions—
Boston Red Sox
(defeated New York Yankees, 4 games to 3)
World Series champions—
Boston Red Sox (defeated St. Louis Cardinals, 4 games to 0)

Eastern Division	W.	L.	Pct.	G.B.
New York Yankees	101	61	.623	—
Boston Red Sox*	98	64	.605	3
Baltimore Orioles	78	84	.481	23
Tampa Bay Devil Rays	70	91	.435	30½
Toronto Blue Jays	67	94	.416	33½

Central Division	W.	L.	Pct.	G.B.
Minnesota Twins	92	70	.568	—
Chicago White Sox	83	79	.512	9
Cleveland Indians	80	82	.494	12
Detroit Tigers	72	90	.444	20
Kansas City Royals	58	104	.358	34

Western Division	W.	L.	Pct.	G.B.
Anaheim Angels	92	70	.568	—
Oakland Athletics	91	71	.562	1
Texas Rangers	89	73	.549	3
Seattle Mariners	63	99	.389	29

Offensive leaders

Batting average	Ichiro Suzuki, Seattle	.372
Runs scored	Vladimir Guerrero, Anaheim	124
Home runs	Manny Ramirez, Boston	43
Runs batted in	Miguel Tejada, Baltimore	150
Hits	Ichiro Suzuki, Seattle	262
Stolen bases	Carl Crawford, Tampa Bay	59
Slugging percentage	Manny Ramirez, Boston	.613

Leading pitchers

Games won	Curt Schilling, Boston	21
Earned run average (162 or more innings)—	Johan Santana, Minnesota	2.61
Strikeouts	Johan Santana, Minnesota	265
Saves	Mariano Rivera, New York	53
Shut-outs	Jeremy Bonderman, Detroit	2
	Tim Hudson, Oakland	2
	Sidney Ponson, Baltimore	2
Complete games	Mark Mulder, Oakland	5
	Sidney Ponson, Baltimore	5
	Jake Westbrook, Cleveland	5

Awards†

Most Valuable Player	Vladimir Guerrero, Anaheim
Cy Young	Johan Santana, Minnesota
Rookie of the Year	Bobby Crosby, Oakland
Manager of the Year	Buck Showalter, Texas

NATIONAL LEAGUE

National League champions—
St. Louis Cardinals (defeated Houston Astros, 4 games to 3)

Eastern Division	W.	L.	Pct.	G.B.
Atlanta Braves	96	66	.593	—
Philadelphia Phillies	86	76	.531	10
Florida Marlins	83	79	.512	13
New York Mets	71	91	.438	25
Montreal Expos	67	95	.414	29

Central Division	W.	L.	Pct.	G.B.
St. Louis Cardinals	105	57	.648	—
Houston Astros*	92	70	.568	13
Chicago Cubs	89	73	.549	16
Cincinnati Reds	76	86	.469	29
Pittsburgh Pirates	72	89	.447	32½
Milwaukee Brewers	67	94	.416	37½

Western Division	W.	L.	Pct.	G.B.
Los Angeles Dodgers	93	69	.574	—
San Francisco Giants	91	71	.562	2
San Diego Padres	87	75	.537	6
Colorado Rockies	68	94	.420	25
Arizona Diamondbacks	51	111	.315	42

Offensive leaders

Batting average	Barry Bonds, San Francisco	.362
Runs scored	Albert Pujols, St. Louis	133
Home runs	Adrian Beltre, Los Angeles	48
Runs batted in	Vinny Castilla, Colorado	131
Hits	Juan Pierre, Florida	221
Stolen bases	Scott Podsednik, Milwaukee	70
Slugging percentage	Barry Bonds, San Francisco	.812

Leading pitchers

Games won	Roy Oswalt, Houston	20
Earned run average (162 or more innings)—	Jake Peavy, San Diego	2.27
Strikeouts	Randy Johnson, Arizona	290
Saves	Armando Benitez, Florida	47
Shut-outs	Cory Lidle, Philadelphia	3
	Jason Schmidt, San Francisco	3
Complete games	Livan Hernandez, Montreal	9

Awards†

Most Valuable Player	Barry Bonds, San Francisco
Cy Young	Roger Clemens, Houston
Rookie of the Year	Jason Bay, Pittsburgh
Manager of the Year	Bobby Cox, Atlanta

*Qualified for wild-card play-off spot.
†Selected by the Baseball Writers Association of America.

Red Sox slugger Manny Ramirez celebrates after hitting a run-scoring single in Game 1 of the World Series on October 23. Ramirez had a terrific series against the St. Louis Cardinals, hitting .412, with 1 home run and 4 RBIs. Ramirez was named Most Valuable Player of the World Series for his efforts, which helped propel the Red Sox to a sweep of the Cardinals.

The Boston Red Sox caught up with history in 2004, winning their first World Series since 1918.

Members of the Boston Red Sox storm the field on October 27, after defeating the St. Louis Cardinals 3-0 in Game 4 of the World Series in St. Louis, Missouri. The Red Sox were led in the play-offs by Manny Ramirez and pitcher Curt Schilling, who underwent an experimental medical procedure to even be able to pitch. The Red Sox went on a historic hot streak in the post-season, becoming the first team to win their last eight games of the season. The victory ended 86 years of frustration for legions of Red Sox fans.

first-of-its-kind surgical procedure to stabilize the ankle. After the procedure, Schilling pitched seven strong innings, giving up only one run. Boston won the game 4-2. It was the first time in major-league post-season history that a team that had fallen behind 0-3 came back to force a Game 7. On October 20, Boston took Game 7, defeating the Yankees 10 to 3 to get to the World Series.

In the National League Division Series, St. Louis eliminated the Los Angeles Dodgers 3 games to 1 while the Houston Astros eliminated the Atlanta Braves 3 games to 2. In the NL Championship Series, St. Louis defeated Houston 4 games to 3. Houston pitcher Roger Clemens performed very well and later earned a record seventh Cy Young Award.

Regular season. The NL West came down to the final weekend, with the Dodgers (93-69), edging the San Francisco Giants by two games. The St. Louis Cardinals ran away with the NL Central, posting a major-league best record of 105-57 to take the division by 13 games over the Houston Astros, who went on a tear at the end of the season, winning their last 18 home games to surge past the slumping Chicago Cubs and win the NL wild card. Atlanta won the NL East by 10 games over the second-place Philadelphia Phillies.

The AL West also came down to the final weekend, with the Anaheim Angels taking two of three games from the Oakland Athletics to win the division by one game. The Yankees held off Boston by three games to win the AL East with a 101-61 mark. The Minnesota Twins easily captured the AL Central by nine games with a record of 92-70.

Barry Bonds. In 2004, Barry Bonds broke three records he had set in 2002. His .609 on-base percentage topped his old mark of .582. He also walked 232 times, 34 more than in 2002 and received 120 intentional walks, nearly twice as many as in 2002. On Sept. 17, 2004, he became the third player to hit 700 home runs. Bonds finished with 703 home runs. Only Babe Ruth (714) and Henry Aaron (755) have hit more.

New hit king. Ichiro Suzuki of the Seattle Mariners established new records for hits in a season and singles in a season. Suzuki finished the season with 262 hits and set major league records for singles in a season (225).

College. California State (Fullerton) won its fourth national championship on June 27, 2004, with a 3-2 victory over the University of Texas (Austin) in the National Collegiate Athletic Association World Series in Omaha, Nebraska.

Youth. On August 29 in Williamsport, Pennsylvania, a team from Willemstad, Curacao, became the first team from a Caribbean nation to win the Little League World Series, defeating a team from Thousand Oaks, California, 5-2. ■ Michael Kates

See also **Building and construction; Deaths; Montreal; People in the news; Sports; Washington.**

Basketball. The Detroit Pistons pulled off perhaps the biggest upset in National Basketball Association (NBA) history, stunning the heavily favored Los Angeles Lakers on June 15, 2004, to capture the team's first NBA title since 1990. The Pistons won in surprisingly easy fashion, 4 games to 1. The Pistons' swarming defense and unselfish play overwhelmed the Lakers. Detroit point guard Chauncey Billups was named the Finals' most valuable player (MVP).

However, the NBA's image was seriously damaged in November 2004 when a brawl broke about between players and fans during a game in Auburn Hills, Michigan. Several players received lengthy suspensions, for the incident, in which players injured several fans.

In college basketball, the University of Connecticut (UConn) became the first Division I team in National Collegiate Athletic Association (NCAA) history to win both the men's and women's national titles.

Lakers star guard Kobe Bryant was involved in a high-profile sexual assault case for the entire 2004 season. However, the case was dismissed in September 2004.

Professional men. Detroit became the first Eastern Conference champion since the Chicago Bulls took the title in 1998. Detroit sealed its championship season with a convincing Game 5 triumph over Los Angeles on June 15, 2004, in Auburn Hills, Michigan. Detroit's Chauncey Billups scored 14 points in the game while teammate Ben Wallace added an 18-point, 22-rebound performance. Richard Hamilton was equally impressive with 21 points as the Pistons built a lead of more than 20 points and glided to a 100-87 victory. Larry Brown won his first championship in 22 years as an NBA coach.

The Lakers barely escaped a sweep, but were fortunate to win Game 2, in Los Angeles. Rallying from six points down with less than 1 minute to play, Kobe Bryant made a clutch three-pointer to force overtime. The Lakers went on to win that game, but could not answer Detroit when the series shifted to Michigan. The Pistons became the first home team to sweep the middle three games since the NBA shifted to the 2-3-2 format in 1985.

Shortly after the season ended, the breakup of the Lakers began. The team's owners decided not to renew Phil Jackson's contract and agreed to Shaquille O'Neale's request for a trade, sending him to the Miami Heat in late July. For a time, it appeared that Kobe Bryant would not return either, but he and the team reached an agreement in July.

Detroit reached the finals by topping the Indiana Pacers 4 games to 2 in the Eastern Conference finals. In Game 2, which Detroit won 72-67, both teams combined for an all-time play-off low of 45

Diana Taurasi of the University of Connecticut (UConn) shoots over Shyra Ely of the University of Tennessee during the championship game of the NCAA tournament on April 6, 2004. UConn won the game 70-61, taking its third straight title.

set an NBA record for holding opponents to fewer than 100 points in 38 consecutive games. They also set a record by holding opponents to fewer than 70 points in five straight games.

In the American Basketball Association, Ashley McElhiney became the first woman coach of a men's professional team when she was named coach of the expansion team the Nashville Rhythm on May 17.

Brawl. On November 19, players and fans fought in the stands during what several commentators called the ugliest brawl in the history of professional sports.

The fight began after a game between the Detroit Pistons and the Indiana Pacers. As the game ended, a Pistons fan threw a beverage at Indiana's Ron Artest, who climbed into the stands throwing punches. Several other players followed him.

Nine fans were injured in the brawl. Artest was suspended for the remainder of the 2004–2005 season. Eight other players also received suspensions ranging from one to 30 games.

Professional women. The Seattle Storm defeated the Connecticut Sun 2 games to 1 to win their first Women's National Basketball Association (WNBA) title on October 12 in Seattle. The Sun won the first game of the series 68-64, but the Storm stormed back to take the final two games in the three-game series for the title. They won Game 3 in convincing fashion, defeating the Sun 74 to 60.

College men. UConn, the preseason No. 1 team in the country, blasted Georgia Tech 82-73 on April 5 in San Antonio, Texas, behind the junior tandem of Emeka Okafor and Ben Gordon. Okafor scored 24 points and added 15 rebounds and earned Most Outstanding Player honors as the Huskies (33-6) built a 25-point lead in the second half. Gordon added 21 points.

The Huskies, the No. 2 seed out of the Phoenix regional, reached the title game by rallying from eight points down with four minutes to go to edge Duke, the No. 1 seed in the Atlanta regional, 79-78 on April 3. Georgia Tech (28-10), the No. 3

field goals and scored a play-off record low 59 combined second-half points. Detroit topped the New Jersey Nets 4 games to 3 in the conference semifinals and defeated the Milwaukee Bucks 4 games to 1 in the first round.

The Lakers earned a Finals berth by toppling the Minnesota Timberwolves 4 games to 2 in the Western Conference finals, beating defending champion the San Antonio Spurs 4 games to 2 in the semifinals and overpowering the Houston Rockets four games to 1 in the first round.

During the regular season, Indiana topped the Central Division with the best record in the NBA, 61 wins and 21 losses. New Jersey won the Atlantic with a 47-35 record. Minnesota, behind league MVP Kevin Garnett, posted the best record in the Western Conference, 58-24, to win the Midwest Division, while the Lakers won the Pacific with a mark of 56-26.

New Jersey interim coach Lawrence Frank set a North American mark for best starts in professional coaching on Feb. 24, 2004, when his team's 86-74 victory over the Toronto Raptors gave him a 13-0 mark as Nets coach. The Pistons

THE 2003-2004 COLLEGE BASKETBALL SEASON

COLLEGE TOURNAMENT CHAMPIONS

NCAA (Men)
Division I:	Connecticut
Division II:	Kennesaw State
Division III:	Wisconsin-Stevens Point

(Women)
Division I:	Connecticut
Division II:	California of Pennsylvania
Division III:	Wilmington (Ohio)

NAIA (Men)
Division I:	Mountain State (W. Virginia)
Division II:	Oregon Institute of Technology

(Women)
Division I:	Southern Nazarene (Oklahoma)
Division II:	Morningside (Iowa)

NIT (Men)   Michigan

MEN'S COLLEGE CHAMPIONS

CONFERENCE	SCHOOL
America East	Boston
	Vermont (tournament)
Atlantic 10	Xavier (tournament)
East Division	Saint Joseph's
West Division	Dayton
Atlantic Coast	Duke
	Maryland (tournament)
Atlantic Sun	Troy State
	Central Florida (tournament)
Big 12	Oklahoma State*
Big East	Pittsburgh
	Connecticut (tournament)
Big Sky	Eastern Washington*
Big South	Birmingham Southern–Liberty* (tie)
Big Ten	Illinois
	Wisconsin (tournament)
Big West	Utah State–Pacific* (tie)
Colonial	Virginia Commonwealth*
Conference USA	DePaul–Memphis–Cincinnati*–
	Alabama (Birmingham)–Charlotte (tie)
Horizon League	Wisconsin (Milwaukee)*
Ivy League	Princeton†
Metro Atlantic	Manhattan*
Mid-American	
East Division	Kent State
West Division	Western Michigan*
Mid-Continent	Valparaiso*
Mid-Eastern	South Carolina State–Florida A&M* (tie)
Missouri Valley	Southern Illinois
	Northern Iowa (tournament)
Mountain West	Air Force
	Utah (tournament)
Northeast	St. Francis (New York)–Monmouth* (tie)
Ohio Valley	Austin Peay
	Murray State (tournament)
Pacific 10	Stanford*
Patriot League	American–Lehigh* (tie)
Southeastern	
Eastern	Kentucky*
Western	Mississippi State
Southern	
North Division	East Tennessee State*
South Division	Georgia Southern–Charleston–
	Davidson (tie)
Southland	Texas (Arlington)–
	Southeastern Louisiana–
	Texas (San Antonio)* (tie)
Southwestern	Mississippi Valley State
	Alabama State (tournament)
Sun Belt	
East Division	Arkansas (Little Rock)
West Division	Lafayette-Louisiana*
West Coast	Gonzaga
Western Athletic	Texas (El Paso)–Nevada* (tie)

*Regular season and conference tournament champion.
†No tournament played.
Sources: National Collegiate Athletic Association (NCAA);
National Association of Intercollegiate Athletics (NAIA);
National Invitation Tournament (NIT); Conference Web sites.

UConn guard Taliek Brown makes a reverse lay-up over defenders from Georgia Tech in the championship game of the NCAA tournament on April 5, 2004. UConn, which had been ranked the best team in the country in the pre-season, defeated Georgia Tech 82-73 to win the title.

NATIONAL BASKETBALL ASSOCIATION STANDINGS

EASTERN CONFERENCE

Atlantic Division	W.	L.	Pct.	G.B.
New Jersey Nets*	47	35	.573	—
Miami Heat*	42	40	.512	5
New York Knicks*	39	43	.476	8
Boston Celtics*	36	46	.439	11
Philadelphia 76ers	33	49	.402	14
Washington Wizards	25	57	.305	22
Orlando Magic	21	61	.256	26

Central Division				
Indiana Pacers*	61	21	.744	—
Detroit Pistons*	54	28	.659	7
New Orleans Hornets*	41	41	.500	20
Milwaukee Bucks*	41	41	.500	20
Cleveland Cavaliers	35	47	.427	26
Toronto Raptors	33	49	.402	28
Atlanta Hawks	28	54	.349	33
Chicago Bulls	23	59	.280	38

WESTERN CONFERENCE

Midwest Division				
Minnesota T'wolves*	58	24	.707	—
San Antonio Spurs*	57	25	.695	1
Dallas Mavericks*	52	30	.634	6
Memphis Grizzlies*	50	32	.610	8
Houston Rockets*	45	37	.549	13
Denver Nuggets*	43	39	.524	15
Utah Jazz*	42	40	.512	16

Pacific Division				
Los Angeles Lakers*	56	26	.683	—
Sacramento Kings*	55	27	.671	1
Portland Trail Blazers	41	41	.500	15
Golden State Warriors	37	45	.451	19
Seattle Supersonics	37	45	.451	19
Phoenix Suns	29	53	.354	27
Los Angeles Clippers	28	54	.341	28

INDIVIDUAL LEADERS

Scoring	G.	F.G.	F.T.M.	Pts.	Avg.
Tracy McGrady, Houston	67	653	398	1,878	28.0
Kevin Garnett, Minnesota	82	804	368	1,987	24.2
Peja Stojakovic, Sacramento	81	665	394	1,964	24.2
Kobe Bryant, L.A. Lakers	65	516	454	1,557	24.0
Paul Pierce, Boston	80	602	517	1,836	23.0
Baron Davis, New Orleans	67	554	237	1,532	22.9
Vince Carter, Toronto	73	608	336	1,645	22.5
Tim Duncan, San Antonio	69	592	352	1,538	22.3
Dirk Nowitzki, Dallas	77	605	371	1,680	21.8
Michael Redd, Milwaukee	82	633	383	1,776	21.7
Shaquille O'Neale, L.A. Lakers	67	554	331	1,439	21.5

Rebounding	G.	Off.	Def.	Tot.	Avg.
Kevin Garnett, Minnesota	82	245	894	1,139	13.9
Tim Duncan, San Antonio	69	227	632	859	12.4
Ben Wallace, Detroit	81	324	682	1,006	12.4
Erick Dampier, Dallas	74	344	543	887	12.0
Carlos Boozer, Utah	75	230	627	857	11.4
Zach Randolph, Portland	81	242	609	851	10.5
Jamaal Magloire, New Orleans	82	268	579	847	10.3
Brad Miller, Sacramento	72	191	552	743	10.3
Marcus Camby, Denver	72	211	516	727	10.1
Kenny Thomas, Philadelphia	74	261	489	750	10.1
Jermaine O'Neal, Indiana	78	193	585	778	10.0

NBA champions—Detroit Pistons
(defeated Los Angeles Lakers, 4 games to 1)

*Made play-offs.

---

seed in the St. Louis regional, reached the title game with a 67-65 win over Oklahoma State, the No. 2 seed out of the East Rutherford, New Jersey, regional.

College women. UConn captured its third consecutive women's title with a 70-61 triumph over the University of Tennessee (Knoxville) on April 6 in New Orleans. It was the second time in as many years that UConn beat Tennessee for the title. UConn (31-4) was led by national player of the year Diana Taurasi, who scored 17 points.

UConn made it to the title game by defeating the surprising Minnesota Golden Gophers 67-58. Tennessee (31-4) reached the title game with a narrow 52-50 victory over Louisiana State University (Baton Rouge).

■ Michael Kates

See also **Sports.**

Belarus. President Aleksandr Lukashenko retained his hold on Belarus in 2004. He reinforced his power through an election that many international observers believed to have been rigged.

In parliamentary elections on October 17, not a single opposition candidate managed to win 1 of the 110 seats in the National Assembly. In a referendum on the same ballot, more than 77 percent of voters approved amending the Belarussian constitution to eliminate the two-term limit on the presidency, clearing the way for Lukashenko to run for a third term in 2006.

The results sparked public protests in the capital, Minsk, causing numerous injuries and dozens of arrests. Prominent opposition leaders such as Anatoly Lebedko, head of the United Civil Party, were taken into custody.

The European Union and the United States joined observers from the Organization for Security and Cooperation in Europe in condemning the election. Allegations included ballot-box stuffing, harassment and detention of opposition candidates, and the use of premarked ballots.

On Oct. 20, 2004, U.S. President George W. Bush signed the Belarus Democracy Act of 2004. The act prevents federal agencies from giving financial aid to Belarus, but encourages aid to nongovernmental organizations and independent media. ■ Juliet Johnson

See also **Europe; Russia.**

Belgium. One of the biggest criminal trials held in Belgium in decades ended in June 2004 with the conviction of Marc Dutroux, an unemployed electrician, for leading a gang that kidnapped and raped six girls, killing four of them, in 1995 and 1996. In addition to kidnapping and rape, Dutroux was convicted of killing two of the girls and one of his accomplices. His former wife, Michelle Martin, was convicted of murder in the deaths of two other girls, aged 8, who died of starvation while being held in a basement prison on one of Dutroux's properties. Dutroux was sentenced to life in prison, and Martin to 30 years in prison. Two other associates were convicted of charges including kidnapping and drug-dealing and received prison sentences.

The case had traumatized Belgians for years, in part because of the serious errors police made while investigating Dutroux, who had previous convictions for abduction and rape. Witnesses at the trial recounted how police had searched Dutroux's house while the 8-year-old girls were being held captive but failed to find them. The errors fueled speculation that the authorities were covering up a wider network of kidnappings and abuse, a theory that Dutroux used to prolong the trial. However, prosecutors said there was no evidence that others had been involved. The case prompted major reforms of Belgium's police and judicial system and the creation of a European agency for missing and sexually abused children.

Far-right gains. The right-wing, anti-immigrant Vlaams Blok party scored major gains in regional elections in Flanders, the economically dominant Dutch-speaking province in the north of Belgium, in June 2004. The party won 24 percent of the vote, the biggest share of any single party, and 32 seats in the regional parliament, up from 22 seats in the previous parliament. The party had campaigned in favor of deporting illegal immigrants, requiring immigrants to speak the Dutch language, and holding a referendum on independence for Flanders. The region's other main parties—the Christian Democrats, Socialists, and two smaller populist parties—banded together to form a coalition government excluding Vlaams Blok.

In April, a Belgian court had convicted three Vlaams Blok fund-raising associations of violating antiracism laws. Vlaams Blok filed an appeal that allowed the party to participate in the June election. In October, the country's high court banned the party, saying leaflets used in campaigns in the 1990's had sought to incite anti-immigrant sentiment. The party responded by relaunching itself as Vlaams Belang, or Flemish Interest. ■ Tom Buerkle

See also **Europe.**
Belize. See **Latin America.**
Benin. See **Africa.**
Bhutan. See **Asia.**

Biology. Surprising findings about the family history of dogs were reported in May 2004. The report came from genetic analyses of dogs by scientists at the Fred Hutchinson Cancer Research Center in Seattle, Washington.

The geneticists compared about 100 different spots on DNA, or *deoxyribonucleic acid* (the molecule that makes up genes), from 414 dogs representing 85 breeds. When they plugged the genetic data describing these spots into a computer program, the program correctly identified the breeds of 410 of the 414 dogs. This indicated that genetic differences between breeds are more significant than previously realized.

The genetic analyses also allowed the scientists to group dog breeds into four main clusters, with each cluster made up of closely related breeds. One cluster consisted of the oldest breeds, including the Siberian husky, Alaskan malamute, shar-pei, and Akita. The scientists said these breeds are the dogs most closely related to wolves. The three other clusters represented old European efforts to breed dogs for specific purposes, according to the researchers. The hunting cluster of dogs included bloodhounds, golden retrievers, and beagles. The guarding cluster included mastiffs, bulldogs, and boxers. The herding cluster included sheepdogs, collies, Saint Bernards, and greyhounds.

A major surprise involved Ibizan and pharaoh hounds, breeds long thought to be descended from similar canines seen in ancient Egyptian art. The genetic analyses, however, indicated that the two modern breeds are later European re-creations of the Egyptian breeds and belong to the hunting cluster.

Mighty marathon mice. Two independent teams of geneticists reported in August that they each had created mice that had extraordinary physical endurance. Both studies had important implications for human health.

In the first study, researchers at the University of California at San Diego used *genetic engineering* (the manipulation of an organism's genes) to delete a mouse gene named HIF-1. This gene normally allows muscles to switch from *aerobic* (oxygen-using) to *anaerobic* (nonoxygen-using) chemical processes when oxygen levels in the muscles run low during vigorous exercise. These anaerobic processes lead to feelings of exhaustion. The muscles of the genetically altered mice, however, relied on aerobic processes throughout various exercise tests. Their muscles worked in the low oxygen conditions without resulting in exhaustion.

The marathon mice were able to swim for an average of 195 minutes, compared with 150 minutes for normal mice, and they could run on a treadmill for at least 60 minutes, compared

Francis Crick:
Father of the Genetics Revolution

Francis Crick, one of the most influential scientists of the 20th century, died on July 29, 2004, at age 88. The British biologist shared the 1962 Nobel Prize in physiology or medicine with American biologist James Watson and British biophysicist Maurice Wilkins for discovering the molecular structure of DNA. (Wilkins also died in 2004.) DNA, or deoxyribonucleic acid, is the double-stranded, spiral-shaped molecule that carries genetic instructions from one generation to the next. This discovery, published in 1953, marked the beginning of the genetics revolution—leading the way to such scientific break-throughs as the development of genetically engineered drugs and foods; genetic screening for disease-causing genes; and the cloning of animals.

Francis Harry Compton Crick was born on June 8, 1916, in Northhampton, England. His original scientific interest was physics, which he studied at University College, London. After designing mines during World War II (1939–1945), Crick turned to studying biology. In 1949, he began research in molecular biology at Cambridge University in England. Watson joined Crick there in 1951.

During the early 1950's, many scientists believed that proteins were the carriers of genetic information. Watson and Crick, however, decided that DNA might direct the formation, growth, and reproduction of cells and organisms after they saw images of the molecule made with X rays. The images, created by Wilkins and British chemist and molecular biologist Rosalind Franklin, inspired Watson and Crick to construct a three-dimensional model of DNA. (Franklin's death in 1958 prevented her from sharing the Nobel Prize with her colleagues.)

The model—built from pieces of cardboard, sheet metal, wire, and colored beads—depicted DNA as consisting of two strands twisted around each other like a spiral-shaped ladder. Watson and Crick proposed that each strand carried chemical instructions for inherited traits. As a cell in a body divides, the strands of the DNA in the cell unwind, with each strand going to a new cell. Each strand then acts as a template to re-create the other strand in the new cell. This explanation revealed how an organism's genetic information is preserved when new cells are made.

During the late 1950's and early 1960's, Crick's continued research shed light on the "rungs" of the DNA "ladder," which are made of four different kinds of units

with 50 minutes for the normal mice. After four days of exercise tests, however, the altered mice developed significant muscle damage—suggesting that normal chemical processes are necessary to maintain muscle health.

In the second study, geneticists at the Salk Institute for Biological Studies in La Jolla, California, used genetic engineering techniques to keep a gene called PPAR-delta continuously active in mice. Normally, this gene is sometimes inactive. The altered mice were able to run twice as far as normal mice and were resistant to weight gain when placed on a high-fat diet.

The scientists explained that the genetic manipulation caused a transformation in skeletal muscle fibers—with an increase in the mass of "slow-twitch" muscle fibers and a decrease in "fast-twitch" fibers. Slow-twitch fibers are more

called bases. Crick explained how the order in which these bases occur on a DNA strand serves as the codes, or instructions, that make up genes. These genetic codes direct the cells of the body to put particular amino acids together to form proteins. The proteins then go on to do all the work that makes life possible—from building the various parts of the body to carrying out the many different functions of the body.

Because of Crick's work, scientists knew by the 1960's that DNA carries the genetic information, and they understood how DNA replicates and codes for protein production. This knowledge opened the door to a flood of scientific achievements that are still bearing fruit— as well as causing controversy.

Many drugs and foods are produced through genetic engineering, the name for various processes in which scientists manipulate and alter the genes of organisms. The genetic engineering of bacteria and certain other living things has enabled scientists to coax these organisms into producing useful proteins and other medications. The use of genetic engineering in agriculture has led to the development of crops that are resistant to diseases and livestock that grow more rapidly.

The discovery of genes that cause or contribute to various diseases has made it possible for physicians to screen patients for these faulty genes. In some cases, scientists have tried to treat or even cure patients with certain immune system disorders and other diseases by replacing the faulty genes with healthy genes. Several experimental, clinical trials of such gene therapy cases had occurred by 2004.

In the 1990's, scientists began to clone—or produce genetic duplicates of—such animals as sheep, cattle, and mice. Cloning promises new breakthroughs in medicine, agriculture, and other areas of scientific research. However, cloning—like most other developments in genetic engineering—also has raised serious questions about ethics and safety that remained subjects of intense debate in 2004. One of the most profound of these debates concerned the cloning of human embryos, from which certain cells, called stem cells, could be extracted for use in medical research.

A number of additional, and somewhat less controversial, areas of science can trace their existence to the famous discovery of Watson and Crick: the identification of criminals based on DNA samples; insights into evolutionary relationships among different species; and even research into the development of computer systems modeled after DNA.

Crick was a man who was always interested in new challenges. In the 1970's— as other biologists were beginning to contribute to the genetics revolution—Crick began pursuing scientific interests of a different nature. At the Salk Institute for Biological Studies in La Jolla, California, Crick conducted groundbreaking research into such mysteries of the brain as the nature of consciousness and the meaning of dreams. He remained involved in this research for the rest of his life.

Francis Crick was considered by most of his colleagues to be one of the true giants of science—on a par with such luminaries as Isaac Newton, Charles Darwin, and Albert Einstein. On the occasion of Crick's death, a heartfelt tribute to him came from the man with whom he had made history. James Watson said, "I will always remember Francis for his extraordinarily focused intelligence. . . He will be sorely missed."

■ Alfred J. Smuskiewicz

resistant to fatigue than fast-twitch fibers. The team observed a similar change when they gave the mice an experimental drug that activates the PPAR-delta gene. The researchers noted that this drug promotes the burning of fat and might prove useful for weight control in humans.

Mice with only moms. Japanese geneticists reported in April that they had created mice using genes from only two female "parents." The creation of offspring without a father had never before been accomplished with mammals.

An individual inherits different versions of the same genes from its mother and father. During some parts of the normal development of an *embryo* (immature organism), the mother's gene versions are needed; during other parts of development, the father's versions are needed.

The geneticists, from the Tokyo University of

The sweat of the hippopotamus contains red and orange pigments made of acidic chemical compounds that have both sunscreen and antibiotic properties. Chemists at Keio University in Japan announced in May that these compounds protect the animals from harmful ultraviolet rays and bacteria.

Agriculture in Japan and the National University College of Medicine in Seoul, South Korea, got around this problem by causing certain *mutations* (genetic changes) in one of the female parents. As a result of these mutations, two of this female's genes acted like male versions, coding for growth-related chemicals normally coded for by the male versions. The scientists combined this mutated DNA with DNA from a normal female in 457 mouse eggs. Only two of these eggs developed into living mice, one of which grew to maturity and was seemingly normal.

The geneticists said their research might find applications in the livestock industry or in other areas of scientific research. They added, however, that such research likely had too many ethical and technical problems to be attempted with human genes.

Sleep-deprived sparrows. Migrating birds remain mentally alert during their long treks, despite the fact that they fly all night, forage for food during the day, and rarely sleep. This finding was reported in July by a team of researchers led by psychiatrist Niels C. Rattenborg of the University of Wisconsin at Madison.

The team studied eight caged white-crowned sparrows for one year. Even while caged indoors, these kinds of birds tend to stay awake all day

and night during the spring and autumn—times when white-crowned sparrows in the wild migrate between breeding grounds in Alaska and wintering sites in southern California. The researchers attached electrical sensors to the heads of the birds to record brain activity during the periods of nighttime activity. The recordings showed that both hemispheres of the birds' brains remained active during these periods. This finding disputed the idea of some scientists that migrating birds "sleep" with one hemisphere of their brain while the other hemisphere remains active.

The team also observed that the caged sparrows could learn new tasks—such as pecking buttons in a specific order to get food—during the sleepless migration periods just as well as they learned tasks during the rest of the year. However, when the researchers disrupted the birds' sleep patterns at times outside of the normal migration seasons, the birds' mental abilities showed a sharp decline.

The scientists concluded that, during migration seasons, normal sleep patterns are not necessary for learning and memory in birds. The team noted that additional research in this area might lead to clues about how humans could make do with less sleep when necessary.

Who's your daddy? Biologists in Japan created trout whose fathers were salmon, according to a study reported in August. The scientists said the technique they invented might be used to boost the world's fish stocks and save endangered species.

The biologists, at the Tokyo University of Marine Science and Technology, removed *primordial germ cells* (cells that can develop into eggs or sperm) from newly hatched rainbow trout. They then implanted these germ cells into masu salmon embryos. In some of these salmon, the cells matured into trout eggs and sperm. One year later, the scientists mixed the trout sperm from the male salmon with eggs from female trout, producing fish that were purebred trout.

The researchers hoped to use this technique to implant primordial germ cells from slowly maturing bluefin tuna—highly valued fish used to make sushi—into quickly maturing mackerel. They believed these mackerel would then produce mature tuna eggs and sperm more quickly than tuna could. The scientists also noted that their technique might be used to increase populations of endangered species by implanting germ cells from such species into more common animals. ■ Thomas H. Maugh II

See also **Ocean.**

Boating. American adventurer Steve Fossett and his 12-person crew set a new record for sailing around the world on April 5, 2004. The crew shattered the previous mark by six days.

Fossett's 125-foot (38-meter) catamaran *Cheyenne* reached the finish on the French island of Quessant after traveling 21,760 miles (35,019 kilometers) in 58 days, 9 hours, 32 minutes, and 45 seconds. Frenchman Bruno Peyron had set the previous record of 64 days and 8 hours in 2002. Later in 2004, Fossett announced his intention to stop competing in international speed sailing events to focus on other projects.

Atlantic record. Frenchman Michel Desjoyeaux smashed the North Atlantic solo crossing record on June 9, winning the 2,800-mile (4,500-kilometer) Transat yachting race from Plymouth, England, to Boston. He finished in a time of 8 days, 29 minutes and 55 seconds. Desjoyeaux, sailing a 60-foot (18-meter) trimaran, led from the start of the race and broke fellow Frenchman Francis Joyon's mark of 9 days, 23 hours, and 21 minutes set in 2000.

America's Cup. Team New Zealand, which lost the 2003 America's Cup to the Swiss syndicate Alinghi, announced in June 2004 that it intends to compete in the 2007 America's Cup races. With the announcement, Team New Zealand joined San Francisco's BMW Oracle Racing, Italy's Puitrentanove syndicate, and South Africa's first-time challenger Team Shosholoza as formal challengers for the 2007 Cup, which was scheduled to be held off the coast of Valencia, Spain.

2004 world championships. Spain's Iker Martinez and Xavier Fernandez took the 49er Gold Fleet title off Athens. Greece. in April; Sweden's Fredrik Loof and Anders Ekstrom won the Star title off Gaeta, Italy, in May; Denmark's Trine Palludan, Christina Otzen, and Ida Hartvig won the Yngling women's title off Santander, Spain, in May; Australians Nathan Wilmot and Malcolm Page won the men's 470 title, and Therese Torgersson and Vendela Zachrisson of Sweden won the women's 470 title off Zadar, Croatia, in May. Italy's Alessandra Sensini captured the Women's Mistral title off Bitez, Turkey, in August. Brazil's Robert Scheidt won the Laser title in that same competition.

Powerboats. Nate Brown piloted Miss Detroit Yacht Club to victory in the 100th running of the Gold Cup race for Unlimited Hydroplanes in Detroit on July 18.

■ Michael Kates

See also **Sports.**

Bolivia. On July 18, 2004, Bolivians approved a national referendum that permitted the export of large quantities of natural gas from Bolivia's vast reserves. Multinational oil and gas corporations, which had invested $3.5 billion in expanding Bolivia's known gas reserves tenfold since 1997, backed the measure. However, the referendum also called for increasing the taxes and royalties paid by the companies to Bolivia's government. In addition, the companies were to provide unspecified benefits to Bolivia's poor people.

President Carlos Diego Mesa Gisbert confronted the daunting task of persuading Congress to pass legislation that would satisfy popular expectations for openness in the handling of future revenues from gas exports. At the same time, he strove to blunt certain demands from labor unions and Indian groups, who wanted a greater role in deciding how energy earnings were spent. These groups called for the renationalization of Bolivia's energy industry.

President Mesa moved ahead on his pledge to convene a special assembly in 2005 to rewrite Bolivia's constitution. Mesa supported providing more autonomy to municipalities serving Bolivia's Indian majority. ■ Nathan A. Haverstock

See also **Latin America.**

Books. See Literature, American; Literature, World; Literature for children; Poetry.

Bosnia-Herzegovina. Bosnian leaders in 2004 achieved some progress in creating a common military establishment for Bosnia-Herzegovina, which consists of two ethnically distinct ministates—the Bosnian Serb Republika Srpska and the Muslim-Croat Federation. The two are linked in a loosely configured national state. In March, the national parliament appointed Nikola Radovanovic, a Bosnian Serb, as Bosnia's first central defense minister and appointed an ethnic Croat and a Muslim as deputy defense ministers. International officials representing the United Nations (UN), European Union (EU), and NATO praised the appointments as a step toward Bosnian nationhood and military reform.

Bosnia continued to be governed under terms of the 1995 Dayton Accords, which ended Bosnia's 1992–1995 civil war. Paddy Ashdown, the UN High Representative in Bosnia, oversaw implementation of the Dayton Accords in 2004.

Crackdown on Serb nationalists. International authorities continued to suspect that extremist Serb nationalists were impeding the capture of war criminals indicted by the UN War Crimes Tribunal in The Hague, Netherlands. The most notorious indictee, Radovan Karadzic, evaded arrest in 2004. He was under indictment for complicity in a 1995 mass killing in Bosnia.

Alleging that officials in the Republika Srpska were helping war criminals remain free, High Representative Ashdown imposed a funding freeze on the nationalist Serb Democratic Party (SDS) in April 2004 and dismissed 60 officials of the Republika Srpska in June. Despite these efforts and police work by NATO officials, Karadzic remained free and the Republika Srpska retained the distinction of being the only political entity of the former Yugoslavia that had not arrested a single war criminal.

NATO rejection. Prior to the NATO summer summit in Istanbul, Turkey, officials of the alliance pointedly did not invite Bosnia-Herzegovina to join the Partnership for Peace (PfP). Countries admitted to PfP generally achieve full NATO membership in time. In a statement, the officials said that Bosnia was not cooperating sufficiently with international authorities.

Economy. Bosnians continued to experience severe economic difficulties in 2004. Unemployment remained above 40 percent throughout the year. At a September conference, international donors pledged $1.2 billion in aid to Bosnia.

EUFOR. In December, an EU-sponsored force of 7,000 troops took over peacekeeping duties in Bosnia from NATO forces. The force, called EUFOR, was the EU's largest military mission to date.   ■ Sharon L. Wolchik

See also **Europe; United Nations.**

Botswana. See Africa.

Bowling. Women made inroads into the men's Professional Bowlers Association (PBA) in 2004, with the financial collapse of the Professional Women's Bowling Association (PWBA) in June 2003. Because of the collapse, Liz Johnson of Cheektowaga, New York, became the first woman to qualify for a PBA tour event at the Uniroyal Tire Classic on Nov. 10, 2004, in Wickliffe, Ohio. However, she lost to the top-seeded Brad Angelo of Lockport, New York.

On March 21, Tom Baker of Buffalo, New York, defeated Mika Koivuniemi 246-239 to win the PBA World Championship in Ypsilanti, Michigan. In May, Koivuniemi, of Ann Arbor, Michigan, was named the 2004 PBA player of the year.

Danny Wiseman of Baltimore won the first major of the 2004-2005 season, earning $100,000 by defeating Patrick Allen 268-183 at the American Bowling Congress Masters in Milwaukee, Wisconsin, on Oct. 31, 2004.

In December, Walter Ray Williams, Jr., led the PBA tour with an average of 228.65, while Danny Wiseman led in earnings with $122,680.

In late 2004, there was hope that a women's tour would return in 2005. Several major bowling organizations, including the Women's International Bowling Congress, which owns the PWBA's assets, merged to form the United States Bowling Congress.   ■ Michael Kates

Boxing. Two former heavyweight champions who had tangled with the law attempted to resurrect their careers in 2004. Mike Tyson tried to fight his way out of a financial crisis, and Riddick Bowe returned to the ring after serving prison time. In other boxing action, Lennox Lewis retired and the career of Roy Jones, Jr., appeared to be ending.

Tyson's travails. Tyson, who was once worth $300 million, dropped a $100-million lawsuit against boxing promoter Don King in exchange for a $14-million settlement. The deal was part of an overall strategy to enable Tyson to emerge from $38.4 million in debts he owes to the Internal Revenue Service, creditors, and his ex-wife. Part of the plan was a series of seven fights over three years that would have allowed him to apply $19.5 million in future purses toward the debt.

However, in his first fight back—and his first since February 2003—Tyson was knocked out in the fourth round by British heavyweight Danny Williams on July 30, 2004, in Louisville, Kentucky. Tyson, who had won the first three rounds, tore cartilage in his left knee during the fight and underwent surgery afterwards. His boxing future —as well as his ability to draw big purses— remained in serious doubt in late 2004.

Bowe's back. Riddick Bowe, who was released from prison on May 17 after serving 17 months for kidnapping his estranged wife and their five children in 1998, successfully returned to the ring on Sept. 25, 2004. Bowe knocked out Marcus Rhode in Shawnee, Oklahoma, in the second round.

De La Hoya knocked out. Bernard Hopkins delivered the first knockout of Oscar De La Hoya's career and retained his middleweight titles on Sept. 18, 2004, in Las Vegas. Prior to his win, Hopkins had successfully defended his middleweight titles 19 straight times. De La Hoya, who made $30 million in the fight, considerably more than Hopkins, had gained weight to fight at the middleweight class. Before the fight, De La Hoya was an underdog for the first time in his career.

Lewis retires. British heavyweight Lennox Lewis, who had defeated Vitali Klitschko in a technical knockout on June 21, 2003, announced his retirement in February 2004. Lewis, only the third heavyweight to retire as champion, said there was no chance that he would return to the ring.

Jones knocked out. International Boxing Federation light heavyweight champion Glen Johnson knocked out Roy Jones, Jr., in the ninth round of their fight on Sept. 25, 2004, in Memphis. Jones, at one time considered to be one of the most talented boxers in the game, had won titles at classes ranging from middleweight to heavyweight. ■ Michael Kates

See also **Sports.**

Ronald "Winky" Wright displays the belts he claimed by defeating Shane Mosely in Las Vegas on March 13, 2004. With his victory, Wright became the undisputed champion in the 154-pound (69.9-kilogram) weight class.

Brazil strengthened its position as an agricultural powerhouse in 2004. Many foreign agricultural companies—especially those from the United States—moved increasing amounts of their production to Brazil, where both land and labor costs were relatively inexpensive.

Cargill Incorporated, an agricultural and pharmaceutical giant headquartered near Minneapolis, Minnesota, was one of the largest foreign companies in Brazil in 2004. Cargill produced much of Brazil's soybeans, orange juice, and chocolate, and it accounted for roughly one-quarter of Brazil's sugar exports. Cargill was also an important player in the trading of commodity contracts in Sao Paulo, Brazil's financial center. Moreover, Cargill executives believed the company was poised to reap enormous profits from the production of ethanol—a nonpolluting, corn-based fuel additive—by its Brazilian subsidiaries. The demand for ethanol surged in 2004 as new regulations on cleaner-burning fuels took effect in the United States.

Record trade surplus. Brazil's exports during the first nine months of 2004 increased by 33 percent, compared with the same period in 2003, according to the nation's Ministry of Trade. In September 2004, Brazil's Central Bank projected that exports would reach a record value of $90 billion by the end of the year—providing Brazil with a $30-billion trade surplus.

WORLD CHAMPION BOXERS

WORLD BOXING ASSOCIATION

Division	Champion	Country	Date won
Heavyweight	John Ruiz	United States	12/03
Light heavyweight	Fabrice Tiozzo	France	3/04
Middleweight	Bernard Hopkins	United States	9/01
Welterweight	Cory Spinks	United States	12/03
Lightweight	Juan Diaz	United States	7/04
Featherweight	Juan Manuel Marquez	Mexico	11/03
Bantamweight	Vacant		
Flyweight	Lorenzo Parra	Venezuela	12/03

WORLD BOXING COUNCIL

Division	Champion	Country	Date won
Heavyweight	Vitali Klitschko	Ukraine	4/04
Light heavyweight	Antonio Tarver	United States	5/04
Middleweight	Bernard Hopkins	United States	4/01
Welterweight	Cory Spinks	United States	12/03
Lightweight	Jose Luis Castillo	Mexico	6/04
Featherweight	Injin Chi	Korea	4/04
Bantamweight	Veeraphol Nakhonluang	Thailand	12/98
Flyweight	Pongsaklek Wonjongkam	Thailand	3/01

With investment forthcoming from China, South Korea, and Italy, the Brazilian Steel Institute, a trade organization, announced plans in May to invest $7.4 billion to boost steel production by 30 percent through 2008. Much of this new production was destined for export to China, Brazil's second largest trading partner.

Companhia Vale do Rio Doce (CVRD) of Brazil announced plans in 2004 to construct a $1.5-billion steel mill in the northeast state of Maranhao with the Baosteel Group of Shanghai. The new steel plant was one of several envisioned by CVRD. CVRD also entered into partnership with Chalco, another Chinese company, to build a $1-billion aluminum refinery in northern Brazil.

Workers' Party scandals. The administration of President Luiz Inacio Lula da Silva was rocked by scandal in February when a newsmagazine Web site showed a videotape of Waldomiro Diniz, the president's chief liaison aide with the Congress, accepting a bribe. On the two-year-old tape, Diniz agreed to rewrite a lottery contract with a gambling kingpin in return for a $100,000 contribution to Workers' Party gubernatorial candidates. President da Silva fired Diniz after the tape was made public.

Also in early 2004, Brazilian prosecutors reopened the investigation into the 2002 murder of Celso Daniel, who was the mayor of Santo Andre and an official in da Silva's presidential campaign. Although Daniel's killing had originally been attributed to a right-wing death squad, evidence surfacing in 2004 linked the murder to disputes over the size of kickbacks paid by bus operators to the Workers' Party.

War on drugs. In June, the Brazilian government authorized the creation of a 2,000-person elite police force to combat urban violence, particularly in slum areas ruled by drug dealers. In addition, the army announced plans to reposition a 3,000-person brigade from Rio de Janeiro to patrol the Colombian and Venezuelan borders for illegal drugs.

Keeping kids in school. The Brazilian government tripled the value of payments to poor parents for keeping their children in school in 2004. Under the Family Grant program, parents received monthly benefits averaging about $24 if their children regularly attended school and received regular medical checkups. The program had been started in 2001 as a small, experimental project. Officials estimated that, by 2006, the Family Grant program would reach an estimated 11.4 million poor families, at a total cost of $7 billion.   ■ Nathan A. Haverstock

See also **Latin America**.

British Columbia. See Canadian provinces.

Brunei. See Asia.

Building and construction. In October 2004, the Council on Tall Buildings and Urban Habitat, a Bethlehem, Pennsylvania-based non-profit organization that evaluates tall buildings, declared newly constructed Taipei 101 in Taipei, Taiwan, to be the world's tallest building. Taipei 101 tops out at 1,667 feet (508 meters) —184 feet (56 meters) higher than the previous titleholder, the Petronas towers in Kuala Lumpur, Malaysia.

Taiwanese architectural firm C. Y. Lee & Partners designed the $1.7-billion skyscraper to withstand Taiwan's frequent typhoons and earthquakes. An earthquake registering 7.0 shook Taiwan in October, but the jolt inflicted no damage on Taipei 101. Earthquake-resistant features of the skyscraper include a complex system of dampers and a huge steel ball suspended by cables inside the upper part of the structure. The ball absorbs quake-generated motion by swinging up to five feet (1.5 meters) in any direction.

Taipei 101's height record is unlikely to stand for long, experts noted. Future candidates for the world's tallest building include New York City's replacement for the World Trade Center, the Freedom Tower, at a proposed 1,776 feet (537 meters); and the Burj Dubai, a 2,314-foot (705-meter) skyscraper planned for Dubayy, United Arab Emirates. Both structures are slated for completion sometime before 2010.

Three Gorges Dam. Work continued throughout 2004 on China's Three Gorges Dam complex—the world's largest construction project. The multipurpose structure—which is 7,549 feet (2,300 meters) long and 607 feet (185 meters) high—is designed to provide flood control and improve navigation on the Yangtze River; the complex will also produce hydroelectric power. Demand for electricity in China is growing by 6.8 percent annually, according to government reports, and the Three Gorges Dam is the centerpiece of China's long-term energy plan.

The dam complex is designed to have a powerhouse on the left and right banks of the river, plus several underground powerhouses. In July, Three Gorges began operating its ninth 700-megawatt generator in the left-bank powerhouse. By the end of 2005, all 14 left-bank generators are expected to be online, officials said.

An 11,000-member crew began work in 2004 on the right bank and underground powerhouses. Collectively, they will house 18 generators, each rated at 700 megawatts. When the dam complex is completed, its electrical output will peak at 22,400 megawatts. In mid-2004, dam officials noted unofficially that they expected to complete the entire project in time for the 2008 Summer Olympic Games in Beijing, one year ahead of schedule.

In August 2004, unusually heavy summer rains

Construction crews complete the span of the Millau Bridge over the Tarn River Valley in southern France on May 28, 2004. With one of the seven piers 1,125 feet (343 meters) high—75 feet (23 meters) higher than the Eiffel Tower in Paris—the structure is the world's highest road bridge. It opened to automobile traffic on December 16.

tested the dam's flood prevention capabilities. In anticipation of flooding, dam operators lowered the reservoir pool from 456 feet (139 meters) to 443 feet (135 meters). After days of rain, flooding occurred in the upriver Yangtze basin, but the filling reservoir of the dam delayed the flood waters and spared downriver communities from major inundation.

New deepwater port. In early 2004, engineers, contractors, and support staff moved onto two recently vacated islands in the Qiqu archipelago off the coast of Shanghai, China, and set up living and working quarters. They were the advance members of a team starting work on the Yangshan Port project, which is to create a new deepwater port for Shanghai, China's largest

city. The new facilities are to provide berths for the world's largest container ships. The original port of Shanghai—on the shallow, heavily silted Yangtze River—will remain in use for smaller river and coastal ships.

In the initial, $2-billion phase of the project, five berths are being built at the terminal plus a bridge-and-causeway road link to the mainland. At its projected completion in 2020, the $20-billion facility will have 32 berths and rail links to the mainland. Shipping experts predict that Shanghai will overtake Singapore and Hong Kong as the world's largest container port.

San Diego's new baseball park. The San Diego Padres opened PETCO Park in April 2004, just in time for the major league baseball season.

The $453-million ballpark, to which San Diego taxpayers contributed approximately $206 million, is the cornerstone of an ambitious urban renewal plan for a downtown community called the East Village.

The collaborating designers on the project included architect Antoine Predock of Albuquerque, New Mexico; HOK, a sports-oriented design firm based in Kansas City, Missouri; and Poirier Landscape Architects of San Diego. Some visitors to the park compared the sandstone-clad stadium and other buildings sited in the 17-acre (6.9-hectare) landscaped park to Aztec ruins or desert mesas.

Millau Bridge. The span of the world's highest road bridge—$410-million Millau Bridge, which was designed by renowned British architect Sir Norman Foster—was completed in 2004 and opened to automobile traffic on December 16. The 8,074-foot (2,460-meter) span stretches over the Tarn River Valley on seven slender masts, or piers. The tallest of the masts rises 1,125 feet (343 meters)—75 feet (23 meters) higher than the Eiffel Tower in Paris. The bridge deck is suspended from cables strung through the tops of the masts. The structure completes France's A75 highway between Bezier and Clermont-Ferrand.
◾ Andrew Wright

See also **Architecture; China.**

Bulgaria. The government led by Prime Minister Simeon Saxe-Coburg-Gotha and his National Movement for Simeon II lost its parliamentary majority in March 2004, with the defection of 11 legislators from the ruling coalition. Despite the losses, the governing coalition survived a vote of no confidence and held onto power.

Bulgaria's economy performed strongly in 2004. The standard of living, which had fallen dramatically after 1989 as non-Communist governments struggled to create a market economy, attained pre-1989 levels again in June 2004, economists reported. Growth in Bulgaria's gross domestic product (GDP)—the value of all goods and services produced in a country in a year—hovered between 5 and 6 percent in 2004.

On March 29, Bulgaria was admitted to the North Atlantic Treaty Oraganization (NATO). In June, Bulgarian officials completed negotiations with the European Union (EU) for Bulgaria's entry into the 25-member economic and political association, tentatively scheduled for 2007. However, EU officials reserved the right to delay Bulgaria's accession if the government lagged on promised reforms.
◾ Sharon L. Wolchik

See also **Europe.**

Burma. See Myanmar.

Bush, George W. See **United States, President of the.**

Cabinet, U.S. Several members of President George W. Bush's Cabinet resigned following his re-election on Nov. 2, 2004.

Attorney General John Ashcroft and Donald L. Evans, secretary of the Department of Commerce, announced their resignations on November 9.

Four Cabinet members submitted their resignations on November 15: Colin L. Powell, secretary of the Department of State; Ann M. Veneman, secretary of the Department of Agriculture; Roderick R. Paige, secretary of the Department of Education; and Spencer Abraham, secretary of the Department of Energy.

On November 30, Thomas J. Ridge, secretary of the Department of Homeland Security, announced his resignation. On December 3, Tommy G. Thompson, secretary of the Department of Health and Human Services, resigned. Anthony J. Principi, secretary of the Department of Veterans Affairs, announced his resignation on December 8.

Nominees. On November 10, the president nominated Alberto R. Gonzalez as attorney general. Gonzalez had been the president's counsel. On November 16, President Bush nominated National Security Adviser Condoleezza Rice as secretary of state. No nominee had been sent to the U.S. Senate for confirmation by the end of 2004.
◾ Tim Frystak

California. See **State government.**

Cambodia. Norodom Sihamoni, a 51-year-old former dancer, was crowned king of Cambodia on Oct. 29, 2004. He was selected by his father, King Norodom Sihanouk. A nine-member Throne Council confirmed Sihanouk's selection.

Sihanouk had announced on October 7 that he would give up the throne, which he had held, off and on, since 1941. The 81-year-old king, who dominated Cambodia in the 1950's and 1960's, was receiving medical treatment in China when he made his announcement. He had left Cambodia in December 2003 after failing to end feuding between Cambodia's political parties.

The new National Assembly approved Hun Sen as prime minister on July 15, 2004. His Cambodian People's Party had won 47 percent of the votes in July 2003. Hun Sen was a former member of the Communist Khmer Rouge, which had run the country from 1975 to 1979 and was responsible for the deaths of more than 1.5 million Cambodians. Prince Norodom Ranariddh, the royalist leader and Sihamoni's half-brother, became head of the Assembly.

On Oct. 4, 2004, the Assembly ratified a 2003 agreement with the United Nations to try surviving leaders of the Khmer Rouge. A deputy prime minister said 10 people would be placed on trial in 2005.
◾ Henry S. Bradsher

See also **Asia; People in the news** (Norodom Sihamoni).

CANADA

Canada underwent dramatic political changes in 2004. The Liberal Party, which held power for two-thirds of the 20th century, was reduced to heading a minority government after an election held on June 28. The voters' rebuke came after the retirement of Prime Minister Jean Chretien and his replacement by Paul Martin in December 2003. The humbling of the Liberals led to a weakened position in a Parliament characterized by a considerably stronger opposition.

The new prime minister, Paul Martin, did not possess the parliamentary experience of his predecessor, Jean Chretien. Chretien, with 36 years in Canada's House of Parliament and more than 10 years as prime minister, had won three successive elections. Martin had been Chretien's finance minister, but his experience in Parliament had only begun in 1988. When he became prime minister in late 2003, he faced the challenging task of leading a government that would have to work with a larger opposition to enact legislation.

A short session of Parliament from February to May 2004 revealed a cautious new administration. Legislation introduced came mostly from the agenda of the Chretien days. One measure, based on the returns of the 2001 census, increased the size of the House of Commons from 301 to 308 members. Ontario received three of the new seats; Alberta and British Columbia received two each. The Patent Act was amended to facilitate access to drugs combating HIV/AIDS in developing countries. Another measure, the Assisted Human Reproduction Act, regulated research in human reproduction to ban human cloning; creating human embryos for research purposes; and in the practice of commercial surrogate motherhood.

Scandal. The Martin government was just beginning to settle into office when news of a damaging scandal in Quebec came to light in February 2004. Following the near-victory of the separatist movement in Quebec, which sought to lead the province from Canada, in a 1995 referendum, the federal government tried to heighten its image in the province. The sum of $250 million was set aside to provide federal sponsorship to community and sporting events in Quebec. The money was paid out to advertising agencies, many of which turned out to be friendly to the Liberal government. The auditor-general, responsible to Parliament, discovered that payments made to the agencies did not follow the provisions of the Financial Administration Act.

Invoices were fictitious, payments were made for little or no service, and proper records were not maintained. Martin took immediate action to deal with the scandal. Alfonso Gagliano, the minister responsible for the distribution of the grants, was dismissed, and the heads of several state corporations involved in the program were suspended and later retired. Some public servants working on the sponsorship plan faced criminal charges. A judicial enquiry began in September 2004, and a lawyer was appointed to recover funds improperly spent.

A wave of anger, especially in Quebec, focused on the Liberals. Martin was accused of being aware of the situation but of taking no action to deal with it. Former Prime Minister Chretien, whose office was ultimately responsible for the sponsorship plan, was felt to be ethically, if not legally, responsible. Martin did his best to defend himself against allegations that he had been remiss in his duty. However, his reputation had suffered from the affair. Nevertheless, Martin pressed ahead with the plan to secure a mandate for his new government through a general election on June 28, 2004.

Election. The Liberals faced a united conservative opposition for the first time in a decade in 2004. The two opposing conservative parties, the historic Progressive Conservative Party, once strong across the country, and the new Canadian Alliance, expressing the viewpoint of the western provinces, had merged in October 2003 to form the Conservative Party of Canada. They elected a leader, Stephen Harper, a former member of Parliament from Alberta, on March 20, 2004. Faced with the prospect of an imminent election, Harper adopted a moderate position in order to appeal to Canadians in every part of the country. He took up the familiar conservative stance of tax relief and balanced budgets, as well as greater transparency in government operations. He espoused publicly funded health care but showed that he was willing to consider a secondary role for private medicine within the public system. He advocated stronger defense forces, proposing to raise armed forces enrollment from 52,000 to 80,000 soldiers. Harper's party favored close relations with the United States, but on a realistic basis. He advocated that Canada should agree with the United States when their interests coincided but express an independent view when their interests were at odds.

Martin found himself in an awkward position as election campaigning got underway. He had been a popular finance minister in the previous administration, achieving five consecutive balanced budgets, but he now hoped to disassociate himself from the tired final administration of Chretien. As the head of a new government, Martin emphasized the need for more solid funding for health care, the creation of a national child care program, and greater support to cities for the heavy costs of public infrastructure. In spite of the large financial demands of this agenda, he promised that balanced budgets would be a hallmark of his government.

Canada's socialist New Democratic Party (NDP) came forward with a social program more extensive than that of the Liberals. It promised major spending on health care, tax relief, and the introduction of an inheritance tax for upper-income Canadians. The party was led by Jack Layton, an urban activist from Toronto, who was chosen leader in 2003. Layton was expected to appeal to urban-dwellers, who had once been a strong NDP constituency.

The federal wing of Quebec separatism, the Bloc Quebecois (BQ), which political experts had considered in decline in recent years, took on new life in the election. It channeled the widespread anger in Quebec about the sponsorship scandal, claiming the Liberal Party in Quebec was corrupt and too interested in helping its friends. The ultimate goal of Quebec separation was played down in 2004 as the party emphasized a social agenda close to that of the Liberals.

Election results. Liberal strength in the House of Commons fell from 176 seats in the 2000 election to 135 in 2004, with a drop in popular support from 41 percent to 37 percent. In Ontario, where Liberals had held all but three seats before the election, the party's standing fell to 75 seats out of 106. It still captured almost all the seats in the larger cities, though Layton and a former leader of the NDP, Ed Broadbent, won in Toronto and Ottawa, respectively.

Nationally, the Conservatives did not do as well as they had hoped, taking 99 seats, compared with 78 before the election. Their 14 seats in Ontario were mostly in smaller towns and in rural areas. The four provinces in Western Canada—Alberta, British Columbia, Manitoba, and Saskatchewan—displayed their conservative roots by giving the new party 68 seats, with the Liberals taking only 14. The conservatives captured 30 percent of the popular vote, lower than in the 2000 election. Building a national base remained a major problem for the new conservative grouping. The NDP increased its popular vote from 9 to 16 percent, winning 19 seats overall, 7 of which were in Ontario.

FEDERAL SPENDING IN CANADA
Estimated budget for fiscal 2004-2005*

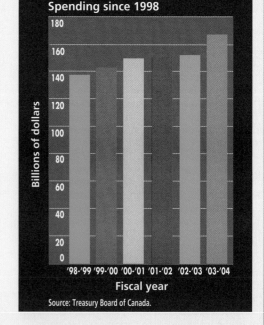

Spending since 1998

Department or agency	Millions of dollars†
Agriculture and agri-food	2,612
Atlantic Canada opportunities agency	489
Canada customs and revenue agency	3,429
Canadian heritage	3,188
Citizenship and immigration	1,131
Environment	3,926
Finance	69,125
Fisheries and oceans	1,471
Foreign affairs and international trade	4,510
Governor general	19
Health	3,927
Human resources and skills development	2,012
Human resources development (social development)	28,554
Indian affairs and northern development	5,762
Industry	4,746
International trade	238
Justice	1,462
National defence	13,300
Natural resources	1,383
Parliament	451
Privy Council	442
Public works and government services	2,411
Solicitor general	4,906
Transport	1,673
Treasury board	2,497
Veterans affairs	2,788
Western economic diversification	391
Total	**166,843**

Source: Treasury Board of Canada.

* April 1, 2004, to March 31, 2005.
† Canadian dollars; $1 = U.S. $0.79 as of Oct. 1, 2004.

The election's most conspicuous surprise occurred in Quebec, where the BQ captured virtually every French-speaking district in the province. The party won 54 seats, compared with the Liberals' 21, many of which came from the island of Montreal. The Liberals won only 33 percent of the provincial popular vote, while the BQ took nearly 50 percent. Political experts noted that while the BQ strategy clearly had paid off, what it might mean for the future prospects for separatism remained unclear. A national base remained a major problem for the new conservative grouping. The stronger opposition made the general election an exciting one for Canadians. However, only 60.5 percent of voters turned out, the lowest number in any Canadian national election.

New Cabinet. Martin announced a new Cabinet on July 20. Six ministers had been defeated so Martin brought in eight new faces. Four stalwarts from the previous Cabinet were given key posts. Anne McLellan from Alberta was named deputy prime minister and minister of public safety and emergency procedures, a position from which she would guide measures for homeland security. Ralph Goodale kept his position as minister of finance, and Bill Graham moved from foreign affairs to national defense. Pierre Pettigrew, a former trade minister, was named minister of foreign affairs. Two new posts were created—minister of state (infrastructure and communities) to deal with the problems of the cities; and minister of state (families and caregivers) responsible for the promised day care program. The Cabinet included 39 members, 8 of whom were junior ministers of state. The Cabinet included nine women.

Health care. Martin faced his first demanding test as prime minister at a meeting with provincial and territorial leaders in Ottawa, the capital, September 13 to 15. The purpose was to discuss public health care, especially Martin's promise to provide more federal funds for the popular program. Health care presents constitutional and political difficulties in Canada. Under the constitution, the provinces possess exclusive jurisdiction for the delivery of social services, such as public health care. The national scheme, 40 years old, requires expenditures from both the provincial and federal governments to be viable. Health costs make up an ever-larger part of provincial budgets, with the result that provinces demand greater assistance from the national government. The provincial governments claim, in fact, that the capital's financial contribution to state medicine has declined in recent years, even though Ottawa's tax base is much broader than that of the provinces. Provincial officials pressed Martin in 2004 to increase the federal contribution substantially.

After three days of hard bargaining, Martin

2004 CANADIAN POPULATION ESTIMATES

PROVINCE AND TERRITORY POPULATIONS

Alberta	3,194,700
British Columbia	4,179,800
Manitoba	1,169,800
New Brunswick	751,400
Newfoundland and Labrador	520,100
Northwest Territories	42,400
Nova Scotia	937,900
Nunavut	30,000
Ontario	12,385,200
Prince Edward Island	138,600
Quebec	7,532,100
Saskatchewan	993,800
Yukon Territory	32,100
Canada	31,907,900

CITY AND METROPOLITAN AREA POPULATIONS

	Metropolitan area	City
Toronto, Ont.	5,080,400	2,541,900
Montreal, Que.	3,564,000	1,837,900
Vancouver, B.C.	2,132,100	566,100
Ottawa-Hull	1,137,300	
Ottawa, Ont.		808,700
Hull, Que.		*
Calgary, Alta.	1,002,900	957,100
Edmonton, Alta.	972,600	698,900
Quebec, Que.	699,400	512,900
Hamilton, Ont.	689,700	504,500
Winnipeg, Man.	685,900	620,186
Kitchener, Ont.	440,800	198,200
London, Ont.	428,100	343,300
St. Catharines-Niagara Falls	392,500	
St. Catharines, Ont.		128,100
Niagara Falls, Ont.		80,000
Halifax, N.S.	370,000	369,400
Windsor, Ont.	322,500	215,200
Victoria, B.C.	318,700	74,500
Oshawa, Ont.	312,200	142,000
Saskatoon, Sask.	232,000	198,700
Regina, Sask.	196,400	176,900
St. John's, Nfld. Lab.	177,600	97,600
Sherbrooke, Que.	157,100	75,400
Chicoutimi-Jonquiere	156,100	
Chicoutimi, Que.		58,300
Jonquiere, Que.		53,900
Greater Sudbury, Ont.	155,500	149,600
Abbotsford, B.C.	152,100	122,200
Trois-Rivieres, Que.	141,400	45,000
Saint John, N.B.	126,800	68,000
Thunder Bay, Ont.	124,900	106,400

*Hull became part of the city of Gatineau in 2002. Gatineau's projected 2004 population was 235,700.

Source: World Book estimates based on data from Statistics Canada.

promised greater assistance than he had mentioned in the election campaign. Over the next 10 years he committed the federal government to a grant of $41.2 billion, with the added feature that an "escalator" clause would provide 6 percent in extra funds. (All amounts are in Canadian dollars.) Evidence-based benchmarks were defined to guide the provinces in reducing waiting times for medical services. Quebec, with a distinct health care system, was allowed to follow

MEMBERS OF THE CANADIAN HOUSE OF COMMONS

The House of Commons of the first session of the 38th Parliament convened on Oct. 5, 2004. As of that date, the House of Commons consisted of the following members: 135 Liberal Party, 54 Bloc Quebecois, 99 Conservative Party of Canada, 19 New Democratic Party, and 1 Independent. This table shows each legislator and party affiliation. An asterisk (*) denotes those who served in the 37th Parliament.

Alberta
Diane Ablonczy, C.P.C.*
Rona Ambrose, C.P.C.
Rob Anders, C.P.C.*
Leon E. Benoit, C.P.C.*
Rick Casson, C.P.C.*
David Chatters, C.P.C.*
Ken Epp, C.P.C.*
Peter Goldring, C.P.C.*
Art Hanger, C.P.C.*
Stephen Harper, C.P.C.*
Rahim Jaffer, C.P.C.*
Brian Jean, C.P.C.
Dale Johnston, C.P.C.*
Jason Kenney, C.P.C.*
David Kilgour, Lib.*
Anne McLellan, Lib.*
Ted Menzies, C.P.C.
Rob Merrifield, C.P.C.*
Bob Mills, C.P.C.*
Deepak Obhrai, C.P.C.*
Charlie Penson, C.P.C.*
Jim Prentice, C.P.C.
James Rajotte, C.P.C.*
Lee Richardson, C.P.C.
Monte Solberg, C.P.C.*
Kevin Sorenson, C.P.C.*
Myron Thompson, C.P.C.*
John Williams, C.P.C.*

British Columbia
Jim Abbott, C.P.C.*
David Anderson, Lib.*
Don Bell, Lib.
Chuck Cadman, Ind.*
Raymond Chan, Lib.
Jean Crowder, N.D.P.
Nathan Cullen, N.D.P.
John Cummins, C.P.C.*
Libby Davies, N.D.P.*
Stockwell Day, C.P.C.*
Ujjal Dosanjh, Lib.
John Duncan, C.P.C.*
David Emerson, Lib.
Paul Forseth, C.P.C.*
Hedy Fry, Lib.*
Jim Gouk, C.P.C.*
Gurmant Grewal, C.P.C.*
Nina Grewal, C.P.C.
Richard Harris, C.P.C.*
Russ Hiebert, C.P.C.
Jay Hill, C.P.C.*
Betty Hinton, C.P.C.*
Peter Julian, N.D.P.
Randy Kamp, C.P.C.
Gary Lunn, C.P.C.*
James Lunney, C.P.C.*
Keith Martin, Lib.*
James Moore, C.P.C.*
Stephen Owen, Lib.*
John Reynolds, C.P.C.*
Werner Schmidt, C.P.C.*
Bill Siksay, N.D.P.
Darrel Stinson, C.P.C.*
Chuck Strahl, C.P.C.*

Mark Warawa, C.P.C.
Randy White, C.P.C.*

Manitoba
Reg Alcock, Lib.*
James Bezan, C.P.C.
Bill Blaikie, N.D.P.*
Bev Desjarlais, N.D.P.*
Steven Fletcher, C.P.C.
Inky Mark, C.P.C.*
Pat Martin, N.D.P.*
Anita Neville, Lib.*
Brian Pallister, C.P.C.*
Raymond Simard, Lib.*
Joy Smith, C.P.C.
Vic Toews, C.P.C.*
Merv Tweed, C.P.C.
Judy Wasylycia-Leis, N.D.P.*

New Brunswick
Claudette Bradshaw, Lib.*
Jean-Claude D'Amours, Lib.
Yvon Godin, N.D.P.*
Charles Hubbard, Lib.*
Dominic LeBlanc, Lib.*
Rob Moore, C.P.C.
Andy Savoy, Lib.*
Andy Scott, Lib.*
Greg Thompson, C.P.C.*
Paul Zed, Lib.

Newfoundland and Labrador
Gerry Byrne, Lib.*
Norman Doyle, C.P.C.*
R. John Efford, Lib.*
Loyola Hearn, C.P.C.*
Bill Matthews, Lib.*
Lawrence D. O'Brien, Lib.*
Scott Simms, Lib.

Northwest Territories
Ethel Blondin-Andrew, Lib.*

Nova Scotia
Scott Brison, Lib.*
Bill Casey, C.P.C.*
Rodger Cuzner, Lib.*
Mark Eyking, Lib.*
Gerald Keddy, C.P.C.*
Peter MacKay, C.P.C.*
Alexa McDonough, N.D.P.*
Geoff Regan, Lib.*
Michael Savage, Lib.
Peter Stoffer, N.D.P.*
Robert Thibault, Lib.*

Nunavut
Nancy Karetak-Lindell, Lib.*

Ontario
Peter Adams, Lib.*
Dean Allison, C.P.C.
Charlie Angus, N.D.P.
Jean Augustine, Lib.*
Navdeep Bains, Lib.

Sue Barnes, Lib.*
Colleen Beaumier, Lib.*
Mauril Belanger, Lib.*
Carolyn Bennett, Lib.*
Maurizio Bevilacqua, Lib.*
Ray Bonin, Lib.*
Ken Boshcoff, Lib.
Don Boudria, Lib.*
Ed Broadbent, N.D.P.
Bonnie Brown, Lib.*
Gord Brown, C.P.C.
Sarmite Bulte, Lib.*
John Cannis, Lib.*
Gary Carr, Lib.
Colin Carrie, C.P.C.
Aileen Carroll, Lib.*
Marlene Catterall, Lib.*
Brenda Chamberlain, Lib.*
Mike Chong, C.P.C.
David Christopherson, N.D.P.
Joe Comartin, N.D.P.*
Joe Comuzzi, Lib.*
Roy Cullen, Lib.*
Paul DeVillers, Lib.*
Barry Devolin, C.P.C.
Ruby Dhalla, Lib.
Ken Dryden, Lib.
Diane Finley, C.P.C.
Joe Fontana, Lib.*
Cheryl Gallant, C.P.C.*
Roger Gallaway, Lib.*
Marc Godbout, Lib.
John Godfrey, Lib.*
Gary Goodyear, C.P.C.
Bill Graham, Lib.*
Albina Guarnieri, Lib.*
Helena Guergis, C.P.C.
Mark Holland, Lib.
Tony Ianno, Lib.*
Susan Kadis, Lib.
Jim Karygiannis, Lib.*
Wajid Khan, Lib.
Daryl Kramp, C.P.C.
Walt Lastewka, Lib.*
Guy Lauzon, C.P.C.
Jack Layton, N.D.P.
Derek Lee, Lib.*
Judi Longfield, Lib.*
Dave Mackenzie, C.P.C.
Paul H. Macklin, Lib.*
Gurbax Malhi, Lib.*
John Maloney, Lib.*
Diane Marleau, Lib.*
Tony Martin, N.D.P.
Brian Masse, N.D.P.*
John McCallum, Lib.*
David McGuinty, Lib.
John McKay, Lib.*
Dan McTeague, Lib.*
Larry Miller, C.P.C.
Peter Milliken, Lib.*
Maria Minna, Lib.*
Andy Mitchell, Lib.*
Lynn Myers, Lib.*
Rob Nicholson, C.P.C.

Pat O'Brien, Lib.*
Gordon O'Connor, C.P.C.
Bev Oda, C.P.C.
Carolyn Parrish, Lib.*
Jim Peterson, Lib.*
Beth Phinney, Lib.*
Jerry Pickard, Lib.*
Pierre Poilievre, C.P.C.
Russ Powers, Lib.
Joe Preston, C.P.C.
Yasmin Ratansi, Lib.
Karen Redman, Lib.*
Scott Reid, C.P.C.*
Anthony Rota, Lib.
Gary Schellenberger, C.P.C.*
Judy Sgro, Lib.*
Mario Silva, Lib.
Lloyd St.-Amand, Lib.
Brent St. Denis, Lib.*
Paul Steckle, Lib.*
Belinda Stronach, C.P.C.
Paul Szabo, Lib.*
Andrew Telegdi, Lib.*
Liu Temelkovski, Lib.
David Tilson, C.P.C.
Alan Tonks, Lib.*
Paddy Torsney, Lib.*
Rose-Marie Ur, Lib.*
Tony Valeri, Lib.*
Roger Valley, Lib.
Peter Van Loan, C.P.C.
Joseph Volpe, Lib.*
Tom Wappel, Lib.*
Jeff Watson, C.P.C.
Bryon Wilfert, Lib.*
Borys Wrzesnewskyj, Lib.

Prince Edward Island
Wayne Easter, Lib.*
Lawrence MacAulay, Lib.*
Joe McGuire, Lib.*
Shawn Murphy, Lib.*

Quebec
Guy Andre, B.Q.
Gerard Asselin, B.Q.*
Claude Bachand, B.Q.*
Eleni Bakopanos, Lib.*
Andre Bellavance, B.Q.
Stephane Bergeron, B.Q.*
Bernard Bigras, B.Q.*
Raynald Blais, B.Q.
Alain Boire, B.Q.
Francoise Boivin, Lib.
France Bonsant, B.Q.
Robert Bouchard, B.Q.
Marc Boulianne, B.Q.
Diane Bourgeois, B.Q.*
Paule Brunelle, B.Q.
Serge Cardin, B.Q.*
Robert Carrier, B.Q.
Roger Clavet, B.Q.
Bernard Cleary, B.Q.
Denis Coderre, Lib.*
Guy Cote, B.Q.
Irwin Cotler, Lib.*

Paul Crete, B.Q.*
Nicole Demers, B.Q.
Johanne Deschamps, B.Q.
Odina Desrochers, B.Q.*
Stephane Dion, Lib.*
Claude Drouin, Lib.*
Gilles Duceppe, B.Q.*
Meili Faille, B.Q.
Raymonde Folco, Lib.*
Liza Frulla, Lib.*
Christiane Gagnon, B.Q.*
Marcel Gagnon, B.Q.*
Sébastien Gagnon, B.Q.*
Roger Gaudet, B.Q.*
Michel Gauthier, B.Q.*
Monique Guay, B.Q.*
Michel Guimond, B.Q.*
Marlene Jennings, Lib.*
Maka Koto, B.Q.
Mario Laframboise, B.Q.*
Francine Lalonde, B.Q.*
Jean-C. Lapierre, Lib.
Real Lapierre, B.Q.
Carole Lavallee, B.Q.
Marc Lemay, B.Q.
Yves Lessard, B.Q.
Yvon Levesque, B.Q.
Yvan Loubier, B.Q.*
Richard Marceau, B.Q.*
Paul Martin, Lib.*
Real Menard, B.Q.*
Serge Menard, B.Q.
Massimo Pacetti, Lib.*
Pierre Paquette, B.Q.*
Denis Paradis, Lib.*
Bernard Patry, Lib.*
Gilles-A. Perron, B.Q.*
Pierre Pettigrew, Lib.*
Pauline Picard, B.Q.*
Louis Plamondon, B.Q.*
Denise Poirer-Rivard, B.Q.
Marcel Proulx, Lib.*
Lucienne Robillard, Lib.*
Pablo Rodriguez, Lib.
Jean-Yves Roy, B.Q.*
Jacques Saada, Lib.*
Benoit Sauvageau, B.Q.*
Francis Scarpaleggia, Lib.
Christian Simard, B.Q.
David Smith, Lib.
Caroline St.-Hilaire, B.Q.*
Louise Thibault, B.Q.
Robert Vincent, B.Q.

Saskatchewan
David Anderson, C.P.C.*
Dave Batters, C.P.C.
Garry Breitkreuz, C.P.C.*
Brian Fitzpatrick, C.P.C.*
Ralph E. Goodale, Lib.*
Jeremy Harrison, C.P.C.
Ed Komarnicki, C.P.C.
Tom Lukiwski, C.P.C.
Gerry Ritz, C.P.C.*
Andrew Scheer, C.P.C.
Carol Skelton, C.P.C.*
Bradley Trost, C.P.C.
Maurice Vellacott, C.P.C.*
Lynne Yelich, C.P.C.*

Yukon Territory
Larry Bagnell, Lib.*

THE MINISTRY OF CANADA*

Paul Martin—prime minister
Jacob Austin—leader of the government in the Senate
Stephane Dion—minister of the environment
Ralph Goodale—minister of finance
Anne McLellan—deputy prime minister and minister of publc safety and emergency preparedness
Lucienne Robillard—president of the Queen's Privy Council for Canada and minister of Intergovernmental Affairs
Pierre Pettigrew—minister of foreign affairs
James Scott Peterson—minister of international trade
Andy Scott—minister of Indian affairs and Northern development and Federal Interlocutor for Metis and Non-Status Indians
Andrew Mitchell—minister of agriculture and agri-food
Claudette Bradshaw—minister of state (human resources development)
Jacques Saada—minister of the Economic Development Agency of Canada for the Regions of Quebec and minister responsible for La Francophonie
Stephen Owen—minister of Western economic diversification and minister of state (sport)
Albina Guarnieri—minister of veterans affairs
Scott Brison—minister of public works and government services
William Graham—minister of national defence
Joseph Volpe—minister of human resources and skills development
Joseph F. Fontana—minister of labour and housing
John McCallum—minister of national revenue
Ujjal Dosanjh—minister of health
Reg Alcock—president of the Treasury Board and minister responsible for the Canadian Wheat Board
Geoff Regan—minister of fisheries and oceans
Jean-C. Lapierre—minister of transport
Tony Valeri—leader of the government in the House of Commons
Irwin Cotler—minister of justice and attorney general of Canada
Judy Sgro—minister of citizenship and immigration
Liza Frulla—minister of Canadian heritage and minister responsible for status of women
John Efford—minister of natural resources
Ken Dryden—minister of social development
David Emerson—minister of industry
Ethel Blondin-Andrew—minister of state (Northern Development)
John F. Godfrey—minister of state (infrastructure and communities)
Raymond Chan—minister of state (multiculturalism)
Joseph Comuzzi—minister of state (Federal Economic Development Initiative for Northern Ontario)
Joseph McGuire—minister of Atlantic Canada Opportunities Agency
Mauril Belanger—deputy leader of the government in the House of Commons; minister responsible for official languages; minister responsible for democratic reform; associate minister of national defence
Carolyn Bennett—minister of state (public health)
Aileen Carroll—minister of international cooperation
Tony Ianno—minister of state (families and caregivers)

*As of December 31, 2004

PREMIERS OF CANADIAN PROVINCES

Province	Premier
Alberta	Ralph Klein
British Columbia	Gordon Campbell
Manitoba	Gary Doer
New Brunswick	Bernard Lord
Newfoundland and Labrador	Danny Williams
Nova Scotia	John Hamm
Ontario	Dalton McGuinty
Prince Edward Island	Patrick George Binns
Quebec	Jean J. Charest
Saskatchewan	Lorne Albert Calvert

GOVERNMENT LEADERS OF TERRITORIES

Northwest Territories	Joe Handley
Nunavut	Paul Okalik
Yukon Territory	Dennis Fentie

its own procedures in working toward common national goals. Martin was criticized for this concession to Quebec but argued that it represented a form of "asymmetrical federalism" recognizing different conditions in different parts of Canada. Similar provisions would be available to other provinces if they desired. It was hoped that the large infusion of funds into state health care would bring about "transformative changes" resulting in a more efficient and cost-conscious system.

Economy. The Canadian economy performed robustly in 2004. The trade surplus stood at a three-year high by the end of the first quarter, with a strong flow of exports to Canada's principal markets in the United States, Japan, and China. (A trade surplus occurs when a country exports more goods and services than it imports.) High demand and increasing prices for crude oil contributed to the positive trade balance. However, the trade surplus shrank over the course of the year. Economists predicted 3-percent growth in the gross domestic product (GDP) for the year. GDP is the total value of all goods and services produced in a given year.

Prices were relatively stable, with a rise in the consumer price index of 1.8 percent on a year-over-year basis recorded in September. The unemployment rate in October stood at 7.1 percent. The Bank for International Settlements in Basel, Switzerland, a respected financial authority, complimented Canada for the best fiscal performance of the Group of Seven (G7) countries, which also includes France, Germany, Italy, Japan, the United Kingdom, and the United States. Deficits had grown worldwide since 2000, but Canada had avoided a financial shortfall. This condition had been achieved by cutting back on expenditures earlier and not relying on an improved economy to boost revenues. The Bank predicted that Canada would be the only G7 nation to achieve a budgetary surplus in 2004 and 2005.

Budget. Finance Minister Ralph Goodale submitted his first budget on March 23, 2004. The careful budget reflected the financial requirements that lay ahead for the government. New spending was fixed at $2.2 billion, a figure lower than in previous budgets. Goodale stated there would be a careful review of all government spending and that the office of comptroller general would be re-established to monitor the financial activities of all branches of government. He estimated the budget surplus for fiscal year 2004 at $1.9 billion. When final figures were available in October, the surplus had climbed to $9.1 billion.

U.S. relations. During the 2004 Summit of the Americas, which took place in January in Monterrey, Mexico, U.S. President George W. Bush announced that Canada would be allowed to bid on Iraqi reconstruction projects, a change from the former U.S. position. Prime Minister Martin made his first official visit to Washington, D.C., on April 29 with the hope of restoring relations that had somewhat deteriorated under Jean Chretien. Martin spoke of the possibility of creating a global leaders forum, modeled on the G-20 group of finance ministers in which he had been a leading participant. The forum would include a broad selection of nations from the industrialized as well as the developing world. The forum's concerns would range from issues of global security and the fight against terrorism to global economic problems. The prime minister discussed bilateral commercial issues, such as softwood lumber and the U.S. ban on Canadian beef imports, without reaching a conclusion with President Bush.

President Bush paid his first official visit to Canada on November 30 and December 1. He pressed Canada to join in the ballistic missile defense of North America.

Security. Participation in the U.S. missile shield for defending North America continued to be a controversial subject in Canada. The BQ proposed a motion in the House of Commons in February 2004, stipulating that Canada would not be prepared to participate. The motion was defeated, 155-71, in a vote held on February 24. Thirty Liberals deserted their party to vote with the Bloc, an action revealing the divisions in Canada over the missile shield. A principal source of concern was that the plan would lead to the dangerous militarization of space.

A redistribution of Canada's more than 1,600 troops abroad was revealed during the summer. A force of about 500 soldiers, as well as 6 helicopters, were withdrawn from security duties in Haiti by the end of August. Canadian police were sent to Haiti to help train a local force after a revolution in February. The final camp of Canadian peacekeepers in Bosnia was closed in November, though 83 Canadians remained to fill staff positions in the multinational United Nations force. In November, Graham announced that Canada would send 700 troops to Afghanistan to join the International Security Assistance Force. Approximately 200 Canadian troops were already serving in Afghanistan.

Gay marriage. Canada's Supreme Court ruled on December 9 that there was nothing in the Canadian constitution that precluded a proposed federal bill that would change the definition of marriage to include same-sex couples. The court's decision opened the way for a federal law legalizing same-sex marriage, which the prime minister's Liberal Party pledged to pass. Two weeks later, Newfoundland and Labrador became the seventh province to allow gay marriage. If the federal bill is passed, Canada will become the third country, after Belgium and the Netherlands, to allow same-sex couples to marry.　　　　　　　▪ David M. L. Farr

See also **Canada, Prime Minister of; Canadian provinces; Canadian territories; Montreal; People in the news** (Paul Martin); **Toronto.**

Canadian Prime Minister Paul Martin waves to supporters as he arrives in Saskatoon, Saskatchewan, on June 21, 2004, to campaign for the June 28 election. Saskatchewan and other western provinces voted for conservative leaders in June elections, forcing Martin, a Liberal, into heading a minority government.

Canada, Prime Minister of.

Paul Martin, Canada's 21st prime minister, completed his first year in office in 2004. He made it clear that his government would push forward a program of ambitious social reform. Canada's public health care system was a priority. Martin responded to provincial health requests with federal financial assistance on an unprecedented scale. His most difficult challenge was to steer his election promises through a divided Parliament. Since his Liberal government did not hold a majority, Martin had to bargain with opposition parties for cooperation.

Martin made his first visit to Washington, D.C., in April. His primary purpose was to improve Canada's relationship with the United States. Ties were strained when Canada refused to take part in the U.S.-led military intervention in Iraq in 2003. Martin assured U.S. President George W. Bush that Canada would cooperate in the struggle against terrorism but by other means than sending troops to Iraq.

Martin's first visit abroad took him to Hungary, France, and Russia in early October 2004. In Hungary, he met with other left-of-center leaders to discuss common values. In Russia, Martin discussed thorny bilateral issues with President Vladimir Putin. Plainly, Martin underwent a rapid initiation into the world of global politics. ■ David M. L. Farr

See also **Canada; Canadian provinces; Canadian territories; People in the news** (Paul Martin).

Canadian provinces.

Canada's 10 provinces faced rising costs in providing education and health services to their citizens in 2004. The obligation strained budgets, causing some provinces to record an operating deficit for the year. Oil-and-gas-rich Alberta, where provincial revenues rose dramatically with higher demand and higher energy prices, proved the exception.

Alberta accomplished the rare feat of retiring its public debt in the 2004 fiscal year, which ends in March 2005. The achievement was announced by Progressive Conservative (PC) premier Ralph Klein on July 12, 2004. A financial surplus, rising through the year from escalating oil and gas revenues, exceeded the $3.7-billion provincial debt. (All amounts are in Canadian dollars.) The debt was to be retired as it became due.

Alberta already had the lowest taxes of any Canadian province, so eliminating the debt further strengthened its financial position. With 3.9-percent economic growth forecast for 2004 by Royal Bank economists in October, Alberta's expansion was well above the national average of 3.1 percent. The province's strong economic position prompted Klein to call a provincial election for November 22. The Progressive Conservatives, who had been in power since 1971, won by a wide margin, and Klein retained his position as premier.

The development of oil sands around Fort McMurray in northern Alberta became an important provincial objective in 2004. The value of projects announced in 2004 for the extraction of oil from the sands amounted to $50 billion. The first large undertaking, the Horizon project, was expected to produce 110,000 barrels of synthetic crude oil a day by mid-2008.

British Columbia. The Pacific province, beset by forest fires and other serious challenges in 2003, nevertheless managed to improve its financial position, primarily by tightly controlling expenditures. In February 2004, Statistics Canada noted that British Columbia's *gross domestic product* (the value of all goods and services produced in the province in a year) grew by 2.5 percent in 2003, higher than the national increase of 2 percent. The budget for fiscal year 2004, announced on February 17, showed a balanced state. In September, the government revised an earlier estimate of its surplus for 2004 from $100 million to $865 million. The Royal Bank forecast in October that economic growth for the province would reach 3.6 percent in the 2004 fiscal year, again surpassing the national average.

An outbreak of avian flu struck poultry farmers in the lower Fraser River Valley in February and March. Although the flu was not the deadly Asian variety, which caused the deaths of more than 30 people in Southeast Asia during 2004, some 19 million birds were slaughtered to bring the epidemic under control.

Beginning on April 25, an illegal strike among support staff in British Columbia's health care system severely disrupted medical services. The walkout occurred as the government attempted to reduce health care costs by contracting out hundreds of jobs to private agencies. Back-to-work legislation less than one week later imposed a 15-percent wage cut over a 2-year contract.

Manitoba. Higher rainfall during 2004 helped improve conditions in the prairie province after several years of drought. The increased rain resulted in greater yields of such high-value crops as barley and canola. In addition, sales of hydro-electric power increased because of the improved water supply. In October, Manitoba's Clean Environment Commission announced a major new hydro project, Wuskwatim Dam, which, when built, was to generate 200 megawatts of power.

Public Health Minister Carolyn Bennett announced in May that a new federal public health agency would be established in the centrally located city of Winnipeg. Modeled on the United States Centers for Disease Control and Prevention, the agency would deal with public health emergencies, such as the outbreak of severe acute respiratory syndrome (SARS), which struck Toronto in 2003.

A new agency, the Manitoba Floodway Expansion Authority, was established in March 2004 to manage the Red River Floodway, a drainage channel around Winnipeg that diverts rising floodwaters from the city. The Authority was to supervise the widening and deepening of the Floodway to prevent future emergencies.

New Brunswick. The provincial budget, unveiled on March 30, emphasized austerity in government operations. The federal equalization grant, paid to ensure that provinces with personal incomes below the national average can provide services comparable with those in other provinces, had been cut in 2003. The reduction resulted in the need to cut 750 jobs from the public payroll over the next two years and eliminate the possibility of wage increases for public sector workers.

New Brunswick fishermen engaged in the lucrative snow crab fishery protested the decision in April 2004 by the federal government to allocate part of the provincial quota to neighboring Prince Edward Island. New Brunswick fishermen claimed that the action represented a loss of $2.1 million to east coast fishermen and $6 million to the provincial economy. Since the early 1990's, New Brunswick's share of the fishery had fallen from 62 percent to 55 percent.

Newfoundland and Labrador. Residents of Canada's poorest province experienced both good and bad news in 2004. The province's brightest economic prospect, construction of a nickel mine at Voisey's Bay on the coast of Labrador, speeded up by six months during the year. Concentrates from the mine were to begin moving to a processing plant at Argentia, on the south coast of the island-province, by late 2005. Finished nickel was to be available one year later. The Voisey's Bay mine is owned by Toronto-based INCO, Limited, one of the world's largest producers of nickel.

Federal Fisheries Minister Geoff Regan announced a small relaxation in the moratorium on cod fishing in May 2004. Newfoundland and Quebec fishermen were to be allowed to take 7,165 tons (6,500 metric tons) of cod from the Gulf of St. Lawrence, though other cod fishing grounds around the province remained closed.

The PC government of Premier Danny Williams, elected in late 2003, expressed concern about the province's financial position and especially the large salary bill for public service workers. The new government's first budget, released on March 30, 2004, estimated a deficit of $840 million for fiscal year 2004-2005, one of the highest in the history of the province. Williams announced that 4,000 public service posts would be eliminated over four years. The result was a strike on April 1, 2004, by 20,000 public service workers, including school support staffs, snowplow operators, and the crews of ferries linking the province with the mainland. During the walkout, workers picketed government buildings and prevented the legislature from sitting. Finally, on May 3, back-to-work legislation laid down a two-year wage freeze, with modest increases for the third and fourth years of the contract.

Nova Scotia. The costs of Hurricane Juan, which swept ashore in Nova Scotia in September 2003, continued to be felt in 2004. The storm caused more than $100 million in damage, resulting in a mammoth clean-up operation. On February 19 and 20, the worst blizzard in 20 years, dubbed "White Juan," struck Nova Scotia and its sister province Prince Edward Island. A state of emergency was declared over three days as fierce winds and tidal surges wreaked havoc along the Atlantic coast. Thirty-seven inches (95 centimeters) of snow fell in Halifax, an all-time record. An estimated 1 million people were affected by the storm, many of whom lost electrical power.

The minority PC government of Premier John Hamm presented a balanced budget on April 22. The $5.9-billion budget estimated a small surplus for 2004-2005, which it achieved through higher equalization grants from the central government and an increase in sales taxes and user fees. Hamm had previously promised a 10-percent cut in personal income taxes, but the move had to be partially rescinded.

Four hundred years of French settlement in North America were marked by a world congress of the Acadian people during the first two weeks of August. (Acadians are descendants of French settlers in the southeastern part of Canada, called Acadia, who were forced by the British to leave the area in the 1700's. Many of them settled in Louisiana.) An estimated 250,000 Acadians held family reunions and celebrated the survival of their culture. At Grande Pre, on the Nova Scotia side of the Bay of Fundy, a large new interpretive center was opened. Grand Pre is associated with the legendary Acadian Evangeline, the heroine of Henry Wadsworth Longfellow's 1847 poem.

Ontario. The new Liberal Party government headed by Dalton McGuinty, elected in October 2003, passed a difficult first year in office. When McGuinty came to power, his government discovered that its PC predecessor—far from balancing the provincial books as it had promised—had run up a $5.6-billion deficit. The Liberal's budget, presented on May 18, 2004, imposed the largest tax increases in Ontario since the early 1990's. The greatest increase was in premiums to the Ontario Health Insurance Plan, a charge totaling

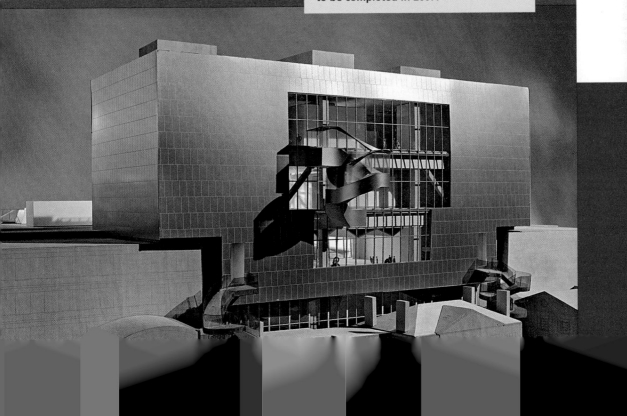

Glass and titanium panels cover the new south facade of the Art Gallery of Ontario in Toronto in an artist's rendering submitted in 2004. The Gallery's renovation and enlargement, designed by Toronto-born, U.S. architect Frank Gehry, was expected to be completed in 2007.

$2.4 billion to be borne by taxpayers. The increase in premiums was graduated according to income and ranged from $300 to $900 in additional health charges each year. The new premium scale was to take effect on July 1, 2004. The announcement sparked a wave of criticism in the province, since McGuinty had promised no tax increases during his first year in office. In addition, rates for hydroelectricity, which had been partially subsidized by the previous government, were allowed to rise.

In spite of the larger revenue, the new government posted a $2.2-billion deficit for fiscal year 2004-2005 and stated that it would be the first of a series of deficits leading, finally, to a balanced budget in 2007-2008. Health care costs represented 45 percent of the provincial budget. McGuinty took satisfaction from the fact that he had successfully led the provincial premiers in demanding larger grants from the central government to meet this expenditure.

Prince Edward Island (P.E.I.), with 55 percent of its population living in rural areas, continued in 2004 to lessen its dependence on farming, fishing, and forestry as an economic base. P.E.I. government economists reported that shipments of manufactured nonfood products, such as aerospace parts and bio-science products, grew by 240 percent from 1993 to 2003. By 2003, tourism had also expanded, in part because of the opening of the Confederation Bridge in 1997, which linked the island with mainland New Brunswick. By 2004, tourism contributed an estimated $350 million annually to P.E.I.'s economy.

The island found a new market in 2004 for its potatoes, P.E.I.'s chief crop. McCain Foods Limited, a leading packager of potato products headquartered in Florenceville, New Brunswick, announced in February that it had sold 8,267 tons (7,500 metric tons) of potatoes to Russia, establishing a new export market. The sale was important in reducing a glut of potatoes on the island.

Also in February, insolvent seafood processor Polar Foods International of Charlottetown, P.E.I., closed six lobster-processing plants on the island, with the loss of 1,200 seasonal jobs. Ocean Choice International Inc., based in St. John's, Newfoundland, bought several of the plants, and in March, it announced that it would reopen two of them.

The PC administration of Premier Pat Binns, re-elected in 2003, faced difficult financial prospects with a reduction in the equalization grant from Ottawa. The March 30, 2004, budget showed a deficit of $85.1 million and projected a deficit for 2004-2005 of $33 million as a result of severe cuts in program spending. The government also enacted new regulations that reduced auto insurance premiums by 12 to 15 percent, in response to an outcry against rapidly rising rates.

Quebec. The Liberal government of Premier Jean Charest, which replaced the separatist Parti Quebecois (PQ) administration in 2003, struggled in 2004 with its plan to reduce state involvement in Quebec's economic affairs. In May, the government announced that it would cut the number of public-sector jobs by 20 percent over 10 years, saving an estimated $700 million a year.

The new government brought down a socially progressive budget on March 30. It had previously promised substantial tax cuts, which proved impossible. Instead, the budget gave $550 million in child assistance to about 1 million low-income families. The assistance was geared to income and was to provide up to $2,000 for families with one child. Larger families would receive larger payments. The work premium initiative provided the budget's second major thrust. About $240 million was to be devoted to assistance to low-income families to encourage them to remain employed. The sales tax was also to be eliminated on such supplies as baby bottles and children's clothing.

Residents of 15 former municipalities on the island of Montreal that had been merged into a "megacity" in 2002 voted in a referendum in June 2004 to break up the integrated metropolis. The previous PQ government had encouraged the formation of the megacity in hopes that sharing common services would reduce expenditures. The "demerger" was to go into effect in 2006.

Saskatchewan. The razor-thin majority won by the New Democratic Party (NDP) government of Premier Lorne Calvert in 2003 elections obliged it to proceed carefully in its fiscal management in 2004. Calvert unveiled the province's 11th balanced budget, which contained a surplus of $42 million, on March 31. The 2004-2005 budget included a sales tax increase from 6 percent to 7 percent and higher taxes on cigarettes and alcohol. Spending for 12 government departments was cut, and about 500 public service workers were to be laid off. Health care and education represented two-thirds of government expenditures.

In May 2004, a herd of 50 purebred bison was released in the Old Man on His Back Conservation Area south of Swift Current. The Canadian prairie had once been the home of countless buffalo, and conservationists hoped that the herd would grow to form a colony of some 300 head. The purebred animals had been trucked into the area, jointly owned by the Nature Conservancy of Canada and the Saskatchewan government, from Elk Island National Park in Alberta in December 2003 and held in paddocks until their release.

■ David M. L. Farr

See also **Canada; Canadian Territories; Montreal; Toronto.**

Canadian territories. Canada's federal territories faced many challenges in 2004. With a population of some 100,000 people scattered over a vast area amounting to more than a third of Canada's land mass, government and economic development was neither easy nor cheap. Although the territories continued moving away from an economy based on traditional hunting and fishing, the outlines of a modern economy were not yet clear in 2004. During this transition period, the tax base remained small, and the territories relied on the federal government for the bulk of their revenue.

Northwest Territories. Diamonds dominated the economy of the Northwest Territories in 2004. With two mines operating and two others being planned, diamonds from the north made Canada the third-largest producer in the world. Canadian diamonds are of high quality and fetch high prices on world markets. De Beers Consolidated Mines Limited of Southdale, South Africa, began constructing its first Canadian mine in 2004, at Snap Lake, near the northern tree line.

A new government, elected in 2003, presented its first budget on March 17, 2004. Diamonds contributed to a 53-percent growth in the Territories' gross domestic product (GDP) over the five years ending in 2003. GDP is the total value of all goods and services produced in a given year. Economists predicted that the Territories' GDP would grow at a rate of 8 percent in 2004.

A spokesperson for Imperial Oil Limited of Toronto announced a cost increase in its projected 758-mile (1,220-kilometer) Mackenzie Valley natural gas pipeline in October. The pipeline, which will extend up the river from its delta on Mackenzie Bay to pipelines in northern Alberta, may cost as much as $7 billion. (All amounts are in Canadian dollars.) The line is expected to carry 1.2 billion cubic feet (34 million cubic meters) of natural gas a day when it goes into operation in 2009. However, the project still faces a complicated approval process, which may take 18 months. Several native groups became partners in the project, but one aboriginal group mounted a legal challenge, claiming that 40 percent of the pipeline route is on the group's land. Construction on the pipeline could not begin until the issue was resolved.

Nunavut. Created in 1999, Nunavut held its second territorial election on Feb. 16, 2004. Ten thousand voters elected 19 people to the territory's assembly. Nunavut has no political parties and manages its affairs by consensus. The legislature, once elected, met to choose a premier and Cabinet. Paul Okalik, a 39-year-old lawyer, was chosen premier on March 5. In his first address to the legislature, Okalik listed priorities for Nunavut—jobs, education, health services, and housing. The budget, announced on May 18, reflected these problems. In the effort to provide essential services, the territo-

rial government amassed a deficit of $13.4 million. In order to clear this deficit, the government needed to use the territory's remaining cash reserves, which would soon be exhausted. The government could only finance current operating costs. Okalik argued that it was essential that the subsidy from the federal government be increased.

The Nunavut economy was not entirely negative in 2004. Diamond prospecting was extremely active, with 1,518 permits, a record number, issued in February. De Beers was granted the largest number, 633. In cooperation with the small Tahera Diamond Corporation of Toronto, De Beers expected to begin production at their first mine, in Jericho, 261 miles (420 kilometers) northeast of Yellowknife, in 2005. Tahera concluded a marketing deal in October 2004 with the famous New York City jeweler Tiffany and Company. Tiffany had previously lent $35 million to Tahera to assist production.

The Conference Board of Canada, an Ottawa-based independent research agency, estimated in 2004 that Nunavut could earn up to $100 million per year by improving its fishing industry. The organization noted that excellent possibilities existed for taking clam and shrimp from Arctic waters.

Canadian sovereignty in the Arctic archipelago was emphasized by a military training operation, Exercise Narwhal, held in late August on Baffin Island. Roughly 600 troops, accompanied by helicopters, naval vessels, and coast guard ships, showed a Canadian presence in the region and practiced cold weather maneuvers that they had not utilized for some years.

Yukon. The Yukon's economy faced a grim future in 2004. With no gold mines in operation, the extraction of *placer gold* (dust, flakes, and nuggets) from the rivers formed the backbone of the industry in 2004. The Yukon's mining industry came into existence during the Klondike gold rush at the end of the 1800's. Forestry, long a standby in the territory, was also in decline in 2004.

Some areas of the Yukon's economy did improve in 2004. True North Gems Inc. of Vancouver announced in August that the company had uncovered emerald deposits at a claim in the Yukon. In October, True North announced that the company had found more emeralds at another Yukon location. Tourism, helped by Alaska cruise visitors, offered another area of growth. A number of First Nations cultural centers opened in 2004, further expanding employment for local people.

The territorial budget, introduced on March 25, showed expenditures of $705 million. The record budget was intended to spur economic renewal through a variety of projects. Yukon and federal officials actively negotiated on a new formula for territorial financing.   ■ David M. L. Farr

See also **Canada.**

Cape Verde. See Africa.

Census. The foreign-born population of the United States remained constant throughout 2003, the U.S. Census Bureau reported on Aug. 5, 2004. The Census Bureau announced that the number of U.S. residents who had been born outside the United States reached approximately 33.5 million people in 2003, 12 percent of the total population. According to the Census Bureau report, 53 percent were born in Latin America; 25 percent were born in Asia; 14 percent were born in Europe; and 8 percent were born in other parts of the world.

In a separate report released on June 14, 2004, the Census Bureau revealed that the U.S. population of Hispanic and Asian ethnic background continued to grow at a faster rate than the population as a whole. The Hispanic population of the United States reached 39.9 million people on July 1, 2003, an increase of about 13 percent since the 2000 census. Hispanics accounted for about 50 percent of the 9.4 million residents added to the U.S. population since 2000. The Asian population of the United States grew 12.5 percent to 13.5 million people, the bureau reported.

On March 18, 2004, the Census Bureau released figures projecting that the Hispanic and Asian populations in the United States would triple by the mid-2000's. Officials projected that the Hispanic population would increase from 35.6 million people in 2000 to 102.6 million people in 2050. The Census Bureau also predicted that the Asian population would increase from 10.7 million people in 2000 to 33.4 million people in 2050. The projections revealed that non-Hispanic whites would account for about 50 percent of the total population in 2050, which is expected to reach 419.9 million people. The U.S. population measured in the 2000 census was 282.1 million people.

Economics. The Census Bureau on March 29, 2004, reported that six industry sectors in the United States had sales or receipts in excess of $1 trillion in 2003. As part of an economic census, Census Bureau officials collected data from more than 7 million business locations in more than 1,000 industries. The report revealed that U.S. wholesale trade had the largest income, with $4.4 trillion in sales or receipts. Wholesale trade involves the purchase of goods in large quantities for resale to merchants who, in turn, sell in smaller quantities to users. Manufacturing was second with $3.8 trillion in sales or receipts; followed by *retail trade* (the sale of goods directly to consumers) with $3.2 trillion; finance and insurance with $2.6 trillion; health care and social assistance with $1.2 trillion; and construction with $1.1 trillion.

The Census Bureau reported in January 2004 that computer system and design related services revenues had declined 7 percent, from $184 bil-lion in 2001 to $172 billion in 2002. Revenues also declined for custom computer programming services, dropping 8 percent from $67 billion in 2001 to $62 billion in 2002.

The data were the first in a series of reports the Census Bureau planned to release through 2006. Bureau officials said that the reports would provide information on business locations, shipments, sales or receipts, payroll, and the employment figures. Future reports would also include economic information for states and population centers. The Bureau has conducted an economic census every five years since the 1950's.

Graduation rates. On June 29, 2004, the Census Bureau released figures revealing that, in 2003, 85 percent of adults aged 25 and older in the United States had completed high school, an all-time high. In addition, 27 percent of adults aged 25 and older had a college degree, another record high. The number of African Americans with a high school diploma or higher rose 10 percent from 1993 to 2003, and non-Hispanic whites had a 5-percent increase over the same period. The Census Bureau assessment also revealed that the number of women with a college degree increased from 19 percent in 1993 to 26 percent in 2003.   ■ Geoffrey A. Campbell

See also **Education: A Special Report; Population.**

Chemistry. A new compound modeled after a complex shape famous in the world of art was described by chemists at the University of California at Los Angeles (UCLA) in May 2004. The compound had the shape of a Borromean knot, a type of knot made of three interlocking rings. Borromean knots are best known from art made by the *Vikings* (people who lived in Scandinavia from the late 700's to about 1100) and from architecture dating to the *Renaissance* (a cultural movement in Europe from the early 1300's to about 1600). The UCLA researchers said their molecular Borromean knot might lead to the production of other complex chemical structures.

To create the knotty new compound, the UCLA team, including chemists Fraser Stoddart and Stuart Cantrill, first experimented with computer simulations of the Borromean structure. The simulations allowed the chemists to test various ways of creating the correct number of chemical bonds in the proper sequence.

Based on these simulations, the chemists created 12 chains of carbon, hydrogen, nitrogen, and oxygen atoms. They then mixed these chains in a solution with zinc *ions* (atoms with electrical charges). The zinc ions acted as a template around which the 12 chains organized themselves, resulting in the spontaneous assembly of the chains into three rings surrounding six ions.

The chemists said the creation of the compound demonstrated the value of combining computer-based "virtual" experimentation with "real-world" laboratory work in the production of new molecular structures. They also noted that the methods used in their research might have practical applications in *nanotechnology*, the manipulation of individual atoms and molecules to create devices for the computer industry and other purposes.

Ammonia alternative. In February 2004, chemists at Cornell University in Ithaca, New York, announced an energy-efficient alternative to a 90-year-old process used to make ammonia-based chemicals, including fertilizers. The new technique involved the production of ammonia at much lower temperatures and pressures than those needed in the Haber-Bosch process. In that industrial process, temperatures greater than 750 °F (400 °C) and pressures hundreds of times greater than the normal atmospheric pressure are used to make ammonia (NH_3) by combining nitrogen with hydrogen. Ammonia is an important ingredient in many fertilizers, because crops take the nitrogen from it and use it for growth.

The extreme conditions of the Haber-Bosch process make it possible to obtain the necessary elemental nitrogen (N) from the molecular nitrogen (N_2) that makes up nitrogen gas. The two nitrogen atoms in a molecule of nitrogen are held together with one of the strongest chemical bonds in nature. This tough bond must be broken to get the nitrogen atoms needed for ammonia production.

Cornell chemist Paul J. Chirik and his colleagues described how they broke the bonds of molecular nitrogen under mild conditions. In their technique, molecular nitrogen first bonded to a compound containing the metal zirconium. This binding resulted in the weakening of the bonds between the nitrogen atoms. The nitrogen bonds broke apart at temperatures as low as 113 °F (45 °C). Then, at about 185 °F (85 °C), the nitrogen combined with hydrogen to form ammonia. These reactions happened at normal atmospheric pressure.

The chemists noted that, because the fertilizer industry has such a huge investment in existing equipment, the new technique was unlikely to replace the Haber-Bosch process in the near future. The researchers added, however, that the technique might be used to produce ammonia for dyes, rocket fuels, and certain other materials.

Shape-shifting molecules. Chemical compounds in medicines can sometimes change shape, making the medicines ineffective or even dangerous. Chemists Michael Ward, Marc Hillmyer, and colleagues at the University of Minnesota at Minneapolis reported in March that

they had developed a way to tame these compounds by forcing them to assume only the shapes that are therapeutically effective.

Compounds change shape when they undergo crystallization, the process by which matter forms crystals, which are composed of atoms arranged in an orderly pattern. A single compound may crystallize into any of several *polymorphs,* varying crystal structures of the same compound. Chemical manufacturers have trouble predicting and controlling the types of polymorphs into which a compound changes. New polymorphs often surprise drugmakers—even after a drug is in production.

The Minnesota chemists controlled the kinds of polymorphs produced by forcing the crystallization of compounds to take place in so-called nanopores. These were tiny holes of different sizes in sheets of glass or plastic. Only a polymorph of a specific kind could form in a nanopore of a particular size. The use of the nanopores allowed the researchers to create pure versions of whatever polymorph they desired.

The chemists said their technique could aid the production of many medicines whose availability has long been hampered by polymorph unpredictability. They added that the technique might also find applications in the agricultural and electronics industries.　　■ Peter Andrews

Chess. In Tripoli, Libya, on July 13, 2004, 24-year-old Rustam Kasimdzhanov of Uzbekistan defeated Michael Adams of the United Kingdom for the world championship title of the Federation Internationale des Echecs (FIDE), the governing body of international chess. In June in Elista, Russia, 25-year-old Antoaneta Stefanova of Bulgaria won the FIDE women's championship.

Tokyo officials detained former world champion Bobby Fischer on July 13; he was traveling with an expired passport. The 61-year-old former world chess champion has lived outside the United States since ignoring instructions from the U.S. government not to play his 1992 match against Russian Boris Spassky in Yugoslavia. Fischer is appealing a decision to deport him.

Chess Olympiad. The Ukrainian team won the gold medal over 128 other nations at the World Chess Olympiad, held in October 2004 in Calvia, Spain. Russia took the silver medal, and Armenia won the bronze, edging out the fourth-place U.S. team at the biennial event. In the 87-team women's division, China won the gold medal, while the United States took silver, its first-ever medal. Russia won the bronze medal.

U.S. events. In 2004, the U.S. Championship brought together 64 players, including women's and children's champions, competing for more than $250,000 in prizes. One notable participant

Gata Kamsky of New York City, the former world championship challenger, had not played a FIDE-rated game since 1999. In the 2004 tournament, 16-year-old Hikaru Nakamura of White Plains, New York, became the youngest U.S. champion since Bobby Fischer, who won at age 14. Rusa Goletiani of Hartsdale, New York, won the women's title at the same event, held in San Diego from November 23 to December 5.

On August 13, FIDE inducted former world champions Alexander Alekhine and Anatoly Karpov, both of Russia, and Max Euwe of the Netherlands into the World Chess Hall of Fame in Miami, Florida. Also on August 13, the U.S. Chess Federation inducted U.S. grandmasters Leonid Shamkovich and Anatoly Lein into the U.S. Chess Hall of Fame, also in Miami. Both Karpov and Lein attended the ceremony.

Young champions. Edward R. Murrow High of New York City won the National High School Championship in April. Catalina Foothills High School of Tucson won the Junior High Championship in May. Hunter College Campus School of New York City won the National Elementary Championship in April. In July, Daniel Ludwig of Orlando, Florida, won the U.S. Cadet Championship, while Lev Milman of New York City clinched the title of 2004 U.S.A. Junior Invitational Chess Champion.　　■ Al Lawrence

Chicago officials formally opened the city's spectacular front-yard playground, Millennium Park, on July 16, 2004. Situated on the east side of downtown commercial artery Michigan Avenue and just north of the city's art museum, the 24.5-acre (9.9-hectare) park revitalizes a stretch of ground once occupied by old railroad yards.

The park showcases a steel-fantasy band shell and pavilion by world-renowned architect Frank Gehry; a highly reflective, curvilinear sculpture by London artist Anish Kapoor; and the twin box-towers of Spaniard Jaume Plensa's digital-age fountain. Amenities include a skating rink, restaurants, gardens, and a commuter bicycle station equipped with showers.

Urban planners consider Millennium Park the most important new U.S. city park in a half-century or more, but it came with a big price tag. The $475-million cost exceeded planners' original 1998 estimate by 300 percent, but a highly successful fund raising campaign brought in $200 million from 91 donors.

Millennium Park sits atop an underground parking garage. Reinforcing the garage roof to provide a solid base for the park was one of the project's biggest challenges and a major factor in cost overruns and delays. As its name implies, the park was originally to have opened in 2000.

O'Hare expansion. In a report submitted to the Federal Aviation Administration (FAA) on Feb. 6, 2004, city officials estimated the cost of the proposed expansion of Chicago's O'Hare International Airport at $14.8 billion—more than doubling the $6.6-billion estimate cited in the original 2001 plan. The FAA requested the new report to evaluate the project's eligibility for federal funding.

Runway limitations at Chicago's major airport have caused backups at O'Hare and slowed air traffic across the United States for years. According to Chicago aviation officials, O'Hare hosted nearly 1 million takeoffs and landings in 2004. The expansion plan proposes building new runways in areas now occupied by suburban developments and reconfiguring existing runways. Officials of the adjacent Illinois suburbs of Elk Grove Village and Bensenville have vigorously opposed the plan, which would require some of their residents to sell their property.

In August, the FAA announced new rules prohibiting new construction near O'Hare and restricting air traffic patterns at regional airports that might impinge on expanded O'Hare traffic. According to Chicago officials, the move was a first step toward approving the O'Hare expansion plan. Federal officials, however, cautioned that the new rules did not guarantee FAA approval. A final FAA decision was expected in late 2005.

Schools. In August 2004, Chicago city officials announced that 74 percent of the city's public schools had improved their scores in state tests administered in the spring of 2004 as compared with 2003. City officials highlighted improvements in math, with especially impressive hikes in scores among third- and fifth-graders.

New look for historic church. On June 13, 2004, members of Fourth Presbyterian Church on Chicago's "Magnificent Mile"—the heavily built commercial district along North Michigan Avenue —voted to sell air rights above part of their 90-year-old neo-Gothic church complex to developers who plan to build a 64-story condo tower. The proposed tower, by architect Lucien Lagrange and Associates, was projected to be completed in 2009. Detractors lamented the loss of open sky around the church and its cloistered courtyard, while church officials hailed the $25-million deal as the means for expanding its outreach to disadvantaged city residents.

Exit. On Feb. 19, 2004, Daniel Barenboim announced that he would step down as music director of the Chicago Symphony Orchestra (CSO) effective at the end of the 2005-2006 season. Barenboim began his CSO tenure in 1991.

■ Harold Henderson

See also **Aviation; Classical music; Deaths.**

Children's books. See Literature for children.

Architect Frank Gehry's stainless steel, whiplash bridge (left at bottom of the aerial photograph) connects lakefront Grant Park with the new Millennium Park dominated by Gehry's music pavilion and sheltered great lawn (left at center). Anish Kapoor's highly reflective sculpture *Cloud Gate* (left at top) rests on a terrace above Michigan Avenue.

Millennium Park opens in downtown Chicago in July 2004 to rave reviews and immediate popularity.

The music pavilion's open air band shell (left) appears to explode around a stage enclosed by a glass curtain wall, which opens for performances. Architect Frank Gehry designed the pavilion for summer concerts and music festivals. An interwoven steel pergola provides a sense of shelter for audiences in regular seats and on the great lawn beyond.

A fountain—consisting of two facing, 50-foot- (1-meter-) high glass-block towers—attracts children to play in a shallow, connecting pool. The towers feature changing video projections of slowly moving faces, which spew water like gargoyles on a gothic cathedral. Spanish artist Jaume Plensa designed the fountain, which is adjacent to Michigan Avenue.

British sculptor Anish Kapoor's *Cloud Gate*, which Chicagoans immediately dubbed "The Bean," rests on a terrace that elevates the music pavilion and a contemporary garden above the bustle of city streets. The sculpture, under which visitors can walk as through a great arch, reflects the city's skyline to the west and parkland and Lake Michigan to the east.

Chile. A Chilean court in August 2004 sentenced four Mapuche Indians and a man in sympathy with their cause to 10 years each in prison after they were convicted of "terrorism by arson." The charges stemmed from the torching of a pine farm on lands that the Indians claimed had been taken from them by timber companies.

Human rights organizations condemned the sentences, claiming that the fire had posed no threat to life or liberty. Moreover, human rights activists maintained it was unfair to convict the Indians on the basis of a law enacted by former dictator Augusto Pinochet Ugarte to silence his political opponents.

Chile's Supreme Court in August stripped Pinochet of his immunity against trial for human rights crimes committed during his dictatorship, from 1973 to 1990. In December 2004, a judge ruled that the 88-year-old general was competent to stand trial, charged him with nine counts of kidnapping and one count of murder, and placed him under house arrest.

In May, President Ricardo Lagos Escobar signed a bill that enabled Chileans to obtain legal divorces for the first time. Previously, couples wishing to separate had to go through a costly legal procedure called a "civil annulment."

■ Nathan A. Haverstock

See also **Latin America.**

China. China's president, Hu Jintao, consolidated his leadership of China on Sept. 19, 2004, by becoming the ruling Communist Party's military chief. He replaced Jiang Zemin, who retired.

Transfer of power. Hu had succeeded Jiang as the party's general secretary in November 2002 and China's president in March 2003. However, Jiang had retained command of the armed forces, the third area of control in the Communist system. Jiang's refusal to retire from all party posts in 2002 had been seen by foreign analysts as an indicator of continuing leadership tensions. Signs later arose of conflict between officials put in office by Jiang and those associated with Hu. Analysts suggested that this conflict was hindering formulation of both economic and foreign policies, though specific disagreements were unclear. Chinese sources denied that there was a power struggle.

Hu made a veiled appeal for Jiang to resign in a speech in August 2004, in which he praised the late Deng Xiaoping, the leader who had tapped them both for future leadership, for having retired before becoming feeble. Jiang's letter resigning the military commission chairmanship was dated September 1, though its contents were not publicly disclosed until September 19, when the Communist Party's Central Committee accepted Jiang's resignation at a meeting in Beijing, the capital. The Committee named Hu, a vice chairman of the commis-

sion, to succeed Jiang. A military officer in charge of propaganda work, Xu Ciahou, replaced Hu as a vice chairman. Defense Minister Cao Gangchuan and General Guo Boxiong also served on the eight-member commission.

At 61, Hu was the youngest Chinese leader since Mao Zedong, who, at the age of 56 in 1949, led the Communist Party to victory in a civil war and established the People's Republic of China. Deng ousted Mao's chosen successor after Mao's death in 1976. Deng's succession plans were upset by a student-led uprising to demand democracy in 1989. Deng then selected Jiang to take over.

Censorship. Chinese authorities tightened control over public discussion of problems and policies during 2004, and Chinese journalists who attempted to write about national problems were pressured into silence. Various kinds of legal charges were made against people who wrote information or opinions that cast an unfavorable light on Communist rule.

In February, a prominent surgeon called for the government to admit that the bloody suppression of the 1989 protestors had been wrong. The physician, Jiang Yanyong, had won acclaim in 2003 by exposing efforts to hide an epidemic of severe acute respiratory syndrome (SARS), leading Hu to discharge two top officials and move quickly to control the problem. The 1989 uprising, however, remained too sensitive for China's leaders to discuss. Jiang, a major general, was detained by the armed forces for 45 days because of his letter seeking reconsideration of the crackdown. He was forced to write what his interrogators took as an admission of error.

Corruption. During the Central Committee session in September 2004, party members were warned that their grip on power was endangered by corruption. Communist Party leaders noted that the fight against corruption was a "life and death struggle" for the party.

The Committee called on members to learn from the loss of power by Communist parties in other countries. The Committee's sentiments reflected statements by Hu on corruption and favoritism as threats to the party's effectiveness. However, emphasis was placed on overcoming reasons that people were disappointed with Communist control, not with loosening it.

Human rights. Under party direction, China's parliament, the National People's Congress (NPC), amended the nation's constitution on March 14. New provisions were worded to protect human rights and private property. Chinese legal experts said the wording was more symbolic than enforceable in a legal system directed by the Communist Party.

China suspended on March 23 talks with U.S. officials on human rights issues amid continuing

charges by the U.S. and international organizations of Chinese violations of human rights. A Chinese official accused the United States of bringing up an "anti-China resolution" at the 60th United Nations (UN) Human Rights meeting in Geneva, Switzerland.

Hong Kong, a special administrative region of China since the United Kingdom returned sovereignty to China in 1997, was told by the NPC on April 26, 2004, that it could not begin direct election of its chief executive in 2007 or its legislature in 2008. The terms of the United Kingdom's handover had made these steps possible. People in Hong Kong responded to the announcement with massive prodemocracy demonstrations.

Prodemocracy parties in Hong Kong won more than 60 percent of votes in Sept. 12, 2004, elections for the region's legislative council, despite official pressure on democracy advocates. However, the democrats won only 25 out of 60 seats in the council under a system that limited the number of seats filled by open balloting. The council, therefore, remained in the hands of those who did not challenge China.

Economic growth created problems for China and for the outside world in 2004. Prime Minister Wen told the NPC on March 14 that "deep-seated problems and imbalances in the economy over the years have not been fundamentally resolved." With China's industrial production annually rising at about 15 percent, officials worried about investment in unneeded facilities and inflation. They

hoped for what economists called "a soft landing" of slowing growth without causing a crash into a *depression* (an extended economic slump). As China in 2004 imported more oil, coal, iron ore, and other materials for its rapid economic growth, worldwide prices of these commodities rose sharply. Shortages loomed in some trade items.

Pollution. Growth also worsened pollution in China. Water supplies in only 6 of China's 27 largest cities met basic health standards in 2004, and water-borne diseases killed large numbers of people. Water shortages became increasingly common across much of the country, limiting growth in some areas. A study by the World Bank, a UN affiliate, reported environmental degradation and resource scarcity were costing between 8 and 12 percent of China's domestic economic production.

Poverty. The World Bank, which defines poverty in developing countries as an income of less than $1 a day, estimated that two decades of Chinese economic growth had lifted 400 million people out of severe poverty—the fastest rate of poverty reduction ever recorded. However, the World Bank estimated that about 200 million Chinese still lived in poverty, and a Chinese newspaper reported in July 2004 that 29 million of China's almost 1.3 billion people lived on less than $77 a year. The public health system established by Mao in the 1950's had virtually collapsed by 2004, and most people lacked access to increasingly expensive medical care.

Taiwan. Chinese officials repeated in 2004 threats to attack Taiwan if the island state, which China claims, moved toward formal independence. However, Chinese officials said that so long as Taiwan recognized that the island and the mainland were part of one China, the two sides could work toward allowing Taiwan "international living space." In July, China conducted its annual military exercises on ways to invade Taiwan, and it continued a buildup of missiles aimed at the island.

The Asian Cup. Angry demonstrations by Chinese fans against foreign teams marred the Asian Cup soccer tournament. The most serious protests occurred in Beijing in August after a Japanese team beat China 3-1 in finals. Chinese fans jeered the Japanese national anthem and waved anti-Japan signs. After the game, Chinese fans rioted, throwing bottles and burning Japanese flags.

The summer rainy season left at least 1,000 people dead, many in mudslides, the government announced on September 22. Rain was especially heavy in the southwest, and the most powerful typhoon in seven years hit the east coast.

■ Henry S. Bradsher

See also **Asia; Building and contruction; Disasters; Korea, North; Taiwan; United Nations.**

City. Cities in the United States in 2004 struggled to balance municipal budgets strained by rising costs and lagging revenues. For an unprecedented third consecutive year, a majority of cities responding to an annual survey by the National League of Cities (NLC) reported declining revenues and deteriorating fiscal conditions. The NLC, based in Washington, D.C., seeks to improve the quality of life in U.S. cities.

According to the survey report, released in November, 63 percent of responding city financial officers said that their city was less able to meet its financial obligations during fiscal year 2004 than during the previous year. (The 2004 fiscal year for state-based governments runs from July 1, 2004, to June 30, 2005.) In addition, 61 percent of the officials predicted worsening conditions in fiscal 2005. The survey report was based on data from 288 cities with a population of at least 50,000.

The report, titled "City Fiscal Conditions in 2004," found that overall city spending for fiscal 2004, adjusted for inflation, was expected to outpace revenues, 3.6 percent to 2.6 percent. City officials cited increases in the cost of employee health benefits, contributions to employee pensions, and infrastructure needs as the biggest demands on municipal budgets. In addition, almost 70 percent of cities reported increased spending on public safety and security.

Reductions in state aid and weakness in local economies also contributed to worsening fiscal conditions, responding officials said. The NLC report noted that at least 80 percent of municipal spending comes from local sources—local income taxes, property taxes, and sales taxes. In the past, NLC officials said, cities relied on state and federal governments to fill budget gaps. Although overall federal aid to the responding cities increased from $3.5 billion in fiscal 2002 to $3.9 billion in fiscal 2004, state aid fell from $9.5 billion to $8.8 billion during the same period.

Regional differences. Although fiscal problems afflicted cities nationwide, some regions were harder hit than others. Only 32 percent of Midwestern financial officials and 33 percent of Western officials predicted a brighter future in fiscal 2005. In contrast, 52 percent of finance officers in the South and 41 percent of those in the Northeast expressed optimism about the future.

Taxing authority—the method by which cities raise revenue—significantly affected the responding cities' fiscal health. About 80 percent of towns and cities that rely exclusively on income taxes for revenue reported worsening conditions. In contrast, 58 percent of cities relying exclusively on property taxes and 52 percent of those relying on sales taxes reported being less able to meet their fiscal obligations. Property tax revenues, buoyed by strong real estate markets, were expected to rise by 5.5 percent in fiscal 2004, the report predicted. Gains from sales taxes were expected to rise by 2.3 percent, while revenues from income taxes were expected to creep up only 1.8 percent.

In response to what the NLC called "grim" conditions, a majority of cities, including 70 percent of the largest municipalities, increased fees and service charges. About 25 percent increased property taxes, up from 17 percent in fiscal 2003. About 40 percent of cities reported increasing employee productivity. In addition, about one-third of cities said they had cut work forces or reduced operating budgets.

Perils of urban sprawl. Two studies released in 2004 provided more evidence linking urban sprawl with health problems among metropolitan residents. The studies emerged as part of a growing focus among community planners on the relationship between health and land-use patterns. Characteristics of sprawling communities include lower population density; separate areas for residences, commerce, and other activities that are located far from each other; and a lack of connected sidewalks and other pedestrian-friendly features.

The first study, released in May, reported that people who live in compact neighborhoods with both residential housing and nearby businesses tend to weigh significantly less than people living

50 LARGEST URBAN CENTERS IN THE WORLD

Rank	Urban center	Population
1.	Tokyo, Japan	26,763,000
2.	Sao Paulo, Brazil	19,245,000
3.	Mexico City, Mexico	18,755,000
4.	Mumbai, India	17,839,000
5.	New York City, U.S.	17,062,000
6.	Dhaka, Bangladesh	15,107,000
7.	Delhi, India	14,655,000
8.	Calcutta, India	14,035,000
9.	Los Angeles, U.S.	13,652,000
10.	Shanghai, China	13,068,000
11.	Jakarta, Indonesia	12,668,000
12.	Buenos Aires, Argentina	12,354,000
13.	Karachi, Pakistan	11,423,000
14.	Rio de Janeiro, Brazil	11,063,000
15.	Osaka, Japan	11,013,000
16.	Beijing, China	10,848,000
17.	Lagos, Nigeria	10,536,000
18.	Manila, Philippines	10,527,000
19.	Cairo, Egypt	9,960,000
20.	Seoul, Republic of Korea	9,888,000
21.	Istanbul, Turkey	9,729,000
22.	Paris, France	9,727,000
23.	Tianjin, China	9,307,000
24.	Moscow, Russia	8,553,000
25.	Lima, Peru	8,025,000
26.	Bangkok, Thailand	7,973,000
27.	London, U.K.	7,640,000
28.	Bogota, Colombia	7,416,000
29.	Tehran, Iran	7,222,000
30.	Hong Kong, China	7,184,000
31.	Chicago, U.S.	7,141,000
32.	Madras, India	6,796,000
33.	Essen, Germany	6,547,000
34.	Bangalore, India	6,315,000
35.	Lahore, Pakistan	6,170,000
36.	Hyderabad, India	5,992,000
37.	Kinshasa, Congo	5,956,000
38.	Wuhan, China	5,815,000
39.	Santiago, Chile	5,782,000
40.	Chongqing, China	5,517,000
41.	Riyadh, Saudi Arabia	5,346,000
42.	Baghdad, Iraq	5,252,000
43.	Toronto, Canada	5,071,000
44.	Ahmedabad, India	5,004,000
45.	Ho Chi Minh City, Vietnam	4,935,000
46.	Shenyang, China	4,898,000
47.	Yangon, Myanmar	4,840,000
48.	St. Petersburg, Russia	4,755,000
49.	Belo Horizonte, Brazil	4,635,000
50.	Philadelphia, U.S.	4,541,000

Source: 2004 estimates based on data from the United Nations.

in spread-out neighborhoods who must drive to their destinations. Researchers led by urban planner Lawrence D. Frank of the University of British Columbia in Vancouver asked nearly 11,000 people living in various neighborhoods of metropolitan Atlanta to record the amount of time they spent walking or driving over a two-day period. The researchers also recorded the participants' body weights and rated their neighborhoods' population density and commercial presence as well as how pedestrian-friendly they were. Frank and his team reported that the likelihood of obesity rose by 3 percent for every half hour spent in a car, regardless of the participant's age, income, or education level.

The second study, reported in October, linked sprawling communities with higher rates of such chronic health problems as high blood pressure, arthritis, and breathing difficulties. Economist Roland Sturm and physician Deborah Cohen of the RAND Corp., a nonprofit research organization based in Santa Monica, California, questioned more than 8,600 people from 38 metropolitan areas about their physical and mental health. They reported that people who lived in more compact cities, such as New York, San Francisco, and Boston, were less likely to report having a broad range of health problems than were people living in more sprawling communities. According to the researchers, regions with the highest level of sprawl include Riverside-San Bernadino, California; Greensboro-Winston-Salem-High Point, North Carolina; Atlanta; Greenville-Spartanburg-Anderson, South Carolina; and West Palm Beach-Boca Raton, Florida. Sturm and Cohen found no connection between sprawl and mental health.

Some planning experts expressed skepticism about the studies. They argued, for example, that slimmer people may prefer to live in compact neighborhoods where they can walk to stores and other destinations.

Economic engines. In 2003, the 318 metropolitan areas in the United States accounted for 85.4 percent of the U.S. gross domestic product (GDP), or $9.4 trillion in goods and services produced, the U.S. Conference of Mayors reported in October 2004. GDP is the total amount of goods and services produced in a country in a given year. In its annual report on metro economies, the nonpartisan organization stated that "metro areas are ... the engines that drive the American economy." The report noted that 84 percent of all people employed in the United States—109 million people—worked in metro areas.

Homeland security aid. A June report issued by the Mayors' Conference revealed that U.S. cities were still experiencing severe delays in obtaining federal funds for homeland security. The report was the third such survey tracking the flow of fed-

50 LARGEST CITIES IN THE UNITED STATES

Rank	City	Population*
1.	New York, N.Y.	8,099,496
2.	Los Angeles, Calif.	3,855,053
3.	Chicago, Ill.	2,856,038
4.	Houston, Tex.	2,018,281
5.	Philadelphia, Pa.	1,469,958
6.	Phoenix, Ariz.	1,408,883
7.	San Diego, Calif.	1,278,941
8.	San Antonio, Tex.	1,236,465
9.	Dallas, Tex.	1,210,754
10.	Detroit, Mich.	901,161
11.	San Jose, Calif.	899,350
12.	Jacksonville, Fla.	786,945
13.	Indianapolis, Ind.	784,116
14.	San Francisco, Calif.	741,520
15.	Columbus, Ohio	733,514
16.	Austin, Tex.	674,355
17.	Memphis, Tenn.	645,333
18.	Baltimore, Md.	620,957
19.	Fort Worth, Tex.	601,793
20.	El Paso, Tex.	592,951
21.	Charlotte, N.C.	592,547
22.	Milwaukee, Wis.	584,257
23.	Boston, Mass.	575,379
24.	Seattle, Wash.	568,931
25.	Washington, D.C.	557,670
26.	Denver, Colo.	556,578
27.	Nashville, Tenn.	544,910
28.	Portland, Ore.	539,348
29.	Oklahoma City, Okla.	529,476
30.	Las Vegas, Nev.	527,603
31.	Tucson, Ariz.	513,566
32.	Long Beach, Calif.	480,590
33.	Albuquerque, N. Mex.	480,527
34.	New Orleans, La.	465,010
35.	Fresno, Calif.	459,211
36.	Sacramento, Calif.	456,832
37.	Cleveland, Ohio	456,153
38.	Virginia Beach, Va.	445,583
39.	Kansas City, Mo.	442,752
40.	Mesa, Ariz.	439,166
41.	Atlanta, Ga.	423,988
42.	Omaha, Nebr.	409,262
43.	Oakland, Calif.	396,727
44.	Tulsa, Okla.	384,727
45.	Honolulu, Hawaii	383,251
46.	Miami, Fla.	381,505
47.	Minneapolis, Minn.	370,511
48.	Colorado Springs, Colo.	369,709
49.	Arlington, Tex.	359,879
50.	Wichita, Kan.	354,979

*2004 World Book estimates based on data from the U.S. Census Bureau.

50 LARGEST METROPOLITAN AREAS IN THE UNITED STATES

Rank	Metropolitan area*	Population†
1.	Los Angeles-Long Beach, Calif.	9,804,254
2.	New York City, N.Y.	9,654,101
3.	Chicago, Ill.	8,663,355
4.	Washington, D.C.-Md.-Va.-W.Va.	5,258,281
5.	Philadelphia, Pa.-N.J.	5,174,782
6.	Atlanta, Ga.	4,790,369
7.	Houston, Tex.	4,625,753
8.	Detroit, Mich.	4,514,842
9.	Dallas, Tex.	3,983,987
10.	Phoenix-Mesa, Ariz.	3,882,378
11.	Riverside-San Bernadino, Calif.	3,602,538
12.	Boston, Mass.	3,482,400
13.	Minneapolis-St. Paul, Minn.-Wis.	3,174,642
14.	Orange County, Calif.	3,058,023
15.	San Diego, Calif.	2,958,353
16.	Nassau-Suffolk, N.Y.	2,815,001
17.	St. Louis, Mo.-Ill.	2,650,789
18.	Baltimore, Md.	2,627,318
19.	Seattle-Bellevue-Everett, Wash.	2,601,380
20.	Tampa-St. Petersburg-Clearwater, Fla.	2,552,055
21.	Oakland, Calif.	2,538,372
22.	Miami, Fla.	2,403,913
23.	Denver, Colo.	2,374,015
24.	Pittsburgh, Pa.	2,344,575
25.	Cleveland-Lorain-Elyria, Ohio	2,270,744
26.	Las Vegas, Nev.-Ariz.	2,152,942
27.	Portland, Ore.-Vancouver, Wash.	2,130,373
28.	Newark, N.J.	2,083,050
29.	Orlando, Fla.	1,882,071
30.	Fort Worth-Arlington, Tex.	1,880,113
31.	Kansas City, Mo.-Kan.	1,864,333
32.	Fort Lauderdale, Fla.	1,821,760
33.	San Francisco, Calif.	1,787,249
34.	Sacramento, Calif.	1,772,803
35.	San Jose, Calif.	1,767,606
36.	San Antonio, Tex.	1,724,999
37.	Indianapolis, Ind.	1,715,560
38.	Cincinnati, Ohio-Ky.-Ind.	1,699,041
39.	Charlotte-Gastonia, N.C.-Rock Hill, S.C.	1,680,924
40.	Columbus, Ohio	1,631,448
41.	Norfolk-Virginia Beach-Newport News, Va.	1,625,522
42.	Milwaukee-Waukesha, Wis.	1,529,763
43.	Austin-San Marcos, Tex.	1,505,828
44.	Salt Lake City-Ogden, Ut.	1,468,947
45.	Bergen-Passaic, N.J.	1,414,266
46.	Raleigh-Durham-Chapel Hill, N.C.	1,383,853
47.	New Orleans, La.	1,359,800
48.	Nashville, Tenn.	1,359,137
49.	Greensboro-Winston-Salem-High Point, N.C.	1,350,429
50.	West Palm Beach-Boca Raton, Fla.	1,278,109

*The U.S. Bureau of the Census defines a metropolitan area as a large population nucleus with adjacent communities having a high degree of economic and social integration.

†2004 World Book estimates based on data from the U.S. Census Bureau.

eral homelands security funds passing through the states to the cities.

According to the June report, 52 percent of the 231 cities surveyed had neither received funds nor been notified that they would receive aid from the First Responder State Block Grant program, the largest homeland security program. This figure, however, represented an improvement over the number of recipient cities in previous surveys. In a report released in January, 76 percent of 215 cities surveyed had said they were still waiting for aid. The first survey report, published in September 2003, found that 90 percent of the 168 cities queried had not received funds or notification.

In October 2004, the Mayors' Conference expressed disappointment with a $400-million cut in funds for the First Responder program contained in the 2005 budget for the Department of Homeland Security. The organization welcomed increased funding for security for transportation and public transit systems and an additional $145 million for cities considered at high risk of terrorist attack. Nevertheless, an NLC spokesperson said, "Our first guard are the police and fire departments. This reduction sends a mixed message." ■ Barbara A. Mayes

See also **Chicago; Houston; Los Angeles; New York City.**

Classical music. Responding to the ongoing problem of declining subscription ticket sales and attendance, symphony orchestras in the United States sought new ways of attracting listeners in 2004. Orchestras also tried new or modified concert formats with the aim of freshening the experience of live classical music.

The Chicago Symphony Orchestra introduced a series of short, informal, early-evening concerts designed to attract office workers before they headed home after work. Other orchestras, including the St. Louis Symphony Orchestra and the Boston Symphony Orchestra, offered specially priced ticket packages aimed at college students and people in their 30's. The Atlanta Symphony Orchestra reported success with free "sampler" concerts comprising highlights of the season's programs. The New York Philharmonic sold 3,500 new subscriptions in a one-week, Internet-only ticket sales drive.

The New York Philharmonic also used video technology—borrowing a device from rock concerts—to lure the younger generation into concert halls. Audience members followed the musical action through images caught by four cameras stationed throughout Avery Fisher Hall and projected onto a large screen hung over the orchestra. A handful of other orchestras also experimented with video technology in 2004.

GRAMMY AWARD WINNERS IN 2004

Classical Album, *Mahler: Symphony No. 3; Kindertotenlieder;* San Francisco Symphony, Michael Tilson Thomas, conductor; Michelle DeYoung, mezzo-soprano; Andreas Neubronner, producer.

Orchestral Performance, *Mahler: Symphony No. 3;* Vienna Philharmonic, Pierre Boulez, conductor.

Opera Recording, *Janacek: Jenufa;* Bernard Haitink, conductor; Jerry Hadley, Karita Mattila, Eva Randova, Anja Silja, Jorma Silvasti, soloists; Wolfram Graul, producer.

Choral Performance, *Sibelius: Cantatas;* Estonian National Symphony Orchestra, Paavo Jarvi, conductor; Ellerhein Girls' Choir and Estonian National Male Choir, Tiia-Ester Loitme and Ants Soots, chorus masters.

Instrumental Soloist with Orchestra, *Britten: Violin Concerto/Walton: Viola Concerto;* London Symphony Orchestra, Mstislav Rostropovich, conductor; Maxim Vengerov, violin and viola.

Instrumental Soloist without Orchestra, *Haydn: Piano Sonatas Nos. 29, 31, 34, 35 & 49;* Emanuel Ax, piano.

Chamber Music Performance, *Berg: Lyric Suite;* Kronos Quartet and Dawn Upshaw, soprano.

Small Ensemble Performance, *Chavez: Suite for Double Quartet;* Southwest Chamber Music, Jeff von der Schmidt, conductor.

Classical Vocal Performance, *Schubert: Lieder with Orchestra;* Thomas Quasthoff, bass-baritone, and Anne Sofie von Otter, mezzo-soprano; Chamber Orchestra of Europe, Claudio Abbado, conductor.

Classical Contemporary Composition, *Argento: Casa Guidi;* Dominick Argento, composer; Frederica von Stade, mezzo-soprano; Eiji Oue; Minnesota Orchestra.

Classical Crossover Album, *Obrigado Brazil;* Jorge Calandrelli, conductor; Yo-Yo Ma, cello; various other artists.

Transitions on the podium. The arrival and departure of music directors at a number of major U.S. symphony orchestras made headlines in 2004. The U.S. conductor James Levine began his first season as music director of the Boston Symphony Orchestra in October, succeeding Seiji Ozawa. Levine was the first conductor of the orchestra who had been born in the United States. He also remained music director of the Metropolitan Opera in New York City. Daniel Barenboim, the director of the Chicago Symphony Orchestra since 1991, announced in February 2004 that he would leave the orchestra when his contract expired at the end of the 2005-2006 season.

In a rare move for a U.S. orchestra, the Pittsburgh Symphony Orchestra in September 2004 appointed a trio of conductors—rather than a single music director—to succeed Mariss Jansons. Musical authority was vested in Sir Andrew Davis as artistic adviser; Yan Pascal Tortelier as principal guest conductor; and Marek Janowski as guest conductor. Andres Cardenes, the concertmaster of the orchestra, explained, "The moniker 'music director' has expectations that one human being cannot possibly fulfill."

Awards. In April, U.S. composer Paul Moravec won the 2004 Pulitzer Prize in Music for his *Tempest Fantasy,* a half-hour "musical meditation" on

Soprano Renee Fleming performs the role of the Countess Madeleine in Richard Strauss's opera *Capriccio* at the Palais Garnier in Paris in June. The production also included mezzo-soprano Anne Sofie von Otter and baritone Dietrich Henschel.

William Shakespeare's play, *The Tempest*. In June, John Adams, one of the most widely revered of American composers, became the first recipient of the Michael Ludwig Nemmers Prize in Musical Composition. American composer George Tsontakis received the prestigious Grawemeyer Award for his *Violin Concerto No. 2* in November.

New orchestral works. Pianist Paul Barnes and the Omaha Symphony Orchestra, under Victor Yampolsky, performed the world premiere of Philip Glass's *Piano Concerto No. 2*, subtitled "After Lewis and Clark," in September. The work commemorated the bicentennial of the historic 1804-1806 expedition into the Pacific Northwest by the American explorers Meriwether Lewis and William Clark. In February 2004, Larry Rachleff led the Providence-based Rhode Island Philharmonic in the premiere of Barbara Kolb's *The Web Spinner*, a 10-minute orchestral piece. In March, *Tangle*, which composer Augusta Read Thomas described as "a colorful, bold fantasy in sound," had its first performance by the Chicago Symphony Orchestra, under David Robertson.

Esa-Pekka Salonen, music director of the Los Angeles Philharmonic, conducted the premieres of two works commissioned to inaugurate the orchestra's new home, the Walt Disney Concert Hall. *Ecstatic Architecture*, by Australian composer Liza Lim, was first heard in May; and *A Scotch Bestiary*, by Scottish composer James MacMillan, had its debut performance in October.

Ellen Taaffe Zwilich's *Rituals*, for five percussionists and orchestra, received its premiere in March by NEXUS, a percussion ensemble based in Toronto, and the Memphis-based IRIS Orchestra, with Michael Stern conducting. In April, the Boston Symphony Orchestra presented the first performance of the Scottish-American composer Thea Musgrave's *Turbulent Landscapes*, a six-movement work based on paintings by the English landscape painter J. M. W. Turner (1775-1851). Grant Llewellyn conducted the orchestra.

New operas. U.S. composer William Bolcom's *A Wedding*, based on the 1978 film by director Robert Altman, received its first performance by the Lyric Opera of Chicago in December 2004. The opera is a comedy about the family secrets that are revealed at the nuptials between the son of a high-society family and the daughter of *nouveau-riche* Kentuckians.

In October, the New York City Opera presented the premiere of *Haroun and the Sea of Stories*, a work with music by Charles Wuorinen and a libretto by James Fenton. The work, a fable about the need for creative freedom, is based on a fantastical novel for children by Salman Rushdie. The

Indian-born author was forced into hiding in 1989 after Islamic leaders sentenced him to death for perceived blasphemy in one of his novels.

Jake Heggie's *The End of the Affair* had its premiere by the Houston Grand Opera in March 2004. Based on British author Graham Greene's 1951 novel of passion, jealousy, and faith, the opera is set against the devastation of the London Blitz, aerial attacks against London by German forces in World War II (1939-1945).

Notable deaths. In October 2004, Robert Merrill, the American baritone who performed for 30 years at the Metropolitan Opera, died at age 85 or 87, depending on the source. The French baritone Gerard Souzay, who reigned as the leading exponent of French art song for three decades after World War II, died in August at age 85. Nicolai Ghiaurov, the Bulgarian-born opera singer with a sumptuous voice who was one of the great basses of the postwar era, died in June at age 74. Robert J. Harth, the visionary artistic and executive director of New York City's Carnegie Hall who guided the institution through two challenging years, died in January at age 47. The Cuban-American composer and pianist Joaquin Nin-Culmell died in January at age 95.   ■ John von Rhein

See also **Deaths; Popular music.**

Clothing. See Fashion.
Coal. See Energy supply.

Colombia. Colombia's major cities were largely peaceful during 2004. The fighting, however, persisted intermittently in much of the country's rugged, rural regions, which were controlled by local warlords, drug traffickers, and self-styled revolutionaries.

In January, some 18,000 United States-trained counterinsurgency troops of the Colombian army began an offensive in the lawless southern part of the country. This area had long been in the hands of Marxist rebels and drug traffickers. The offensive—the largest sustained operation in Colombia's 40-year-old civil conflict—was intended to "strike a decisive blow against narco-terrorists," according to General James Hill, commander of the U.S. Southern Command. Another objective of the offensive was to provide the necessary safety for Colombian and foreign-owned oil corporations to operate in the region, thought to contain potentially vast oil reserves.

Increased U.S. involvement. In October, the U.S. Congress doubled from 400 to 800 the number of American military personnel the U.S. Department of Defense was allowed to maintain in Colombia. Congress also raised the ceiling on U.S. civilian employees under contract with the U.S. government from 400 to 600. The measures were part of a defense bill for fiscal year 2005, which began in October 2004.

Proponents of the increased U.S. role in Colombia justified the actions as necessary to prosecute the global war on illegal drugs. Opponents of the measures objected to the diversion of U.S. funds to aid the Colombian government in its half-century effort to root out armed political rivals. Opponents also objected to the use of the funds to benefit private corporations.

A case in point involved Occidental Petroleum Corporation of Los Angeles, which owned a 500-mile (805-kilometer) pipeline in northeastern Colombia that was protected by U.S.-trained Colombian elite battalions. These units, like the troops that mounted the offensive in southern Colombia in 2004, were supported by U.S.-supplied military advisers, helicopters, and high-tech surveillance equipment.

Peace talks. In early July, the administration of President Alvaro Uribe entered into peace talks with 10 negotiators from the United Self-Defense Forces of Colombia (AUC), a right-wing paramilitary group. However, three weeks later, the U.S. government, which classified the AUC as a terrorist organization, charged two of these negotiators with trafficking in cocaine bound for the United States.

When the peace talks were in progress, three AUC leaders took advantage of a 48-hour safe-conduct pass in July to appear before the Colombian Congress in Bogota, the capital. The three paramilitary leaders excused well-documented atrocities committed by the AUC as "acts of patriotism." Still, they said they were willing to lay down their arms, provided that they would not face trial for crimes in violation of human rights. They also demanded that they not be *extradited* (turned over) to the United States, where several AUC leaders had been indicted on charges of drug trafficking. In early November, the government announced that the AUC had agreed to disarm more than 3,000 fighters by the end of 2004.

Horrors of war. In May, the National Museum of Colombia in Bogota opened an exhibit of recent paintings by Fernando Botero, one of Latin America's most celebrated living artists. In sharp contrast with his previous works, which had often depicted cheery, corpulent people, Botero's new works depicted in horrific detail the brutal, drug-fueled conflict that had raged for so long in Colombia.

■ Nathan A. Haverstock

See also **Latin America.**

Colorado. See State government.
Common Market. See Europe.
Commonwealth of Independent States. See Asia; Azerbaijan; Belarus; Georgia; Kazakhstan; Russia; Ukraine.
Comoros. See Africa.

Computer. Competition in the *search engine* (software that explores the Internet or other collections of information and indexes the findings) marketplace grew heated in 2004. In August, the industry leader, Google Inc. of Mountain View, California, offered its stock to the public for the first time in a sale known as an initial public offering (IPO). Google's IPO was among the most eagerly anticipated in the computer industry. During the first day's trading the company's shares rose from the offering price of $85 to more than $100 per share, raising an estimated $27 billion.

Redmond, Washington-based Microsoft Corporation fought back on November 11, when it launched a test version of its new search engine, MSN Search, capable of scanning some 5 billion pages on the World Wide Web, the Internet's main information repository. Google countered with the announcement that its search engine was capable of searching 8 billion pages.

In October, Google broadened its product beyond the Internet with the the Desktop Search program. Desktop Search uses Google technology to index and search material stored on a personal computer. Those searches can then be combined with searches of the Internet.

Microsoft problems and delays. Security vulnerabilities in both operating system (OS) and Internet browsing software plagued Microsoft in 2004. The vulnerabilities allowed computer viruses and other unwanted bits of software to make their way into computers using Microsoft's Windows-based operating systems. Microsoft issued regular security upgrades throughout the year and, in August, released Windows XP Service Pack 2, a collection of several repairs known as patches. In part because of the time spent on security upgrades, Microsoft announced in August that its much-anticipated overhaul of the Windows OS, code-named "Longhorn," would be delayed until mid-2006.

World's fastest computer. In November 2004, two computers in the United States were proclaimed the world's fastest. The Blue Gene/L, produced by International Business Machines of Armonk, New York, led the race, with a capability of 70.72 trillion calculations per second. In second place was the Columbia computer system from Silicon Graphics Inc. of Mountain View, California, which could perform 51.87 trillion calculations per second. The previous record holder was the Japan Earth Simulator built in 2002 by NEC Corporation of Tokyo, capable of performing 36 trillion calculations per second. ■ Keith Ferrell

See also **Computer: A Special Reprt; Electronics; Internet; Telecommunications.**

Steve Jobs, chief executive officer of Cupertino, California-based Apple Computer, Inc., introduces the new iPod mini at the Macworld Conference and Expo in San Francisco on Jan. 6, 2004. The iPod mini, about the size of a business card, yet capable of holding about 1,000 digital songs, was an immediate hit with the public.

SEARCH ENGINES

Driving the Information Age

Bigger and better search engines are
helping computer users locate
information faster and more effectively.

By Dave Wilson

Google Inc. of Mountain View, California, a company that provides services for searching the World Wide Web, offered its stock to the public for the first time in August 2004. At the close of the initial day of trading, the stock stood at $100 a share. The company had a market capitalization of $27.2 billion. On that first day of trading, the market value of Google Inc. exceeded that of AT&T or General Motors. Google already had achieved the ultimate in market branding. Users had transformed Google's name into a verb, meaning "To search for information on the Web, particularly by using the Google search engine." How could a company have grown so valuable and famous in just eight years? Quite simply, Sergey Brin and Larry Page, two students at Stanford University in Stanford, California, had built a better mousetrap. In this case, the mousetrap was a computer program.

Brin and Page's program allowed users to quickly and efficiently search through more than 8 billion pages on the World Wide Web, a system of computer files linked together on the Internet. The Internet itself connects computers and computer networks around the world. The Web is made up of electronic addresses, called Web sites, that contain Web pages that hold multimedia information—illustrations, sounds, and moving pictures—in addition to text. These sites and their pages reside in computers connected to the Internet.

A search engine user types one or more keywords in a designated space on the computer screen. The typed word or words relate to the subject on which the user wants information. The engine responds by matching that keyword or words with keywords in its index file, a master list of keywords and the Web pages on which they occur. The search engine returns to the user a list of all the Web pages that feature the keyword or words. The best search engines are very fast and provide highly relevant information.

Without search engines, the usefulness of the Internet would be comparable to an enormous library with all books scattered randomly. To avoid such chaos, librarians assign a specific set of numbers to a book based on the information in that book. They use the set of numbers to organize books on the shelves and then provide library patrons with a card catalog, or its computer equivalent, that gives users the information they need to find a specific book. Instead of such highly organized classification systems, Internet users have search engines.

The dawn of the search engine

The first search engines predate the World Wide Web, which began to be widely used on the Internet in 1993. Before 1993, much of the data on the Internet was shared via a technology known as *FTP* (*f*ile *t*ransfer *p*rotocol). However, the only way to know that a file had been placed on an FTP site was to learn about it through another FTP user. Responding to the limitation, users developed electronic lists of files available on FTP sites. However, the number of files on FTP sites grew so rapidly that the lists quickly became too outdated to be of much use.

In 1990, Alan Emtage, a student at McGill University in Montreal, Canada, developed the Internet's first search engine. He named the program "Archie," a shortening of the word "archives" and a reference to the *Archie* comic books that focused on a fictional group of high school students. Archie was a great help to Internet users who needed to find specific files. However, it was very limited compared with newer search engines.

One of Archie's limitations was that it only searched file names. A user who typed in "floods" would get a list of files with "flood" or "floods" in the title. If the name of a file was not perfectly descriptive, users would have a hard time finding the information for which they were searching. Another problem was the fact that computer systems limited file names to a certain number of characters. Authors responded to the limitation by using abbreviations in their titles. A file about the Johnstown Flood of 1889 might be titled "Jtn_Flood_1889" and be lost in an Archie search for "Johnstown Flood."

Search engines kept evolving as the Internet evolved, and Archie was followed by Veronica and Jughead, also named for Archie comic book characters. Veronica (*Very Easy Rodent-Oriented Netwide Index to Computerized Archives*) was developed at the University of Nevada at Reno by the school's System Computing Services group. Jughead (*Jonzy's Universal Gopher Hierarchy Excavation and Display*) was developed by Rhett Jones at the University of Utah in Salt Lake City. Both programs shared many of Archie's limitations.

Enter the Web

Yahoo!, an acronym for *Yet Another Hierarchical Officious Oracle*, was an early search engine designed specifically to hunt for information on the World Wide Web. In the beginning it was very simple. In February 1994, David Filo and Jerry Yang, two Stanford University students, launched a Web site called "Jerry's Guide to the World Wide Web" that was simply a list of other sites. Soon their friends were using it as an index to the Web. Within eight months, more than 100,000 people were using the site. Eventually "Jerry's Guide," renamed Yahoo!, evolved beyond simple listings to incorporate actual searches for words within the contents of a Web page. This critical capacity allowed users to quickly find specific information on the Web, rather than a list of sites that conceivably might contain the needed information.

AltaVista, a search engine that appeared near the end of 1995, offered advanced search capabilities. In addition to searching by standard keywords, for example, "Columbus America," AltaVista allowed users to search by typing questions using natural language— "What year did Columbus land in America?" AltaVista also allowed users to specify more complex queries by adding *Boolean operators* (connecting words such as "and," "or," or "not"), which greatly improved the efficiency of searches. For example, to avoid Web pages mentioning the city of Columbus, Missouri, the AltaVista user could type "Columbus America NOT Missouri."

Search engine results became increasingly cumbersome as more and more Web pages were posted on the Internet. Thousands were personal Web pages containing information of little or no interest to researchers. As a result, search engine users often sifted through hundreds of results

The author:
Dave Wilson is a producer at Cable News Network (CNN).

to find pages that would prove useful. In 1998, Brin and Page launched Google. The name was a play on "googol," a word representing the numeral 1 followed by 100 zeros. Brin and Page's use of the term reflected their intention to organize the seemingly infinite amount of information available on the Web.

Google was unique because of its ability to "rank" Web pages. The software Brin and Page developed takes advantage of the very nature of the Web—its interconnectedness. It utilizes the Web's vast link structure as an indicator of the value of an individual page. Google's page ranking system sees a link from Web page A to page B as page A's recommendation for page B. For example, Google's software assumes that a Web page about Christopher Columbus that is linked to by many other Web pages is likely to be more relevant to the user's search than a Web page with fewer inbound links. Google, therefore, ranks the page with more incoming links toward the top of the results list. Google also rates the page that made the recommendation. Links from "important" pages, for example, from educational or government sites, are given a higher page rank, which the software considers each time it conducts a search.

Spiders and robots

Most search engines use programs called spiders that "crawl" through each page of the World Wide Web. The spider records every word on a Web page, along with links to other Web pages. The spider returns to the search engine that sent it out, saving the information it finds in a large storage file called an index or catalog. Spiders constantly crawl around the Web, searching out changes made to Web pages and noting those changes in the search engines. However, the process is not instantaneous. It may be days or even weeks before a Web page is indexed or any changes made to that Web page are recorded. Until the spider makes a new entry in the index file, anyone searching for a specific Web page with that search engine will not be able to find it.

Larry Page (left) and Sergey Brin co-founded and developed Google, one of the Internet's most popular search engines.

Not all Web pages are indexed. If a Web page is not linked to other pages, the developer must submit it to the search engine. Alternately, programmers can tell spiders not to add certain pages to their index files. Web page designers can designate pages as off limits by putting special computer code called a "robots" tag on the page. This tag tells the spider what content on the page to index and what to ignore. For example, such newspapers as *The New York Times* may place robots tags on stories that are over one month old and charge users for access to those stories. The robots tags tell spiders not to index such stories.

Each search engine uses a specific set of requirements to evaluate how well a Web page matches a request. Factors that influence the results include the relationship of keywords to each other in the text, whether the keywords appear in critical places such as a headline, and the frequency with which those words occur on a page. When keywords are some distance from each other on a page, that page is usually less relevant than a page where keywords are close together.

Search engines also use unique sets of criteria in an attempt to present the most relevant results for each search. Each search engine keeps the criteria it uses to rank Web pages a secret, so that the developers of other search engines cannot copy them. As a result, entering the same search in different search engines often produces different results.

HOW A SEARCH ENGINE WORKS

When a user types a term into a search engine, the search engine produces a list of Web pages that contain that word or phrase. However, before that can happen, an indexer program has to create an *index file*, a list of Web pages and the keywords they contain. The indexer automatically scanned Web pages for keywords—terms for which people are likely to search. It stored this information in an index file, which acts similarly to an index in a book. Each search engine has its own unique index file. This is why searching for the same term on different search engines can produce different results.

When a user enters a search term into a search engine, the search engine scans the index file for that term. This ensures that the search engine will return results quickly. It is much quicker to find a subject in a book by checking the index rather than skimming through the book. Similarly, a search engine can scan an index file much faster than it can look through millions of Web pages for a specific term.

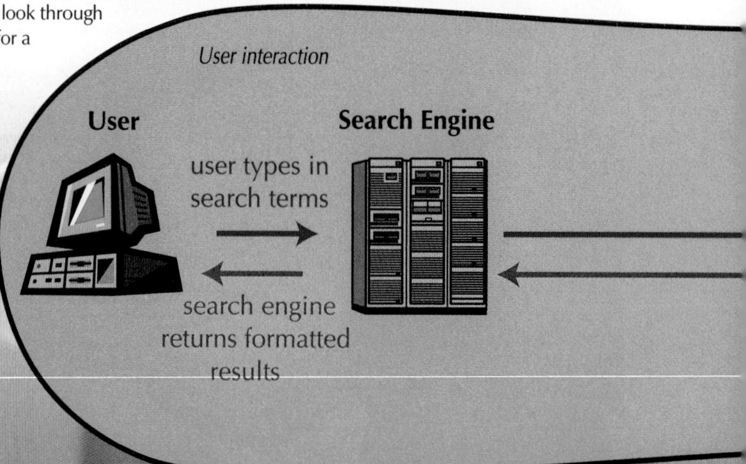

User interaction

User **Search Engine**

user types in
search terms

search engine
returns formatted
results

The owners of many commercial Web pages attempt to figure out the ways search engines rank pages. They do this to get a better ranking in search engine results and more traffic to their sites. Some Web site developers advertise on public commentary sites so that they appear more popular than they really are. Search engine programmers are aware of such tactics and attempt to counter them.

Who pays the bill?

Companies that run Internet search engines make much of their profit though advertising. Many search engines sell keywords to advertisers. If someone searches for "camera," for example, some search engines will display advertisements on the results page in addition to the search results. Advertisers assume that consumers searching for "camera" are often shopping for cameras. Advertisers bid for their advertisements, offering to pay, for example, twenty-five cents or $1 for each time a user links to the advertiser's Web site via the ad. The more advertisers are willing to bid, the better placement their ad receives on the results page. Google officials acknowledge that roughly 95 percent of their revenue comes from such advertising fees. According to eMarketer, a marketing research company based in New York City, U.S. fees for such advertisements totaled about $2.5 billion in 2003 and were expected to rise to $3.2 billion in 2004.

Image of the future

Today's search engines can only search for words. When users search for a photograph or a song using a search engine, they are searching for words that have been attached to the image or sound file by a human being. In the future, search engines will be able to interpret both sounds and images. In April 2004, researchers from Purdue University in West Lafayette, Indiana, announced that they had developed a search engine that returns results based on an image. A user submits a sketch or image, and the engine analyzes it and returns results that resemble the sketch. Such advanced search engines should make the Internet even more useful and, perhaps, spawn another Internet revolution.

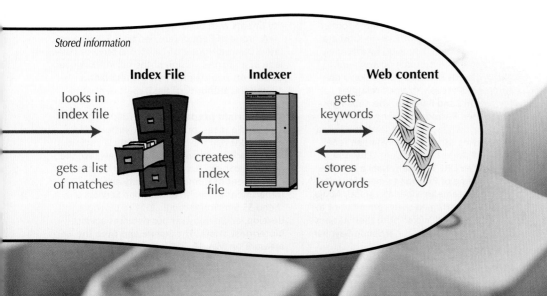

Stored information

Index File   **Indexer**   **Web content**

looks in index file

gets a list of matches

creates index file

gets keywords

stores keywords

Congo (Kinshasa).

In 2004, the coalition government headed by Joseph Kabila—established by a 2003 peace accord ending a five-year civil war—struggled to assert its authority over the Democratic Republic of Congo (DRC). The peace pact was to bring opposing factions together in a power-sharing transitional government that, aided by more than 10,000 United Nations peacekeepers, would bring peace and prepare the way for elections. However, instability in the DRC threatened these objectives.

Coup attempts. On March 28, 2004, rebel soldiers attacked military installations in the capital, Kinshasa, in an attempted coup (overthrow) against the Kabila government. Loyalist troops defeated the rebels. Eleven weeks later, on June 11, members of the presidential guard staged a second coup attempt, which also was foiled.

Fighting between DRC army factions broke out in late May in the eastern city of Bukavu. On June 2, troops commanded by General Laurent Nkunda occupied the city. Nkunda is associated with the Rwanda-backed Congolese Rally for Democracy (RCD), once the main rebel group in the east but, since the 2003 accord, a participant in the transitional government. After a week, regular DRC troops recaptured Bukavu.

In an offensive mounted by the Kabila government in September 2004, loyalist troops advanced into North Kivu province to pursue Nkunda's renegade army. The fighting drove up to 100,000 civilians from their houses.

Defection. On August 23, RCD leader and transitional government Vice President Azarias Ruberwa announced he was withdrawing from the governing coalition. Ruberwa's decision jeopardized the power-sharing arrangement prescribed by the 2003 peace accord. According to that plan, President Kabila retained the presidency—which he had assumed in 2001—but shared administration with four vice presidents, each representing a rebel faction in the former civil war. Senior RCD party officials in Kinshasa preserved the coalition, however, by affirming their loyalty to the transitional government.

Relations with Rwanda. The Bukavu episode in June 2004 deeply strained relations between the DRC and Rwanda. The Kabila government accused Rwanda of aiding Nkunda's renegade army, while Rwandan leaders accused the DRC of giving sanctuary to Rwandan rebels.

On June 18, Nigerian President Olusegun Obasanjo invited DRC President Kabila and President Paul Kagame of Rwanda to meet for talks. The two leaders came to Nigeria's capital, Abuja, and on June 25 reaffirmed their commitment to the 2003 peace accord, which both their nations had signed.   ■ Simon Baynham

See also **Africa**.

Congress of the United States.

The U.S. Congress wrangled over a number of issues in 2004, ranging from an overhaul of the U.S. intelligence community and the Iraq War to whether to extend a ban on assault weapons. Republicans in Congress extended their majority following general elections in November, while one congressman was criticized for not complying with the rules and standards of conduct for elected officials.

Iraq War. The Senate Intelligence Committee on July 9 issued a report criticizing the Central Intelligence Agency (CIA) for faulty intelligence on Iraq prior to the start of the Iraq War in 2003. The committee concluded that the threat from chemical and biological weapons in the hands of former Iraqi President Saddam Hussein had been exaggerated. The authors of the report wrote that U.S. President George W. Bush and Congress had relied upon "flawed" information provided by the intelligence community when the president, backed by Congress, decided to commit U.S. forces to topple the Iraqi government. No chemical, biological, or nuclear weapons were found in Iraq, leading many to question why it was imperative for the United States to invade Iraq.

Intelligence legislation. The House and the Senate agreed in December 2004 on legislation that would overhaul U.S. intelligence agencies and create the position of national intelligence director. The House voted 336 to 75 on December 7 to approve the legislation. The Senate approved the legislation by a vote of 89 to 2 on December 8. The bill was signed by President Bush on December 17.

Among other provisions, the legislation authorizes the creation of a National Counterterrorism Center to act as a clearinghouse for terrorism intelligence information and requires agencies such as the CIA to share their surveillance and intelligence information about national security threats with other government agencies.

A group of Republicans, led by U.S. Representative Duncan Hunter of California, blocked passage of an earlier version of the bill in November. Opponents had claimed that the legislation diluted the authority of the Department of Defense.

Terrorism preparedness. In 2004, Congress approved a measure intended to increase U.S. preparedness in the case of a chemical, radiological, or nuclear terrorist attack. The new law, the Project BioShield Act of 2004, authorizes the Department of Homeland Security and the Department of Health and Human Services to spend $5.6 billion through 2014 to purchase, develop, and deploy various defenses against bioterrorist attack. The Senate approved the measure on May 19, 2004, and the House

MEMBERS OF THE UNITED STATES SENATE

The Senate of the first session of the 109th Congress consisted of 44 Democrats, 55 Republicans, and 1 Independent when it convened on Jan. 4, 2005. The first date in each listing shows when the senator's term began. The second date in each listing shows when the senator's term expires.

STATE	TERM	STATE	TERM	STATE	TERM
Alabama		**Louisiana**		**Ohio**	
Richard C. Shelby, R.	1987-2011	Mary L. Landrieu, D.	1997-2009	Mike DeWine, R.	1995-2007
Jeff Sessions, R.	1997-2009	David Vitter, R.	2005-2011	George V. Voinovich, R.	1999-2011
Alaska		**Maine**		**Oklahoma**	
Theodore F. Stevens, R.	1968-2009	Olympia Snowe, R.	1995-2007	James M. Inhofe, R.	1994-2009
Lisa Murkowski, R.	2003-2011	Susan M. Collins, R.	1997-2009	Tom Coburn, R.	2005-2011
Arizona		**Maryland**		**Oregon**	
John McCain III, R.	1987-2011	Paul S. Sarbanes, D.	1977-2007	Ron Wyden, D.	1996-2011
Jon Kyl, R.	1995-2007	Barbara A. Mikulski, D.	1987-2011	Gordon Smith, R.	1997-2009
Arkansas		**Massachusetts**		**Pennsylvania**	
Blanche Lambert Lincoln, D.	1999-2011	Edward M. Kennedy, D.	1962-2007	Arlen Specter, R.	1981-2011
Mark Pryor, D.	2003-2009	John F. Kerry, D.	1985-2009	Rick Santorum, R.	1995-2007
California		**Michigan**		**Rhode Island**	
Dianne Feinstein, D.	1992-2007	Carl Levin, D.	1979-2009	Jack Reed, D.	1997-2009
Barbara Boxer, D.	1993-2011	Debbie Stabenow, D.	2001-2007	Lincoln D. Chafee, R.	1999-2007
Colorado		**Minnesota**		**South Carolina**	
Wayne Allard, R.	1997-2009	Mark Dayton, D.	2001-2007	Lindsey Graham, R.	2003-2009
Ken Salazar, D.	2005-2011	Norm Coleman, R.	2003-2009	Jim DeMint, R.	2005-2011
Connecticut		**Mississippi**		**South Dakota**	
Christopher J. Dodd, D.	1981-2011	Thad Cochran, R.	1978-2009	Tim Johnson, D.	1997-2009
Joseph I. Lieberman, D.	1989-2007	Trent Lott, R.	1989-2007	John Thune, R.	2005-2011
Delaware		**Missouri**		**Tennessee**	
Joseph R. Biden, Jr., D.	1973-2009	Christopher S. (Kit) Bond, R.	1987-2011	Bill Frist, R.	1995-2007
Thomas Carper, D.	2001-2007	Jim Talent, R.	2003-2009	Lamar Alexander, R.	2003-2009
Florida		**Montana**		**Texas**	
Bill Nelson, D.	2001-2007	Max Baucus, D.	1978-2009	Kay Bailey Hutchison, R.	1993-2007
Mel Martinez, R.	2005-2011	Conrad Burns, R.	1989-2007	John Cornyn, R.	2003-2009
Georgia		**Nebraska**		**Utah**	
Saxby Chambliss, R.	2003-2009	Chuck Hagel, R.	1997-2009	Orrin G. Hatch, R.	1977-2007
Johnny Isakson, R.	2005-2011	Ben Nelson, D.	2001-2007	Robert F. Bennett, R.	1993-2011
Hawaii		**Nevada**		**Vermont**	
Daniel K. Inouye, D.	1963-2011	Harry M. Reid, D.	1987-2011	Patrick J. Leahy, D.	1975-2011
Daniel K. Akaka, D.	1990-2007	John Ensign, R.	2001-2007	James M. Jeffords, I.	1989-2007
Idaho		**New Hampshire**		**Virginia**	
Larry E. Craig, R.	1991-2009	Judd Gregg, R.	1993-2011	John W. Warner, R.	1979-2009
Mike Crapo, R.	1999-2011	John E. Sununu, R.	2003-2009	George F. Allen, R.	2001-2007
Illinois		**New Jersey**		**Washington**	
Richard J. Durbin, D.	1997-2009	Jon S. Corzine, D.	2001-2007	Patty Murray, D.	1993-2011
Barack Obama, D.	2005-2011	Frank R. Lautenberg, D.	2003-2009	Maria Cantwell, D.	2001-2007
Indiana		**New Mexico**		**West Virginia**	
Richard G. Lugar, R.	1977-2007	Pete V. Domenici, R.	1973-2009	Robert C. Byrd, D.	1959-2007
Evan Bayh, D.	1999-2011	Jeff Bingaman, D.	1983-2007	John D. Rockefeller IV, D.	1985-2009
Iowa		**New York**		**Wisconsin**	
Charles E. Grassley, R.	1981-2011	Charles E. Schumer, D.	1999-2011	Herbert Kohl, D.	1989-2007
Tom Harkin, D.	1985-2009	Hillary Rodham Clinton, D.	2001-2007	Russell D. Feingold, D.	1993-2011
Kansas		**North Carolina**		**Wyoming**	
Sam Brownback, R.	1996-2011	Elizabeth Dole, R.	2003-2009	Craig Thomas, R.	1995-2007
Pat Roberts, R.	1997-2009	Richard Burr, R.	2005-2011	Mike Enzi, R.	1997-2009
Kentucky		**North Dakota**			
Mitch McConnell, R.	1985-2009	Kent Conrad, D.	1987-2007		
Jim Bunning, R.	1999-2011	Byron L. Dorgan, D.	1992-2011		

MEMBERS OF THE UNITED STATES HOUSE OF REPRESENTATIVES

The House of Representatives of the first session of the 109th Congress consisted of 202 Democrats, 232 Republicans, and 1 Independent (not including representatives from American Samoa, the District of Columbia, Guam, Puerto Rico, and the Virgin Islands) when it convened on Jan. 4, 2005. This table shows congressional district, legislator, and party affiliation. Asterisk (*) denotes those who served in the 108th Congress; dagger (†) denotes "at large."

Alabama
1. Jo Bonner, R.*
2. Terry Everett, R.*
3. Mike Rogers, R.*
4. Robert Aderholt, R.*
5. Bud Cramer, D.*
6. Spencer Bachus, R.*
7. Artur Davis, D.*

Alaska
†Donald E. Young, R.*

Arizona
1. Rick Renzi, R.*
2. Trent Franks, R.*
3. John Shadegg, R.*
4. Ed Pastor, D.*
5. J. D. Hayworth, R.*
6. Jeff Flake, R.*
7. Raul Grijalva, D.*
8. Jim Kolbe, R.*

Arkansas
1. Marion Berry, D.*
2. Vic Snyder, D.*
3. John Boozman, R.*
4. Mike Ross, D.*

California
1. Mike Thompson, D.*
2. Wally Herger, R.*
3. Dan Lungren, R.
4. John Doolittle, R.*
5. Robert T. Matsui, D.**
6. Lynn Woolsey, D.*
7. George E. Miller, D.*
8. Nancy Pelosi, D.*
9. Barbara Lee, D.*
10. Ellen Tauscher, D.*
11. Richard Pombo, R.*
12. Tom Lantos, D.*
13. Pete Stark, D.*
14. Anna Eshoo, D.*
15. Mike Honda, D.*
16. Zoe Lofgren, D.*
17. Sam Farr, D.*
18. Dennis Cardoza, D.*
19. George Radanovich, R.*
20. Jim Costa, D.
21. Devin Nunes, R.*
22. Bill Thomas, R.*
23. Lois Capps, D.*
24. Elton Gallegly, R.*
25. Howard McKeon, R.*
26. David Dreier, R.*
27. Brad Sherman, D.*
28. Howard Berman, D.*
29. Adam Schiff, D.*
30. Henry Waxman, D.*
31. Xavier Becerra, D.*
32. Hilda Solis, D.*
33. Diane Watson, D.*
34. Lucille Roybal-Allard, D.*
35. Maxine Waters, D.*

36. Jane Harman, D.*
37. Juanita Millender-McDonald, D.*
38. Grace Napolitano, D.*
39. Linda Sanchez, D.*
40. Ed Royce, R.*
41. Jerry Lewis, R.*
42. Gary Miller, R.*
43. Joe Baca, D.*
44. Ken Calvert, R.*
45. Mary Bono, R.*
46. Dana Rohrabacher, R.*
47. Loretta Sanchez, D.*
48. Christopher Cox, R.*
49. Darrell Issa, R.*
50. Randy Cunningham, R.*
51. Bob Filner, D.*
52. Duncan Hunter, R.*
53. Susan Davis, D.*

Colorado
1. Diana DeGette, D.*
2. Mark Udall, D.*
3. John Salazar, D.
4. Marilyn Musgrave, R.*
5. Joel Hefley, R.*
6. Tom Tancredo, R.*
7. Bob Beauprez, R.*

Connecticut
1. John Larson, D.*
2. Rob Simmons, R.*
3. Rosa DeLauro, D.*
4. Christopher Shays, R.*
5. Nancy L. Johnson, R.*

Delaware
†Michael Castle, R.*

Florida
1. Jeff Miller, R.*
2. Allen Boyd, D.*
3. Corrine Brown, D.*
4. Ander Crenshaw, R.*
5. Virginia Brown-Waite, R.*
6. Clifford B. Stearns, R.*
7. John Mica, R.*
8. Ric Keller, R.*
9. Michael Bilirakis, R.*
10. C. W. Bill Young, R.*
11. Jim Davis, D.*
12. Adam Putnam, R.*
13. Katherine Harris, R.*
14. Connie Mack, R.
15. Dave Weldon, R.*
16. Mark Foley, R.*
17. Kendrick Meek, D.*
18. Ileana Ros-Lehtinen, R.*
19. Robert Wexler, D.*
20. Debbie Wasserman Schultz, D.
21. Lincoln Diaz-Balart, R.*
22. E. Clay Shaw, Jr., R.*
23. Alcee Hastings, D.*
24. Tom Feeney, R.*
25. Mario Diaz-Balart, R.*

Georgia
1. Jack Kingston, R.*
2. Sanford Bishop, Jr., D.*
3. Jim Marshall, D.*
4. Cynthia McKinney, D.
5. John Lewis, D.*
6. Tom Price, R.
7. John Linder, R.*
8. Lynn Westmoreland, R.
9. Charles Norwood, R.*
10. Nathan Deal, R.*
11. Phil Gingrey, R.*
12. John Barrow, D.
13. David Scott, D.*

Hawaii
1. Neil Abercrombie, D.*
2. Ed Case, D.*

Idaho
1. C. L. Otter, R.*
2. Mike Simpson, R.*

Illinois
1. Bobby Rush, D.*
2. Jesse L. Jackson, Jr., D.*
3. Daniel Lipinski, D.
4. Luis Gutierrez, D.*
5. Rahm Emanuel, D.*
6. Henry J. Hyde, R.*
7. Danny Davis, D.*
8. Melissa Bean, D.
9. Janice Schakowsky, D.*
10. Mark Kirk, R.*
11. Gerald Weller, R.*
12. Jerry F. Costello, D.*
13. Judy Biggert, R.*
14. J. Dennis Hastert, R.*
15. Timothy Johnson, R.*
16. Donald Manzullo, R.*
17. Lane A. Evans, R.*
18. Ray LaHood, R.*
19. John Shimkus, R.*

Indiana
1. Peter J. Visclosky, D.*
2. Chris Chocola, R.*
3. Mark Souder, R.*
4. Steve Buyer, R.*
5. Dan Burton, R.*
6. Mike Pence, R.*
7. Julia Carson, D.*
8. John Hostettler, R.*
9. Mike Sodrel, R.

Iowa
1. Jim Nussle, R.*
2. Jim Leach, R.*
3. Leonard Boswell, D.*
4. Thomas Latham, R.*
5. Steve King, R.*

Kansas
1. Jerry Moran, R.*
2. Jim Ryun, R.*

3. Dennis Moore, D.*
4. Todd Tiahrt, R.*

Kentucky
1. Edward Whitfield, R.*
2. Ron Lewis, R.*
3. Anne Northup, R.*
4. Geoff Davis, R.
5. Harold (Hal) Rogers, R.*
6. Ben Chandler, D.*

Louisiana
1. Bobby Jindal, R.
2. William J. Jefferson, D.*
3. Charles Melancon, D.
4. Jim McCrery, R.*
5. Rodney Alexander, R.
6. Richard Hugh Baker, R.*
7. Charles Boustany, Jr., R.

Maine
1. Thomas Allen, D.*
2. Michael Michaud, D.*

Maryland
1. Wayne T. Gilchrest, R.*
2. C. A. Ruppersberger, D.*
3. Benjamin L. Cardin, D.*
4. Albert Wynn, D.*
5. Steny H. Hoyer, D.*
6. Roscoe Bartlett, R.*
7. Elijah Cummings, D.*
8. Chris Van Hollen, D.*

Massachusetts
1. John W. Olver, D.*
2. Richard E. Neal, D.*
3. James McGovern, D.*
4. Barney Frank, D.*
5. Martin Meehan, D.*
6. John Tierney, D.*
7. Edward J. Markey, D.*
8. Michael Capuano, D.*
9. Stephen F. Lynch, D.*
10. William Delahunt, D.*

Michigan
1. Bart Stupak, D.*
2. Peter Hoekstra, R.*
3. Vernon Ehlers, R.*
4. Dave Camp, R.*
5. Dale Kildee, D.*
6. Frederick S. Upton, R.*
7. Joe Schwarz, R.
8. Mike Rogers, R.*
9. Joseph Knollenberg, R.*
10. Candice Miller, R.*
11. Thaddeus McCotter, R.*
12. Sander M. Levin, D.*
13. Carolyn Kilpatrick, D.*
14. John Conyers, Jr., D.*
15. John Dingell, D.*

Minnesota
1. Gil Gutknecht, R.*
2. John Kline, R.*

**Died Jan. 1, 2005

3. Jim Ramstad, R.*
4. Betty McCollum, D.*
5. Martin O. Sabo, D.*
6. Mark Kennedy, R.*
7. Collin C. Peterson, D.*
8. James L. Oberstar, D.*

Mississippi
1. Roger Wicker, R.*
2. Bennie Thompson, D.*
3. Charles Pickering, R.*
4. Gene Taylor, D.*

Missouri
1. William Clay, D.*
2. Todd Akin, R.*
3. Russ Carnahan, D.
4. Ike Skelton, D.*
5. Emanuel Cleaver, D.
6. Samuel Graves, R.*
7. Roy Blunt, R.*
8. Jo Ann Emerson, R.*
9. Kenny Hulshof, R.*

Montana
†Dennis Rehberg, R.*

Nebraska
1. Jeff Fortenberry, R.
2. Lee Terry, R.*
3. Tom Osborne, R.*

Nevada
1. Shelley Berkley, D.*
2. Jim Gibbons, R.*
3. Jon Porter, Sr., R.*

New Hampshire
1. Jeb Bradley, R.*
2. Charles Bass, R.*

New Jersey
1. Robert E. Andrews, D.*
2. Frank LoBiondo, R.*
3. H. James Saxton, R.*
4. Christopher H. Smith, R.*
5. Scott Garrett, R.*
6. Frank Pallone, Jr., D.*
7. Mike Ferguson, R.*
8. William Pascrell, Jr., D.*
9. Steven Rothman, D.*
10. Donald M. Payne, D.*
11. Rodney Frelinghuysen, R.*
12. Rush Holt, D.*
13. Robert Menendez, D.*

New Mexico
1. Heather Wilson, R.*
2. Steve Pearce, R.*
3. Thomas Udall, D.*

New York
1. Tim Bishop, D.*
2. Steve Israel, D.*
3. Peter King, R.*
4. Carolyn McCarthy, D.*
5. Gary L. Ackerman, D.*
6. Gregory Meeks, D.*
7. Joseph Crowley, D.*
8. Jerrold Nadler, D.*
9. Anthony Weiner, D.*
10. Edolphus Towns, D.*
11. Major R. Owens, D.*

12. Nydia Velazquez, D.*
13. Vito J. Fossella, R.*
14. Carolyn Maloney, D.*
15. Charles B. Rangel, D.*
16. Jose E. Serrano, D.*
17. Eliot L. Engel, D.*
18. Nita M. Lowey, D.*
19. Sue Kelly, R.*
20. John Sweeney, R.*
21. Michael R. McNulty, D.*
22. Maurice Hinchey, D.*
23. John McHugh, R.*
24. Sherwood Boehlert, R.*
25. James Walsh, R.*
26. Thomas Reynolds, R.*
27. Brian Higgins, D.
28. Louise M. Slaughter, D.*
29. Randy Kuhl, R.

North Carolina
1. G. K. Butterfield, D.*
2. Bob Etheridge, D.*
3. Walter Jones, Jr., R.*
4. David Price, D.*
5. Virginia Foxx, R.
6. Howard Coble, R.*
7. Mike McIntyre, D.*
8. Robin Hayes, R.*
9. Sue Myrick, R.*
10. Patrick McHenry, R.
11. Charles H. Taylor, R.*
12. Melvin Watt, D.*
13. Brad Miller, D.*

North Dakota
†Earl Pomeroy, D.*

Ohio
1. Steve Chabot, R.*
2. Rob Portman, R.*
3. Michael Turner, R.*
4. Michael G. Oxley, R.*
5. Paul E. Gillmor, R.*
6. Ted Strickland, D.*
7. David L. Hobson, R.*
8. John A. Boehner, R.*
9. Marcy Kaptur, D.*
10. Dennis Kucinich, D.*
11. Stephanie Tubbs Jones, D.*
12. Pat Tiberi, R.*
13. Sherrod Brown, D.*
14. Steven LaTourette, R.*
15. Deborah Pryce, R.*
16. Ralph Regula, R.*
17. Timothy Ryan, D.*
18. Bob Ney, R.*

Oklahoma
1. John Sullivan, R.*
2. Dan Boren, D.
3. Frank Lucas, R.*
4. Tom Cole, R.*
5. Ernest Jim Istook, R.*

Oregon
1. David Wu, D.*
2. Greg Walden, R.*
3. Earl Blumenauer, D.*
4. Peter A. DeFazio, D.*
5. Darlene Hooley, D.*

Pennsylvania
1. Robert Brady, D.*
2. Chaka Fattah, D.*
3. Philip English, R.*
4. Melissa Hart, R.*
5. John Peterson, R.*
6. Jim Gerlach, R.*
7. W. Curtis Weldon, R.*
8. Michael Fitzpatrick, R.
9. Bill Shuster, R.*
10. Donald Sherwood, R.*
11. Paul E. Kanjorski, D.*
12. John P. Murtha, D.*
13. Allyson Schwartz, D.
14. Michael Doyle, D.*
15. Charles Dent, R.
16. Joseph Pitts, R.*
17. Tim Holden, D.*
18. Tim Murphy, R.*
19. Todd Platts, R.*

Rhode Island
1. Patrick Kennedy, D.*
2. James Langevin, D.*

South Carolina
1. Henry Brown, Jr., R.*
2. Joe Wilson, R.*
3. J. Gresham Barrett, R.*
4. Bob Inglis, R.
5. John M. Spratt, Jr., D.*
6. James Clyburn, D.*

South Dakota
†Stephanie Herseth, D.*

Tennessee
1. William Jenkins, R.*
2. John J. Duncan, Jr., R.*
3. Zach Wamp, R.*
4. Lincoln Davis, D.*
5. Jim Cooper, D.*
6. Bart Gordon, D.*
7. Marsha Blackburn, R.*
8. John S. Tanner, D.*
9. Harold E. Ford, Jr., D.*

Texas
1. Louis Gohmert, R.
2. Ted Poe, R.
3. Sam Johnson, R.*
4. Ralph M. Hall, R.*
5. Jeb Hensarling, R.*
6. Joe Barton, R.*
7. John Culberson, R.*
8. Kevin Brady, R.*
9. Al Green, D.
10. Michael McCaul, R.
11. Mike Conaway, R.
12. Kay Granger, R.*
13. Mac Thornberry, R.*
14. Ron Paul, R.*
15. Ruben Hinojosa, D.*
16. Silvestre Reyes, D.*
17. Chet Edwards, D.*
18. Sheila Jackson Lee, D.*
19. Randy Neugebauer, R.*
20. Charlie Gonzalez, D.*
21. Lamar S. Smith, R.*
22. Tom DeLay, R.*
23. Henry Bonilla, R.*
24. Kenny Marchant, R.

25. Lloyd Doggett, D.*
26. Michael Burgess, R.*
27. Solomon P. Ortiz, D.*
28. Henry Cuellar, D.
29. Gene Green, D.*
30. Eddie Bernice Johnson, D.*
31. John Carter, R.*
32. Pete Sessions, R.*

Utah
1. Rob Bishop, R.*
2. Jim Matheson, D.*
3. Christopher Cannon, R.*

Vermont
†Bernard Sanders, Ind.*

Virginia
1. Jo Ann Davis, R.*
2. Thelma Drake, R.
3. Robert Scott, D.*
4. J. Randy Forbes, R.*
5. Virgil Goode, Jr., R.*
6. Robert Goodlatte, R.*
7. Eric Cantor, R.*
8. James P. Moran, Jr., D.*
9. Rick C. Boucher, D.*
10. Frank R. Wolf, R.*
11. Tom Davis, R.*

Washington
1. Jay Inslee, D.*
2. Rick Larsen, D.*
3. Brian Baird, D.*
4. Doc Hastings, R.*
5. Cathy McMorris, R.
6. Norman D. Dicks, D.*
7. Jim McDermott, D.*
8. Dave Reichert, R.
9. Adam Smith, D.*

West Virginia
1. Alan B. Mollohan, D.*
2. Shelley Moore Capito, R.*
3. Nick J. Rahall II, D.*

Wisconsin
1. Paul Ryan, R.*
2. Tammy Baldwin, D.*
3. Ron Kind, D.*
4. Gwen Moore, D.
5. James Sensenbrenner, Jr., R.*
6. Thomas E. Petri, R.*
7. David R. Obey, D.*
8. Mark Green, R.*

Wyoming
†Barbara Cubin, R.*

Nonvoting representatives

American Samoa
Eni F. H. Faleomavaega, D.*

District of Columbia
Eleanor Holmes Norton, D.*

Guam
Madeleine Bordallo, D.*

Puerto Rico
Luis Fortuno, R.

Virgin Islands
Donna M. Christensen, D.*

approved the bill on July 14. President Bush signed the measure on July 21.

Fetal protection. The Senate approved legislation in March making it a separate criminal offense to harm a fetus in a federal crime committed against a pregnant woman. The Unborn Victims of Violence Act is based on the idea that an attack on a pregnant woman harms both the mother and the unborn child. Detractors expressed concern that definitions used in the law could then be raised to attack abortion rights. Advocates of the measure, however, said that the legislation was specifically targeted at those who attack pregnant women. President Bush signed the legislation on April 1.

Student athletes. In September, the House and the Senate approved a bill prohibiting sports agents from engaging in unscrupulous practices when recruiting student athletes. Under the legislation, which President Bush signed on September 24, sports agents may not entice student athletes into signing an agency contract through false or misleading information or by providing anything of value to the athletes. Sports agents must also clearly indicate that should a student enter into an agency contract, he or she may lose eligibility to compete as a student athlete. Once an agency contract has been signed, the athlete and agent are required to notify the school's athletic director within 72 hours, or prior to the athlete's next event, that a contract has been signed.

Taxation. The Senate voted 69 to 17 on October 11 to approve $136 billion in corporate tax cuts. The legislation also included $42.6 billion in tax breaks for multinational companies and $10 billion in assistance for U.S. tobacco farmers. The tax breaks were made in response to a World Trade Organization (WTO) ruling that found that a $5-billion annual subsidy to U.S. exporters was against WTO rules. The WTO is an international organization that promotes trade in goods and services among nations. President Bush signed the legislation on October 22.

Spending bills. Congress approved only 4 of the 13 required spending bills by the end of the fiscal year 2004 (Oct. 1, 2003, to Sept. 30, 2004). In June, Congress gave final approval to a spending bill for defense. President Bush signed the $417-billion defense bill on August 5. A military construction appropriations bill was given final congressional approval in September and signed into law October 13. Legislation providing funding for homeland security was approved on September 14 and became law on October 15.

On November 20, both the House and the Senate approved a $388-billion spending bill that included federal money for several local projects, including $1 million to help Missouri hog farmers

convert their animals' waste to energy; $1 million to construct a museum honoring blues musician B. B. King in Indianola, Mississippi; and $1 million for a project called the Wild American Shrimp Initiative, a plan that incurred the wrath of U.S. Senator John McCain III (R., Arizona), who publicly rebuked his fellow members of Congress for setting aside money for such projects.

"Why does the U.S. taxpayer need to fund this 'no shrimp left behind' act," McCain asked during debates in the Senate. "I am hoping that the appropriators could explain to me why we need $1 million for this—are American shrimp unruly and lacking initiative?"

CIA director. The Senate on Sept. 22, 2004, voted 77 to 17 to confirm U.S. Representative Porter Goss (R., Florida) to head the Central Intelligence Agency. Goss replaced George Tennet, who resigned in June. As a congressman, Goss had been chairman of the House Intelligence Committee. Some Senate Democrats criticized Goss's selection as CIA director, claiming that he was too closely tied to the Republican Party to remain neutral as head of the CIA.

Weapons ban. Legislation banning the sale of 19 types of semiautomatic weapons expired on September 13, when neither the House nor the Senate acted to extend it. The assault weapons ban was passed in 1994 but had a 10-year expiration date. Republican leaders in both the House and Senate claimed that they allowed the law to lapse because there were not enough votes to support an extension. Public opinion polls conducted on the topic, however, showed that the majority of U.S. residents supported the assault weapons ban. Even so, critics of the ban maintained the legislation did little to stem the sale of the high-powered weapons because easy alterations to the guns made them technically legal.

Rule change. On November 17, Republicans in the House voted to abandon a rule requiring its leaders to temporarily step aside if indicted on criminal charges. House Democrats argued that the rule was rescinded to protect House Majority Leader Tom DeLay, whom some experts said may be prosecuted in Texas on charges that he used corporate funds to help Republicans win state legislative races in 2002. The increased strength of Republicans in the Texas legislature helped DeLay execute a congressional redistricting plan that added five seats to the Republican majority in the House in the November 2004 election.

Admonishment. The House Ethics Committee admonished DeLay twice in 2004 and warned him to comply with House rules and standards of conduct. On September 30, the committee admonished him for offering to endorse the son of

U.S. Representative Nick Smith (R., Michigan) in a primary election if Smith voted for legislation adding prescription drug coverage to Medicare. Smith ultimately voted against the measure, and his son lost his Republican primary race. The ethics panel likewise admonished Smith himself for "making public statements that risked impugning the reputation of the House." The admonishment was based on a newspaper column Smith wrote in which he said that Republican leaders had offered him bribes of campaign help for his son in exchange for his vote on the Medicare bill.

On October 6, the committee again admonished DeLay on two allegations: for hosting a fundraiser in 2002 for energy company officials while Congress was considering energy legislation; and for contacting the Federal Aviation Administration to track an aircraft carrying Texas Democratic legislators during a debate over a redrawing of the state's congressional district map in 2003.

Elections. Republicans in both the House and the Senate expanded their control following elections on November 2. Republicans gained four Senate seats to give the party a 55-44 majority. (One member of the Senate, James Jeffords of Vermont, is an independent and not affiliated with either party.) The biggest victory for the Republican Party took place in South Dakota, where John Thune, a former congressman, defeated Senator Tom Daschle, the leader of the Senate Democrats. Daschle was first elected in 1986 and had led the Senate Democrats since 1995. Daschle became the first Senate leader to be voted out of office since 1952, when Republican Barry Goldwater defeated Senator Ernest McFarland of Arizona.

The November 2004 elections gave Republicans 232 seats in the House, compared with the Democrats' 202 seats. One representative, Bernard Sanders of Vermont, was an independent not affiliated with either party.

The biggest loss for Republicans came in Illinois, where U.S. Representative Philip Crane was defeated by Democrat Melissa Bean after he had served in the House since 1969.

That loss, however, was tempered by the redistricting plan in Texas, heavily aided, if not planned, by DeLay. The redistricting resulted in 21 Texas Republicans holding House seats in the next session, the largest Republican delegation in Congress.

Same-sex marriage amendment. Congress in 2004 tried unsuccessfully to muster support for an amendment to the U.S. Constitution that would ban same-sex marriage. Such an amendment needs a two-thirds majority in both the House and the Senate and ratification by 38 of the 50 states. In February, President Bush endorsed the premise of a constitutional amendment that would restrict marriage to a man and a woman.

Ricin scare. Senate office buildings in Washington, D.C., closed on February 2 in response to the discovery of an envelope containing the toxin ricin in a mailroom at the Dirksen Senate Office Building. The envelope was addressed to Senator Bill Frist (R., Tennessee), the Senate majority leader.

Commemorative coins. Congress on July 20 directed the Department of the Treasury to create commemorative coins to celebrate the anniversaries of historical events. The coins commemorated the 400th anniversary of the 1607 Jamestown settlement in Virginia, the first permanent English settlement in North America; the 250th anniversary of former U.S. Supreme Court Chief Justice John Marshall's birth in 1755; and the 230th anniversary of the creation of the U.S. Marine Corps in 1775.   ■ Geoffrey A. Campbell

See also **Armed forces; Cabinet, U.S.; Democratic Party; Elections; People in the news** (John Edwards; John Kerry; Barack Obama); **Republican Party; State government; Taxation; United States, Government of the; United States, President of the.**

Connecticut. See State government.

Conservation. Conservation efforts in 2004 continued to focus largely on saving such spectacular species as the large cats and great apes. Increasingly, however, the conservation spotlight also shone on lesser-known species.

"10 Most Wanted Species." A few of these more obscure species were on the list of "10 Most Wanted Species" released in September by the World Wide Fund for Nature (WWF), an international conservation organization headquartered in Gland, Switzerland. The list featured the animals and plants most threatened by illegal international trade: the tiger, Asian elephant, irrawaddy dolphin, pig-nosed turtle, leaf-tailed gecko, yellow-crested cockatoo, great white shark, humphead wrasse, ramin trees, and Asian yew trees.

The WWF report noted that the humphead wrasse, a fish native to the coral reefs of the Indian and Pacific oceans, had become a trendy table delicacy in East Asia. The large lips of the fish fetched hundreds of dollars. The fish is caught by stunning it with cyanide, which damages the reef ecosystem. The WWF warned that trade in the humphead wrasse and other species on the list needed tighter regulation.

CITES meeting. The issue of trade in endangered species dominated the October meeting of the Convention on International Trade in Endangered Species (CITES) in Bangkok, Thailand. CITES is an agency of the United Nations that regulates trade in imperiled species. At the meeting, delegates from more than 160 nations updated trade rules and other protective regulations for a range of animal and plant species.

Delegates voted to require special trade permits for ramin trees, agarwood trees, the great white shark, and the humpback wrasse. The permits would prove that these organisms were obtained legally. Delegates also voted to ban all trade in the irrawaddy dolphin, and they strengthened trade rules for a number of plants with medicinal purposes. In addition, member nations agreed to crack down on unregulated domestic markets in elephant ivory.

"Co-endangered" species. In September, an international study offered more evidence that no matter how obscure a species is, once it becomes extinct, many other species may also disappear. Scientists from universities in Tennessee, Singapore, and Alberta, Canada, examined a list of more than 12,000 threatened or endangered species. The researchers then studied other species that were dependent upon the organisms on the list.

The investigators concluded that more than 6,000 additional species would vanish if the 12,000 species on the list were lost. They described these additional plants and animals as "co-endangered."

Jaguars and tigers. The Wildlife Conservation Society (WCS), a conservation organization based in New York City, announced promising developments involving two big cats in 2004.

A WCS report in May described how biologists discovered that Kaa-Iya Gran Chaco National Park in Bolivia contains approximately 1,000 jaguars. This population estimate, based on evidence from remote cameras, meant that the park was home to more jaguars than any other protected area on Earth. The report noted that the vast area of the park, which spreads across more than 13,000 square miles (34,000 square kilometers), favored the success of the big cats, which need large, unbroken expanses of land to thrive.

An April report by the WCS explained how tigers would benefit from the establishment of the world's largest tiger reserve in Myanmar. The Hukawng Valley Tiger Reserve, which covers about 8,400 square miles (22,000 square kilometers), was home to between 80 and 100 tigers in 2004. Eventually, according to the WCS report, the park could hold 10 times those numbers—provided that protection and management plans are carried out properly.

Mountain gorillas. The number of mountain gorillas in the Virunga Mountains—straddling the borders of Rwanda, Uganda, and the Democratic Republic of Congo (DRC)—increased by 17 percent between 1989 and 2004, according to new census figures released in January. The figures, compiled by the International Gorilla Conservation Program, showed that 380 gorillas lived in the Virunga area in 2004.

The Virunga population is one of only two existing groups of wild mountain gorillas. Along with the other group, which lives in Uganda's Bwindi Impenetrable Forest National Park, the total number of mountain gorillas stood at about 700 in 2004.

In May, thousands of squatters swarmed into the DRC's Virunga National Park, deforesting several square miles of key gorilla habitat. They then brought in livestock and began farming the cleared area. The squatters were reportedly paid by wealthy Rwandan land speculators.

Authorities soon halted the illegal clearing of the Virunga forests and drove out the squatters. However, conservationists feared that the forest destruction might happen again. In July, the United Nations urged the three countries containing the gorilla habitat to do a better job of protecting it.

Sea turtle law. Sea turtles received a boost in July when United States President George W. Bush signed the Marine Turtle Conservation Act into law. The act funded conservation efforts to fight turtle poaching and to protect turtle habitat, including beaches in Florida and other regions where these reptiles nest. Poachers often take adult sea turtles and turtle eggs for food. The U.S Fish and Wildlife Service classifies six of the seven sea turtle species as endangered.

Land conservation. In March, the Trust for Public Land (TPL) announced that it had saved a 640-acre (260-hectare) tract in the foothills of the Cascade Range of Washington state from development. The TPL is a national land conservation organization based in San Francisco. The preserved land and water habitats link two other tracts, protecting 40 endangered and threatened species, including salmon and trout. The trust and organizations working with it hoped to eventually save 600,000 acres (243,000 hectares) in the Cascades foothills.

The U.S. Department of Agriculture reported in January that 329,000 acres (133,000 hectares) of Maine forest would be protected under the department's Forest Legacy Program. The program allows timber to be cut under strict management plans, and it permits such recreational activities as hunting, fishing, and hiking. However, commercial development of forests is banned. ■ Edward R. Ricciuti

See also **Biology; Zoos.**

Costa Rica. See Latin America.
Cote d'Ivoire. See Africa.

Courts. The Massachusetts Supreme Judicial Court on Feb. 4, 2004, removed the last roadblock to same-sex marriage in that state. The 4-to-3 advisory opinion came in response to a question by the Massachusetts Senate—whether granting same-sex couples the same rights and benefits of marriage, while calling the relationship a civil union, would be constitutional. The justices ruled that it would not be constitutional. The first same-sex marriages took place in the state in May.

Courts in two other states also tackled the issue of same-sex marriages in 2004. The California State Supreme Court in August nullified nearly 4,000 marriage licenses to same-sex couples that had been issued in San Francisco. The justices ruled that the licenses violated a state law prohibiting such unions. A circuit court judge ordered officials in a Portland, Oregon, county to stop issuing same-sex marriage licenses in April. Multnomah County officials had issued marriage licenses to approximately 3,000 same-sex couples.

Assisted suicide. The United States Court of Appeals for the Ninth Circuit in San Francisco upheld Oregon's Death with Dignity Act in May. The law allows physicians to assist terminally ill patients commit suicide. Attorney General John Ashcroft announced in 2001 that physicians assisting patients under the state law, which went into effect in 1997, would be prosecuted. The justices, in their 2-to-1 decision in 2004, ruled that the federal government did not have the authority to punish the physicians and that state governments should regulate medical conduct.

Conviction overturned. United States District Judge Gerald E. Rosen on September 2 overturned the convictions of two Arab immigrants after the U.S. Department of Justice requested the dismissal. In 2003, Justice Department officials had applauded the convictions of Abdel Ilah-Elmardoudi and Karim Koubriti as major legal victories in the U.S.-led war against terrorism. The Justice Department, however, later learned that the lead prosecutor in the case, Richard G. Convertino, may have withheld numerous documents from defense attorneys that would have been favorable to the defendants. Convertino claimed that he never withheld crucial evidence.

Although their terrorism convictions were overturned, Rosen ordered that the men be retried on document fraud charges.

Secret searches overturned. United States District Judge Victor Marrero struck down part of the USA PATRIOT Act on Sept. 29, 2004. The act, passed in 2001, gave law enforcement the power to detain for seven days—or in some cases indefinitely—any noncitizen suspected of being a risk to national security. The provision that was struck down allowed the Federal Bureau of Investigation (FBI) to force Internet service providers and phone companies to turn over certain records of some customers. The FBI could then bar companies from admitting that such a search had taken place. In his decision, Marrero said that personal security was equal in importance to national security.

Beltway snipers. A judge in Manassas, Virginia, on March 9, 2004, sentenced John Allen Muhammad to death for the murder of 1 of 10 people who had been killed in a series of sniper attacks in the Washington, D.C., area in 2002. On March 10, 2004, a judge in Chesapeake, Virginia, sentenced Lee Boyd Malvo, an accomplice in the shooting spree, to life in prison without parole for his role in a second shooting.

Martha Stewart. A jury in New York City found Martha Stewart, a media personality specializing in advice about homemaking, guilty on March 5 of lying about the reasons she sold her shares of stock in a biotechnology company. The jury found her guilty of conspiracy, obstruction of justice, and two counts of making false statements in connection with an investigation into the sale.

In 2001, Stewart sold approximately 4,000 shares of stock in ImClone Systems Inc. one day before the U.S. Food and Drug Administration rejected approval of a cancer drug produced by the company. Prosecutors argued that Stewart had advance knowledge that the stock would be dropping in value. U.S. District Judge Miriam Goldman Cedarbaum on July 16, 2004, sentenced Stewart to five months in prison, five months home confinement, and two years of probation in addition to a $30,000 fine. Stewart entered prison on October 8.

The jury also convicted Peter Bacanovic, Stewart's former stockbroker, of obstructing justice, perjury, conspiracy, and making false statements. He was sentenced to five months in prison, two years of probation, and fined $4,000.

Oklahoma City bombing. On May 26, a jury in McAlester, Oklahoma, convicted Terry L. Nichols on 161 state murder counts for his role in the 1995 bombing of the Alfred P. Murrah Federal Building in Oklahoma City, Oklahoma. The jury on June 11, 2004, deadlocked over whether Nichols should be sentenced to death. The impasse meant that Nichols was spared the death penalty. Federal District Judge Steven Taylor on August 9 sentenced Nichols to life in prison.

The state of Oklahoma brought murder charges against Nichols for the deaths of the 161 civilian victims in the bombing. A federal jury convicted Nichols in 1997 of conspiracy and involuntary manslaughter in the deaths of eight law enforcement officials, but he was acquitted of murder. In 1998, a jury sentenced him to life in prison without the possibility of parole.

■ Geoffrey A. Campbell

See also **Crime; State government; Supreme Court of the United States; Terrorism.**

Cricket. Pakistan enjoyed a year of uninterrupted international cricket in 2004, after having had problems with security the previous two years. The highlight, India's tour of Pakistan in March and April, was the first visit by India since 1998. Most observers considered the matches a sign of improving relations between the two countries, which have been divided by a bitter border dispute.

In Zimbabwe, political issues continued to create problems for the country's cricket team. Critics accused Zimbabwe's government of human rights abuses and political repression, and many Britons opposed England's scheduled tour of Zimbabwe in 2004. The situation was complicated in April when Zimbabwe's captain, Heath Streak, who is white, was dismissed after disagreeing with the Zimbabwe Cricket Union (ZCU) over which players were selected for the team. He was supported by other white players who withdrew from the test squad amid allegations that players were being selected because of their race. In May, the players who supported Streak were dismissed.

In October, the International Cricket Council (ICC) cleared the ZCU of the charge of racism. However, the Zimbabwe side was so weakened by the departure of many of its experienced players that the ICC suspended Zimbabwe from test matches through the end of 2004. However, it ruled that the planned one-day international series would be played. In July, England agreed to play five one-day internationals in Zimbabwe in November, though it permitted players to refuse to tour if they had moral objections.

Test cricket. In January, India came as close as any team in the past 11 years to defeating Australia on their home soil. The series finished level at 1-1, with two matches drawn. In the final match,

Indian bowler Laxmipathy Balaji delivers the ball during a test match between India and Pakistan in April 2004. Observers viewed the series, the first between the two countries since 1998, as a sign of improved relations between the two countries.

India's Sachin Tendulkar made 241 not out, his highest test score until his 248 not out against Bangladesh in December.

The match was Australian captain Steve Waugh's last test, and his score of 80 in Australia's second innings helped to prevent an Indian victory. Waugh played in a record 168 test matches. Between 1999 and 2004, he became the most successful test captain in cricket history, winning 41 matches out of 57, with only 9 defeats. Best known as a batsman, Waugh scored 10,927 runs at an average of 51.06, the second-highest aggregate in test cricket.

The West Indies, a side in transition, lost a home series to England 3-0 in March and April. However, despite the loss, in the last match West Indies captain Brian Lara piled up an amazing 400 not out, the highest individual score in test match history.

New Zealand entertained South Africa in March. The series, which ended 1-1, with one match drawn, was the last for Gary Kirsten, one of South Africa's most dependable players. On their historic tour of Pakistan in March and April, India won the closely fought three-match test series by 2-1. The victory was India's first in a series in Pakistan.

500 wickets. In March, two players passed the 500-wicket mark in the same series within five days of each other. Australia's Shane Warne reached the milestone on March 12, and Sri Lanka's Muttiah Muralitharan did so on March 16. On May 8 against Zimbabwe, Muralitharan passed West Indian Courtney Walsh's record aggregate of 519 test wickets.

In the first home of its summer series in May, England beat New Zealand 3-0. At the end of the match, New Zealand's Chris Cairns, who had taken nine wickets in the game, announced his retirement from test cricket. Also in May, Nasser Hussain retired from test cricket. In his last match, Hussain scored the winning century.

In August, England defeated the West Indies by 4-0. For England, fast bowler Steve Harmison continued to impress, while Andrew Flintoff emerged as a major international all-rounder. By September, England had risen to second place after Australia in the test match rankings.

In June and July, Sri Lanka visited Australia. Australia won the first test at Darwin, but the second test was drawn. On July 13, Shane Warne took his 527th wicket, equaling Muralitharan's record. In October and November, Australia toured India, where they reasserted their supremacy by winning the series 2-1, with one match drawn. The series victory was Australia's first in India since 1969-1970. During the series, Shane Warne took his 534th wicket, passing Muralitharan. However, Warne's record was not expected to last because Muralitharan, who was injured late in the season, was expected to return to action.

One-Day Internationals. Of the many one-day international series, the most important was the ICC Champions Trophy, which was described as a mini-World Cup.

England upset the favored Australians in the semi-finals, but the West Indies beat England by two wickets in an exciting final. The series, which took place in the United Kingdom in September, involved the 10 test-match-playing countries, plus Kenya and the United States.

New Zealand defeated the West Indies to take the Natwest series in England in June and July. Sri Lanka also had a good year, winning the Asia Cup in Sri Lanka in July and the Paktel Cup in Pakistan in October.

Death. Keith Miller, one of cricket's greatest all-rounders, died October 11. Between 1946 and 1956, Miller played 55 tests for Australia, scoring 2,958 runs at an average of 36.97 and taking 170 wickets. ■ Keith Lye

Crime. Violent crime in the United States fell by 3 percent, despite a small increase in the murder rate, the Federal Bureau of Investigation (FBI) announced in October 2004. In its annual report, the FBI's Uniform Crime Reporting (UCR) Program estimated that 1.38 million violent offenses occurred in 2003, down from an estimated 1.42 million in 2002. The number of property crimes fell by 0.2 percent over 2002 levels. The UCR Program collects data from about 17,000 U.S. law enforcement agencies on four types of violent crime—murder and non-negligent homicide; forcible rape; robbery; and aggravated assault—and three types of property crime—burglary, larceny-theft, and motor vehicle theft.

According to the report, an estimated 16,503 murders took place in 2003, an increase of 1.7 percent over 2002. About 90 percent of the victims were adults, and about 78 percent were males. Firearms were involved in nearly 71 percent of those murders in which law enforcement officers identified the type of weapon used. In about 55 percent of murders, the victim and the offender had a relationship. Among these, about 32 percent of the victims were women killed by a husband or boyfriend.

The UCR Program report listed an estimated 93,433 forcible rapes in 2003, down by 2.7 percent over 2002 levels. Robberies, which accounted for 30 percent of all violent offenses in 2003, dropped by 1.8 percent from 2002 levels. The estimated number of aggravated assaults fell by 3.8 percent in 2003, the 10th consecutive year of declines, the FBI noted. The report also stated that law en-forcement agencies nationwide made 597,026 arrests for violent crimes, which accounted for about 4.4 percent of all arrests.

An estimated 7 million property crimes oc-cured in the United States in 2003, a figure 0.3 percent below 2002 levels. The loss to victims totaled an estimated $17 billion. Larceny-theft, which includes purse-snatching, shoplifting, and bicycle theft, rose slightly, accounting for about 67 percent of all property crimes and about 71 percent of property-crime arrests in 2003.

Hate crimes. The number of hate crimes in the United States in 2003 remained almost un-changed from 2002 levels, according to a UCR Program report released in November 2004. Law enforcement agencies reported 7,489 bias-motivated incidents involving 9,100 individuals. In 2002, there were 7,462 incidents involving 9,222 individuals. Of the 2003 offenses, about 51 percent resulted from racial bias; 18 percent were motivated by religious bias; 17 percent resulted from bias against a sexual orientation; and 14 percent were motivated by a bias against a dis-ability. Fourteen of the victims died. Among this number were five victims of an antiblack bias and six victims of a bias against male homosexuals, the report stated.

Peterson conviction. A jury in Redwood City, California, on Nov. 12, 2004, found Scott Peterson guilty of first-degree murder with spe-cial circumstances in the death of his pregnant wife, Laci, who had vanished on Dec. 24, 2002. He was also convicted of second-degree murder for the death of the unborn child. On Dec. 13, 2004, a jury sentenced Peterson to death for the mur-ders of his wife and unborn child. Laci Peterson's remains and those of the couple's eight-month-old fetus washed up along San Francisco Bay in spring 2003. Peterson, who had been involved in a relationship with another woman, claimed he had returned from a fishing trip to find his wife gone.

Smuggling trial. Three people charged in what may be the deadliest human smuggling case in U.S. history went on trial in Houston in November 2004. The defendants were accused of participating in an attempt to smuggle at least 70 illegal immigrants across Texas in an unheated, poorly ventilated trailer in May 2003. Nineteen of the immigrants suffocated or died of dehydration or *hyperthermia* (overheating). In June 2004, Karla Chavez Joya, identified by law enforcement officials as the leader of the smuggling ring, pled guilty to conspiring to transport illegal immi-grants in a manner that led to deaths. In Decem-ber, charges against one of the three defendants were dismissed.

Etan Patz case. On April 19, a judge in a New York City civil court found convicted child molester Jose A. Ramos responsible for the wrongful death of Etan Patz, who disappeared in 1979 at age 6. The highly publicized search for him helped launch national programs for missing children. In 2001, a court had declared Patz, whose body remains missing, legally dead. Ramos remained imprisoned in 2004 on an unre-lated molestation conviction.

Bid-rigging lawsuit. Marsh & McLennan, the world's largest insurance broker by revenue, became the object of a civil lawsuit filed by New York State Attorney General Eliot Spitzer on Oct. 14, 2004. Spitzer charged the New York City-based firm with cheating clients out of millions of dollars in a bid-rigging scheme. The complaint alleged that the company collected kickbacks from favored insurance companies to whom it steered clients seeking insurance policies. In response to the lawsuit, Marsh & McLennan sus-pended a number of top executives and halted certain business practices pending the outcome of Spitzer's investigation. ■ Barbara A. Mayes

See also **Civil rights; Courts; Prison; Stocks and bonds; Terrorism.**

Croatia. The European Commission, the administrative arm of the European Union (EU), recommended in October 2004 that EU officials start membership negotiations with Croatia early in 2005. Croatian leaders voiced the hope that Croatia would be ready for *accession* (entry) into the EU in 2007, though EU officials expressed skepticism that Croatia would achieve that goal.

War crimes tribunal. In March 2004, two Croatian generals under indictment by the war crimes tribunal in The Hague, Netherlands, turned themselves in. The generals, Ivan Cermak and Mladen Markac, were charged with crimes allegedly committed in a 1995 offensive in which Croatia sought to recover territory seized earlier by Serbia (formerly Yugoslavia). EU officials com-mended Croatia's government for its role in the generals' surrender but continued to press for the arrest of General Ante Gotovina, another indicted war criminal. Croatian officials insisted that Gotovina was no longer in Croatia.

Regional relations. In September 2004, Croatian border police arrested a Slovenian polit-ical leader in the disputed Piran Bay border area between Croatia and Slovenia. Since 1991, the two countries have contested their mutual bor-der along Piran Bay on the Adriatic coast.

Slovenia's foreign minister, calling the politi-cian's arrest "totally unacceptable," recalled the

Slovenian ambassador from Zagreb, Croatia's capital, and reported the incident to Javier Solana, chief foreign policy official of the EU. Slovenia, an EU member since May 2004, withdrew support for Croatia's EU candidacy.

Croatia's economy grew at a rate of 4.2 percent in the first quarter of 2004 and 3.8 percent in the second quarter, compared with 4.3 percent in 2003. Inflation continued to fluctuate between 1.5 and 2.5 percent, one of the lowest rates in Europe. The percentage of unemployed Croatians, which had topped 20 percent for most of 2003, declined to 17.6 percent in late 2004.

Relations with the United States. Prime Minister Ivo Sanader, who came to power in December 2003, sought to improve Croatia's relations with the United States in 2004. Croatia's previous government, led by Ivica Racan, had criticized the administration of U.S. President George W. Bush for going to war in Iraq in March 2003 without United Nations approval. Croatia did not participate in military operations in Iraq. In a February 2004 meeting in Zagreb, U.S. Secretary of Defense Donald Rumsfeld encouraged Croatian officials to follow through with defense reforms to position the country for eventual membership in the North Atlantic Treaty Organization. ■ Sharon L. Wolchik

See also **Europe; United Nations.**

Cuba. The worst drought in 40 years affected the eastern Cuban provinces of Camaguey and Las Tunas in 2004, causing reservoirs serving Holguin, Cuba's fourth largest city, to dry up by midyear. The drought was followed by a severe hurricane season in which more than 1 million people in western Cuba were temporarily displaced. The harsh weather caused widespread damage to houses, businesses, and crops.

Hard-line U.S. policy. In May, the Commission for Assistance to a Free Cuba called for a "more proactive, integrated and disciplined approach to undermine the survival strategies of the [Cuban President Fidel] Castro regime. . . ." The commission was a panel of United States officials chaired by U.S. Secretary of State Colin Powell. The panel affirmed a central U.S. role in Cuban affairs—including government, education, public health, and economic policy—during an eventual post-Castro transition period.

In line with the panel's report, U.S. President George W. Bush ordered further economic restrictions against Cuba aimed at destabilizing the Cuban economy and reducing the government's access to U.S. dollars. Under the restrictions, Cuban exiles living in the United States were limited to visiting Cuba once every three years and to spending only $50 a day during their visits. President Bush also announced plans to

provide $36 million to support dissidents in Cuba and another $18 million to broadcast jam-proof anti-Castro television and radio programs to Cuba from a military aircraft circling the island.

Economic disarray. The new restrictions succeeded in destabilizing the Cuban economy, which had become dependent on the estimated $1 billion a year that Cubans living in the United States sent to friends and relatives on the island. President Castro responded to the U.S. actions in October by announcing that the U.S. dollar would be banned from all commercial transactions in Cuba, beginning in November. He said that Cubans would need to exchange their dollars for pesos, which would replace the dollar as the primary currency in Cuba. These pesos were valueless outside of Cuba, but they could be converted into other currencies, such as euros, British pounds, and Canadian dollars.

Embargo exemption. CancerVax Corp., a biotechnology company headquartered in Carlsbad, California, announced in July that U.S. authorities had licensed the firm to test three cancer drugs that had been developed in Cuba. The license was a rare exemption from the 44-year-old U.S. trade embargo against Cuba.
■ Nathan A. Haverstock

See also **Latin America; Weather.**

Cyprus. See Middle East.

Czech Republic. The Czech Republic officially became a member of the European Union (EU) on May 1, 2004. In mid-June, Czechs went to the polls to elect their 24 representatives to the European Parliament (EP). The EP, part of the EU governmental structure, is a 700-plus-member advisory body that meets in Strasbourg, France.

The election results bolstered Czech opposition parties. The Civic Democratic Party—the right-of-center main opposition party—took 30 percent of the vote to win 9 EP seats. The Communist Party garnered 11 percent and 3 seats. Running fifth, Prime Minister Vladimir Spidla's ruling Social Democratic Party gathered less than 9 percent of the vote and only 2 seats.

Turnout among Czechs for the EP elections was low—about 28 percent of eligible voters. Analysts attributed low turnout and strong showings by politicians wary of a strong EU government—dubbed "Eurosceptics"—to a wait-and-see attitude. According to the analysts, voters in the Czech Republic and elsewhere in Eastern Europe wanted economic conditions to improve substantially before committing themselves to the EU.

New prime minister. In the wake of the ruling party's poor performance in the EP elections, pressure mounted on Prime Minister Spidla to step down, and he resigned on June 26. To form a new government, President Vaclav Klaus

Fireworks burst above St. Vitus Cathedral in Prague, Czech Republic, on May 1, as Czech citizens celebrate their country's entry into the European Union. The Czech Republic was 1 of 10 nations admitted to the European organization in 2004.

called on 34-year-old Stanislav Gross, the outgoing Spidla's deputy prime minister, emergent leader of the Social Democrats, and a popular politician in his own right. President Klaus, who is aligned with the opposition Civic Democratic party, admonished Gross to build a coalition based on a "credible majority."

Gross, with some difficulty, assembled a governing coalition made up of the same parties that had participated in the previous coalition under Spidla. President Klaus approved the new government on August 4, ending a six-week period of political uncertainty.

Economy. The Czech finance ministry reported in late 2004 that the nation's gross domestic product—the value of all goods and services produced in a year—had grown by an average of 3.8 percent during 2004, up from 2.5 percent in mid-2003. Inflation was running at 3.4 percent in mid-2004, and unemployment registered 9.3 percent.

War on terror. A 100-member Czech military police force served in Iraq throughout 2004. The Czech parliament had voted in December 2003 to send the force to Iraq to help U.S.-led coalition members train Iraqi police. The Czech force was deployed at a British-run base near the city of Al Basrah in southern Iraq in late 2003.

■ Sharon L. Wolchik

See also **Europe; Iraq: A Special Report.**

Dallas. City Manager Ted Benavides announced on May 26, 2004, that he would step down in November after serving in that position since September 1998. Political analysts viewed Benavides's exit as the outcome of a power struggle with Dallas Mayor Laura Miller.

Conflict between the mayor and city manager prompted a number of city officials and activists to lobby for structural changes in the Dallas city government, which is based on the council-manager plan. In that plan, an elected mayor with relatively few powers heads an elected city council, but the day-to-day running of government is delegated to a professional city manager hired by the council. Mayor Miller advocated retaining the city manager position but increasing the mayor's powers.

In late 2004, Beth Ann Blackwood, an activist and a city council candidate, led a petition movement to put the issue on the ballot in elections scheduled for May 2005. Blackwood advocated abolishing the city-manager system and replacing it with a strong-mayor form of city government. The petition drive collected enough certified signatures by November 2004 to ensure the proposal's inclusion on the May 2005 ballot.

Superintendent quits. Superintendent Mike Moses of the Dallas Independent School District announced his resignation in July 2004. During Moses's 3½-year tenure, the school district won voter approval for a $1.3-billion bond issue, settled a 31-year-old school desegregation lawsuit, and improved student test scores. On July 26, Dallas school trustees named Larry Groppel interim school superintendent.

Parks. On June 9, the Dallas City Council approved a downtown master parks plan that would significantly increase open space in the center of the city. Officials estimated the cost of developing the parks at $21 million. In a May 2003 bond issue, voters had approved $5 million to purchase land for the parks.

New police chief. David Kunkle was sworn in on June 24, 2004, as Dallas police chief. Kunkle had served as deputy city manager of suburban Arlington, Texas, 15 miles (24 kilometers) west of Dallas, and was a former Arlington police chief. In his first months as Dallas police chief, Kunkle reorganized his command staff and emphasized officer accountability and street patrolling.

Cowboys stadium. In 2004, Dallas lost an opportunity to bring the Dallas Cowboys football team back into the center city. The team has played at Texas Stadium in suburban Irving since 1971. In June 2004, Dallas county officials failed to reach a financing agreement with the team's owners on a plan to relocate near downtown Dallas. Team officials then negotiated a deal with Arlington officials, and Arlington voters approved the plan in the November elections. The Cowboys' new stadium in Arlington was scheduled to open in 2009.

Public housing crackdown. In early September 2004, officials of the Dallas Housing Authority (DHA) notified 900 residents of low-income housing that their rent subsidies would be cut off at the end of the month. Background checks had revealed that persons with criminal records were living in the renters' households. DHA officials said the policy was part of a national campaign to improve safety in federally funded housing.

The Texas Tenants Union, a Dallas tenants' advocacy group, accused the DHA of using the federal policy to reduce expenditures. The DHA had about 16,000 households in its federally funded Section 8 housing program in 2004.

In predawn raids during the last week of September, law enforcement officers arrested more than 30 DHA tenants suspected of defrauding federally funded housing assistance programs. The Dallas County district attorney's office charged the suspects with underreporting their income to obtain higher rental subsidies. DHA officials said the raids were part of a national crackdown ordered by the U.S. Department of Housing and Urban Development, which partially funds the rent subsidy programs. ■ Henry Tatum

See also **City.**

Dance. In 2004, ballet companies around the world celebrated the 100th anniversary of George Balanchine's birth. Balanchine—who was born on Jan. 22, 1904, in St. Petersburg, Russia, and who died on April 30, 1983, in New York City—was one of the greatest of choreographers and is credited with transforming ballet into a modern art form.

New York City Ballet. Top honors for the centennial observance went to the New York City Ballet, which Balanchine founded in 1948 and led until his death. The company's 20004 winter season, in January and February at the New York State Theater in Lincoln Center, approached Balanchine's repertory from a thematic point of view: The company danced ballets in which the influence of master 19th-century choreographers could be seen and then moved on to Balanchine's early works. The spring season, in May and June 2004, divided the repertory of Balanchine, as well as other choreographers, into three mini-festivals of American, European, and Russian composers.

In keeping with New York City Ballet's policy of producing new work, ballet master in chief Peter Martins commissioned a number of world premieres. Two of them proved to be the most controversial of the Balanchine centennial festivities because they lacked the classical ideals that formed the basis of Balanchine's work. On January 23, Susan Stroman's *Double Feature* premiered, set to music by Irving Berlin and Walter Donaldson. A veteran of Broadway musicals, Stroman, who directed and choreographed *The Producers*, fashioned an homage to silent films that was theatrically vivid but thin in actual dancing. Her two-part work, the first a melodrama and the second a comic romp inspired by Buster Keaton movies, was nonetheless a box office hit. Boris Eifman's *Musagete,* which debuted June 18, treated Balanchine biographically. The three muses in *Musagete* might represent Balanchine's ballerinas—including his former wife Tanaquil LeClercq, who was paralyzed by polio at the age of 27; and Suzanne Farrell, who some considered to be Balanchine's ideal ballerina. Many critics did note, however, that Eifman's depiction of the master as a tormented soul was not accurate and that some of the dances were so graphic as to be offensive.

Tetsuya Kumakawa of the K-Ballet Company of Tokyo dances in *Rhapsody* as part of the tribute to English choreographer Sir Frederick Ashton at the Metropolitan Opera House in New York City in July 2004. The performance marked the debut of the K-Ballet Company in the United States.

More Balanchine remembrances. Thirty-two troupes in the United States and 30 troupes from China, South Africa, and Europe joined in the celebration not only by performing Balanchine's ballets but by hosting conferences about his work in 2004. A Russian-American Balanchine Symposium was held in St. Petersburg, Russia, at the Maryinsky Theatre, where Balanchine spent his youth. While Russian troupes performed Balanchine's ballets at a six-day festival, other dancers and scholars discussed his legacy. The State Hermitage Museum in St. Petersburg mounted an exhibit of material pertaining to Balanchine's days as a student and fledgling choreographer.

In the United States, the most interesting Balanchine exhibit in 2004 was at the Harvard Theatre Collection in Cambridge, Massachusetts. The exhibit displayed for the first time memorabilia from its Balanchine Archive, deposited there after Balanchine's death. Among the items on display were letters from Balanchine's parents in the former Soviet Union to their son in the United States during the 1930's. The U.S. Postal Service commemorated the Balanchine centennial by issuing stamps honoring American choreographers. In addition to Balanchine, Alvin Ailey, Agnes de Mille, and Martha Graham were honored.

Ashton performances. The 100th birthday of the great English choreographer Sir Frederick Ashton, who died in 1988, also was celebrated in 2004. The San Francisco Ballet and Joffrey Ballet of Chicago marked the occasion with minifestivals. The main event took place July 6 to 17 in New York City at the Metropolitan Opera House as part of the Lincoln Center Festival. The Joffrey Ballet was joined by K-Ballet Company of Tokyo and by the English companies Birmingham Royal

Ballet and the Royal Ballet, where Ashton was resident choreographer for most of his professional life.

Dance critics noted that the most interesting repertory was from the Birmingham Royal Ballet troupe, which performed *Dante Sonata, The Two Pigeons,* and Ashton's masterpiece, *Enigma Variations.* Since Ashton's ballets were rarely seen in the United States, the festival, which presented 11 complete Ashton ballets plus several excerpts, was especially revelatory.

Two modern-dance troupes celebrated milestones in 2004. The Bill T. Jones/Arnie Zane Dance Company observed the 20th anniversary of its founding with three new works and a heavy tour schedule in the United States; in Ottawa, Toronto, and Montreal in Canada; and in five cities in the United Kingdom in June. The Paul Taylor Dance Company's 50th anniversary celebration began in March at the Yerba Buena Center for the Arts in San Francisco, with the premiere of Taylor's *Dante Variations.* Set to music by Gyorgy Ligeti, the dance was one of Taylor's darker pieces, suggesting the futility of mechanistic human relations. The company will perform in all 50 states through 2006.

Mark Morris, though trained in modern dance, has created many works for classical ballet troupes. His ongoing relationship with the San Francisco Ballet resulted in the first American production of the full-length *Sylvia,* set to French composer Leo Delibes's 1876 score. Critics were charmed by Morris's straightforward approach to the mythological story and the musicality of the dancing. *Sylvia* premiered at the War Memorial Opera House on April 30, 2004. Morris created for his own troupe a new piece set to a commissioned score by the American jazz trio The Bad Plus. Called *Violet Cavern,* it premiered June 8 at the Brooklyn Academy of Music and was next seen in October at Zellerbach Auditorium in Berkeley, California.

The Dance Theatre of Harlem, founded in 1969 by Arthur Mitchell and Karel Shook, announced in May 2004 that it was disbanding until June 2005 due to a debt of more than $2 million and a long history of financial troubles. On Oct. 16, 2004, the company closed its school, which served some 1,000 students, primarily African American children from the community in the New York City neighborhood of Harlem. However, the school reopened on December 4, after receiving a donation of $1.6 million, largely from New York City Mayor Michael Bloomberg. A new executive director, Laveen Naidu, was appointed to run the company.

The Pacific Northwest Ballet, in November, named Peter Boal as its new artistic director, effective in July 2005.   ■ Nancy Goldner

DEATHS

in 2004 included those listed below, who were Americans unless otherwise indicated.

Adair, Paul "Red" (1915–August 7), gas and oil field firefighter who capped 119 Kuwaiti wells in six months in 1991 and whose earlier exploits inspired the 1968 John Wayne movie *Hellfighters*.

Adams, Eddie (1933–September 19), photojournalist who won the Pulitzer Prize for his photo of a Communist guerrilla being executed in a Saigon street during the Vietnam War.

Aiken, Joan (1924–January 4), English author of more than 100 books, including *The Wolves of Willoughby Chase* series and *Night Fall* (1970). She was the daughter of the American poet and novelist Conrad Aiken.

Arafat, Yasir (1929–November 11), controversial Palestinian leader who personified his people's yearning for a homeland. See Middle East.

Avedon, Richard (1923–September 29), photographer who revolutionized fashion photography and whose images helped define American culture in the second half of the 20th century.

Babbitt, Harry (1913–April 9), big-band singer whose hits with the Kay Kyser orchestra included "The White Cliffs of Dover," "On a Slow Boat to China," and "Three Little Fishies."

Bank, Aaron (1902–April 1), retired U.S. Army colonel who was known as the "father of the Green Berets" for organizing and serving as first commander of the special force.

Barnes, Edward Larrabee (1922–September 21), architect of notable modernist structures, including the Walker Art Center in Minneapolis and IBM corporate headquarters in New York City.

Beene, Geoffrey (1927–September 28), award-winning designer of simple, classic clothes who with Bill Blass pioneered the American sportswear fashion.

Bemer, Bob (1920–June 22), computer pioneer who helped invent the ASCII coding system and other innovations that played a major role in how computers operate.

Bergstrom, Sune (1916–August 15), Swedish biochemist who was awarded the

Fanny Blankers-Koen, Dutch athlete

1982 Nobel Prize in Medicine and Physiology for uncovering the origin and chemisty of prostaglandins, a family of hormones.

Bernhard, Prince (1911–December 1), controversial German-born consort of Queen Juliana of the Netherlands and father of the current queen, Beatrix.

Bernstein, Elmer (1922–August 18), Academy Award-winning film composer of scores of hundreds of television shows and movies, including *Man with the Golden Arm* (1955), *The Ten Commandments* (1956), *Sweet Smell of Success* (1957), and *The Magnificent Seven* (1960).

Berry, Jan (1941–March 26), singer/lyricist and creative force in the 1960's "surf sound" who wrote the Jan & Dean hits "Dead Man's Curve," "Surf City," and "The Little Old Lady (From Pasadena)."

Birchfield, Robert (1923–July 5), influential New Zealand-born lexicographer who as chief editor of the *Oxford English Dictionary* added some 60,000 new words.

Blankers-Koen, Fanny (1918–January 25), Dutch athlete who won a record four gold medals in track and field at the 1948 London Olympics and who in 1999 was named the best female athlete of the 20th century.

Bloch, Richard (1926–July 21), businessman who, with his brother, Henry, founded the H & R Block tax preparation company.

Boone, Ray (1923–October 16), American League infielder who was the patriarch of major league baseball's first three-generation family, which included son Bob Boone and grandsons Bret and Aaron Boone.

Boorstin, Daniel J. (1914–February 28), scholar, social historian, and author of the award-winning *The Americans* trilogy (1958, 1965, 1973). Boorstin served as librarian of Congress from 1975 to 1987.

Bracheen, Harry "the Cat" (1914–January 17), St. Louis Cardinals pitcher who won three games over the Boston Red Sox in the 1946 World Series.

Brando, Marlon (1924–July 1), actor whose performances in *A Streetcar Named Desire* (1951), *On the Waterfront* (1954), *The Godfather* (1972), *Last Tango in Paris* (1972), and *Apocalypse Now* (1979) forged a new realistic style of acting that forever changed film art. See Portrait at Motion pictures.

Brown, Roosevelt (1932–June 9), Hall of Fame football player whose career with the New York Giants included 13 seasons as an offensive tackle and 40 years as an assistant coach and scout.

Brunn, Francis (1922–May 28), German-born circus performer who was the first juggler in history to work the center ring when he was featured as a solo headliner by the Ringling Brothers and Barnum & Bailey Circus.

Bucher, Lloyd "Pete" (1927–January 28), Former U.S. Naval officer who commanded the spy ship *U.S.S. Pueblo* when it was captured by North Korea in

1968. Bucher helped his crew survive 11 months of brutal captivity only to be faced with a possible court martial upon his return.

Bush, Richard E. (1923–June 7), U.S. marine in World War II who received the Congressional Medal of Honor for leading a charge in the battle for Okinawa and then fell on a hand grenade to protect fellow marines.

Byers, Clark (1914?–February 19), man who changed the rural landscape by painting "See Rock City"—an advertisement for a Chattanooga, Tennessee, tourist attraction—on the roofs of some 900 barns across the United States.

Caminiti, Ken (1963–October 10), baseball player who was elected most valuable player of the National League in 1996.

Cartier-Bresson, Henri (1908–August 3), French artist whose photos capturing what he described as "the decisive moment" were among the greatest images of the 20th century, setting a new standard for the art of photography.

Casals-Ariet, Jordi (1911–February 10), epidemiolo-

Julia Child, chef and TV personality

Gordon Cooper, astronaut

Rodney Dangerfield, comedian

gist who headed the team of Yale University researchers who in 1969 discovered the hemorrhagic virus that causes Lassa fever.

Charles, Ray (1930–June 10), singer whose fusion of gospel, soul, jazz, and country profoundly changed American popular music. See Portrait at Popular music.

Child, Julia (1912–August 13), cooking instructor and author of *Mastering the Art of French Cooking*—the definitive French cookbook in English. Child is credited with launching an epicurean craze that changed U.S. cuisine while incidentally popularizing public television.

Chodorov, Jerome (1911–September 12), playwright and librettist who co-wrote the play *My Sister Eileen* (1940) and its musical version *Wonderful Town* (1953).

Clausen, Raymond (1947–May 30), U.S. marine who during the Vietnam War was awarded the Con-

gressional Medal of Honor for crossing a minefield six times to rescue casualties.

Cooke, Alistair (1908–March 29), urbane British-born journalist who introduced English culture to America as host of the public television series "Masterpiece Theater" and American culture to the English on the BBC's "Letter from America." See Portrait at Radio.

Cooper, Leroy Gordon (1927–October 4), astronaut who in the last of the original Mercury missions stayed aloft long enough to demonstrate the feasibility of a trip to the moon.

Cox, Archibald (1912–May 29), law professor whom President Richard Nixon fired because Cox refused to limit his investigation of the Watergate scandal. The 1973 dismissal precipitated the infamous "Saturday Night Massacre" and Nixon's downfall.

Crick, Francis (1916–July 28), English scientist who shared the 1962 Nobel Price in physiology and medicine with James Watson for their discovery of the double-helical structure of DNA. See Portrait at Biology.

Dangerfield, Rodney (Jacob Cohen) (1921–October 5), comedian whose stage persona as a middle-aged everyman who got no respect transferred succesfully to the screen in such movies as *Caddyshack* (1980) and *Back to School* (1986).

Dark, Danny (Daniel Melville Croskery) (1925–June 13). voice-over artist who was the voice of the NBC TV network, the "Bonanza" and "Bewitched" TV shows, Superman on "Super Friends," and hundreds of commercials, most memorably StarKist's "Charlie Tuna."

Dash, Sam (1925?–May 29), law professor who

as chief counsel of the Senate Select Committee on Watergate became nationally known for his penetrating questions during the 1973 and 1974 hearings.

Da Silva, Leonidas (1913–January 24), Brazilian soccer legend who was credited with inventing the bicycle kick.

Davis, Skeeter (Mary Frances Penick) (1931–September 19), country-music singer whose long career included the 1963 hit "The End of the World" and more than 40 years on the "Grand Ole Opry" radio program.

Dee, Frances (1907–March 6), film actress who played opposite many male film stars of the 1930's, including Ronald Coleman, Gary Cooper, and her husband, Joel McCrea.

Derrida, Jacques (1930–October 8), Algerian-born French intellectual whose deconstruction theory—that absolute truth and meaning is impossible because of the confusion and contradiction inherent in langugae—made him one of the most celebrated, and reviled, philosophers of the late 20th century.

De Sapio, Carmine (1908–July 27), last of New York City's Tammany Hall bosses whose enormous power in the 1950's dissolved in allegations of massive corruption.

Devonshire, Duke of (Andrew Robert Buxton Cavendish) (1920–May 3), British war hero and Cabinet minister who turned his family estate, Chatsworth, into a profitable enterprise and paid off $20 million in inheritance tax.

Dorfman, Steven (1955–January 4), trivia expert who wrote questions, that is, answers, for the TV game show "Jeopardy!" for nearly 20 years.

Ebb, Fred (1928?–September 11), Tony Award-winning lyricist who with composer John Kander wrote the scores for the Broadway musicals *Cabaret* (1967), *Chicago* (1975), *Woman of the Year* (1981), and *Kiss of the Spider Woman* (1993).

Fong, Hiram L. (1906–August 18), millionaire businessman and civil rights advocate who was the first Asian American to serve in the U.S. Senate.

Frey, Viola (1933–July 26), sculptor whose larger-than-life figures blended Abstract Expressionism with Pop Art while pushing at the boundaries of the ceramics medium.

Genevieve (Ginette Marguerite Auger) (1921?–March 14), French chanteuse and comedian whose fractured English delighted audiences of Jack Paar's "The Tonight Show."

Ghiaurov, Nicolai (1929–June 2), Bulgarian-born opera singer whom critics considered one of the great basses of the second half of the 20th century.

Gold, Joe (1922–July 12), legendary body builder and workout equipment designer who founded the original Gold's Gym, in Venice Beach, California, and the World Gym franchise.

Gold, Thomas (1920–June 22), astronomer and physicist who theorized that pulsars were neutron stars emitting radio waves.

Goldsmith, Jerry (1929–July 21), composer of classic television scores—"Gunsmoke," "Perry Mason," "The Twilight Zone"—and the film scores for *Chinatown* (1974), *L.A. Confidential* (1997), and the *Star Trek* series.

Goldstine, Herman (1913–June 16), mathematician who helped develop ENIAC, the first computer, and continued work on computer development as one of IBM's chief scientists.

Gravely, Samuel (1922–October 22), U.S. Navy vice admiral who made history as the first African American to command a warship and a U.S. Navy fleet.

Gray, Spalding (1941–January 10?), actor/writer who presented the events of his life in such self-scrutinizing theatrical monologues as "Swimming to Cambodia" and "It's a Slippery Slope."

Grey, Virginia (1917–July 31), character actress whose long career began in silent films and included appearances in more than 100 movies and 40 television shows.

Hagen, Uta (1919–January 14), German-born drama teacher and stage actress who most famously played Desdemona opposite Paul Robson's *Othello* and Martha in the original 1962 production of Edward Albee's *Who's Afraid of Virginia Woolf?*

Hailey, Arthur (1920–November 24), British-born author of *Airport* and *Hotel* and other successful, if formulaic, novels made into movies.

Hale, Fred, Sr. (1890–November 19), the world's oldest man according to *Guinness World Records*. Hale died 12 days short of his 114th birthday.

Halpin, Bonnie Jo (1939–March 31), whom Hugh Hefner described as the prototype of the Playboy

Elroy "Crazylegs" Hirsch, football player

bunny. Halpin was hired as the first "door bunny" at the first Playboy Club, in Chicago.

Hart, C. J. (1911–June 25), businessman who created the first commercial drag strip after organizing the first commercial drag race, which took place on a runway at the Orange County (California) Airport in June 1950.

Hawkins, Willis M. (1913–September 28), engineer who was the principal desinger of the C-130 Hercules cargo and military transport plane that remains in production after 50 years, longer than any aircraft in history.

Heatley, Norman (1911–January 5), British biochemist who helped revolutionize medicine by isolating from mold the active substance of penicillin so it could be converted into the first antibiotic drug.

Hirsch, Elroy "Crazylegs" (1923–January 28), 1950's Hall of Fame receiver for the Los Angeles Rams whose pro career statistics included 387 receptions, 7,029 yards, and 60 touchdowns.

Bob Keeshan, Captain Kangaroo

Hoff, Syd (1912–May 12), *New Yorker* cartoonist and prolific children's book illustrator whose best-known work, *Danny and the Dinosaur*, sold more than 10 million copies.

Hounsfield, Sir Godfrey (1919–August 12), English electrical engineer who was awarded the Nobel Prize in Physiology or Medicine in 1979 for his work in creating the CAT scan.

Howard, Bart (Howard Joseph Gustafson) (1915–February 21), composer of "Fly Me to the Moon" and other songs popularized by cabaret artist Mabel Mercer, whom Howard accompanied.

Jacquet, Illinois (1922–July 22), tenor saxophonist who played with several jazz legends, including Lionel Hampton and Court Basie, and defined the jazz style "screeching."

James, Rick (James Amrose Johnson) (1948– August 6), singer whose widely acclaimed 1981 hit "Super Freak" catapulted him into the forefront of the funk movement.

Jarrett, Vernon (1921–May 23), journalist who became a prominent commentator on African American history and race relations.

Johnston, Verona (1890–December 1), at age 114, the oldest person in the United States. Johnston voted in every election since women were allowed to vote in 1920.

Jones, Elvin (1927–May 18), innovative drummer whose explosive style powered a number of jazz ensembles, including the highly influential and controversial John Coltrane Quartet of the 1960's.

Jones, Fay (1921-August 30), "organic" architect whose Thorncrown Chapel in the Arkansas Ozarks was voted the fourth best building of the 20th century by the American Institute of Architects.

Jordan, James (1930–February 4), premier advertising sloganeer who coined "Wisk beats ring around the collar," "Tareyton smokers would rather fight than switch," and "Zest-fully clean."

Jordan, Ramona Trinidad Iglesias (1889–May 29), woman whom the *Guinness World Records* recognized as the world's oldest person.

Juliana of the Netherlands (1909–March 20), former queen whose social causes and common touch moved the Dutch monarchy closer to the people. Juliana abdicated in favor of her daughter Beatrix in 1980.

Justice, Herb (1925–August 6), Pulitzer Prize-winning poet whose precise language and strain of melancholy resulted in formalist and highly musical verse acclaimed for its individuality.

Kalber, Floyd (1924–May 13), Emmy Award-winning news anchor whose career included highly rated programs in Chicago and the "Today" show on NBC.

Kaye, M. M. (1908–January 29), British author of the bestselling novel *The Far Pavilions* (1978) who also wrote children's books—the *Potter Pinner* series (1937-1941) and *Black Bramble Wood* (1938)—under the name Mollie Kaye.

Keel, Howard (Harold Clifford Leek) (1919–November 7), broad-shouldered baritone who capped a career in MGM musicals—*Show Boat* (1951), *Kiss Me Kate* (1953), *Seven Brides for Seven Brothers* (1954)—with a 10-year run on the TV soap "Dallas."

Keeshan, Bob (1927–January 23), TV personality who created Captain Kangaroo, gentle host of the childrens' program that ran on CBS from 1955 to 1984 and on public television for an additional six years.

Kiley, Dan (1912–February 21), pre-eminent U.S. landscape architect who completed some 1,000

Elizabeth Kubler-Ross, psychiatrist

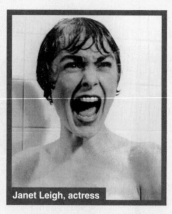

Janet Leigh, actress

projects, including landscapes at the National Gallery in Washington, D.C., the Gateway Arch in St. Louis, and the Art Institute in Chicago.

King, Alan (Irwin Alan Kniberg) (1927–May 9), stand-up comedian, character actor, and Broadway and film producer whose wry take on marriage and life in general entertained generations.

Kleiber, Carlos (1930–July 13), eccentric, independent Austrian conductor whom many critics and musicians regarded as one of the greatest conductors of the second half of the 20th century.

Koenig, Pierre (1925–April 4), architect whose designs for two houses—Case Study Nos. 21 and 22—completed in 1959 and 1960, became world renowned icons of post-World War II modernism.

Kubler-Ross, Elizabeth (1926–August 24), Swiss-born psychiatrist and author of *On Death and Dying* whose investigation of the dying process sparked the hospice movement in the United States and markedly changed the nation's perception of death.

Kucher, Karol Kennedy (1932–June 25), figure skater who, teamed with brother Peter Kennedy, became the first U.S. pair to win a world championship when they took the gold medal in 1950 and went on to capture the silver medal at the 1952 Winter Olympics.

Lacy, Steve (Steven Lackritz) (1934–June 4), jazz musician and avant-garde composer whom critics considered one of the greatest of soprano saxophonists.

Lampert, Harry (1916–November 13), illustrator who drew the 1940's-era superhero The Flash for DC Comics.

LaRue, Fred (1928–July 24), shadowy Nixon administration figure known to be the "bagman" who delivered payoffs to participants in the Watergate break-in.

Lauder, Estee (Josephine Esther Mentzer Lauter) (1906?–April 24), founder of the cosmetic empire that bears her name. Lauder's drive and marketing innovations led *Time* to name her as the only woman on the magazine's list of 20 geniuses of business of the 20th century.

Lawrence, Jerome (1915–February 29), playwright who with collaborator Robert E. Lee wrote 39 plays, including *Inherit the Wind* (1955) and *Auntie Mame* (1956).

Lee, Anna (1913–May 14) (Joan Boniface Winnifrith), English-born actress who appeared in a number of John Ford films and who played the same role on the soap opera "General Hospital" for 30 years.

Leigh, Janet (Jeanette Helen Morrison) (1927–October 3), actress who won acclaim for her roles in *Touch of Evil* (1958) and *The Manchurian Candidate* (1962) but achieved film immortality as the ill-fated Marion Crane in Alfred Hitchcock's *Psycho* (1960).

Lewis, Edward B. (1918–July 21), geneticist who received the 1995 Nobel Prize in Physiology or Medicine for the "colinearity principle," which derived from his discovery that the linear arrangement of genes on chromosomes in fruit flies is in an order corresponding to body parts.

Manchester, William (1922–June 1), best-selling writer whose richly detailed biographies—Douglas MacArthur in *American Caesar* and John F.

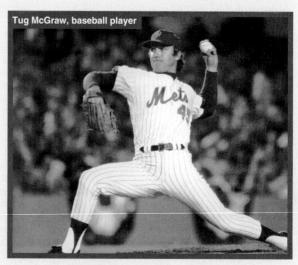

Tug McGraw, baseball player

Kennedy in *Death of a President*—culminated in the first two volumes of the unfinished Winston Churchill trilogy *The Last Lion*.

Markova, Alicia (Lillian Alicia Marks) (1910–December 2), British ballerina who was renowned for her delicacy and simplicity of movement, particularly in *Giselle*, her signature role.

Maxwell, Brian (1953–March 19), British-born Canadian marathoner who created the Power-Bar, which he turned into a multimillion dollar business.

McCambridge, Mercedes (1916–March 2), actress who won an Academy Award for *All the King's Men* (1949) and a cult following for *Johnny Guitar* (1954), *Touch of Evil* (1958), and *The Exorcist* (1973). Orson Wells called her "the world's greatest living radio actress."

McGraw, Tug (Frank Edwin McGraw, Jr.) (1944–January 5), colorful, left-handed pitcher who helped the New York Mets capture the 1969 world series and the Philadelphia Phillies take the 1980 title by striking out Kansas City's Willie Wilson with the bases loaded.

McGrory, Mary (1918–April 21), newspaper columnist whose "tell-it-like-it–is" commentary, written in exquisite prose, won her a Pulitzer Prize and a place on the Nixon administration's "enemies list."

McWhirter, Norris (1925–April 19), British writer and editor who cofounded the *Guinness Book of Records*—original published by the Guinness brewery to settle trivia disputes in pubs.

Merrill, Robert (1917–October 23), powerful baritone and leading Verdi interpreter who was a favorite with Metropolitan Opera patrons from 1945 until 1976.

Meyer, Russ (1922–September 18), writer/director known as "King Leer" for his "sexploitation" films, including *Faster Pussycat, Kill! Kill!* (1965), *Vixen* (1968), and *Beyond the Valley of the Dolls* (1970).

Miller, Ann (Johnnie Lucille Collier) (1923–January 22), actress and dancer whose machine-gun tap routines made her a standout in film musicals, such as *Easter Parade* (1948), *On the Town* (1949), and *Kiss Me Kate* (1953), and on Broadway in the long-running *Sugar Babies*.

Miller, J. Irwin (1909–August 16), industrialist and philanthropist who guided the Cummins Engine Co. into the world's leading maker of large diesel engines and transformed his hometown, Columbus, Indiana, into a showcase of modern architecture.

Milosz, Czeslaw (1911–August 14), Polish poet who won the 1980 Nobel Prize in Literature for his powerful dissections of the impact of historical immorality on the spiritual values of the individual.

Minor, Jan (1917–February 15), actress who for 26 years portrayed Madge the manicurist in Palmolive detergent commercials.

Mitchelson, Marvin M. (1928–September 18), divorce lawyer who pioneered "palimony," alimony for nonmarried live-in partners.

Morgan, Robert (1918–May 15), commander of the famed Memphis Belle B-17 bomber that flew 25 combat missions over France and Germany during World War II.

Mydans, Carl (1907–August 16), *Life* magazine photographer who was acclaimed for his World

Ann Miller, dancer and actress

War II pictures, including General Douglas MacArthur wading ashore on Luzon in 1945.

Newton, Helmut (1920–January 23), German-born fashion photographer whose glamorous and edgy photos were a staple at *Vogue* and other magazines for more than 30 years.

Nitze, Paul H. (1907–October 19), military treaty negotiator and Cold War strategist who advised Presidents Roosevelt, Truman, Kennedy, Johnson, Nixon, and Reagan.

O'Neil, Ron (1937–January 14), actor who starred in the 1972 hit *Superfly* and went on to ride a wave of "blaxploitation" films.

Orbach, Jerry (1935–December 28), actor who found equal success on television, as the cynical cop Lennie on "Law and Order," as he had as a song-and-dance man in the original casts of *The Fantasticks, Promises, Promises, Chicago,* and *42nd Street*.

Osmond, Humphry (1917–February 6), British psychiatrist who coined the word "psychedelic" to describe a type of drugs, such as LSD and mescaline, which he used in the treatment of psychological ailments.

Parr, Jack (1918–January 27), television personality who hosted "The Tonight Show" from 1957 to 1962, holding the nation's attention with a blend of brashness, sentimentality, and wit. See Portrait at Television.

Partridge, Francis (1900–February 5), British diarist who was the last surviving member of the Bloomsbury literary circle that included Virginia Woolf, Lytton Strachey, John Maynard Keynes, and E. M. Forster.

Paschke, Ed (1939–November 25), artist whose haunting urban images and powerfully colored portraits made him a leading figure among the Chicago fantasists known as Imagists.

Pastorelli, Robert (1954–March 7?), actor who played Murphy Brown's live-in house painter, Eldin, on the "Murphy Brown" television series.

Peel, John (John Ravenscroft) (1939–October 25), influential British disc jockey who championed new and experimental music on his live "Peel session" BBC radio programs.

Pickering, William (1910–March 15), New Zealand-born space scientist who was a former director of NASA's Jet Propulsion Laboratory and led the first successful U.S. satellite launch.

series as "December Bride" and "Pete and Gladys."

Rakosi, Carl (1903–June 25), prolific San Francisco writer who at the age of 100 was called "the nation's oldest major poet."

Raksin, David (1912–August 9), composer who wrote the scores for more than 160 films, most notably the haunting theme for *Laura* (1944) and *The Bad and the Beautiful* (1952).

Ramone, Johnny (John Cummings) (1948–September 15), guitarist and cofounder of The Ramones, the influential rock band.

Randall, Tony (Leonard Rosenberg) (1920–May 17), actor and talk-show raconteur who specialized in fastidious characters, most famously the "best friend" in Rock Hudson-Doris Day comedies and the obsessive Felix Unger on "The Odd Couple" TV series.

Randolph, John (Emanuel Hirsch Cohen) (1915–February 24), Tony Award-winning character actor who appeared in some 90 films, including *The Naked City* (1948), *Serpico* (1973), and *You've Got Mail* (1998).

Reagan, Ronald (1911–June 5), 40th president of the United States. See Special Report at United States, President of

Reeve, Christopher (1952–October 10), actor—*Superman* (1978), *Deathtrap* (1982), and *The Remains of the Day* (1993)—who inspired millions with his activism and struggle to overcome total paralysis resulting from a riding acident.

Rey, Alvino (1908–February 24), swing-era band-leader who popularized the electrified steel guitar.

Robinson, Arthur H. (1915–October 10), Canadian-born geographer who created the Robinson projection, a widely adopted improvement of the Mercator flat projection of the round world.

Rockefeller, Laurance S. (1910–July 11), third of the five grandsons of John D. Rockefeller and prominent conservationist who donated thousands of acres for state and national parks and built resorts credited with launching ecotourism.

Tony Randall, actor

Christopher Reeve, actor and activist

Pople, Sir John A. (1925–March 15), British-born mathematician and chemist who was awarded a Noble Prize in 1998 for a widely used computer program that predicts the properties and movement of molecules in chemical reactions.

Pugh, Alfred (1895–January 7), the last known U.S. veteran to have been wounded in combat in World War I.

Rafferty, Frances (1922–April 18), B-movie actress who moved into early television in such comedy

Sagan, Francoise (Francoise Quoirez) (1935–September 24), French author whose first novel, *Bonjour Tristesse* (1954), rocketed her to fame at the age of 18.

Salinger, Pierre (1925 October 16), journalist who served as press secretary to President John F. Kennedy.

Susan Sontag, writer

Jan Sterling, actress

mathematical models from game theory into the study of behavior and investigated evolutionary reasons for sexual reproduction.

Sontag, Susan (1933–December 28), novelist, essayist, and intellectual who synthesized high and popular culture, the avantgarde, and politics in such works as "Notes on Camp" (1964), *Against Interpretation* (1966), and *AIDS and Its Metaphors* (1989).

Stepanek, Mattie (1990–June 22), child poet whose five "Heartsong" books made him a best-selling author and a prominent advocate for people with muscular dystrophy.

Sterling, Jan (Jane Sterling Adriance) (1921–March 26), actress who most memorably played tramps in such noir films as *Appointment with Danger* (1951) and *Ace in the Hole* (1951).

Straus, Roger, Jr., (1917–May 25), publisher who cofounded the respected publishing house Farrar, Straus & Giroux.

Strickland, Shirley (1925–February 17), Australian runner who won seven Olympic medals, including three golds, an Australian record, at the 1948, 1952, and 1956 games.

Taylor, June (1918?–May 16), choreographer whose extravagant chorus line numbers on "The Jackie Gleason Show" brought the kaleidoscopic patterns of a Busby Berkeley production to television.

Tcherina, Ludmilla (1924–March 21), French ballet star and artist who appeared in 22 films, including *The Red Shoes* (1948).

Tebaldi, Renata (1922–December 19), Italian soprano whose rich, flexible voice and consummate artistry made her one of the great opera divas of the second half of the 20th century.

Thomas, Franklin (1912–September 8), one of the Walt Disney Studios' famed "nine old men," the artists who animated the classic Disney films of the 1930's through the 1950's. Most notably, Thomas created the seven dwarfs in *Snow White* (1937) and the spaghetti love scene in *Lady and the Tramp* (1955).

Thulin, Ingrid (1926–January 7), Swedish actress who appeared in the Ingmar Bergman classics *Wild Strawberries* (1957) and *Cries and Whispers* (1972).

Sanache, Frank (1918?–August 21), last of the Meskwaki "code talkers" who used elements of their native language to encrypt walkie-talkie communications during World War II.

Sanford, Isabel (1917–July 9), Emmy Award winning actress who played the stoic Louise Jefferson on the TV sitcoms "All in the Family" and "The Jeffersons."

Scavullo, Francesco (1921–January 6), photographer whose highly glamorized images of women graced the covers of *Cosmopolitan* and other magazines for more than 30 years.

Schwartz, Julius (1915–February 8), DC comic book editor whose flair for science fiction and revival of the superhero is credited with saving the industry and launching its "silver age" in the 1950's.

Shaw, Artie (Arthur Arshawsky) (1910–December 30), big-band leader and influential jazz clarinetist whose recordings of "Begin the Beguine," "Lady Be Good," and "Stardust" remain standards.

Sheridan, David S. (1909?–April 29), self-taught inventor who is credited with saving millions of lives with the development of the first modern disposable catheter; the first cardiac catheter; an endotracheal tube routinely used in surgery; the Saratoga Sump Drain; and the Salem Stomach Sump Drain.

Shifriss, Oved (1915?–June 25), Palestinian-born plant breeder and geneticist who in 1949 developed the Big Boy tomato, which revolutionized home gardening.

Smith, Jeff (1939–July 7), Protestant minister whose "Frugal Gourmet" dominated public television cooking programs in the 1980's.

Smith, John Maynard (1920–April 19), influential English environmental biologist who introduced

Tillman, Pat (1976–April 22), former NFL safety who quit football to join the U.S. Army. Tillman was killed in combat in Afghanistan.

Toland, John (1912–January 4), historian who wrote the best-selling *Adolf Hitler: The Definitive Biography* (1976) and won the 1971 Pulitzer Prize for *The Rising Sun, a History of the Japanese Empire between 1936 and 1945*.

Troy, Doris (Doris Higginson), (1937–February 16), soul singer who achieved fame with the 1963 hit "Just One Look" and whose life inspired the musical *Mamma, I Want to Sing* (1983).

Ustinov, Peter (1921–March 28), British-born novelist, playwright, raconteur, and character actor who won Academy Awards for *Spartacus* (1960) and *Topkapi* (1964).

Ward, Rodger (1921–July 5), race car driver who won the Indianapolis 500 in 1959 and 1962.

Westphal, James A. (1930–September 8), self-tutored astronomer who directed the Palomar Observatory and led the team that built the first camera for the Hubble Space Telescope.

Whalen, Eleanor Holm, (1913?–January 31), Olympic swimming champion who parlayed her notoriety for being expelled from the 1936 Berlin games into a show business career, most famously in husband Billy Rose's "Acquacade" at the 1939-1940 New York World's Fair.

Whipple, Fred L., (1906–August 30), astronomer who revolutionized the study of comets with the idea that they are made of ice and rock.

White, Reggie (1961–December 26), defensive end for the Philadelphia Eagles, Green Bay Packers, and Carolina Panthers who was twice

Fay Wray, actress

physiology with James Watson and Francis Crick for determining the structure of DNA.

Williams, Claude (1908–April 25), pioneering jazz violinist who played with Ben Webster, Lester Young, and Count Basie among others.

Winfield, Paul (1941–March 7), actor who won accolades for roles in the film *Sounder* (1972), the TV special "Go Tell It on the Mountain," and his portrait of Martin Luther King, Jr., in a 1978 miniseries.

Wotherspoon, Adella (1903–January 26), last survivor of the 1904 *General Slocum* disaster in which 1,021 New Yorkers died when the ship burned in the East River.

Wray, Fay (1907–August 8), Canadian-born actress who appeared in 90-plus films but gained immortality in the grasp of a giant ape atop the Empire State Building in the 1933 classic *King Kong*.

Yardley, George (1928–August 12), Hall of Fame forward who was the first NBA player to score 2,000 points in a single season (1957–1958).

Peter Ustinov, actor

Paul Winfield, actor

NFL defensive player of the year and was elected to the Pro Bowl a record 13 straight times.

Whitehead, John (1949?–May 11), Rhythm and Blues artist who was best known for his 1974 hit "Ain't No Stoppin' Us Now."

Wilkins, Maurice (1916–October 5), British scientist who shared the Nobel Prize for medicine or

Zayed bin Sultan al-Nahayan (1918?–November 2), Abu Dhabi sheik who modernized his own country and successfully consolidated seven city states into the United Arab Emirates.

Zimmermann, Joseph J., Jr. (1912–March 31), inventor of the first commercially successful answering machine—the Electronic Secretary.

Democratic Party. The Democratic Party lost further ground to the Republican Party in the Nov. 2, 2004, general elections. Democrats lost the presidential race and seats in both the United States Senate and House of Representatives.

President election. Senator John Kerry (D., Massachusetts) lost his bid to unseat President George W. Bush on November 2. The president captured 286 electoral votes, compared with Kerry's 252 electoral votes. President Bush won the popular vote with 60.6 million votes, compared with 57.2 million votes for Kerry. An estimated 119.8 million people voted in the 2004 election.

Democratic primaries. Kerry's capture of the Democratic Party's nomination for president in the 2004 election was the culmination of a lengthy series of primaries in which a number of Democrats fought to become the party's presidential candidate. Former Vermont Governor Howard Dean entered the primaries as the Democratic frontrunner. However, as the primary season got under way, Dean's lead in the polls failed to translate into delegates.

The first Democratic Party primary, the Iowa caucuses, was held on January 19, with Kerry claiming victory, Senator John Edwards (D., North Carolina) finishing second, Dean capturing third, U.S. Representative Richard A. Gephardt (D., Missouri) taking fourth, and U.S. Representative Dennis Kucinich (D., Ohio) in fifth place. Gephardt's poor showing in Iowa prompted him to drop out of the race on January 20.

Kerry's campaign continued to roll with victories in January in New Hampshire, and in February in Arizona, Delaware, Maine, Michigan, Missouri, New Mexico, North Dakota, and Washington state. Wesley Clark, a retired U.S. Army general and former supreme allied commander of the North Atlantic Treaty Organization, won the February 3 Oklahoma primary, while Edwards picked up his only victory in the February 3 primary in South Carolina.

On February 9, Clark abandoned his bid for the nomination. Continued poor showings in primaries held in February prompted Dean to end his quest for the presidential

nomination on February 18. Edwards dropped out of the race on March 3. Kerry captured the Democratic nomination after taking the Illinois primary on March 16.

Democratic National Convention. On July 6, Kerry selected John Edwards as his running mate. Democrats convened in Boston in late July, formally nominating Kerry as their candidate on July 29. In accepting the nomination, Kerry criticized President Bush for leading the United States into war and for administration policies that Kerry said put the U.S. environment and economy at risk.

U.S. Senate elections. The Democrats lost four U.S. Senate seats in the November election, falling to a 55-44 minority. (One senator, James M. Jeffords of Vermont, is an independent and not affiliated with either party.) Democrats lost seats in Florida, Georgia, Louisiana, North Carolina, and South Carolina. In South Dakota, Sen-

Barack Obama acknowledges the crowd during his widely acclaimed keynote speech at the Democratic National Convention in Boston in July 2004. Obama was elected to the U.S. Senate from Illinois in a landslide victory on November 2.

ator Tom Daschle, the leader of the Senate Democrats, lost to Republican John Thune, a former congressman. Daschle was first elected in 1986 and had led Senate Democrats since 1995.

Democrats applauded Barack Obama's landslide victory in Illinois in 2004. Obama captured 70 percent of the vote to defeat Alan Keyes, a former Republican presidential candidate, in the race to succeed Senator Peter Fitzgerald (R., Illinois). Fitzgerald had chosen not to seek re-election.

Voters in Colorado elected Colorado Attorney General Ken Salazar, a Democrat, to succeed Senator Ben Nighthorse Campbell, a Republican.

Incumbent Democrats re-elected to the Senate included Evan Bayh of Indiana; Christopher J. Dodd of Connecticut; Byron L. Dorgan of North Dakota; Blanche Lambert Lincoln of Arkansas; Patrick J. Leahy of Vermont; Barbara J. Mikulski of Maryland; Harry M. Reid of Nevada; and Charles E. Schumer of New York.

U.S. House of Representatives. Democrats also lost ground in the House of Representatives in November, where they fell to a 232 to 202 minority. One independent in the House, Bernard Sanders of Vermont, was re-elected.

Gubernatorial races. Democrats won 6 of 11 races for governor in November. Voters re-elected Delaware Governor Ruth Minner and North Carolina Governor Michael Easley. In Montana, voters elected Brian Schweitzer governor. In New Hampshire, Democratic challenger John Lynch unseated Republican Governor Craig Benson. West Virginia voters elected Secretary of State Joe Manchin III as their next governor. State Attorney General Christine Gregoire, a Democrat, narrowly defeated Dino Rossi, a Republican, in the race for the governor of Washington.

New Jersey Governor James E. McGreevey, a Democrat, resigned on November 15 after admitting to having had an extramarital same-sex relationship with a former aide. Richard J. Codey, a Democrat and president of the state senate, was sworn in as acting governor.

Fundraising. Political party fundraising increased in 2004. The Democratic National Committee, Democratic Senatorial Campaign Committee, and the Democratic Congressional Campaign Committee raised $451.8 million in donations through mid-October, according to the Federal Election Commission (FEC). The Republican National Committee, the National Republican Senatorial Committee, and the National Republican Congressional Committee raised $554.7 million.

■ Geoffrey A. Campbell

See also **Congress of the United States; Elections; People in the news** (John Edwards; John Kerry; Barack Obama); **Republican Party; State government; United States, Government of the; United States, President of the.**

Denmark. The government of Prime Minister Anders Fogh Rasmussen continued to support the United States-led intervention in Iraq despite several controversies in 2004. On November 26, the parliament voted to extend the tours of duty of the roughly 500 Danish troops serving in Iraq by six months, to the end of June 2005. Although several European countries withdrew troops in 2004 or announced plans to do so, Rasmussen said Denmark would provide security so Iraqis could regain control of their country. Parliament also increased the Danish peacekeeping force in Afghanistan to 225 troops from 50 and extended their term of deployment by six months.

Abuse allegations. In August 2004, the defense ministry recalled four Danish commanders from Iraq over allegations that they had abused Iraqi prisoners by denying them water and forcing them to stay in stressful positions during interrogations. Investigators found the treatment violated interrogation rules of warfare but did not amount to torture.

The Danish economy improved significantly in 2004, helped by a government decision to accelerate tax cuts. The reductions, which had been scheduled to be phased in between 2005 and 2007, amounted to more than $900 for many Danes or a total of $1.5 billion in 2004. The government decided in March to implement the tax cuts immediately to stimulate the economy, which was close to recession. Growth picked up during the year, and economic output was forecast to increase by 2.3 percent, up from 0.5 percent in 2003. Unemployment was expected to edge up to 5.8 percent from 5.6 percent.

Hippy enclave. Police cracked down on the cannabis trade in the Copenhagen neighborhood of Christiania in 2004. The neighborhood has been a counter-culture haven since the early 1970's, when hippies moved into an abandoned army base and established a commune with the right of self-rule. Seeking to stop the drug trade, police raided Christiania in March 2004 and arrested 48 people for possession or sale of the drug. In June, politicians agreed on a law to let residents remain as long as they pay for gas and electricity, allow the creation of an independent committee to run the area, and build 300 new houses in the area.

Royal family. Crown Prince Frederik, the heir to the Danish throne, married Mary Elizabeth Donaldson in Copenhagen on May 14. Donaldson, an Australian, gave up her native citizenship and converted to Denmark's official Lutheran Church for the marriage. Frederik's younger brother, Prince Joachim, and his wife, Alexandra, announced their intention to divorce on September 16. ■ Tom Buerkle

See also **Europe; Iraq: A Special Report.**

Dinosaur. See Paleontology.

Crown Prince Frederik, the heir to the Danish throne, and his bride, Australian Mary Elizabeth Donaldson, leave Our Lady's Church in Copenhagen following their wedding ceremony on May 14. Donaldson renounced her Australian and British citizenships to marry the Danish prince.

Disability. In a 5-to-4 decision, the United States Supreme Court ruled on May 17, 2004, that states can be sued for damages under federal disability law in certain circumstances. Previous Supreme Court decisions had given states broad immunity from such suits, based on the 11th Amendment to the Constitution, which bars lawsuits against states in federal court. The new ruling cited the fact that Congress has the right to cancel the states' immunity if it is doing so to ensure the right of citizens to equal protection and due process guaranteed in the 14th Amendment. According to the decision, Congress did exactly that in enacting the Americans with Disabilities Act (ADA) in 1990.

The case before the court involved six people from Tennessee and centered on the inaccessibility of state courthouses to people with physical disabilities. One of the individuals, George Lane, was unable to reach a second-floor courtroom in his wheelchair and was charged by the state with failure to appear at a hearing. When Lane sued the state of Tennessee over the matter in 1998, a lower-level court ruled that the state was immune from the suit. The Supreme Court justices ruled that such a suit is permissible but emphasized that disabled citizens can only sue states in matters involving access to state courts.

Updated accessibility guidelines. On July 23, 2004, the U.S. Access Board released a long-awaited revision to the ADA Accessibility Guidelines, which were first published in 1991. The revision updated construction guidelines for amenities that provide people with disabilities easier access to public, commercial, and federally financed facilities. The Access Board is composed of representatives of federal government agencies and members of disability rights groups and businesses appointed by the U.S. president.

The purpose of the Accessibility Guidelines is to help builders and building managers comply with ADA regulations and with those specified in the Architectural Barriers Act of 1968. The guidelines serve as the basis for standards that are enforced by other federal agencies, such as the U.S. Department of Justice.

The revised guidelines covered accessibility to a variety of services for people with varying disabilities. For example, the guidelines specified that hotels must make one-sixth of their parking spaces usable by vans and install shower sprays and vanities accessible by people in a wheelchair. In the banking industry, automated teller machines (ATM's) must include voice duplication of visual displays and either headsets or earphone jacks for users who do not want other people to hear the information being spoken to them.

■ Kristina Vaicikonis

See also **Supreme Court of the United States.**

Disasters. The deadliest disaster of 2004 was a December 26 earthquake that triggered tsunamis that struck the coasts of several Asian and African nations. At least 125,000 people were confirmed dead by December 31. Disasters that resulted in 25 or more deaths include the following:

Aircraft crashes

January 3—Egypt. An Air Flash Boeing 737 jet, en route from the resort of Sharm ash Shaykh on the southern tip of Egypt's Sinai Peninsula, crashes into the Red Sea minutes after takeoff. All 135 passengers, most of whom are French tourists, and the 6 Egyptian crew members are killed.

January 13—Uzbekistan. An Uzbekistan Airways Yakovlev-40 jet crashes in heavy fog on approach to the airport at Tashkent, the capital. All 37 people aboard are killed, including the top United Nations official in Uzbekistan. The jet was en route to Tashkent from Termez, a major hub for humanitarian aid flowing into Afghanistan.

November 21—China. All 53 people aboard a China Eastern Airlines commuter plane, and one person on the ground, are killed when the plane crashes shortly after takeoff into a frozen lake in Baotou, northern China.

Earthquakes

February 24—Morocco. As many as 600 people are killed and hundreds of others are injured when an earthquake rocks the area surrounding the port city of Al Hoceima in northern Morocco. Neighboring villages, in which many of the dwellings are built of mud-brick, are the hardest hit.

May 28—Iran. At least 35 people are killed and more than 350 others are injured as an earthquake of 6.2 magnitude strikes northern and central Iran. More than 80 villages are heavily damaged in an area centered about 40 miles (64 kilometers) north of Tehran, the capital.

October 23—Japan. An earthquake of 6.8 magnitude centered in Niigata, about 160 miles (260 kilometers) northwest of Tokyo, causes the deaths of 39 people and injures more than 2,000 others.

December 26—Asia and Africa. An earthquake of 9.0 magnitude about 100 miles (160 kilometers) off the coast of Sumatra triggers tsunamis that strike Asian and African nations, from Malaysia to Tanzania. At least 125,000 people are confirmed dead by December 31.

Explosions and fires

February 15—China. A fire in a crowded shopping mall in Jilin, 590 miles (950 kilometers) northeast of Beijing, the capital, kills more than 53 people and injures at least 70 others.

February 18—Iran. More than 300 people are killed and as many as 450 others are injured when

DISASTER IN SOUTH ASIA

A December 26 undersea earthquake off Sumatra generates tsunamis that devastate coastal areas in southern Asia, including Thailand's Phi Phi Island (below). A father mourns the death of his 8-year-old son (left) in India, where the tsunamis left thousands of people dead and hundreds of thousands of others homeless.

train cars carrying fuel and chemicals derail and explode in Khorasan province, east of Tehran. The blast destroys five villages and registers on seismographs as the equivalent of a 3.6-magnitude earthquake.

March 16—Russia. A natural gas explosion shears off part of an apartment building in Arkhangelsk, about 600 miles (1,000 kilometers) north of Moscow. At least 58 residents are killed. Authorities believe the explosion was caused by two homeless men who allegedly removed bronze fittings from gas pipes to sell for scrap.

April 22—North Korea. Two railroad cars filled with liquid chemicals are caught in overhead live electrical wires in a rail station at Ryongchon, North Korea, 90 miles (145 kilometers) north of the capital, Pyongyang. The subsequent explosion kills as many as 160 people and leaves more than 1,300 others injured.

June 24—Iran. A tanker truck carrying 4,500 gallons (17,000 liters) of gasoline crashes into six buses at a police checkpoint in Nosratabad, about 690 miles (1,100 kilometers) southeast of Tehran, the capital. The resulting fireball kills at least 90 passengers and injures 114 others.

July 16—India. A fire in a school in Kumbakonam in the southern state of Tamil Nadu leaves 90 children dead and more than 30 others injured. The fire began when a thatched roof caught fire and collapsed.

August 1—Paraguay. A fire in a supermarket in a suburb of Asuncion, the capital, kills 464 people and injures hundreds of others. A security guard was reportedly ordered to lock the doors as the fire began to prevent theft.

December 30—Argentina. A fire during a rock concert at a nightclub in Buenos Aires, the capital, leaves more than 165 people dead and injures at least 375 others.

Mine disasters

April 10—Russia. At least 40 miners are killed when methane gas explodes in a coal mine in the Kemerovo region of western Siberia, about 1,850 miles (2.977 kilometers) east of Moscow.

July 19—Ukraine. A massive methane gas explosion kills at least 31 miners in Ukraine's eastern Donetsk region, considered to be one of the world's deadliest coal-mining areas.

December 1—China. The Chinese state media company confirms that at least 166 miners died in a gas explosion in a state-owned coal mine in China's Shaanxi province on November 28, the deadliest mining disaster in at least 10 years. Nearly 150 Chinese miners were killed in a similar blast October 20. According to Chinese government statistics, 4,153 people died in mining accidents in China during the first nine months of 2004.

Shipwrecks

May 23—Bangladesh. Two ferries traveling about half a mile (1 kilometer) apart along the

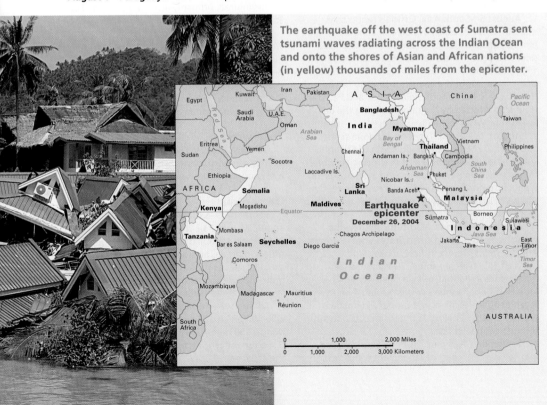

The earthquake off the west coast of Sumatra sent tsunami waves radiating across the Indian Ocean and onto the shores of Asian and African nations (in yellow) thousands of miles from the epicenter.

River Meghna near Chandpur, 106 miles (170 kilometers) southeast of Dhaka, the capital, sink during a storm. More than 80 of the estimated 300 people aboard the two vessels are killed.

Storms and floods

March 7-9—Madagascar. Rescue service officials report that nearly 200 people were killed and more than 200,000 others were left homeless when Cyclone Gafilo struck northern Madagascar and then turned to strike the southern part of the island. Among the dead were passengers on a ferry traveling from the Comoros Islands that capsized in seas described as "mountainous."

April 5—Mexico. Torrential rains turn Mexico's Escondido River, a tributary of the Rio Grande, into a raging flood that inundates the border city of Piedras Negras. At least 36 people are killed, and hundreds of houses are destroyed.

May 25—West Indies. Two weeks of torrential rain cause flooding and mudslides on the Caribbean island of Hispaniola, leaving at least 3,300 people dead in Haiti and the Dominican Republic.

July 2—Asia. Typhoon Mindulle hits the Philippines with gusts up to 118 miles (190 kilometers) per hour, killing at least 30 people and forcing thousands of others to flee flood waters. Twenty-nine people were killed when the storm struck Taiwan on July 1, causing major flooding and damage to crops totaling an estimated $65.4 million. Mindulle traveled on to China, where its heavy rains killed two people on July 3.

August 5—South Asia. Officials report that more than 600 people have died in Bangladesh and more than 30 million others have been displaced since mid-June in massive flooding and landslides triggered by the heaviest monsoons in years. More than two-thirds of the country was engulfed by flood waters. Portions of India, Nepal, and Pakistan were also affected by the rains, bringing the death toll in South Asia to 1,883.

August 12—China. Typhoon Rananim slams into China's Zhejiang province, south of Shanghai, killing at least 164 people and destroying tens of thousands of houses. Rananim, the most powerful typhoon to hit China in 50 years, brushed over the northeastern tip of Taiwan earlier in the day, killing one person.

August 13—Florida. Hurricane Charley, the worst storm to hit the United States since Hurricane Andrew struck Florida in 1992, makes landfall with 145-mile-per-hour (230-kilometer-per-hour) winds at Punta Gorda, a small city on Charlotte Harbor on Florida's western coast. Twenty-seven people are killed, and property damage is estimated at $7.4 billion as the storm cuts a swath through central Florida.

September 7—Japan. Typhoon Songda slams into the western coast of Japan with winds as high as 135 miles (215 kilometers) per hour, killing 31 people and injuring about 900 others. The typhoon is the seventh to hit Japan in 2004, the highest number since 1951.

September 15—Alabama. Hurricane Ivan barrels ashore near the Gulf Coast resort town of Gulf Shores with winds of 130 miles (209 kilometers) per hour. The storm wreaks havoc across Alabama, the Florida Panhandle, and other southern and northeastern states. Fifty-two people are killed and more than 1.8 million others are without power across nine states. Days earlier, Ivan caused the deaths of 70 people in the Caribbean.

September 19—Haiti. Tropical Storm Jeanne's 13 inches (33 centimers) of rain trigger flooding and landslides that kill more than 2,000 people and leave 300,000 others homeless, most of them in Gonaives, Haiti's third-largest city located on the country's western coast. Another 26 people died as Jeanne cut through the Dominican Republic and Puerto Rico days earlier.

September 22—China. Government officials announce that at least 1,029 people throughout China have died in mudslides and floods during the year's rainy season. Similar seasonal floods left a record 4,150 people dead in 1998, before the government invested in reinforcing dikes and building a network of flood warning stations.

October 20—Japan. Typhoon Tokage strikes western Japan with high winds and heavy rains, leaving at least 80 people dead and hundreds of others injured, primarily around the city of Toyooka in Hyogo Prefecture.

December 2—Philippines. Four powerful storms strike the northern Philippines in one month, bringing flash floods and mudslides that cause the deaths of more than 1,000 people and leave hundreds of thousands of others homeless. Tropical Storm Winnie, on November 29, takes the highest toll, killing more than 800 people.

Train wrecks

July 22—Turkey. Five cars on a high-speed train overturn in northwestern Turkey, killing 37 people and causing injuries to more than 80 others.

Other disasters

February 1—Saudi Arabia. A stampede at the annual Muslim *hajj,* the pilgrimage to Mecca, leaves 251 people trampled to death and hundreds of others injured. The stampede took place during a ritual known as the stoning of the devil, when pilgrims throw rocks at three stone pillars to demonstrate disdain for Satan.

February 2—Turkey. At least 89 people are killed when an apartment building collapses in Konya, 150 miles (250 kilometers) south of Ankara. Government officials blame shoddy construction for the collapse.

February 5—China. Thirty-seven people are killed and more than a dozen others are injured when a crowd stampedes over a bridge during the annual spring Lantern Festival in Miyun County, outside Beijing.

February 14—Russia. At least 25 people are killed and dozens of others are injured when the roof of a water park on the outskirts of Moscow collapses. City officials suspect faulty construction.

June 7—Pakistan. Forty people are killed when the truck in which they are returning from a pilgrimage to the shrine of a Muslim saint plunges into a ravine at Nathiagali, about 50 miles (80 kilometers) northwest of Islamabad, the capital.

June 7—India. A bus filled with wedding guests plunges into the Bagmati River near Runisaitpur, in eastern India's Bihar state, killing 25 of the 32 people aboard. The accident takes place near a spot where, hours earlier, a boat ferrying primarily women and children from Dubaghat to a nearby village capsized, killing some 40 people.

June 25—Iran. A bus is hit by a fuel tanker and bursts into flames in southeastern Iran, killing at least 90 people and injuring dozens of others. The tanker hit the bus and other vehicles stopped at a police post outside Zahedan on the road from Bam, near the Pakistani border. ■ Kristina Vaicikonis

See also **Haiti: A Special Report.**

Drug abuse.
In 2003, 119 million Americans—about half of the U.S. population age 12 or older—were current drinkers, 70.8 million were current smokers of cigarettes, and 19.5 million were illegal drug users, according to the National Survey on Drug Use and Health (NSDUH), released in September 2004. The figures were based on past-month use of the substances, according to the Substance Abuse and Mental Health Services Administration (SAMHSA), which conducts the survey annually.

Alcohol. Out of the 119 million users of alcohol in the United States, 54 million reported engaging in binge drinking in the previous month, the NSDUH survey reported. The survey revealed the highest levels of binge drinking among youths aged 18 to 25. Health experts have warned that alcohol abuse—especially binge drinking—during adolescence and early adulthood can pose long-term risks to health.

A poster in Kabul warns Afghans of the dangers of drug addiction. In 2004, the United Nations warned that Afghanistan is on the verge of becoming a "narco-state." At least 87 percent of the world's opium was produced in Afghanistan in 2004, with 2.3 million Afghans—10 percent of the entire work force—engaged in some aspect of the trade.

Tobacco. The 2003 NSDUH survey found that, among the general population, cigarette smoking decreased from 26.0 percent in 2002 to 25.4 percent in 2003. Among young smokers, aged 12 to 17, cigarette smoking decreased from 13.0 percent in 2002 to 12.2 percent in 2003. The figures are based on respondents having smoked at least one time in the prior month.

The Monitoring the Future Survey (MTF), an annual study focusing on 8th-, 10th-, and 12th-graders, showed declines in smoking among high-school students in 2002–2003, but at smaller rates than in previous years. The MTF survey is sponsored annually by the National Institute on Drug Abuse and conducted by the University of Michigan Institute for Social Research. Despite recent declines in youth smoking, research data show that a fourth of U.S. youth smoke by the time they leave high school.

Illegal drugs. According to the NSDUH survey, 19.5 million Americans (8.2 percent) were illicit drug users in 2003—that is, they had used an illegal drug such as ecstasy, marijuana, heroin, or crack/cocaine. The figure changed little from the 2002 survey. Among youth ages 12 to 17, NSDUH found 11.2 percent of respondents reporting they had used an illegal drug in the prior month.

The NSDUH survey indicated that marijuana predominated in illegal drug use. More than 70 percent of illegal drug users used marijuana, though not necessarily exclusively. Cocaine and heroin use showed up in the survey, at rates essentially unchanged from the previous year.

The MTF survey revealed that use of the illegal drug ecstasy among high school students—which had surged in the 1990's—dropped 50 percent between 2001 and 2003. Ecstasy, or MDMA, is a mild hallucinogen dubbed the "club" or "rave" drug among youth.

■ David C. Lewis

See also **Drugs.**

Drugs. Pharmaceutical companies and the United States Food and Drug Administration (FDA) came under fierce criticism in 2004 from the U.S. Congress, health care experts, and public advocacy groups on charges of suppressing negative information about widely used and profitable drugs. The FDA is the government agency charged, in part, with administering federal laws designed to ensure the safety and effectiveness of drugs. The controversy led a number of groups to offer plans to increase *transparency* (openness) in clinical trials of new

drugs. A clinical trial is a scientific evaluation of a new medical treatment in which living people participate.

In June, New York Attorney General Eliot Spitzer sued British-based GlaxoSmithKline, alleging that the company had fraudulently withheld negative results from clinical trials of the antidepressant Paxil. Spitzer charged that at least four unpublished studies indicated that the drug was no more effective than a *placebo* (inactive substance) for children under age 18 and, in some cases, had increased the risk of suicidal thoughts among teen-aged participants. In August, the company settled the case by agreeing to pay $2.5 million in fines and to create a publicly accessible Web site offering summaries of company trials conducted since December 2000.

In September 2004, a House of Representatives subcommittee questioned FDA officials and drug company executives about their speed in revealing negative findings about antidepressant use in children. Senate investigators also explored charges that FDA officials had tried to silence an agency scientist whose research had concluded that high doses of the hugely successful arthritis

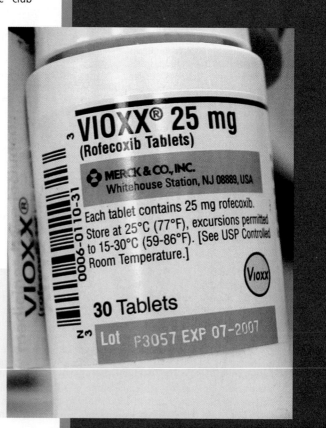

New Jersey-based Merck & Co. pulled its widely popular arthritis drug Vioxx from the market on Sept. 30, 2004. The company took the action after a new study revealed that Vioxx doubled the risk of heart attack and stroke in people who had been taking it for more than 18 months.

drug Vioxx doubled the risk of heart problems among users after 18 months. The warning came several months before Merck & Co., which is based in New Jersey, pulled Vioxx from the market on September 30.

The New York City-based pharmaceutical company Pfizer Inc. announced on December 15 that its arthritis painkiller Celebrex may increase cardiovascular problems. New study results indicated that the drug may more than double the risk of major heart problems. However, a second study did not corroborate that finding.

In November, the FDA announced an investigation of German-based Bayer AG after the *Journal of the American Medical Association* published an article accusing the drugmaker of waiting for more than a year to warn physicians and patients that people taking the anticholesterol drug Baycol had a risk of developing a rare muscle-wasting disease. Bayer had voluntarily withdrawn Baycol from use in August 2001.

In October, the Pharmaceutical Researchers and Manufacturers of America, a drug industry group, launched its own online database to register clinical trial by members.

Antidepressant warnings. A strong, new warning about the dangers of antidepressant use in children and adolescents must appear on all package inserts accompanying these medications, the FDA ordered on October 15. The order for the warning—the strongest possible—followed a recommendation from an FDA advisory panel, which analyzed 23 pediatric clinical studies of 9 antidepressants.

The panel had reported that children under age 18 who took antidepressants were about twice as likely to exhibit suicidal behaviors as were study participants taking a placebo. The FDA warning also states that for the first few months following the beginning of antidepressant treatment, minors should be observed closely for worsening symptoms.

Many mental health experts supported the decision to issue the warning. Some experts, however, worried that the warning would discourage the treatment of children with serious depression or other psychiatric disorders.

Race-specific drug? A fixed combination of two well-known drugs sharply reduced death rates among African Americans with heart failure in the first nationwide study ever conducted solely on this group. In the study, which was reported in November 2004, participants who took the drug BiDil along with drugs commonly prescribed for heart failure were 43 percent less likely to die of this condition than participants who took standard drugs alone.

Heart failure is a disorder in which the heart does not pump efficiently because of any of a number of diseases. Blacks are 2½ times more likely than whites to develop this condition and less likely to benefit from the drugs commonly used to treat heart failure, called ACE inhibitors.

BiDil, produced by Massachusetts-based NitroMed Inc., boosts blood levels of nitric oxide, a signalling molecule that helps regulate heart function. NitroMed had previously failed to obtain FDA approval for BiDil because clinical studies showed little benefit for participants, most of whom were white. A two-year study of the drug involving 1,050 African Americans, however, revealed not only lower death rates but also a 33-percent reduction in first hospitalizations for heart failure. At year-end, NitroMed was awaiting FDA approval to market the drug.

Some medical experts applauded the idea of tailoring medical treatments to groups most likely to benefit from them. Others, however, worried about the effects of treatment based on appearance or stated ethnic group. They argued that race is an arbitrary distinction with no biological basis and treatment should focus on genetic factors instead.   ■ Barbara A. Mayes

See also **AIDS; Health care issues; Medicine.**

Eastern Orthodox Churches.

Orthodox Christians in Africa in 2004 mourned the death of their spiritual leader, the Patriarch of Alexandria, Petros VII. Petros was killed on September 11 when a Greek government helicopter on which he and 16 other people were traveling crashed into the Aegean Sea. The group was on its way to the monastic community of Mount Athos in northern Greece.

Ecumenical Patriarchate. A long-festering dispute between the Ecumenical Patriarchate of Constantinople, based in Istanbul, Turkey, and the Orthodox Church of Greece about supervision of local *metropolises* (dioceses) in Greece reached a crisis in 2004. In April, Ecumenical Patriarch Bartholomew I—the acknowledged spiritual leader of the estimated 200 million Orthodox Christians throughout the world—suspended relations with the Greek Orthodox Church. Greek government officials resolved the issue through mediation.

Jerusalem. The Israeli government recognized Eirenaios I as the Greek Orthodox Patriarch of Jerusalem in March 2004. Eirenaios had been elected Patriarch in 2001. However, his selection required the approval of the secular rulers of the nations of the Holy Land. The government of Jordan and the Palestinian Authority approved the appointment, but Israel long refused to grant approval because of Eirenaios's perceived support of the Palestinians.

Russia. In February 2004, meetings between representatives of the Russian Orthodox Church and the Vatican were held in Moscow in an

Russian Orthodox worshippers gather in Holy Trinity Cathedral in St. Petersburg in June to venerate the Tikhvin Mother of God icon. According to tradition, the icon was painted by St. Luke. It was returned to Russia in 2004, after decades in the United States, where it had been taken for safekeeping after the Russian Revolution of 1917.

attempt to better relations. Russian Orthodox leaders had accused the Roman Catholic Church of aggressive *proselytizing* (attempting to win converts) in the traditionally Orthodox nation.

United States. A group of lay worshipers sued the Greek Orthodox Archdiocese of America, headquartered in New York City, in February 2004, claiming that church leaders had violated the group's 1978 charter by creating a new one in 2002. The old charter gave American laity more power. In August 2004, the New York State Supreme Court dismissed the lawsuit, stating that the church is a hierarchy and, as such, has the right to make decisions regarding its organization.

Greece. Archbishop Christodoulos announced in September 2004 that, for a trial period, modern Greek would be used in the Divine Liturgy in Athens. Church leaders hoped that the switch from Byzantine Greek, the old form of the national language, would attract more young people to the services.

Cuba. President Fidel Castro turned over the key to the government-built Greek Orthodox Cathedral of St. Nicholas in Havana to Patriarch Bartholomew I in January 2004. Cuba had officially been an atheist nation since Castro's take-over in 1959, but the government had since removed references to atheism from the country's constitution.
∎ Stanley Samuel Harakas

Economics. The world economy underwent such widespread growth in 2004 that, for the first time in years, regional economies were competing for industrial raw materials and bidding up the price of many *commodities* (natural resources that are traded in markets). Central banks—institutions that control money supply and interest rates for national or multinational areas—began to raise interest rates to curb growth. For several years prior to 2004, most central banks had been cutting their interest rates to encourage economic growth.

Meanwhile, steep price rises for crude oil and related fuels began to exert a brake on the pace of economic growth in mid- to late-2004. Some economists began to see fuel costs as a potential drag on world economies in 2005.

Tightening commodities. Heightened competition tightened supply of a number of commodities in the global market in 2004. A major factor in the scramble for resources, according to economists, was especially strong demand from China. The huge East Asian country, with a population of 1.2 billion, invested heavily in industrial projects as its economy boomed. The competition for both materials and services helped bid up worldwide prices for oil, steel, and other key materials and strained freight transportation systems already limited in capacity and struggling to deliver surging volumes of finished goods as well as raw materials.

The crude oil market. On the New York commodities market, crude oil had been priced at under $35 a barrel in January 2004. The price hit a record high of $48.70 a barrel on August 19 before sliding and then rising again. In October, the price hit a new peak at nearly $56 a barrel. Analysts said that strong worldwide demand, tight supplies, and uncertainty in the Middle East—especially in Iraq—were strong factors in high oil prices. In the United States, Hurricane Ivan's rampage through the eastern Gulf of Mexico in September put pressure on oil production and distribution systems. However, favorable news about world oil supplies in early December pushed oil prices down sharply, to below $43 a barrel.

Interest rates. Against the backdrop of strengthened demand, capacity constraints, and intense resource competition, major central banks raised interest rates repeatedly during 2004 to avert overheating of economies. The Federal Reserve Bank (the Fed), the central bank of the United States, posted its first interest-rate hike in four years on June 30; it raised the short-term rate one-quarter of a percent. The Fed followed up with three more rate quarter-point hikes as the year progressed.

Global outlook. The International Monetary Fund (IMF)—a United Nations-affiliated organization that provides short-term credit to member nations—forecast in September that global economic output would increase by 5 percent for 2004, after gains of 3.9 percent in 2003 and 3 percent in 2002. The forecast was part of the organization's "World Economic Outlook," an analysis of world economic trends prepared twice a year by IMF economists. The report also predicted that the pace of global economic growth would slow slightly to a still-strong rate of 4.3 percent in 2005. However, if oil prices remained high or resumed an upward spiral, IMF economists warned, worldwide economic growth could slow still further.

World economies. Although growth in the U.S. economy was uneven in 2004, the IMF forecast a solid 4.3-percent increase in the nation's gross domestic product (GDP)—the value of all goods and services produced in a country in a year—for the whole of 2004. The manufacturing sector of the U.S. economy grew throughout 2004, but the pace of expansion slowed in the second half of the year, due mainly to increased fuel costs and price inflation of other commodities. For 2005, the IMF forecast a slightly more modest 3.5-percent increase in GDP for the United States.

SELECTED KEY U.S. ECONOMIC INDICATORS

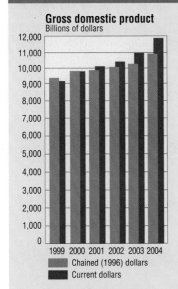

Gross domestic product
Billions of dollars

1999 2000 2001 2002 2003 2004

■ Chained (1996) dollars
■ Current dollars

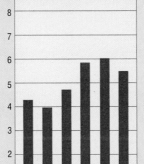
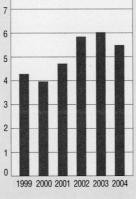

Unemployment rate
Percent of labor force

1999 2000 2001 2002 2003 2004

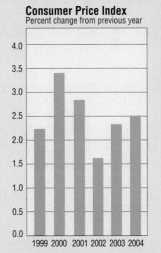

Consumer Price Index
Percent change from previous year

1999 2000 2001 2002 2003 2004

Sources: U.S. Department of Commerce and U.S. Department of Labor, except 2004 figures, which are estimates from The Conference Board.

The gross domestic product (GDP) measures the value in current prices of all goods and services produced within a country in a year. Many economists believe the GDP is an accurate measure of the nation's total economic performance. Chained dollars show the amount adjusted for inflation. The unemployment rate is the percentage of the total labor force that is unemployed and actively seeking work. The Consumer Price Index measures inflation by showing the change in prices of selected goods and services consumed by urban families and individuals.

The two biggest economies in East Asia, China and Japan, performed strongly in 2004. IMF economists forecast that the huge economy of China would grow by 9 percent in 2004, just slightly behind its growth rate for 2003. In its September "World Economic Outlook," the IMF singled out China as a major engine of world economic growth, along with the United States. Japan, after years of economic stagnation, would post a healthy 4.4-percent rate of growth for 2004, IMF economists forecast. In 2003, Japan's economy had grown by 2.5 percent.

Another huge Asian economy, India, surged in 2004. Economists forecast a 6.4-percent growth rate—down from the 8-percent rate of 2003, but still impressive. Analysts said that exceptionally strong performance in the manufacturing and service sectors was driving India's economic engine.

Many other world regions experienced economic growth in 2004. Most Latin American countries improved on previous lackluster years. The largest economies in the region, Argentina, Brazil, Chile, and Mexico, all grew at rates of 4 percent or higher in 2004.

IMF economists, in the September "World Economic Outlook," advised government officials in Latin America to "seize the moment" to introduce fiscal reforms to reduce their nation's debt levels. The economists noted that solid economic growth and relatively positive global economic conditions in 2004 created unusually favorable conditions for Latin American policymakers.

Nations of central and eastern Europe maintained solid economic growth or improved on earlier weakness in 2004. According to IMF forecasts, the Russian economy would grow by 7.3 percent in 2004 and 6.6 percent in 2005.

Similarly, most countries in the Middle East and Africa conformed to the global trend of economic growth. In sub-Saharan Africa, IMF economists forecast GDP growth of nearly 5 percent for 2004 and predicted a 5.8-percent rate of growth for 2005.

The lackluster Eurozone. While all world regions experienced recovery in 2004, IMF economists reported that recovery in the Eurozone—the group of 12 EU member nations using the euro as their common currency—was "relatively weak." Economies in the Eurozone were heavily dependent on the stimulus of foreign demand, the economists noted. Economic growth in Germany—Europe's largest national economy and a member of the Eurozone—would reach just 2 percent in 2004 following a 0.1-percent decline in 2003, the IMF economists forecast.

■ John D. Boyd

See also **Bank; Energy supply; Interna-tional trade; Manufacturing.**

Ecuador. In November 2004, President Lucio Edwin Gutierrez narrowly avoided being impeached by Ecuador's Congress, where his leftist Patriotic Society Party held just 6 of 100 seats. The effort to remove the president failed by only three votes. Gutierrez was accused of being responsible for corruption and unlawful use of government vehicles by his party's candidates.

In August, inspectors began sampling the soil and groundwater in La Joya de las Sachas, a village in Ecuador's eastern Amazonian region, as part of a trial against ChevronTexaco Inc., the United States oil giant. The trial was to determine whether the company would be forced to pay an estimated $6 billion to clean up pollution in the region, where it maintained oil-drilling operations between 1972 and 1992. The plaintiffs in the case were 88 local residents representing some 30,000 subsistence farmers.

Oil industry spokespeople blamed disputes between foreign oil companies and President Gutierrez in 2004 for Ecuador's failure to realize the potential of the recently completed trans-Andean pipeline. The pipeline, which linked Amazonian oil fields with ports on the Pacific coast, carried only about 180,000 barrels a day in 2004—far less than the 450,000 barrels for which it was designed. ■ Nathan A. Haverstock

See also **Latin America.**

Education. About 48.2 million students enrolled in public schools in the United States in 2004, in pre-kindergarten through 12th grade, as record numbers of immigrants and the children of post-World War II *baby boomers* (people born between 1946 and 1964) showed up for classes. The U.S. Department of Education, which had been predicting that enrollment would peak in the early 2000's, forecast that the number of school children would continue to grow until at least 2013, when, it predicted, 49.7 million children would enroll in public schools. In addition, 6.3 million students enrolled in private schools in 2004, an increase of 1 million in three years. Another 1.1 million students were home schooled, an increase of about 250,000 since the Education Department's 1999 home schooling survey.

College enrollment rose to an estimated record 14.1 million students in 2004. As the baby bulge worked its way through school, the Education Department predicted that college enrollment would reach 15.6 million in 2013. Four-year colleges and universities enrolled 56 percent of those students, while the rest attended two-year junior and community colleges. Public colleges enrolled about 80 percent of all students, and 57 percent of students were women.

No Child Left Behind, the federal government's sweeping school-reform law, underwent another rocky year in 2004. The law, which was signed by President George W. Bush in 2002, required the states to give mathematics and reading tests to public school children in grades 3 through 8. Each state was allowed to define what "proficient" meant and set yearly improvement goals. Schools were judged by the percentage of children who tested proficient in each subject, with a goal of having all children reach proficiency by 2014. Schools that failed to meet yearly learning requirements for two years in a row were required to allow their students to transfer to a better-performing public school, with the home school paying their transportation bills. After three years, failing schools were to offer students private tutors; and after five years, such schools faced being closed and reopened with a new staff and curriculum.

Problems arose because the law required schools to "disaggregate" students by race and gender and by whether the students are English-language learners, poor, or in special education classes. All subgroups must make equal progress toward proficiency goals. The Education Department relaxed the requirements for English-language learners and learning-disabled students in 2004. However, it was still fairly easy for a school to miss its goal. If not enough Hispanic third-graders passed reading or not enough white fifth-graders passed math, for example, the whole school could be held "in need of improvement."

Another part of the No Child Left Behind law required that all teachers in all public schools be "highly qualified" by the 2005-2006 school year. The definition of "highly qualified" was left up to each state. University of Pennsylvania education professor Richard Ingersoll reported that, based on a survey of staffing for the 1999-2000 school year, 44 percent of middle-school classes are assigned to teachers who do not have either a college major or minor in the subject they teach. In their teacher-quality reports to the Education Department in 2004, however, the states varied widely in the percentage of their classes taught by highly qualified teachers—Wisconsin reported 98 percent; California, 48 percent; and Alaska, 16 percent.

The testing requirements, high rates of school failure, and the cost of providing new services to struggling schools fanned opposition to No Child Left Behind in state legislatures. In their 2004 legislative sessions, 20 states introduced resolutions or bills opposing the law. Democrats in the U.S. Congress also attacked U.S. President George W. Bush over No Child Left Behind, charging that his administration did not budget sufficient funds to help schools reach the law's goals. The administration countered that since President Bush came to office, he has increased school spending to $38.7 billion in the fiscal year that began in October 2004. Nevertheless, both parties in Congress continued to support the law.

Voucher supporters experienced both setbacks and victory in 2004. In February, the U.S. Supreme Court ruled that the state of Washington was within its rights to refuse a taxpayer-funded college scholarship to a student who was studying to be a minister. Constitutions in Washington and in 36 other states ban public spending on religious education. The U.S. Supreme Court ruled in 2002 that publicly funded vouchers could be used to pay tuition at religious schools, but amendments in the state constitutions helped stall the passage of voucher laws in the legislatures.

Colorado was the only state to have passed a voucher law since the high court's ruling. However, in June 2004, the Colorado Supreme Court overturned that plan, which would have paid $4,500 in private-school tuition for low-income students from failing schools. The court ruled that the law stripped local school boards of control over their students' education.

In November, an appeals court struck down Florida's first-in-the-nation voucher plan on the grounds that it violated the state constitution by allowing taxpayer money to be spent on religious schools. Nevertheless, vouchers were allowed to be used by about 700 students in 2004 while the Florida Supreme Court prepared to make a final decision.

In a victory for vouchers, the U.S. Congress agreed in January to fund a $14-million voucher program for Washington, D.C., students. That program was the first ever financed by the federal government and paid up to $7,500 in private-school tuition for children from low-income families. Congressional supporters had predicted that up to 1,600 children a year would receive vouchers, but private schools enrolled only 1,000 voucher students in September, one-quarter of whom had already been attending private schools.

College admissions test scores rose slightly in 2004. On the College Board's SAT exam, which is most popular with students on the East and West coasts, the average math score fell 1 point from 2003, to 518 out of a possible 800. The score on the verbal test rose 1 point, to 508. The combined average score—1026—thus remained the same as the year before. On ACT Inc.'s ACT exam, which is most commonly used in the Midwest and in the mountain states, the composite national average was 20.9 out of a possible 36 in 2004, up from 20.8 in the previous year. Scores on the English, math, reading, and science tests, which make up the four-part ACT, each rose 0.1 point. Both tests were to add writing exams in 2005.

■ June Kronholz

See also **Education: A Special Report; Supreme Court of the United States.**

BROKEN PROMISES: THE CRISIS IN HIGHER EDUCATION

By June Kronholz

By 2004, educators were already calling it "the college crisis." In an increasingly knowledge-based economy, a college education had never been more important. Yet at the same time, getting into college had never been more difficult, and paying for it had become tougher than ever. Public universities in the United States had long made an implicit promise to high school students: "Work hard, get good grades, and we'll welcome you to campus." With the college-age population growing, state budgets under stress, and tuition rising, that promise had begun to fray.

The U.S. Department of Education estimated that 14.1 million undergraduates were enrolled in degree-granting two- or four-year colleges in 2004, up from 10.6 million in 1984. The number of college students was expected to grow annually, reaching about 15.6 million in 2013. The increase has been fueled primarily by *echo boomers,* the children of the post-World War II baby boom generation (people born between 1946 and 1964), and by record-high immigration. The number of babies born each year increased about 32 percent between 1975 and 1990, when it peaked. Meanwhile, the immigrant population nearly tripled between 1970 and 2000.

Population growth has not been the only factor causing the enrollment boom. The value of a college education had spiraled since the 1970's, as jobs began requiring advanced skills. The U.S. Census Bureau estimated that employees with a college education could expect to earn an average $49,900 in 2003, compared with $30,800 for those with only a high school diploma. Even workers who attended college for only one year could expect to earn almost $5,000 more annually than high school graduates. College graduates were also about half as likely to be unemployed as high school graduates.

Such statistics lured record numbers of laid-off workers back to school in search of new skills and prompted young people who once might have gone straight from high school to a job or marriage to enroll in college. The Department of Education reported that about two-thirds of high school graduates enrolled directly in college in 2001, compared with one-half of graduates in 1980.

More and more students are competing for limited spaces—and limited funds— at U.S. colleges and universities. Who deserves to get in?

Women led the rush to campus as their career opportunities expanded. About 8 million women enrolled in college in fall 2004, compared with about 5.5 million in 1980. Enrollment of women was expected to increase to an estimated 8.9 million in 2013. Minority enrollment also rose. About 55 percent of African American high school graduates enrolled in college in 2001, compared with 40 percent in 1980. The share of Hispanics going to college stalled at about half of all Hispanic high school graduates in 2002. Nevertheless, the number of

The author:

June Kronholz is a reporter for *The Wall Street Journal* and has written extensively on education issues.

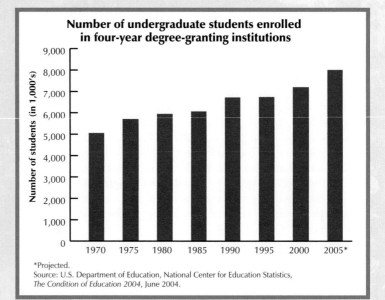

Number of undergraduate students enrolled in four-year degree-granting institutions

*Projected.
Source: U.S. Department of Education, National Center for Education Statistics, *The Condition of Education 2004*, June 2004.

The number of undergraduate students enrolled in four-year colleges and universities rose significantly between 1970 and the early 2000's.

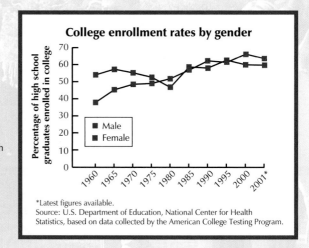

College enrollment rates by gender

*Latest figures available.
Source: U.S. Department of Education, National Center for Health Statistics, based on data collected by the American College Testing Program.

While the percentage of male high school graduates who enrolled in college increased only slightly between 1960 and 2001—from 54 percent to 59.7 percent—the percentage of female graduates who enrolled jumped from 37.9 percent to 63.6 percent.

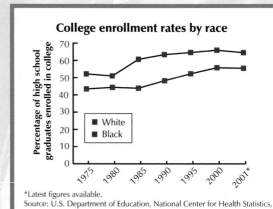

College enrollment rates by race

*Latest figures available.
Source: U.S. Department of Education, National Center for Health Statistics, based on data collected by the American College Testing Program.

College enrollment rates among both white and black students increased during the 1990's. By 2001, 64.2 percent of white high school graduates and 54.6 percent of black high school graduates were enrolling in college, compared with 51.1 percent of whites and 41.7 percent of blacks in 1975.

Hispanics enrolled in college had doubled between 1980 and 2000, to 159,000.

Meanwhile, the number of part-time students rose as young people increasingly worked their way through school, juggled families and classes, or returned to school for additional courses. Just under 5.5 million students enrolled to study part-time in fall 2004, compared with slightly fewer than 8.7 million students attending school full-time. Part-time students generally take six years or more to finish a four-year course. As they stay longer on campus, they crowd out new students trying to get in.

Increased competition for spaces

The University of Michigan at Ann Arbor received 26,000 applications for 5,553 seats in the 2003 freshman class; the University of Virginia in Charlottesville received 14,800 applications for 3,100 spots; and the University of Texas at Austin turned away three applicants for each of the 6,500 students it enrolled. Administrators in Florida, Texas, and Virginia, among others, began diverting qualified students to community colleges, deferring some student admissions to later in the year, or turning students away altogether. For decades, the California State University system had promised to enroll all students who graduated in the top third of their class, while the University of California system was open to those in the top one-eighth. In 2003, California administrators announced that the California State University system would start rejecting qualified applicants in fall 2004. After last-minute negotiations with the state legislature, the system announced

Although the number of students applying to the University of California's various campuses rose sharply between 1995 and 2003, the number admitted did not increase significantly at all locations.

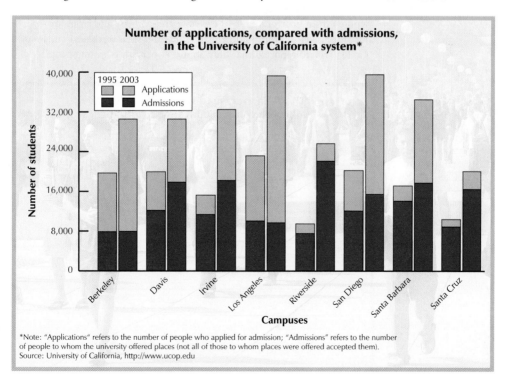

Number of applications, compared with admissions, in the University of California system*

Y-axis: Number of students (0; 8,000; 16,000; 24,000; 32,000; 40,000)

Legend: 1995 2003 Applications / Admissions

X-axis (Campuses): Berkeley, Davis, Irvine, Los Angeles, Riverside, San Diego, Santa Barbara, Santa Cruz

*Note: "Applications" refers to the number of people who applied for admission; "Admissions" refers to the number of people to whom the university offered places (not all of those to whom places were offered accepted them).
Source: University of California, http://www.ucop.edu

that 7,500 rejected applicants would be accepted after all, but only in spring 2005. (The problem was not as acute in states with slow-growing populations and in regional universities—North and South Dakota, Maine, and Montana all expected their number of high school graduates to drop in the 2000's; nor did smaller state universities without national reputations face enrollment gluts.)

The increased competition for seats naturally benefited better-prepared students. The University of Virginia disclosed that 85 percent of its 2003 freshmen had graduated in the top one-tenth of their high school class, and the University of Michigan reported that half of its freshman class had scored between 1200 and 1410 on the 1600-point SAT college admissions exam.

The increased competition also raised the prospect of college campuses increasingly filling up with white, middle-class students from suburban households. The New York City-based College Board and the Iowa City, Iowa-based ACT Inc.—owners of the two major college-admissions tests—reported that white test takers are more likely than minorities to have the sort of qualifications to get them into college: the completion of advanced-math courses; high grade-point averages; and high test scores. Children whose parents have a college education and earn more than $80,000 a year—a profile that fits more whites than minorities—do best of all on the tests. The College Board also reported that suburban students outscored rural students 1066 to 1009 on the SAT in 2004, while students from big cities scored 1000.

A 2003 U.S. Supreme Court decision allowed public universities to consider race when deciding whom to admit. Most universities also looked for geographic and economic diversity—that is, young men and women from different parts of the state and country and from low-income as well as from middle-class households. Nevertheless, the College Board reported that only about 54 percent of young people

The average cost of tuition and fees soared at private four-year colleges and universities between the mid-1970's and 2004. Costs at public four-year colleges and universities rose as well, though not as dramatically.

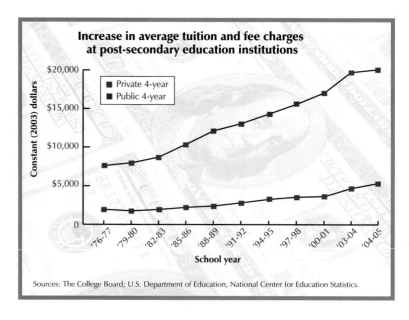

Increase in average tuition and fee charges at post-secondary education institutions

■ Private 4-year
■ Public 4-year

Constant (2003) dollars

School year

Sources: The College Board; U.S. Department of Education, National Center for Education Statistics.

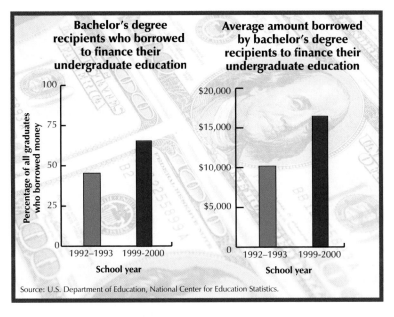

Bachelor's degree recipients who borrowed to finance their undergraduate education

Percentage of all graduates who borrowed money

School year

Average amount borrowed by bachelor's degree recipients to finance their undergraduate education

School year

Source: U.S. Department of Education, National Center for Education Statistics.

The percentage of bachelor's degree recipients who borrowed money to finance their education increased from 46.4 percent during the 1992-1993 school year to 63.4 percent during the 1999-2000 school year (the latest for which figures were available). The average amount of money that bachelor's degree recipients borrowed to finance their education increased from $10,300 in the 1992-1993 school year to $16,800 in the 1999-2000 school year.

from low-income families attended college in 2001, compared with about 82 percent from high-income families.

Rising costs

As colleges became harder to enter, they also became more expensive. The College Board reported that in the 2004-2005 academic year, tuition averaged $5,132 at public four-year colleges, which educate about 80 percent of U.S. undergraduates. The 2004-2005 figure represented a 10.5-percent increase over the 2003-2004 academic year. The average tuition was $3,796 in 2000, when the 2004-2005 college

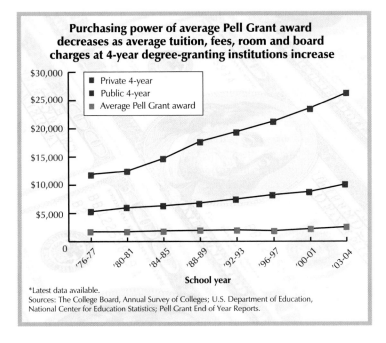

Purchasing power of average Pell Grant award decreases as average tuition, fees, room and board charges at 4-year degree-granting institutions increase

- ■ Private 4-year
- ■ Public 4-year
- ■ Average Pell Grant award

School year

*Latest data available.
Sources: The College Board, Annual Survey of Colleges; U.S. Department of Education, National Center for Education Statistics; Pell Grant End of Year Reports.

Although the average Pell Grant award showed virtually no increase from 1976 to 2003 (in constant dollars), tuition and other associated college costs rose significantly at public and private four-year degree-granting institutions.

freshmen entered high school. When room and board were added, the College Board estimated a year at a public university cost $11,354, while a year at a private college averaged $27,516.

State legislatures generally set public college tuition prices. The more the states give their universities in aid, the lower student tuition bills are. However, the share of college budgets that comes from state funds has been falling for decades. States paid about one-third of state college costs in 2000, down from an average of about one half in 1980.

The states' share of college costs fell even further during the recession that followed the bursting of the stock market bubble in 2000 and the terrorist attacks on the United States on Sept. 11, 2001. States collected less money in taxes, and legislatures reasoned that tuition increases could make up for cuts in state funds. In addition, there was a growing feeling in state capitals that students should shoulder a bigger share of the cost of their education, because of the higher income that education would earn them down the road.

State economies were expected to improve in 2005, but the tuition increases did not appear to be over. A research project at Illinois State University that tracks appropriations to higher education calculated that states collectively cut their funding of higher education by 2.1 percent in their 2004 fiscal year over 2003 and by 4 percent since 1999. With data available from about 40 states, Illinois State reported that higher education appropriations may grow by 1 percent to 2.5 percent in the 2005 fiscal year. But some states, including Michigan and Minnesota, have announced another year of small cuts, and other states have proposed increases so small that they may not keep up with enrollment growth.

Increase in student aid

There was one bright spot amid rising college costs. A record $122 billion was available in student aid in the 2003-2004 school year, up 11 percent from the year before. Full-time students, including graduate students, received an average $10,500 each in aid, or about $1,000 more than in 2002-2003, according to the College Board. The silver lining came wrapped in a fairly dark cloud, however. Just 38 percent of the aid—about $4,000 per student—was awarded as grants in 2003-2004, down from 46 percent in 1993-1994. Another 56 percent of the aid was in the form of loans, which must be repaid. Work-study earnings accounted for 1 percent of aid, and the remaining 5 percent was in the form of credits that the parents of low- and middle-income families could take against their taxes.

The federal government's major commitment to student grant aid is the Pell Grant program, which in 2003-2004 provided 5.1 million low-income students with $12.7 billion to help pay for college. Federal spending for Pell Grants nearly doubled between 1995 and 2003. However, because of the weak economy after 2000, the number of students qualifying for aid also increased—by 1.2 million between the 2000-2001 and the 2003-2004 school years. The average Pell Grant—$2,466 in 2003-2004—covered less than one-quarter of a year's tuition, fees, and room and board at a public university, down from about one half in 1975-1976. It covered less than 9 percent of expenses at a private university.

The states and individual colleges and universities increased their aid

as tuition rose, but much of that money was merit-based aid rather than need-based. About half of the states had programs in 2004 that rewarded good students with free or reduced tuition. These programs are designed to encourage students to remain residents after graduation, raising the education level of the workforce and attracting employers. Georgia's Hope Scholarships, for example, paid full tuition at one of the state's public universities, or partial tuition at an in-state private college, to any Georgia high school student who graduated with a B average. Florida's Bright Futures scholarships paid three-quarters of the tuition at the state's public universities and partial tuition at its private universities for students with a B average and an SAT score of 970 or an ACT score of 20. The National Association of State Student Grant and Aid Programs, which tracks state-funded student aid, reported that in the 2002-2003 school year, states gave undergraduate students $1.9 billion in aid based at least in part on merit. That figure was down slightly from the year before, but up from $1.2 billion in 1998-1999. Of all state-based undergraduate aid, the group noted, 22 percent was based on student qualities other than need.

Colleges and universities also frequently used their own scholarship money to attract students with good grades or special talents, regardless of need. Top-level students attract other top students and top-flight teachers, who in turn attract research grants and big gifts from alumni. Private colleges in 2000 paid out about $4 in scholarships for every $10 they took in as tuition revenue—up from $2.70 in 1990. Two-thirds of that aid was non-need based. Public universities also gave two-thirds of their aid for reasons other than need.

Loan increases are not the answer

Federal student loans, which must be repaid after students graduate, made up about $55.5 billion of all student aid in the 2003-2004 school year. Any student who is a U.S. citizen (or a non-citizen who meets

A new laboratory facility, the Neuroscience Research Building, rises on the Westwood campus of the University of California at Los Angeles in 2004. Some colleges hoped that modern facilities would attract more academically gifted students to campus, which in turn would result in greater alumni support. Nevertheless, most colleges could not afford major new building projects.

certain criteria) is entitled to a federal loan. For low-income families, the government defers interest while the student is in school. In 2002, 6.2 million students attended college on federal student loans. However, the loans did not stretch as far as they once did.

A freshman in 2004 was allowed to borrow a maximum of $2,625, and the loan limit was to increase slightly each subsequent school year. But in 2004 the freshman loan covered less than 25 percent of average yearly costs at a public college and less than 10 percent at a private school. President George W. Bush proposed lifting the federal loan limit to $3,000 during his 2004 re-election campaign, but even student groups were cool to that plan. Raising the loan limit would raise student indebtedness. About two-thirds of students borrow to help pay for their education. Students who completed public four-year colleges or universities in 2002 graduated with an average of $16,800 in federal student-loan debt.

A park ranger at the John Day Fossil Beds National Monument headquarters near Dayville, Oregon, participates in an online course at Eastern Oregon University. By the early 2000's, about 90 percent of U.S. colleges and universities offered such courses, which helped many students hold down jobs while attending school and also somewhat eased overcrowding on campuses.

The shortage of grant and scholarship funds has forced more students to work their way through school. The U. S. Department of Education reported in 2004 that about 80 percent of U.S. college students held jobs. According to the Government Accountability Office (GAO), about half of those students worked 25 or more hours per week. The GAO added that the more students work, the less likely they are to graduate. About 66 percent of students who work fewer than 20 hours a week graduate. The rate drops to 28 percent for students who work 32 hours a week or more.

All of these factors have created a devastating effect on the ability of low- and moderate-income students to attend college. The College Board estimated that total annual charges at a public university in 2003 represented 70 percent of the annual income of a family making less

than $25,000, compared with about 40 percent in 1975. Even for families making between $43,000 and $65,000, a year in college took 20 percent of annual income.

In 2002, a Department of Education advisory committee on financial aid warned that 400,000 students who were qualified to attend four-year colleges could not afford to attend. Of those, 170,000 could not afford even a community college. Between 2001 and 2010, an estimated 2 million qualified students would not be able to attend college. "For the nation, the loss of human capital will exact a serious economic and social toll for much of this century," the committee added in its final report, which carried the title, *Empty Promises: The Myth of College Access in America.*

How colleges are dealing with the problem

Colleges have acknowledged that they face problems, both in finding places for all the students who want to attend and in helping them pay for their education. Universities in some states began efforts to increase the number of students they could admit by using their campuses more efficiently. The University of Oregon, for example, tried to ease the strain on crowded buildings by offering discounts to students who took classes at unpopular times; for example, late afternoons or early mornings. Florida State University and other state universities in Florida required students to attend classes during the summer—traditionally a time when many students work instead of attending school—during at least one of their years in college. The University of California system encouraged students to spend their freshman and sophomore years at one of the state's community colleges. However, California's community colleges were already full, and juggling classroom use and schedules only marginally eased the crowding.

Building new campuses was hugely expensive and an option for very few colleges. The federal government had stopped underwriting the kind of campus construction it had engaged in after World War II (1939-1945) or in the 1960's, when record numbers of war veterans and, later, their baby-boomer offspring, enrolled. The University of California, with 200,000 students, planned to add a tenth campus, in Merced, in 2005. Arizona State University, with 55,000 students, planned to double enrollment by building an additional campus in Phoenix.

New campuses were exceptions, however, and even they were not expected to relieve the pressure for college seats in the fastest-growing states. The Western Interstate Commission for Higher Education, a regional association made up of 15 member states based in Boulder, Colorado, predicted that California's public high schools will graduate 375,000 students in 2008, up from about 350,000 in 2005 and 250,000 in 1994. The commission predicted similarly rapid growth for Arizona—73,000 graduates in 2018, or almost 50 percent more than in 2005. In both states, more than half those graduates were expected to come from families earning less than $50,000 a year.

Many colleges tried to accommodate more students in less space through the use of "distance learning," or online courses. The U.S.

Department of Education reported that about 90 percent of two-year and four-year public colleges and universities offered online courses in 2000-2001. Students enrolled in 2.9 million such college-level online courses. Only about half those public colleges, however, offered degree programs that students could take entirely online—that is, at half the schools, students were still required to take some on-campus courses. Many of those online programs also offered only graduate degrees or professional certificates. Only about one-fifth of colleges that had distance-education programs offered an undergraduate degree that a student could take entirely online.

Congress offered only modest proposals for increasing the number of college seats. In 2004, Republicans proposed extending federal student loans to students at for-profit colleges—including vocational and trade schools—and to online colleges. Legislators also suggested making it easier to transfer credits from for-profit schools to non-profit colleges. The idea was to make for-profit schools, which tend to be more expensive than public universities, more attractive to students, reducing the pressure on public universities.

Some colleges tried to make themselves more affordable to more students by raising their fees and using the extra funds for aid to low-income students. Miami University in Oxford, Ohio, adopted a policy in 2003 in which both in-state and out-of-state students paid the same tuition. All Ohio students received an automatic $5,000 yearly "residency" scholarship. Some students were then awarded other scholarships—funded with the additional tuition funds—to help offset the remainder of the $4,000 tuition increase. Private colleges have had a long-standing practice of stating their tuition price in public literature but then "discounting" it heavily for students they want to attract. Whether such discounts—which tend to go to high-achieving and minority students—would be politically acceptable at public universities supported by tax dollars remained to be seen.

Ways the government may help

In 2004, Congress also considered the idea of punishing colleges that institute big tuition increases by withholding some federal student aid. Colleges campaigned against the idea, calling it "price control" and pointing out that students would bear the brunt of the punishment. In an attempt to soften the proposal, Republicans suggested requiring colleges to rate themselves on an "affordability index" that would compare their tuition increases against the inflation rate. Such an index may create public pressure on the colleges to keep any tuition increases smaller.

In fact, there is little Congress can do about college bills without deepening the federal deficit. Democrats in Congress and on the campaign trail called for major boosts in Pell Grant funding, but so many students qualified for the loans in the 2003 school year that the program was $2.7 billion short, according to the Department of Education. That figure was expected to climb to $3.7 billion in the 2004 school year. Raising grants enough to cover just the increase in tuition, room, and board in 2004 would cost another $4.6 billion.

Even letting students borrow more to pay for college would be costly because the government would have to borrow the money and pay interest on it. The government in 2002-2003 guaranteed about $42 billion in annual student loans and allowed many students to defer their interest payments until they graduated. President Bush campaigned for reelection on a promise to allow students to borrow up to $30,000 over their college careers, up from $23,000. Even doing that would cost the government $20 billion over 10 years, the Congressional Budget Office stated.

The "college crisis"—the fact that middle-class voters felt squeezed by college costs—was not lost in 2004 on either President Bush or Senator John Kerry, his Democratic challenger. On the campaign trail, President Bush talked about offering an extra $1,000 Pell Grant to students who would take "rigorous" courses in high school. In his 2004 State of the Union message, the president asked Congress for $33 million for the program, but that sum would cover only 33,000 of the 14.1 million students who attended college in 2004. The president also campaigned on a pledge to give community colleges an additional $250 million. However, the money was aimed at developing job-retraining programs, not at building classrooms and campuses, and would not go far among the country's 1,200 community colleges.

Kerry promoted a $13-billion plan that would pay the college costs of 200,000 students who would work for two years in "troubled schools," on "improving our homeland security," or in such jobs as elder care or "keeping our water and parks more clean." Another 300,000 students would get college aid in return for helping in pre-school, reading, and college-readiness programs. Kerry planned to pay for those public-service jobs by changing the role that commercial banks play in the student-loan program.

Students borrow money for college either directly from the government or from banks, with the government guaranteeing and subsidizing both kinds of loans. Critics of that system say commercial banks earn huge profits from student loans. Kerry's plan was to make the banks bid for the right to offer the loans, thereby paying the federal government for the business. The banks, however, had powerful supporters in Congress who had derailed other changes to the student-loan program, and Kerry did not say how he would get his program passed.

Ironically, the two candidates' plans to improve public elementary and high schools promised to make the college crisis even worse. President Bush's campaign pointed out that for every 100 ninth graders, only 68 graduate on time, 38 go on to college, and 18 earn a degree. The numbers for minority students were even worse. However, as state and federal education-reform efforts begin to work, high school graduation rates are likely to increase, producing even more college-ready students than educators had anticipated.

That would be good news, of course. Education is the bedrock on which American prosperity is built. It is the great equalizer in a diverse, melting-pot society and a vehicle for upward mobility. But for many students in the early 2000's, a college education was becoming a far-off goal. In many ways, America would become a poorer country if they never reached it.

Egypt. On July 14, 2004, Egyptian President Hosni Mubarak presided over the swearing in of a new Cabinet headed by Prime Minister Ahmad Nazif. Fourteen of the 34 ministers were new to the government.

Prime Minister Nazif emphasized the importance to Egypt's economy of continuing to develop modern information technology, noting that tens of thousands of Egyptians were working and training in the field. He also pledged that his Cabinet would tackle the persistent problem of high unemployment, as well as the low wages of the 6.5 million employees of the public sector.

Nazif said the solutions for these problems would come through better promotion of private enterprise in Egypt's economy.

Terrorist attacks. Three car bombings on October 7 in resort areas on the Red Sea left at least 35 people dead and more than 160 others wounded. The Taba Hilton, a hotel frequented by Israeli tourists, sustained the largest blast. Most terrorism experts believed that the Islamic terrorist network al-Qa'ida was behind the bombings.

Israeli-Palestinian peace process. President Mubarak dispatched Umar Sulayman, the head of the Egyptian Intelligence Service, to the West Bank and Israel in June to meet with top Palestinian and Israeli officials. The officials discussed the many roadblocks to peace.

In April, President Mubarak met with United States President George W. Bush at Bush's ranch in Crawford, Texas. The main subject of discussion

The restored *sarcophagus* (stone coffin) of Pharaoh Ramses VI in his tomb in Egypt's ancient Valley of the Kings was unveiled in March. Archaeologists believe that tomb robbers shattered the sarcophagus to get to golden ornaments that likely had been placed on the mummified remains of the king, who ruled during the mid-1100's B.C. Restorers from Egypt, Canada, and the United States reconstructed the elaborate coffin by piecing together some 250 stone fragments.

was the proposed Israeli withdrawal from Gaza, a piece of land administered by the Palestinians but also the site of numerous Israeli settlements. President Mubarak told President Bush he considered the impending Israeli withdrawal to be a crucial step in the "roadmap for peace" devised by the so-called Quartet—a group made up of the United States, Russia, the European Union, and the United Nations.

Arafat's funeral. President Mubarak hosted the official funeral of Palestinian leader Yasir Arafat in the Egyptian capital, Cairo, on November 12. A large number of Arab and Muslim leaders—including King Abdullah II of Jordan, President Bashar al-Assad of Syria, and Crown Prince Abdullah of Saudi Arabia—attended the funeral.

Son as successor? The ruling National Democratic Party's annual congress convened in September with President Mubarak's 41-year-old son, Gamal, presiding. Gamal Mubarak, who was the chief of the party's policies committee, had gotten several of his reform-minded supporters appointed to the Cabinet in July. Political observers said the September congress boosted Gamal's prospects to succeed his ailing 76-year-old father as Egypt's president.

■ Marius Deeb

See also **Israel; Middle East.**

Elections.

Elections. The 2004 presidential election in the United States was among the most contentious in modern American history, with President George W. Bush on November 2 realizing a narrow victory over his challenger, Senator John Kerry (D., Massachusetts). President Bush compiled 286 electoral votes, while Kerry finished with 252 electoral votes. The president received 60.6 million popular votes compared with Kerry's 57.2 million. Approximately 119.8 million Americans voted in the presidential election, the largest turnout since 1968.

The nominating process. As an incumbent president, Bush's nomination as the Republican presidential candidate was essentially uncontested. The Republican Party formally nominated him for re-election on Sept. 2, 2004, at the Republican National Convention in New York City. The president once again selected Vice President Dick Cheney as his running mate.

The battle for the Democratic Party's nomination, however, was hotly contested. Former Vermont Governor Howard Dean entered 2004 as the Democratic front runner, outpacing rivals in the polls. As the primary season began, Dean's lead failed to translate into delegates. The first Democratic Party primary, a caucus, was held on January 19 in Iowa, with Kerry winning 38 percent of the vote. Senator John Edwards of North

Carolina took 32 percent; Dean captured 18 percent; U.S. Representative Richard A. Gephardt of Missouri took 11 percent; and U.S. Representative Dennis Kucinich of Ohio mustered 1 percent. Gephardt's poor showing in Iowa prompted him to drop out of the race on January 20.

Kerry's campaign continued to roll with wins on January 27 in New Hampshire and on February 3 in Arizona, Delaware, Missouri, New Mexico, and North Dakota. A retired U.S. Army general and former supreme allied commander of the North Atlantic Treaty Organization, Wesley Clark, won the February 3 Oklahoma primary, while Edwards picked up a victory in the February 3 primary in South Carolina.

Kerry went on to take the February primaries in Maine, Michigan, and Washington state. On February 9, Clark announced that he was abandoning his bid for the nomination. Continued poor showings in primaries held in February prompted Dean to end his quest on February 18. Edwards, who generally finished a distant second to Kerry in most primaries, dropped out of the race on March 3. On March 16, Kerry won the Illinois primary, giving him the delegates needed to secure the Democratic nomination for president.

On July 6, Kerry selected John Edwards as his running mate. The Democratic Party nominated Kerry at its convention in Boston on July 28.

The debates. The candidates clashed in a series of three nationally televised debates. The first, held on October 1 at the University of Miami in Florida, focused on foreign policy and homeland security. The second debate, held October 8 at Washington University in St. Louis, Missouri, featured a town hall format in which audience members asked the candidates a variety of questions, ranging from the war in Iraq to abortion. In the third debate, held October 13 at Arizona State University in Tempe, Arizona, the candidates wrangled over domestic issues.

Too close to call. Polls conducted across the United States in the days leading up to the November election showed that voters appeared to be virtually deadlocked. Among voters who believed it was appropriate for the United States to invade Iraq, President Bush was the clear choice. Those who were against the war, particularly voters in the urban Northeast and Northwest, favored Kerry. Voters who expressed concern over the U.S. economy also tended to favor Kerry. Supporters said they believed Kerry would be the better choice to create jobs and revamp the health care system.

Political fault lines also emerged over moral values, particularly in the South and Midwest. According to exit polls, voters who supported bans on same-sex marriage and abortion tended to support President Bush.

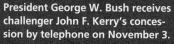

ELECTIONS

President George W. Bush receives challenger John F. Kerry's concession by telephone on November 3.

The 2004 elections tighten Republican control of the United States government.

President George W. Bush, the Republican candidate, defeated Senator John F. Kerry of Massachusetts, the Democratic candidate, in both popular and electoral votes in the Nov. 2, 2004, presidential election. In legislative races, the Republican Party widened its majority in both the House of Representatives and the Senate.

POPULAR VOTES

STATE	BUSH	KERRY
Alabama	1,176,221	693,288
Alaska	151,876	86,064
Arizona	908,211	735,327
Arkansas	566,678	464,157
California	5,114,795	6,250,561
Colorado	1,068,233	960,666
Connecticut	686,923	847,666
Delaware	171,531	199,887
Florida	3,955,656	3,574,509
Georgia	1,890,166	1,345,366
Hawaii	194,109	231,318
Idaho	408,254	180,920
Illinois	2,336,253	2,866,307
Indiana	1,477,807	967,346
Iowa	746,600	733,102
Kansas	717,507	420,846
Kentucky	1,068,741	712,431
Louisiana	1,101,871	819,150
Maine	330,416	395,462
Maryland	951,892	1,223,813
Massachusetts	1,067,163	1,793,916
Michigan	2,310,803	2,475,046
Minnesota	1,345,175	1,443,619
Mississippi	671,084	445,608
Missouri	1,452,715	1,253,879
Montana	265,473	173,363
Nebraska	508,794	251,626
Nevada	414,939	393,372
New Hampshire	330,848	340,019
New Jersey	1,594,204	1,812,956
New Mexico	376,940	370,893
New York	2,798,220	3,998,196
North Carolina	1,911,574	1,484,471
North Dakota	195,998	110,662
Ohio	2,796,147	2,659,664
Oklahoma	959,655	504,077
Oregon	823,210	890,698
Pennsylvania	2,756,904	2,885,773
Rhode Island	161,654	247,407
South Carolina	924,170	650,350
South Dakota	232,545	149,225
Tennessee	1,381,937	1,033,176
Texas	4,518,491	2,825,723
Utah	612,623	227,286
Vermont	120,710	183,621
Virginia	1,667,198	1,400,254
Washington	1,304,894	1,510,201
West Virginia	417,516	322,276
Wisconsin	1,477,122	1,488,935
Wyoming	167,129	70,620

ELECTORAL VOTES

| 286 | George W. Bush | 252 | John F. Kerry |

Wash. 11 · Oregon 7 · Montana 3 · Idaho 4 · Wyoming 3 · North Dakota 3 · South Dakota 3 · Minn. 10 · Wisconsin 10 · Michigan 17 · Vermont 3 · Maine 4 · New York 31 · N.H. 4 · Mass. 12 · R.I. 4 · Conn. 7 · Pennsylvania 21 · New Jersey 15 · Nevada 5 · Utah 5 · Colorado 9 · Nebraska 5 · Iowa 7 · Illinois 21 · Ind. 11 · Ohio 20 · W.Va. 5 · D.C. 3 · Delaware 3 · Maryland 10 · California 55 · Kansas 6 · Missouri 11 · Kentucky 8 · Virginia 13 · North Carolina 15 · Arizona 10 · New Mexico 5 · Oklahoma 7 · Arkansas 6 · Tennessee 11 · South Carolina 8 · Miss. 6 · Alabama 9 · Georgia 15 · Texas 34 · Louisiana 9 · Florida 27 · Alaska 3 · Hawaii 4

Senator John F. Kerry of Massachusetts, the Democratic candidate for U.S. president, speaks with supporters in Boston after conceding defeat in the 2004 election.

HOUSE

Party	Total	Gain/Loss
Republican	232	+3
Democrat	202	-3
Independent	1	0

SENATE

Party	Total	Gain/Loss
Republican	55	+4
Democrat	44	-4
Independent	1	0

Early exit polls indicated that Kerry had the edge. However, as returns rolled in, the race for the presidency tightened, and Kerry conceded on the morning of November 3.

U.S. Senate elections. Republicans expanded the party's control of the U.S. Senate following the November election, gaining four seats to give the party a 55-44 majority. Senator James M. Jeffords of Vermont was an independent and not affiliated with either party. Republicans picked up Senate seats held by Democrats in Florida, Georgia, Louisiana, North Carolina, and South Carolina. Republicans also won hotly contested seats in Alaska, Kentucky, and Oklahoma.

Democratic candidates did win a few major contests in the November election. In Illinois, state Senator Barack Obama won the race to replace Senator Peter Fitzgerald, a Republican, who did not seek re-election. Obama defeated Republican Alan Keyes, a former presidential candidate, in a landslide. Obama had been lauded as one of the party's rising stars after giving a widely applauded keynote speech at the Democratic National Convention. Colorado Attorney General Ken Salazar, a Democrat, defeated Pete Coors to succeed Senator Ben Nighthorse Campbell, a Republican.

Incumbent Democratic senators winning re-election included Evan Bayh of Indiana; Christopher J. Dodd of Connecticut; Byron L. Dorgan of North Dakota; Blanche Lambert Lincoln of Arkansas; Patrick J. Leahy of Vermont; Barbara J. Mikulski of Maryland; Harry M. Reid of Nevada; and Charles E. Schumer of New York.

Republicans claimed several narrow victories in November, enabling the party to increase its control in the Senate. In Kentucky, Senator Jim Bunning narrowly won re-election over Daniel Mongiardo, a Democrat. Bunning saw his once formidable lead in the race evaporate in the weeks before the election but managed to pull out a victory. In Oklahoma, former congressman Tom Coburn, a Republican, won a close election against U.S. Representative Brad Carson (D., Oklahoma) to succeed Senator Don Nickles, a Republican, who did not seek re-election. Senator Lisa Murkowsi (R., Alaska) fended off a challenge by Democrat Tony Knowles, a former Alaska governor.

Handily re-elected incumbents included senators Christopher S. Bond of Missouri; Sam Brownback of Kansas; Charles E. Grassley of Iowa; Judd Gregg of New Hampshire; John McCain III of Arizona; Richard C. Shelby of Alabama; and George V. Voinovich of Ohio.

In Louisiana, U.S. Representative David Vitter, a Republican, was elected to succeed Senator John Breaux, a Democrat. In Georgia, U.S. Representative Johnny Isakson, a Republican, easily won the Senate seat vacated by Senator Zell Miller, a conservative Democrat.

The biggest coup for Republicans took place in South Dakota, where John Thune, a former congressman, defeated Senator Tom Daschle, the leader of the Senate Democrats. Daschle was first elected in 1986 and had been the Democratic leader since 1995.

U.S. House of Representatives. Republicans extended control of the House of Representatives in 2004, gaining a 232 to 202 advantage over Democrats. One independent in the House, Bernard Sanders of Vermont, was also re-elected.

Gubernatorial races. Eleven states elected governors in November. Party control of the governor's office switched in four states, leaving the Republican Party in control of 28 states.

In New Hampshire, Democratic challenger John Lynch unseated Republican Governor Craig Benson. Voters elected West Virginia Secretary of State Joe Manchin III, a Democrat, as the state's next governor. Manchin defeated Republican Monty Warner. In Montana, Democrat Brian Schweitzer edged out Republican Bob Brown in the governor's race. Washington state Attorney General Christine Gregoire, a Democrat, narrowly won the Washington governor's race. She defeated Republican Dino Rossi by 130 votes.

Republican Mitch Daniels, who had served as budget director in the Bush administration, defeated Indiana Governor Joseph Kernan for re-election. Republican Matt Blunt, Missouri's secretary of state, defeated Democrat Claire McCaskill, Missouri's state auditor, in the race for governor. Republican Jon Hunstman, Jr., defeated Democrat Scott Matheson in Utah's gubernatorial contest. Voters re-elected Delaware Governor Ruth Minner and North Carolina Governor Michael Easley, both Democrats. Voters also re-elected North Dakota Governor John Hoeven and Vermont Governor Jim Douglas, both Republicans.

Same-sex marriage bans. Voters in 11 states approved initiatives in November to ban the marriage of same-sex couples. Voters in Arkansas, Georgia, Kentucky, Michigan, Mississippi, Montana, North Dakota, Ohio, Oklahoma, Oregon, and Utah adopted marriage amendments.

Stem cells. Voters in California approved an initiative to spend $3 billion on embryonic stem cell research. Stem cells are taken from human embryos and can develop into any of the different cell types that make up the tissues and organs of the body. Such research has been decried on moral grounds. Supporters counter that the research may hold the potential for important medical advances.   ■ Geoffrey A. Campbell

See also **Congress of the United States; Democratic Party; People in the news** (John Edwards; John Kerry; Barack Obama); **Republican Party; State government; United States, Government of the; United States, President of the.**

Electronics. Digital music devices became one of the bright spots in electronics during 2004. The iPod music player and iTunes music service from Apple Computer, Inc., of Cupertino, California, drove this trend.

Digital music had long been a matter of much concern in the music industry because of the ease with which such music could be copied illegally and then distributed over the Internet. Apple's introduction of the iTunes Music Store in 2003 helped to calm those fears by providing a legal commercial music source online. The Apple iTunes store offered millions of songs, most at a cost of less than $1 apiece. By November 2004, the Apple iTunes store had sold more than 150 million songs. After being launched in Europe in June 2004, the iTunes Music Store sold more than 800,000 songs during its first week of operation.

The iPod itself was an adaptation of computer technology, employing a small hard disk to store up to 10,000 separate songs. The latest versions of the device were introduced in July 2004 and included simplified navigation of stored songs, longer battery life, and more sophisticated software for listening. The new iPods ranged in price from $299 to $399, depending on features, primarily the storage capacity of the player's hard disk.

Apple's iPod proved to be one of the hottest holiday gifts in 2004. Just in time for the Christmas season, a U2 special edition iPod became available to customers in November. Priced at $349, this red-and-black iPod featured, on its flip side, reproductions of autographs from members of the U2 band.

Apple's success with the iPod music player, which dramatically turned around the fortunes of the computer maker, was noticed by the electronics industry and other computer manufacturers. Dell Inc. of Round Rock, Texas, had launched its own music player, the $249 Dell Digital Jukebox, in October 2003, partnering with digital songs provider Musicmatch, Inc., of San Diego, California. Musicmatch offered a library of more than 800,000 songs. In June 2004, Dell tried to entice potential customers by offering a $100 rebate to buyers who mailed their iPods to Dell for recycling.

Search engine company Yahoo! Inc., of Sunnyvale, California, announced in September that it was acquiring Musicmatch, paying approximately $160 million for the online music source. Industry experts considered the acquisition another example of the convergence of the computer industry and digital electronics, including music.

Personal video recorders. The same advances in hard disk technology that made possible such music devices as the iPod helped ignite the video recording market in 2004. More than 4 million personal video recorders (PVRs) were sold worldwide in 2003, and 11 million were expected to be sold in 2004.

In addition to increased capacity, PVRs could store between 40 and 160 hours of recorded programming. The sales growth was powered by cable and satellite television providers, who include PVR technology in many of the decoder boxes that carry their signals to the subscriber's television. PVR capabilities were also being included in many DVD players and recorders.

Personal television directions. In August, Sony Corporation of Tokyo announced the development of a special chip that would give viewers control over images on their televisions. The new Digital Reality Creation Multifunction v2 chip, or DRC-MFv2, takes advantage of the digital nature of high-definition television (HDTV) images. It allows users to alter the perspective from which they view an image, without losing any of the image's level of detail. Viewers could zoom, *pan* (move) across the width of an image, or tilt the image to a different angle.

While DRC-MFv2 chip-equipped televisions were demonstrated by Sony, the technology was not expected to be widely available in the marketplace for several years.   ■ Keith Ferrell

See also **Computer; Telecommunications.**

El Salvador. Elias Antonio (Tony) Saca, of the Nationalist Republican Alliance (ARENA), was sworn to a five-year term as El Salvador's president on June 1, 2004. Saca, owner of a network of radio stations, had won a landslide victory over Schafik Handal, of the left-wing Farabundo Marti National Liberation Front, in March. Saca pledged to follow the privatization and pro-United States policies of the three previous ARENA administrations.

President Saca also vowed to persuade the U.S. government to continue allowing 300,000 Salvadorans working in the United States to send money transfers to El Salvador. Salvadorans living in the United States sent an estimated $2 billion to families and friends in El Salvador in 2003—equivalent to 14 percent of El Salvador's *gross national product* (the value of all goods and services produced in a country in a given year).

More than 30 prisoners were killed and at least 24 others were wounded during a riot at a jail in San Salvador, the capital, on Aug. 18, 2004. The riot began when members of a prison gang beat an inmate to death. More than 3,000 inmates were confined in the jail, which was built to house 800 inmates.   ■ Nathan A. Haverstock

See also **Latin America.**

Employment. See Labor and employment.
Endangered species. See Conservation.

Energy supply. Costs of energy surged in 2004 as rising world demand threatened to exceed supplies of many fuels. Global economic growth contributed to increased fuel use, with China's growing thirst for oil and other commodities a major factor. The use of other energy, including coal, rose in the wake of the petroleum demand.

In the past, additional production of energy, particularly oil and natural gas, would have kept prices relatively stable despite the higher demand. In 2004, the added supplies were limited and failed to match the rise in demand in some cases.

Storms disrupted production of oil and natural gas from the Gulf of Mexico to onshore areas of the United States in August and September. Volatile conditions in petroleum fields abroad, mainly around the Persian Gulf, raised new fears of supply disruptions from that prolific region.

Supply worries. Most of the 11 member nations of the Organization of the Petroleum Exporting Countries (OPEC), the cartel that accounts for much of the world's oil trade, produced at full capacity as demand and the prices of their oil grew to record levels. However, in war-torn Iraq, one of the founders of OPEC, sabotage kept output well below expected levels. Political turmoil in some other OPEC member nations, including Venezuela and Nigeria, also restricted oil supplies.

OPEC itself had contributed to the build-up of supply worries in 2004 by limiting production when prices of petroleum were much cheaper. As fears mounted in 2004 of a possible world oil shortage, OPEC rushed to expand production. Its output reached more than 30 million barrels a day, the highest volume in more than 20 years. However, the expanded production left the cartel with little spare capacity to meet any further jumps in global oil demand.

Price surges. No natural resource shortages occurred in 2004. Nevertheless, speculators rushed into the oil markets because of the possibility of a supply crunch, which drove energy prices even higher. As a result, crude oil, which had cost around $30 a barrel for much of 2003, reached $55 a barrel for the first time in history in October 2004.

A barrel consists of 42 gallons (158.97 liters), and per-gallon prices of fuels, such as gasoline and heating oil, reflected the jumps in the cost of crude oil. Gasoline, which had spiked beyond $1.80 at the pump in 2003, rose further in 2004 to hover around $2 a gallon. From July to September, the price of natural gas at the wellhead was around $5.90 per 1,000 cubic feet, up from $5.29 for the same months in 2003. By December 2004,

Gasoline prices climbed to more than $2 a gallon in the United States in 2004, a record high. The price of crude oil reached $55 a barrel for the first time in history in October 2004.

wholesale prices of home heating oil delivered to New York Harbor were around $1.43 a gallon, compared with approximately 82 cents in 2003.

Petroleum consumption worldwide exceeded 82 million barrels a day in 2004, more than 3 percent higher than 2003 oil use. The United States was the world's biggest consumer of petroleum in 2004. According to the Energy Information Administration (EIA), U.S. petroleum demand averaged some 20.5 million barrels a day in 2004, up 2 percent from 2003. The EIA is a statistical agency of the U.S. Department of Energy.

Gasoline continued to dominate U.S. fuel use in 2004, accounting for nearly one-half of all the petroleum products consumed. In November, gasoline supplied to U.S. motorists averaged 9.1 million barrels a day, up 1 percent from the same month in 2003.

Alternate fuels. A renewed focus on alternate fuels proved to be the one positive development from 2004's high energy costs and concerns over possible oil or gas shortages. Still, so-called renewable energy accounted for only 6.6 percent of the total energy used in the United States in 2004. Vehicles powered by fuel cells or other more-efficient energy means were still years away in 2004. However, buyer waiting lists existed for hybrid cars, which have both gasoline and electric engines for better gas mileage.

Natural gas. Experts continue to view natural gas as the fuel of choice because it is less polluting than other hydrocarbon energy sources, such as coal or oil. However, because of mild weather and high prices, the volume of gas burned in the United States in 2004 was flat for the second straight year. According to EIA estimates for 2004, consumption of natural gas in the United States totaled about 22.5 trillion cubic feet (642.9 billion cubic meters).

Experts expected natural gas to be increasingly important in the U.S. energy picture, despite the indicated slow growth in demand in 2004. As for future supplies, the high prices of 2004 triggered increased exploration and drilling. Also, more oil and gas companies planned to build ports and plants for the shipping of liquefied natural gas to the United States from the Middle East and elsewhere.

Electricity. The EIA estimated that U.S. electricity demand rose by 1.7 percent in 2004. The increase led to greater consumption of coal, which is used to generate more than one-half of the electrical power needs of the United States. According to the EIA, coal demand grew by some 3.7 percent in 2004, to approximately 1.1 billion tons (1 billion metric tons).   ■ James Tanner

Engineering. See Building and construction.

England. See United Kingdom.

Environmental pollution. In 2004, scientists continued to monitor signs of climate change. A number of studies published during the year contributed to the growing body of data documenting climate-related changes and possible links between the changes and human-related activities.

Antarctic glaciers. In September 2004, National Aeronautic and Space Administration (NASA) scientists reported an acceleration in the seaward flow of glaciers following the breakup of the Larsen B ice shelf on the Antarctic Peninsula. An ice shelf is an extension of the Antarctic ice cap that forms a ledge over water. The scientists detected the changes in glacial flow by studying satellite images. Their studies were published in the September 2004 issue of the *Geophysical Research Letters*.

The Larsen B ice shelf, measuring 1,255 square miles (3,250 square kilometers) and weighing 500 billion tons (454 billion metric tons), disintegrated dramatically over the course of 35 days in 2002. A nearby shelf, Larsen A, had collapsed in 1995.

The NASA scientists theorized that ice shelves act as a kind of brake for the glaciers in their gradual flow from higher to lower elevations toward the seacoasts. Without the braking action of the Larsen shelves, three glaciers on the Antarctic Peninsula began to slide toward the Weddell Sea at a rate eight times faster than before the most recent Larsen breakup. Moreover, scientists detected a 125-foot (38-meter) drop in the height of the glaciers over a six-month period.

Many scientists believe that the build-up of carbon dioxide and other greenhouse gases in the atmosphere, brought about by human technologies, is causing global warming. The accelerated breakup of polar ice, they theorize, is an important indicator of climate change. According to meteorological records, the Antarctic Peninsula has warmed more than 4.5 °F (2.5 °C) since the mid-1900's. The Antarctic contains more than 90 percent of the world's ice. If that ice were all to melt, world sea levels could rise by as much as 260 feet (80 meters).

Arctic ice. Scientists in 2004 also found ample evidence of global warming at the opposite end of the world, the Arctic. A study sponsored by the Arctic Council and released in November documented rising temperatures and many resulting changes in the Arctic environment. The Arctic Council is a cooperative association comprised of governmental representatives of Canada, Denmark, Finland, Iceland, Norway, Russia, Sweden, the United States, and Arctic indigenous groups.

According to the findings of the four-year study involving hundreds of scientists, average temperatures in the Arctic rose by nearly 2 °F (1.1 °C) in the 20th century, while average winter temperatures have risen by nearly 4 °F (2.2 °C). In every year since 2000, scientists have measured smaller areas of ocean ice coverage in the Arctic Ocean.

The study contained ample indirect and anecdotal evidence of changes caused by the warming trend. Arctic hunters reported falling through melting sea ice, while people living in more settled Arctic regions reported many structural problems related to the thawing of *permafrost* (permanently frozen ground).

Species extinctions. One-quarter or more of all land animals and plants, amounting to more than 1 million species, could die off by 2050 if presently accepted models of climate change prove to be true. A 19-member international team led by conservation biologist Chris Thomas of the University of Leeds in the United Kingdom reported that conclusion of their study in the January 2004 issue of the journal *Nature*.

Using widely accepted models that predict an average increase in the Earth's temperature of between 2.5 °F (1.4 °C) and 10.4 °F (5.8 °C) by 2100, the Thomas team surveyed habitat decline for 1,103 plant and animal species in widely scattered world regions representing 20 percent of Earth's land area. The team then made broader estimates of species decline relying on a fundamental principle of ecology—that dwindling habitat supports a shrinking number of species.

The researchers called for prompt action to curtail emissions of greenhouse gases and reduce the magnitude of likely species extinction. Some scientists disputed the study's conclusions, suggesting that many species would adapt to new conditions and thereby escape extinction.

Kyoto victory. In late 2004, Russia approved the Kyoto Treaty, the global agreement to set limits on the emission of carbon dioxide and other greenhouse gases. Russia's approval achieved the threshold needed to bring the treaty into force and left only Australia and the United States among the world's most developed countries as nonsigners. The United States is the world's largest producer of greenhouse gases.

Corporations and climate change. The Conference Board—a New York City-based consortium of about 2,000 companies—issued a report in September 2004 predicting "increased pressure" on corporate boards to address the problem of climate change in response to mounting scientific evidence that human-induced global warming was occurring on the planet. The report said that governments and markets were becoming more and more sensitized to the debate over climate change and warned that businesses intent on ignoring the issue would do so "at their own peril."

California demands cleaner autos. In September, the California Air Resources Board, a regulatory agency appointed by the state's governor, approved rules requiring automakers to cut polluting emissions by an average of 29 percent in vehicles introduced between model years 2009 and 2016. According to industry experts, California's action imposed the world's most rigorous fuel economy standards on automakers. New York and six other states were poised to follow California's lead, the experts noted.

In December 2004, nine automakers filed suit to block the California ruling. If the regulations were to stand, automakers would be compelled to boost fuel efficiency on millions of vehicles, because California's huge economy generates one-fifth of all U.S. automobile sales. California Governor Arnold Schwarzenegger promised to defend the regulations.

Pollution and snow. Snowflakes formed within polluted clouds are likely to contain less water mass than those formed in cleaner clouds, researchers with the University of Nevada's Desert Research Institute at Reno concluded in a study released in September 2004. The scientists, Douglas Lowenthal and Randy Borys, spent 10 years studying snowflakes in a mountaintop laboratory near Steamboat Springs, Colorado. They found that snow clouds packed with particulates from vehicle emissions, coal-burning power plants, and other polluting sources produce snowflakes with 50 percent less water mass than "clean" snowflakes. The study could have profound implications for the water-starved urban Southwest, which depends largely on meltwater from mountain snows for its water supply.

Suit settlement. In September, E. I. du Pont de Nemours and Company of Wilmington, Delaware, settled a class-action lawsuit with more than 50,000 West Virginia and Ohio residents. The suit alleged that chemicals used to manufacture Teflon at a factory near Parkersburg, West Virginia, entered water supplies and may have exposed area residents to unsafe levels of perfluorooctanoic acid, also known as PFOA.

Du Pont officials maintained that PFOA does not pose serious human health risks, and they denied any liability on the part of the company. Under the settlement, du Pont agreed to help area water treatment districts reduce PFOA concentrations and to pay up to $350 million in cash awards, legal fees, and medical monitoring for area residents.   ■ Andrew Hoffman

See also **Automobile; Conservation.**

Equatorial Guinea. See Africa.

Eritrea. See Africa.

Estonia. See Baltic states; Europe.

Ethiopia. See Africa.

EUROPE

The European Union (EU), Europe's main political and economic bloc, underwent dramatic changes in 2004. In the largest expansion of its 47-year history, the EU admitted 10 new members, including 8 former satellite states of the Soviet Union. The EU also agreed to open membership negotiations with Turkey. EU leaders reached agreement on a new constitution designed to strengthen political cooperation within the bloc and streamline governing procedures.

EU enlargement. The EU admitted 10 new member nations on May 1, formally ending the Cold War division of Europe some 15 years after the fall of the Berlin Wall signalled the end of Communism. (The Cold War was a period of intense rivalry between United States allies and Communist nations that began after World War II [1939-1945] and ended with the collapse of the Soviet Union in 1991.) The new members included five former members of the Soviet-dominated Warsaw Pact: the Czech Republic, Hungary, Poland, Slovakia, and Slovenia; three former Soviet republics, Estonia, Latvia, and Lithuania; and the Mediterranean island states of Cyprus and Malta.

The 75 million people in the 10 new member states increased the EU's total population by 20

The Old Bridge connects the two sides of the city of Mostar, Bosnia-Herzegovina, after its reconstruction was completed in July 2004. The bridge across the Neretva River had been destroyed in 1993, during Bosnia's civil war. Preservationists used original building methods and materials discovered at the bottom of the river to reconstruct the more than 500-year-old structure.

Country	Population	Government	Monetary unit*	Foreign trade (million U.S.$)	
				Exports[†]	Imports[†]
Albania	3,214,000	President Alfred Moisiu; Prime Minister Fatos Nano	lek (100.50 = $1)	425	1,760
Andorra	71,000	Co-sovereigns bishop of Urgel, Spain, and the president of France; Prime Minister Marc Forne Molne	euro (0.81 = $1)	58	1,077
Austria	8,041,000	President Heinz Fischer; Chancellor Wolfgang Schuessel	euro (0.81 = $1)	83,450	81,590
Belarus	9,885,000	President Aleksandr Lukashenko	ruble (2,172.90 = $1)	9,413	11,090
Belgium	10,286,000	King Albert II; Prime Minister Guy Verhofstadt	euro (0.81 = $1)	182,900	173,000
Bosnia-Herzegovina	4,160,000	Chairman of the collective presidency Sulejman Tihic	marka (1.61 = $1)	1,280	4,700
Bulgaria	7,742,000	President Georgi Purvanov; Prime Minister Simeon Saxe-Coburg-Gotha	lev (1.58 = $1)	7,337	9,723
Croatia	4,385,000	President Stjepan Mesic; Prime Minister Ivo Sanader	kuna (6.12 = $1)	6,355	12,860
Czech Republic	10,262,000	President Vaclav Klaus; Prime Minister Stanislav Gross	koruna (25.43 = $1)	46,770	50,400
Denmark	5,375,000	Queen Margrethe II; Prime Minister Anders Fogh Rasmussen	krone (6.00 = $1)	64,160	54,470
Estonia	1,309,000	President Arnold Ruutel; Prime Minister Juhan Parts	kroon (12.61 = $1)	4,075	5,535
Finland	5,214,000	President Tarja Halonen; Prime Minister Matti Taneli Vanhanen	euro (0.81 = $1)	54,280	37,350
France	59,579,000	President Jacques Chirac; Prime Minister Jean-Pierre Raffarin	euro (0.81 = $1)	346,500	339,900
Germany	81,886,000	President Horst Koehler; Chancellor Gerhard Schroeder	euro (0.81 = $1)	696,900	585,000
Greece	10,953,000	President Konstandinos Stephanopoulos; Prime Minister Konstandinos Karamanlis	euro (0.81 = $1)	13,195	44,375
Hungary	9,770,000	President Ferenc Madl; Prime Minister Peter Medgyessy	forint (198.33 = $1)	42,030	46,190
Iceland	287,000	President Olafur Grimsson; Prime Minister Halldor Asgrimsson	krona (70.76 = $1)	2,379	2,590
Ireland	3,875,000	President Mary McAleese; Prime Minister Bertie Ahern	euro (0.81 = $1)	98,310	57,540
Italy	57,231,000	President Carlo Azeglio Ciampi; Prime Minister Silvio Berlusconi	euro (0.81 = $1)	278,100	271,100 (includes San Marino)
Latvia	2,367,000	President Vaira Vike-Freiberga; Prime Minister Aigars Kalvitis	lat (0.54 = $1)	3,000	4,921
Liechtenstein	34,000	Prince Hans Adam II; Prime Minister Otmar Hasler	Swiss franc (1.25 = $1)	2,470	917

percent, to 453 million. The living standards of the new members ranged from 41 percent of the EU average in Latvia to 83 percent in Cyprus. Economic output in most of the new member nations was expected to grow between 3.5 percent to 7.5 percent in 2004, compared with 2.3 percent in the original 15 EU members, according to the European Commission, the executive agency that monitors EU economies.

The new members continued to attract signifi-cant investment from Western European compa-nies because of their lower wage and tax levels, causing political tension within the EU. The fi-nance ministers of France and Germany proposed setting a minimum standard corporate tax rate for EU nations. However, they failed to win the back-ing to enact the proposal.

The EU also completed membership negotia-tions with Bulgaria in June 2004 and with Roma-nia in December. The two countries were invited

Country	Population	Government	Monetary unit*	Foreign trade (million U.S.$)	
				Exports[†]	Imports[†]
Lithuania	3,661,000	President Valdas Adamkus; Prime Minister Algirdas Mykolas Brazauskas	litas (2.78 = $1)	7,890	9,200
Luxembourg	458,000	Grand Duke Henri; Prime Minister Jean-Claude Juncker	euro (0.81 = $1)	8,571	11,610
Macedonia	2,059,000	President Branko Crvenkovski	denar (50.15 = $1)	1,346	2,184
Malta	396,000	President Edward Fenech Adami; Prime Minister Lawrence Gonzi	lira (0.35 = $1)	2,175	2,761
Moldova	4,251,000	President Vladimir Voronin; Prime Minister Vasile Tarlev	leu (12.17 = $1)	790	1,340
Monaco	33,000	Prince Rainier III	euro (0.81 = $1)	no statistics available	
Netherlands	16,087,000	Queen Beatrix; Prime Minister Jan Peter Balkenende	euro (0.81 = $1)	253,200	217,700
Norway	4,536,000	King Harald V; Prime Minister Kjell Magne Bondevik	krone (6.68 = $1)	67,270	40,190
Poland	38,466,000	President Aleksander Kwasniewski; Prime Minister Marek Belka	zloty (3.50 = $1)	57,600	63,650
Portugal	10,068,000	President Jorge Sampaio; Prime Minister Pedro Santana Lopes**	euro (0.81 = $1)	31,130	43,730
Romania	22,206,000	President Traian Basescu; Prime Minister Calin Popescu Tariceanu	leu (33,158.00 = $1)	17,630	22,170
Russia	141,802,000	President Vladimir Putin	ruble (29.21 = $1)	134,400	74,800
San Marino	28,000	2 captains regent appointed by Grand Council every 6 months	euro (0.81 = $1)	278,100	271,000 (includes Italy)
Serbia and Montenegro	10,489,000	President Svetozar Marovic	euro (0.81 = $1) new dinar (65.00 = $1)	2,667	7,144
Slovakia	5,416,000	President Ivan Gasparovic; Prime Minister Mikulas Dzurinda	koruna (32.28 = $1)	21,250	21,900
Slovenia	1,978,000	President Janez Drnovsek; Prime Minister Anton Rop	tolar (193.40 = $1)	11,980	12,630
Spain	39,878,000	King Juan Carlos I; President of the Government (Prime Minister) José Luis Rodríguez Zapatero	euro (0.81 = $1)	159,400	197,100
Sweden	8,796,000	King Carl XVI Gustaf; Prime Minister Goran Persson	krona (7.27 = $1)	102,800	83,270
Switzerland	7,153,000	President Joseph Deiss	franc (1.25 = $1)	110,000	102,200
Turkey	71,455,000	President Ahmet Necdet Sezer; Prime Minister Recep Tayyip Erdogan	lira (1,515,152.00 = $1)	49,120	62,430
Ukraine	47,730,000	President Viktor Yushchenko	hryvna (5.32 = $1)	23,630	23,580
United Kingdom	59,107,000	Queen Elizabeth II; Prime Minister Tony Blair	pound (0.56 = $1)	304,500	363,600

*Exchange rates as of Oct. 1, 2004, or latest available data.   [†]Latest available data.

**The government of Prime Minister Pedro Santana Lopes resigned on Dec. 11, 2004. Santana Lopes agreed to head a caretaker government until the next general election, scheduled for Feb. 20, 2005.

to sign treaties of accession in 2005 and were due to join the EU in 2007. Romania's invitation was conditional on EU demands that it strengthen its judicial system and attack corruption.

Talks with Turkey. EU leaders agreed in December 2004 to open membership negotiations with Turkey in October 2005, a controversial and potentially historic step. The leaders said their decision was a recognition of efforts by the government of Prime Minister Recep Tayyip Erdogan to strengthen Turkey's democracy, protect human rights, and modernize the economy. Supporters of Turkish membership claimed it would enhance EU influence in the Middle East and reduce the threat of Islamic fundamentalism by making Turkey a model for moderate governments in the region.

Many Europeans opposed the move, however, fearing that a predominantly Muslim country such as Turkey would not integrate with a primarily Christian Europe. Opponents also feared that

Turkey's large population of 71 million people and its relative poverty—with average incomes one-fourth of EU levels—would lead to uncontrolled immigration. The opposition Christian Democratic Union in Germany vowed to block the negotiations if the party came to power. President Jacques Chirac of France bowed to opposition in his country by promising to submit Turkish membership to a referendum. The negotiations were expected to last about 10 years, during which EU leaders hoped opposition would fade.

The EU also agreed in December to open membership negotiations with Croatia in April 2005, making Croatia the first country from the former Yugoslavia to move toward EU membership. The offer was conditional on Croatia's helping the International Criminal Tribunal for the former Yugoslavia to prosecute people suspected of committing war crimes during the country's civil war in the 1990's.

NATO expansion. The North Atlantic Treaty Organization (NATO) took in seven new members in Eastern Europe in 2004. Bulgaria, Estonia, Latvia, Lithuania, Romania, Slovakia, and Slovenia joined NATO, the military alliance between the United States and Europe, on March 29, when the prime ministers of the seven nations submitted accession documents to U.S. government officials in Washington, D.C. The expansion raised the number of member countries to 26.

EU constitution. The EU's leaders reached agreement on a draft constitution in 2004 in an effort to improve the EU's decision-making capability. The constitution expands the number of policy areas in which the EU could make decisions by majority vote, rather than unanimity, and increases EU powers in areas such as criminal justice and immigration. It creates the position of EU president, to be appointed by the member countries every 30 months, to give the bloc stronger leadership. It also creates the post of foreign minister to enable the EU to act more forcefully in international affairs. The constitution contains a Charter of Fundamental Rights, similar to the U.S. Bill of Rights.

The agreement, reached at a summit meeting of EU leaders in Brussels in June and signed at a ceremony in Rome in October, came after more than two years of hard-fought negotiations. At least 10 countries planned to hold referenda on the constitution in 2005 or 2006. Many Europeans, including many people in the United Kingdom (U.K.), worried that the document would shift power from their nations to the EU.

Commission controversy. Political tensions erupted in 2004 over the choice of a new European Commission, the EU executive agency. EU leaders failed in their first attempt to agree on a president to lead the commission when the U.K.

threatened to block Guy Verhofstadt, the Belgian prime minister who was the favored candidate of France and Germany. U.K. officials feared Verhofstadt would try to centralize too much power in the EU at the expense of member nations. At a special summit in Brussels on June 29, EU leaders agreed to nominate the Portuguese prime minister, Jose Manuel Durao Barroso, for the post.

Durao Barroso's credibility immediately came into question when he encountered difficulties in forming the 25-member commission. Italy had nominated Rocco Buttiglione for its seat on the commission. Buttiglione, a conservative who served as the country's European affairs minister, stirred controversy at his confirmation hearing in the European Parliament by saying he considered homosexuality a sin and that marriage was designed for women to have children. Parliament threatened to reject the commission, forcing Italy to withdraw Buttiglione and replace him with Foreign Minister Franco Frattini.

Terrorism. Europe took several measures to combat terrorism in 2004 following attacks by Islamic militants. The biggest attack occurred in Madrid, where a series of 10 bombs exploded on four commuter trains on March 11, killing 191 people. The attack was the worst in Europe since the downing of a Pan Am jetliner over Lockerbie, Scotland, in 1988 killed 270 people. Concerns about terrorism also increased after the murder of a Dutch film director, Theo van Gogh, apparently over a television film he made about abuse against Islamic women.

In the wake of the Madrid attack, EU leaders agreed at a meeting in Brussels on March 25, 2004, to adopt a measure requiring member countries to provide mutual assistance in the case of a terror attack; appoint an official to coordinate anti-terrorist efforts; improve the sharing of intelligence information; establish an EU database on terrorists; and allow an arrest warrant issued by one EU country to be served in another.

Several EU countries also cracked down on radical Islamic clerics suspected of condoning or inciting terrorism. France deported a cleric to Algeria after the man, Abdelkader Bouziane, condoned the beating and stoning of wives. The U.K. stripped the citizenship of Abu Hamza al-Masri, an Egyptian-born cleric, and charged him with supporting al-Qa'ida and inciting racial hatred. Denmark tightened its immigration rules to deny entry to radical Islamic clerics.

Foreign policy. The EU played an active role in international affairs in 2004. An EU delegation, including the foreign ministers of France, Germany, and the United Kingdom, reached an agreement with Iran in November that required Iran to suspend the enrichment of uranium in return for increased trade opportunities. (Enriched uranium is used to make fuel for nuclear reactors and can be used to make nuclear weapons.) The EU wanted to prevent Iran from developing nuclear weapons. The United States had argued for tougher action, including the threat of sanctions, if Iran did not halt its nuclear activities, but the failure to find weapons of mass destruction in Iraq—one of the main reasons for going to war—weakened the U.S. position.

The EU took steps to resolve internal differences over Iraq, an issue that had split the bloc during 2003. EU leaders invited Iraq's prime minister, Ayad Allawi, to a summit meeting in Brussels on Nov. 5, 2004, and agreed to provide $39 million to train Iraqi election workers, police, and lawyers. Several EU countries announced plans to cut their support for the U.S.-led military intervention. Spain withdrew its 1,300 troops after the Socialist Party, which had opposed the war, defeated the conservative Popular Party in elections in March. Hungary withdrew the last of its 300 troops from Iraq on December 20. The Netherlands planned to pull its 1,350 troops sometime after Iraqi elections scheduled for January 2005. Poland also announced that it would begin withdrawing its 2,500 troops in 2005.

EU leaders agreed in December 2004 to work toward lifting the bloc's arms embargo against China, a move supported by France and Germany. The Europeans imposed the embargo in 1989, after the Chinese crackdown on prodemocracy protestors in Beijing. The United States opposed lifting the embargo, arguing that arms sales could help China threaten Taiwan and upset the military balance of power in Asia.

An EU-led military force took over the peacekeeping mission in Bosnia-Herzegovina from NATO on Dec. 2, 2004. The force of 7,000 troops, called EUFOR, was the largest military mission ever undertaken by the EU, which had built up its capacity to take joint military actions.

Economy. Europe enjoyed an economic recovery in 2004. A strong global economy boosted demand for EU exports, while low interest rates supported demand within Europe, especially in the housing market. *Gross domestic product* (GDP, the total value of goods and services produced in a year) was expected to increase by an average of 2.5 percent in the EU in 2004, according to the European Commission, compared with 1.0 percent in 2003. Unemployment remained high in 2004 at 9.1 percent of the work force.

Currency worries. The sharp decline in the U.S. dollar against the euro late in 2004 threatened to undermine Europe's recovery and increase tensions with the United States. On November 16, EU finance ministers urged the United States to take action to support the dollar and reduce the U.S. budget and current account

deficits. No action was taken, however, and many economists believed that the administration of U.S. President George W. Bush was content to allow the dollar to decline in order to boost overseas demand for U.S. products.

Trade dispute. The EU engaged in several trade disputes with the United States in 2004. In March, the EU imposed tariffs on a wide range of U.S. exports, including jewelry, refrigerators, and paper, to retaliate against U.S. tax subsidies for exporters. The World Trade Organization, the Geneva-based body that regulates global trade, had found in 2003 that the U.S. subsidies violated trade rules. The EU suspended the sanctions in October 2004 after President Bush signed a bill eliminating the subsidies.

In October, the Bush administration filed a complaint with the WTO to stop EU governments from providing development subsidies to Airbus Industrie, the European aircraft consortium. The move followed strong gains in market share by Airbus in recent years. The EU filed a counter complaint to stop U.S. support for Chicago-based Boeing Corp. The two sides, which have argued about aircraft subsidies for years, agreed in December to suspend the WTO complaints and seek a negotiated settlement.   ■ Tom Buerkle

See also **Economics; Iraq: A Special Report; Terrorism;** and various European country articles.

Fashion. The grand era of *haute couture* (expensive, made-to-order clothes) came to an end in 2004, fashion experts noted. The factors affecting sales of high-fashion clothing included the sluggish economy of the United States and the rise in the value of the euro, compared with the value of the U.S. dollar. The high value of the euro increased the cost of European-made clothes for Americans.

Haute couture. Several major houses announced they would no longer produce haute couture collections in 2004. In addition to Hanae Mori, the Japanese designer who retired, the French houses of Ungaro and Givenchy and the Italian house of Versace abandoned their couture lines. Jean Paul Gaultier considered a shift to a couture that required only one fitting instead of the many fittings usually needed. Such a move would cut the expense and time required to make a garment.

The fashions designed by couture houses had become more prestigious than profitable by 2004. Fashion experts estimated that only some 500 women worldwide paid the five-figure prices required for these items—clothing that is largely made by hand of the most expensive materials. These clothes did, however, inspire buyers to purchase the more attainable make-up, belts, handbags, and other items that carried the brand name.

Tom Ford, who built the Gucci line into a major player in the fashion industry, left his design job with that house in 2004. However, he left in triumph with two highly praised shows in the spring—one for Gucci and one for the Gucci-owned Yves Saint Laurent line.

Despite these closings, new designers, who may be the major players of the future, did turn up in store displays in 2004. Among these were Bryan Bradley of Tuleh, Lazaro Hernandez and Jack McCollough of Proenza Schouler, and Alber Elbaz, who joined Lanvin after working for Geoffrey Beene.

Street fashion. Designers continued to dabble in inexpensive clothing for mass markets in 2004. Karl Lagerfeld designed a collection for Swedish retailer Hennes & Mauritz (H&M), which included T-shirts priced as low as $6. Isaac Mizrahi's special collection for Target, the Minneapolis-based discount retail chain, continued to do well in 2004.

Most of the action in fashion was indeed taking place at lower price points. Increasingly, people did not object to mixing a fashion piece with something more mundane—pairing a cashmere sweater with pants from The Gap or Old Navy, both part of the San Francisco-based specialty retailer Gap Inc. This trend reflected only the fringes of the fashion market, because many people in 2004 wore T-shirts and jeans except for the most formal of occasions. Sneakers were the preferred footgear, varied only by sandals.

A Brazilian flip-flop sandal became very popular in 2004. By spring and summer, flip-flops, which had previously been beach attire, were worn by younger men and women almost everywhere, even in some casual business environments.

The crocheted poncho, a nod to the 1970's, was another item popular with women in 2004. The latest version, however, was somewhat narrower than the earlier one and came only to the waist.

Other fashion trends. Color was big in 2004, with pink a big contender, even in shirt designs for men. Prints often showed up in flouncy skirts. Uneven hemlines and sparkly embroidery were important in dressy clothing for women, and trench coats in bright colors were also popular.

Low-rise pants remained popular, though by summer, those in the know on the coasts were no longer baring their midriff, and waistlines on pants and skirts began to rise. After many years of a grunge or hip hop, urban look for teen women, clothing that revisited the preppie look of the 1980's—including plaid skirts, cable-knit sweaters, and polo shirts—reappeared in 2004.

By fall, women's clothing began to look more polished as suits, jackets, and pencil skirts, especially made of tweed, became popular. Women's shoes, which had previously shown pointed toes with a very high heel, changed to a rounded toe with a less extravagant heel.

Men, usually younger men, began wearing dress clothes in a more casual way. Fashionable young men wore the tails of their dress shirts untucked, either over khaki pants or with a suit, and with loosely knotted ties.

Deaths. Two great fashion innovators died in 2004. Designer Geoffrey Beene died on September 28. He was noted for his technical ability to make two-dimensional fabric conform to a three-dimensional body. Beene won the Coty Fashion Critics' Award eight times.

Richard Avedon, who died on September 29, elevated fashion photography to an art form. His later work shifted from fashion to portraits, particularly portraits of celebrities.

■ Bernadine Morris

Dress shirts with unbuttoned cuffs, worn untucked, combined with spiked hair to form a look popular with men in 2004. Capris, sandals, and plastic-framed sunglasses harkened back to 1950's and 1960's women's fashion.

Finland. The former prime minister of Finland was acquitted of charges of illegally obtaining secret documents in a trial that dominated Finnish political life in 2004. Anneli Jaatteenmaki had led Finland's Center Party to victory in parliamentary elections in March 2003 after opposing the United States-led invasion of Iraq. She claimed that her opponent, then-Prime Minister Paavo Liipponen, had promised to support the invasion in violation of Finland's neutrality. Jaatteenmaki was forced to resign as prime minister in June 2003 after only two months in office, however, over allegations that she had illegally obtained secret foreign ministry documents about Iraq. The documents, which appeared to support her campaign stance, were then leaked to the press.

After a two-week trial, a Helsinki court found Jaatteenmaki not guilty on March 19, 2004, saying there was no evidence she had instigated the leak. The court did find a former presidential aide guilty of leaking the documents, however, and fined the aide 80 days' salary. Jaatteenmaki, who had been Finland's first female prime minister, revived her political career in June by winning election to the European Parliament.

The economy improved significantly in 2004 as part of a Europe-wide recovery. The European Commission, which monitors the economies of the European Union (EU), forecast that Finland's output of goods and services would grow by 3 percent in 2004, up from 1.9 percent in 2003 and well ahead of the 2.5 percent average of the 25 EU nations. Unemployment remained stubbornly high at almost 9 percent of the labor force, however.

Business investment remained a relative weak spot in the economy. Investment declined in 2002 and 2003 because of a slump in the country's high-technology and telecommunications industries, and it recovered only slightly in 2004. In an effort to stimulate investment, the government in August announced it would reduce the corporate income tax rate from 29 percent to 26 percent, effective in 2005. The move was partly a response to growing competition from countries in Eastern Europe, which have used lower tax rates to attract investment from Western Europe.

Speeding fine. One of Finland's richest men received a record fine of $215,000 for speeding. Jussi Salonoja, the 27-year-old heir to a family sausage business, was fined in 2004 after being caught driving at 50 miles (80 kilometers) per hour in a 25-mile- (40-kilometer) per-hour zone. Finland sets traffic fines according to the income of the person convicted of an offense, and Salonoja's most recent declared annual income was more than $6.6 million. ■ Tom Buerkle

See also **Europe; Iraq: A Special Report.**

Food. Proposed guidelines to update the United States government's diet and health recommendations were published on Aug. 27, 2004, by the departments of Health and Human Services (HHS) and Agriculture (USDA). The previous guidelines were published in 2000.

The Dietary Guidelines for Americans included these recommendations: consume a variety of foods from the basic food groups; control calorie intake to control weight; include at least 30 minutes of moderate physical activity daily; increase daily intake of fruits and vegetables, whole grains, and nonfat or low-fat milk and milk products; choose fats and carbohydrates wisely, restricting the amount of trans fats (found in many baked goods and fast foods); choose and prepare foods with little salt; drink alcoholic beverages only in moderation; and wash and cook food properly to avoid food-borne illnesses. The final guidelines were to be released early in 2005.

U.S. beef and "mad cow disease." New USDA rules to strengthen protections against bovine spongiform encephalopathy (BSE), or "mad cow disease," took effect Jan. 12, 2004, following the first report of a BSE-infected cow in the United States in December 2003. BSE is a fatal brain disorder in cattle that scientists believe is related to a brain degenerative disease in people called variant Creutzfeldt-Jakob disease. The rules require holding meat from cattle tested for BSE until negative test results are received; and prohibiting the air-injection stunning of cattle, a process during which brain matter may become mixed with meat.

On March 15, 2004, the USDA announced expanded testing plans to test thousands of cattle considered to be at "high risk" for BSE over an 18-month period. Animals exhibiting nervous system disorders, cattle that cannot walk, and those that died of unknown causes were to be tested.

On April 27, the USDA launched the National Animal Identification System (NAIS). The purpose of the voluntary program was to enable the government to track specific animals and to quickly · quarantine such potential food contamination sites as ranches and feedlots.

Bioterrorism safeguards. On May 27, the U.S. Food and Drug Administration (FDA) announced a final rule establishing procedures for detaining food under the Public Health Security and Bioterrorism Preparedness and Response Act of 2002. Under the rule, the FDA may detain a food product based on credible evidence or information that it threatens serious negative health consequences or death to people or animals. Previous regulations implementing the Bioterrorism Act were issued in 2003, requiring all meat and food processing plants to register with the FDA and to provide prior notification of foodstuffs being imported into the United States.

Low-carb diets in 2004 continued to influence consumers to reduce carbohydrates and increase protein. Grocery store meat and egg sales rose sharply, while pasta, rice, and bakery product sales suffered. New products, including low-carb beer and low-carb chocolate, brought increased revenue for such companies as Anheuser-Busch of St. Louis, Missouri, maker of Michelob Ultra, and Hershey, Pennsylvania-based Hershey Foods Corp., maker of 1 g Sugar Carb bars. Interstate Bakeries Corp. of Kansas City, Missouri, maker of Twinkies and Wonder Bread, faced declining demand and filed for bankruptcy.

However, the low-carb craze appeared to be moderating by midyear. Atkins Nutritionals Inc. of Ronkonkoma, New York, announced in mid-September that it would lay off employees and eliminate at least one distribution facility, as declining sales indicated that the number of people on carb-restricted diets had begun to drop.

Grocery costs. In September, ACNielsen of Stamford, Connecticut, reported the results of a survey that compared the cost of the top 50 grocery products over a period of 12 months at a variety of stores. The same items cost $82.57 at a supermarket; $83.90 at a club store (such as Sam's Club or Costco); and $78.05 at a drug chain or supercenter, such as Wal-Mart Supercenter.

■ Robert C. Gatty

Football. The organizers of the Bowl Championship Series (BCS), which was designed to determine the best college football team in the United States, suffered another embarrassment in 2004 when three teams from major conferences—the University of Southern California (USC), the University of Oklahoma (Norman), and Auburn University—finished the season without a loss. Since only two teams could play for the national title, the outcome renewed critics' calls for a play-off system. Fortunately for the BCS system, USC averted a split national title by defeating Oklahoma 55-19 in the Orange Bowl on Jan. 4, 2005, giving USC a second consecutive title and the 11th in the team's history.

In the National Football League (NFL), the New England Patriots won their final 15 games of the regular season and play-offs, culminating with their second Super Bowl title in three years, a dramatic 32-29 victory in Super Bowl XXXVIII over the Carolina Panthers on Feb. 1, 2004, in Houston, Texas.

BCS mess—again. The BCS system, which involves both polls and six computer rankings to determine the best teams, took another beating in 2004. In 2003, the system produced a split championship—precisely the outcome it was designed to avoid. Louisiana State University (LSU) topped the *USA Today* coaches' poll, while USC topped the Associated Press (AP) poll. As a result, BCS officials changed the formula.

The BCS increased the importance of the AP and coaches' polls, eliminated a separate strength of schedule component, and reduced the role of the computer polls. However, these changes did not alter the fact that three teams ended the season without a loss, and therefore, each had a claim to play in the title game.

In an attempt to include more smaller schools in the BCS bowl picture, organizers in February 2004 announced plans to add a fifth BCS bowl in 2006. Smaller schools had long complained that the BCS system did not give them a fair chance to compete for the national title.

College. On Jan. 4, 2005, USC trounced Oklahoma 55-19 to take the BCS national football title. USC's Heisman Trophy-winning quarterback Matt Leinart led his team's unstoppable offense, throwing for 332 yards and an Orange Bowl record 5 touchdown passes.

Before the game, there was a possibility of a split championship if the AP poll voters selected undefeated Auburn to be the top team. However, because of its resounding victory, USC received all but three first-place AP votes.

In other major BCS bowls, the University of Texas (Austin) defeated the University of Michigan (Ann Arbor) 38-37 in the Rose Bowl on January 1 in Pasadena, California. The University of Utah defeated the University of Pittsburgh 45-7 in the Fiesta Bowl on January 2 in Tempe, Arizona. Auburn defeated Virginia Tech 16-13 in the Sugar Bowl in Baton Rouge, Louisiana, on January 3.

Heisman Trophy. USC quarterback Matt Leinart captured the Heisman Trophy, awarded on December 11 at the Downtown Athletic Club in New York City. Leinart received 267 first-place votes, easily beating University of Oklahoma freshman Adrian Peterson.

Milestones. University of Hawaii quarterback Timmy Chang smashed the all-time National Collegiate Athletic Association (NCAA) passing record in 2004. Chang passed for 17,072 yards, topping the 15,031-yards record set by Ty Detmer at Brigham Young University from 1988 to 1991.

The University of Nebraska (Lincoln), a perennial power in the Big 12, took a tumble in 2004. The team finished with a record of 5-6, its worst since 1961.

Clarett denied. A federal appeals court on May 24, 2004, denied Ohio State sophomore Maurice Clarett's attempt to declare for early entry into the NFL draft. The court ruled that federal labor policy allows NFL teams to determine when players can enter the league.

2004 NATIONAL FOOTBALL LEAGUE FINAL STANDINGS

AMERICAN CONFERENCE

North Division	W.	L.	T.	Pct.
Pittsburgh Steelers*	15	1	0	.938
Baltimore Ravens	9	7	0	.562
Cincinnati Bengals	8	8	0	.500
Cleveland Browns	4	12	0	.250

East Division	W.	L.	T.	Pct.
New England Patriots*	14	2	0	.875
New York Jets*	10	6	0	.625
Buffalo Bills	9	7	0	.562
Miami Dolphins	4	12	0	.250

South Division	W.	L.	T.	Pct.
Indianapolis Colts*	12	4	0	.750
Jacksonville Jaguars	9	7	0	.562
Houston Texans	7	9	0	.438
Tennessee Titans	5	11	0	.312

West Division	W.	L.	T.	Pct.
San Diego Chargers*	12	4	0	.750
Denver Broncos*	10	6	0	.625
Kansas City Chiefs	7	9	0	.438
Oakland Raiders	5	11	0	.312

*Made play-offs

NATIONAL CONFERENCE

North Division	W.	L.	T.	Pct.
Green Bay Packers*	10	6	0	.625
Minnesota Vikings*	8	8	0	.500
Detroit Lions	6	10	0	.375
Chicago Bears	5	11	0	.312

East Division	W.	L.	T.	Pct.
Philadelphia Eagles*	13	3	0	.812
New York Giants	6	10	0	.375
Dallas Cowboys	6	10	0	.375
Washington Redskins	6	10	0	.375

South Division	W.	L.	T.	Pct.
Atlanta Falcons*	11	5	0	.688
New Orleans Saints	8	8	0	.500
Carolina Panthers	7	9	0	.438
Tampa Bay Buccaneers	5	11	0	.312

West Division	W.	L.	T.	Pct.
Seattle Seahawks*	9	7	0	.562
St. Louis Rams*	8	8	0	.500
Arizona Cardinals	6	10	0	.375
San Francisco 49ers	2	14	0	.125

*Made play-offs

TEAM STATISTICS

Leading offenses (yards gained)	Yards	Per game
Kansas City	6,695	418.4
Indianapolis	6,475	404.7
Denver	6,332	395.8
New England	5,722	357.6
San Diego	5,552	347.0

Leading defenses	Avg. points against	Yards per game
Pittsburgh	15.7	258.4
Buffalo	17.8	264.2
Denver	19.0	278.7
Baltimore	16.8	300.2
New York	16.3	304,9

TEAM STATISTICS

Leading offenses (yards gained)	Yards	Per game
Green Bay	6,349	396.8
Minnesota	6,339	396.2
St. Louis	5,877	367.3
Seattle	5,634	352.1
Philadelphia	5,618	351.1

Leading defenses	Avg. points against	Yards per game
Washington	16.6	267.6
Tampa Bay	19.0	284.5
Philadelphia	16.2	319.7
Arizona	20.1	321.3
New York	21,7	324.2

INDIVIDUAL STATISTICS

Leading scorers, touchdowns	TD's	Rush	Rec.	Ret.
LaDainian Tomlinson, San Diego	18	17	1	0
Marvin Harrison, Indianapolis	15	0	15	0
Priest Holmes, Kansas City	15	14	1	0
Curtis Martin, New York	14	12	2	0

Leading kickers	PAT made/att.	FG made/att.	Longest FG	Pts.
Adam Vinatieri, New England	48/48	31/33	48	141
Matt Stover, Baltimore	30/30	29/32	50	117
Jason Elam, Denver	42/42	29/34	52	129
Jeff Reed, Pittsburgh	40/40	28/33	51	124

Leading quarterbacks	Att.	Comp.	Yds.	TD's	Ints.
Trent Green, Kansas City	556	369	4,591	27	17
Peyton Manning, Indianapolis	497	336	4,557	49	10
Jake Plummer, Denver	521	303	4,089	27	20
Tom Brady, New England	474	288	3,692	28	14
David Carr, Houston	466	285	3,531	16	14

Leading receivers	Passes caught	Rec. yards	Avg. gain	TD's
Chad Johnson, Cincinnati	95	1,274	13.4	9
Tony Gonzalez, Kansas City	102	1,258	12.3	7
Drew Bennett, Tennessee	80	1,247	15.6	11
Reggie Wayne, Indianapolis	77	1,210	15.7	12

Leading rushers	Rushes	Yards	Avg.	TD's
Curtis Martin, New York	371	1,697	4.6	12
Corey Dillon, New England	345	1,635	4.7	12
Edgerrin James, Indianapolis	334	1,548	4.6	9
Rudi Johnson, Cincinnati	361	1,454	4.0	12

Leading punters	Punts	Yards	Avg.	Longest
Shane Lechler, Oakland	73	3,409	46.7	67
Hunter Smith, Indianapolis	54	2,443	45.2	62
Brian Moorman, Buffalo	77	3,325	43.2	80
Mike Scifres, San Diego	69	2,974	43.1	60

INDIVIDUAL STATISTICS

Leading scorers, touchdowns	TD's	Rush	Rec.	Ret.
Shaun Alexander, Seattle	20	16	4	0
Muhsin Muhammad, Carolina	16	0	16	0
Tiki Barber, New York	15	13	2	0
Terrell Owens, Philadelphia	14	0	14	0

Leading kickers	PAT made/att.	FG made/att.	Longest FG	Pts.
David Akers, Philadelphia	41/42	27/32	51	122
Ryan Longwell, Green Bay	48/48	24/28	53	120
Jason Hanson, Detroit	28/28	24/28	48	100
Josh Brown, Seattle	40/40	23/25	54	109

Leading quarterbacks	Att.	Comp.	Yds.	TD's	Ints.
Daunte Culpepper, Minnesota	548	379	4,717	39	11
Brett Favre, Green Bay	540	346	4,088	30	17
Marc Bulger, St. Louis	485	321	3,964	21	14
Jake Delhomme, Carolina	533	310	3,886	29	15
Donovan McNabb, Philadelphia	469	300	3,875	31	8

Leading receivers	Passes caught	Rec. yards	Avg. gain	TD's
Muhsin Muhammad, Carolina	93	1,405	15.1	16
Joe Horn, New Orleans	94	1,399	14.9	11
Javon Walker, Green Bay	89	1,382	15.5	12
Torry Holt, St. Louis	94	1,372	14.6	10

Leading rushers	Rushes	Yards	Avg.	TD's
Shaun Alexander, Seattle	353	1,696	4.8	16
Tiki Barber, New York	322	1,518	4.7	13
Clinton Portis, Washington	343	1,315	3.8	5
Ahman Green, Green Bay	259	1,163	4.5	7

Leading punters	Punts	Yards	Avg.	Longest
Tom Tupa, Washington	103	4,544	44.1	61
Todd Sauerbrun, Carolina	76	3,351	44.1	65
Mitch Berger, New Orleans	85	3,704	43.6	63
Scott Player, Arizona	98	4,230	43.2	57

THE 2004 COLLEGE FOOTBALL SEASON

NATIONAL CHAMPIONS

NCAA Div. I-A	Southern California	55	Oklahoma	19
NCAA Div. I-AA	James Madison	31	Montana	21
NCAA Div. II	Valdosta State	36	Pittsburgh	31
NCAA Div. III	Linfield	28	Mary Hardin-Baylor	21
NAIA	Carroll College	15	St. Francis (Ind.)	13

BOWL CHAMPIONSHIP SERIES GAMES

BOWL	RESULT			
Orange	Southern California	55	Oklahoma	19
Sugar	Auburn	16	Virginia Tech	13
Fiesta	Utah	35	Pittsburgh	7
Rose	Texas	38	Michigan	37

OTHER BOWL GAMES

Alamo	Ohio State	33	Oklahoma State	7
Capital One	Iowa	30	Louisiana State	25
Champs Sports	Georgia Tech	51	Syracuse	14
Continental	Boston College	37	North Carolina	24
Cotton	Tennessee	38	Texas A&M	7
Ft. Worth	Cincinnati	32	Marshall	14
Emerald	Navy	34	New Mexico	19
GMAC	Bowling Green	52	Memphis	35
Gator	Florida State	30	West Virginia	18
Hawaii	Hawaii	59	UAB	40
Holiday	Texas Tech	45	California	31
Houston	Colorado	33	Texas (El Paso)	28
Independence	Iowa State	17	Miami (Ohio)	13
Insight	Oregon State	38	Notre Dame	21
Las Vegas	Wyoming	24	UCLA	21
Liberty	Louisville	44	Boise State	40
MPC Computers	Fresno State	37	Virginia	34
Motor City	Connecticut	39	Toledo	10
Music City	Minnesota	20	Alabama	16
New Orleans	S. Mississippi	31	North Texas	10
Outback	Georgia	24	Wisconsin	21
Peach	Miami	27	Florida	10
Silicon Valley	Northern Illinois	34	Troy	21
Sun	Arizona State	27	Purdue	23

CONFERENCE CHAMPIONS

NCAA DIVISION I-A

CONFERENCE	SCHOOL
Atlantic Coast	Virginia Tech
Big 12	Oklahoma
Big East	Pittsburgh
Big Ten	Iowa—Michigan (tie)
Conference USA	Louisville
Mid-American	Toledo
Mountain West	Utah
Pacific 10	Southern California
Southeastern	Auburn
Sun Belt	North Texas
Western Athletic	Boise State

NCAA DIVISION I-AA

CONFERENCE	SCHOOL
Atlantic 10	James Madison
Big Sky	Montana—Eastern Washington (tie)
Big South	Coastal Carolina
Gateway	Illinois State
Great West	California Polytechnic
Ivy League	Harvard
Metro Atlantic	Duquesne
Mid-Eastern	Hampton—South Carolina State (tie)
Northeast	Monmouth—Central Connecticut State (tie)
Ohio Valley	Jacksonville State
Patriot	Lafeyette—Lehigh (tie)
Pioneer	Drake
Southern	Furman
Southland	Northwestern State—Sam Houston (tie)
Southwestern	Alabama State

Clarett, who starred as a freshman on the Ohio State team that won the national title at the end of the 2002 season, had been suspended from the team in 2003 for violating bylaws of the NCAA, including receiving improper benefits and lying to investigators. NFL rules specify that a player must be out of high school for three years to qualify.

NFL. On Feb. 1, 2004, the New England Patriots defeated the Carolina Panthers 32-29, winning their second Super Bowl title the same way they won their first in 2002—on a dramatic last-second field goal by kicker Adam Vinatieri. The game started slowly, with the two teams going a Super Bowl-record 26 minutes, 55 seconds without scoring. However, the ending made up for the slow beginning.

The Patriots led 14-10 at half-time. Neither team scored in the third quarter, but combined for a record 37 points in the fourth. Carolina took a 22-21 lead on the longest pass play in Super Bowl history—an 85-yard bomb from Jake Delhomme to Muhsin Muhammad. The Panthers fell behind 29-22 and then tied the game at 29 with 1 minute, 8 seconds to play.

New England quarterback Tom Brady, who later received his second Super Bowl Most Valuable Player trophy, took over at his own 40 yard line. He marched his team downfield into position for Vinatieri to kick his 41-yard game-winning field goal with 4 seconds remaining. Brady completed a Super Bowl record 32 passes on 48 attempts for 354 yards, three touchdowns, and one interception.

Play-offs. In the American Football Conference (AFC) wild-card play-offs, the Tennessee Titans edged past the Baltimore Ravens 20-17 on January 3 while the Indianapolis Colts

ALL-AMERICA TEAM (as chosen by the Associated Press)

OFFENSE
Quarterback—Matt Leinart, Southern California
Running backs—Adrian Peterson, Oklahoma;
 J. J. Arrington, California
Wide receivers—Braylon Edwards, Michigan;
 Taylor Stubblefield, Purdue
Tight end—Heath Miller, Virginia
Center—David Baas, Michigan
Other linemen—Jammal Brown, Oklahoma; Alex Barron, Florida
 State; Elton Brown, Virginia; Michael Munoz, Tennessee
All-purpose player—Reggie Bush, Southern California
Place-kicker—Mike Nugent, Ohio State

DEFENSE
Linemen—Erasmus James, Wisconsin; David Pollack, Georgia;
 Shaun Cody, Southern California; Marcus Spears, Louisiana State
Linebackers—Derrick Johnson, Texas; Matt Grootegoed, Southern
 California; A. J. Hawk, Ohio State
Backs—Carlos Rogers, Auburn; Antrel Rolle, Miami;
 Marlin Jackson, Michigan; Ernest Shazor, Michigan
Punter—Brandon Fields, Michigan State

PLAYER AWARDS
Heisman Trophy (best player)—Matt Leinart, Southern California
Bednarik Trophy (best defensive player)—David Pollack, Georgia
Lombardi Award (best lineman)—David Pollack, Georgia

Matt Leinart, quarterback for the University of Southern California (USC.), was awarded the Heisman Trophy on December 11, which is given to the outstanding college football player in the United States. On Jan. 4, 2005, he led USC to a national football title by throwing for 332 yards and 5 touchdown passes to win the Orange Bowl 55-19 against the University of Oklahoma.

routed the visiting Denver Broncos 41-10 on January 4 behind quarterback Peyton Manning's five touchdown passes. The following weekend, New England edged visiting Tennessee 17-14 in bitter cold conditions while Indianapolis beat the Kansas City Chiefs 38-31. New England defeated Indianapolis 24-14 in the AFC championship game on January 18 in Foxboro, Massachusetts.

In the National Football Conference (NFC) wild-card play-offs, the Carolina Panthers stomped the visiting Dallas Cowboys 29-10 on January 3, while host Green Bay Packers up-ended the Seattle Seahawks 33-27 in overtime. The following weekend, Carolina stunned host St. Louis Rams 29-23 in double overtime, and the Philadelphia Eagles edged visiting Green Bay 20-17 in overtime. In the NFC title game, Carolina's defense smothered Philadelphia at home for a 14-3 win on January 18.

Streak over. On October 31, the Pittsburgh Steelers defeated the New England Patriots 34-20, snapping New England's record run of 21 straight victories, dating to Sept. 28, 2003.

Troubles. The Miami Dolphins in 2004 suffered a series of injuries and embarrassments. In July, one week before training camp, star running back Ricky Williams announced that he was retiring at the age of 27. Williams later admitted that the NFL was about to suspend him for four games for failing his third drug test for marijuana. In September, an arbitrator ruled Williams owed the Dolphins $8.6 million for breach of contract. On November 9, with a record of 1-9, coach Dave Wannstedt resigned.

Baltimore running back Jamal Lewis, who led the NFL in rushing with 2,066 yards in 2003, was indicted in February 2004 on drug charges. He later pleaded guilty to having used a telephone to facilitate a drug purchase in 2000.

Milestones. Indianapolis Colts quarterback Peyton Manning on Dec. 26, 2004, broke one of the most revered records in football. Manning threw his 49th touchdown pass of the season, breaking the record of 48 held by Dan Marino of the Miami Dolphins since 1984. Manning's record-breaking touchdown pass came in dramatic fashion, tying the San Diego Chargers with 56 seconds left in the game. The Colts won the game in overtime.

Legendary receiver Jerry Rice saw his streak of 274 games with a reception end on Sept. 19, 2004. Rice failed to catch a pass in three of the first five games of the season with the Oakland Raiders and was traded to Seattle in October at his request.

Canadian Football League. The Toronto Argonauts captured their first Grey Cup title since 1997 with a 27-19 victory over the British Columbia Lions in Ottawa on Nov. 21, 2004.

■ Michael Kates

See also **Sports.**

France. The government of Prime Minister Jean-Pierre Raffarin suffered several electoral setbacks in 2004 amid rising public protests over budgetary cutbacks and economic reforms. The government had to make cutbacks to reduce its budget deficit, which in 2004 exceeded the limit for countries using the euro for the third consecutive year. Hospital workers, teachers, and scientific researchers staged a series of strikes and protest marches against budget cuts early in the year.

Raffarin's center-right governing Union for the Presidential Marjority, known by its French acronym UMP, suffered a major defeat in regional elections on March 28. The party captured just 37 percent of the vote and won control of the governing council in only 1 of France's 22 regions. The opposition Socialists won 50 percent of the vote and gained control of councils in 21 regions.

Government shakeup. Raffarin reshuffled his Cabinet following the election, replacing Finance Minister Francis Mer with Nicolas Sarkozy, the former interior minister. Sarkozy was the government's most popular member, but his openly declared ambition of running for president in 2007 created tension with President Jacques Chirac, who was eligible for re-election.

Sarkozy sought to boost the economy by offering tax incentives for first-time home buyers, easing France's 35-hour work week law to enable people to work longer hours. He also offered tax breaks to companies that create jobs. To reduce the deficit, he introduced a two-year freeze on government spending and sold off stakes in several state-owned companies. In June, the government raised $1.5 billion by selling a 35-percent stake in the aircraft engine maker Snecma on the stock market. Sarkozy also raised $6.2 billion in September by selling a stake of 10.85 percent in France Telecom, the national phone company.

In July, the government passed a law paving the way for the privatization of two main energy utilities, Electricite de France and Gaz de France, in 2005. Unions opposed the move, which they feared would lead to job cuts.

Sarkozy resigned as minister in November 2004 to become chairman of the UMP party after Chirac ruled that he could not hold both jobs at the same time. Sarkozy hoped the party leadership would position him to run for the presidency in 2007.

The economy improved in line with a general European recovery in 2004, but the upturn failed to reduce unemployment. European Union economists forecast that France's output would grow by 2.4 percent, up from 0.5 percent in 2003. Joblessness increased slightly to 9.6 percent from 9.4 percent.

Corruption case. Former Prime Minister Alain Juppe, a close ally of Chirac, was found guilty of corruption in 2004. A court found that Juppe had allowed party employees to be put on the city of Paris payroll when he was deputy mayor in the 1980's and early 1990's. Chirac was mayor at the time. In January 2004, Juppe received an 18-month suspended sentence and was barred from holding political office for 10 years. The verdict forced Juppe to resign his position as UMP chairman. In December, an appeals court reduced the sentence to 14 months and the ban on holding political office to 1 year.

Headscarf ban. A new law banning the wearing of headscarves in schools aroused tensions in France's Muslim community, the largest Muslim community in Europe. The law, which was adopted by the French parliament in March, outlawed the wearing of overt religious symbols, including large Christian crosses, Jewish skullcaps, and Sikh turbans. Nevertheless, it was aimed primarily at Islamic headscarves. The government insisted the law was necessary to defend the secular, or non-religious, nature of French state schools, particularly from the threat of Islamic fundamentalism. Opponents criticized the ban as a violation of human rights. A small number of Muslim students who defied the ban when it went into effect in September were expelled from school.

Cote d'Ivoire. France stepped up its military intervention in Cote d'Ivoire, a West African former French colony torn by civil war since 2002. In November 2004, Cote d'Ivoire government forces killed nine French peacekeeping troops while attacking rebels in the country's north. In re-sponse, French forces destroyed Cote d'Ivoire's tiny air force. In December, demonstrators called for the withdrawal of the approximately 5,000 French troops deployed in Cote d'Ivoire.

Health reforms. The government approved a package of controversial measures designed to reduce France's high health care costs. The measures, approved by parliament in July 2004, increased fees paid by patients and companies, cut spending on brand-name prescription drugs, and aimed to cut waste and fraud. The reforms were to eliminate a deficit of about $16 billion in the state health care system.

Industrial policy. The government played an active role to rescue and promote French industrial companies in 2004. In April, the French pharmaceutical company Sanofi-Synthelabo agreed to acquire its Franco-German rival, Aventis, for $64 billion in cash and stock. The deal was encouraged by the government after the Swiss company Novartis sought to acquire Aventis. The merged company, Sanofi-Aventis, became the world's third-largest drug company. In July, the government completed a $2.75-billion financial rescue of Alstom, a French maker of trains and power-generation equipment whose debts had threatened it with bankruptcy. ■ Tom Buerkle

See also **Europe.**

City residents and tourists enjoy "Paris Beach," an installation along the Seine River, in July 2004. The attraction —which was in its third year—included palm trees, tons of sand, showers, beach chairs, and a swimming pool along the stone embankments that line the river.

Gardening. Invasive plants, diseases, and insect pests continued to bedevil experts and cause consternation for nurseries and gardeners alike in 2004. Invasive plants—whether weedy species such as star thistle or popular garden plants like butterfly bush and English ivy—cost the United States economy more than $30 billion a year, according to researchers at the Department of Ecology and Evolutionary Biology of Cornell University in Ithaca, New York.

During 2004, the American Nursery & Landscape Association and the U.S. Department of Agriculture (USDA) entered into a partnership to encourage research on new ways of combatting invasive plants. Rather than endorsing plant bans, the initiative was to concentrate on front-end solutions such as breeding for noninvasive traits.

Trends. As more gardeners embraced organic methods in 2004, companies that offer gardening products responded by rolling out new lines of organic pesticides, fertilizers, and soil amendments. One of the most popular of these organic products was compost tea, a concentrated solution made in mechanical brewers that bubble water through compost fortified with nutrient additives. SoilSoup, Inc., of Edmonds, Washington, the first company to market a home compost brewer, introduced its smallest system, capable of brewing 6.5 gallons (24.5 liters). Gardeners could also buy compost tea ready-made at nurseries. Compost tea provides a number of nutrients to plants and introduces beneficial microbes that foster soil health and help prevent diseases.

Tropical gardening, container gardening, and water features were still popular among gardeners, but the hottest trend in 2004 was "Mediterranean lush courtyards." The style, which evoked the sunny climes and warm colors of Italy and the south of France, featured tile-decorated surfaces and a central tile or stucco fountain; containers stuffed with tropical plants; plant materials common to Mediterranean areas, such as ornamental grasses, salvias, and olive trees; and stone and gravel surfaces in lieu of grass lawn.

Weather. As scientists debated global warming versus natural climate shifts, gardeners experienced the havoc wrought on their landscapes by atypical weather patterns in 2004. Meanwhile, gardeners awaited a new issue of the USDA's Plant Hardiness Zone Map, the weather bible of plant growers. A draft version of the new map, which incorporated more zones and modified zones in many areas, was made available for review in 2003. However, reviewers with the USDA and the American Horticultural Society, partners in the map development project, rejected the draft. The USDA promised a new map in 2004, but as of early December, gardeners were still waiting.

Saving water. Even in moisture-drenched places like the Pacific Northwest, drought-tolerant gardening—also known as xeriscape gardening—gained popularity in 2004. Rising water bills in many parts of the country enhanced the appeal of xeriscape gardening. To design a drought-tolerant landscape, gardeners search out plants with low water requirements, group them according to their needs, and install drip irrigation and soaker systems that use far less water than sprinklers. Many water-friendly gardeners also opt to replace a portion or all of their water-greedy lawns with low-water ground covers.

■ Kym Pokorny

Gas and gasoline. See Energy supply.
Genetic engineering. See Biology; Medicine.

Geology. As coastal development increases at unprecedented rates, most of the world's shorelines are eroding and retreating—setting the stage for disaster. This was the conclusion reported in March 2004 by geologists Orrin Pilkey of Duke University in Durham, North Carolina, and J. Andrew Cooper of the University of Ulster in the United Kingdom. Pilkey and Cooper also concluded that existing computer models of coastal retreat, in which scientists use computer simulations to try to understand the phenomenon better, are so flawed that they may actually be a "hazard to society."

Scientists believe there are two main reasons for global coastal erosion, both the result of *global warming,* an increase in the average temperature of Earth's lower atmosphere and surface. One reason is that sea level is rising due to the melting of icecaps and glaciers, which produces runoff that enters the sea. The other reason is *thermal expansion* of the ocean—that is, the expansion and rising of the ocean caused directly by higher temperatures.

Pilkey and Cooper pointed out that there are many unknowns when it comes to making predictions of future shoreline positions. Shoreline retreat is controlled by numerous complex factors besides sea level rise, including the frequency and magnitude of large storms; the distribution of sand on a shore; and various geological characteristics unique to each region. The geologists suggested that coastal planners should recognize and accept the limitations and uncertainties in predicting shoreline retreat due to sea level rise. Because of these uncertainties, the scientists advocated changes in coastal management policies to reduce the chances that large numbers of people would be affected by shoreline erosion.

New Geologic Time Scale. A revised Geologic Time Scale was published in August by the International Commission on Stratigraphy, an international scientific organization concerned with *stratigraphy,* or layers of geological deposits. The commission had been working for several years on the revision of the time scale, which shows the times when the various eras and periods of Earth's geological history began and ended. The previous version of the scale had been released in 1989. The new revision was an attempt to clear up the confusion caused by different scientists using different dates for the 91 geological divisions.

Since 1972, geologists have been seeking to firm up the boundaries of geological periods by finding *global standard stratotype-section and points (GSSP's)*—also referred to as "golden spikes." These are locations where strong evidence of ancient, worldwide geological events—such as volcanic eruptions; meteorite impacts; or the appearance or disappearance of certain fossils—can be found. As of 2004, geologists had found golden spikes to establish reliable dates for 50 of the 91 geological divisions.

Geologists hoped to have golden spikes for all 91 divisions by 2008. Nevertheless, the exact timing of many of the boundaries between periods is likely to remain the subject of debate for years to come.

Instant ice age? The Hollywood disaster film *The Day After Tomorrow* received a mixed review for scientific accuracy in August. In the film, an abrupt change in deep-sea circulation caused by global warming triggers an instantaneous ice age that wreaks havoc on society. A group of scientists led by oceanographer Bogi Hansen of the Faeroese Fisheries Laboratories on the Faroe Islands, in the North Atlantic Ocean, evaluated the movie's assumptions about *thermohaline circulation,* vertical currents that move from the sea surface to the deep sea and back again.

The near-bottom waters in thermohaline circulation originate at high latitudes, such as in the Norwegian Sea, where cooling and sea-ice formation increase the density of surface waters. These dense waters then sink to the bottom and spread out toward the equator. Moving in the opposite direction, warm surface waters flow toward the polar regions to take the place of the cold, sinking waters. These warm currents help moderate the climate in many areas.

If the downward flow of cold water was somehow reduced or stopped—as in the film,

when melting fresh water from ice sheets decreases the density of the salty seawater— the climate-moderating warm currents might also be slowed or stopped. Hansen's team concluded that this type of change in ocean circulation could lead to at least regional cooling in Western Europe. However, his team pointed out that such changes would be unlikely to lead to a global ice age as depicted in the film; there are decades worth of deep, cool waters stored in the ocean basins, and these waters would continue to drive thermohaline circulation.

Massive earthquake. On December 26, a magnitude-9.0 earthquake off the coast of the Indonesian island of Sumatra generated enormous tsunamis that left tens of thousands of people dead in several nations bordering the Indian Ocean. The tremor was the most powerful earthquake recorded in 40 years. Enzo Boschi, head of Italy's National Institute of Geophysics, noted that the quake was strong enough to have disturbed the wobble in Earth's rotation about its axis.   ■ Henry T. Mullins

See also **Disasters; Oceanography.**

Georgia. Opposition leader and United States-educated lawyer Mikhail Saakashvili swept to victory in Georgia's presidential election on Jan. 4, 2004, completing Georgia's so-called "Rose Revolution." The Rose Revolution, named for the flower that became a symbol of its peaceful nature, began in November 2003, when Saakashvili led large-scale protests in the Georgian capital of Tbilisi in response to a parliamentary election that observers believed to have been rigged. The protests eventually forced President Eduard Shevardnadze from power.

Elections. The 36-year-old Saakashvili, with no serious competitors, won a stunning 96 percent of the vote and was sworn in as president on Jan. 25, 2004. The U.S. government hailed Saakashvili's victory as a step forward for democracy, while Russia took a dimmer view of the political transition. The United States and Russia competed fiercely for political and economic influence in Georgia, a vital link for a major U.S.-backed oil pipeline.

In parliamentary elections on March 28, Saakashvili's ruling coalition National Movement-Democrats received more than 67 percent of the vote, winning 135 of the 150 contested party-list seats. The opposition bloc New Rightists-Industrialists, the only other group to surpass the 7-percent support threshold necessary to enter parliament, won the 15 remaining seats. The election was a partial re-run of the disputed November 2003 parliamentary elections.

Separatists. Saakashvili's immediate domestic challenge was regaining control over Georgia's separatist regions of Abkhazia, Adjaria, and South Ossetia. Under Shevardnadze, the three regions had assumed nearly complete autonomy from the central government.

After troops loyal to Adjarian leader Aslan Abashidze prevented Saakashvili from entering Adjaria on March 14, Saakashvili gave Abashidze a one-day deadline to disarm and acknowledge the authority of the Georgian government. When Abashidze failed to do so, Georgia imposed economic sanctions on Adjaria, which forced Abashidze to back down. The crisis resumed on May 2 as Abashidze's troops blew up bridges connecting Adjaria to the rest of Georgia in response to Georgian military maneuvers near the border. Following another ultimatum and massive anti-Abashidze protests in Batumi, the Adjarian capital, Abashidze fled to Moscow on May 6, ceding Adjaria to Georgian government control.

Saakashvili also increased pressure on Abkhazia and South Ossetia to recognize his government's authority. However, no significant progress was made in either region. ■ Juliet Johnson

See also **Asia; Russia.**

Georgia. See State government.

Germany. The government of Chancellor Gerhard Schroeder continued to implement welfare and labor reforms in 2004. The reforms were intended to increase Germany's competitiveness by promoting growth and job creation. The economy remained sluggish, however, and the reforms sparked protests and contributed to electoral defeats for Schroeder's Social Democratic Party.

Reforms. The Bundestag, the lower house of parliament, passed legislation in July to trim unemployment benefits for many of Germany's 4 million jobless people. The law, scheduled to take effect in 2005, was the last of a series of measures implemented to scale back Germany's generous welfare system and encourage more people to work.

The reforms proved especially controversial in eastern Germany, where the unemployment rate in 2004 was higher than 18 percent. Beginning in July, tens of thousands of Germans took to the streets weekly in major cities in so-called Monday demonstrations to protest the welfare cutbacks.

The discontent also fueled support for radical parties. In regional elections on September 19, the Party of Democratic Socialism (the former Communist Party) won 28 percent of the vote in the state of Brandenburg, while the extreme right-wing National Democratic Party (NDP) won 9 percent of the vote in Saxony. The score gave the NDP its first seats in any state parliament since 1968.

Electoral losses. Opposition to the welfare reforms contributed to a string of defeats for Schroeder's Social Democrats. On Feb. 29, 2004, the party was routed in a parliamentary election in Hamburg, a former stronghold, winning just 30.5 percent of the vote, compared with 47.2 percent for the center-right Christian Democratic Union (CDU). In June, the Social Democrats won just 21.5 percent of the vote in elections for the European Parliament, compared with 44.5 percent for the CDU and its Bavarian sister party, the Christian Socialist Union (CSU).

New president. Horst Koehler, a former finance ministry official who served as managing director of the International Monetary Fund, was elected as Germany's president on May 23, 2004. Koehler was the candidate of the opposition CDU and CSU parties. He succeeded Johannes Rau, a Social Democrat, in the largely ceremonial post.

The German economy picked up modestly as part of a European-wide recovery in 2004. European Union (EU) economists forecast that Germany's *gross domestic product* (GDP—the total output of goods and services produced in a country in a year) would grow by 1.9 percent in 2004, the strongest rate since 2000 but below the average rate of 2.5 percent for the 25 EU countries. German unemployment edged up, however, to 9.7 percent, from 9.6 percent in 2003.

The sluggish economy caused Germany's high budget deficit to persist. The deficit was forecast to amount to 3.9 percent of GDP in 2004, the third consecutive year in which it exceeded the 3-percent limit for countries using the euro.

Relations with the United States improved in 2004, following sharp disagreements in 2003 over the war in Iraq, which Germany opposed. Chancellor Schroeder met with U.S. President George W. Bush at the White House in Washington, D.C., on Feb. 27, 2004, and both men promised to improve cooperation. In June, Germany consented to a U.S. plan to have the North Atlantic Treaty Organization train Iraqi security forces, though the government refused to send German troops to Iraq as part of the effort.

Immigration law. The Schroeder government and the opposition agreed in June on Germany's first immigration law. The controversial measure allowed a certain number of skilled workers to enter the country; required legal immigrants to learn the German language; and provided for the deportation of illegal immigrants.

Corporate cutbacks. Several large companies won significant concessions from their workers in 2004. Siemens AG, a global electronics and engineering company based in Munich, reached an agreement in July under which 4,000 workers at two German factories would work 40 hours a week, up from 35 previously, without a pay raise. The company had threatened to move its mobile telephone assembly operations to Hungary, where wages are lower than in Germany.

Also in July, workers at Stuttgart-based auto-

Crowds gather before the newly restored Church of Our Lady in Dresden on June 22, 2004, as the cupola and gold cross are positioned atop the Protestant cathedral. The original 18th-century, Baroque structure—along with much of the rest of the city—was destroyed in firebombing by Allied forces at the end of World War II (1939-1945).

maker DaimlerChrysler agreed to work longer hours and give up some benefits to save 6,000 jobs at a factory near Stuttgart. Several other companies struck similar deals with their workers, claiming that the concessions were necessary to keep German manufacturing competitive.

Workers at U.S. automaker General Motors Corp.'s (GM) German subsidiary, Adam Opel, staged brief strikes after GM announced in October plans to cut 12,000 jobs in Europe, mostly in Germany. Similar strikes affected Wolfsburg-based automaker Volkswagen. In November, the company guaranteed jobs for 100,000 workers through 2011 in exchange for a pay freeze until 2007.

Banker trial. The chief executive of Frankfurt-based Deutsche Bank, Josef Ackermann, was acquitted in July 2004 of illegally approving $94 million in bonuses to executives of Dusseldorf-based mobile telephone company Mannesmann AG after they agreed to the acquisition of the company by Britain's Vodafone. The $190-billion deal was the world's biggest takeover in 2000. Many Germans disliked the use of huge, U.S.-style bonus payments, but a court in Dusseldorf found the payments were not illegal.   ■ Tom Buerkle

See also **Europe; Iraq: A Special Report.**

Global warming. See **Environmental pollution.**

Golf. Vijay Singh of Fiji dominated the men's Professional Golfers' Association (PGA) in 2004, winning nine tournaments, including a major, the PGA Championship. Singh, known for his work ethic and demanding practice schedule, bumped Eldrick "Tiger" Woods from the world No. 1 spot and became the first player to win $10 million in a season.

PGA. Phil Mickelson shook the label of being the best player never to win a major when he drained his 18-foot (5.5-meter) birdie putt on the final hole to win the Masters in Augusta, Georgia, on April 11. Mickelson birdied five of the final seven holes, shooting a 31 on the back nine to finish at 9-under-par and win by one stroke. Mickelson also became just the fourth player in Masters history to win with a birdie on the final shot of the tournament. Ernie Els of South Africa, who had an eagle, a birdie, and some tough pars down the stretch, finished at 8-under-par.

Retief Goosen of South Africa captured his second U.S. Open in four years with a two-shot victory in Southampton, New York, on June 20. Goosen finished at 4-under 276.

Todd Hamilton of the United States held off Els in a play-off to win the British Open on July 18, 2004, in Troon, Scotland. Both men finished 72 holes at 10-under 274, one shot ahead of Mickelson, but Hamilton beat Els by one stroke in the play-off.

Singh won the PGA Championship on August 15 in Haven, Wisconsin, edging Chris DiMarco and Justin Leonard in a three-hole play-off after all three finished regulation at 8-under-par 280.

LPGA. Grace Park won her first Ladies Professional Golf Association (LPGA) major when she drained a six-foot (1.8-meter) putt to capture the Kraft Nabisco Championship in Rancho Mirage, California, on March 28.

Annika Sorenstam of Sweden captured her seventh career major on June 13, winning the LPGA Championship in Wilmington, Delaware.

Meg Mallon won the U.S. Women's Open in South Hadley, Massachusetts, on July 4 with a final round 65 (6-under), the lowest final round by a champion in the 59-year history of the event.

Karen Stupples of the United Kingdom won her first major title at the Women's British Open on August 1 in Berkshire, England. Stupples's score of 19-under-par 269 tied the record total for an LPGA major tournament. Stupples shot an 8-under-par 64 on the last day to win by five strokes over Rachel Teske of Australia. The round of the tournament, however, went to Minea

Todd Hamilton of the United States watches his tee shot during the final round of the British Open at Royal Troon Golf Club in Troon, Scotland, on July 18, 2004. Hamilton, a rookie on the PGA Tour, outdueled veteran Ernie Els in a play-off to win.

Blomqvist, 19, of Finland, who on July 31 carded a 10-under-par 62, the lowest single-round score ever in a major, men's or women's.

Champions Tour. On the circuit for professional men more than 50 years old, Hale Irwin captured the Senior PGA Championship in Louisville, Kentucky, on May 31 with a birdie on the final hole to finish at 8-under, one stroke ahead of Jay Haas, who was playing in his first senior event.

Mark James of the United Kingdom became the first European to win a Senior major when he took the Senior Players Championship on July 10 in Dearborn, Michigan.

Peter Oakley, who had to qualify into the Senior British Open, won that event in Portrush, Northern Ireland, on July 25. On the final day, Oakley shot a 2-under-par round to finish the tournament at 4-under-par.

Peter Jacobsen won the U.S. Senior Open in St. Louis, Missouri, to finish at 12-under, one stroke ahead of Irwin. The players were forced to play 36 holes on the final day after rain washed out the second round.

Craig Stadler birdied the last four holes to win the Tradition on August 30 by one shot for his second major title in two years on the tour.
■ Michael Kates

See also **Sports.**

Greece. Voters elected a new conservative government in 2004, ending nearly two decades of Socialist rule. The country also staged a successful Summer Olympic Games, but the cost of the event was expected to burden Greece for years.

Change of power. The conservative New Democracy party swept to victory in elections on March 7. Party leader Costas Karamanlis campaigned against alleged corruption under the Socialists, who had ruled the country for 19 of the past 23 years. He also promised to cut taxes and spur job creation. In February, unemployment in Greece was estimated to stand at 9 percent.

New Democracy captured a majority of 165 seats in the 300-seat parliament, making Karamanlis prime minister. The result signaled a return to power for one of Greece's biggest political dynasties. Karamanlis's uncle, Constantine Karamanlis, founded New Democracy and served as prime minister five times between 1955 and 1980. The Socialists won 117 seats in parliament.

The government's first task was to prepare for the Olympics. Work on many of the facilities, including the Olympic Stadium, had been plagued by delays. Athens was ready in time for the Aug. 13, 2004, opening day, however, and the games were successful. A record 11,099 athletes from 202 countries participated, and television ratings exceeded those of the 2000 games in Sydney.

Deficit woes. Two months after taking office, Karamanlis announced that Greece's budget deficit in 2003 had reached 3.2 percent of *gross domestic product* (GDP—the total amount of goods and services produced in a country in a year), nearly double the 1.7 percent of GDP reported by the previous government. Karamanlis blamed the Socialists for underreporting military spending and overestimating Social Security surpluses.

By September 2004, it had become clear that the previous government had underreported the deficit each year from 1997 to 2003. In addition, Karamanlis announced that the deficit would increase to 5.3 percent of GDP in 2004 largely because of the Olympics, which cost an estimated $11.6 billion. The European Union (EU) criticized Greece because the deficits exceeded the 3-percent ceiling for EU countries using the euro.

Soccer victory. Greece's soccer team scored a huge upset by winning the European Championship in July 2004. Greece, which had never before won a single game in an international tournament, defeated Portugal 1-0 in the final in Lisbon on July 4. The victory prompted massive celebrations throughout the country.   ■ Tom Buerkle

See also **Eastern Orthodox Churches; Europe; Olympics: A Special Report; People in the news** (Gianna Angelopoulos-Daskalaki); **Soccer.**

Grenada. See Latin America.

Guatemala. Oscar Berger Perdomo, of the Great National Alliance coalition, was sworn in to a four-year term as president of Guatemala on Jan. 14, 2004. President Berger pledged to increase employment through stepped-up private investment.

In July, President Berger ordered 1,600 soldiers to patrol the streets of Guatemala City, the capital. During the first six months of 2004, some 2,000 people living in large Guatemalan cities were murdered—most of them by urban street gangs.

The Guatemalan government in July paid $3.5 million to victims and their families for the loss of life and property resulting from state-sponsored oppression during the 1960-1996 civil war. President Berger said the payments constituted "explicit recognition of the suffering of thousands of Guatemalans. . . ."

In January 2004, Guatemala's Supreme Court sentenced Juan Valencia Osorio, a former army colonel, to 30 years in prison for ordering the 1990 murder of Myrna Mack Chang. Mack, a renowned Guatemalan anthropologist, had been investigating abuses of Maya Indians by the Guatemalan army.   ■ Nathan A. Haverstock

See also **Latin America.**

Guinea. See Africa.

Guyana. See Latin America.

Can Haiti, with international assistance, overcome its troubled legacy of poverty, misrule, and environmental destruction?

By Nathan A. Haverstock

Haiti
In Search of Higher Ground

A man tries to salvage his belongings in the city of Gonaives after Tropical Storm Jeanne caused massive flooding in September that left more than 2,000 Haitians dead and tens of thousands homeless.

Supporters of President Jean-Bertrand Aristide demonstrate in Haiti's capital, Port-au-Prince, in the midst of a coup that forced him from office in late February.

Tropical Storm Jeanne, on September 18, 2004, dropped 13 inches (330 millimeters) of rain on Haiti, triggering massive flooding. In the country's fourth largest city, Gonaives, on the west coast, flood-waters crested at 9 feet (2.7 meters), affecting 80,000 of the 100,000 residents. In all, the storm left more than 2,000 Haitians dead and hundreds of thousands of others homeless. It was Haiti's second natural disaster in just four months. In May, seasonal storms had caused flooding that killed more than 3,300 people in the southeastern part of the country. It was "like the flood in the Bible," said Fernando Gueren, a poor farmer, who lost his parents and a son to raging floodwaters 5 feet (1.5 meters) deep. In the Haitian town of Mapou, 1,600 people drowned in their sleep, when a nearby river overflowed its banks.

Fortunately, well-equipped foreign troops were on hand and transported by road or airlifted by helicopter tons of emergency food, medicine, clothing, and temporary shelter to the people afflicted by the flooding. The troops belonged to a United Nations (UN) peacekeeping mission whose original job, beginning in late February, was to restore order after a popular uprising forced President Jean-Bertrand Aristide to resign and flee the country. The political crisis—Haiti's 15th change of government in 18 years—had prompted the United Nations to dispatch soldiers to Haiti for the second time in less than 10 years. "This time, let us get it right," said UN Secretary General Kofi Annan on June 1, the day the United Nations assumed responsibility for restoring democracy.

France, which once had ruled Haiti as a colony, and the United States, which had intervened several times in Haiti's affairs, were the first foreign countries to send troops to reestablish order in 2004. Concerned for the welfare of Haitians and anxious to prevent a massive exodus of Haitian refugees to the United States, President George W. Bush dispatched a team of 1,600 marines in March. The international assistance would test, once more, whether Haiti could, with help from abroad, overcome its legacy of poverty, misrule, and ecological disaster.

Haiti's troubled history

The legacy is centuries old. Spaniards rushed to Hispaniola in the early 1500's after Christopher Columbus discovered gold on the island. (Haiti shares the island of Hispaniola with the Dominican

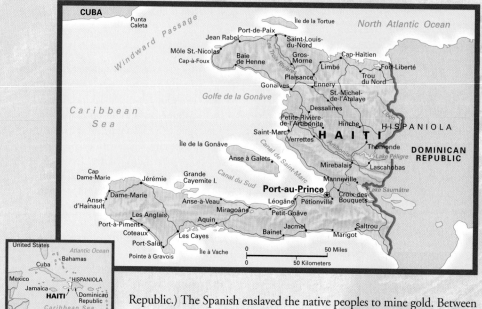

A 1791 slave revolt on the island of Hispaniola, depicted in this 19th-century engraving, led to the creation of Haiti, the first independent black nation in the Western hemisphere.

Republic.) The Spanish enslaved the native peoples to mine gold. Between mistreatment and disease, only a few hundred Indians remained alive by 1530. Africans were then imported as slaves. When the gold petered out, most of the Spanish colonists left, bent on exploiting the vastly richer gold reserves of Mexico and Peru. In 1606, King Philip III of Spain ordered those who remained to relocate to the eastern side of Hispaniola, where he could better assure their safety.

Over time, a motley assortment of English, French, and Dutch settlers, including pirates, moved into abandoned areas on Hispaniola's northern and western coasts. In 1697, Spain officially recognized French control of the western third of the island. French emigrants subsequently established large and lucrative sugar cane plantations cultivated by enslaved Africans.

Haitian dictator Francois "Papa Doc" Duvalier, in constant fear for his life, traveled by car with a rifle between his legs. His brutal regime and that of his son lasted from 1957 to 1986.

The French colonial period, which lasted for a century, gave rise to enduring racial tensions between Haiti's mixed population of Europeans; people of pure African descent; and people of mixed European and African descent, who eventually became an "elite" class who controlled much of the wealth.

In 1791, Haitians of African descent, who by then outnumbered European colonists 8 to 1, rebelled. Emboldened by the ideals of the French Revolution (1789-1799), Toussaint L'Ouverture, a former slave, assumed control of the colony's government. Napoleon I responded by sending an army to restore French rule. Toussaint was captured in 1802 and imprisoned in France, where he died of starvation and cold. Nevertheless, his cause prevailed, and the French, diminished by yellow fever, were eventually defeated. General Jean-Jacques Dessalines, another former slave, proclaimed the colony an independent country on Jan. 1, 1804, and named it Haiti, an Indian word meaning "high ground." Unfortunately, independence did not provide immediate or lasting freedom to the people.

Haiti was ruled by tyrannical, corrupt, or ineffective leaders—most of them drawn from the elite, mixed-race class—for much of its subsequent history. During a period of particularly violent political upheaval in 1915, U.S. President Woodrow Wilson sent marines to Haiti to forestall the possibility of an intervention by some European power. Thereafter, the United States administered Haiti until 1934 under a constitution drafted by Wilson's assistant secretary of the Navy, Franklin D. Roosevelt.

In 1950, Haiti adopted a constitution of its own making, which paved the way for democratic elections. However, tensions persisted between the wealthy, mixed-race elite and the people of pure African descent, who constituted 95 percent of population. The latter rejoiced when one of their own, Francois "Papa Doc" Duvalier, won the presidency in 1957.

The author:

Nathan A. Haverstock is an affiliate scholar at Oberlin College in Oberlin, Ohio.

Haitians cheer rebels arriving in Port-au-Prince, the capital, on February 29 after the downfall of President Jean-Bertrand Aristide.

Duvalier, a conservative, black, country physician soon assumed dictatorial powers with the support of Haiti's armed forces. Duvalier, who died in 1971, and his son, Jean-Claude "Baby Doc," ruled Haiti with an iron hand. Their secret police—the *Tontons Macoutes* (bogeymen)—terrified and terrorized the Haitian people from 1957 to 1986, when the younger Duvalier was ousted in a popular uprising. The Duvaliers reportedly looted the treasury to the tune of $900 million, leaving Haiti an outcast among nations, unable to meet the needs of its people or its international financial obligations.

The presidency of Jean-Bertrand Aristide

Haiti's long history of corrupt misrule appeared to be at an end in 1990 when another black leader, Jean-Bertrand Aristide, a former Roman Catholic priest, was elected president on his pledge to help the poor. He was, however, soon ousted in a military coup, to the dismay of numerous supporters at home and abroad, who rallied to his cause. In response to the public outcry, President Bill Clinton sent troops to Haiti in 1994, and Aristide was forcibly restored to power without the loss of a single life.

Once again in power, Aristide was soon charged with human rights violations and corruption, and his re-election in 2000 was widely regarded as fraudulent. When the Organization of American States—an association of 35 American countries that promotes regional cooperation—later confirmed that the election had indeed been rigged, foreign donors, including the United States, cut off monetary aid to Haiti.

Without foreign aid, Aristide's government essentially was without operating funds, and political paralysis set in. Conditions got even worse for the poor, and their widespread misery fueled rebellion.

An outlaw faction, with local popular support, took up arms and captured Gonaives on Feb. 5, 2004. Other factions took to the field under the banner of the National Revolutionary Front for the Liberation of Haiti. While former Haitian soldiers, furious that Aristide had disbanded the army in 1995, helped lead the rebellion, armed gangs carried out the fighting on both sides.

In a confusing campaign that developed episodically, the Gonaives-based Cannibal Army, which had previously supported Aristide, captured Cap-Haitien, on the north coast, on February 22, and Port-de-Paix, in the northwest, two days later. Their rapid progress was facilitated by support from local people, by Aristide's political opponents among the elite, and by both of Haiti's major opposition parties, though political leaders denied any involvement.

Aristide—under enormous pressure to resign from the rebels who were marching on the capital, Port-au-Prince; from his political foes; and from the governments of the United States and France—resigned on February 29. He later charged that the Bush administration had forced him out of office—had, in fact, "abducted him."

The allegation, though ridiculed by the Bush administration, elicited some sympathy from African Americans in the Black Caucus of the U.S. Congress. They accused President Bush of having undermined Aristide's government by blocking humanitarian assistance to one of the world's poorest countries, thereby destabilizing its fragile economy. Bush critics conceded, however, that Aristide had imposed an increasingly corrupt and oppressive regime upon being restored to power.

Rebuilding the government

Once American and French forces were firmly in control of the situation on the ground in early March, Boniface Alexandre, Haiti's chief justice, was sworn in as interim president, as mandated by Haiti's constitution. "We are all in the same boat. If it sinks, we all sink together," he said, appealing to Haitians for calm during the turbulent political storm. The rebels and opposition parties pledged their support to Alexandre.

On March 9, a seven-member council of eminent Haitians, convened by the U.S. government, named Gerard Latortue prime minister. A prominent economist and former Haitian foreign minister, Latortue was living in exile in Florida. He selected for his Cabinet, for the most part, technically well-qualified people who did not belong to Haiti's bitterly divided political parties. Similarly, he worked with UN officials to recruit an Electoral Council that would oversee elections scheduled for 2005.

In June 2004, Lieutenant-General Augusto Heleno Ribeiro Pereira, of the Brazilian army, assumed command of the United Nations peacekeeping force that

A Haitian farmer burns vegetation from his land in preparation for planting crops, a widespread practice that has created an ecological disaster.

was to provide Haiti with the security necessary for the transitional government to function. His immediate and most daunting task was to remove from circulation arms and ammunition whose proliferation had created a climate of fear and anxiety everywhere in Haiti. The weapons were in the hands of outlaw gangs, which had fought in the recent rebellion, and drug traffickers, who had made Haiti a key transit point in the flow of illicit narcotics between Latin America and the United States.

Prime Minister Latortue's government faced an even greater challenge—dealing with the poverty produced by two centuries of misrule and ruthless disregard for the land. In 2004, Haiti was the poorest nation in the Western Hemisphere. Two-thirds of the work force was unemployed, and most Haitians lived on less than $1 a day. The per capita gross domestic product (GDP) was $1,600, compared with Haiti's neighbor, the Dominican Republic, which had a per capita GDP of $6,000. (GDP is the value of all goods and services produced in a country in a given year.) In 2004, Haiti led the hemisphere in the number of cases of AIDS per capita, and life expectancy was little more than 50 years.

In addition, government was confronted with a collapsed economy, a looming deficit of $100 million, and a treasury without enough money on hand to cover one month's expenses. "We are faced with an impossible situation," said Henri Bazin, the new finance minister. "We need $100 million immediately … to do the bare minimum of what the government should be doing. But we don't know where that money will come from."

Garbage rots in Cite Soleil, a vast slum in Port-au-Prince. Deforestation and the erosion of once-fertile land in rural areas have forced hundreds of thousands of Haitians off the land and into city slums.

An ecological disaster

The poverty of the Haitian people and the massive flooding in May and September are both directly related to a single problem: deforestation.

Deforestation, and the soil erosion that results from deforestation, have wreaked havoc on Haiti's preindustrial, predominantly agricultural society. Prime Minister Latortue noted in May, "The root of the problem is that we have to go and reforest the hills and until we do that ... the same thing could happen again."

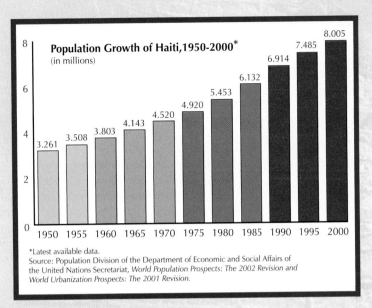

Population Growth of Haiti, 1950-2000*
(in millions)

3.261 | 3.508 | 3.803 | 4.143 | 4.520 | 4.920 | 5.453 | 6.132 | 6.914 | 7.485 | 8.005
1950 | 1955 | 1960 | 1965 | 1970 | 1975 | 1980 | 1985 | 1990 | 1995 | 2000

*Latest available data.
Source: Population Division of the Department of Economic and Social Affairs of the United Nations Secretariat, *World Population Prospects: The 2002 Revision and World Urbanization Prospects: The 2001 Revision.*

The cutting of trees on the once lush island of Hispaniola began in the 1600's when the French cleared land to plant the cane that would make Haiti the world's largest producer of sugar. More trees were cut to fuel the mills that processed the cane into sugar. Later, entire forests of mahogany were felled and shipped off to France to make furniture. In the 20th century, trees were cut to produce charcoal, which supplies more than 70 percent of Haiti's energy needs. By 2004, an estimated 98 percent of all trees in Haiti had been cut, and even avocado and mango trees were beginning to disappear, threatening a vital food source.

Without vegetation to hold the land, Haiti's shallow tropical soil washed down hillsides, silting up streams and rivers. Because trees emit water vapor into the air, their loss also resulted in less-regular rain. Less rain lowered the water table, which in turn reduced crop yields. The lower yields impoverished Haiti's farmers, the backbone of the country's agrarian economy.

Haitian law made the farmers' problems even worse. Under the law, land must be divided among a farmer's heirs, dividing family holdings into smaller and smaller pieces. In 2004, the average land holding in Haiti was only slightly more than 0.5 acre (0.2 hectare), which is insufficient to support a family in the best of years. As a result, a formerly self-reliant nation, which once managed to produce enough rice to feed its population, now imports even this basic staple of the Haitian diet.

By 2004, approximately 6 million of Haiti's 7.6 million people lived in run-down, litter-strewn villages or ramshackle houses on the land, attempting to eke out a living as subsistence farmers on largely barren, mountainous terrain. Their own numbers made their plight worse. The population of Haiti quadrupled between 1940 and 2000, despite the migration of hundreds of thousands of people to the United States and other nations in the 1980's and 1990's.

Between 1950 and 2000, the population of Haiti almost tripled, intensifying the poverty of the people.

Addressing environmental problems

Attempts have been made to reverse the damage to the land. The Agency for International Development (AID), which manages U.S.

foreign assistance programs, has overseen the planting of 60 million trees in Haiti over the last 20 years—3 million per year. However, as David Adams, director of the AID program in Haiti, pointed out, poor people annually chop down from 10 million to 20 million trees per year—more than can be planted.

Still some experts, such as Ron Pierre, a board member of the Illinois-based charitable organization Double Harvest, are more optimistic about restoring the land. Double Harvest, launched in 1981 to help Haitians help themselves, maintains a 200-acre (80-hectare) plot of land where Haitians are taught how to grow enough to become self-sufficient. "Haiti has two things going for it—water and climate," Pierre emphasized. According to Pierre, restoring the productivity of the land depends on allowing the soil "to breathe." For this purpose, Double Harvest mixes into its planting beds a waste product of local sugar cultivation called bagasse—the dried pulp left over after the juice is extracted from the stalks of cane—that can be used to properly ventilate the soil.

Double Harvest has devoted its acreage to the labor-intensive production of crops for which a local distribution network was already in place, or for which there was strong local demand, such as seedlings for trees. In 2004, the organization employed 400 Haitians, who grew tomatoes, peppers, okra, carrots, lettuce, cucumbers, papaya, manioc, and bananas for local consumption.

Bereft of effective national health care, social security, and welfare systems, Haitians had long looked for help from international relief agencies such as Double Harvest, which is sponsored by the Evangelical Baptist Missions of the United States. When the UN force arrived in Haiti in 2004, foreign-based relief agencies—such as CARE, the Catholic Relief Services, the International Red Cross, Save the Children, and World Vision International, plus various private local foundations—attended to the urgent daily needs of as many as 1 million desperately poor Haitians.

Humanitarian programs supported by various Protestant churches also played a prominent role in helping Haiti's poor. Wallace Turnbull, who with his wife Eleanor served for more than 50 years as a Baptist missionary near the Haitian town of Fermathe, dated this Protestant presence in Haiti to the dictatorship of Francois Duvalier. "Duvalier threw wide open Haiti's doors to Protestant Evangelical missionaries," Turnbull noted, "as a means of curbing the then-dominant influence of the Roman Catholic Church." In recent years Turnbull's mission added a sizeable greenhouse to its network of primary schools—where more than 50,000 children annually received a healthy start on life—and worked with their parents to reverse environmental degradation by planting trees.

Aid from the international community

Privately operated charitable organizations cannot single-handedly raise Haiti out of poverty, even when supplemented by the vital monetary support provided by Haitians living abroad to their families and friends. This assistance amounted to $800 million in 2003, with a large portion coming from the 600,000 Haitians residing in the United States.

Haiti still needed a substantial amount of aid from the international community, according to U.S. Secretary of State Colin Powell. In July, he urged representatives at a World Bank conference in Washington, D.C., to be more generous in helping Haiti's new government build a stable democracy. Moreover, he assured the representatives of donor nations that the interim government led by Prime Minister Latortue was determined to fashion a better future for the people of Haiti.

At the conference, U.S. officials pledged $230 million toward Haiti in 2004 and 2005, including $19 million targeted for helping Haitians combat AIDS. The pledges of 30 countries and 32 international organizations at the conference brought the total international assistance package to more than $1 billion.

Rebuilding the Haitian spirit

In Haiti, the commander of the UN peacekeeping force, General Heleno, faced another kind of challenge—restoring the spirit of people severely plagued by what a Haitian proverb characterizes as a "big devil called discouragement." Upon assuming his command in Haiti, Heleno emphasized the need to reawaken "the desire to rebuild" and rekindle hope among the Haitian people, most immediately by establishing and maintaining an orderly society. The challenge involves not only removing a massive number of weapons from the streets, but fostering the resumption of business and banking and returning some sense of normalcy. International affairs experts speculated that "to get it right this time" might require a UN presence of modest proportions in Haiti for as long as 20 years. With luck, Haitians during this period will witness the revival both of their soils and spirit—and the preservation of a unique and endangered culture. Despite a year of political and natural disasters, Haitians in 2004 found renewed pride in celebrating the 200th anniversary of the founding of the world's first black republic—the product of history's only successful slave rebellion.

UN peacekeeping troops from Brazil block a street in Port-au-Prince in June in an attempt to keep order in the capital. A coup in February prompted the UN to dispatch troops to Haiti for the second time in less than 10 years.

Health care issues. Activity related to health policy in the United States was largely focused on prescription drugs in 2004; particularly on whether Americans should be allowed to "reimport" U.S.-manufactured prescription drugs from Canada, where prices were lower. In 2004, several cities—Boston, Revere, and Springfield, Massachusetts—and states—Illinois, Iowa, Kansas, Maine, Minnesota, Missouri, New Hampshire, Washington, and Wisconsin—attempted to buy reimported drugs for employees or to assist residents to buy such drugs on their own. The federal Food and Drug Administration (FDA), which is charged with overseeing the safety of food and drugs, opposed these programs. Citing concerns about potential dangers of reimported drugs, the FDA warned public officials that the purchase of such drugs violated federal law. The FDA did not, however, attempt to shut down the programs. Nevertheless, Vermont sued the FDA for the right to purchase drugs from Canada.

The FDA came under fire after prescription drug maker Merck & Co., of New Jersey, withdrew Vioxx from the market in October. The popular arthritis painkiller was withdrawn because of concerns that it increased the risk of heart attack and stroke. Critics charged that the FDA had known for years about the drug's potential dangers and chose not to act. Defenders noted that the FDA is limited in terms of what it can do to protect the public.

On December 17, the FDA announced that study participants taking Celebrex, a drug similar to Vioxx, but manufactured by Pfizer, Inc., of New York City, had twice as high a risk of heart attack as participants not taking the drug. Pfizer announced on December 19 that it would keep Celebrex on the market but stop advertising it.

The FDA issued an order in October requiring that antidepressants, drugs taken to relieve depression, must be labeled with strong warnings about possible ill effects the drugs may have on patients younger than 18 years.

Election issues. President George W. Bush and Senator John Kerry (D., Massachusetts) both campaigned in 2004 for the U.S. presidency on health issues, including the reimportation of drugs; the number of U.S. citizens without health coverage; and the high cost of medical malpractice insurance. After winning re-election in November, President Bush announced that top priorities for his second term included malpractice insurance reform and the implementation of changes to the Medicare program, which covers many health care costs for people over 65. The changes cover some prescription drug benefits.

Various health care issues were on state ballots in November. California voters narrowly defeated a proposition that would have required most employers to offer health insurance to their workers. Cali-

fornians did approve annual funding of nearly $300 million for stem-cell research. Colorado, Montana, and Oklahoma citizens voted to increase tobacco taxes. Montana voters approved a measure to legalize the use of marijuana for medical purposes.

Insurance issues. In August, the U.S. Census Bureau reported that almost 16 percent of U.S. citizens did not have health insurance in 2003, compared with 14.2 percent in 2000, raising the total of uninsured to 45 million Americans. The greatest number of people without health insurance live in Texas, New Mexico, Louisiana, Oklahoma, and Nevada. In 2004, one state, Maine, launched a program, Dirigo Health, that was designed to offer coverage to all state uninsured residents and to control health care costs.

Infant mortality. In February, the U.S. Centers for Disease Control and Prevention reported that the U.S. infant mortality rate had risen for the first time in 40 years. The rate climbed from 6.8 deaths per 1,000 live births in 2001 to 7.0 deaths in 2002—a 3-percent increase.

Changes at the top. On Dec. 3, 2004, Tommy Thompson resigned as secretary of the U.S. Department of Health and Human Services. President Bush nominated Mike Leavitt, current director of the Environmental Protection Agency, to head the department. ■ Emily Friedman

See also **Drugs; Medicine; Public health.**

Hockey. The Tampa Bay Lightning, for the first time in the franchise's 12-year history, won the National Hockey League (NHL) Stanley Cup championship on June 7, 2004. The Lightning, down 3 games to 2 to the Calgary Flames, rallied for the title with a heart-stopping 2-1 victory in Game 7 in Tampa Bay.

Calgary, a sixth seed out of the Western Conference, had led the series 3 games to 2, but Tampa Bay, one of the worst teams in the NHL for most of the past decade, won in overtime on June 5 in Calgary to force a Game 7. The Lightning's Ruslan Fedotenko scored both goals to win Game 7.

Tampa Bay's Brad Richards won the Conn Smythe Award as play-off Most Valuable Player (MVP), while teammate Martin St. Louis won the Hart Trophy as regular season MVP and the Lester B. Pearson Award for best player as voted by other players. Tampa Bay coach John Tortorella was named coach of the year.

Regular season. In the Western Conference, the Detroit Red Wings rolled to the league's best record with 48 wins and 109 points to win the Central Division. The San Jose Sharks won the Pacific with 104 points, and the Vancouver Canucks won the Northwest with 101. In a heated race for the Eastern Conference's best mark, Tampa Bay came out on top, winning the

NATIONAL HOCKEY LEAGUE STANDINGS

WESTERN CONFERENCE

Central Division

	W.	L.	T.	†OTL.	Pts.
Detroit Red Wings*	48	21	11	2	109
St. Louis Blues*	39	30	11	2	91
Nashville Predators*	38	29	11	4	91
Columbus Blue Jackets	25	45	8	4	62
Chicago Blackhawks	20	43	11	8	59

Northwest Division

	W.	L.	T.	OTL.	Pts.
Vancouver Canucks*	43	24	10	5	101
Colorado Avalanche*	40	22	13	7	100
Calgary Flames*	42	30	7	3	94
Edmonton Oilers	36	29	12	5	89
Minnesota Wild	30	29	20	3	83

Pacific Division

	W.	L.	T.	OTL.	Pts.
San Jose Sharks*	43	21	12	6	104
Dallas Stars*	41	26	13	2	97
Los Angeles Kings	28	29	16	9	81
Anaheim Mighty Ducks	29	35	10	8	76
Phoenix Coyotes	22	36	18	6	68

EASTERN CONFERENCE

Northeast Division

	W.	L.	T.	OTL.	Pts.
Boston Bruins*	41	19	15	7	104
Toronto Maple Leafs*	45	24	10	3	103
Ottawa Senators*	43	23	10	6	102
Montreal Canadiens*	41	30	7	4	93
Buffalo Sabres	37	34	7	4	85

Atlantic Division

	W.	L.	T.	OTL.	Pts.
Philadelphia Flyers*	40	21	15	6	101
New Jersey Devils*	43	25	12	2	100
New York Islanders*	38	29	11	4	91
New York Rangers	27	40	7	8	69
Pittsburgh Penguins	23	47	8	4	58

Southeast Division

	W.	L.	T.	OTL.	Pts.
Tampa Bay Lightning*	46	22	8	6	106
Atlanta Thrashers	33	37	8	4	78
Carolina Hurricanes	28	34	14	6	76
Florida Panthers	28	35	15	4	75
Washington Capitals	23	46	10	3	59

*Made play-offs   †Overtime losses

STANLEY CUP CHAMPIONS—Tampa Bay Lightning
(defeated Calgary Flames, 4 games to 3)

LEADING SCORERS	Games	Goals	Assists	Pts.
Martin St. Louis, Tampa Bay	82	38	56	94
Ilya Kovalchuk, Atlanta	81	41	46	87
Joe Sakic, Colorado	81	33	54	87
Markus Naslund, Vancouver	78	35	49	84
Marian Hossa, Ottawa	81	36	46	82

LEADING GOALIES (26 or more games)	Games	Goals against	Avg.
Miikka Kiprusoff, Calgary	38	65	1.69
Dwayne Roloson, Minnesota	48	89	1.88
Marty Turco, Dallas	73	144	1.98
Martin Brodeur, New Jersey	75	154	2.03
Robert Esche, Philadelphia	40	79	2.04

AWARDS

Adams Award (coach of the year)—John Tortorella, Tampa Bay
Calder Trophy (best rookie)—Andrew Raycroft, Boston
Hart Trophy (most valuable player)—Martin St. Louis, Tampa Bay
Jennings Trophy (team[s] with fewest goals against)—Martin Brodeur, New Jersey
Lady Byng Trophy (sportsmanship)—Brad Richards, Tampa Bay
Masterton Trophy (perseverance, dedication to hockey)—Bryan Berard, Chicago
Norris Trophy (best defenseman)—Scott Niedermayer, New Jersey
Pearson Award (best player as voted by NHL players)—Martin St. Louis, Tampa Bay
Ross Trophy (leading scorer)—Martin St. Louis, Tampa Bay
Selke Trophy (best defensive forward)—Kris Draper, Detroit
Smythe Trophy (most valuable player in Stanley Cup)—Brad Richards, Tampa Bay
Vezina Trophy (best goalkeeper)—Martin Brodeur, New Jersey

Andrei Nikolishin of the Colorado Avalanche tries to pull Vancouver Canuck Todd Bertuzzi (#44) off of injured teammate Steve Moore during a game in Vancouver, Canada, on March 8. Bertuzzi, who had seriously injured Moore by hitting him from behind and driving his head into the ice, was later suspended for the rest of the season and faced criminal charges for the incident.

Southeast with 106 points and 46 wins. The Boston Bruins won the Northeast with 104 points, and the Philadelphia Flyers took the Atlantic with 101 points.

Play-offs. Tampa Bay slipped past Philadelphia 4 games to 3 in the Eastern Conference finals to gain the Stanley Cup finals. Tampa Bay ousted the New York Islanders 4 games to 1 in the first round and swept the Montreal Canadiens in the semifinals. Calgary defeated Vancouver 4 games to 3 in the first round, stunned top-seeded Detroit 4 games to 2 in the semifinals, and defeated San Jose 4 games to 2 in the Western Conference finals.

World championships. Canada defeated Sweden 5-3 in Prague on May 9 to win its second straight men's world title. The United States team took the bronze. In women's hockey, Canada topped the United States 2-0 in Halifax, Nova Scotia, on April 6 to win the gold.

College. The University of Denver won its first men's National Collegiate Athletic Association Division I title since 1969 with a 1-0 victory over the University of Maine (Orono) on April 10, 2004, in Boston.

Lockout. On September 15, NHL owners followed lock outed the players, shutting down the league after the owners and players failed to reach a new labor agreement. Observers speculated the lockout could last the entire 2004-2005 season.   ■ Michael Kates

Horse racing. In 2004, Smarty Jones, a colt from Pennsylvania, became the 18th horse in history to win the first two legs of the Triple Crown—the Kentucky Derby and the Preakness Stakes—only to lose the Belmont Stakes.

Smarty Jones achieved superstar status in 2004. The popular colt was the main reason that a crowd of more than 120,000 people came out to watch the Belmont Stakes in Elmont, New York, on June 5. The crowd was the largest ever to attend a sports event in New York State. Smarty Jones was just the fifth undefeated horse to win the Kentucky Derby and the first since Seattle Slew in 1977.

For the first time in the 130-year history of the Kentucky Derby, jockeys were allowed to wear advertising on their uniforms, after a federal judge ruled on June 3, 2004, that the Kentucky Horse Racing Authority's rule barring the ads was unconstitutional. The ruling prevented a threatened walkout by jockeys.

Three-year-olds. Smarty Jones overtook Lion Heart and won the Kentucky Derby by 2¾ lengths on May 1, 2004, in Louisville, Kentucky. With the victory, Stewart Elliott became the first jockey to win the Kentucky Derby in his first attempt since Ronnie Franklin did so riding Spectacular Bid in 1979.

MAJOR HORSE RACES OF 2004

THOROUGHBRED RACING

Race	Winner	Value to Winner
Atto Mile (Canada)	Soaring Free	$600,000
Belmont Stakes	Birdstone	$600,000
Blue Grass Stakes	The Cliff's Edge	$465,000
Breeders' Cup Classic	Ghostzapper	$2,080,000
Breeders' Cup Distaff	Ashado	$1,040,000
Breeders' Cup Filly & Mare Turf	Ouija Board	$733,200
Breeders' Cup Juvenile	Wilko	$780,000
Breeders' Cup Juvenile Fillies	Sweet Catomine	$520,000
Breeders' Cup Mile	Singletary	$873,600
Breeders' Cup Sprint	Speightstown	$551,200
Breeders' Cup Turf	Better Talk Now	$1,040,000
Canadian International Stakes	Sulamani	$900,000
Dubai World Cup (United Arab Emirates)	Pleasantly Perfect	$3,600,000
Derby Stakes (United Kingdom)	North Light	£800,000
Haskell Invitational Handicap	Lion Heart	$600,000
Hollywood Gold Cup	Total Impact	$450,000
Irish Derby (Ireland)	Grey Swallow	£736,000
Jockey Club Gold Cup	Funny Cide	$600,000
Kentucky Derby	Smarty Jones	$854,500
Kentucky Oaks	Ashado	$354,640
King George VI and Queen Elizabeth Diamond Stakes (United Kingdom)	Doyen	£435,000
Oaklawn Handicap	Peace Rules	$300,000
Pacific Classic	Pleasantly Perfect	$600,000
Preakness Stakes	Smarty Jones	$650,000
Prix de l'Arc de Triomphe (France)	Bago	915,000 euros
Santa Anita Derby	Castledale	$450,000
Santa Anita Handicap	Southern Image	$600,000
Lane's End Stakes	Sinister G	$300,000
Stephen H. Foster Handicap	Colonial Colony	$502,665
Travers Stakes	Birdstone	$600,000

HARNESS RACING

Race	Winner	Value to Winner
Cane Pace	Timesareachanging/ Western Terror (tie)	$125,577 (each)
Hambletonian	Windsong's Legacy	$500,000
Kentucky Futurity	Windsong's Legacy	$196,650
Little Brown Jug	Timesareachanging	$226,885
Meadowlands Pace	Holborn Hanover	$500,000
Messenger Stakes	Metropolitan	$126,472
Woodrow Wilson	Village Jolt	$216,000
Yonkers Trot	Windsong's Legacy	$195,600

Sources: *The Blood Horse Magazine* and U.S. Trotting Association.

On May 15, 2004, Smarty Jones dominated the Preakness Stakes at Baltimore's Pimlico Race Course. Smarty Jones won by 11½ lengths, the largest margin of victory in the 129-year history of the race.

Smarty Jones's quest to be the first horse since Affirmed in 1978 to win the Triple Crown ended when Birdstone, a long shot, chased him down on the final stretch to win the Belmont Stakes.

International. On March 27, 2004, Pleasantly Perfect rallied past Medaglia d'Oro to capture the world's richest horse race, the $6-million Dubai

Smarty Jones (left), ridden by Stewart Elliott, makes his move on Lion Heart in the final turn of the Kentucky Derby at Churchill Downs in Louisville on May 1, 2004. Smarty Jones won the race, becoming the fifth undefeated horse ever to win the Kentucky Derby.

World Cup, held in the United Arab Emirates. Bago captured the Prix de l'Arc de Triomphe on October 3 in Paris; North Light won the Vodafone Derby Stakes on June 5 in Epsom, England.

Harness racing. Windsong's Legacy became the seventh winner of the Triple Crown for trotters by winning the Kentucky Futurity in Lexington on October 9. Windsong's Legacy had previously won the Hambletonian in East Rutherford, New Jersey, and the Yonkers Trot at Hawthorne Race Course in Stickney, Illinois.

Timesareachanging and Western Terror finished in a dead heat in the Cane Pace on September 6, the first time there has been a dead heat in the 50-year history of the race. On July 18, Holborn Hanover became the longest shot to win the Meadowlands Pace, beating odds of 58-1.

■ Michael Kates

See also **Sports.**

Hospital. See Health care issues.

Housing. See Building and construction.

Houston. A historic rift in 2004 divided two of the founding institutions of the Texas Medical Center, a long-time economic and research powerhouse in Houston. In April, Baylor College of Medicine and The Methodist Hospital ended a 50-year partnership in which Methodist had served as a classroom for Baylor medical students. Methodist also had provided Baylor with patients for medical studies.

The two institutions split after Baylor announced it would build a new, one-stop adult outpatient clinic for its faculty and patients. Methodist objected, noting that the move might have a negative impact on its own outpatient operations. Baylor then chose St. Luke's Episcopal Hospital, a rival of Methodist, to become its new primary teaching hospital. In June, Methodist announced a new relationship with Weill Medical College of Cornell University in New York City.

The bickering between Baylor and Methodist grew more intense as 2004 went on. Baylor claimed that Methodist was trying to steal physicians under contract, which Methodist denied. In addition, some Baylor researchers refused to move to St. Luke's, while some Methodist physicians objected to the collaboration with Weill.

MetroRail trouble. Houston's new 7.5-mile

(12-kilometer) light rail line gained a reputation for crashes in 2004. The $324-million MetroRail Main Street line, which began operating in October 2003, runs from downtown Houston to the Astrodome and Reliant Stadium.

By September 2004, the trains of the line had been involved in more than 60 collisions with automobiles or pedestrians. Each resulted in at least one injury or $1,000 in property damage.

To reduce the number of crashes, the Metropolitan Transit Authority implemented several safety measures in 2004. These measures included adding more warning signs at intersections and redesigning problematic crossings.

Police crime lab scandal. The problems with Houston's police crime lab, where DNA testing had been suspended in 2002 amid questions about the quality and accuracy of the work, worsened in 2004. In May, Texas Governor Rick Perry pardoned Josiah Sutton, an inmate who had been imprisoned for more than four years on a rape conviction, after new DNA tests discredited the original tests that had been performed at the crime lab. In October, inmate George Rodriguez was released from prison because of improper DNA testing at the lab. A court had sentenced Rodriguez to 60 years in prison in 1987 for the kidnapping and rape of a 14-year-old girl.

Earlier in 2004, an internal investigation revealed that the crime lab had misplaced evidence from more than 8,000 cases between 1979 and 1991. Investigators discovered more than 280 boxes of evidence that had been abandoned.

As the scandal widened, many prisoner advocates called for a moratorium on death-penalty cases that had been investigated by the crime lab. In October 2004, Judge Tom Price, an eight-year veteran of the Texas Court of Criminal Appeals, urged that no more executions take place until questions about the crime lab's work were resolved.

Sports renaissance. Houston hosted its second Super Bowl in February at the newly built Reliant Stadium, home of the Houston Texans football team. National Football League officials praised the city for its efforts to entertain visiting dignitaries and celebrities. Civic leaders hoped to join the rotation of mostly Southern cities that host the competition every six to eight years.

Houston also hosted major league baseball's All-Star Game in July at Minute Maid Park, home of the Houston Astros baseball team. By attracting such marquee sporting events, city and county leaders argued that the $1 billion spent during the previous six years building Minute Maid Park, Reliant Stadium, and Toyota Center (a basketball arena) was justified.   ■ Eric Berger

See also **Baseball; Football; Immigration.**

Human rights. The fight against terrorism had broad repercussions for human rights globally in 2004. In addition, human rights violations by governments also dominated headlines and provoked international outrage. One of the most widely publicized controversies of 2004 arose after United States soldiers were accused of violating the human rights of captured Iraqis.

Abu Ghraib prison abuse. The U.S. armed forces were embarrassed in April by revelations that military guards at the Abu Ghraib prison in Iraq had abused Iraqi prisoners of war, subjecting them to physical and psychological abuse. Reports and photos of the abuse angered human rights advocates around the world.

United States President George W. Bush appeared on Arab television in May and expressed regret about the prison abuse. Without offering a direct apology, the president said the abuse of Iraqi prisoners "does not represent the America that I know." The next day, President Bush, during an appearance at the White House with King Abdullah II of Jordan, said he had told the Jordanian leader he was sorry for the humiliation suffered by the Iraqi prisoners. On May 7, Donald Rumsfeld, secretary of the U.S. Department of Defense, also accepted blame for the abuse and offered an apology to Iraqis abused by the U.S. soldiers.

A U.S. Army report released in August painted a picture of confusion and poor training that led to the abuse. A classified portion of the report, obtained and published by *The New York Times,* revealed that Lieutenant General Ricardo S. Sanchez, the top military commander in Iraq, had approved the use of severe interrogation techniques of prisoners. Such interrogation methods had been intended for use only against members of the al-Qa'ida terrorist network. The techniques included isolating prisoners and using dogs to intimidate them during questioning.

The report maintained that "at Abu Ghraib, isolation conditions sometimes included being kept naked in very hot or very cold, small rooms, and/or completely darkened rooms, clearly in violation of the Geneva Conventions." The Geneva Conventions are a series of treaties providing for the humane treatment of civilians, prisoners, and wounded people in wartime.

International Criminal Court. The Bush administration on June 23 abandoned efforts to establish immunity for U.S. troops from prosecution by the International Criminal Court (ICC). The ICC is a permanent court located in The Hague, Netherlands, for the prosecution of individuals accused of committing *genocide* (the deliberate and systematic mistreatment or extermination of a national, racial, political, religious, or cultural group), war crimes, and crimes against humanity.

Since the court was established in 2002, the United Nations' Security Council had passed resolutions exempting U.S. troops from such prosecutions. In the wake of the Abu Ghraib prison scandal, however, several members of the 15-member Security Council had increasingly opposed the exemptions. UN Secretary General Kofi Annan also opposed an exemption. The Bush administration had claimed that the United States needed the exemption to shield U.S. armed forces from politically motivated war-crime charges.

Racial profiling practices by law enforcement officials in the United States have increased as part of the federal government's war on terrorism. Amnesty International USA, a human rights organization headquartered in New York City, announced that finding in September 2004. Racial profiling is the act of targeting a person for criminal investigation primarily because of racial or ethnic characteristics. According to the report, approximately 32 million Americans had been questioned by law enforcement officials based solely on their race, ethnicity, or religious practices.

Sudan crisis. United States Secretary of State Colin L. Powell told the Senate Foreign Relations Committee on September 9 that killings, rapes, and property destruction in Sudan represented genocide and should be dealt with by the UN Security Council. Powell said he had reached the conclusion that genocide had occurred in Sudan—and may still have been taking place in 2004—after reviewing evidence compiled by State Department investigators. Powell blamed the Sudanese government and a government-sponsored militia for the attacks against civilians in the western region of Darfur. Sudanese officials claimed that the accusations were false.

Religious discrimination. The U.S. Department of Justice on March 30 intervened in a lawsuit against a Muskogee, Oklahoma, public school district in support of a sixth-grade Muslim girl who had been suspended for refusing to remove a headscarf. The girl and her family argued that the headscarf, called a hijab, was a traditional religious head covering. The district argued that the headwear violated its student dress code, which prohibited students from wearing hats, caps, bandannas, or jacket hoods inside school buildings. Justice Department officials said students should not be forced to choose between following their faith and receiving a public education. School district officials agreed on May 19 to allow the girl to wear the headscarf and revise its student dress code policy to accommodate exceptions for religious reasons.

■ Geoffrey A. Campbell

See also **Armed forces; Courts; Government of the United States; Iraq: A Special Report; State government; Sudan; Supreme Court of the United States; United Nations.**

Hungary joined the European Union (EU) on May 1, 2004. On June 13, Hungarians went to the polls to elect their 24 representatives to the European Parliament (EP). The EP, part of the EU governmental structure, is a 700-plus-member advisory body that meets in Strasbourg, France. The chief opposition party in Hungary's parliament, Hungarian Civic Alliance, took nearly half the vote and won 12 of the EP seats. The ruling Socialist party trailed at 34 percent, taking 9 seats.

In August, Socialist Prime Minister Peter Medgyessy resigned after a dispute with members of his governing coalition. Socialists chose Ferenc Gyurcsany to replace Medgyessy, and parliament confirmed the new prime minister in September.

Economic growth in Hungary accelerated in 2004. Gross domestic product—the value of all goods and services produced in a year—grew by 4.1 percent in the first half of the year, compared with 2.9 percent in 2003. In May 2004, Hungarian officials announced the government's goal of adopting the euro by 2010. The euro is the common currency of 12 of the 25 members of the EU.

In November 2004, the Hungarian parliament rejected the government's proposal to extend deployment of Hungary's 300 troops in Iraq into 2005. The soldiers went to Iraq in August 2003.

■ Sharon L. Wolchik

See also **Europe; Iraq: A Special Report.**

Ice skating. Shizuka Arakawa on March 27, 2004, became the third Japanese woman, after Yuka Sato and Midori Ito, to win a world championship. Arakawa's victory denied a sixth title to Michelle Kwan of the United States, who had been favored to win.

The International Skating Union, the sport's governing body, adopted a new scoring system in June in response to a judging scandal at the 2002 Winter Olympics in Salt Lake City, Utah. The new scoring system uses points, with every technical element assigned a value based on its difficulty. The 12 judges also give 5 artistic marks that are totaled; then a computer randomly selects 9 of the scores and throws out the high and low ones.

U.S. championships. Kwan captured her eighth U.S. title, her record-breaking seventh in a row, easily taking the gold at the championships on Jan. 10, 2004, in Atlanta, Georgia. Sasha Cohen finished second, and Jennifer Kirk took third. Also on January 10, Johnny Weir captured his first U.S. title, topping three-time winner Michael Weiss, who took the silver. Matthew Savoie came in third. Rena Inoue and John Baldwin, Jr., won their first pairs gold on January 9 as did ice dancers Tanith Belbin and Ben Agosto.

European championships. Brian Joubert became the first Frenchman in four decades to win the European title with his victory on Febru-

Chinese skaters Qing Pang and Jian Tong perform at the World Figure Skating Championships in Dortmund, Germany, on March 24, 2004. The pair received bronze medals for their performance, behind Russians Tatiana Totmianina and Maxim Marinin (gold) and China's Shen Xue and Hongbo Zhao (silver).

ary 5 in Budapest, Hungary. Joubert defeated Russians Evgeni Plushenko (silver) and Ilia Klimkin (bronze).

On Feb. 7, 2004, Julia Sebestyen became the first Hungarian woman to win the European title, beating Ukrainian Elena Liashenko (silver) and Russian Elena Sokolova (bronze). Russians Tatiana Totmianina and Maxim Marinin captured their third straight title. Russians Tatiana Navka and Roman Kostomarov took the ice dancing gold.

World championships. Arakawa, who finished third in her nation's championship competition, took the world championship in Dortmund, Germany, in March. She landed seven triple jumps in her free skate despite a strained thigh muscle. Cohen took the silver, and Kwan claimed the bronze.

Plushenko gained his third career title on March 25, with phenomenal jumping that earned him four perfect 6.0's despite a fall. Joubert took the silver, and German Stefan Lindemann won the bronze.

On March 24, Totmianina and Marinin captured the pairs gold medal, upending the two-time defending champions Shen Xue and Hongbo Zhao of China. On March 26, Navka and Kostomarov won their first world ice dancing title.   ■ Michael Kates

See also **Sports.**

Immigration. Officials with the United States Citizenship and Immigration Services (USCIS) announced in June 2004 that the bureau was streamlining the way immigration benefits are delivered. The streamlining is to eliminate a large backlog of requests while enhancing national security. The USCIS, which is part of the U.S. Department of Homeland Security, oversees immigration services, including the review and processing of citizenship applications and requests for work permits.

The USCIS hopes to eliminate a backlog of more than 3 million cases of people with outstanding immigration applications by the end of 2006. In 2003, the USCIS, which receives approximately 6 million applications a year, had a backlog of 3.7 million cases.

To eliminate the backlog, USCIS officials in 2004 began streamlining the application process, allowing officials to identify low-risk cases and process them more quickly. Applications from individuals thought to pose a higher security risk can also be identified more quickly, providing officials with the opportunity to subject them to a higher level of scrutiny at an earlier time.

Another streamlining plan allows people to make appointments with immigration information officers online, instead of waiting in line at

USCIS district offices. The USCIS launched the online appointment system, InfoPass, in Miami in 2003. It was in use in several cities and states by mid-2004, including Dallas, Detroit, and upstate New York. USCIS officials said the program would be offered nationwide by the end of 2004. USCIS Director Eduardo Aguirre reported that the bureau had a dramatic decrease in the length of lines, shortening the amount of time that people had to wait.

Air security. As part of the Homeland Security Department's effort to ensure public safety from terrorist attack at high-profile sporting events, U.S. Immigration and Customs Enforcement (ICE) took part in securing the airspace of Minute Maid Park in Houston for Major League Baseball's All-Star game on July 12. ICE aircraft enforced flight restrictions that forbade either commercial or private aircraft from flying over the stadium. Aircraft from the bureau's Air and Marine Operations division similarly provided security support for other high-profile events, including the 2004 Super Bowl, and around-the-clock protection in Washington, D.C.

Detention alternatives. ICE officials announced a new program in June designed to provide an alternative to detaining *aliens* (noncitizens) awaiting immigration court appearances. Under the program, aliens who do not pose a threat to either the local community or national security can be released if they post $1,500 bond or, in some cases, agree to appear at their next court appearance. Aliens awaiting court appearances may also be released if they wear electronic monitoring devices or agree to a variety of monitoring methods ranging from home and work visits to regular phone calls to case specialists. The program is being tested in Baltimore; Denver, Colorado; Kansas City, Kansas; Miami, Florida; Philadelphia; Portland, Oregon; St. Paul, Minnesota; and San Francisco.

Operation Predator. Immigration officials announced in July 2004 that more than 3,200 people had been arrested since mid-2003 as part of a federal program to safeguard children from sexual predators. Border and Transportation Security officials and ICE representatives said that 3,247 arrests had been made across the United States. Foreign law enforcement agencies had made another 500 arrests based on information from the U.S. government.

Called Operation Predator, the government program coordinates investigative and intelligence resources to protect children from *pedophiles* (adults who are sexually attracted to children) in countries outside the United States, human traffickers, international sex tourists, and Internet pornographers.

■ Geoffrey A. Campbell

India. The Congress Party, which had governed India through most of the 57 years since it gained independence in 1947, won an upset victory in parliamentary elections and returned to power in May 2004. The Congress Party defeated the Bharatiya Janata Party (BJP), which had led India since 1998. The BJP leader, Atal Bihari Vajpayee, resigned as prime minister and was succeeded by Manmohan Singh, who headed a coalition of Congress and other parties.

The BJP called the elections ahead of schedule in hopes of benefiting from a strengthened economy. The party, which emphasized Hindu nationalism, campaigned on a slogan of "India shining" to claim credit for prosperity. Opinion polls and analysts all indicated a BJP victory.

The Congress Party campaigned under the leadership of Sonia Gandhi, the Italian-born widow of former Prime Minister Rajiv Gandhi, who was the son and grandson of earlier Congress prime ministers. Sonia Gandhi's daughter, Priyanka, and son, Rahul, the family's fourth generation of party leaders, also played prominent roles in the campaign.

Congress, with 26.7 percent of the national vote, won 145 of the 543 seats in the Lok Sabha, the lower house of Parliament from which governments are formed. The party had held only 112 seats after the previous election in 1999.

Fall of the BJP. The BJP's support fell from 24 percent of the vote in 1999 to 22 percent in 2004; its Lok Sabha seats fell from 182 to 138. The party had governed with a coalition called the National Democratic Alliance.

Indian political commentators said rural voters had reacted against BJP claiming credit for a prosperity from which they had not benefited. Although India's economy had fared well under BJP rule, the agriculture sector, which employs nearly two-thirds of the population, performed poorly. Commentators also said many voters failed to support BJP efforts to intensify the Hindu character of Indian public life. The BJP was also accused of not working to prevent religious violence.

In two south Indian states noted for booming technological industries, Andhra Pradesh and Karnataka, voters tossed out governments that had failed to bring progress to farming areas. Both states had suffered from severe droughts in recent years, and leaders who had been widely praised for urban economic reforms were blamed for not alleviating rural misery.

BJP leaders began adopting a more radical position. The party was torn between reasserting its Hindu nationalistic nature and appealing to moderate center voters. Vajpayee, a moderate, began to fade as the more fanatical Lal Krishna Advani assumed party leadership in the Lok Sabha. Advani became president of the BJP after Venkaiah Naidu resigned on October 18. Party members complained

Election officials transport ballot boxes by elephant in rural India before national parliamentary elections in April. In a stunning upset, Indian voters turned the Bharatiya Janata Party out of office and returned the Congress Party to power.

religion, he became India's first non-Hindu leader. He held a doctorate in economics from Oxford University in Oxford, England. As finance minister in a Congress government from 1991 to 1996, he had launched economic liberalization that was widely credited with

about efforts of the new government to halt its revision of textbooks, which the BJP was rewriting to emphasize Hindu elements in history.

United Progressive Alliance. With the largest number of Lok Sabha seats, Congress put together a coalition—the United Progressive Alliance—to run the government. Communists, who won 61 seats, supported the coalition but did not join it.

Sonia Gandhi, as Congress Party president, was expected to become prime minister, despite BJP campaigning that denounced her as foreign born and not a Hindu. She decided to stand aside and support Manmohan Singh, rejecting emotional pleas from supporters to change her mind.

New prime minister. Singh was sworn in as prime minister on May 22. An adherent of the Sikh

breaking decades of stagnation caused by overly rigid government controls and with setting India on the road to more rapid economic growth. As prime minister, Singh promised more emphasis on "the human element" in public policy and greater help to poor farmers and unemployed youth. Singh also pushed for India to receive a permanent seat on the United Nations Security Council.

Singh's government resumed earlier efforts to resolve a dispute with Pakistan over Kashmir. India and Pakistan have been in conflict over control of the Indian state of Jammu and Kashmir since 1947, when the two countries gained independence. Singh and Pakistani President Pervez Musharraf met in New York City on Sept. 24, 2004, but made little progress.

Northern violence. Violence again flared in Kashmir in 2004. In the state of Jammu and Kashmir, where guerrilla fighters have long sought to loosen India's control of the predominately Muslim region, sporadic bombings took place in 2004. On April 17, suspected militants threw a hand grenade into a crowd during an election rally, wounding the state ministers of finance and tourism. On May 23, a land mine killed 28 Indian soldiers and their families on a bus.

Tsunamis disaster. A magnitude-9.0 earthquake off the northern coast of the Indonesian island of Sumatra on December 26 triggered tsunamis that crashed into several Asian countries, including India. Waves as high as 30 feet (10 meters) swamped more than 1,200 miles (2,000 kilometers) of southern coast in the states of Tamil Nadu, Andhra Pradesh, and Kerala. Madras, capital of Tamil Nadu, was particularly hard hit. On December 31, more than 10,000 people were confirmed dead in India.

Famous bandit killed. Veerappan, India's most famous bandit, was shot and killed on October 18. A task force created by the state of Tamil Nadu took 11 years to catch Veerappan, whom many of India's poor regarded as a hero and Robin Hood figure. ■ Henry S. Bradsher

See also **Asia; Disasters; Islam; Pakistan; People in the news** (Sonia Gandhi, Manmohan Singh).

Indian, American.
A new museum celebrating both the ancient traditions of American Indians and their own modern interpretations of their culture opened in Washington, D.C., on Sept. 21, 2004. The National Museum of the American Indian (NMAI) was built on the last open land on the National Mall, between the Capitol and the Washington Monument. Although it was not the first national Indian museum—the Museum of the American Indian had been established in New York City by banker George Gustav Heye in 1916—the new museum was the largest. Heye's museum had fallen into disrepair and been taken over by the Smithsonian Institution in 1989. The NMAI also became a part of the Smithsonian. The Institution, headquartered in Washington, D.C., is a nonprofit organization that operates numerous scientific, educational, and cultural museums.

The NMAI is housed in a five-story structure built of North American hardwoods, Canadian granite, and buff-colored Minnesota limestone. Its rounded exterior reflects the curves of Earth, sun, and moon. The entrance faces east toward the rising sun. The building is set on 4 acres (1.6 hectares) and is surrounded by 700 native trees and shrubs, a wetlands area, native crops, and boulders from Canada.

At its opening, the museum featured between 7,000 and 8,000 objects in five major exhibitions.

The remainder of the museum's collection—some 800,000 objects acquired by Heye—was to remain in storage in Suitland, Maryland, at NMAI's Cultural Resource Center. All of the displayed and stored objects, representing nearly 1,000 indigenous cultures, were to remain permanently accessible to visiting American Indians. Tribes could arrange to borrow and use specific objects or to conduct ceremonies or offerings to sacred objects on the museum premises. Rather than a static display, museum director W. Richard West, Jr., a Southern Cheyenne, and the tribal committees with which he consulted sought to create a dynamic representation of Native American life.

Trust accounts. In April 2004, representatives of the U.S. government and of Indians involved in a $137-billion class-action lawsuit against the government agreed on the selection of mediators. Charles Renfrew, a former federal judge and chairman of the board of the nonprofit CPR Institute for Dispute Resolution in New York City, and John Bickerman, an attorney, mediator, and secretary of the Dispute Resolution Section of the American Bar Association, were to attempt to negotiate a settlement over the matter.

The suit was brought in 1996 by Elouise Cobell, a banker and member of the Montana Blackfeet tribe, on behalf of some 500,000 Indians. The suit demanded that the U.S. Department of the Interior account for billions of dollars collected and managed for Indians by the government since the late 1800's. It also called for establishing a more accurate accounting system to monitor the funds. Although the Interior Department acknowledged the mismanagement, department representatives claimed the amount of the loss was overstated.

The trust funds had been established in 1887, after the U.S. government divided reservations into parcels and allotted the land to individual Indians and tribes. Proceeds from mining, oil, and gas extraction; timber cutting; and grazing were to be held in trust for the individual owners.

Apology. Senators Sam Brownback (R., Kansas), Daniel K. Inouye (D., Hawaii), and Ben Nighthorse Campbell (R., Colorado) introduced a resolution in Congress in May 2004 that would extend an apology "to all Native Peoples on behalf of the United States" for past government misdeeds. The proposed resolution acknowledged the suffering of American Indians during such injustices as the Trail of Tears (the forced march of Cherokee from North Carolina to Oklahoma in 1838 and 1839) and the Wounded Knee Massacre of 1890. The legislation did not suggest compensation or reparations for the tribes. By the end of 2004, Congress had not acted on the resolution.

■ Kristina Vaicikonis

See also **People in the news** (Elouise Cobell).

Indiana. See State government.

A new museum celebrates ancient traditions and modern interpretations of American Indian culture.

The National Museum of the American Indian (above) was built on the last open land on the National Mall, between the Capitol and the Washington Monument. The five-story structure (right) is made of North American woods, Canadian granite, and buff-colored Minnesota limestone. Its rounded facade reflects the curves of sun, Earth, and moon. The museum is set on 4 acres (1.6 hectares) and is surrounded by native trees and shrubs; a wetlands area; native crops including corn, beans, squash, and tobacco; and boulders from Canada.

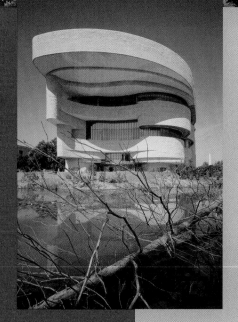

W. Richard West, Jr., the director of the National Museum of the American Indian (far left) and Senator Ben Nighthorse Campbell (R., Colorado), both Native Americans, preside over dedication ceremonies at the new museum on Sept. 21, 2004.

The Potomac (right), a 120-foot- (37-meter-) wide rotunda, is a central feature of the museum's interior space. It soars 120 feet from the circular hardwood floor to the concentric rings of the dome and was designed to be used for Native American ceremonies and performances.

A bronze sculpture titled *May We Have Peace* by Allan Houser and an oil painting called *Passage* by George Morrison are featured in an exhibit of Native American artists during the opening of the museum.

Indonesia. A 9.0-magnitude earthquake struck Indonesia on Dec. 26, 2004. The greatest damage was on Sumatra, which was closest to the epicenter. Dozens of buildings were destroyed in the initial tremor, which generated tsunamis up to 40 feet (14 meters) in height. The huge walls of water hit the provinces of Aceh and North Sumatra. On December 31, Indonesian officials estimated that at least 80,000 people had been killed and more than 1 million others had been left homeless.

Elections. Susilo Bambang Yudhoyono became president of Indonesia on October 20, succeeding Megawati Sukarnoputri. He defeated her in a run-off on September 20 with 61 percent of the vote.

Yudhoyono, a retired army general, had served as security minister, dealing with terrorism and regional separatist problems, before resigning in early 2004 after a disagreement with the president. Yudhoyono completed work on a doctorate degree in agricultural economics days before his election.

Yudhoyono became Indonesia's first popularly chosen president during a year of elections that established a democracy in Indonesia after decades of dictatorship and the indirect selection of leaders. He was Indonesia's fifth president in just over six tumultuous years.

In parliamentary elections on April 5, the Golkar party of former president Suharto took 21.6 percent of the vote. Megawati's party won 18.5 per-cent—a drop from 34 percent in the 1999 vote. Yudhoyono's new Democrat party came in a sur-prisingly strong fifth place. Golkar then chose as its presidential candidate a general and former secu-rity minister, Wiranto. He had been charged by a United Nations-backed court with crimes against humanity in East Timor, which Indonesia controlled from 1975 to 1999. In the first round of presidential polling on July 5, 2004, Wiranto ran third behind Yudhoyono and Megawati.

Megawati only indirectly conceded the Septem-ber 20 vote. After losing, she apologized for failing during her three-year term to solve problems of unemployment, poverty, and education. Econo-mists estimated that Indonesia had about 40 million people unemployed or underemployed in 2004, with more than half its people living on less than $2 a day and more than 6 million children too poor to attend school.

Terrorism. In Jakarta, the capital, a bomb ex-ploded outside the Australian embassy on Septem-ber 9. Australia had helped Indonesia fight terror-ism. The bomb killed 11 people and wounded more than 180 others. Police blamed Jemaah Islamiyah (JI), an affiliate of the al-Qa'ida terrorism network. JI had been blamed for a Bali nightclub bombing in 2002 that killed 202 people and a Jakarta hotel bombing in August 2003 that killed 12 people. On Nov. 24, 2004, Indonesian police announced that

Two members of the Indonesian royal family, Princess Tjokorda Istri Muter and Ibu Henny Sudharsana, are cremated on Bali in July atop a traditional funeral pyre featuring a Balinese mask. The cremation was the last of many ceremonies honoring the princess, who died at the age of 94.

they had arrested four extremists in connection with the hotel and embassy bombings.

Abu Bakar Bashir went on trial October 28 on charges of being the spiritual leader of JI and inciting the hotel bombing. He earlier had been cleared of terrorism charges but was still held in jail when the Australian embassy was bombed. He faced a possible death sentence in the new trial.

The Constitutional Court ruled on July 24 that antiterrorism laws passed after the 2002 Bali bombing could not be used against those accused of that bombing. Nevertheless, the court did not reverse the death sentence of three men who had been sentenced under those laws for their roles in the Bali bombing. The men subsequently filed appeals. In August 2004, a JI militant was sentenced to death for the hotel bombing under the new laws.

East Timor verdicts. On August 6, an appeals court overturned the convictions of four officers for violence during Indonesia's withdrawal of its army in 1999. An army rampage following East Timor's independence left some 1,500 people dead. On Nov. 5, 2004, Abilio Soares, who was governor of East Timor at the time of the violence, was acquitted of crimes against humanity. Indonesia's Supreme Court ruled that because the military was in charge of East Timor at the time, Soares could not be held responsible. ■ Henry S. Bradsher

See also **Asia; Terrorism.**

International trade of goods and services surged during 2004 to the highest levels since the major industrial nations slid into recession in 2001. Trade growth was a direct result of a worldwide economic recovery, which gathered strength in late 2003 and early 2004.

Global economic expansion put new pressures on the availability and prices of raw materials and on such services as freight shipping and ocean port operations. Competition for resources and limited freight-hauling capacity threatened to constrain growth and spur price inflation. In response, many nations, including giant traders such as China and the United States, raised interest rates to help ease price pressures.

The price of crude oil soared to record heights as strong worldwide growth pushed demand near the limits of global output. Supply disruptions in many major oil-producing countries added to the scarcity. The jump in oil prices—to a peak of nearly $56 a barrel in October 2004 from $30 a year earlier—raised the overall value of traded goods. It also acted as a tax on consumers, economists noted, and was likely to slow the rate of economic growth in 2005.

In a statement issued on Oct. 25, 2004, World Trade Organization Director-General Supachai Panitchpakdi tried to allay fears of a global economic slowdown due to high oil prices. The direc-

tor-general emphasized strong growth in trade and output in China, Japan, and a number of economies in Latin America and Africa. Panitchpakdi suggested that these trends would counteract restraints exercised by high fuel prices. The World Trade Organization (WTO) is a Geneva, Switzerland-based group that oversees global trade agreements and arbitrates disputes among member countries.

The International Monetary Fund (IMF) in its September 2004 "World Economic Outlook" projected that the combined volume of global trade in goods and services would grow by 8.8 percent in 2004 before slowing to 7.2 percent in 2005, mainly as a result of higher energy costs. The IMF is a United Nations-affiliated organization based in Washington, D.C., that provides short-term credit to member nations and performs analyses of world economies. The IMF forecasts compared favorably with the 5.1-percent growth in trade volume reported in 2003 and the 3.3-percent growth reported in 2002.

Doha revival. Trade ministers of nations within the WTO signed an agreement on July 31, 2004, that put the so-called Doha Round back on track. The Doha Round is named for a November 2001 meeting of WTO ministers in Doha, Qatar, in which the participants agreed on a framework for cutting trade tariffs and eliminating agricultural subsidies. Economists have said that protectionist farm subsidies in highly developed economies, such as those of the United States and Western Europe, make agricultural products of developing countries less competitive, and leaders of the developing countries have called for an end to such subsidies.

A September 2003 meeting of WTO trade ministers in Cancun, Mexico, had ended in disarray, casting doubt on the future of the Doha initiative. At the July 2004 meeting, however, participants set aside the original deadline for completion of the Doha Round—Jan. 31, 2005—and set a series of interim deadlines for specific actions in 2005. Most significantly, trade representatives of the United States and the European Union (EU) agreed in principle to a phasing out of their agricultural subsidies. Trade analysts predicted that the entire Doha suite of negotiations would be completed in 2006 or 2007.

Threats to trade growth. In making their forecasts for 2005, economists at both the WTO and IMF cautioned that the huge U.S. trade deficit posed risks to economic growth. The enormous U.S. consumer economy had in 2003–2004 acted as a locomotive for the broader world economy by pulling in a much higher level of imports than the value of goods and services the United States was exporting. Economists expressed concerns that a future slowing of the U.S.

economy could derail the economies of countries whose growth depended more heavily on export sales than on domestic demand.

One gauge of the magnitude of the overall U.S. trade deficit was a series of monthly trade deficits the United States ran up in agricultural products during the summer of 2004. Not since 1986 had the country imported more agricultural goods than it exported. Economists urged the U.S. government to pursue policies that would moderate its trade deficit while urging other nations to try to achieve more balance between domestic and trade-based growth.

The weakening dollar. Financial markets also reflected widespread worries that the large U.S. federal budget deficit presented an imbalance that could threaten long-term economic growth. Starting on the day after the U.S. presidential election of Nov. 2, 2004, global currency markets began driving the U.S. dollar down to record lows. Analysts speculated that many currency investors held the view that the administration of U.S. President George W. Bush welcomed a weaker dollar. Some economists predicted that the president would do little to address the twin budget and trade deficits, even though Bush had pledged in his campaign to cut the budget deficit in half.

A weaker currency helps a country's producers sell their goods and services abroad, by automatically making their prices lower in foreign markets. Likewise, a weak currency protects domestic companies by raising the cost of imported goods, making those goods less competitive. A rising currency, on the other hand, has the opposite effect; it raises the cost of a country's exports to foreign markets. The situation presented by the dollar-euro instability, therefore, caused special concern to European nations experiencing an export-based economic recovery.

By mid-November, the U.S. dollar was trading at a 12-year low against the currency of Canada —the largest single U.S. trading partner—and at a record low against the euro, the currency of 12 nations within the EU. In late November, the euro was trading at above $1.30 U.S. As recently as early 2003, the two currencies had been trading approximately on par.

On Nov. 23, 2004, a statement by an official with the Russian central bank hinting that Russia might transfer some of its foreign reserves from dollars to euros spurred speculation that other nations might also shift their foreign reserves toward euro holdings. That possibility amplified concerns about the impact of the U.S. trade and budget deficits on financial markets.

■ John D. Boyd

See also **Agriculture; China; Economics; Europe; Latin America.**

Internet. The number of people in the United States with home access to the Internet in 2004 rose to 204.3 million, or nearly 75 percent of the population, according to statistics compiled by Nielsen//NetRatings. That figure represented a 9-percent increase over 2003. Nielsen//NetRatings is an Internet audience measuring service of NetRatings, Inc., of New York City.

High-speed access grows. The number of home computer users with access to high-speed Internet connections, known as broadband, increased by 60 percent between March 2003 and February 2004. The big increase was revealed in a February survey by the Pew Internet & American Life Project, a research organization in Washington, D.C.

According to the survey, 48 million Americans had broadband connections at home—which was equivalent to 39 percent of adult U.S. Internet users, or 24 percent of all adult Americans. The survey also showed that, for the first time, a majority of college-educated people age 35 or younger had a high-speed Internet connection at home. A total of 52 percent of those Americans had broadband at home.

About 68 million Americans had high-speed Internet connections either at home or at work in 2004. That figure represented roughly 55 percent of adult U.S. Internet users, or 34 percent of adult Americans.

Spam remains a problem. A U.S. law called the CAN-SPAM Act, which prohibited companies from sending unsolicited e-mails known as *spam,* went into effect in January. Congress had passed the law in December 2003 in response to public complaints about spam, which advertises everything from weight-loss programs to pornography. Spam had become a huge problem, forcing many people to delete hundreds of e-mails every day. Attempts to develop technical solutions to the problem by blocking spam had proven largely ineffective.

The CAN-SPAM Act required *spammers,* that is, companies that send spam, to follow certain rules, such as honoring the requests of computer users who ask the spammers to stop. However, critics of the act charged that the legislation was too weak. They pointed out that most spammers simply ignored the new law. According to statistics compiled by the Denver-based Internet security company MX Logic Inc., only 3 percent of unsolicited e-mails were in compliance with the law in April 2004, and this figure fell to 1 percent in May.

Analysts noted that a failure to apply serious penalties against spammers, such as fines or jail terms, likely encouraged spammers to continue operating. Law enforcement officials began to counter the spammers by mid-2004 by preparing legal cases, based on the CAN-SPAM Act, against major spam operations. They hoped that those cases would eventually convince other spammers to comply with the act.

Internet security. Internet thieves stole $2.4 billion from nearly 2 million Americans between April 2003 and April 2004, according to estimates made by the research firm Gartner Inc., of Stamford, Connecticut. Most of these thefts involved illegal access to the checking accounts of computer users.

The thieves accomplished their crimes with two main techniques: by using *phishing* and *spyware.* In phishing, spam is designed to trick an Internet user into visiting a Web site that appears to be legitimate, such as the site of the user's bank. However, the site is actually operated by the thief, who uses the site to collect personal information about the user, such as a password and checking account number. Spyware arrives in what looks like innocent e-mail, but if opened, the e-mail secretly installs software that records keystrokes made by the user. The thief can then gather passwords and other private data.

Software scans of more than 2 million computers during the first half of 2004 detected nearly 55 million examples of spyware installed in the computers. The scans were conducted by EarthLink Inc., an Internet service provider based in Atlanta, Georgia, and Webroot Software Inc., a producer of protective software in Boulder, Colorado. The companies noted, however, that fewer than 1 million of those infections were so serious that they could have led to financial losses like those described in the Gartner report.

Internet piracy. The number of songs available for free, unauthorized downloading off the Internet increased to 1 billion in June 2004, compared with 820 million in June 2003. These statistics were compiled by the online market research company BigChampagne, of Los Angeles. CacheLogic, a technology firm in Cambridge, England, reported in July 2004 that Internet users downloaded twice as many movies, computer programs, and music each day in 2004 as they did in 2003.

The increase in Internet piracy came despite a series of high-profile lawsuits filed by recording industry groups against people who had allegedly violated copyright law by sharing songs with other people over the Internet. The continued thefts also came despite of the success of legitimate, subscription download sites, such as the iTunes Music Store, operated by Apple Computer Inc., of Cupertino, California.

■ Dave Wilson

See also **Computer: A Special Report; Telecommunications.**

Iowa. See **State government.**

Iran. In negotiations with representatives of the governments of the United Kingdom, France, and Germany in November 2004, Iranian authorities made a commitment to abide by the Nuclear Nonproliferation Treaty and, thereby, not seek to acquire nuclear weapons. Iran also agreed to cooperate with the International Atomic Energy Agency (IAEA), a Vienna-based organization that promotes the safe and peaceful use of nuclear energy. Later in November, Iranian authorities said they would temporarily suspend uranium enrichment activities—activities that produce fuel that could be used either in civilian nuclear reactors or nuclear bombs.

Iran's moves appeared to head off potential sanctions by the United Nations Security Council. Despite the Iranian pledges, however, officials with the IAEA, as well as the governments of the United States and some other countries, continued to be concerned that Iran might be involved in covert activities to build nuclear weapons.

Reversal for reformers. Conservatives defeated reformers in February parliamentary elections, giving the conservatives a majority of approximately 180 seats in the 290-seat *Majlis* (the main legislative body). The Majlis had been controlled by reformers since the 2000 parliamentary elections.

The reversal of fortunes for reformers was due to the fact that the 12-member Council of Guardians had disqualified more than 2,000 candidates, most of whom belonged to the reformist camp. The Council of Guardians, made up of Muslim religious leaders, has the power to both disqualify candidates and veto legislation passed by the parliament. One of the candidates that the council barred from running was Mohammad Reza Khatami, the brother of President Mohammad Khatami-Ardakani and the leader of the reformist party, Islamic Iran Participation Front.

Election boycott. The results of the parliamentary elections, in addition to the continued blocking of reforms by the Council of Guardians, led to the rise of a movement of passive resistance among Iranian youth in 2004. The Office to Consolidate Unity—the largest student organization—launched a campaign to persuade the public to boycott the presidential elections of May 2005.

Cultural contact. James H. Billington, the head of the U.S. Library of Congress, led a small U.S. delegation to Iran for a six-day visit in October and November 2004. Billington, who was the highest-ranking U.S. official to visit Iran since the two countries severed diplomatic relations in 1980, had been invited by Mohammed Bojnourdi, the director of the Iranian National Library.

■ Marius Deeb

See also **Middle East; United Nations.**

Iraq

A Quest for Political Identity in a Second Year of War

By Christine Moss Helms

The nightmare came true on April 4, 2004. The al-Mahdi Army, a militia of Shiah Muslims, launched an uprising against the United States-led occupation in Iraq. (The Shiah are one of two great sects of Islam; the Sunnis are the other.) With a wide array of weapons, including rocket-propelled grenades, the militia attacked U.S. forces in Sadr City, a vast Baghdad slum of 2 million people. The fighting quickly spread to the cities of An Najaf, Al Kufah, and Al Amarah in south-central Iraq. The uprising had been unleashed by a militant, young Shiah cleric, Moqtada al-Sadr, who in 2003 had called for the formation of an al-Mahdi, or Islamic, Army to oust occupation forces. Hours after al-Sadr urged his followers to "terrorize your enemy," members of the militia took control of police stations and government buildings in cities across the predominantly Shiah region south of Baghdad, the capital. The U.S.-led occupation was now fighting insurrections involving both Shiah and Sunni Muslims, two of Iraq's three main population groups.

The following day, April 5, U.S. Marines sealed off Al Fallujah in an operation designed to crush the insurrection in the so-called Sunni Triangle. This is an area largely north and west of Baghdad from which

The author: Christine Moss Helms has written some 500 journal articles on international affairs. She twice interviewed Saddam Hussein in preparation for her book *Iraq: Eastern Flank of the Arab World.*

Sunni militants, Saddam Hussein loyalists, and foreign terrorists launched near-daily attacks on coalition forces and other targets in 2004.

To the north, in a region largely populated by ethnic Kurds—Iraq's third major population group—a suicide bomber detonated an explosive device in his car outside Kirkuk. The explosion killed an American soldier and severely wounded six others. Near the city of Mosul, in the northwest, militants detonated a bomb alongside a road as a military convoy drove past, killing another U.S. soldier on April 5.

The events of April 4 and April 5 provide a microcosm of Iraq through 2004—bombings and sabotage in the north; continuing insurrection in the Sunni Triangle; near-daily car bombings in Baghdad; and an on-again, off-again insurrection in the Shiah south. In April, insurgents staged 50 to 70 attacks per day on average, with car bombings, particularly suicide bombings, growing ever more frequent. Victims were often civilians, even children, and a recognizable pattern of attacks on police and Iraqi national guard headquarters emerged.

During the same period, militants unveiled a new tactic—kidnapping. The threat of killing hostages was used to coerce foreign corporations and coalition partners into pulling out of Iraq. Many victims, in fact, were beheaded, with video recordings of their murders placed on the Internet to magnify the horror.

Little was known about the insurgents. According to terrorism experts, militant Iraqis and foreigners drawn to the war apparently fought in small units that may, or may not, have been connected to organized bands functioning under the coordination of a leader. Unlike Palestinian

militant groups, the insurgents in Iraq rarely claimed responsibility for bombings and almost never disclosed the names of suicide bombers. A major exception—Unification and Jihad—was associated with Jordanian extremist Abu Mussab al-Zarqawi. Members changed the organization's name to "Qa'ida of Jihad" in October after pledging their loyalty to al-Qa'ida leader Osama bin Laden. Al-Zarqawi and his followers became the object of an intense manhunt in 2004.

In April, U.S. forces made an incursion into Al Fallujah, in an ill-fated attempt to root out al-Zarqawi and other insurgents. On September 7, Donald Rumsfeld, secretary of the U.S. Department of Defense, acknowledged that insurgents remained in control of much of the Sunni Triangle. The following day, a Defense Department spokesperson reported that the number of deaths of U.S. military personnel in Iraq had surpassed the 1,000 mark. Nearly 7,000 American troops had been wounded. Estimates of the number of Iraqis who had died since the war began in March 2003 ranged from 10,000 to 100,000. In October and November 2004, U.S. and Iraqi forces launched another major offensive into Al Fallujah and successfully retook control of the city. However, the incursion touched off insurgent counteroffensives in Mosul, Kirkuk, Baqubah, and other Iraqi cities, resulting in hundreds of deaths.

A U.S. soldier, standing before the main mosque in Samarra, scans his sector of the city after U.S. and Iraqi forces re-took Samarra from insurgents in early October. The incursion was part of a larger offensive to regain control of the Sunni Triangle in anticipation of national elections scheduled for January 2005.

A country difficult to govern

The swift collapse of Iraqi President Saddam Hussein's Baath Party regime in 2003 had fostered hopes that Iraqis would forge a new national identity and provide a democratic model for the Middle East.

Vehicles burn at the scene of a car bombing in Baghdad in June. Bombings, particularly suicide car bombings, became a favorite tool of insurgents in Iraq in 2004, resulting in the deaths of hundreds of soldiers and civilians.

Those hopes dimmed in the violence that engulfed the country as ethnic and religious communities, distrustful of the U.S.-led coalition, jockeyed to secure rights and prerogatives. More troubling, Iraq's many ethnic and religious communities became both victims and perpetrators of the violence, raising the specter of civil war.

Iraq has always been difficult to govern. It is one of the most *pluralistic* (diverse) of Middle Eastern countries. Although its 25 million people are mainly Arab and Muslim, different Islamic sects, ethnic ties, and complex population patterns have produced a vibrant, if complicated social fabric. Iraq's non-Muslim population, though small, is remarkable for its diversity. Ethnic groups include Yazidis, Sabeans, and Shabaks. There are also Christian groups and a community of Jews.

Iraq's diversity is a legacy of geography and a history that stretches back to the world's earliest civilization. The region's rich resources and strategic position, astride the great river systems of the Tigris and Euphrates, were magnets for trade as well as for conquest. Iraq's extraordinary archaeological heritage, a record of many successive empires, testifies to the fleeting nature of politics; while its religious shrines, some a thousand years old, annually attract millions of pilgrims in an awesome demonstration of the durability of religion and ethnicity.

No one yet knows whether Iraqis can craft a democratic state to accommodate this diversity. While religion and ethnicity have often stirred deep and passionate divisions in Iraq, they have also acted as a powerful cohesive force. Several times during the 20th century, Iraqis rose up in unison to oust a foreign power.

Iraq's colonial past

The modern nations of the Middle East were forged in colonialism. The Ottomans—a Turkish Muslim empire—wielded power over the region's predominantly Arab Muslim populations beginning in the 1600's. Victorious European colonial powers divided the territory after the Ottomans were defeated in World War I (1914-1918). The Europeans drew largely artificial boundaries to demarcate their new spheres of influence. The United Kingdom laid claim to a number of former Ottoman territories, including the three provinces—Baghdad, Mosul, and Al Basrah—that became modern Iraq. The British designated Baghdad the capital.

The colonization of the Middle East by non-Muslim Europeans unleashed a turbulent struggle for independence. Aspiring political groups within each colonial state soon realized that independence would be won more readily if an *ideology* (doctrine of a political movement) could be developed with a sufficiently broad appeal that could transcend national borders and ethnic and religious divisions. Arab nationalism developed into an obvious force for unity during this period.

Arab nationalism, or Pan-Arabism, as the ideology came to be called, quickly became a standardbearer in the struggle for independence in the Middle East, especially in highly urbanized and pluralistic colonial states, such as Iraq. Advocates of Pan-Arabism believed that Arab countries should strive for political unity and be free of outside influence. Pan-Arabism, a *secular* (nonreligious) ideology, appealed to non-Muslims and even to Muslims, because it bridged differences within Islam and with other religions.

The struggle for independence took different forms in different colonial states. In Iraq, the struggle was particularly violent. The United Kingdom had set up a new government in 1921, renamed the country

Bomb victims are cared for at a hospital in Baqubah in July. The men had been in line to apply for jobs when they were injured by a suicide bomber who detonated a explosive device outside a police station, killing at least 51 Iraqis. Police and national guard headquarters were frequent targets of insurgent attack in 2004.

Iraq, and installed a Hashemite monarch, King Faisal I. (Hashemite refers to the royal dynasty of the kingdom of Jordan, which claimed direct descent from the Prophet Muhammad, the founder of Islam.) In 1958, Iraqis—distrustful of the monarchy's English sponsorship and Jordanian roots—rose up in a violent anticolonial revolution and killed King Faisal as well as his son, Prince Abdul Ilah.

A succession of colonial states in the Middle East broke free from European colonial powers in the mid-20th century. This wave of independence reinforced public confidence in Pan-Arabism, which Middle Easterners came to regard as the intellectual force that had freed

Hooded gunmen threaten the life of a hostage in a video broadcast on the Arab-speaking Al-Jazeera satellite television channel. Insurgents in Iraq used the very real threat of killing kidnapping victims to try to coerce foreign corporations and governments to pull out of Iraq.

them from colonialism and protected them against further foreign intervention. The embrace of Arab nationalism took many forms. Baathism, or the Reawakening, proved to be one of the more successful. Branches of the party eventually gained power in Syria and Iraq, where Saddam Hussein became the chief proponent. Iraq's Baath Party initially was dominated by Kurds and then by the country's Shiah majority, which still made up some 60 percent of rank-and-file when Hussein was overthrown in 2003.

Ironically, the appeal of Pan-Arabism was also its undoing. Political elites and ethnic and religious groups all used Arab nationalism as a tool to secure power. When they continued to use it to justify corrupt, incompetent leadership, the people of the Middle East quickly grew disenchanted. The disenchantment was fed by a series of wars between Arab nations and Israel that led to disastrous defeats for the Arabs. The allure of Arab nationalism also was tarnished by the failure of entrenched elites to deliver on promises of economic prosperity amid massive corruption and widespread *nepotism* (favor by one in power to relatives).

By the 1980's, most Arab governments, even those still professing Arabism, devoted significant effort to encouraging social cohesion within their countries and justifying their own political legitimacy. Saddam Hussein, for example, used Iraq's vast oil resources to fund massive development projects within Iraq. He called upon all Iraqis—whether ethnic Arabs or Kurds, Sunni or Shiah Muslims, and men or women—to put aside their differences for the greater good of the country. Hussein eventually preached that Iraqi nationalism, rather than Arab nationalism, transcended all other forms of identification, ethnic or religious. To this end, he invoked the names of historic leaders, most notably King Sargon of Akkad, who in the 2300's B.C., founded one of the first great empires by unifying northern and southern Mesopotamia (now Iraq).

Arab governments, while striving for political unity, found themselves overwhelmed by the rapid pace of social change in the last decades of the 20th century. High population growth swelled the ranks of the unemployed, especially among the region's ever more restive

An Iraqi boy holds aloft a leaflet that reads "Al Fallujah, the cemetery of the Americans," as Iraqis rejoice in the murder and mutilation of four private U.S. security guards in late March. The incident led to an unsuccessful U.S. incursion into the Sunni Triangle city in an attempt to subdue the insurgency.

A rebel carries a portrait of militant Shiah cleric Moqtada al-Sadr through the streets of a Baghdad slum in April. Al-Sadr unleashed Shiah insurrections against the U.S.-led coalition in Baghdad and in the cities of south-central Iraq in April and August.

youth. Blaming Pan-Arabism for their plight, many people sought solace in Islam. Young Iraqis turned to religion after two decades of war and a series of international sanctions had left their country politically isolated and economically debilitated. Saddam Hussein, ever the shrewd politician, began in the mid-1990's to restore Iraq's Islamic shrines and build new mosques. He added "God is Great" to the national flag during this period. His overthrow in 2003 reopened a Pandora's box of regional conflicts, both religious and ethnic.

Iraq's Kurdish-Arab equation

Ethnic Kurds, who make up approximately 15 to 20 percent of the population of Iraq, offer one of the most difficult roadblocks in the quest for unity. The major drawback to Arab nationalism was its failure to address the political aspirations of two large non-Arab minorities—the Berber people of North Africa and the Kurds of northern Arabia. These groups, whose cultures and languages became sublimated to Arab culture and language, have nursed grievances for decades. Northern Iraq, where more Kurds live than in any other Arab nation, is often called Kurdistan. However, the name is misleading. Although Kurds predominate in various areas of northern Iraq, roughly half of the region's population is Arab. The north also has major clusters of ethnic Turkomans. All three ethnic groups are primarily Sunni Muslims.

Saddam Hussein's overthrow opened a new chapter in Kurdish-Arab relations, one that has been marred by deep suspicions on both sides. Kurds had enjoyed relative *autonomy* (self-government) since 1991 when Allied forces, after the the Gulf War, set up a safety zone in northern Iraq to protect the Kurds from Saddam Hussein. (Hussein's troops had brutally put down a Kurdish rebellion stirred by the war.) After the fall of Hussein in 2003, many Kurds demanded a federal state. The Kurds feared a centralized government in Baghdad would again relegate them to minority status. Kurdish politicians also demanded greater control over Iraq's northern oil resources and the right to veto constitutional amendments that might dilute their role in future power-sharing arrangements.

Many non-Kurdish Iraqis feared that the Kurd's demands, including calls for independence, would fragment the country. Those fears were sparked when Kurdish militias in 2003 evicted thousands of Arabs from their residences, especially in oil-rich Kirkuk. Kurds claimed they were retaking property seized when the Baath Party began relocating Arabs to the north in the late 1960's. Arabs, claiming to constitute a majority in Kirkuk, countered that the 2003 expulsions were intended to alter the region's political landscape prior to the formation of a new government. Kurdish actions also alarmed the north's minority Turks and Assyrian Christians. Resentment festered when the U.S.-led coalition allowed Kurdish militias to keep their heavy weapons while demanding that Sunni- and Shiah-dominated militias disarm.

Kurdish political aspirations also threatened to embroil neighboring Turkey and Iran. Leaders in both nations feared that allowing Kurds

Members of Kurdish militias stand guard in northern Iraq in February. A coalition decision to allow the Kurds to maintain their militias while attempting to disarm Sunni and Shiah paramilitary groups fostered mistrust of U.S. motives in Iraq.

greater autonomy, let alone independence, could ignite discontent among the significant Kurdish populations in both countries. In Turkey, militant Kurdish nationalists, some of whom have taken refuge in northern Iraq, have waged a protracted war for independence.

Shiah Muslims test their strength

The religious beliefs of Iraqi people always complicate the nation's political situation. Although nearly all Iraqis, including both Arabs and Kurds, are Muslim, roughly 65 percent of Iraqis adhere to the Shiah branch of Islam. Neighboring Iran, whose 65 million people are almost wholly Shiah, is the only Middle Eastern nation with a larger Shiah population than Iraq, but the people of Iran are Persian, not Arab. Elsewhere in the Middle East, the overwhelming majority of Arab people are Sunni Muslims, the dominant branch of Islam.

The Shiah branch lost its struggle for preeminence in the Muslim world in the A.D. 600's in what is now Iraq. The most revered of Shiah shrines—generally glorifying sacrifice and martyrdom—are in the Iraqi cities of An Najaf and Karbala. Of these, the Imam Ali Mosque, built over the tomb of the son-in-law and cousin of the Prophet Muhammad, is preeminent. During the Iran-Iraq War (1980-1988), Iranian tanks went into battle inscribed with the words "to An Najaf." Many international affairs experts have suggested that the Iran-Iraq War, despite its many causes, could be regarded as a struggle between Arab nationalism and the potent new force of political or militant Islam.

In the early chaos following the fall of Hussein in 2003, Shiah leaders successfully restored calm to the Shiah communities of southern Iraq. While relieved by the relative calm, the U.S.-led coalition feared the numerical strength of Iraq's Shiah majority and the many links between Shiah leaders in Iraq and their counterparts in Iran. The situation seemed ripe for the imposition in Iraq of an anti-American *theocracy* (a government ruled by religious leaders), like the cleric-controlled government in Iran. Those fears intensified in 2003 after two moderate Shiah clerics were assassinated in An Najaf within days of their return from exile.

Shiah political and religious leaders, in turn, were antagonized by various actions taken by the U.S.-led Coalition Provisional Authority (CPA) in Iraq. In 2003, the CPA delayed national elections while crafting an interim Iraqi Governing Council. The 25 members of the council were largely Iraqi exiles, many of whom had been financially and politically supported by the United States. Many Shiites suspected that the United States was orchestrating a future Iraqi government that would minimize Shiah influence.

The passions of Iraqi Shiites were ignited in April 2004 when the CPA ordered the arrest of Moqtada al-Sadr for the murder of Abdel Majid al-Khoei, one of the two clerics assassinated in 2003. Al Sadr was the son of the highly revered Grand Ayatollah Mohammed Sadiq al-Sadr, who was assassinated in 1999. Despite being young and lacking scholarly credentials, Moqtada al-Sadr ignited the first clashes between Shiah and coalition forces. His rhetoric, which was notably nationalist in sentiment, tapped into a major reservoir of discontent among young

Iraqi males, some 65 percent of whom found themselves unemployed in the postwar period. This situation was especially true in Sadr City, the Baghdad slum that had been renamed for al-Sadr's father after the fall of Hussein. As early as April 2003, al-Sadr's followers briefly surrounded a compound in An Najaf where Grand Ayatollah Ali Sistani, Iraq's most revered and influential cleric, lived and worked. Islamic authorities took this rather threatening gesture as a signal that al-Sadr might have aspirations to control the Hawza —the powerful Shiah religious establishment headed by al-Sistani. Clerics with Persian origins, such as al-Sistani, have long dominated the Hawza in Arab Iraq.

Al-Sistani, whom religious authorities generally viewed as a recluse who advocated separation of politics and religion, proved himself a formidable foe for the CPA and, eventually, al-Sadr. According to some experts, al-Sistani entered the political arena to counter al-Sadr's radical appeal. The older cleric issued a written call for early elections. Bowing to al-Sistani's prestige, the CPA sought the help of the United Nations to craft a plan for implementing the transition to democracy sooner than originally planned. The result was the interim Iraqi government, which assumed sovereignty from the U.S.-led occupation on June 28, 2004, and the scheduling of national elections on or before Jan. 31, 2005. Analysts in both Iraq and the United States questioned whether these elections would take place on schedule, given the threat of violence and the large areas under insurgent control.

Events took a dramatic new turn in August 2004 when al-Sistani sought medical treatment in London. During his absence, al-Sadr's militia, which had clashed with U.S. forces in April, again took up arms in An Najaf and other southern cities. The renewed fighting devastated much of the old, central part of An Najaf, threatening the 1,000-year-old Imam Ali Mosque where Sadr's supporters had taken up positions.

An Iraqi woman kisses a giant poster of Grand Ayatollah Ali al-Sistani outside his house in An Najaf in March. The most revered Shiah cleric in Iraq, al-Sistani brokered a cease-fire of the Shiah insurrection in Iraq in August. He also prompted the U.S.-led coalition to create the interim Iraqi government and schedule national elections for 2005.

Al-Sistani, returning at the height of the crisis, brokered a deal that spared further destruction and loss of life. Although some members of Iraq's new interim government hoped al-Sadr might eventually join the mainstream political process, others feared he retained the power to yet again mobilize the forces of the restive "Muslim street," that is, the young and disaffected.

Sunnis in the postwar period

Iraq's Sunni Muslims, though a minority, wielded significant power under Saddam Hussein. Hussein, himself a Sunni, relied heavily, but not exclusively, on their support. In the early postwar period, the insurgency against the U.S.-led coalition was confined mainly to central Iraq, where Sunnis and Hussein loyalists predominated. Some observers attributed the insurgency to the CPA's decision in 2003 to disband the Iraqi army and to ban former Baath Party members from government jobs, regardless of their qualifications or reasons for joining the party. (The CPA, believing Sunnis were behind the original insurgency, eventually eased these regulations in the hope of dampening the rebellion.) The extent to which former Baathists participated in or fostered the insurgency remains unknown. However, young Sunni males shared the same high unemployment statistics as Shiites. Military affairs experts believed these youth likely formed the core membership of at least 30 radical Sunni insurgent groups hatched in the postwar period.

Mainstream Sunni Muslim leaders were no less affected by the political competition of the postwar period than their Shiah and Kurd counterparts. However, because of their connections with Saddam Hussein, they had no strong political parties prior to 2003. The Council of Islamic Scholars, composed of preeminent Sunni leaders, was the most prominent of new political organizations to emerge in 2004.

Minorities and tribes complicate the political equation

Iraq's other minorities and tribes complicated Iraq's future. Christians, who constitute 3 percent of the population, are mostly concentrated in northern Iraq and Baghdad, where they have lived peacefully. In the postwar period, however, Christian-owned liquor stores were torched. In August 2004, five Christian churches were bombed in a single day. The unprecedented attacks, though condemned by Muslim clerics, spurred a Christian exodus. Other minorities watched with trepidation.

Iraq also has more than 150 Iraqi tribes. Although colonial and Arab governments sought to manipulate the tribes or diminish their strength, tribal leaders continued to exert strong influence in 2004. As his power waned, Saddam Hussein had tried to revitalize tribal identities.

Foreign extremists

An influx of foreign Muslim extremists further stirred Iraq's political cauldron in 2004. Estimates of their strength varied from hundreds to thousands. Their primary goals were to oust the coalition and create an Islamic nation. However, the group headed by al-Zarqawi also fostered strife between Sunnis and Shiahs. Al-Zarqawi apparently viewed the Shiahs as U.S. collaborators, at least until the Shiah themselves had launched insurrections. Although some terrorist experts questioned whether al-Zarqawi remained alive in late 2004, the radical group or groups operating under his name claimed responsibility for significant violence.

A tortuous path

The postwar violence prompted some Westerners to suggest dividing Iraq into separate Kurdish, Shiah, and Sunni countries, a proposal most Iraqis viewed as unworkable. Although a particular group may predominate in a given region, Iraq's ethnic and religious groups are intermixed. Rapid urbanization in recent decades has made inter-marriage between Shiah and Sunni Iraqis increasingly common. Baghdad, located in primarily Sunni territory, is a vast, multicultural "melting pot." Historic oddities also exist. One large Iraqi tribe is primarily Sunni, though its sheiks, or tribal leaders, are Shiah.

The division of Iraq's water and oil resources would also create nearly insurmountable problems that could possibly embroil neighboring nations. International affairs experts have suggested that a southern Shiah state could end up impoverished due to its dependence upon water supplies from the north. This weakness could invite Iranian and perhaps Saudi intervention. Despite Kurdish demands for independence, a Kurdish state would be landlocked and invite intervention from Turkey and Iran.

There is little doubt that Iraq's path to democracy will continue to be tortuous. The composition of the interim government established on June 28 reflected Iraq's complex realities. A Shiah prime minister, Ayad Allawi, was appointed, with various other key posts apportioned among urban, provincial, ethnic, political, and religious groups. Everyone had to be pleased or at least appeased. In August, a national conference of 1,100 Iraqis, chosen by caucuses overseen by the coalition, voted for a 100-member advisory council. The conference was a raucous affair in which prominent Kurdish, Shiah, and Sunni political parties pushed aside the less powerful parties, many minority groups, and some traditional tribal leaders. Many Iraqis also were disturbed that 19 former Iraqi Governing Council members who had been excluded from the interim government—for being too closely allied with the United States—ended up on the advisory council.

While differences remained among Iraq's diverse communities, signs of growing nationalism began to emerge in 2004—a reminder that Iraqis had united more than once to oppose a foreign power. An increasing discontent among nearly all Iraqis with the U.S.-led coalition became clearly visible in the face of the escalating insurrection. When U.S. troops prepared to attack Sunni insurgents in Al Fallujah in April, Shiah Muslims poured into the city to support fellow Iraqis. When insurgents captured and executed 49 freshly trained Iraqi soldiers on October 26, Iraq's interim prime minister, Ayad Allawi, did not condemn the insurgents. Instead, he blamed the United States for not providing Iraqis with sufficient security. Never before had a member of the interim Iraqi government, empowered by the U.S.-led coalition, dared to publicly criticize the government of the United States.

Ireland. In 2004, the Fianna Fail government of *Taioseach* (prime minister) Bertie Ahern, which had come to power in 1997, and been re-elected in 2002, had a turbulent year with major electoral setbacks. However, the Irish economy underwent a year of strong growth. Bank of Ireland economists forecast that the economy would grow by up to 6 percent during 2004, with unemployment averaging only 4.5 percent and inflation averaging 2.3 percent. During the first half of the year, Ahern, on behalf of the Irish Republic, held the rotating six-month presidency of the European Union.

Elections. The governing Fianna Fail party was heavily defeated in June in local elections and in elections for representatives to the European Parliament. Fianna Fail lost 20 percent of its local council seats, and its number of European Parliament seats was reduced from six to four. The opposition party, Fine Gael, obtained five. The result was blamed on opposition to the government's indirect tax increases and cuts in public expenditure. The nationalist movement Sinn Fein (which aims to unite the Irish Republic with the British province of Northern Ireland) achieved a surge of support and won its first seat in the European Parliament, indicating that it was now increasingly seen as a mainstream party in the Irish Republic. Bertie Ahern, however, maintained his economic policies, including low direct taxation, and promised that he would lead his party in the next general election.

Reshuffle. On September 29, Ahern reshuffled his Cabinet. Charlie McCreevy, who had been finance minister, became a European commissioner and was replaced by the former foreign minister, Brian Cowen. Cowen in turn was replaced by Dermot Ahern (no relation to Bertie Ahern). The *tanaiste* (deputy prime minister), Mary Harney, whose Progressive Democrats were part of the governing coalition with Fianna Fail, took over the department of health to introduce reforms. The purpose of the reshuffle was to provide the government with a more caring public image.

Irish President Mary McAleese retained her position for a second seven-year term after she ran unopposed in October. McAleese had proved extremely popular with people of all parties.

Referendum. On June 11, voters in a referendum overwhelmingly chose to remove the automatic right of citizenship for children born in the Irish Republic. The resolution was supported by the government, which claimed it would bring Ireland into line with the rest of the European Union and maintained that foreigners deliberately came to Ireland to have children and claim benefits. Opponents of the proposal, including the Irish Labour party, argued it would increase racism and hatred of foreigners.   ■ Rohan McWilliam

See also **Europe; Northern Ireland.**

Islam. Iraq remained at the center of Muslim attention in 2004, and events there vividly shaped European and American views of Islam. By mid-2004, Iraq clearly had become a magnet for Islamic terrorists, with the insurgency mobilizing thousands of disaffected Muslims around the world. *Jihad* (religious struggle) had become the dominant theme of resistance to the United States-led occupation and assumed a prominence in Islamic discourse unknown since the Crusades (Christian-Muslim warfare in the Holy Land from 1096 to 1270).

Denominational violence between Iraq's Sunni and Shiah Muslims, including assassinations of significant clerics, increased in 2004 despite a Sunni-Shiah agreement in April to promote the concept of "one Islam in Iraq." Tensions also were fueled by a new constitution that promised majority rule to Shiites for the first time. Fear of losing power stimulated Sunni support for the insurgency.

Resistance to the U.S.-led occupation was further inflamed by the Abu Ghraib Prison scandal. Muslim groups everywhere condemned the abuse of Iraqi prisoners by U.S military guards. Experts noted that the exposure in April of photographs of prisoners being physically abused and humiliated led many Muslims to regard the occupation as specifically designed to humiliate Arabs in particular and Muslims in general.

In April, a minor Shiah cleric, Moqtada al-Sadr, launched an insurgency in the Shiah holy cities of Karbala and An Najaf. His militia, the Mahdi Army, held those cities for several months. In a demonstration of power, Grand Ayatollah Ali al-Sistani returned to Iraq after having heart surgery in London, and on August 25 led a march into An Najaf and brokered a truce between al-Sadr and U.S. forces.

Define and control. Terrorism became the public face of Islam in Europe as well as Iraq after Islamic militants detonated bombs on commuter trains in Madrid, Spain, in March, killing 191 people. Responding to such attacks, the governments of European and Muslim nations in 2004 attempted to define and control "acceptable Islam": authorities in Egypt mandated that calls to prayer be broadcast by the state, rather than by local imams; Saudi Arabia tried to rein in Wahhabi scholars by silencing those whose sermons criticized national policy or supported terrorism; Morocco required that religious edicts be submitted to a council of scholars, and ultimately to the king, for approval; and the president of Yemen called for revising and controlling the curriculum in the *madrasas* (religious schools).

In Europe, Germany established a university-based imam training school. France created the French Council of the Muslim Faith to supervise religious activities. France also implemented a ban on "symbols of religious identity" in schools; the ban was aimed primarily at Muslim women wearing headscarves. In December, the French interior minister announced that, beginning in September 2005, French imams would have to study law, civics, history, and French at French universities.

United States authorities' monitoring of ports of entry for potential terrorists stirred controversy when officials detained Muslims widely regarded as moderates. On May 6, 2004, federal authorities arrested Brandon Mayfield, an Oregon lawyer and convert to Islam, on suspicion of involvement in the Madrid bombings. After two weeks in custody, he was cleared of any wrongdoing and released. His case drew the attention of American Muslims, who felt increasingly scrutinized by the U.S. government after the September 2001 terrorist attacks on the United States.

In August 2004, prominent, moderate Islamic cleric Tariq Ramadan was refused entry to the United States to teach at Notre Dame University's Institute of Peace in South Bend, Indiana. In September, Yusuf al-Islam—known before his conversion to Islam as Cat Stevens, the singer—was escorted off a diverted transatlantic flight and returned to the United Kingdom "on national security grounds." Both men denied any connection to terrorists.   ■ A. Kevin Reinhart

See also **France; Human rights; Iraq: A Special Report; Pakistan; Terrorism.**

Israel. In October 2004, the Israeli *Knesset* (parliament) voted in favor of Prime Minister Ariel Sharon's plan to remove all 8,000 Israeli settlers from Gaza and turn complete control of the territory over to the Palestinian people. Although Sharon's Likud Party was divided on the vote, the opposition Labor Party supported the plan, hoping that it would help resolve the decades-long Israeli-Palestinian conflict. The Gaza settlements, as well as four small Israeli settlements in the West Bank, were scheduled to be dismantled by the end of 2005.

International criticism of Israel. The United Nations (UN) General Assembly voted 150-6 in July 2004 to condemn the barrier that Israel was building to separate Israelis from Palestinians in the West Bank. British Foreign Secretary Jack Straw expressed his strong disapproval with the part-fence, part-wall barrier. According to Straw, "The construction of this barrier on occupied territory, with the destruction of property and hardship that it entails, is unlawful."

In October, the New York City-based Human Rights Watch criticized Israeli military incursions into southern Gaza over the previous four years. A report by the organization stated, "The pattern

Israeli police and rescue workers surround the scorched shell of a bus in Jerusalem after a Palestinian suicide bomber blew it up on January 29. The bomber and at least 10 passengers were killed in the attack.

Palestinians carry coffins bearing the bodies of Sheik Ahmed Yassin, the leader of the Islamic militant group Hamas, and his aides on March 22. The men were killed in an Israeli missile strike, part of an Israeli policy to target leaders of radical Palestinian organizations.

of destruction strongly suggests Israeli forces demolished homes wholesale, regardless of whether they posed a specific threat, in violation of international law." A spokesman for the Israeli Foreign Ministry responded to this report by claiming that Israel was doing its "utmost to minimize damage to the civilian population."

War on terrorism. As part of efforts to undermine the four-year-old Palestinian *Intifada* (uprising), Israel continued its policy of eliminating the leaders of Islamic militant organizations, such as Hamas, in 2004. On April 17, an Israeli helicopter missile strike killed Hamas leader Abdel Aziz Rantisi. The strike came less than one month after Rantisi took over the Hamas leadership from Sheik Ahmed Yassin, who was killed in an Israeli missile strike on March 22.

In retaliation for the two assassinations, Hamas militants bombed two buses in Beersheba on August 31, killing at least 12 people. Consequently, Israel targeted the Hamas member responsible for these bombings—Izz Eldine Subhi Sheik Khalil, who was killed by a car bomb on September 26 in Damascus, Syria. Experts in international affairs noted that the assassination was likely meant to send a message to Syria that Israel would not allow the Syrian government to grant

safe haven to members of radical Palestinian organizations.

On October 7, three car bombings struck holiday resort areas frequented by Israeli tourists in the Taba region of Egypt. At least 35 people were killed in the attacks, which Israeli authorities blamed on the al-Qa'ida terrorist network, led by Osama bin Laden.

Future prospects for peace? Following the death of Palestinian leader Yasir Arafat in November, many Middle East experts said prospects for peace between Palestinians and Israelis may have improved. They noted that Israelis might be more willing to support negotiations with new Palestinian leaders who were opposed to the Intifada. Elections for a new Palestinian president were scheduled for Jan. 9, 2005. Mahmoud Abbas, a former Palestinian prime minister considered to be a moderate, was favored to win the post.

Relations with France. Michel Barnier, the foreign minister of France, made an official visit to Israel in October 2004. Barnier met with Prime Minister Sharon, as well as several Israeli business leaders and academicians, in an attempt to mend fences with Israel in the wake of controversial comments by Sharon that rising anti-Semitism had made France unsafe for Jews.

Economy. Twenty-two percent of Israelis lived in poverty in 2003, according to a November 2004 report by the World Bank, an affiliate of the United Nations.   ■ Marius Deeb

See also **Judaism; Middle East; Terrorism.**

Italy. The government of Prime Minister Silvio Berlusconi set a record for longevity in 2004. Berlusconi completed his third year in office since his 2001 election victory, beating the post-World War II (1939-1945) record set by Bettino Craxi in 1986. Despite the record, tensions grew within his four-party, center-right coalition throughout the year.

A weak economy, budget cutbacks, and the unpopularity of the government's support for the United States-led war in Iraq weakened Berlusconi's political position. In elections for the European Parliament in June 2004, his Forza Italia party won 16 seats, a loss of 4 from the previous parliament. Berlusconi's coalition partners—the National Alliance, the Northern League, and the Christian Democrats—increased their seats by 2, to 18. In regional elections in June, Forza Italia lost control of the governorship of the Milan region, Berlusconi's home base, to its center-left opponents.

Coalition tensions. The election results strained tensions within the government coalition. When Economy Minister Giulio Tremonti proposed big spending cuts to reduce Italy's budget deficit, the National Alliance opposed the plans and forced Tremonti to resign on July 3. Domenico Siniscalco, an economist who headed the treasury, replaced Tremonti. Also in July, Umberto Bossi, the head of the Northern League, resigned as Cabinet minister for reform.

The economy remained sluggish in 2004 despite a modest upturn. The European Commission (EC), the executive agency of the 25-nation European Union (EU), forecast that Italy's *gross domestic product* (GDP, the total output of goods and services produced in a country in a year) would grow by just 1.3 percent, compared with an average of 2.5 percent growth for the 25 EU countries.

The weak economy aggravated Italy's budget deficit, forcing the government to adopt fresh austerity measures. The EC requested the measures after warning that Italy's deficit risked exceeding 3 percent of GDP—the limit for countries using the euro. In September, the government approved a budget for 2005 that contained $31.6 billion in spending cuts and tax increases. The package aimed to reduce the deficit to 2.7 percent of GDP in 2005 from 2.9 percent in 2004. In November, Berlusconi's coalition added $8.6 billion in tax cuts to the 2005 budget, in order to fulfill a key election promise. Unions staged a national strike on Nov. 30, 2004, shutting down much of the country, to protest the tax cuts, which they claimed would help the rich and hurt public services.

Pension reform. Parliament passed a hotly debated reform of the country's retirement pension system on July 28. The law will raise the retirement age in stages to 60 from 57. Berlusconi argued that the reforms were needed to reduce the budget deficit and the national debt.

Berlusconi trial. The prime minister was put back on trial on corruption charges in 2004 after the country's Constitutional Court rejected a law granting him immunity from prosecution. That law, passed in 2003, had forced the suspension of an earlier trial. In the new trial, which opened in Milan in April 2004, Berlusconi was accused of bribing judges in the 1980's in order to block a business rival and gain control of state-owned food company SME. Berlusconi denied the charges. In December 2004, a three-judge panel in Milan ruled that Berlusconi indeed had kept judges on his payroll. However, the statute of limitations on one charge had expired, and he was acquitted of a second charge.

Media controversy. The parliament passed a controversial law on media ownership in April that limits the amount of television and radio advertising revenue that any one media company can earn. The opposition complained that the law would not affect Berlusconi's dominance of Italian media because the limits were set too high and did not cover publishing. Berlusconi's Fininvest company owns more than 90 percent of the country's commercial television channels and controls several newspapers. Lilli Gruber, a leading news presenter at the state-owned broadcaster Rai, resigned to protest Berlusconi's influence and won election to the European Parliament in June as a member of the opposition Olive Tree Coalition.

EU dispute. Berlusconi sparked a controversy within the EU when he nominated his European affairs minister, Rocco Buttiglione, to serve as Italy's member of the EU Commission. Buttiglione, a conservative Roman Catholic, said at his confirmation hearing in the European Parliament that he considered homosexuality a sin and that the aim of marriage was to allow women to have children. The parliament threatened to block confirmation of the Commission in October, forcing Berlusconi to replace Buttiglione with Franco Frattini, his foreign minister. Gianfranco Fini, the head of the National Alliance, became foreign minister.

Corporate scandal. Italy continued to grapple with the accounting fraud at Parmalat SpA, a dairy company that collapsed in Europe's largest-ever bankruptcy in December 2003. Auditors estimated the company's debts at around $18 billion in January 2004. Later in the year, the company's court-appointed administrators sued the auditing firms Deloitte & Touche and Grant Thornton International, as well as U.S. banking giants Bank of America and Citigroup, claiming they had helped the company conceal the fraud. The government introduced a package of reforms designed to prevent future frauds.   ■ Tom Buerkle

See also **Europe; Iraq: A Special Report.**

Ivory Coast. See Cote d'Ivoire in **Africa.**

Jamaica. See **West Indies.**

Japan. The governing Liberal Democratic Party (LDP) won only 49 of 121 seats being contested in elections for half of the upper house of parliament on July 11, 2004. The opposition Democratic Party of Japan (DPJ) took 50 seats. In proportional representation voting, the DPJ received 21 million votes, compared with fewer than 17 million for the long-dominant LDP. The election for the upper house was the first since 1989 in which the opposition had beaten the LDP. Despite this setback, the LDP led by Prime Minister Junichiro Koizumi retained a majority in the upper house through coalition allies. The LDP's real majority remained intact in the lower house. After the election, opinion polls showed Koizumi's popularity at its lowest level since he became prime minister in 2001. Political experts attributed the LDP's poor showing at the polls and Koizumi's loss of popularity to scandals.

Pension scandals. The scandals involved payments into the national pension plan. In 2004, the average age of Japan's population was one of the oldest in the industrial world and rising rapidly. At the same time, the work force was shrinking. In 2002, the pension plan began paying out more than it took in, and the government estimated a shortfall of $580 billion by 2025.

Resisting the idea of raising sales taxes to help fund the pension plan, the LDP government on May 11, 2004, passed an unpopular new law that raises workers' premiums and cuts benefits between 2005 and 2017. Many tried to evade the payments, especially the self-employed, because they expected to get back less than they had paid.

In 2004, the media revealed that several members of Koizumi's Cabinet had not made pension plan payments in past years, even before the unpopular new law. DPJ leader Naoto Kan responded with severe criticism of LDP members, and Yasuo Fukuda, the chief Cabinet secretary, was forced to resign. Then Kan admitted that he, too, had missed payments and was forced to give up DPJ leadership. Koizumi also conceded that he had failed to pay into the plan in several periods prior to 1986. However, the prime minister rode out the storm in 2004 as public attention shifted away from the scandal.

The DPJ chose Katsuya Okada to succeed Kan. Okada capitalized on his party's purge to lead the DPJ to victory in the upper house elections.

Iraq. The first Japanese troops to be deployed in a combat area since World War II (1939-1945) arrived in Samawah, in southern Iraq, in January 2004. The members of Japan's Self-Defense Force (SDF) were sent after a controversial decision to help the United States try to stabilize Iraq. Some Japanese argued the deployment violated the country's constitution, but opinion polls showed 53 percent of the public supported the move.

The 550 soldiers, including some air and naval personnel, were authorized to return fire if at-tacked. Nearby Dutch troops were assigned to aid the Japanese if they were attacked, but the SDF troops had no reciprocal duty to aid the Dutch. The SDF's humanitarian mission included making improvements to the local water supply, distributing medicine, erecting buildings, and generally helping the people of Samawah.

On April 8, an Iraqi group calling itself the Mujahideen Brigades announced that it was holding three Japanese hostages and would kill them if Koizumi did not withdraw the SDF troops. Koizumi refused. Japanese commentators suggested he was risking the fall of his government. However, the hostages were released unharmed, reportedly because members of a Sunni Muslim organization called the Committee of Muslim Scholars had intervened for the three—an aid volunteer, an antiwar researcher, and a photojournalist. In October, a radical Islamic group kidnapped a Japanese student sightseeing in Iraq in another attempt to convince Koizumi to withdraw the SDF troops. When Koizumi refused, the student was beheaded.

Foreign relations. Koizumi argued that the deployment in Iraq was part of Japan's assuming a world role comparable with its economic power. Japan intensified its efforts to obtain a permanent seat on the United Nations (UN) Security Council. The five permanent members since the UN's founding in 1945 primarily were nations that had defeated Japan in World War II, but Japan contended that circumstances now gave it a right to a seat.

At the end of that war, the Soviet Union seized from Japan two small islands and two groups of outcrops in the Kuril chain northeast of Japan's Hokkaido island. The two countries never signed a peace treaty because Japan demanded the return of the islands. On Sept. 2, 2004, Koizumi sailed along the mist-enshrouded islands to reassert Japan's claims.

Relations with China were troubled by a dispute over small, rocky islands northeast of Taiwan. Japan calls the islands the Senkakus, and China calls them the Diaoyu. Among various confrontations over the islands, Japanese officials arrested and deported in March seven Chinese activists who had landed on one of the islands to stake a claim.

Japan agreed in March to participate in a ballistic missile defense system under the leadership of the United States. The system was designed to defend the United States and Japan against possible attack by China or North Korea.

North Korea remained a major concern for Japan in 2004. North Korea's missile developments, efforts to make nuclear weapons, and alleged smuggling of narcotics led Japan to take part in international attempts to soften the Communist country's policies.

In 2002, North Korea admitted having kidnapped Japanese citizens in the 1970's to tutor North Korean spies. Koizumi subsequently visited North Korea and, in return for aid, was allowed to return to Japan with five of the kidnap victims, but not with the victims' North Korean spouses or children. The prime minister returned to North Korea on May 22, 2004, and promised to increase food and medical aid. In return, he was allowed to take five children of kidnap victims back to Japan. Some 60 percent of Japan's people told pollsters Koizumi had done the right thing, but media critics said it was a defeat to pay ransom for the children.

An American accused of deserting the U.S. Army in South Korea in 1965, Charles Robert Jenkins, had married a Japanese kidnap victim in North Korea and had appeared in propaganda films. His wife returned to Japan in 2002. Jenkins and their two daughters were allowed to leave North Korea in July 2004, and in September, he surrendered to the U.S. Army in Japan. On November 3, he pled guilty to desertion and aiding the enemy in a U.S. Army court-martial at Camp Zama, the United States Army headquarters in Japan. Jenkins was given a dishonorable discharge and a 30-day jail sentence.

Nuclear accident. An accident killed four people and seriously injured seven others on August 9 at a nuclear power plant at Mihama on the Sea of Japan. A cooling pipe that had not been inspected in the 28 years since the reactor was completed burst due to corrosion—four days before an inspection was scheduled. No nuclear contamination resulted. However, the accident further damaged public trust in Japan's nuclear power industry. In 2003, the Tokyo Electric Power Company, which operates 17 nuclear power plants, admitted having falsified their safety records for more than a decade.

Terrorism. On Feb. 27, 2004, a Tokyo court sentenced Shoko Asahara to death for masterminding the 1995 release of poison gas in a subway that killed 12 people and sickened some 5,500 others. Asahara, head of the Aum Shinrikyo cult, was the 12th cult member to be sentenced to death. His incoherent statements in court failed to explain why the cult had made the deadly attacks.

Typhoons. The Pacific Ocean generated more typhoons than normal in 2004. Ten of the storms swept across Japan, the highest number since record keeping began in 1951. Tokage, the deadliest typhoon to hit Japan in 25 years, killed at least 80 people when it pounded much of the country on Oct. 20, 2004. Later that week, a 6.8-magnitude earthquake shook the region around Niigata. It was the deadliest quake to strike Japan in 10 years, killing 39 people. ■ Henry S. Bradsher

See also **Asia; Disasters; Korea, North.**

Militants in Iraq display three Japanese hostages on an Arab-speaking television network on April 8, 2004. The militants threatened to kill the hostages if Japanese troops were not immediately withdrawn from Iraq. Prime Minister Koizumi refused to comply, and the three eventually were released.

Jordan. Jordanian authorities reported in April 2004 that they had impounded five trucks laden with chemical explosives that had entered Jordan from Syria. The authorities said that several militants who were arrested in a series of raids after the truck seizures were linked with al Qa'ida, the terrorist network led by Osama bin Laden. The militants had planned to attack the Jordanian General Intelligence Department headquarters, the prime minister's office, and the United States embassy—all in the capital, Amman.

On April 29, Queen Rania joined an estimated 80,000 Jordanians in Amman to protest the terrorist plot. The queen noted that the "silent majority has started to speak out against terrorism in a first-of-its-kind demonstration in the Arab and Islamic world ... "

Muslim Brotherhood. In September, Jordanian authorities arrested 11 clerics of the Muslim Brotherhood, an international Islamic fundamentalist organization. The clerics were accused of preaching sermons that "incite violence against Western targets and inflame anti-U.S. feelings." Following a meeting between Prime Minister Faisal al-Fayez and leaders of the Islamic Action Front, the political arm of the Muslim Brotherhood, authorities released most of the detained clerics. Although the clerics had to agree to abide by a law that regulates the contents of sermons, few observers expected the clerics to stop speaking out against the presence of U.S. troops in Iraq and the normalization of relations with Israel.

Arab-Israeli peace process. King Abdullah II met in Israel with Israeli Prime Minister Ariel Sharon on March 18, in an attempt to boost the quest for peace between the Israelis and Palestinians. The king also met a number of times with Palestinian Prime Minister Ahmad Quray in 2004.

In May, King Abdullah visited Washington, D.C., to meet with U.S. President George W. Bush. President Bush gave the king a letter of assurance emphasizing that the planned Israeli withdrawal from Gaza—a strip of land administered by the Palestinians, but the site of numerous Israeli settlements—was an essential part of the peace process.

King Abdullah attended the funeral of Palestinian leader Yasir Arafat in the Egyptian capital, Cairo, on November 12.

Women's rights setback. In June, the National Assembly voted down a proposed law that would have granted women the right to divorce their husbands. A deputy of the Islamic Action Front argued against the law, stating that "women who initiate divorce proceedings under this law are often women of comfort and leisure who don't care about their families."

■ Marius Deeb

See also **Iraq: A Special Report; Israel.**

Judaism. On Oct. 26, 2004, the Knesset, Israel's parliament, narrowly approved a plan for a phased withdrawal of all Jewish settlers from Gaza. The plan, sponsored by Prime Minister Ariel Sharon, was to be part of an eventual total withdrawal by Israel from Gaza. A majority of Israelis supported the plan, but it faced strong opposition from Jewish settlers, rabbis representing religious parties, and Sharon's own Likud Party.

Civilian deaths from terror attacks in Israel fell sharply in 2004. Some experts attributed the drop to policies of Sharon's government, including a campaign against the Palestinian militant group Hamas. In March, an Israeli missile attack in Gaza killed top Hamas leader Sheik Ahmed Yassin and, in April, an Israeli helicopter attack killed his successor, Abdel Aziz Rantissi. Many vacationing Israelis were killed on October 7 in a terrorist attack on Taba, an Egyptian resort.

Terrorist experts also said that the security barrier Israel was building to fence off the West Bank may have prevented some acts of terror. Nevertheless, the barrier drew a serious rebuke when on July 9, the International Court of Justice in The Hague, Netherlands, issued a ruling in which judges called the barrier "illegal" and ordered it to be dismantled. Sharon's government and the United States rejected the ruling.

Palestinian Authority Chairman Yasir Arafat died in Paris on November 11. He was succeeded by Mahmoud Abbas, a former Palestinian prime minister. Analysts speculated that with the combative Arafat gone, Israelis and Palestinians might be able to restart the peace process.

Israel's improved security situation encouraged a rebound of tourism in 2004. According to Israel's Tourism Ministry, the country hosted 136,000 visitors in April, nearly doubling the figure for April 2003.

United States. Jews celebrated the 350th anniversary of American Jewish life in 2004. In the late summer of 1654, 23 Jewish refugees from Recife, Brazil, stepped off a boat in New Amsterdam, the Dutch settlement that was to become New York City. Those Jews, forerunners of the Jewish community in the future United States, found religious tolerance and freedom from persecution in North America, as did the millions of Jews who followed them over the next three and one-half centuries.

Cities and towns all over the United States staged celebrations of the anniversary. In Washington, D.C., the Library of Congress mounted a major exhibit on Jewish life in America, which opened on Sept. 8, 2004.

Mel Gibson's controversial film, *The Passion of the Christ*, stirred fears of anti-Semitism among American Jews, since it appeared to blame them for Jesus's crucifixion and seemingly ran counter

A man examines a headstone desecrated by anti-Semitic symbols in a cemetery in Herrlisheim, France, on April 30, 2004. According to a report by the Israeli government, the number of anti-Semitic incidents in France in 2004 nearly doubled, compared with 2003.

to recent Roman Catholic teachings concerning how the Passion should be portrayed. To the consternation of Jews, many Catholic and Evangelical Protestant leaders defended the film, which was widely popular. Christian-Jewish relations were also strained by the decision of the Presbyterian Church (U.S.A.) to divest from firms doing business with Israel. Evangelical ties with the Jewish community improved, thanks to those churches' vocal support for the Jewish state of Israel.

Europe. According to an Israeli report released in January, incidents of anti-Semitism declined in much of the world in 2003 but nearly doubled in France. Prime Minister Sharon stirred controversy in July 2004 when he urged French Jews to immigrate "immediately" to Israel.

Jonathan Joseph, president of the European Council of Jewish Communities, noted at a May "General Assembly" of European Jewry, which included over 1,000 leaders representing more than 40 countries, that 90 percent of Jews' image in Europe was defined by anti-Semitism, the Holocaust, and defense of Israel, but that these issues did not define 90 percent of Jews' lives. To drive home the point, speakers cited hundreds of Jewish exhibitions, concerts, publications, festivals, and Jewish museums opening across Europe.

■ Jonathan D. Sarna and Jonathan J. Golden
See also **Israel; Middle East; Terrorism.**

Kazakhstan. President Nursultan Nazarbayev continued to dominate Kazakh politics in 2004. His Otan party won 42 of the 77 seats in the Mazhilis, the Kazakh legislature's lower chamber, in two-part elections in September and October. Other propresidential parties also gained representation, with 11 seats going to a bloc formed by the progovernment Agrarian and Civic parties; 4 seats to the Asar Party of the president's daughter Dariga Nazarbayeva; and 1 seat to the Democratic Party of Kazakhstan. Independent candidates garnered 18 seats, while the opposition party Ak Zhol took just one seat.

The election was widely criticized as neither free nor fair. Foreign observers noted irregularities during the vote count and pressure on voters to support progovernment parties. Mazhilis speaker Zharmakhan Tuyakbay of the Otan party resigned in protest over the conduct of the elections, signaling divisions within the country's leadership. Ak Zhol also gave up its Mazhilis seat and party co-chairman Altynbek Sarsenbayev resigned his position as information minister in the Nazarbayev government. Despite these tensions, Nazarbayev declared his intention to run for another seven-year term as president in 2006.

■ Juliet Johnson
See also **Asia.**

Kentucky. See State government.

Kenya. President Mwai Kibaki's ruling National Rainbow Coalition (NARC) faced a crisis in 2004 over delays in drafting a promised new constitution. Terrorism and corruption also lingered as major concerns for Kenya's government.

Kibaki had won election as president in 2002 on a reform platform. He replaced Daniel arap Moi, widely regarded as corrupt and autocratic.

Stalled reform. On June 28, 2004, President Kibaki postponed the introduction of a new constitution designed to limit presidential power, provoking riots in Nairobi, the capital, and other cities. Upon taking office in January 2003, Kibaki had set a June 2004 deadline for implementing a new constitution.

Kenya's original 1963 Constitution, with subsequent amendments, gives the president wide powers. Reformers within the NARC coalition wanted a government that distributed more power to parliament. However, some members of Kibaki's National Alliance of Kenya, also part of NARC, wished to retain a strong presidency. Opinion polls in 2004 showed strong support among Kenyans for the reformist position.

Corruption. In July, the United Kingdom's high commissioner in Kenya, Sir Edward Clay, alleged that corrupt Kenyan officials had pocketed more than $190 million of public funds. Representatives of other donor nations also voiced alarm over the scale of corruption in Kenya's administration. Kenya relied on donors for about half of its governmental budget in 2004.

Terrorism. In January, President Kibaki responded to a letter from Islamic leaders who objected to proposed antiterror legislation. The leaders charged that the Suppression of Terrorism Bill, designed to heighten security, would lead to harassment of Muslims. About 6 percent of Kenyans are Muslims, most of whom live on the Indian Ocean coast or in Nairobi. Kibaki promised the leaders that the bill would be modified to protect Muslims. The revised bill awaited passage by Kenya's parliament in late 2004.

The threat of terrorism continued to loom large in Kenya during 2004. Major attacks in the country in 1998 and 2002 sharply reduced tourism, a vital sector of the economy, and prompted international pressure to tighten security measures. The United States Department of State in 2004 reissued travel advisories discouraging Americans from traveling to Kenya.

Trials. On February 2, four Kenyans charged with killing 13 people in the November 2002 terror attack on an Israeli-owned hotel in Mombasa went on trial in a Nairobi court. Some of the defendants were also implicated in the August 1998 attack on the U.S. embassy in Nairobi.

■ Simon Baynham

See also **Africa; Terrorism.**

Korea, North. International efforts to force North Korea to give up its nuclear weapons program in return for security guarantees and economic aid failed in 2004. The North Korean government accused the United States of hostile policies that made further talks impossible. Delegates from the United States, China, North and South Korea, Japan, and Russia met for four rounds of talks in Beijing beginning in August 2003. In August 2004, representatives of North Korea declared that they would not attend another meeting.

China, which provides essential food and fuel for impoverished North Korea, had pressed the North Korean government to participate in talks intended to reduce regional tensions. In April, North Korean leader Kim Jong-Il visited China and firmly committed himself to flexibility in the talks, according to Chinese reports. However, in August, U.S. President George W. Bush called Kim a tyrant, angering the North Koreans.

Signs that North Korea had tested a nuclear bomb on September 9 caused international concern. However, what looked like the mushroom cloud from a nuclear explosion was later explained as an unusual cloud formation occurring at the same time as a conventional blast to clear land for a hydroelectric dam in northern North Korea.

International aid. North Korea has remained heavily dependent upon donated food since a 1990's famine, which was the product of both bad weather and government mismanagement. Foreign aid workers and diplomats noted that the North Korean government in 2004 was tightening restrictions on incoming aid, making it harder for foreigners to be sure their help was reaching those most in need. Malnutrition remained widespread in North Korea in 2004.

Refugees. The dire economic situation, plus police state abuses, caused a continuing stream of North Koreans to try to flee into China in 2004, despite tight border controls. Up to 300,000 refugees were reported living illegally in China and nearby countries.

In 2003, more than 1,250 northerners reached South Korea through third countries. By September 2004, another 1,500 had gotten to South Korea, including some 460 North Koreans who followed a smuggling route through China to Vietnam. They were airlifted from Vietnam to South Korea in July. The North accused the South of "abduction and terrorism" in helping these refugees join thousands of other northern refugees and defectors living there.

Accident. A train loaded with liquid chemicals exploded on April 22 in the town of Ryongchon. The blast destroyed buildings over a radius of 2½ miles (4 kilometers), killed as many as 160 people, and wounded 1,300 others. ■ Henry S. Bradsher

See also **Asia; China; Disasters; Korea, South.**

Korea, South. The National Assembly voted on March 12, 2004, to impeach President Roh Moo-hyun. He was charged with violating a law banning presidents from campaigning in legislative elections. The charges were brought after Roh publicly supported the new Uri Party in scheduled Assembly elections. Roh was also accused of corruption and incompetence.

Prime Minister Goh Kun assumed presidential duties pending a decision of the Constitutional Court on the impeachment. Large crowds turned out to support Roh, and opinion polls showed about 70 percent of voters opposed the impeachment. The two parties that had backed impeachment lost the Assembly election on April 15. Uri won 152 of the 299 seats, giving parliamentary control to a younger generation of liberals after a half century of conservative control. Polls showed that South Koreans considered the election a vote of confidence in Roh, who had had low public approval ratings before being impeached. On May 14, the Constitutional Court dismissed the impeachment case, restoring Roh to office.

Nuclear experiments. South Korea's government admitted on August 23 that scientists in 2000 had secretly enriched a small amount of uranium to approximately the quality needed to make nuclear weapons. In September 2004, the government admitted to having conducted a plutonium-based nuclear experiment in 1982. Officials insisted South Korea would uphold its commitment not to make nuclear weapons. However, the experiments raised suspicions abroad about South Korea's intentions at a time when international efforts were being made to limit North Korea's nuclear ambitions.

U.S. Army reductions. The United States announced in June 2004 that it would reduce its armed forces in South Korea from 37,000 to 24,500 troops by the end of 2008. The first 5,000 soldiers left for Iraq in 2004. South Korea, which counts on the U.S. military to help protect it from North Korea, objected. However, it welcomed plans to move the 7,000 troops stationed in Seoul to Pyongtaek, 50 miles (80 kilometers) south of the capital.

Translator murdered. Iraqi extremists in Baghdad murdered a South Korean translator in June 2004. Despite protests, Roh stuck to plans to deploy another 3,000 soldiers to Iraq, joining 600 military medics and engineers in reconstruction work.

Koguryo dispute. South Korea argued with China in September over the Koguryo kingdom that ruled northern Korea and adjacent China from 37 B.C. until 668 A.D. A Chinese magazine article claimed the kingdom was part of Chinese history. South Korea objected, claiming the kingdom as part of Korean history. Later in September 2004, the Peoples' Education Press of China issued a retraction.   ■ Henry S. Bradsher

See also **Asia; Korea, North.**

Kuwait. See **Middle East.**

Members of South Korea's National Assembly attempt to protect Speaker Park Kwan-yong from a shoe thrown at him after he announced on March 12 that the assembly has impeached South Korea's President, Roh Moo-hyun. South Korea's Constitutional Court later dismissed the impeachment as politically motivated.

Labor and employment.

The United States economy began to generate new jobs in 2004, following the so-called "jobless recovery" from the 2001 recession. Of the 2.6 million payroll jobs that had been lost as a result of the recession and the terrorist attacks of Sept. 11, 2001, the economy recovered about 2 million jobs in 2004. As of October, almost 140 million U.S. workers were employed. The unemployment rate was 5.5 percent.

Unemployment rates declined in all major regions of the United States in 2004, according to data compiled by the Bureau of Labor Statistics (BLS). Unemployment rates in October were lowest in the South, at 4.9 percent; 5 percent in the Northeast; 5.5 percent in the Midwest; and 5.6 percent in the West.

Compensation of civilian workers—that is, wages, salaries, and benefits—rose 3.8 percent in the 12 months ending in September 2004, according to the BLS's Employment Cost Index. The Consumer Price Index, which shows the effect of prices on workers' purchasing power, rose 3.2 percent in the 12 months ending in October 2004. This represented a slight upward trend in prices from the unusually low rate of inflation of the previous several years.

Trends in collective bargaining. Companies and unions engaged in difficult bargaining over health costs, pay of new workers, and length of contracts in 2004. Many employers wanted workers to pick up more of the cost of health care premiums, to pay higher co-payments for medical and prescription drug services, or to accept higher deductibles before receiving insured services. Another trend of collective bargaining in 2004 included giving larger pay increases to full-time workers and current employees, compared with part-time workers and new employees.

Communications industry. SBC Corporation, Inc., of San Antonio, Texas, and the Communication Workers of America concluded a five-year agreement in May after a four-day strike. The agreement included four separate pacts covering a total of 102,000 workers in 13 states. Wages were to rise 11.5 percent over the life of the contract. The Communication Workers also won a continuation of the employer-paid health care premiums for both active and retired workers. In addition, the bargainers agreed there would be no layoffs over the contract's life.

SBC Corporation concluded a five-year agreement with the International Brotherhood of Electrical Workers in June. Under the contract, wages were to increase 12 percent across the board, with a cost-of-living adjustment to be activated in the fourth and fifth years. Both current employees and retirees were required to pay higher co-payments for medical services. This provision, however, was partially offset by cash payments of $1,000 to active employees and $2,500 to retirees.

In August, Verizon Communications, Inc., of New York City, and the Communication Workers of America reached agreement on a five-year contract covering 3,400 employees in Texas. Under the agreement's terms, workers were to receive raises of between 1 and 2.5 percent each year. In addition, workers were to get a 4-percent bonus in the first year and improved pension, health care, and vacation benefits.

Also in August, Bell South Corporation of Atlanta, Georgia, and the Communication Workers agreed on a five-year contract covering 45,000 workers in nine states. Wages were to rise by 10.5 percent, and workers were to receive a 4-percent lump sum payment upon contract ratification, which happened in September.

Entertainment industry. In February, the Screen Actors Guild and the American Federation of Television and Radio Artists agreed with the Alliance of Motion Picture and Television Producers (AMPTP) to extend their contract for one year beyond the scheduled expiration of June 30. The extension provided that minimum salaries would increase 2.5 percent, and employers would pay an additional half-percent into the union health fund.

The Writers Guild of America announced a three-year agreement with the AMPTP and four television networks—ABC, CBS, NBC, and Fox—in October. The 11,000 guild members were to receive a 3-percent increase in wages each year, beginning November 1. Under the contract, employer contributions to the health care fund were to rise from 7.5 percent to 8.5 percent.

In November, members of the UNITE HERE union approved a five-year contract that had been reached with seven hotels/casinos in Atlantic City, New Jersey. UNITE HERE was the name members chose to represent the labor association created by the July merger of the Union of Needletrades, Industrial, and Textile Employees and the Hotel Employees and Restaurant Employees. The pact provided continuation of employer-paid health care premiums. Wages were frozen in the first year of the contract for all workers. Workers with more than eight years seniority would receive bonuses in the second and third years of the contract, with wage increases in the final two years.

Retail trade industry. In February, five United Food and Commercial Workers union locals ratified a three-year contract with Stop & Shop Supermarket Company, Inc., based in Quincy, Massachusetts. The agreement, which covered 42,000 workers in Connecticut, Massachusetts, and Rhode Island, was reached after the company withdrew a proposal requiring workers to pay 20 percent of their health care premium costs. The contract increased wages $25 a week for full-time employees, with lesser increases for part-time workers.

In March, 70,000 California members of the United Food and Commercial Workers approved a three-year contract, ending a four-month strike and lockout at various large grocery chains. The strike and lockout resulted from the bargainers' failure to agree on the terms of health coverage. Under the pact, the companies were to pay full health premiums for the first two years of the contract, with employees paying between $5 and $15 a week in the third year—if the health fund trustees found such contributions to be necessary. In addition, workers were to receive lump sum payments instead of wage increases, and new hires were to come onboard at lower wages.

Also in March, United Food and Commercial Workers members in Washington, D.C., and Baltimore ratified a four-year agreement with Giant Foods, Inc., of Landover, Maryland, and Safeway Stores, Inc., of Pleasanton, California. The same union concluded a three-year agreement with 86 Kroger stores in Michigan in June.

In February, the International Brotherhood of Teamsters approved a three-year contract with Costco Companies, Inc., based in Issaquah, Washington. Under the agreement, which covered 12,000 workers in California, hourly wages were to increase by $1.50 over the pact's life, with annual bonuses ranging from $2,800 to $5,500. The employer's pension contributions and health premium payments were also increased.

Automobile industry. The United Automobile Workers (UAW) ratified a four-year agreement with American Axle & Manufacturing, Inc., of Detroit, following a one-day strike in March. The agreement, covering 6,700 workers, provided a $5,000 signing bonus to each employee, but it introduced a lower pay rate for new hires. The contract also provided for 2-percent performance bonuses and $1,000 holiday bonuses in each year from 2005 to 2007.

Delphi Corporation of Troy, Michigan, finalized a seven-year supplemental agreement with the UAW in April 2004. The agreement, which covered 30,000 workers, provided that new hires would start work at $14 an hour, compared with $16.51 for current employees. The UAW and Visteon Corporation of Van Buren Township, Michigan, reached a similar agreement covering 21,000 workers.

Longshore industry. In June, members of the International Longshoremen's Association ratified a six-year master contract with the United States Maritime Alliance, Ltd., of Iselin, New Jersey. The contract covered 15,000 workers

CHANGES IN THE UNITED STATES LABOR FORCE

	2003	2004*
Civilian labor force	146,516,000	147,113,000
Total employment	137,739,000	138,929,000
Unemployment	8,777,000	8,184,000
Unemployment rate	6.0%	5.5%
Change in weekly earnings of production and nonsupervisory workers (nonfarm business sector)		
Current dollars	+1.2%	+2.9%
Constant (1982) dollars	-0.5%	-0.4%
Change in output per employee hour (nonfarm business sector)	+4.4%	+3.1%

*All 2004 data are through the third quarter of 2004 (preliminary data).
Source: *World Book* estimates based on data from the U.S. Bureau of Labor Statistics.

on East and Gulf coast docks. Workers earning more than $21 an hour were to receive wage increases totaling $4 per hour; those earning less than $21 an hour were to get increases totaling $7 an hour. In addition, pension funding and job security were improved.

Airline industry. The turbulence affecting the airline industry since the terrorist attacks of Sept. 11, 2001, continued through 2004. In October, a bankruptcy judge granted US Airways of Arlington, Virginia, the authority to impose a 21-percent cut in wages through February 2005. The airline had gone to court after the unions refused to accept a 23-percent pay cut. Later in October 2004, members of the Airline Pilots Association (APA) ratified salary cuts of 18 percent with U.S. Airways as part of a five-year contract—thereby making them exempt from the temporary 21-percent cut.

Also in October, the APA and Northwest Airlines Corp. of Eagan, Minnesota, announced agreement on creating $300 million in savings, including $265 million from labor cost reductions. In November, the APA approved an agreement with Delta Airlines of Atlanta to cut pilots' pay by 32.5 percent and to freeze retirement benefits over five years.

In contrast to these concessions, the APA ratified a three-year contract in January with America West Airlines of Phoenix that provided an 11-percent pay increase, effective immediately. Another 3-percent boost was scheduled for the end of the contract.

Union membership. The BLS reported in

January that U.S. membership in unions stood at 15.8 million, or 12.9 percent of the labor force, in 2003. This represented a drop of 369,000 unionized workers from 2002, when such workers represented 13.3 percent of the U.S. labor force.

In September 2004, delegates at the convention of the International Association of Machinists (IAM) in Cincinnati, Ohio, overwhelmingly approved a resolution that would allow the union to withdraw from the American Federation of Labor and Congress of Industrial Organizations (AFL-CIO). IAM leaders hoped the resolution would send a strong message of concern about recent AFL-CIO operations and decisions. The IAM delegates were highly critical of the AFL-CIO's support for the so-called "New Unity Partnership" movement. This partnership—made up of UNITE HERE, the Service Employees International Union, the Laborers International Union, and the International Brotherhood of Carpenters and Joiners—pushed for new directions and initiatives by labor, including larger mergers of unions to confront corporate mergers.

Federal government. In January, U.S. President George W. Bush proposed a "Guest Worker Program" under which U.S. companies would be allowed to hire temporary immigrant workers if American workers were not available for the jobs. Congress, however, had not acted on the proposal by the end of 2004.

U.S. Department of Labor regulations took effect in August that added new jobs to those exempted from overtime pay and the minimum wage. To previous exemptions for executive, administrative, professional, and outside sales personnel, the new regulations added certain occupations in computer fields. The new exemptions provoked strong opposition from labor unions and many members of Congress.

International unemployment in the 30 nations of the Organization for Economic Co-operation and Development (OECD) stood at 6.8 percent in September 2004, down from 7.1 percent in 2003. The highest unemployment rates in OECD countries were 18.7 percent in Poland and 18 percent in the Slovak Republic. The lowest rates were 4.3 percent in Luxembourg and 4.4 percent in Ireland. September unemployment rates in the larger European members nations of the OECD were significantly higher than those in the United States (5.4 percent) and Japan (4.6 percent). The unemployment rate in Germany was 9.9 percent; and in France, 9.6 percent.   ■ Robert W. Fisher

See also **Aviation; Economics; Telecommunications; Transportation.**
Laos. See Asia.

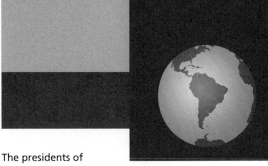

The presidents of three South American nations—Argentina, Brazil, and Venezuela—proved themselves forceful leaders on the world stage in 2004 by confronting wealthy, industrialized nations on issues of global agricultural trade, international finance, and national control over petroleum revenues. Their efforts stood to benefit many Latin American farmers, who depend heavily on exports to make a living.

Reducing farm subsidies. President Luiz Inacio Lula da Silva of Brazil championed a series of trade negotiations within the World Trade Organization (WTO), an international body based in Geneva, Switzerland. In July, the WTO ruled that the subsidies paid by the governments of wealthy, industrialized nations—including the United States—to their farmers to grow such crops as sugar and cotton constituted unfair competition. "This is the beginning of the end of subsidies," said a hopeful Celso Amorim, Brazil's foreign minister, who led the group of developing nations at the WTO negotiations.

Restructuring Argentine debt. President Nestor Kirchner of Argentina faced down the International Monetary Fund (IMF), a United Nations agency that provides financial assistance to financially troubled nations. As Argentina lifted itself out of the worst depression in its history, President Kirchner insisted that he would not impose further hardships on the Argentine people in exchange for immediate IMF assistance. In August, the president won IMF approval of a process for restructuring Argentina's $100-billion external debt that allowed him to conduct his own negotiations with Argentina's foreign creditors. Previously, the IMF had handled such negotiations. By carrying out his own negotiations, President Kirchner hoped to drive a better bargain for Argentina and avoid transferring the burden for settling debts to Argentina's taxpayers.

Chavez controls oil revenues. President Hugo Chavez Frias of Venezuela completed the overhaul of his nation's petroleum industry in 2004 in the face of daunting resistance from international oil corporations. The objective of the overhaul was to make the state-owned oil company, which had long operated independently, more responsive to direction by the Venezuelan government. During 2004, President Chavez redirected a substantial share of the windfall profits from oil exports to increased spending on social programs and public projects beneficial to low

LATIN AMERICA

Thousands of Venezuelans march in Caracas, the capital, on June 6 in a massive show of support for President Hugo Chavez Frias. On August 15, voters soundly rejected a referendum that would have recalled the controversial leftist president from office.

Country	Population	Government	Monetary unit*	Foreign trade (million U.S.$) Exports[†]	Imports[†]
Antigua and Barbuda	78,000	Governor General James B. Carlisle; Prime Minister Baldwin Spencer	dollar (2.67 = $1)	40	357
Argentina	37,533,000	President Nestor Kirchner	peso (2.98 = $1)	29,570	13,270
Bahamas	320,000	Governor General Ivy Dumont; Prime Minister Perry Christie	dollar (1.00 = $1)	617	1,614
Barbados	271,000	Governor General Sir Clifford Husbands; Prime Minister Owen Arthur	dollar (1.99 = $1)	206	1,039
Belize	259,000	Governor General Sir Colville Young; Prime Minister Said Wilbert Musa	dollar (1.97 = $1)	208	501
Bolivia	9,069,000	President Carlos Diego Mesa Gisbert	boliviano (7.98 = $1)	1,495	1,505
Brazil	177,971,000	President Luiz Inacio Lula da Silva	real (2.84 = $1)	73,280	48,250
Chile	15,942,000	President Ricardo Lagos Escobar	peso (604.59= $1)	20,440	17,400
Colombia	44,847,000	President Alvaro Uribe Vélez	peso (2,630.20 = $1)	12,960	13,060
Costa Rica	4,129,000	President Abel Pacheco de la Espriella	colon (448.34 = $1)	6,176	7,057
Cuba	11,334,000	President Fidel Castro	peso (1.00 = $1)	1,467	4,531
Dominica	72,000	President Nicholas J. O. Liverpool; Prime Minister Roosevelt Skerrit	dollar (2.67 = $1)	39	98
Dominican Republic	8,887,000	President Leonel Fernandez Reyna	peso (28.40 = $1)	5,524	7,911
Ecuador	13,549,000	President Lucio Gutierrez Borbua	U.S. dollar	6,073	6,220
El Salvador	6,748,000	President Elias Antonio Saca	colon (8.75 = $1)	3,162	5,466
Grenada	102,000	Governor General Daniel Williams; Prime Minister Keith Mitchell	dollar (2.67 = $1)	46	208
Guatemala	12,606,000	President Oscar Berger	quetzal (7.88 = $1)	2,763	5,749
Guyana	767,000	President Bharrat Jagdeo	dollar (179.00 = $1)	512	612
Haiti	7,636,000	Interim President Boniface Alexandre; Prime Minister Gerard Latortue	gourde (35.25 = $1)	321	1,028
Honduras	7,028,000	President Ricardo Maduro	lempira (18.46 = $1)	1,370	3,110
Jamaica	2,669,000	Governor General Sir Howard Cooke; Prime Minister P. J. Patterson	dollar (61.28= $1)	1,355	3,265
Mexico	103,011,000	President Vicente Fox Quesada	new peso (11.33 = $1)	164,800	168,900
Nicaragua	5,617,000	President Enrique Bolanos Geyer	gold cordoba (16.04 = $1)	632	1,658
Panama	3,005,000	President Martin Torrijos Espino	balboa (1.00 = $1)	5,237	6,622
Paraguay	6,057,000	President Nicanor Duarte Frutos	guarani (5,945.00 = $1)	2,727	2,770
Peru	27,344,000	President Alejandro Toledo; Prime Minister Carlos Ferrero Costa	new sol (3.35 = $1)	8,954	8,244
Puerto Rico	3,944,000	Governor Sila Maria Calderon	U.S. dollar	46,900	29,100
St. Kitts and Nevis	37,000	Governor General Cuthbert Montraville Sebastian; Prime Minister Denzil Douglas	dollar (2.67 = $1)	70	195
St. Lucia	163,000	Governor General Pearlette Louisy; Prime Minister Kenny Anthony	dollar (2.67 = $1)	66	267
St. Vincent and the Grenadines	116,000	Governor General Sir Frederick Nathaniel Ballantyne; Prime Minister Ralph Gonsalves	dollar (2.67 = $1)	38	174
Suriname	424,000	President Runaldo Ronald Venetiaan	guilder (2,515.00 = $1)	495	604
Trinidad and Tobago	1,317,000	President George Maxwell Richards; Prime Minister Patrick Manning	dollar (6.23 = $1)	4,900	3,917
Uruguay	3,431,000	President Jorge Batlle	peso (27.25 = $1)	2,164	1,989
Venezuela	23,950,000	President Hugo Chavez Frias	bolivar (1,919.40 = $1)	25,860	10,710

*Exchange rates as of Oct. 1, 2004, or latest available data.   [†]Latest available data.

income Venezuelans. Political observers noted that Chavez's actions aided him in defeating a national recall referendum on his presidency in August.

President Chavez also pushed for regional solidarity on energy issues and advocated the eventual creation of a transnational Latin American company called Petroamerica. Such a company, he argued, would bolster South America's influence on international gas and oil issues. In line with this strategy, Colombia and Venezuela agreed in July to construct a jointly owned, $200-million natural gas pipeline as part of a network to supply consumers in California and Asia.

Expanding trade with China. China increasingly turned to Latin America for raw materials to stoke the expanding Chinese economy in 2004. China obtained iron ore, soybeans, timber, and other materials from Brazil; tin from Bolivia; oil from Venezuela; and copper from Chile.

Chinese leader Hu Jintao toured Argentina, Brazil, Chile, and Cuba for two weeks in November. He announced $30 billion in new Chinese investment in the region, including $20 billion for railways, oil and gas exploration, construction, and communications satellites in Argentina. Jintao also signed long-term contracts to guarantee a steady future supply of Latin American natural resources for China.

Brazil's President da Silva led a delegation of some 500 Brazilian business leaders to Beijing, the capital of China, for a six-day visit in May. "We are two giants without historical, political, or economic differences," he assured his hosts, following a year in which Brazil's trade with China doubled to $4.5 billion.

The Macao International Trade and Investment Fair, held on China's southern coast in October, featured several large exhibits highlighting China's increasing trade with Portuguese-speaking nations, including Brazil. The International gathering helped Macao position itself as a gateway for lucrative trade with Latin America.

Leftists win key elections. In Uruguay, Tabare Vazquez, an *oncologist* (cancer specialist) and former mayor of Montevideo, the capital, was elected president in October. Vazquez, a socialist, was the candidate of a coalition called the Progressive-Encounter-Broad-Front-New-Majority. The largest component of this coalition comprised former Tupamaros—Marxist rebels who had terrorized Uruguay in the late 1960's and early 1970's. Vazquez, the first leftist ever elected president of Uruguay, pledged to closely align his administration with the left-leaning governments of Argentina, Brazil, Chile, and Venezuela. He also promised to restore diplomatic relations with Cuba.

In Panama, Martin Torrijos Espino, the candidate of the left-of-center New Homeland Alliance, became president in September 2004. Torrijos was the son of the widely revered General Omar Torrijos Herrera, the Panamanian leader who had negotiated the 1977 treaties with the United States that ceded control of the Panama Canal to Panama in 1999.

Rightist victories. In two other Latin American countries, right-of-center leaders won election in 2004. In El Salvador, Elias Antonio (Tony) Saca, of the *incumbent* (ruling) Nationalist Republican Alliance, took office in June. Saca pledged to pursue pro-U.S. policies.

In the Dominican Republic, Leonel Fernandez Reyna, of the Dominican Liberation Party, began his second term in mid-August. He had previously served from 1996 to 2000. Fernandez confronted a Dominican economy that was a shambles because of the $2.2 billion drained from the national treasury to bail out the country's second largest bank.

Continued corruption. Fresh revelations of corruption in high places came to the fore from one end of Latin America to the other in 2004. A lengthy series of trials involving Vladimiro Montesinos, the former chief of Peru's intelligence agency, and some 1,300 codefendants captivated public attention throughout 2004. The defendants faced charges of money laundering, drugs and arms smuggling, and other crimes in the largest corruption scandal in Latin American history.

In Mexico, videotapes broadcast in March showed a key political operative of Manuel Lopez Obrador, the popular leftist mayor of the capital, Mexico City, stuffing his pockets with money that was allegedly an illegal campaign contribution from a wealthy businessman. At first, the video seemed to spell the end of a political career that had made Lopez Obrador the front-runner for the 2006 presidential election. However, in late August 2004, hundreds of thousands of the mayor's supporters rallied to his defense, marching through the streets of Mexico City. Many of the marchers wore stickers proclaiming, "Say what you want to, I am with Lopez Obrador."

In October 2004, former Costa Rican President Miguel Angel Rodriguez resigned as secretary general of the Organization of American States (OAS), less than two weeks after being elected. The OAS is an association of American countries dedicated to regional cooperation. Costa Rican authorities took Rodriguez into custody to answer charges of having accepted a bribe from a French telecommunications company in return for lucrative cell-phone contracts while he was president in 2001.

Another former Costa Rican president, Rafael Angel Calderon, was also arrested in October 2004. Prosecutors charged Calderon with accepting a $450,000 kickback, while president, to help a company obtain a contract to sell medical equipment to the government in the early 1990's.

Indians become activists. The *indigenous* (native) people of several Latin American countries mobilized to make their views known on national and local issues in 2004. In southwestern Colombia, some 40,000 Indians belonging mostly to the Paez and Guambiana tribes marched along the Pan American Highway to the city of Cali in September. Their demonstration was in protest of the 40-year-long civil conflict raging in Colombia. The conflict had long trapped the Indians in the middle of fighting between Marxist rebels, right-wing paramilitaries, and drug traffickers. The fighting in the Indians' ancestral lands increased in 2004 due to a U.S.-supported government offensive to assert control over the region, which has large oil reserves.

In June, Indians in a remote Bolivian town lynched the mayor, whom they had accused of corruption. In August, a mob of Tzotzil Indians in San Juan Chamula, Mexico, jailed the mayor, police chief, and other officials, alleging that they had embezzled public funds. The Indians released their captives only after assurances from officials of the state government of Chiapas that there would be a thorough investigation of the matter.

Wal-Mart in Mexico. Wal-Mart Stores, Inc., the U.S. merchandising giant, unveiled plans in February to open 77 new stores in Mexico by 2005. Wal-Mart was Mexico's largest private employer in 2004. The Mexican revenues of the company exceeded $11 billion annually—more than its top three Mexican competitors combined.

In late October, one of the new Wal-Mart stores, which employed 185 workers, opened near the historic ruins at Teotihuacan. Many Mexicans opposed the construction of the store, which was less than 1 mile (1.6 kilometer) from the ancient pyramids of the sun and moon. In the words of the Mexican poet Homero Aridjis, the Wal-Mart store amounted to "driving the stake of globalization into the heart of Mexican antiquity."

Dollars sent back home. Latin Americans living in the United States were expected to send more than $30 billion to families and friends in their countries of origin in 2004, according to a May report by the Inter-American Development Bank (IDB). The IDB, a regional organization based in Washington, D.C., that supports social and economic projects, said this sum exceeded the amount Latin America received in foreign aid and investment in 2004.

The IDB's Multilateral Investment Fund conducted the pioneering survey, which was based on U.S. Census data and extensive research on Latin Americans in the United States. "We want to bring this [information] out of the shadows so

people understand the critical contributions these hard-working people are making," said Donald F. Terry, manager of the fund.

Habitat conservation. Two U.S. institutions joined forces in 2004 to preserve a vast old-growth forest in Latin America. The investment firm Goldman Sachs and the Bronx Zoo's Wildlife Conservation Society, both headquartered in New York City, established a reserve of more than 680,000 acres (275,000 hectares) on pristine lands on Tierra del Fuego, an island at the southern tip of South America.

"This is really a unique area with lots of ecological possibilities," said Steven Sanderson, the Conservation Society's president. The reserve, he noted, comprised unique high-latitude forests, grasslands, peat bogs, rivers, and wetlands. Thousands of rare animal and plant species inhabited the reserve, including the guanaco, a New World relative of the camel. The guanaco's population was rebounding in 2004 thanks to decades of conservation efforts. The new reserve was expected to help ensure the survival of this and many other species. ■ Nathan A. Haverstock

See also the various Latin American countries; **China; Haiti: A Special Report.**

Latvia. See Europe.

Law. See Courts; Supreme Court of the United States; United States, Government of the.

Lebanon. The United Nations Security Council passed a resolution in September 2004 calling for nations to respect the *sovereignty* (independence from control by another government) of Lebanon and for foreign troops to withdraw from Lebanon. The resolution was directed at Syria, which had occupied and dominated Lebanon since 1976. Syria, however, ignored the Security Council's wishes. Through its control of the Lebanese parliament, Syria extended the term of Emile Lahoud, Syria's hand-picked president of Lebanon, for three additional years. The Security Council called again on Syria to withdraw its troops from Lebanon in October 2004.

Militias. The September UN resolution also called for the disbanding of all Lebanese and non-Lebanese militias in Lebanon. This included the heavily armed Hezbollah terrorist organization, which served both Syria and Iran by continuing to launch attacks against Israel from southern Lebanon in 2004. These attacks came despite the complete withdrawal of Israeli troops from southern Lebanon in 2000. Hasan Nasrallah, the leader of Hezbollah, rejected the resolution.

Prisoner exchange. In January 2004, German mediators arranged an exchange of prisoners between Hezbollah and Israel. Hezbollah obtained the release of 423 Lebanese and other Arab prisoners, as well as the remains of 59

Lebanese guerrillas. In exchange, Israel accepted the return of one prisoner and the bodies of three soldiers.

New prime minister. Omar Karami, the new, pro-Syrian prime minister of Lebanon, formed a 30-member Cabinet in October, which for the first time included two women ministers. Syria picked virtually all the Cabinet ministers. Karami replaced Rafiq Hariri, who had been prime minister for a total of 10 years.

Assassination attempt. Marwan Hamadeh, who had resigned as a Lebanese Cabinet minister because he opposed Syrian domination, was the target of an assassination attempt on October 1. Hamadeh was wounded, and his bodyguard was killed.

Student protest. On November 19, thousands of Lebanese students and other activists defied the government's ban on protests by demonstrating against Syrian domination. At least 3,000 protestors, mostly Christians, marched from their universities to downtown Beirut shouting "Syrians out." One placard read, "Bush help us save Lebanon"—reflecting a desire for greater involvement in Lebanese affairs by President George W. Bush of the United States.

■ Marius Deeb

See also **Israel; Middle East; Syria.**

Lesotho. See Africa.

Library.
A sluggish economy continued to affect libraries in the United States in 2004. Budget shortfalls forced large and small libraries to cut hours, decrease purchases of library materials, and reduce staff. Many of the nation's largest systems were hardest hit. The New York (City) Public Library launched a campaign to raise $18 million to counteract cuts enacted over the past two years. The Minneapolis Public Library used a week-long shut-down to make up a $1.5-million shortfall. The Anchorage (Alaska) Public Library eliminated 2 percent of the staff due to "unprecedented financial pressure." The Seattle Public Library—just before opening a $165.5-million central library by Dutch architect Rem Koolhaas—shut down for the third time in two years.

Academic libraries also were forced to slash budgets to rein in costs. West Contra Costa Unified School District in California eliminated district school libraries entirely, in a bid to save $16.5 million in order to avoid bankruptcy. Even prestigious universities were forced into cutting acquisition funding.

There were some signs of recovery in 2004. Hawaii restored $450 million in previously made state funding cuts, which allowed the Public Library System to return to a full schedule and begin filling 86 staff vacancies. Voters in Dallas and San Antonio approved tax increases to build

or upgrade city libraries. In California, San Jose and San Jose State University opened the Dr. Martin Luther King, Jr., public library, the first to be jointly funded, managed, and operated by a city and a major university.

Federal assistance to libraries. The 2003 Museum and Library Services Act boosted federal funds to libraries in 2004. The legislation allocated $232 million to libraries in fiscal 2004 (which began in October 2003), up from $150 million in fiscal 2003; $10 million was earmarked to recruit and train librarians.

CIPA. The Federal Communications Commission (FCC) set July 1, 2004, as the date by which libraries needed to certify compliance with the Children's Internet Protection Act (CIPA) of 2000. The U.S. Supreme Court—after legal challenges by the American Library Association (ALA), the American Civil Liberties Union, and other groups—ruled in 2003 that CIPA was constitutional, and the court ordered the FCC to set forth rules for dispensing so-called e-rate funds to libraries that installed and maintained content filters on library computers. CIPA mandates the use of filtering software on public-access computers to prevent young people from viewing Web site content considered objectionable. Libraries not in compliance with CIPA lose federal e-rate funding—generated by a tax on phone companies—that helps pay for computers and Internet connections.

The ALA developed a response strategy to CIPA and similar laws passed by some states. The ALA strategy focused on providing libraries with accurate and authoritative information about requirements. As the deadline for compliance approached, a number of libraries announced they would forego e-rate funding in order to remain filter-free; others complied.

The House Committee on Energy and Finance, which oversees the FCC, investigated allegations of fraud in the e-rate program in 2004. Substantial violations were uncovered, prompting the FCC to request more auditors. The Texas-based telecommunications giant SBC was forced to return $8.8 million in federal funds for networking equipment that SBC had failed to deliver to the Chicago Public School system.

Radio frequency identification (RFID) tagging by libraries stirred controversy in 2004. RFID tags—widely used by retailers—are gummed labels that contain a microchip that stores information about the object to which it is attached. The San Francisco Public Library announced in March that RFID was being used on library materials to facilitate reshelving and automated checkout. This prompted privacy advocates to call for an investigation into how RFID tagging might affect patron privacy.   ■ Rob Carlson

See **Internet; News bytes.**

Libyan leader Muammar Muhammad al-Qadhafi (right) meets with British Prime Minister Tony Blair in Tripoli in March. The United Kingdom was one of several nations that mended ties with Libya in 2004, after Qadhafi renounced the use of weapons of mass destruction.

Libya. The United States and European nations lifted a number of sanctions against Libya throughout 2004. The moves followed the December 2003 declaration by Libyan leader Muammar Muhammad al-Qadhafi that Libya would end all of its programs aimed at developing weapons of mass destruction (WMD's). In January 2004, Libya ratified the Comprehensive Nuclear Test Ban Treaty.

U.S. relations. In April, the United States Department of the Treasury lifted a long-time ban on travel by U.S. citizens to Libya. However, certain restrictions remained, including a prohibition on Americans flying on Libyan airlines. Later in April, U.S. President George W. Bush opened the door for U.S. oil companies to resume commercial activities in Libya after an 18-year absence. President Bush also authorized the establishment of a U.S. diplomatic mission in Libya—the first since 1980.

In September 2004, President Bush signed an executive order lifting the remaining commercial sanctions against Libya. The move paved the way for reinstating normal air travel between the United States and Libya and unblocking approximately $1.2 billion in frozen Libyan assets. However, President Bush stopped short of removing Libya from the U.S. State Department list of nations that sponsor terrorism.

British relations. In February, Libya's foreign minister, Abd al-Rahman Muhammad Shalgam, made an official visit to the United Kingdom—the first such visit in more than 20 years. Meeting with British Prime Minister Tony Blair and Foreign Secretary Jack Straw, Shalgam discussed the dismantling of Libya's WMD program, cooperation on the war on terrorism, and bilateral relations. In March, Prime Minister Blair made the first official visit to Libya by a British prime minister since the 1969 Libyan Revolution that brought Qadhafi to power. During the visit, Blair announced that BAE Systems, a major British defense manufacturer, was discussing aviation projects with Libya.

Germany. In October 2004, German Chancellor Gerhard Schroeder visited Libya. The visit came after Libyan leader Qadhafi pledged to pay $35 million in compensation to the victims of the 1986 bombing of a Berlin discotheque.

European Union. The European Union (EU) lifted its 18-year arms embargo on Libya in October 2004. Pressure had been placed on the EU by the Italian government, which sought better relations with Libya in order to help the African nation patrol its coastline and prevent illegal immigrants from sailing to Europe.

■ Mary-Jane Deeb

See also **Europe; Middle East; Terrorism.**

Liechtenstein. See Europe.

Literature, American.

Established writers such as Joyce Carol Oates, Philip Roth, Anne Tyler, John Updike, and Tom Wolfe all came out with new books in 2004. With the exception of Wolfe and Roth, most were overshadowed by new voices. Nonfiction books, particularly political screeds and several well-received biographies, garnered more attention than most fiction.

Notables. Philip Roth's *The Plot Against America* was greeted with both acclaim and derision. Roth's novel imagines life in an America that signed nonaggression treaties with Adolf Hitler and Japan's Emperor Hirohito in 1940. While some critics read it as a moving indictment of current political philosophy, others saw it as little more than a literary trick. In order to write *I Am Charlotte Simmons,* Tom Wolfe visited college campuses across the country and interviewed hundreds of students. Some found his tale of a naive freshman who struggles through the college world of alcohol, athletes, and sexual encounters a scathing satire, while other critics thought it had nothing new to say.

Adam Langer was heralded as a writer to watch with the publication of his debut novel, *Crossing California.* The book takes place in Chicago's West Rogers Park neighborhood in 1979, where California Avenue divides the rich from the poor. Langer told the overlapping tales of three neighborhood families in a novel that won him comparisons with Saul Bellow and Stuart Dybek. Celebrated short story writer Dan Chaon viewed a fragmented family through interwoven flashbacks and colliding memories in his first novel, *You Remind Me of Me.*

The first two volumes of *The Complete Peanuts,* a collection of the Charles Schulz comic strip, were published in 2004. The volumes, covering 1950-1952 and 1953-1954, portray Linus and Lucy as infants, and Snoopy as a puppy. Twenty-three more volumes are scheduled for release at the rate of two per year.

Politics. The 2004 presidential election campaign season spawned dozens of political works. The most anticipated, and best received, was former President Bill Clinton's autobiography, *My Life.* Part memoir, part political analysis, the book debuted at the top of the best-seller lists, where it remained for much of the year.

The presidency of George W. Bush and the Iraq War provided fertile ground for political writers. Bob Woodward weighed in with *Plan of Attack,* an analysis of decisions leading to the war, written with the cooperation of key members of the Bush administration, including Secretary of State Colin Powell, Secretary of Defense Donald Rumsfeld, and the president himself. Although Woodward echoed claims made by opponents of the administration—that planning for the war began early in November 2001 and that the Bush administration had targeted Iraq from its first days in office—his approach to the material was even-handed and was applauded by readers on both the right and left of the political spectrum.

Other books proved far more critical of the administration. In *Against All Enemies: Inside America's War on Terror,* Richard Clarke, former adviser to Presidents George H. W. Bush and George W. Bush, as well as to Bill Clinton and Ronald Reagan, accused the Bush administration of turning a blind eye to the threat of terrorism before the attacks of Sept. 11, 2001. Craig Unger's *House of Bush, House of Saud* traced the relationship between the Bush family and the Saudi royal family and drew connections between that relationship and the growth of terror. In *The Price of Loyalty,* Ron Suskind followed the downfall of former Treasury Secretary and National Security Council member Paul O'Neill as an object lesson in the fate suffered by opposition within the administration. In *Worse Than Watergate,* John Dean, a member of President Richard Nixon's staff, compared the secrecy of the Bush administration with the Nixon administration.

President Bush's opponent in the 2004 election, Senator John Kerry (D., Massachusetts), also found himself under attack. *Unfit for Command,* by longtime Kerry opponent John O'Neill, accused Kerry of inappropriate behavior while in service during the Vietnam War (1957-1975) and criticized him for his later work with Vietnam Veterans Against the War. Historian Douglas Brinkley's *Tour of Duty* provided a less political view of the same events.

America (The Book): A Citizen's Guide to Democracy Inaction presented a lighter view of American politics. Written by Jon Stewart and the staff of his television program, "The Daily Show," the book took a satiric look at the democratic process and quickly became a best-seller.

Pulitzer Prizes. Edward P. Jones won the Pulitzer Prize for fiction for *The Known World,* his novel of a former slave who becomes a plantation proprietor and slave owner in antebellum Virginia and of the chaos that ensues following his death. *American Woman* by Susan Choi and *Evidence of Things Unseen* by Marianne Wiggins were also nominated as finalists in the fiction category.

Anne Applebaum's *Gulag: A History* was awarded the Pulitzer Prize for nonfiction. Using the many memoirs and studies that have been published since the collapse of the Soviet Union in 1991, Applebaum's book is the first fully documented history of the Soviet prison camp system. Other finalists in the nonfiction category included *Rembrandt's Jews* by Steven Nadler and *The Mission: Waging War and Keeping Peace with America's Military* by Dana Priest.

National Book Awards. Controversy surrounded the finalists for the 2004 National Book Award in fiction. An article in *The New Yorker* magazine railed against the obscurity of the nominated books, noting that only one of the five had sold more than 2,000 copies. Novelist Thomas McGuane pointed out that the nominees were all women from New York City and suggested that the award "should be called the Municipal Book Awards." A past chair of the fiction committee, McGuane admitted that few judges read the nominated books in their entirety and said that the winner is generally reached by compromise: "three people's second-favorite book." The controversy continued the complaint of the 2003 honorary winner, Stephen King, who had once accused the Foundation of snobbery against popular writers.

Lily Tuck, the winner in the fiction category for *The News from Paraguay,* accepted her award by saying, "I'd like to acknowledge my fellow 'unknown' finalists." Her book, the fictionalized account of Ella Lynch, the Irish-born mistress of 19th-century Paraguayan leader Francisco Solano Lopez, is told from multiple points of view. Finalists in the fiction category included Sarah Shun-lien Bynum with her debut novel *Madeleine is Sleeping,* a fairy tale-like dreamscape, which follows its main character down a path of discovery. Christine Schutt's *Florida* also follows a path of self-discovery as Alice, abandoned at age 10, is shuttled between various relatives in what she calls her "sleep-over life." *Ideas of Heaven* by Joan Silber and Kate Walbert's *Our Kind* are both collections of connected stories.

The 9/11 Commission Report was the surprise nonfiction nominee. Critics said the report, which traces the roots of the terrorist attacks on the United States on Sept. 11, 2001, was written well enough to engage the general public. Stephen Greenblatt's *Will in the World* was another best-selling nominee. Greenblatt combined his extensive Elizabethan scholarship with an ability to write about Shakespeare's world in a way that brought that world alive for a modern reader. Both books lost to Kevin Boyle's *Arc of Justice,* the story of Ossian Sweet, an African American physician accused of killing a white man in 1920's Detroit. Critics called *Arc of Justice* both an important history and a compelling courtroom drama. David Hackett Fischer's *Washington's Crossing,* about George Washington's crossing of the Delaware River, and *Life on the Outside: The Prison Odyssey of Elaine Bartlett* by Jennifer Gonnerman were also nominated.

The 2004 Medal for Distinguished Contribution to American Letters went to Judy Blume, the popular author of such children's fiction as *Are You There God? It's Me, Margaret,* and the "Fudge" books. Blume's work has been both widely praised and widely censored, a fact she acknowledged, saying, "It makes me sad and very angry that encouraging people to think for themselves is subversive."

■ Brian Bouldrey

See also **Literature, World; Literature for children; Poetry; Pulitzer Prizes.**

Literature, World. The Nobel Prize for literature in 2004 was awarded to Elfriede Jelinek, "for her musical flow of voices and counter-voices in novels and plays that with extraordinary linguistic zeal reveal the absurdity of society's cliches and their subjugating power." Born in 1946 in the province of Styria in Austria, Jelinek was educated in music and art. Influenced by the radical groups with which she spent much of her young adulthood, her early writings are satirical and her early novels form a sustained attack on popular culture. Jelinek's writing, which often changes from poetry to prose, alternates between extreme wit and graphic violence.

Jelinek is not well known outside of Austria and Germany, and only the most prominent of her prose works have been translated into English: *The Piano Teacher; Wonderful, Wonderful Times; Lust;* and *Women as Lovers.* She is considered a controversial figure in her native Austria because of her social criticisms aimed against her own native culture, especially regarding the role of women.

Other former Nobel Prize-winners continued to publish in 2004, and a number of new works were offered to English-speaking readers for the first time. Portuguese Laureate Jose Saramago's *The Double* is a parablelike tale concerning a man who sees his exact look-alike on television and tries to meet him. Trinidad native V. S. Naipaul offered *Magic Seeds,* a sequel to his autobiographical novel *Half a Life.* West Indian poet Derek Walcott published a fictional autobiography in verse in his book-length poem *The Prodigal.*

Hungarian Imre Kertesz, perhaps as obscure to international audiences as Jelinek until receiving the Nobel Prize in 2002, enjoyed growing fame after the publication in 2004 of the English translation of *Liquidation,* a novel about a book editor who publishes the last manuscript of an old writer friend 10 years after the friend's suicide. Chinese writer Gao Xingjian's short stories were collected and translated in 2004 in a volume entitled *Buying a Fishing Rod for My Grandfather.*

Near neighbors. Canadian writers published several outstanding works in 2004, most notably short story master Alice Munro, whose collection *Runaway* shows her growing ability to write long yet tightly crafted stories. Yann Martel, whose novel *Life of Pi* was awarded the 2002 Booker Prize, gave readers a story collection entitled *The Facts Behind the Helsinki Roccamatios.*

Ghana emigre Esi Edugyan published *The Second Life of Samuel Tyne* in 2004, a novel about family and racial strife as a West African family moves to the Canadian province of Alberta.

Several young Mexican writers emerged on the international scene in 2004. Ignacio Padilla published *Shadow Without a Name,* a complex novel in which characters based on real people change identities while playing chess at several different points in history. Elena Poniatowska offered *The Skin of the Sky,* about a Mexican astronomer with conflicting loyalties. Mexican American novelist Francisco Goldman mined his experiences growing up Jewish in Mexico and the United States to pen *The Divine Husband,* the tale of a strong-willed woman of mixed heritage living in Central America and New York City in the late 19th century.

Whitbread Prizes. The Whitbread Prizes are given annually to citizens of the United Kingdom for best first novel, best novel, best poetry, best biography, and best new book of the year. In 2004, the best new book prize was awarded to Mark Haddon for *The Curious Incident of the Dog in the Night-Time.* The novel, which also received the award for best novel, tells the story of an autistic boy who, inspired by Sherlock Holmes, tries to find out who killed his neighbor's dog. Other nominees for best novel included Rachel Cusk's *The Lucky Ones,* Shena Mackay's *Heligoland,* and *Frankie & Stankie* by Barbara Trapido.

The Whitbread Prize for best first novel was given to DBC Pierre for *Vernon God Little,* a satirical novel about a young man who is wrongfully accused of killing a group of students at his high school. The Whitbread Prize for best first novel is often used as a barometer for future literary success. The three other contenders for the best first novel prize were *Buddha Da* by Scottish writer Anne Donovan, *An Evening of Long Goodbyes* by Irish writer Paul Murray, and *An Empty Room* by London native Talitha Stevenson.

Man Booker Prize. The Man Booker Prize, sponsored until 2007 by the Man Group, a British securities fund, is the United Kingdom's most prestigious literary award. The prize competition is restricted to books published by writers from member nations of the British Commonwealth and from the Republic of Ireland. The 2004 prize went to British writer Alan Hollinghurst for his novel *The Line of Beauty.* This sequel to another distinguished novel by Hollinghurst, *The Swimming-Pool Library,* is the story of a gay man who moves into an attic room in the house of a conservative member of the British Parliament and his family.

The other nominees, all strong contenders in a year with many fine books published in the United Kingdom, included Irish writer Colm Toibin's *The Master,* a novel about the author Henry James; *The Electric Michelangelo* by British writer Sarah Hall; South African writer Achmat Dangor's *Bitter Fruit;* British writer Gerard Woodward's *I'll Go to Bed at Noon;* and *Cloud Atlas* by British author David Mitchell.

In 2004, the Man Booker Prize launched an International Prize for novels published in English or translated into English. The first International Prize will be given in 2005.

Prix Goncourt. France's Prix Goncourt, named for two French brothers who were literary collaborators, is given annually to the best novel written in French. In 2004, the prize was awarded to Laurent Gaude for *Le Soleil des Scorta* (*The Sun of the Scortas*). The multigenerational epic tells of a family trying to escape poverty in southern Italy.

New translations. Important newly translated works written by both distinguished and new international writers include Italian Umberto Eco's *History of Beauty,* a discussion of how every era of human history has different standards of beauty. *The Last Night of a Damned Soul,* by Algerian-born French writer Slimane Benaissa, was translated into English in 2004. The novel is about a young Arab American who joins a Muslim fundamentalist group and helps plot a terrorist attack.

The relations between East and West formed the backdrop of several important novels in 2004. Turkish author Orhan Pamuk's novel *Snow* describes the clash between Eastern and Western cultures as seen through the eyes of a Turkish poet returning from a 12-year exile. *Persepolis 2* is Marjane Satrapi's autobiographical graphic novel about her life in exile in Austria and subsequent return to her native Iran. Yasmina Khadra, an Algerian army officer, wrote *The Swallows of Kabul,* a novel of life in Afghanistan under the Taliban government.

Translations of classics. Stephen Mitchell, known for his translations of the *Tao Te Ching* and the *Bhagavad-Gita,* published a new translation of *Gilgamesh,* one of the oldest epics in world literature. Previous translations of *Gilgamesh* were primarily scholarly works, but Mitchell's version was lauded for its poetic quality.

Irish Nobel laureate Seamus Heaney, who has become as noted for his translations as he is for his own poetry, offered a version of the Greek tragedy *Antigone* called *The Burial at Thebes.* New translations of Marcel Proust's seven-volume *In Search of Lost Time* continued in 2004 with the publication of the second volume, *In the Shadow of Young Girls in Flower,* translated by James Grieve. ■ Brian Bouldrey

See also **Australia; Literature, American; Literature for children; Nobel prizes; Poetry.**

Literature for children.

Literature for children. Fantasy and young adult books were among the strongest genres of the year. Some of the outstanding books of 2004 included the following:

Picture books. *La La Rose* by Satomi Ichikawa (Philomel Books). Delicate watercolors illustrate the story of a little girl in Paris who leaves her beloved stuffed rabbit, La La Rose, behind in a park, but then recovers it. Ages 3 to 5.

Tiny's Big Adventure by Martin Waddell, illustrated by John Lawrence (Candlewick). Terrific woodcuts accompany the tale of Tiny, a little mouse who is afraid to go into the big wheat field until his sister Katy leads him through. Ages 4 to 7.

Knuffle Bunny by Mo Willems (Hyperion). Cartoonlike figures are computer-blended with black-and-white photographs in the story of a little girl and her father who go to the Laundromat and leave her beloved bunny behind. Ages 4 to 7.

Science Verse by Jon Scieszka, illustrated by Lane Smith (Viking). The well-known team is at its zany best again, with poems about science based on the works of such familiar poets as Robert Frost and Edgar Allan Poe. It's not "Casey" but the "Scientific Method at the Bat." Ages 10 to 14.

Kitten's First Full Moon by Kevin Henkes (Greenwillow). Henkes chooses black, white, and grays to tell the story of a kitten that mistakes the full moon for a bowl of milk but cannot reach it. Ages 3 to 5.

The Boy on Fairfield Street by Kathleen Krull, illustrated by Steve Johnson and Lou Fancher (Random House). Krull traces the early life of Theodore Geisel, or Dr. Seuss, providing insight about his shyness, his energy, and his interest in zoo animals, all of which can be seen in his artistic creations. Ages 8 to 11.

September Roses by Jeanette Winter (Farrar, Straus and Giroux). Two South African sisters, bringing their roses to a flower show, are stranded in New York City during the aftermath of the terrorist attacks on Sept. 11, 2001. They use the roses to make a memorial at Ground Zero. Winter's illustrations move from colors to grays and back to colors, reflecting the emotions surrounding that day. Ages 9 to 12.

You're All My Favorites by Sam McBratney, illustrated by Anita Jeram (Candlewick). Three baby bears are reassured that they are "the most wonderful baby bears in the whole wide world!" Ages 3 to 5.

Fiction. *Chasing Vermeer* by Blue Balliett (Scholastic). Readers solve puzzles and problems as they follow two sixth-graders, Petra and Calder, involved in tracking down a stolen painting by Dutch master Jan Vermeer. Ages 9 to 13.

Indigo's Star by Hilary McKay (McElderry Books). British teen-ager Indigo, whose parents are artists and have named all of their children after paint colors, is a victim of bullies at school. He is befriended by a visiting American, Tom, and both of them are watched over by Indigo's fearless 8-year-old sister, Rose. Ages 11 to 14.

Bucking the Sarge by Christopher Paul Curtis (Wendy Lamb Books). Fifteen-year-old Luther wants to be at Harvard University, not in Flint, Michigan, where he is vying for a middle-school science fair prize. His mother, "the Sarge," dominates his life and gives him no choice about working in the group homes she runs. Luther's friend Sparky wants out of Flint, too, though his dreams of how to go about it are less legal. Ages 11 to 14.

How I Live Now by Meg Rosoff (Wendy Lamb Books). Daisy, an anorexic teen who hates her stepmother, is sent to live with cousins in the United Kingdom. When London is attacked by unnamed enemies and a war breaks out, the family is separated, and Daisy struggles to help her youngest cousin survive. Ages 11 to 14.

Here Today by Ann M. Martin (Scholastic). All the kids on Witch Tree Lane, a run-down and isolated neighborhood, have trouble at school. Ellie Dingman has trouble at home, too, as the fall of 1963 begins. Her mother, Doris, wants to be a movie star, and Ellie learns she cannot make the world perfect. Ages 9 to 12.

Kissing the Rain by Kevin Brooks (Chicken House). Moo, a fat outcast, hides out by watching traffic on a bridge. When he becomes the only witness to a crime there, he is pressured from all sides. Both telling the truth and lying have serious consequences. Ages 11 to 14.

Fantasy. *A Hat Full of Sky* by Terry Pratchett (Harper Collins). In a humor-filled sequel to *The Wee Free Men,* a small, blue, and irritable group of fairies watches over Tiffany Aching, an 11-year-old girl learning to be a witch. Tiffany is pursued by a demon who wants to possess her. Ages 10 to 14.

The Gift by Ursula K. Le Guin (Harcourt). Le Guin's first full-length young adult novel since *Tehanu* (1990) deals with the fate of two young people, from the Uplands of Earthsea, who possess special powers. Orrec has "the gift of unmaking," or destroying other living things, and Gry can call animals to come. Slowly, they learn to use their gifts in ways other than domination. Ages 11 to 14.

The Haunting of Alaizabel Cray by Chris Wooding (Orchard). In a futuristic London, where wolves and wych-kin terrorize the dwellers, 17-year-old Thaniel, a famed wych-hunter, encounters a mysterious young woman, haunted from within. Thaniel, his guardian, and their allies battle to save the world from the evil forces. Ages 12 to 15.

The Oracle Betrayed by Catherine Fisher (Greenwillow). Two Lands, a mythic desert country, resembles both ancient Egypt and Greece. Mirany, servant to the treacherous Speaker, is caught up in webs of political intrigue and religious beliefs. First

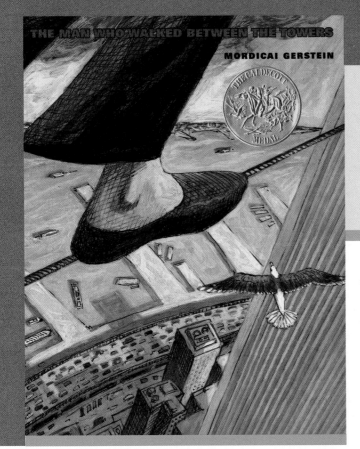

THE MAN WHO WALKED BETWEEN THE TOWERS

MORDICAI GERSTEIN

Hiram College in Ohio to the rain forests of French Guiana, explaining what he does, how he lives, and how he works. Ages 8 to 12.

The Voice That Challenged a Nation: Marian Anderson and the Struggle for Equal Rights by Russell Freedman (Clarion Books). Contemporary photographs accompany the story of Marian Anderson and her 1939 Washington, D.C., concert on the steps of the Lincoln Memorial, which brought racial injustice into the public view. Ages 9 to 12.

Old Hickory: Andrew Jackson and the American People by Albert Marrin (Dutton). Marrin helps readers understand the complicated man who became the seventh president of the United States. Courageous, stubborn, committed to preserving the union yet unquestionably prejudiced against Native Americans and himself a slave owner, Jackson's actions were important in shaping the wild and tough nation that the United States was at that time. Ages 12 to 15.

Awards. The 2004 Newbery Medal was awarded to Kate DiCamillo for *The Tale of Despereaux*. The award is given by the American Library Association (ALA) for "the most distinguished contribution to children's literature" published the previous year. The ALA's Caldecott Medal for "the most distinguished American picture book" was awarded to Mordicai Gerstein for *The Man Who Walked Between the Towers*. The Michael L. Printz Award for excellence in literature for young adults, sponsored by the ALA's Young Adult Library Services Association, went to Angela Johnson for *The First Part Last*.

■ Mary Harris Russell

published in the United Kingdom as *The Oracle* in 2003. Ages 10 to 14.

The Golem's Eye by Jonathan Stroud (Miramax Kids). Bartimaeus, a djinn from long ago, is called up in Book II of the Bartimaeus Trilogy to help his master, apprentice magician Nathaniel. London is being devastated by a towering golem, the magicians are vying for power, and Kitty Jones, a young commoner, has joined the struggle against the ruling magician class. Ages 10 to 14.

Predator's Gold by Philip Reeve (Eos). In Book II of The Hungry City Chronicles, the futuristic world of predatory cities on wheels grinds on. Young Hester and Tom have been living in an airship above the fray, but now events in the frozen city of Arkangel, a nonpredator ruled by Freya, draw them dangerously back in. Ages 12 to 15.

Informational books. *Top-Secret: A Handbook of Codes, Ciphers, and Secret Writing* by Paul B. Janeczko (Candlewick). Janeczko explains the origins—and the need for—code-making and breaking throughout history and provides detailed information to re-create centuries-old coding devices. Ages 9 to 14.

Tarantula Scientist by Sy Montgomery (Houghton Mifflin). Photographs and text follow tarantula scientist Sam Marshall from his lab at

See also **Literature, American.**

Lithuania. See Baltic States; Europe.

Los Angeles city officials and developers moved ahead in 2004 with long-delayed plans to revitalize the downtown area. Anschutz Entertainment Group, based in Denver, announced plans in July for a $1-billion project surrounding the south-central Staples Center sports complex. The new construction was to include a convention hotel, theater, retail businesses, and residences.

In August, officials chose developer Related Cos. of New York City to modernize areas of Bunker Hill east and south of the Walt Disney Concert Hall, which opened in 2003. Plans called for adding 3.2 million square feet (297,000 square meters) of housing, office, retail, and entertainment space at an estimated cost of $1.2 billion.

Economy. On May 17, 2004, the Los Angeles City Council approved Mayor James K. Hahn's $5.3-billion budget. The budget included funds for hiring a modest number of new police officers and paramedics and allocated money for maintaining street repairs and increasing after-school programs. Hahn announced plans to run for a second, and final, term as mayor on the March 2005 ballot.

Los Angeles County Supervisors approved a $17.3-billion budget in June 2004. The 2004-2005 budget, a 1-percent increase in spending over the 2003-2004 budget, included a $30-million cut for the Department of Mental Health, jeopardizing treatment for uninsured patients. Although the budget did include some additional funding for the sheriff's department, the board of supervisors agreed in July 2004 to include Sheriff Lee Baca's demand for a half-cent sales tax measure to expand police services on the November ballot. The measure, which would have boosted the sales tax from 8.25 percent to 8.75 percent, failed to muster the two-thirds majority needed for passage.

A bitter grocery strike in southern California that began in October 2003 and ended in February 2004 had a strong negative impact on the Los Angeles economy. Nearly 60,000 workers at Safeway, Inc., of Pleasanton, California; Kroger Co. of Cincinnati, Ohio; and Albertsons, Inc., of Boise, Idaho, participated in the strike over potential benefit losses. Industry analysts estimated that the grocery owners lost about $700 million in profits while the workers failed to prevent most losses.

Police scandal. Seeking to stop allegations of police brutality, Los Angeles Police Chief William J. Bratton announced in August 2004 that he would replace officers' large, metal flashlights with smaller, rubber-coated ones. The decision was the result of an internationally televised incident on June 23 during which an officer beat an African American car theft suspect with a flashlight. The incident prompted comparisons with the 1991 videotaped beating of a black motorist by LAPD officers.

Education. The first new high school to be built in the Los Angeles Unified School District in 14 years—Orthopaedic Hospital Medical Magnet School—opened on Aug. 5, 2004, south of downtown. Orthopaedic Hospital donated a portion of the land for the school and planned to offer students internships, health care jobs, and research opportunities. The magnet school was one of 160 schools that the district planned to build by 2012 to ease overcrowding.

Housing demand continued to outpace supply in a market boosted by rising population and low mortgage rates. The median price for a house in Los Angeles County in June 2004 was $445,140, up 31.6 percent over 2003, according to the Los Angeles Economic Development Corporation.

Ports. Los Angeles/Long Beach remained the largest container shipping port in the United States and the third largest in the world, behind Hong Kong and Singapore, in 2003, with traffic up 11.3 percent. The trend was expected to continue in 2004 with four new shipping lines docking at Los Angeles/Long Beach. Congestion was increased by the arrival in June of the West Coast's first super cargo ship from China. The vessel, with a capacity 40 percent greater than that of the average freighter, represented a new trend in cargo ships.   ■ Margaret A. Kilgore

See also **City**.

Louisiana. See **State government**.
Luxembourg. See **Europe**.

Macedonia. On Feb. 26, 2004, Macedonian President Boris Trajkovski died when his plane crashed in Bosnia-Herzegovina. Trajkovski's support for peaceful resolution of ethnic conflict between majority Macedonians and the Albanian minority contributed to stability in Macedonia, noted political analysts.

In April elections, Branko Crvenkovski, then serving as prime minister, won election as president. Crvenkovski nominated interior minister Hari Kostov to succeed him as prime minister, and parliament confirmed his choice.

Macedonian and Albanian relations continued to dominate political life in Macedonia in 2004. Many Albanian and Macedonian leaders reaffirmed support for the 2001 Ohrid Agreement, which had ended a six-month-long rebellion by Macedonia-based ethnic Albanians. The agreement promised broader rights and greater political power to the Albanian minority.

In August 2004, the Macedonian parliament enacted a key reform endorsed in the Ohrid Agreement—a redistricting of local administrative regions designed to give greater autonomy to predominantly Albanian communities. The resulting Law on Territorial Organization drew sharp protests from opposition nationalist politicians, who charged that the changes would disenfranchise ethnic Macedonians liv-

Macedonian soldiers lead a massive funeral procession on March 5, 2004, for President Boris Trajkovski. The Macedonian leader died on February 26 when his plane crashed in Bosnia-Herzegovina, killing all aboard.

ing in Albanian-majority locales.

Opponents gathered enough signatures on petitions to put the law to the voters in a referendum. The referendum, held on November 7, failed to overturn the law.

Foreign affairs. Admiral Gregory Johnson, the North Atlantic Treaty Organization commander in southern Europe, praised Macedonia in August for the "huge progress" the country had made in reforming its military establishment. Johnson's comments boosted Macedonian officials' hopes for admission to NATO in 2006.

On March 22, 2004, Macedonia submitted a formal application for membership in the European Union. The milestone represented the first step in a lengthy process that the officials hoped would result in accession by 2010.

Name recognition. In November 2004, the United States Department of State recognized the replacement of the name, "Former Yugoslav Republic of Macedonia" (FYROM), with "Republic of Macedonia." When the United Nations admitted newly independent Macedonia in 1993, it did so as FYROM to distinguish the new nation from the region of Macedonia in Greece, at the Greek government's insistence. Republic of Macedonia officials hailed the U.S. move as a boost to the nation's pride.   ■ Sharon L. Wolchik

See also **Europe.**

Magazine publishers in 2004 continued to create new publications based on celebrities and entertainment shows—despite some high-profile failures. Many of these magazines were designed to appeal to women.

In October, the final issue of *Lifetime* magazine was published by Hearst Magazines of New York City and The Walt Disney Co. of Burbank, California. The magazine had been launched in April 2003 to reach the same female audience attracted to the cable television channel Lifetime. The magazine increased its *rate base,* the amount of circulation guaranteed to advertisers, from 500,000 at its launch to 600,000 by April 2004. Nevertheless, the circulation of *Lifetime* proved disappointing when compared with *O: The Oprah Magazine,* Hearst's popular joint venture with television talk-show host Oprah Winfrey.

In April, American Media Inc. of Boca Raton, Florida, launched a monthly entitled *Thalia.* The magazine, targeted to young Hispanic women, was named after Latin music pop star Thalia Sodi.

Sales in stores. Newsstand sales of the 100 top-selling magazines declined by 36 percent between 1993 and 2003, reported *Folio,* a publication for the magazine industry, in April 2004.

Magazines sold at Wal-Mart stores accounted for an estimated 15 percent of all magazine newsstand sales in 2004. In September, Time Inc.

of New York City launched a magazine that could be purchased only at Wal-Mart stores. The women's monthly, titled *All You,* had an initial rate base of 500,000.

Too many teen 'zines. Gruner & Jahr (G&J) USA Publishing of New York City relaunched *YM,* its five-year-old magazine for girls, as a publication for older teen-agers in July. Industry analysts noted that the move was an attempt to differentiate *YM* in the overcrowded market of teen-oriented magazines.

The competitive market forced *Teen People,* published by Time Inc., to cut its rate base from 1.6 million to 1.45 million in 2004. *Seventeen,* published by Hearst, reduced its rate base from 2.35 million to 2.1 million.

Changes. *Life* magazine—after four years off the newsstands—returned in October as a weekly supplement distributed in newspapers. *Life,* which had once been an industry giant acclaimed for its photography and feature stories, debuted in 1936 and was a popular weekly until 1972. From 1978 to 2000, it was published monthly.

World Press Review, which had featured translated articles from foreign newspapers and magazines, ceased publication in April 2004 with its 30th-anniversary issue.   ■ Mark Fitzgerald

Maine. See **State government.**

Malawi. See **Africa.**

Malaysia. Five months after becoming prime minister, Abdullah bin Ahmad Badawi led the National Front coalition to victory on March 21, 2004, winning a record number of parliamentary seats. With 64 percent of votes, the party won 90 percent of parliament seats plus control of 11 of the country's 12 states. Abdullah campaigned for a more open, efficient government, with promises to end the corruption associated with his predecessor, Mahathir bin Mohamad.

Malaysia's highest court on September 2 overturned Anwar Ibrahim conviction on a sodomy charge. Anwar had been Mahathir's deputy until the two disagreed on the Asian financial crisis of 1997. His conviction in 1998 was believed by many Malaysians to have been engineered by Mahathir. The court refused to overturn another suspect sentence, for corruption, which Anwar had already served. Abdullah's political party refused to allow Anwar, once its star, to rejoin the organization.

A massive earthquake off Sumatra on Dec. 26, 2004, generated giant tsunamis that smashed into the coastal states of Kedah and Perak and the northern island of Penang, where scores of people were swept from beaches.   ■ Henry S. Bradsher

See also **Asia.**

Maldives. See **Asia.**

Malta. See **Europe.**

Manitoba. See **Canadian provinces.**

Manufacturing. Factories across the United States during 2004 experienced the most robust growth in output since before the recession of 2001, as the U.S. economy continued to expand and demand for goods kept manufacturers busy. As the year progressed, however, the pace of the industrial recovery slackened as overall consumer demand weakened in response to mounting energy prices and an uneven economic recovery.

Meanwhile, manufacturers grappled with shortages and high prices for materials, such as steel, with soaring fuel prices that added to production costs, and with strains on capacity within the trucking and rail sectors. Manufacturers are highly dependent on trucking and railroads to deliver raw materials to factories and to ship finished goods.

Manufacturing growth. Apart from elevated consumer demand, economists attributed the expansion in manufacturing in 2004 to the effects of federal tax cuts on investment and record-low interest rates. The Institute for Supply Management (ISM)—a professional organization based in Tempe, Arizona, of U.S. purchasing managers—reported in January that its index of overall factory activity registered a robust 63.6 points. The gauge indicates economic contraction below 50 and expansion above that reading. In June, officials with the Federal Reserve (the Fed), the nation's central bank, reported that U.S. factory output in May had attained a level that was just 0.3 percent below the prerecession peak of June 2000.

Growth in the manufacturing sector softened, however, later in 2004. In November, the ISM index registered overall factory activity at 57.8, marking the 18th consecutive month of expansion for the sector but settling substantially below the January level. Through the first 10 months of 2004, the monthly ISM reports revealed fairly consistent slowing of the rate of growth—though the index remained in positive territory, and the November data showed some gains after three months in which the index had slid.

Threats to growth. An unusually large number of strong tropical storms and hurricanes in August and September repeatedly ravaged parts of Florida and caused destruction in the Southeast, the mid-Atlantic states, and into the Northeast. Effects of the storms on residences, businesses, and infrastructure—as well as large-scale evacuations of residents—greatly disrupted normal business activities.

One especially powerful storm, Hurricane Ivan, swept through the eastern Gulf of Mexico to come ashore September 16 near the Florida-Alabama border. Ivan disrupted oil production and pipeline deliveries in and around the Gulf of Mexico for months, adding to already spiraling prices for crude oil. Those prices rose above $48 a barrel in August and hit a peak of nearly $56 a barrel in late October. As recently as late 2003, crude oil had traded at prices slightly above $30 a barrel. By early December 2004, oil prices were back down in the low $40's, but economists warned that disruptions in oil production in unstable regions of the world or increasing demand on the world market could send prices back up. Some analysts even speculated about the possibility of a recession in 2005 if energy prices spiked again and stayed high for too long.

Norbert J. Ore, chairman of ISM's business survey committee and group director for strategic sourcing and procurement at Atlanta-based Georgia-Pacific Corp., said in late 2004 that high energy prices and broader commodity price inflation had become major concerns for manufacturers worried that costs were eroding profits. The price of steel—a material particularly important in many manufacturing processes—increased by as much as 50 percent in 2004.

Interest rates. After several years of record-low interest rates, the Fed repeatedly raised the prime rate in 2004. On June 30, policymakers led by Chairman Alan Greenspan announced that the economy was strong enough to remove the monetary stimulus of the record-low rates, and they raised the federal funds rate, an overnight lending rate among commercial banks, by 0.25 percent. The Fed hiked rates again by the same percentage on August 10, September 20, November 10, and December 14, bringing the funds rate up to 2.25 percent at year end. Industry experts noted that the hikes were not enough to discourage investment in manufacturing, but that business leaders would be keeping close tabs on future actions by the Fed.

Transportation challenges. Disruptions in the trucking industry and the rail shipping industry during 2004 caused great concern among manufacturers. Much large-scale manufacturing in the United States is conducted according to "just-in-time" (JIT) principles in which factories receive all necessary inputs to a manufacturing process just before the start of an operation. The system eliminates the necessity of warehousing large quantities of materials, thus cutting costs for manufacturers. Given the JIT system, delays in shipments have the potential of seriously disrupting production.

Implementation in January 2004 of new federal regulations for commercial bus and truck drivers added to strains on trucking service and warehouse operations. The new federal rules allowed an extra hour of driving per shift but trimmed an hour from a trucker's overall work shift, which includes nondriving tasks such as loading and unloading cargoes. According to

industry experts, new rules mandating how shift time must be calculated caused even greater problems. Truckers could no longer shut off the clock for meal breaks, nap breaks, idle waiting time at loading docks, or other driving downtime. As a result, factories had to change their loading and unloading procedures to get truck drivers in and out more quickly.

During 2004, freight railroad companies in the United States were swamped with demand that stretched their resources to the limit and led to widespread backups and delays. Based on volume in the first eight months of 2004, representatives of the Association of American Railroads, a Washington, D.C.-based organization that represents railroad freight companies, predicted that U.S. rail traffic would set an all-time record for the year. In the summer and fall, import volumes surged, causing freight backups on the West Coast, while the August-September succession of hurricanes in the East delayed freight deliveries in that part of the country. All of these developments sent manufacturers scrambling to meet transportation needs for their supplies or finished goods. ■ John D. Boyd

See also **Economics; Transportation; Weather.**

Maryland. See **State government.**

Massachusetts. See **State government.**

Mauritania. See **Africa.**

Mauritius. Analysts predicted in 2004 that the ruling coalition government would remain firmly in power in Mauritius until after the next general elections, due to take place by September 2005. The coalition consisted of the Militant Mauritian Movement (MMM), headed by Prime Minister Paul Berenger; and the Militant Socialist Movement (MSM), headed by Deputy Prime Minister Pravind Jugnauth.

The island's economy expanded by approximately 4.7 percent in 2004, down only slightly from the 2003 figure of 5 percent. However, economists highlighted the country's growing budget deficit as cause for concern. Increased state borrowing and growing inflationary pressures cut into resources available for social spending, the economists noted.

Regional relations. In August 2004, Mauritius hosted the annual summit of the Southern African Development Community (SADC) at the seaside resort of Grande Baie. SADC is an association of 14 African nations, including Mauritius. Prime Minister Berenger was chosen chairman of the organization for 2005. In a speech, Berenger said he intended to push for the adoption of a charter promoting free and democratic elections in member countries.

Chagos developments. During 2004, a long-standing dispute continued between Mauritius and the United Kingdom over the status of several thousand islanders who had been forcibly evicted from the British Indian Ocean Territory more than 30 years earlier. The territory is a 65-island archipelago also known as the Chagos Islands. Between 1967 and 1973, British officials removed the Chagossians—mainly to Mauritius, 1,200 miles (1,930 kilometers) to the southwest—to make room for a huge United States military base on Diego Garcia, the biggest and only inhabited island in the chain. Under a 1966 agreement, the United Kingdom leased the island to the U.S. government until at least 2016.

In 2001, many of the Chagossians living in Mauritius, which had been a British colony until 1968, staged demonstrations to demand British citizenship. The Mauritian government, which disputes the British claim to the Chagos Islands, rejected the islanders' demands.

Prime Minister Paul Berenger announced in 2004 that he intended to bring the case of the Chagos Islands' sovereignty before the International Court of Justice in The Hague, Netherlands. In July 2004, a British court upheld a lower court's ruling that the Chagos Islanders were not entitled to compensation from the British government, due to a legal technicality.

■ Simon Baynham

See also **Africa**.

Medicine.

Medicine. An implantable computer chip that would enable health care providers to quickly access a patient's medical record won approval from the United States Food and Drug Administration on Oct. 13, 2004. The device, called the VeriChip, resembles chips implanted in millions of pets and livestock for identification purposes. Privacy advocates warned, however, that the chip could threaten the confidentiality of personal medical information.

The chip, manufactured by Applied Digital Solutions Inc. of Delray Beach, Florida, is about the size of a grain of rice. It would be injected under a patient's skin using a syringe. The Veri-Chip itself does not hold information. Instead, it stores a code, revealed when a scanner passes over it, that allows access to a secure medical-records database. Health care providers would be able to update information on the database. Applied Digital Solutions argued that the chip would improve medical care in emergencies and for people under treatment by several physicians.

Rare blood infection in soldiers. An unexplained increase in the number of injured U.S. soldiers infected with the rare and antibiotic-resistant bacterium *Acinetobacter baumannii* was reported by the Centers for Disease Control and Prevention in Atlanta, Georgia, on November 19. Most of the infections occurred in soldiers who had been injured in Iraq or Afghanistan. Military health officials said 102 soldiers were diagnosed with the infection from Jan. 1, 2002, to Aug. 31, 2004. Previously, military hospitals had recorded about one case of the bacterial infection per year. Military officials said they had no evidence linking the infections to biochemical agents.

New vaccines. For the first time, a vaccine against malaria proved effective at reducing infection rates as well as the severity of the disease among children, researchers reported on October 15. Malaria is the leading cause of death among children ages 1 to 5 in Africa. In addition, children account for about 70 percent of all annual deaths due to malaria worldwide.

The researchers reported that the vaccine, called Mosquirix, reduced malaria infections by almost 30 percent among the 2,022 children in the study. The vaccine, manufactured by British-based GlaxoSmithKline, also reduced the number of severe malaria infections by 58 percent.

An experimental vaccine already shown to offer short-term protection against cervical cancer may provide long-term protection as well, according to research reported on November 1. The vaccine, produced by New Jersey-based Merck & Co., provides immunity against sexually transmitted human papilloma virus (HPV)-16, which causes most cases of cervical cancer.

In a study reported in 2002, researchers from the University of Washington in Seattle found that none of the 768 women who received the vaccine had become infected with HPV-16 after 18 months. The new study, also by Washington researchers, followed 755 of these women for another two years. They found that seven of the women had become infected with the virus, but none had developed either cervical cancer or precancerous conditions. About 470,000 women worldwide develop cervical cancer annually; about half of them die of the disease.

Rising osteoporosis rates. The number of people in the United States diagnosed with osteoporosis rose from an estimated 500,000 in 1994 to an estimated 3.6 million in 2003, according to a study published on July 26, 2004. Osteoporosis is a condition in which bones become abnormally fragile. Scientists from the Stanford Prevention Research Center in Palo Alto, California, based their findings on data from a survey of physicians conducted by a health care information company. According to the researchers, the number of osteoporosis-related physician visits jumped from 1.3 million to 6.3 million during the same period. They associated the rise in both diagnoses and physician visits with an increased awareness of osteoporosis based on the introduction of new medications.   ■ Barbara A. Mayes

See also **Health care issues; Public health.**

Mental health. The use of antidepressants in children and adolescents continued to come under sharp government scrutiny in 2004. In September, the United States Food and Drug Administration (FDA) warned consumers that antidepressants could cause suicidal thoughts and behaviors in children under age 18.

Antidepressant benefit. Mental health experts who favor the use of medication for treating depression found support for their point of view in a major study reported in August. Researchers led by psychiatrist John March of Duke University in Durham, North Carolina, concluded that a combination of medication and psychotherapy ranked as the most effective treatment. The study, sponsored by the National Institute of Mental Health, was the first large, federally funded investigation of antidepressant use for adolescents with major depression.

The study tracked 439 adolescents between the ages of 12 and 17. The researchers found an improvement in the mental health of 71 percent of the participants who received fluoxetine, the only antidepressant approved by the FDA for use by children and adolescents, as well as cognitive-behavioral therapy (CBT). CBT is a form of psychotherapy that emphasizes the importance of thinking in how people feel and behave. Nearly 61 percent of the teen-agers who received only fluoxetine improved. In contrast, only 43 percent of those treated with CBT alone and 39 percent of those receiving a *placebo* (an inactive substance) showed improvement.

The researchers also noted that at the beginning of the study, 29 percent of the participants reported having had clinically significant suicidal thoughts. This problem diminished in all groups, though the decline was greatest among adolescents receiving both medication and CBT.

Mental illness in the United States. An estimated 19.6 million adults in the United States—9.2 percent of all those over age 18—had a serious mental illness (SMI) in 2003, according to the 2003 National Survey on Drug Use and Health. The report was released in September 2004 by the Substance Abuse and Mental Health Services Administration (SAMHSA), an agency of the U.S. Department of Health and Human Services. In 2002, SAMHSA said, an estimated 8.3 percent of U.S. adults had SMI, which is defined, in part, as a disorder that substantially interferes with a person's major life activities.

Researchers found that adults ages 18 to 25 had the highest rates of SMI—13.9 percent. Adults age 50 or older had the lowest rate—5.9 percent—though this group showed the largest increase over 2002 levels. The study also revealed that adults with SMI were more than twice as likely as those without SMI to have used an illegal drug in the past year—27.3 percent compared with 12.5 percent.

Mental illness worldwide. Preliminary findings from the largest international survey on mental health ever conducted, published in June 2004, revealed that mental illness is both widespread and seriously under treated. The two-year survey was conducted by researchers from the World Health Organization in Geneva, Switzerland, and Harvard Medical School in Cambridge, Massachusetts.

The researchers found that in most countries from 9 to 17 percent of those surveyed reported experiencing an episode of mental illness in the previous year. Anxiety disorder was the most common problem. In general, mild disorders outnumbered moderate or severe problems. However, people with moderate or serious disorders reported losing as many days of work as people with cancer or other serious physical illnesses.

The results emerged from 60,643 face-to-face interviews with adults in 14 countries. Eight of the countries, including the United States, were defined as wealthy. The researchers reported that in rich countries, from 35 to 50 percent of people with SMI received no treatment for their condition. In poorer countries, this number rose to from 76 to 80 percent. ■ Barbara A. Mayes

See also **Drugs; Medicine.**

Mexico. The performance of President Vicente Fox Quesada and his National Action Party (PAN) proved increasingly disillusioning to many Mexicans in 2004. President Fox remained unable to persuade the Mexican Congress, which was controlled by the opposition Institutional Revolutionary Party (PRI), to pass his promised reforms, including tax and energy measures.

The help that President Fox had anticipated from United States President George W. Bush failed to materialize in 2004. President Bush was unable to obtain approval by the U.S. Congress for measures to allow more Mexicans to work legally in the United States. President Fox had hoped that such measures would help relieve severe unemployment in Mexico.

Furthermore, many economists noted that the Mexican economy had not benefited significantly from the North American Free Trade Agreement (NAFTA), a 1994 pact that united Mexico, Canada, and the United States in a free-trade zone. This was partly due to the downturn of the U.S. economy during President Fox's administration.

In his state-of-the-union message in September 2004, President Fox steered clear of divisive issues of reform. Instead, he invited his opponents to join him in expanding medical insur-

In one of the largest demonstrations in Mexican history, an estimated 250,000 people march through the capital, Mexico City, on June 27 to protest soaring rates of kidnapping and homicide. Many of the demonstrators, dressed in white, carried photos of loved ones lost to street crime.

Durazo of Sahagun's perceived political ambitions to succeed her husband.

"Mexico is ready to be governed by a woman," Sahagun fired back one week later. "Nevertheless, I wish to affirm that I will not be a candidate for the presidency [in 2006]," she added in response to criticism that her political aspirations were damaging her husband's presidency.

Marching against crime. Masked gunmen killed Francisco Ortiz Franco, deputy editor of the weekly newspaper *Zeta*, in Tijuana on June 22, 2004. On June 27, hundreds of thousands of Mexicans took to the streets in several cities to express their anger over skyrocketing rates of kidnapping and homicide in urban areas. One of the largest demonstrations in Mexican history occurred in Mexico City, the capital, where a huge throng of people from all walks of life and political persuasions filled the streets.

Former president indicted. In July, Ignacio Carrillo Prieto, a special federal prosecutor, filed charges against 82-year-old former President Luis Echeverria Alvarez, two of his aides, and three generals for the killing of dozens of student protestors in 1971. The charges marked the first time in Mexican history that a former president had been charged with criminal activities.

The day after the charges were filed, the judge overseeing the case threw out the indictment, ruling that the statute of limitations on the alleged crimes had expired. The administration of President Fox, who had pledged to prosecute perpetrators of past misdeeds, requested that the Mexican Supreme Court review the case. In October 2004, the Supreme Court agreed to hear the charges against former President Echeverria and the other officials.　　■ Nathan A. Haverstock

ance to all Mexicans and providing computers to all fifth- and sixth-grade classrooms.

PRI comeback. The PRI, which had been in power for 71 straight years before President Fox's election in 2000, was well positioned for a political comeback in 2004. In July, the PRI captured the mayoral office in the border city of Ciudad Juarez, which had been governed by two consecutive PAN administrations. In August, the PRI reclaimed the mayoral seat in Tijuana for the first time since 1989. PRI candidates also won a number of governor races in 2004.

The surge in PRI's political fortunes was assisted by infighting within the Fox administration. In a scorching letter of resignation in July, President Fox's chief of staff, Alfonso Durazo, charged the president's wife, Marta Sahagun Fox, with exerting undue influence over the government. Mexico was "not prepared to have the president leave the presidency to his wife," said

See also Latin America.

Michigan. See **Detroit; State government.**

MIDDLE EAST

The Coalition Provisional Authority, which began governing Iraq after United States-led forces ousted Iraqi leader Saddam Hussein in April 2003, was dissolved on June 28, 2004. Chief U.S. administrator L. Paul Bremer III transferred power to the interim Iraqi government, led by President Ghazi al-Ujayl al-Yawr and Prime Minister Ayad Allawi. An advisory council of Iraqi officials had appointed these leaders on June 1. Elections for a permanent government were scheduled for Jan. 30, 2005.

Fighting between coalition forces and Iraqi insurgents increased throughout 2004. The number of insurgent attacks on coalition troops grew from 700 in October 2003 to 2,400 in October 2004. In November, U.S. troop fatalities reached the highest one-month level since the preceding April—at least 135 troops were killed in each of those months.

Coalition forces launched a major offensive in November to capture the insurgent stronghold of Al Fallujah. Although Al Fallujah was successfully retaken, much of the city was destroyed in the battle. In addition, coalition troops captured few fighters and found no trace of insurgent leader Abu Mussab al-Zarqawi, who was presumed to have escaped.

Pressure builds on Syria. President George W. Bush of the United States signed an executive order in May implementing economic and trade sanctions on Syria. The sanctions were meant to punish Syria for supporting terrorist organizations, such as the Lebanese group

Egyptian students in Cairo, the capital of Egypt, burn flags representing the United States, the United Kingdom, and Israel in April to protest Israel's assassination of Abdel Aziz Rantisi. Rantisi was the second leader of Hamas, a Palestinian militant organization, to be killed by an Israeli missile strike within a month.

Yasir Arafat

1929-2004

regions after Israel officially came into being and was immediately attacked by surrounding Arab countries.

Israel's occupation of Gaza and the West Bank after 1967 further inflamed Arab-Israeli tensions, causing Palestinian nationalism to become more radical. After the war, Fatah and other guerrilla groups gained control of the Palestine Liberation Organization (PLO), which Arab leaders had established to represent the Palestinians. In 1969, Arafat was elected chairman of the PLO, which he controlled for the rest of his life.

His self-reinvention from guerrilla fighter to statesman began in 1974, when he became the first person to address the United Nations (UN) as a leader of a liberation movement rather than a UN member state. After his appearance before the General Assembly, the UN recognized the PLO as the representative of the Palestinian people.

In 1993, Arafat and Israeli Prime Minister Yitzhak Rabin signed a limited peace treaty—the Oslo Accords—that established a framework and timetable for the Middle East peace process. The process included the gradual transfer of control of parts of the West Bank and the Gaza Strip to the Palestinian Authority, which Arafat headed. That year, both men shared the Nobel Peace Prize with Israeli leader Shimon Peres for the Oslo Accords.

Seven years later, Arafat turned his back on the accords and rejected the biggest compromise Israel had ever offered. At the time of his death, he had become largely marginalized, with neither Israel nor the United States willing to negotiate directly with him. He had, one too many times, rejected the opportunity to forge a lasting peace in the Israeli-Palestinian conflict.

Yasir Arafat's legacy is ambiguous at best. He died without achieving any of the goals he had championed at various times in his life—the destruction of Israel; then peace with Israel, which he backed after 1988; and an independent Palestinian nation with Jerusalem as its capital. He did, however, succeed in forging a nationalist movement among Palestinians, and he placed his people and their situation at the absolute center of world politics.　　■ Scott Thomas

Yasir Arafat was an enigmatic man. To most Palestinians, he was the father of a nation that remained yet unborn at the time of his death, Nov. 11, 2004. To many Israelis, he was a terrorist who endorsed peace as a tactic simply to destroy Israel. Whatever the reality, he was, unmistakably, the embodiment of the Palestinian people and their longing for a homeland in the historic region of Palestine (Israel, the Gaza Strip, and the West Bank).

Ironically, the man who was so closely associated with the Palestinian people was probably born in Egypt, on Aug. 24, 1929, of Palestinian parents. After his mother's death when Arafat was 4 years old, he was shuttled back and forth among relatives in Cairo, Gaza, and Jerusalem.

Arafat became politically active at Cairo University in 1949 and joined in Palestinian nationalist activities in 1957. In 1959, he and three other Palestinians founded Fatah, "the Conquest," a clandestine organization dedicated to the creation of a Palestinian state, presumably through the destruction of Israel. As the leader of Fatah, Arafat launched a series of high-profile acts of anti-Israel terrorism. According to Middle East experts, he masterminded the kidnapping that resulted in the deaths of Israeli athletes at the 1972 Olympics in Munich, Germany.

In 1967, Israel had defeated Arab countries in a war and occupied the West Bank and Gaza Strip, where many Palestinians had lived since 1948. The Palestinians had moved into these

Hezbollah, and for continuing to occupy Lebanon, which Syria had invaded in 1976. The United States also accused Syria of seeking weapons of mass destruction and serving as a passageway for foreign fighters entering Iraq.

International pressure on Syria increased in September 2004, when the United Nations Security Council passed a resolution sponsored by the United States and France that reaffirmed the territorial integrity of Lebanon and called for all foreign troops to evacuate the country. Popular discontent with the Syrian military occupation grew in 2004, especially among Lebanese Christians. On November 19, thousands of Lebanese students and activists demonstrated in Beirut, the capital, shouting, "Syrians out!"

Hardliners score in Iran. Conservative hardliners scored victories over reformers in February elections for the Iranian parliament. The Council of Guardians, a group of religious leaders with authority to disqualify candidates and veto legislation, had disqualified more than 2,000 reformist candidates prior to the elections.

A nonviolent movement arose among Iranian youth in 2004 in response to the continued blocking of reforms. This movement was spearheaded by student groups, which called for the boycotting of the May 2005 presidential election to demonstrate the illegitimacy of the government.

Nuclear negotiations. Following negotiations with France, Germany, and the United Kingdom, Iranian authorities agreed in November 2004 to fully cooperate with the International Atomic Energy Agency (IAEA), a Vienna-based organization that promotes the peaceful use of nuclear energy, and to temporarily halt Iran's uranium enrichment program. Such a program could produce fuel for use in either nuclear reactors or nuclear bombs. However, some European and U.S. officials expressed doubts about Iran's commitment to the agreement.

Al-Qa'ida attacks. Terrorists affiliated with al-Qa'ida, the terrorist network led by Osama bin Laden, targeted Saudi Arabia several times in 2004. In April, a car-bomb attack on the national police headquarters in Riyadh, the capital, marked the first time terrorists hit Saudi security forces. In May, in the Yanbu region, a petrochemical company partly owned by Exxon-Mobil Corporation of Irving, Texas, was attacked and seven people were killed. Also in May, an attack on a compound in Khobar housing foreign employees of oil companies left 22 people dead.

In June, after terrorists beheaded Paul Johnson, an American engineer working for Lockheed Martin Corp. of Bethesda, Maryland, the Saudi government launched a major offensive against the militants. The government killed Abdulaziz al-Moqrin, the leader of al-Qa'ida in Saudi Ara-

bia; closed down charities suspected of financing al-Qa'ida; and offered incentives for information on militants operating covertly in the kingdom.

Al-Qa'ida militants attacked the U.S. Consulate in Jidda, Saudi Arabia, on December 6. The resulting shootout left at least nine people dead.

The Israeli government suspected that al-Qa'ida was behind three car bombings on resorts frequented by Israeli tourists in the Taba region of Egypt on October 7. At least 35 people were killed in the coordinated attacks.

Despite the efforts of the United States and other powers to hunt down bin Laden and his deputy Ayman el-Zawahiri, the two terrorist leaders remained at large in 2004.

Israeli-Palestinian conflict. Terrorist operations against Israeli civilians declined in 2004, compared with 2003. Nevertheless, the Israeli government's policy of targeting leaders of Palestinian militant organizations continued in 2004. An Israeli helicopter missile strike killed Sheik Ahmed Yassin, the leader of the militant group Hamas, on March 22. A second such strike killed Yassin's successor, Abdel Aziz Rantisi, on April 17.

In a political victory for Israeli Prime Minister Ariel Sharon, the Israeli *Knesset* (parliament) voted in October to support the withdrawal of all Israeli settlers from the Palestinian area of Gaza and from various settlements in the West Bank. The planned withdrawal, which drew strong opposition from the settlers and their supporters, was scheduled to take place by the end of 2005.

The death of Palestinian leader Yasir Arafat in November 2004 opened new opportunities for peace between the Israelis and Palestinians, according to Middle East experts. Representatives of both sides expressed hopes to resume long-stalled peace negotiations.

Libya and the West. After Libyan leader Muammar Muhammad al-Qadhafi renounced the production of weapons of mass destruction in December 2003, Western leaders began flocking to Libya to renew relations with the North African nation. Italian Prime Minister Silvio Berlusconi—the closest Western ally of Qadhafi—was the first to arrive, in February 2004. British Prime Minister Tony Blair followed in March, in the first visit by a British prime minister since Qadhafi came to power in 1969. In October 2004—after the Libyan government agreed to pay $35 million in compensation to the victims of the Libyan bombing of a Berlin discotheque in 1986—German Chancellor Gerhard Schroeder came to Libya. French President Jacques Chirac paid an official visit to Libya in November 2004.

The U.S. government opened a liaison office in Tripoli, the Libyan capital, in June, after a visit to Libya by Assistant Secretary of State William J. Burns.

Country	Population	Government	Monetary unit*	Foreign trade (million U.S.$)	
				Exports†	Imports†
Bahrain	673,000	King Hamad bin Isa Al Khalifa; Prime Minister Khalifa bin Salman Al Khalifa	dinar (0.38 = $1)	6,492	5,126
Cyprus	773,000	President Tassos Papadopoulos; (Turkish Republic of Northern Cyprus: President Rauf R. Denktash)	pound (0.46 = $1)	1,100	4,938
Egypt	72,534,000	President Hosni Mubarak; Prime Minister Ahmed Mohamed Nazif	pound (6.24 = $1)	8,759	14,750
Iran	74,293,000	Supreme Leader Ayatollah Ali Hoseini-Khamenei; President Mohammad Khatami-Ardakani	rial (8,759.00 = $1)	29,880	25,260
Iraq	25,576,000	President Ghazi al-Ujayl al-Yawr; Prime Minister Ayad Allawi	new dinar (1,890.00 = $1)	7,542	6,521
Israel	6,543,000	President Moshe Katzav; Prime Minister Ariel Sharon	shekel (4.47 = $1)	29,320	32,270
Jordan	5,506,000	King Abdullah II; Prime Minister Faisal al-Fayez	dinar (0.71 = $1)	2,908	4,946
Kuwait	2,118,000	Amir Jabir al-Ahmad al-Jabir Al Sabah; Prime Minister Sabah al-Ahmad al-Jabir Al Sabah	dinar (0.29 = $1)	22,290	9,606
Lebanon	3,718,000	President Emile Lahoud; Prime Minister Omar Karami	pound (1,514.50 = $1)	1,359	6,073
Oman	2,887,000	Sultan Qaboos bin Said Al Said	rial (0.39 = $1)	11,700	5,659
Qatar	600,000	Amir Hamad bin Khalifa Al Thani; Prime Minister Abdallah bin Khalifa Al Thani	riyal (3.64 = $1)	12,360	5,711
Saudi Arabia	22,998,000	King & Prime Minister Fahd bin Abd al-Aziz Al Saud	riyal (3.75 = $1)	86,530	30,380
Sudan	34,056,000	President Umar Hasan Ahmad al-Bashir	dinar (258.64 = $1) pound (2,586.40 = $1)	2,450	2,383
Syria	17,905,000	President Bashar al-Assad; Prime Minister Muhammad al-Utri	pound (51.85 = $1)	5,143	4,845
Turkey	71,455,000	President Ahmet Necdet Sezer; Prime Minister Recep Tayyip Erdogan	lira (1,515,152.00 = $1)	49,120	62,430
United Arab Emirates	2,790,000	President Zayid bin Sultan Al Nuhayyan; Prime Minister Maktum bin Rashid al-Maktum	dirham (3.67 = $1)	56,730	37,160
Yemen	21,524,000	President Ali Abdallah Salih; Prime Minister Abd al-Qadir Ba Jamal	rial (184.50 = $1)	3,920	3,042

*Exchange rates as of Oct. 1, 2004, or latest available data.
†Latest available data.

Humanitarian crisis in Darfur. A humanitarian crisis plagued the western Sudanese region of Darfur in 2004. The crisis was sparked by violent conflict between the government-supported Arab "Janjaweed" militia and two rebel groups—the Sudan Liberation Army and the Justice and Equality Movement. The conflict began in February 2003. As a result of the fighting, more than 70,000 Sudanese had been killed and 1.6 million others had been displaced by December 2004, according to United Nations (UN) estimates.

In November, the UN-based World Food Program was forced to suspend a large part of its food relief operations because of the worsening conflict. The suspension left tens of thousands of refugees without food. Many observers of the worsening situation in Darfur urged the United Nations, the United States, and the European powers to exert greater efforts to resolve the crisis.   ■ Marius Deeb

See also **Africa; Iraq: A Special Report; Terrorism;** the various Middle East country articles.

Mining. See Energy supply.

Minnesota. See State government.

Mississippi. See State government.

Missouri. See State government.

Moldova. Tensions flared in Moldova in 2004 over the status of the breakaway Trans-Dniester region. Trans-Dniester's government on July 15 ordered the closure of six schools that taught in the Latin, rather than Russian Cyrillic, alphabet. Trans-Dniester, populated primarily by ethnic Russians, declared independence in 1990 from Moldova, then the Soviet republic of Moldavia. The ethnic Russians feared that Moldova's Romanian-speaking majority might seek reunification with neighboring Romania. The school closing order caused tension on both sides, as Moldova threatened economic sanctions against Trans-Dniester.

The dispute continued until Sept. 29, 2004, when the Trans-Dniesterian government declared that it would reopen the schools. Talks between Moldova and Trans-Dniester mediated by the Organization for Security and Cooperation in Europe stalled following the school closures. Tensions were further inflamed by the presence of Russian troops who had remained stationed in Trans-Dneister since the collapse of the Soviet Union in 1991. Although the troops quelled a violent conflict between Moldova and Trans-Dniester in 1992, they were by 2004 regarded as a partisan force supporting the Trans-Dniesterian government.   ■ Juliet Johnson

See also **Europe**; **Russia**.

Mongolia. See Asia.

Montana. See State government.

Montreal prepared in 2004 to lose its "one island, one city" status, after residents of 15 former municipalities voted in a June referendum to split from the "megacity." The megacity had been created in 2002, after the provincial legislature passed a law merging 28 municipalities on the Island of Montreal and some adjacent islands. The goal of the merger, supported by the then-ruling Parti Quebecois, was to reduce spending by eliminating duplications in government administration and services. The "demerger" was scheduled to go into effect Jan. 1, 2006.

"Superbug." Reports in June 2004 of a high number of deaths from infections of *Clostridium difficile* bacteria raised concerns that a "superbug" may be spreading in Montreal hospitals. *C. difficile* is a bacterium that most people carry in the stomach and colon. In people who are taking antibiotics and stomach acid reducers called proton pump inhibitors—particularly the elderly and those who are ill—*C. difficile* can cause an infectious diarrhea. The bacterium can usually be controlled with antibiotics. However, doctors speculated that the strain in Montreal hospitals, which caused perforation or rupture of the colon, may be especially deadly. Some 80 patients died of *C. difficile* infection during an 18-month period in 2002 and 2003.

Reputed Montreal Mafia godfathers Vito Rizzuto and Frank Cotroni were back in the headlines in 2004. At the request of United States authorities, Rizzuto was arrested at his Montreal residence in January. He was charged with racketeering in the 1981 murders of three Mafia captains from the Bonnano crime family of New York City. Rizzuto fought extradition throughout 2004.

In August, Frank Cotroni, who with his late brothers Vincenzo (Vic) and Giuseppe (Pep or Pepe) allegedly controlled many illegal Quebec rackets, died of brain cancer. As recently as 2002, Cotroni had completed a prison sentence for conspiracy to import cocaine.

Brewery merger. Company officials in July 2004 announced the merger of Montreal-based Molson, Inc., and Golden, Colorado-based Adolph Coors Company. Molson, founded in 1786, is the oldest brewery in North America. The new firm, to be called the Molson Coors Brewery Company, would become the world's fifth-largest beer maker. Shareholders were to vote on the plan in 2005.

Air Canada, the country's largest airline, emerged from bankruptcy in September 2004. The Montreal-based carrier had filed for bankruptcy in April 2003. Unsecured creditors voted in August 2004 in favor of the company's financial restructuring plan. The plan could result in the creditors owning as much as 88 percent of the carrier.

Mont Tremblant. The Intrawest Corp. of Vancouver revealed plans in August to spend $1 billion over 10 years to nearly double the capacity of its Mont Tremblant ski and golf resort in the Laurentian Mountains north of Montreal. (All amounts are in Canadian dollars.) The Canadian and Quebec governments agreed to contribute $47.5 million each toward the expansion project for infrastructure development.

Days later, a minority stakeholder in the neighboring Gray Rocks Inn confirmed that he would buy the historic resort and keep it open through the 2004-2005 season. Former owner Phillip Robinson had indicated in June that he would be forced to close for the winter because of mounting losses.

The Montreal Symphony Orchestra (MSO) announced in March 2004 that it had hired Kent Nagano as a replacement for its celebrated conductor, Charles Dutoit. Nagano's contract stipulated that he take over as musical director in September 2006 for six years. Dutoit had resigned abruptly in 2002 after members of the Quebec Musicians Guild had filed complaints against him. He had served as maestro for nearly 25 years.

The Montreal Expos, which in 1969 became the first Major League Baseball franchise awarded outside of the United States, played its final game on Canadian soil on Sept. 29, 2004. That same day, the team confirmed that it was moving to Washington, D.C., for the 2005 season.   ■ Mike King

See also **Canada**; **City**; **Washington, D.C.**

Morocco. See Africa.

Motion pictures. Ties binding motion pictures and political debate were stronger and more controversial than ever during the United States presidential election in 2004. The release of a number of technically innovative animated or partially animated features in 2004 met with mixed receptions.

Political documentaries. Michael Moore's *Fahrenheit 9/11* became the centerpiece in 2004 of a new sub-genre of films, the partisan "anti-Bush documentary." Moore's incendiary film was an international success and the first documentary to surpass $100 million in U.S. box office receipts. Highly critical of U.S. President George W. Bush, the film questioned the Bush administration's agenda following the terrorist attacks on the United States on Sept. 11, 2001, emphasizing the Bush family's alleged financial connections to the royal house of Saudi Arabia.

Fahrenheit 9/11 was the highly controversial winner of the 2004 International Film Festival's Golden Palm Award. Some critics argued that the festival's jury had selected the film because of its political message. Members of the jury responded that the film won the award not for its politics, but because they believed it to be well made. The prestigious festival is an annual motion-picture exhibition and competition held in the resort city of Cannes, on the French Riviera.

Films critical of the Bush administration and its politics were in abundance in 2004. Joseph Mealey and Michael Shoob's *Bush's Brain* was a chilling portrait of President Bush's political strategist Karl Rove. Robert Greenwald's *Uncovered: The War on Iraq* included interviews with U.S. intelligence and defense officials who took a skeptical view of the decision to invade Iraq.

Documentaries supporting President Bush also sprang up during the 2004 campaign. Michael Wilson's *Michael Moore Hates America* criticized Moore's filmmaking techniques in *Fahrenheit 9/11* as well as in his earlier documentaries, *Bowling for Columbine* and *Roger & Me*. While Wilson's film took a relatively good-natured spin on Moore's work, Kevin Knoblock's *Celsius 41.11* offered a much harsher condemnation of Moore and presidential nominee Senator John Kerry (D., Massachusetts).

Another documentary, Jehane Noujaim's *Control Room,* examined the war in Iraq from an Arab perspective. The film provides a behind-the-scenes look at the Arabic news network Al Jazeera, which has been accused of both providing a pro-Iraqi insurgent viewpoint and of being the mouthpiece of the United States. The film also follows an American press officer trying to reconcile the differences between official statements and what he witnesses.

Controversy. Earlier in 2004, another controversial film, Mel Gibson's *The Passion of the Christ,* made headlines. A graphic depiction of the torture and crucifixion of Jesus, the film stirred controversy for its extreme violence and for its depiction of Jews as being partially responsible for the crucifixion. Starring James Caviezel as Jesus and with a production budget of about $30 million, the movie became a huge box-office success, grossing $370 million in the United States. It was particularly popular with fundamentalist religious groups, attracting viewers who ordinarily do not attend movies.

ACADEMY AWARD WINNERS IN 2004

The following winners of the 2003 Academy Awards were announced in February 2004:

Best Picture, *The Lord of the Rings: The Return of the King*

Best Actor, Sean Penn, *Mystic River*

Best Actress, Charlize Theron, *Monster*

Best Supporting Actor, Tim Robbins, *Mystic River*

Best Supporting Actress, Renee Zellweger, *Cold Mountain*

Best Director, Peter Jackson, *The Lord of the Rings: The Return of the King*

Best Original Screenplay, Sofia Coppola, *Lost in Translation*

Best Screenplay Adaptation, Fran Walsh, Philippa Boyens, and Peter Jackson, *The Lord of the Rings: The Return of the King*

Best Animated Feature, Andrew Stanton, *Finding Nemo*

Best Cinematography, Russell Boyd, *Master and Commander: The Far Side of the World*

Best Film Editing, Jamie Selkirk, *The Lord of the Rings: The Return of the King*

Best Original Score, Howard Shore, *The Lord of the Rings: The Return of the King*

Best Original Song, Fran Walsh, Howard Shore, and Annie Lennox, "Into the West" from *The Lord of the Rings: The Return of the King*

Best Foreign-Language Film, *The Barbarian Invasions* (Canada)

Best Art Direction, Grant Major, Dan Hennah, and Alan Lee, *The Lord of the Rings: The Return of the King*

Best Costume Design, Ngila Dickson and Richard Taylor, *The Lord of the Rings: The Return of the King*

Best Sound Mixing, Christopher Boyes, Michael Semanick, Michael Hedges, and Hammond Peek, *The Lord of the Rings: The Return of the King*

Best Sound Editing, Richard King, *Master and Commander: The Far Side of the World*

Best Makeup, Richard Taylor and Peter King, *The Lord of the Rings: The Return of the King*

Best Visual Effects, *The Lord of the Rings: The Return of the King*

Best Animated Short Film, *Harvie Krumpet*

Best Live-Action Short Film, *Two Soldiers*

Best Feature Documentary, *The Fog of War*

Best Short Subject Documentary, *Chernobyl Heart*

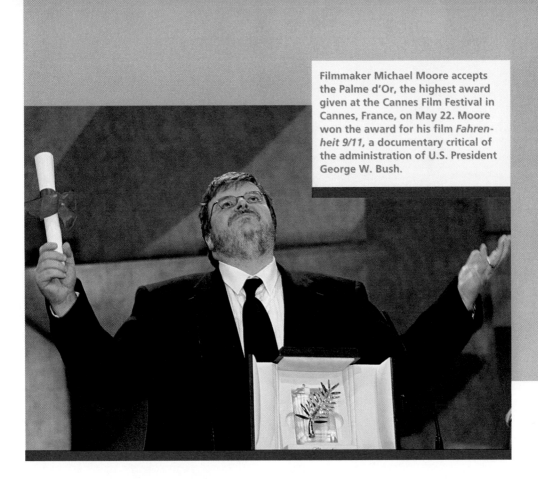

Filmmaker Michael Moore accepts the Palme d'Or, the highest award given at the Cannes Film Festival in Cannes, France, on May 22. Moore won the award for his film *Fahrenheit 9/11*, a documentary critical of the administration of U.S. President George W. Bush.

Biographies and history. In addition to the once-taboo subjects of politics and religion, moviemakers also produced a number of biographies in 2004, a genre whose popularity had waxed and waned over time. Jamie Foxx earned some of 2004's most glowing reviews as legendary musician Ray Charles in *Ray.* Liam Neeson was lauded for his role as sex researcher Alfred Kinsey in *Kinsey,* while Kevin Kline received praise for his personification of composer Cole Porter in *De-Lovely.* Two of 2004's most anticipated ventures, both dealing with historical figures and directed by provocative filmmakers, were released near the end of 2004. Oliver Stone's *Alexander,* featuring Colin Farrell as the Macedonian conqueror Alexander the Great, was widely panned. Martin Scorsese's *The Aviator,* starring Leonardo DiCaprio as Howard Hughes, received mostly positive reviews.

The Alamo, the year's most anticipated historical drama—another genre of fluctuating popularity—was a major disappointment. A critical and commercial flop, the Texas epic starred Billy Bob Thornton as Davy Crockett and Dennis Quaid as Sam Houston.

Sequels and remakes were plentiful in 2004, as usual. *Spider-Man 2* and *Shrek 2* ranked as smash hits, while *Harry Potter and the Prisoner of Azkaban* and *The Bourne Supremacy* were solid

box-office draws. *Spider-Man 2* earned stronger reviews than its predecessor, but some viewers felt alienated by its hero's sad-sack demeanor.

Such remakes as *The Stepford Wives* and *The Manchurian Candidate* fell short of expectations, though Meryl Streep's raw-nerved performance as the devious mother in the latter was greatly admired. *Alfie,* starring Jude Law in an update of the 1966 film that made a star of Michael Caine, won praise for Law and tepid overall reviews.

Quentin Tarantino, who skyrocketed to fame with 1994's *Pulp Fiction,* released *Kill Bill: Vol. 2,* the second installment of his two-part, ultra-violent martial-arts celebration. The film finished the story of a woman known as The Bride, played by Uma Thurman, and her quest for revenge against the people who attempted to kill her on her wedding day. Some critics praised the second film more than the original, *Kill Bill: Vol. 1* (2003), which was itself a box-office smash.

Richard Linklater's *Before Sunset* was the sequel to his 1995 film *Before Sunrise. Before Sunset* featured Ethan Hawke as an American author who runs into a woman, played by Julie Delpy, whom he had met briefly nine years earlier. The pair walk around Paris, discussing life and love.

Several smaller films garnered praise in 2004. David O. Russell's *I Heart Huckabees,* a philo-

The Lord of the Rings: The Return of the King, the final installment of director Peter Jackson's adaptation of J. R. R. Tolkien's trilogy of epic fantasy novels, won 11 Academy Awards, including one award for best visual effects. The film also won best picture and best director.

The 2004 Academy Awards recognized character-driven dramas and a major fantasy epic.

Sean Penn, *center*, portrays Jimmy Markum, a convenience store owner trying to cope with the death of his daughter in Clint Eastwood's *Mystic River*. Penn won an Academy Award for best actor for his performance, and Tim Robbins won the Academy Award for best supporting actor for his portrayal of Jimmy's friend Dave Boyle.

Charlize Theron portrays Aileen Wuornos in *Monster,* for which she won the Academy Award for best actress. The film is the true story of a woman who becomes a serial murderer in an attempt to forge a better life for herself. Theron was praised for her complete transformation into her character.

sophical comedy, was lauded for its offbeat, heady humor. The film featured Jason Schwartzman as an ecological activist searching for meaning with the help of "existential detectives," played by Dustin Hoffman and Lily Tomlin. Michel Gondry won rave reviews for his oddball comedy-drama *Eternal Sunshine of the Spotless Mind.* Written by Charlie Kaufman, the film featured Jim Carrey and Kate Winslet as a couple who undergo a procedure to erase each other from their memories.

Year-end surprises. The year's most widely praised films released at the end of 2004 included *Sideways, Finding Neverland, Being Julia,* and *The Machinist.* In Alexander Payne's perceptive comedy-drama *Sideways,* Paul Giamatti and Thomas Haden Church gave superb performances as two former college roommates who discover new relationships while visiting California wineries. Marc Forster's *Finding Neverland* chronicled the events that led Sir James M. Barrie to write the classic *Peter Pan,* with Johnny Depp delivering a much-lauded portrayal of the gentle author.

Annette Bening's performance as an aging actress in *Being Julia* drew some of the best reviews of her career. Christian Bale received rave reviews for his performance of an insomniac industrial worker in Brad Anderson's psychological thriller *The Machinist.* For this role, Bale lost 63 pounds (28.6 kilograms), and reviewers suggested that his emaciated appearance made his performance in the film genuinely ghostly. Clint Eastwood's *Million Dollar Baby* was praised for bringing genuine human emotion back to the boxing film genre, which tends to fall into melodrama. The film featured Eastwood, Morgan Freeman, and Hilary Swank.

Women filmgoers, often neglected by mainstream Hollywood, responded warmly to the sentimental romance *The Notebook,* featuring relative newcomers Ryan Gosling and Rachel McAdams as well as veterans James Garner and Gena Rowlands. *Shall We Dance,* starring Richard Gere, Susan Sarandon, and Jennifer Lopez in a remake of a 1996 Japanese film about a tired businessman rejuvenated by dance lessons, also met with an enthusiastic response.

Family films. Three films aimed at family audiences used advanced technology to mixed results. Although it earned some positive reviews, Kerry Conran's *Sky Captain and the World of Tomorrow* failed to meet box office expectations. The film was shot entirely on a blue screen, and actors were superimposed over a wonderfully stylish 1930's world that was produced wholly on computers. Brad Bird's *The Incredibles,* a joint release by Disney and Pixar Animation Studios, was a huge success, breaking opening weekend records set by the previous Disney/Pixar release, 2003's *Finding Nemo. The Incredibles* tells the story of a family of superheroes trying to live a quiet suburban life but who come out of retirement to save the world. The film featured the voices of Craig T. Nelson and Holly Hunter. Robert Zemeckis's adaptation of Chris Van Allsburg's children's book *The Polar Express,* starring Tom Hanks, won praise for its vivid computer-generated animation. Other critics found the film lacking in emotional depth and noted that it failed to live up to the hype surrounding its November release.

International. World War II (1939-1945) provided the background for 2004's most discussed German film, Oliver Hirschbiegel's *The Downfall,* which starred Bruno Ganz as Adolf Hitler. The feature depicted the final days of Hitler and his close associates. *The Downfall* broke box-office records in Berlin, and critical reaction was generally positive. However, some viewers felt that the film was too sympathetic in its depiction of Hitler.

Sentimental romance resurfaced in Japan, where *Crying Out for Love from the Center of the World* was a giant hit. The film, which cost $3.5 million to make and earned more than $70 million at the box office, told of a man about to be married who cannot erase memories of a tragic high-school romance.

Night Watch, a Russian science-fiction thriller directed by Timur Bekmambetov, became one of the most successful films in Russia's movie history, grossing about $15 million. In the tradition of American thrillers, *Night Watch* is to be followed by two sequels, *Day Watch* and *Dusk Watch.*

One of Taiwan's most popular films of the year, the gay comedy *Formula 17,* told of the relationship between a sensitive teen and a philandering bachelor. The film contained no heterosexual or female characters.

Thailand's big 2004 hit was the monster film *Paksa Wayu (The Garuda),* about a prehistoric bird stalking users of the Bangkok subway. The film was Thailand's first all-digital movie.

The visually stirring British-German documentary *Deep Blue,* which explored seldom seen corners of the sea, was a major hit internationally. The feature was hugely popular in Japan, where it drew more viewers than most Hollywood blockbusters.

Film receipts for the 2004 summer box-office season in the United States—Memorial Day to Labor Day—totaled just under $4 billion, an increase of 3 percent from the same period in 2003. However, studio executives noted that, with higher ticket prices, the total number of tickets sold decreased when compared with the summer of 2003.   ■ Philip Wuntch

See also **People in the news** (Michael Moore, Sean Penn, Charlize Theron).

Mozambique. See Africa.

Marlon Brando:
The Method and the Man

Actor Marlon Brando died at a Los Angeles hospital on July 1, 2004, at the age of 80. Colleagues and critics considered him to be one of the most influential actors of his generation. A reluctant celebrity, Brando gained a reputation for being as rebellious offscreen as many of the memorable characters he portrayed onscreen.

Brando represented a completely different kind of leading man. Previous Hollywood leading men, such as Cary Grant, were suave gentlemen. In his casual appearance and often combative behavior with directors, Brando seemed to take his cue from the motorcycle gang leader he portrayed in *The Wild One* (1953). When asked what he was rebelling against, his character replied, "What've ya got?" While Hollywood leading men in the early 1950's typically presented a more glamorous appearance, Brando dressed in T-shirts and jeans. He rarely gave interviews or attended film premieres.

From the beginning of his career, Brando appeared in challenging, diverse roles. He portrayed a disabled veteran in *The Men* (1950), his screen debut. He earned Oscar nominations as a Mexican revolutionary in *Viva Zapata!* (1952) and Marc Antony in *Julius Caesar* (1953). He portrayed a gay Army officer in *Reflections in a Golden Eye* (1967), and a renegade Green Beret colonel in *Apocalypse Now* (1979).

However, it was his breakthrough, Oscar-nominated performance as brutish Stanley Kowalski in *A Streetcar Named Desire* (1951), a role he originated on the Broadway stage, that changed the face of American acting. Brando was a disciple of Method acting, taught in the United States by actor Lee Strasberg and acting coach Stella Adler. This style of acting required actors to tap into their own memories and emotions to add psychological complexity to a character. In Bernardo Bertolucci's controversial drama *Last Tango in Paris* (1972), Brando portrayed an emotionally shattered character. He improvised much of his dialogue that drew upon memories of the unhappy childhood he chronicled in his 1994 autobiography, *Songs My Mother Taught Me.*

Brando won the Academy Award for his role as the conflicted, mob-connected longshoreman Terry Malloy in *On the Waterfront* (1954). In 1972, he won a second Oscar, which he refused, for his portrayal of mob kingpin Don Vito Corleone in *The Godfather* (1972). He was also honored with an Emmy Award for his role as American Nazi George Lincoln Rockwell in the television miniseries *Roots: The Next Generations* (1979).

In some interviews, Brando spoke of taking jobs solely for the money. For his small role as Superman's father in *Superman* (1978), he reportedly was paid between $3 million and $4 million for a few weeks' work.

Brando, in his later years, showed flashes of his early brilliance. He was nominated for an Oscar for his performance as an antiapartheid lawyer in *A Dry White Season* (1989). He also appeared opposite actors who acknowledged his influence on their careers, including Johnny Depp in *Don Juan DeMarco* (1995) and Robert De Niro in *The Score* (2001).

Although Brando showed contempt for his profession in his later years, his legacy in the American cinema cannot be denied. He was truly the godfather of a new breed of actors. ■ Donald Liebenson

BLOCKBUSTER:
THE NEW FACE OF AMERICAN MUSEUMS

Large-scale shows are changing the
traditional missions of many museums in
the United States.

By David Yezzi

Art purists were aghast. Curators at the Solomon R. Guggenheim Museum in New York City had wrapped the internal spiral of the Frank Lloyd Wright designed museum on Fifth Avenue with stainless steel and had filled its galleries with more than 100 vintage motorcycles. According to the curators, "The Art of the Motorcycle," as the exhibit was called, celebrated the motorcycle as a cultural icon. According to most art critics, "The Art of the Motorcycle" shamelessly pandered to popular taste and to corporate culture. (The show was sponsored by a motor company that manufactures motorcycles.) Nevertheless, "The Art of the Motorcycle" was the most popular exhibition in the history of the Guggenheim. It attracted crowds of people who had never before entered the museum, which is famous for its collection of modern and abstract paintings and sculpture. The 1998 show made a great deal of money and generated enormous publicity for the museum. "The Art of the Motorcycle" later traveled to the Field Museum of Natural History in Chicago, the Guggenheim Museum in Spain, and the Guggenheim Las Vegas in Nevada. In every way, "The Art of the Motorcycle" was a real blockbuster of a show.

Such large-scale museum shows have changed the traditional missions of many museums in the United States. More and more American museums use eye-catching subjects and marquee names to attract bigger audiences and higher ticket sales. Some are from a given historical period, such as "The Quest for Immortality: Treasures of Ancient Egypt" presented by the Milwaukee Public Museum in Wisconsin, in 2004. Others focus on the career of a single "superstar" artist, for example, "Monet at Giverny: Masterpieces from the Musée Marmottan" at the Albright-Knox Art Gallery in Buffalo, New York, in 1999. Increasingly dependent on blockbuster shows for revenue, many museum officials have broadened their traditional role of educating and delighting the public to include the presentation of objects and themes drawn from popular culture. In 2000, Chicago's Field Museum presented "Star Wars: The Magic of Myth," which featured art works, props, models, and costumes from the motion picture *Star Wars* (1977) and its two sequels. The Museum of Science in Boston scheduled "Star Wars: Where Science Meets Imagination" to open for an extended run in 2005.

Two types of blockbusters

As two prominent blockbusters from 2004 made clear, what constitutes objects worthy of museum display depends on both the taste of a museum curator and on the exhibit's potential drawing power. New York City's highly respected Metropolitan Museum of Art hosted an example of a traditional museum exhibition—"Byzantium: Faith and Power (1261-1557)" from March through July 2004. (Byzantium, the capital of the Byzantine Empire, is now the city of Istanbul, Turkey.) "Byzantium: Faith and Power," which took seven years to organize, was the third of three blockbuster shows at the Metropolitan focusing on Byzantine and early Christian art. The series began in 1978 with "The Age of Spirituality." This was followed in 1997 by "The Glory of Byzantium, A.D. 843-1261," an exhibition that drew nearly 500,000 visitors.

"Byzantium: Faith and Power" consisted of some of the world's most prized examples of art of the late Middle Ages (the period of European history between 1300 and 1500). It encompassed over 350 works gathered from approximately 30 countries, including Bulgaria, Egypt, France, Greece, Italy, Macedonia, Romania, Russia, and Turkey. According to some estimates, the cost of mounting the show ran to nearly $4 million, making it one of the most expensive exhibits in the Metropolitan's history.

While many critics applauded the exhibit's scholarly integrity and aesthetic richness, some viewers complained about the media hype surrounding it. Others argued that the exhibit's size—objects spanned nearly 300 years of cultural and artistic history—was too large to see at

The author:
David Yezzi is an editor and writer. He is also director of the Unterberg Poetry Center in New York City.

just one viewing. Jed Perl, art critic of *The New Republic* magazine, praised the show in a May 2004 article, pointing out that its curators "worked hard to achieve the supercharged atmosphere that animates the exhibition, and the exhilaration that we feel is the real thing, for here are great objects presented not only beautifully but also intelligently."

Perl, however, qualified his admiration later in his article, suggesting certain difficulties inherent in all blockbuster exhibitions. "Some museum goers," he wrote, might feel "that the show promises far more than it delivers, or that it is really three or four shows awkwardly cobbled together, or that the groupings of icons from different areas begin to feel like teasers for more specialized exhibitions."

A second exhibition of 2004 also sought to capture attention by presenting objects of great interest. Critics, however, questioned the decidedly less historical and artistic significance of "Jacqueline Kennedy: The White House Years" at Chicago's Field Museum. The exhibit included more than 70 articles of clothing and other objects belonging to the wife of President John F. Kennedy. According to critics, the exhibit relied less on scholarly interest than on the public's lingering fascination with the mystique surrounding Jacqueline Kennedy Onassis.

"Jacqueline Kennedy: The White House Years" was the latest of a variety of blockbuster exhibitions presented by the Field Museum that reflected a wider mission and a new image. In 1893, the Field Museum of Natural History was incorporated as a museum of natural history and anthropology. In the 1990's, the museum shortened its name to the Field Museum in press relations and marketing messages. By the early

The blockbuster "Jacqueline Kennedy: The White House Years" opened at Chicago's Field Museum in November 2004 with an exhibit of *couture* (high fashion) gowns worn by the first lady during her husband's presidency. Critics questioned the exhibit's connection to the museum's research and education programs.

2000's, it began staging shows on topics somewhat outside natural history and anthropology—including Cleopatra, baseball in America, chocolate, motion-picture props, and pearls.

Although some museum purists claimed these exhibits strayed from the historic purpose of a museum, museum officials countered that each exhibit has a natural history component. For example, "Chocolate" reflected botany and zoology by discussing how cacao trees grow and how they are fertilized by insects. It also focused on anthropology by discussing the importance of chocolate to many of the world's cultures.

The exhibition of Mrs. Onassis's personal items struck critics as unlikely fare for the Field Museum or, for that matter, the Metropolitan Museum of Art, where the same show drew huge crowds in 2001. However, the popular appeal of the exhibition and the media attention devoted to it were typical of certain blockbuster exhibitions. According to officials at the Field, the motivation for such programming was largely financial. In a 2003 article in *Crain's Chicago Business*, a business-oriented weekly newspaper, Field Museum President John W. McCarter, Jr., said that to fulfill its mission the museum needs "to hit 2 million admissions a year, and blockbusters make that happen." Echoing that sentiment, many museum executives have stated that they rely on blockbusters that lie outside their museums' standard purview to afford smaller shows more in line with traditional museum missions.

Although some people have condemned the growing reliance on the products of popular culture to stir audience interest in museums, museum executives and trustees admit that they would have a difficult time meeting their annual financial goals without the blockbuster. During an interview for the same 2003 article in *Crain's Chicago Business*, Marshall Field V, a Field Museum trustee, described the museum's blockbuster strategy as a short-term solution to the widespread economic challenges that museums and other not-for-profit cultural organizations face: chiefly a downturn in overall attendance coupled with steeply rising operating costs and reduced government and private funding. Despite such challenges, the Field Museum has maintained its position as a major research institution, with anthropological and natural history research projects underway in more than 90 countries.

The history of the modern blockbuster

The genesis of the museum blockbuster dates to an exhibition in 1976 of 55 objects from the tomb of King Tutankhamun, or King Tut, as he is commonly called. Tutankhamun (sometimes spelled Tutankhamen) was pharaoh, or king, of Egypt from about 1347 B.C. until his death in 1339 B.C. His tomb, discovered in 1922, is the only burial chamber of an ancient Egyptian king to be discovered almost completely undamaged. "Treasures of Tutankhamun" was initially displayed at the National Gallery of Art, in Washington, D.C., and ran from Nov. 17, 1976, to March 15, 1977. National Gallery curators described the exhibition as, "a combination of the age-old fascination with ancient Egypt, the legendary allure of gold and precious stones, and the funeral trappings of the boy-king."

More than 800,000 visitors made their way to the National Gallery during the 117 days of the exhibition. After closing at the National Gallery, "Treasures of Tutankhamun" went on the road for several years, playing to packed houses at the Field Museum, the New Orleans Museum of Art, Los Angeles Museum of Art, the Seattle Museum, and the Metropolitan Museum of Art. "Treasures of Tutankhamun" drew huge crowds and generated revenue everywhere it was mounted—facts not lost on the directors and trustees of other museums.

What makes a blockbuster?

Blockbuster exhibitions are large collections of objects of great artistic or popular appeal that exist apart from a museum's permanent collection, though a blockbuster may include relevant works gathered from a museum's holdings. Blockbusters are made up largely of works on loan from other museums, which are then shipped from museum to museum as the blockbuster tours different cities. Through partnerships struck between host museums, blockbuster shows routinely travel to three or more cities in the United States and other cities around the world.

Such touring exhibitions are extremely expensive to produce because of their size. The high cost of transporting, insuring, and, in many cases, conserving the objects on display make blockbusters something of a financial gamble for most museums. As a result, additional expenses are often incurred to launch far-reaching advertising campaigns as a means to encourage audience turnout. To a certain extent, blockbusters are as

A full-scale prop of a Naboo Royal N-1 Starfighter is displayed at the Museum of Science in Boston in 2004 to promote the exhibit "Star Wars: Where Science Meets Imagination." The exhibit, scheduled to open in 2005, used the *Star Wars* saga as a gateway to examining real-world technology.

much the creation of publicists, sponsors, and media companies, as they are of the museum curators responsible for the objects included in a given exhibition. To boost attendance and sales, museums typically rely on extensive media campaigns to generate excitement and a sense of anticipation. This sense of excitement, or hype, creates a "must-see" atmosphere around a given show. Blockbusters are rare opportunities to appreciate works of art assembled for the first time in unprecedented numbers, allowing museum-goers special insight into a particular period or artist's body of work. John Russell, visual art critic for *The Times* of London, concocted a wry formula for the creation of blockbusters: "Assemble as many works by the master (artist) as you can, put them together in the most stylish and easy-to-take manner possible, tour the result to not more than three major centres of art, advertise so heavily that no one could feel cultivated unless they had seen the show, and wait for the *queues* (lines) to form."

When they are successful, blockbusters are responsible for a record number of museum visits, with attendance figures approaching or exceeding 1 million people. "Henri Matisse: A Retrospective," shown at the Museum of Modern Art (MoMA) in New York City in 1992 and 1993, boasted a total attendance of some 900,000 patrons. More than 1.2 million people visited the Museum of Science and Industry in Chicago in 2000 to view "Titanic: The Exhibition." The first real blockbuster, "The Treasures of Tutankhamun," pulled 1.3 million people into the Field Museum during its stay in the late 1970's.

The payoff from the sales of a million or more tickets can be substantial. Most blockbuster exhibitions require a special fee on top of the museum's general admission price. The admission price for "Gauguin Tahiti," a 2004 retrospective of late work of French artist Paul Gauguin at the Museum of Fine Arts in Boston hit $20. Tickets for a revival of the Tutankhamun blockbuster scheduled to open in 2005 were priced at $30. Admission tickets, which can usually be purchased through commercial agencies for an added handling surcharge, generally restrict patrons to a particular time.

Museum gift shops also generate big revenue during blockbuster shows by stocking items—books, clothing, postcards, tote bags, umbrellas, and assorted giftware—related to the show. Often, museums set up a separate gift shop stocked only with merchandise related to the show. These temporary shops are frequently located in a space through which exhibition patrons must walk after exiting the gallery.

Beyond ticket and merchandise sales, which constitute an exhibition's earned

The 3,000-year-old gold death mask of Tutankhamun was among the items that attracted millions of visitors in the 1970's to "Treasures of Tutankhamun," the first real museum blockbuster.

income, blockbusters attract an array of financial support, or contributed income, from corporate and government sources. The museums that exhibited "Treasures of Tutankhamun," for example, received gifts from Exxon Corporation, a New York City-based oil company, and the Robert Wood Johnson Jr. Charitable Trust. These contributions were matched by grants from the National Endowment for the Humanities, based in Washington, D.C.

A conservator at the Museum of Fine Arts in Boston in 2004 examines the condition of *Where Do We Come From? What Are We? Where Are We Going?* a painting by French artist Paul Gauguin. Preservation remains a core mission of most museums.

Museums and their mission

Historically, the mission of a museum was to collect, document, preserve, and exhibit objects illustrating art, history, natural history, science, or other subjects of human study or endeavor. Museums, generally founded around a group of objects called a collection, were responsible for preserving the works in their possession. Beyond preservation and exhibition, museums also carefully documented their holdings and often conducted related research into the periods or cultures that produced the works.

The International Council of Museums, a private organization based in Paris and associated with the United Nations' Economic and Social Council, defines a museum as "a nonprofit making, permanent institution in the service of society and of its development, and open to the public, which acquires, conserves, researches, communicates and exhibits, for purposes of study, education and enjoyment, material evidence of people and their environment. . . ." The definition is the product of more than 50 years of thought about what constitutes a museum, though it reflects a number of ideas fundamental to museums that have evolved over centuries.

A conservator discusses a painting with museum patrons at the J. Paul Getty Museum in Los Angeles in 1997. Public education constitutes one of the traditional roles of museums.

The word museum derives from the Ancient Greek word *mouseion*, which means "place of the Muses." The muses were nine goddesses of the arts and sciences in Greek mythology. The first museums, which were largely centers of contemplation and philosophical discussion, date back to the Museum of Alexandria in ancient Egypt, founded sometime after 331 B.C. In the 1400's, the word *museum* was used in Europe to refer to the personal art collection of Lorenzo de' Medici, who ruled the Italian city-state of Florence from 1469 until his death in 1492. The world's first public museum, the Ashmolean, opened at Oxford University in Oxford, England, in 1683.

The modern notion of a museum as a building or physical place where objects are displayed for the general public developed in the 1800's. From 1850 to 1900, some of the world's most distinguished museums opened in the United States. These included the American Museum of Natural History, founded in 1869, and the Metropolitan Museum of Art, founded in 1870, both in New York City. By 1876, the United States had more than 200 museums.

While blockbusters are common across the spectrum of museums, those generating the most controversy have tended to be staged by art museums whose missions involve offering the public an aesthetic experience. Like "The Art of the Motorcycle," another recent show at the Guggenheim in New York City exemplifies how blockbusters frequently shift emphasis away from a museum's permanent holdings, which in the case of the Guggenheim is modern art. In 2000 and 2001, the Guggenheim presented an exhibition of fashion entitled "Giorgio Armani." Curated by the avant-garde artist Robert Wilson, the show featured a retrospective of clothing by the popular Italian designer. The

Guggenheim received criticism on a number of counts, among them the idea that fashion was considered a dubious subject for presentation by an art museum, as well as the fact that the museum received a donation from Armani of a reported $15 million. Some critics claimed the donation constituted a conflict of interest for the museum, suggesting museum officials had prioritized money over curatorial integrity. In response to these detractors, Thomas Krens, director of the Guggenheim, stated that he has "expanded the concept of what a museum/gallery is. . . . I see a museum as a research and education institution, as well as a theme park—I say theme park not in a pejorative manner." The idea of a museum as a "theme park" struck many art critics and traditional museum curators as a distortion of the museum's traditional function.

Changing role of museums

The motivation behind the changing role of art museums—from places that cater to a relatively modest number of art lovers to ones designed to host throngs of people drawn to popular subjects—may be largely a financial one. As sources of public funding have leveled off and even stopped, museums increasingly have had to rely on the sale of admission tickets to meet the costs of collecting, transporting, and exhibiting works of art, which might amount to many hundreds of thousands of dollars for a single show. Experts maintain that the rise of massive public relations campaigns, corporate partnerships, trendy subjects, and

The motorcycle ridden by Peter Fonda in the motion picture *Easy Rider* (1969) is displayed at the Solomon R. Guggenheim Museum in New York City as part of "The Art of the Motorcycle" exhibit in 1998.

celebrity endorsements reflect a desire on the part of museum officials to bring more paying customers through their doors.

When "The Art of the Motorcycle" opened at the Guggenheim Las Vegas, a branch of the New York City museum, officials created 60-foot (18-meter) long billboards at McCarran International Airport in Las Vegas depicting celebrities Lauren Hutton and Samuel L. Jackson riding motorcycles. Similarly, in 2001, the Museum of Contemporary Art in Los Angeles enlarged its public profile when it partnered with an advertising agency to launch a brand-awareness campaign. The museum was marketed much like the firm's other clients, which ranged from a battery manufacturer to a fast-food restaurant chain. Large ads for the museum were placed on billboards and even on the sides of public buses. Thomas Krens, who is credited with increasing attendance at the Guggenheim museums by 600 percent over a 10-year period, has stated that for museums "life is promotion."

Even museum buildings are being redesigned to cater to the masses attracted by blockbuster shows. By 2004, many leading museums across the United States had undergone extensive renovations specifically designed to accommodate larger crowds. Typically, the remodeling involved closing original front entrances and lobbies and crafting new entrances, often underground, through which large numbers of people could be channeled to specialized galleries. Such a trend appeared as early as the 1980's. In a 1984 magazine article, art critic Hilton Kramer of *The New Criterion* noted that renovations at the Museum of Modern Art were done to bring more people to the museum, even though some of those individuals might have little or no interest in the art world in general but would still attend a blockbuster exhibit. "The . . . museum is designed, we may say, for a public nurtured on blockbuster exhibitions—exhibitions that are as much media events as they are art events, and have the inevitable effect of arousing, by means of high-intensity publicity campaigns, the kind of interest which art in and of itself can probably never satisfy," wrote Kramer.

Critics warned that such a shift in focus by museums from connoisseurship to popular taste may have a detrimental effect. In some cases, opponents claim, fashion and flash have displaced the thoughtful and illuminating presentation of art works of true aesthetic value. Graham Beal, the director of the Detroit Institute of Arts in Detroit, Michigan, said in an interview on National Public Radio in April 2004, "Very, very quickly, we found that we had, in a way, turned ourselves into coming attractions places, and the permanent collection that the exhibitions were supposed to illuminate seemed to have taken a back seat."

The blockbuster's questionable future

Blockbuster museum shows, ironically, may at the height of their popularity be turning into dinosaurs. Blockbusters are very expensive to mount. They operate on the notion that it takes money—usually money from corporate sponsors—to make money. They came of age during the financial boom of the 1980's, when corporate sponsorship was relatively

plentiful. In the sluggish economic conditions that followed the turn of the millennium, sponsorship is much harder to come by.

In addition, museum costs associated with shipping and insuring art have skyrocketed since the terrorist attacks on the United States on Sept. 11, 2001. The attacks made it more difficult for museum curators to develop blockbusters, which typically are assembled with works borrowed from around the world. From 2003 to 2004, museum insurance rates went up as much as 50 percent in New York City, as museums sought to protect themselves against the aftereffects of a terrorist attack. Fearing for the safety of prized works in a period of international troubles, museum curators have also become reluctant to allow their artwork to be moved. Higher operating costs for fuel and security also have forced freight companies used to transport art works to increase their prices.

In response to higher costs, a number of museums in 2004 opted to return to their roots and focus attention again on their permanent collections. Officials at the Art Institute of Chicago planned to expand their current exhibition galleries by approximately 60,000 feet (18,000 meters) to accommodate the growth of its collections, which in 2004 were cramped for space. Neal Benezra, director of the San Francisco Museum of Modern Art, was similarly concerned to showcase his museum's holdings in newly configured galleries. While the rejuvenation of permanent collections is unlikely to displace the ever-present blockbuster, it may well restore to prominence the notion, as Benezra said in a July 2004 newspaper interview, that "a great museum is measured by its collections."

Museums capitalize on blockbuster exhibits with specialized gift stores that offer merchandise related to the exhibit. In 1998, Boston's Museum of Fine Arts marketed merchandise that ranged from books to tote bags to stuffed frogs in connection to its "Monet in the Twentieth Century" show.

Myanmar. The military government convened a constitutional convention on May 17, 2004, which the National League for Democracy (NLD) boycotted. The convention recessed on July 9 without having made progress. The NLD won 1990 elections for parliament, but the country's military *junta* government said a new constitution had to be written before parliament could open. With the NLD boycott, the 1,088 convention delegates represented only ethnic minorities and junta supporters. Ethnic minorities make up 35 percent of Myanmar's population.

A constitutional convention in session from 1993 to 1996 failed to agree on a constitution because the junta insisted on provisions that would guarantee their continued dominance. In 2004, the junta continued to require such provisions. They also refused to release from house arrest the NLD's leader, Nobel Peace Prize winner Aung San Suu Kyi.

On October 19, Thailand's prime minister, Thaksin Shinawatra, alleged that Myanmar's prime minister, General Khin Nyunt, had been ousted by the junta. Later that day, Myanmar's state media announced that Khin Nyunt had, in fact, resigned, but for health reasons. He was replaced by Lieutenant General Soe Win.   ■ Henry S. Bradsher

See also **Asia.**

Namibia. See **Africa.**

Nebraska. See **State government.**

Nepal was torn by conflict in 2004. Maoist guerrillas fought to abolish the monarchy, and demonstrators demanded free and fair elections for a new parliament to replace one dissolved by King Gyanendra Bir Bikram Shah Dev in October 2002.

The eight-year-long Maoist insurgency had resulted in the loss of roughly 10,000 lives by late 2004. On March 20, rebels attacked the western town of Beni, with more than 150 deaths reported.

The Maoists announced in August a blockade of the capital, Kathmandu. The blockade, which involved roadblocks, sparked protest demonstrations and led to some violence. The rebels lifted the blockade after a week, but their threats forced some private companies to close indefinitely. On September 24, rebels rejected a government call to resume peace talks that the rebels had broken off in August 2003. In November 2004, a clash between Maoists and army troops left around 30 people dead.

Demonstrations by the five-party opposition alliance that opposed the king's rule surged through Kathmandu repeatedly, defying bans on protests. In April 2004, they called for King Gyanendra to observe a 1990 constitutional settlement that limited the power of the monarchy. The king promised elections by March 2005, but protests continued.   ■ Henry S. Bradsher

See also **Asia.**

Riot police charge supporters of a demonstration against King Gyanendra in Kathmandu, Nepal, on April 4. About 30,000 demonstrators demanded that the king allow a democratic government. King Gyanendra promised elections by March 2005.

The royal hearse carries the remains of former Dutch Queen Juliana past crowds of mourners in Delft on March 30, 2004. Juliana, who died at the age of 94, reigned from 1948 to 1980.

Netherlands continued to struggle with economic difficulties in 2004, despite recovering from the country's worst recession in 20 years. While the Netherlands benefited from a European-wide upturn in activity in 2004, the recovery was weak, with unemployment rising to 4.6 percent in 2004 from 3.8 percent in 2003. European Union (EU) economists forecast that Dutch economic output would grow by 1.4 percent in 2004, compared with a decline of 0.9 percent in 2003.

Budget protests. The government of Prime Minister Jan Peter Balkenende adopted austerity measures in 2004 to reduce the budget deficit. The measures, announced in May and September and totaling nearly $2.9 billion, included the elimination of benefits for workers retiring early, the tightening of eligibility requirements for unemployment benefits, and several tax increases. The government also indicated it would seek to raise the retirement age to 66 or 67, from 65, and lengthen the average working week from 36 hours to 40 hours. The deficit in 2004 was expected to be 2.9 percent of *gross domestic product* (GDP—the total value of goods and services produced in a country in a year).

The cutbacks sparked demonstrations across the Netherlands. An estimated 200,000 people attended a rally in Amsterdam on October 2 to protest the cutbacks. Strikes by unions shut down the port of Rotterdam and brought trains and buses to a halt across the country on October 14.

Muslim tensions. The murder of a controversial Dutch film director inflamed tensions with the country's Muslim population. Theo van Gogh was shot and stabbed to death on an Amsterdam street on November 2. The director, a distant relative of artist Vincent van Gogh, had made a film for Dutch television criticizing the treatment of women under Islam. A man with dual Dutch and Moroccan citizenship was arrested and charged with the murder, as well as with several terrorism-related counts. The man's six associates were also charged.

Former Queen Juliana, who reigned from 1948 until her abdication in favor of her daughter, Queen Beatrix, in 1980, died on March 20, 2004, at the age of 94. Juliana presided over the reconstruction of the Netherlands after World War II (1939-1945) and the dismantling of the Dutch empire shortly thereafter. Her husband, Prince Bernhard, died on Dec. 1, 2004. ■ Tom Buerkle

See also **Deaths; Europe.**

Nevada. See State government.
New Brunswick. See Canadian provinces.
New Hampshire. See State government.
New Jersey. See State government.
New Mexico. See State government.
New York. See State government.

New York City. More than 50,000 conventioneers converged on Manhattan for the Aug. 30, 2004, opening of the Republican National Convention, the party's first-ever gathering in historically Democratic New York City. While the convention at Madison Square Garden closely followed a scripted schedule right up to President George W. Bush's acceptance speech on September 2, tens of thousands of demonstrators filled nearby streets in a series of largely orderly protests against the Iraq War.

New York City police arrested and detained nearly 1,800 protestors, but most were released without being charged. Prosecutors later dismissed charges brought against 227 protestors. Civil libertarians contended that police strategy was simply to detain protestors until after President Bush left the Garden.

The tourist bureau estimated that the four-day convention generated $282 million in revenues for city businesses. Critics complained that the delegates actually spent little money and discouraged tourists from coming into the city.

Sports venues. Proposals for three new sports stadiums in New York City boroughs stirred controversy during 2004. The proposals concerned venues for the New York Jets football team; the New Jersey Nets basketball team; and the New York Yankees baseball team.

A plan to build a new stadium for the Jets on Manhattan's West Side turned into a personal battle between James Dolan, head of New York City-based telecommunications giant Cablevision Systems Corp., and New York City Mayor Michael R. Bloomberg. In March, the mayor un-

The *Queen Mary 2* (QM2), the world's largest ocean liner, embarks on its return voyage to Southampton, England, on April 25, after arriving in New York City on its maiden voyage on April 22. The QM2 offered regular transatlantic service between the United Kingdom and the United States, with 12 crossings in 2004 and 26 scheduled for 2005.

veiled his plan to bring the Jets back to New York City from their New Jersey venue. Bloomberg also championed the plan as a way to attract the 2012 Olympics to New York City. The mayor's plan included expanding the adjacent Jacob Javits Convention Center, extending a subway line to the site, and building commercial and residential buildings in the area as a stimulus to private development. The Jets were to contribute $800 million and the city and state $600 million of the $1.4-billion total cost.

Dolan spearheaded a television and radio advertising blitz against the plan, claiming that supporters had exaggerated its benefits and that the project would end up costing the city too much. Stadium proponents accused Dolan of fighting the plan because the stadium would compete for lucrative events with Madison Square Garden, which Cablevision owns. Bloomberg allies voiced hopes that construction on the stadium could begin in mid-2005.

On Aug. 11, 2004, developer Bruce C. Ratner won approval from the National Basketball Association Board of Governors for the $300-million purchase of the New Jersey Nets. The purchase was part of a long-range plan to move the Nets to a new Brooklyn arena to be designed by world-famous architect Frank Gehry. Since the Dodgers baseball team moved to Los Angeles in 1957, Brooklyn has been without a Major League franchise.

Bronx Borough President Adolfo Carrion, Jr., unveiled a proposal on Oct. 19, 2004, for a new Yankee Stadium, home of the New York Yankees baseball team. The $700-million plan called for a new ballpark in the Bronx to be built across the street from the 1923 stadium currently used by the Yankees. Yankees watchers speculated whether team owner George Steinbrenner would sign onto the plan or offer an alternate proposal for the stadium.

The Museum of Modern Art, known as MoMA, reopened its enlarged and renovated midtown Manhattan museum on Nov. 20, 2004, ending a temporary, two-year exile in Queens. The museum expansion, one of the largest projects ever undertaken by a cultural institution, cost $858 million, including costs of relocating the museum in 2002 and bringing it home in 2004.

Movie studio. On September 28, comedian Mel Brooks opened Steiner Studios, the largest movie studio on the East Coast, at the site of the former Brooklyn Navy Yard. Brooks gave New York state credit for making incentives available to attract filmmakers to its premier city. Filmmakers produced nearly 200 films in New York City in 2003. ■ Owen Moritz

See also **Architecture; Art; Republican Party.**

New Zealand. The indigenous Maori people continued in 2004 to confront the New Zealand government with a claim to ownership of New Zealand's foreshore and seabed—that is, the country's shorelines and the seabeds of its territorial ocean waters. To secure the government's sovereignty over these resources, Parliament in November 2004 passed the landmark Foreshore and Seabed Bill, which Prime Minister Helen Clark's Labour government had sponsored in response to a 2003 court ruling.

In June 2003, the New Zealand Court of Appeal ruled that Maoris could press land claims based on their assertion that Maori ancestors had not relinquished rights to the foreshore and seabed when they signed the Treaty of Waitangi in 1840. That treaty, regarded as New Zealand's founding document, defined legal relationships between European settlers and Maori peoples.

Debate over the Foreshore and Seabed Bill dominated political life in New Zealand for much of 2004. Maori leaders condemned the bill, and in April, 20,000 Maoris massed in Wellington, the capital, for a protest march. A key Maori government official, Associate Maori Affairs Minister Turiana Turia, resigned in May and founded the Maori Party. On the other side of the political divide, Don Brash, leader of the opposition National Party, decried "special treatment" for Maori and proposed abolishing the seven set-aside seats for Maori in Parliament.

New Zealand's new Supreme Court convened for the first time on July 1, amid controversy. While the court replaces England's Privy Council as New Zealanders' court of last appeal, the judges are not empowered to review legislation, as do Supreme Court justices in the United States, for example. Chief Justice Dame Sian Elias expressed concern that the relationship between the Supreme Court and New Zealand's government was imprecise and that judicial independence might be threatened. In November, Prime Minister Clark set up a parliamentary committee to consider these and other constitutional issues.

Economy. In 2004, New Zealand recorded one of the lowest unemployment rates in the developed world—3.8 percent—reflecting a strong domestic economy. In the first half of 2004, the economy grew by 4.4 percent, and economists predicted an annual growth rate of 5 percent into 2005.

Gay rights. In December 2004, the New Zealand Parliament passed a law that allows gay and Lesbian couples to enter into civil unions that confer the same legal rights as marriage. ■ Gavin Ellis

See also **Pacific Islands.**

Newfoundland. See **Canadian provinces.**

Selected news from 2004:

Super-sized donation. The Salvation Army, an international Christian religious and charitable organization headquartered in London, announced in January that Joan Kroc, widow of the founder of the McDonald's restaurant chain, had bequeathed $1.5 billion to the organization. It was the largest gift ever given to a charity. The Salvation Army earmarked the donation for the construction and operation of more than 25 community centers across the United States.

Gone in a flash. One of the largest manufacturers of photographic equipment announced in January that the company would stop selling film cameras in several countries. Officials at Eastman Kodak Company, headquartered in Rochester, New York, said that the company would phase out sales of reloadable film-based cameras in the United States, Canada, and Europe by 2005. The company planned to continue selling traditional rolls of film and disposable single-use cameras but claimed that digital cameras, which store images on microchips, had undermined the sales of film cameras.

American businessman George Eastman founded the company in 1880 and marketed the first camera in 1888. In 1900, Kodak introduced the Brownie, an inexpensive camera that made photography affordable for millions of people.

The Eastman Kodak Company planned to continue selling traditional film cameras as well as introduce

Eastman Kodak announced in 2004 that the Rochester, New York-based company was phasing out production of reloadable film-based cameras because of the popularity of the digital camera, such as the Kodak Easyshare LS743 (bottom left). Kodak's inexpensive Brownie (top left) made photography affordable for millions of people throughout the 20th century.

The "Lilies of the Valley" Easter egg, created for Czar Nicholas II in 1898, is displayed in Moscow in May 2004 for the first time since 1917. A Russian businessman purchased nine Faberge eggs in February 2004 and returned them to Russia for public display.

six new camera models in China, Eastern Europe, India, and Latin America, where sales remained strong in 2004.

Imperial treasures. Victor Vekselberg, a Russian businessman, paid an undisclosed sum of money in February 2004 for a collection of nine Faberge eggs and several other pieces of Faberge artwork from the family of publisher Malcolm Forbes, who died in 1990. The items had been slated for auction in April 2004 and were estimated to bring in at least $90 million. Vekselberg planned to return the items to Russia for display.

Peter Carl Faberge, a Russian goldsmith and jeweler, created the elaborately decorated eggs in the late 1800's and early 1900's for the Russian royal family. Among the treasures acquired from the Forbes estate was the "Coronation Egg," which Czar Nicholas II of Russia gave to his wife, Alexandra, in 1897 to commemorate his ascension to the throne, and the "Cuckoo Egg," which the czar presented to his mother in 1900.

Following the Russian Revolution of 1917, in which the Russian people rebelled against Nicholas II, the collection of approximately 50 eggs disappeared. They later appeared for sale in art circles after presumably being smuggled out of Russia or sold to fund the revolution. Nineteen of the eggs had been returned to Russia by 2004. Eight remained unaccounted for. The rest are in museums and private collections.

Deadly duel. In July, descendants of Alexander Hamilton and Aaron Burr commemorated the 200th anniversary of their deadly duel with a reenactment of one of the more fascinating episodes of American history.

On July 11, 1804, Burr, the vice president under President Thomas Jefferson, squared off against Hamilton, the former secretary of the Department of the Treasury and a political opponent of Jefferson. The men faced each other with pistols in Weehawken, New Jersey. Burr fatally wounded Hamilton with one shot. A New Jersey grand jury indicted

The William J. Clinton Presidential Library opened in November in Little Rock, Arkansas. Part of the glass-and-steel structure is cantilevered over the banks of the Arkansas River, playing off the adjacent railroad bridge.

him for murder, but he was never arrested.

More than 1,000 people watched as Antonio Burr, a descendant of Aaron Burr's cousin, and Douglas Hamilton, a fifth-great-grandson of Alexander Hamilton, donned period costumes and faced each other at a site in Weehawken near the Hudson River. Burr fired a replica of the .54-caliber pistol used to wound Hamilton.

"It wasn't something on my top 100 list, but it was nice to meet Antonio Burr," Douglas Hamilton noted. "He seems to be a very nice man, though I'm not sure I'm going to be on his Christmas card list."

Two presidential libraries opened to the public in 2004. The Abraham Lincoln Presidential Library opened on October 14 in Springfield, Illinois. The three-story facility, which also houses the Illinois State Historical Society, contains 47,000 artifacts related to Lincoln, 1,500 manuscripts written by the former president, and more than 200 personal and family items. The library's goal is to make the artifacts more easily available to researchers and scholars.

The William J. Clinton Presidential Library opened in Little Rock, Arkansas, on November 18. President George W. Bush joined former President Clinton and former Presidents Jimmy Carter and George H. W. Bush at the dedication.

The library's collection features nearly 2 million photographs, 80 million pages of paper documents, and 75,000 artifacts, including a collection of saxophones

belonging to former President Clinton.

Exhibits at the library and presidential center delve into the Clinton presidency, including his impeachment and a brief mention of his acknowledged relationship with a former intern.

Dogs get their day. The Congregation of Canons of the Great Saint Bernard in Geneva, Switzerland, announced plans in October 2004 to sell their St. Bernard dogs. The large dogs became famous for rescuing lost travelers over hundreds of years, but the five monks who operate St. Bernard's Hospice in the Swiss Alps said that the 18 adult dogs and 16 pups had become too costly and time-consuming to maintain. The monks wanted to sell the dogs in order to devote more time to needy people.

A group of monks developed the dogs in the 1600's. At the time, many people traveled in the Alps on foot, and some became lost or buried in sudden snowdrifts and snowstorms. The St. Bernard was trained to use its keen sense of smell to find lost travelers and call for help by barking.

Madison, Wisconsin-based Schwinn reintroduced a limited number of Sting-Ray bicycles (below, right) in June 2004. The bicycle's unique design was based upon the original Sting-Ray (below, left), which was all the rage in the 1960's and 1970's.

The dogs saved approximately 2,000 travelers since the 1800's on the Saint Bernard Pass, located in the Alps between the borders of Switzerland and Italy. The dogs have not been used on a rescue mission since 1975 and had not actually rescued a traveler since the 1950's. However, they remained a popular tourist attraction.

The monks planned to sell their dogs, which each eat up to 4 pounds (1.8 kilograms) of meat a day, to associations rather than individual owners. Buyers will be required to return the dogs to the monks' care during the summer to satisfy the tourist trade.

Bartman ball. In February 2004, the owners of Harry Caray's Restaurant in Chicago, a popular watering hole named for the late sports announcer, used electrically triggered explosives to exorcise a supposed curse on the Chicago Cubs. As part of a publicity stunt to raise money for juvenile diabetes research, the owners arranged to publicly destroy the "Bartman ball," a baseball some fans blamed for derailing the Cubs' run at the 2003 World Series. The restaurant owners paid $113,824.16 for the baseball during an auction in 2003.

The Cubs last won a World Series in 1908 and have not played in one since 1945. According to legend, a bar owner cursed the team after he and his goat were denied entry to the 1945 World Series at Wrigley Field in Chicago.

In 2003, the Cubs were leading by three runs and were five outs away during Game 6 of the National League Championship Series (NLCS) at Wrigley Field when a fan, Steve Bartman, grabbed at a foul ball that likely would have been caught for an out. The Cubs lost momentum and later lost the NLCS to the Florida Marlins.

Auctions. Popular culture memorabilia commanded high prices at several different auctions in 2004.

A Fender Stratocaster guitar used from 1970 to the mid-1980's by rock guitarist Eric Clapton sold for a record $959,500 at an auction in June 2004. Clapton made the guitar, nicknamed Blackie, from a number of different Stratocasters he owned.

More than 700 items belonging to Johnny Cash, one of popular music's most influential figures, and his wife, singer June Carter Cash, brought in more than $3.9 million at an auction in September. Both Cash and his wife died in 2003. Fans paid $27,600 for one of Cash's signature black fringed coats; $78,000 for one of his elaborately carved wooden canes; $131,200 for a guitar inlaid with abalone; and $187,200 for his 1986 Grammy Award.

In December 2004, an anonymous sports memorabilia collector paid $1.26 million for the baseball bat with which Babe Ruth slammed the first home run at Yankee Stadium in New York City on April 18, 1923. Ruth had autographed and donated the bat to a newspaper contest as the top prize for a high school home-run hitting contest. The boy who won that contest had kept the bat for nearly 80 years. ■ Tim Frystak

Popular music items commanded high prices at auctions in 2004. Items used by singer Johnny Cash (top left), including an acoustic guitar and a long black coat, sold for more than $3.9 million at an auction in September. Guitarist Eric Clapton (left) plays Blackie, a Stratocaster guitar that he had used for more than 15 years. Blackie sold for $959,500 at an auction in June.

Newspaper circulation scandals surfaced in June 2004 when executives at the *Chicago Sun-Times* revealed the newspaper had overstated its sales to the Audit Bureau of Circulations (ABC), an industry trade group in Schaumburg, Illinois. *Sun-Times* officials said on October 5 that its actual daily circulation was about 50,000 copies fewer than the circulation of about 487,000 copies it had claimed.

On June 17, the Chicago-based Tribune Company announced that it had overstated the circulation of its two New York daily newspapers, *Newsday* and the Spanish-language *Hoy*. An internal investigation concluded on September 10 that *Newsday*'s weekday circulation was 17 percent lower than the 579,729 copies reported to ABC. Tribune officials said *Hoy*'s daily circulation was at least 50 percent lower than the 92,604 copies reported to ABC.

Officials with the Belo Corporation on August 5 also said that *The Dallas Morning News* had overstated its circulation by 5 percent on Sundays and 1.5 percent on weekdays.

Officials at all the newspapers said they would set aside money to compensate advertisers who may have overpaid for advertisements based on the false circulation figures. Tribune officials announced that the company would set aside between $80 million and $95 million to compensate advertisers who may have overpaid for advertisements based on the false circulation figures. *Chicago Sun-Times* executives said $27 million had been set aside. *Morning News* officials said $23 million would be paid.

A financial scandal worsened in 2004 at Hollinger International Inc., owner of the *Chicago Sun-Times* and other newspapers. In 2003, the company's chief executive, Conrad Black, resigned along with several other executives after Hollinger officials said the group had received more than $15.6 million in unauthorized payments. On August 30, a committee comprised of members of the company's board of directors accused Black and others of "looting" Hollinger of $400 million, the equivalent of 95 percent of its profits from 1997 to 2003. Black said in September 2004 that the report was "laced with outright lies."

Attorneys representing Hollinger International filed a lawsuit against Black and others in October, demanding $542 million in compensation and damages for the alleged unauthorized payments. On November 2, Black resigned as chairman and chief executive of the holding company that controls Hollinger International, but he remained its controlling shareholder with a 68-percent voting stake in the publishing company.

■ Mark Fitzgerald

See also **Radio; Telecommunications.**

Nicaragua. Nicaragua's comptroller's office recommended in October 2004 that the National Assembly impeach President Enrique Bolanos Geyer for his refusal to disclose the sources of funding for his 2001 election victory. President Bolanos responded by accusing opposition leaders, who had an 8-to-1 majority in the National Assembly, of plotting a *coup* (overthrow) to force him from office.

The Organization of American States (OAS), a regional body headquartered in Washington, D.C., dispatched a delegation to Nicaragua in October 2004 to try to resolve the political crisis. The OAS sought to mediate a solution short of a lengthy impeachment process. President Bolanos worked with the OAS to plan a national dialogue that included all parties in Nicaragua.

In September, the United States Department of State joined Italy, the Netherlands, and Spain to express concern over the failure of Nicaragua's National Assembly to pass legislation eliminating Bolanos's opponents' stranglehold over the country's judicial system. The State Department accused the Nicaraguan courts of being corrupt and politically influenced. Bolanos had denounced several court rulings as "harmful" to the cause of justice. ■ Nathan A. Haverstock

See also **Latin America.**

Niger. See Africa.

Nigeria. On May 2, 2004, an ethnic Tarok Christian militia stormed Yelwa, a predominantly Muslim community in central Nigeria, killing 630 villagers, according to Red Cross workers. Weeks later, a Muslim Fulani militia raided Tarok towns, killing hundreds of Christians.

The violence was the latest in a series of ethnic and religious clashes that have plagued northern and central Nigeria in recent years, raising fears of widespread bloodshed between Christians and Muslims. Northern Nigeria has a largely Muslim population, while the south is mainly Christian. Migration of northern-based Fulani and Hausa people into central Nigeria has heightened ethnic and religious tensions.

Emergency declared. On May 18, President Olusegun Obasanjo declared a state of emergency in Plateau, the central Nigerian state where the Yelwa massacre occurred. The emergency measure involved suspending the civilian government and appointing a military governor. The action marked the first time that Obasanjo, a former military ruler, had invoked emergency powers as president. Nigerians had elected Obasanjo in 1999, re-establishing a civilian executive after years of military dictatorship.

Nuclear ambitions. In March 2004, an announcement issued by the Nigerian defense ministry—and an abruptly issued correction—

A boy tries to remove a damaged motorcycle from the front of a burned-out building in Kano, Nigeria, following riots in the city on May 12, 2004. Mobs of Muslim youth instigated the riots by attacking Christian residents. They were acting to avenge earlier attacks by armed Christian bands on Muslims.

raised suspicions in international circles about Nigeria's nuclear ambitions. After a meeting between Nigerian and Pakistani officials in Abuja, Nigeria's capital, the Nigerian defense ministry issued a statement saying, in part, that the Pakistani officials had outlined ways to help Nigeria "acquire nuclear power." However, the next day, a spokesperson from Nigeria's defense ministry said that the statement contained a "typographical error" and that nuclear weapons had not been discussed. Two months earlier, Nigerian officials had raised international hackles by discussing with a high-ranking North Korean official the possibility of purchasing ballistic missiles from North Korea.

Oil tanker disappears. Nigerian officials admitted to a "national embarrassment" in September, after a Russian tanker with 30,000 barrels of oil vanished from the Nigerian navy's custody. The vessel had been seized in Nigerian territorial waters in 2003 on suspicion of oil smuggling. Nigeria is Africa's largest oil producer, earning over 90 percent of its hard currency from daily exports of 2 million barrels.

Delta violence. According to human rights observers, more than 500 people were killed in September 2004 as rival militias, vying for control of illegal oil smuggling operations, clashed with government troops in the oil-rich Niger Delta. Some of the militia members claimed to be fighting for the right of the Ijaw people, the Delta's largest ethnic group, to exercise control over oil revenues.   ■ Simon Baynham

See also **Africa.**

Nobel prizes in literature, peace, the sciences, and economics were awarded in October 2004 by the Norwegian Storting (parliament) in Oslo and by the Royal Swedish Academy of Sciences, the Karolinska Institute, and the Swedish Academy of Literature, all in Stockholm. Each prize was worth about $1.3 million.

The 2004 Nobel Prize in literature went to Austrian novelist and playwright Elfriede Jelinek, widely known in the German-speaking world for grim, unconventional works condemning the oppression of women and right-wing extremism. Jelinek first won literary acclaim with her 1975 novel *Women as Lovers*. Her other works include *Wonderful, Wonderful Times* (1980), *The Piano Teacher* (1983), and *Lust* (1989). Jelinek's plays include *Bambiland* (2003), a highly critical look at United States actions in Iraq.

The 2004 Nobel Peace Prize was awarded to Wangari Maathai, a Kenyan environmentalist and political advocate for women's rights and democracy in her native country. She is the first African woman to win the peace prize.

In 1977, Maathai founded the Green Belt Movement, a grass-roots organization dedicated to environmental conservation and community development. The group is best known for its program of having helped poor women in Kenya plant at least 20 million trees to prevent soil erosion and provide fuel for cooking fires. In announcing her award, the Nobel Committee noted that, "Peace on earth depends on our ability to secure our living environment."

The 2004 Nobel Prize in physiology or medicine was awarded to medical researcher Richard Axel of Columbia University in New York City and immunologist Linda B. Buck of the Fred Hutchinson Cancer Research Center and the University of Washington, both in Seattle. The two scientists were honored for solving the mystery of how human beings can distinguish and remember about 10,000 different odors.

In a pioneering study published in 1991, Axel and Buck identified a family of genes responsible for receptor proteins found on olfactory nerve cells. In later independent research, the scientists identified about 1,000 olfactory genes, about 350 of which are found in people. They also discovered that each olfactory nerve has only one type of receptor and that the molecules in a specific odor attach to a particular combination of receptors. These interactions cause the nerve cells to signal the brain, which combines the signals to identify an odor by its characteristic signature.

The 2004 Nobel Prize in economic science went to Edward C. Prescott of Arizona State University in Tempe and the Federal Reserve Bank of Minneapolis and to Norwegian-born Finn E. Kyd-

land of Carnegie Mellon University in Pittsburgh, Pennsylvania, and the University of California, Santa Barbara (UCSB). The two economists won for important contributions to macroeconomics, the study of an economy as a whole.

A major part of Prescott and Kydland's research examined the effects of government policies on national economies. Their research indicated that governments are more effective at promoting economic stability if they follow consistent, long-term policies, even at the expense of short-term problems for some parts of an economy. Prescott and Kydland also challenged economists' traditional focus on demand, especially consumer demand, with their explorations of how technological developments and changes in supply, such as shortages, act as driving forces in business cycles.

The 2004 Nobel Prize in chemistry was awarded to cancer researcher Irwin A. Rose of the University of California, Irvine, and Israeli biochemists Aaron Ciechanover and Avram Hershko of the Technion-Israel Institute of Technology in Haifa. They were recognized for their discovery of the way cells break down damaged or unneeded proteins.

Rose, Ciechanover, and Hershko found that proteins marked for destruction are tagged with a molecular label that the scientists named ubiquitin because it is found in every tissue of nearly every organism. The tagged proteins are then carried to the cells' waste disposal areas to be destroyed. Just before the doomed cells enter a disposal area, the ubiquitin molecule is detached for reuse. A breakdown in this process may result in such diseases as cystic fibrosis or cervical cancer.

The 2004 Nobel Prize in physics went to David J. Gross of UCSB; H. David Politzer of the California Institute of Technology in Pasadena; and Frank Wilczek of the Massachusetts Institute of Technology in Cambridge. The three physicists were honored for their independent discoveries of a phenomenon that explains the strong force, one of the four fundamental forces of nature. The strong force binds together elementary particles called quarks that scientists believe make up the protons and neutrons in an atom's nucleus.

The scientists discovered that the strong force varies according to the distance between quarks, becoming stronger when quarks move apart and weaker when they move closer together. This finding has enabled physicists to predict the types of subatomic particles emitted in high-energy collisions. ■ Barbara A. Mayes

See also **Deaths; Literature, World; People in the news** (Wangari Maathai).

North Carolina. See **State government.**
North Dakota. See **State government.**

Northern Ireland. During 2004, leaders from all sides attempted to restart the Northern Ireland Assembly. The power-sharing government had been suspended in 2002 and replaced by direct rule from London.

Northern Ireland, a province of the United Kingdom (U.K.), has been torn since 1969 by violence between the Protestant majority, who want to remain united with the U.K., and the minority Roman Catholic population, many of whom wish to join the Irish Republic in the south. The Good Friday Agreement of 1998 resulted in peace and the formation of the Northern Ireland Assembly, through which the province was to govern itself and in which all sides would be represented. However, allegations about a spy ring of the Irish Republican Army (IRA—the military wing of the Catholic nationalist Sinn Fein party) and its failure to disarm led to the suspension of the Assembly in October 2002.

In the November 2003 election, moderate parties on both sides—David Trimble's Ulster Unionists (which had previously been the most popular Protestant party) and the Catholic Social Democratic and Labour Party (SDLP)—lost seats to the more extreme parties, Ian Paisley's Democratic Unionist Party (DUP) and the Catholic Sinn Fein. The DUP refused to share power with Sinn Fein, preventing the restoration of devolved rule. The stand-off was reinforced by elections to the European Parliament on June 14, 2004. The DUP increased its share of the vote, and Sinn Fein came in second, winning its first European Parliament seat.

Ulster Unionists. In January, Trimble's rival in the Ulster Unionist Party, Jeffrey Donaldson, defected to the DUP with two colleagues. Because all three men were members of the Northern Ireland Assembly, the move made Paisley's DUP the majority Unionist party with a total of 33 seats.

In March, Trimble was re-elected leader of the Ulster Unionists. Earlier that month, he had withdrawn from peace talks because the IRA had allegedly broken the cease-fire through its involvement in the attempted kidnapping of dissident republican Bobby Tohill in February. Trimble demanded that the U.K. and Irish governments expel Sinn Fein from the talks. U.K. Prime Minister Tony Blair attacked Sinn Fein for violating human rights. In April, the U.K. Northern Ireland Secretary Paul Murphy withheld the government's grant for political expenses to Sinn Fein and the Progressive Unionist Party because of violence by both sides.

Peace talks in Belfast in February and Dublin in May failed to restore devolution. In September, talks hosted by the U.K. and Irish governments were held at Leeds Castle in Kent in England in an attempt to make Paisley's DUP cooperate with Sinn Fein. Sinn Fein offered its strongest assurances to date that the IRA would disarm.

However, Paisley expressed doubt that the promises were sincere. He argued for abandoning the power sharing structure at the heart of the Good Friday agreement and returning to majority Unionist rule. The talks ended without agreement.

Cory Report. The British government announced in 2004 that it would begin public inquiries into the possible involvement of U.K. security forces in the murders of Catholic Robert Hamill, Loyalist leader Billy Wright, human rights lawyer Rosemary Nelson, and Catholic lawyer Pat Finucane, which took place between 1989 and 1999. The announcements came as the result of a report in April 2004 by Canadian Judge Peter Cory, who had been appointed by the British and Irish governments to review the cases. Cory uncovered evidence that British security forces knew about possible plans to assassinate Finucane (who had represented a number of leading republicans) but had done nothing to block the killing.

John Hume, the founder and former leader of the SDLP, announced his retirement in 2004. Hume was acknowledged as one of the key figures in the peace process and an architect of the Good Friday agreement. He shared the Nobel Peace Prize in 1998 with David Trimble.   ■ Rohan McWilliam

See also **Ireland; United Kingdom.**

Northwest Territories. See Canadian territories.

Norway enjoyed a resurgent economy in 2004 as a result of the sharp increase in world oil prices. The government forecast that economic output would increase by a little more than 3 percent for the year, compared with just 0.4 percent in 2003.

Labor tensions in the industry caused a brief reduction in oil production, however. Oil industry workers went on strike for eight days in June 2004, shutting down about 12 percent of production. The government halted the strike, which was over better retirement benefits and job security, on June 25 by ordering workers and employers to submit to binding arbitration.

Tax reform. The government launched a tax reform package designed to encourage more Norwegians to work. The changes, announced on October 6 and due to take effect in 2005 and 2006, were to reduce income tax rates while increasing value-added tax and taxes on dividends and capital gains. The net effect of the measures was to reduce overall taxes by $270 million.

Bribery case. Norway's largest company, Statoil, was found guilty of making illegal payments in an attempt to win business contracts in Iran. The country's economic crime investigator ruled in June 2004 that Statoil had violated an antibribery law by paying $15 million to a consultancy controlled by Mehdi Hashemi Rafsanjani, son of the former Iranian President Akbar Hashemi Rafsanjani. The company was fined $2.9 million. Disclosure of the payments forced Statoil's chairman and chief executive to resign in 2003.

Museum heist. Armed robbers stole one of Norway's most famous paintings in a daytime raid on Oslo's Munch Museum on Aug. 22, 2004. The theft of *The Scream,* one of four versions of the painting created by Edvard Munch in 1893, along with a second work sparked debate about the level of security in Norwegian museums. Another version of *The Scream* was stolen from the National Gallery in 1994 but later recovered.

A smoking ban, passed by parliament in May 2003, went into effect in Norway's restaurants and bars on June 1, 2004. The ban was the second in Europe, following a similar move by Ireland in March.

Royal birth. The heir to the Norwegian throne, Crown Prince Haakon, and his wife, Crown Princess Mette-Marit, had a baby girl on January 22. The baby, Ingrid Alexandra, is in line to become Norway's first female head of state in over 600 years. A 1990 constitutional amendment stipulates that the throne passes to the first-born child, regardless of sex. ■ Tom Buerkle

See also **Art; Europe.**

Nova Scotia. See Canadian provinces.

Nuclear energy. See Energy supply.

Nutrition. See Food.

Ocean. More than 100 dolphins were found dead on beaches in the Florida Panhandle in March and April 2004, the largest dolphin die-off in the region since early 2000, when more than 160 dolphins were found dead. Between 10 and 20 dolphins die along the Florida Panhandle in an average year.

Biologists with the National Oceanic and Atmospheric Administration (NOAA) in Washington, D.C., tested body tissues from some of the dolphin carcasses. The NOAA scientists found the presence of a dangerous *toxin* (poison) produced during a red tide that likely killed the dolphins. A red tide is a sudden surge in the populations of one-celled organisms called dinoflagellates. Large numbers of the organisms turn waters chocolate brown or red.

The dinoflagellates in red tides produce various chemicals that are poisonous to some living organisms, including human beings. Some fish, however, can feed on the dinoflagellates and accumulate toxins without becoming sick. When birds and mammals, such as dolphins, eat the contaminated fish they become ill and die.

Ocean commission report. The 16-member United States Commission on Ocean Policy urged the overhaul of U.S. ocean policies to reverse decades of destructive overfishing and pollution. The findings were part of a preliminary report

released in April 2004. The commission's recommendations were presented in a report to the nation's 50 governors, a first step in a review process that was to involve President George W. Bush and the U.S. Congress.

The preliminary report included nearly 200 specific recommendations for action by the Bush administration, Congress, and state governments. The commission's recommendations included a plan to streamline the activities of the various state and federal agencies that manage ocean resources and to increase funding of ocean and marine science. Funding for new ocean programs would come from royalties on offshore drilling profits earned by oil and gas companies. A final report was expected in early 2005.

Largest no-fishing zone. On July 1, 2004, commercial and recreational fishing became illegal in about one-third of the Great Barrier Reef Marine Park in Queensland, Australia, creating the largest no-fishing zone in the world. The Great Barrier Reef is the world's largest system of coral reefs. It is made up of more than 2,000 individual reefs that extend about 1,240 miles (2,000 kilometers). The park that surrounds the reefs encompasses about 128,960 square miles (334,000 square kilometers).

Two-thirds of the park was closed to a destructive form of fishing known as bottom trawling, in which weighted nets are dragged along the seabed. The practice can rip apart *ecosystems* (the biological and physical environments of an area) that take hundreds of years to grow.

The Australian Parliament passed the ban to protect coral reefs, sea grass beds, and sponge gardens in the park, to preserve the value of ecotourism, and to sustain fishing in the region.

Australian fishing crews criticized the legislation, claiming the no-take zone would decrease their profits. Biologists argued that setting aside key habitats would prevent fishery collapses in the future by protecting large sexually mature fishes and their breeding areas.

Deadly tsunamis. Walls of water reported to be as high as 40 feet (14 meters) crashed into several Asian and African countries along the Indian Ocean on December 26. The tsunamis were the result of a 9.0-magnitude earthquake about 100 miles (160 kilometers) off the northern coast of the Indonesian island of Sumatra. Scientists said that some of ths tsunamis reached as far as 3,000 miles (5,000 kilometers) from the quake's epicenter, with the waves washing more than a ½ mile (1 kilometer) inland.

■ Christina S. Johnson

Ohio. See State government.

Oklahoma. See State government.

Old age. See Social Security.

THE 2004 OLYMPICS

The Olympic Games returned to Greece with the world's greatest athletes gathered in Athens in August 2004 to compete in the XXVIII Olympiad of the modern era.

ARCHERY

Men's individual
GOLD Marco Galiazzo, Italy
SILVER Hiroshi Yamamoto, Japan
BRONZE Tim Cuddihy, Australia

Men's team
GOLD South Korea
SILVER Taiwan
BRONZE Ukraine

Women's individual
GOLD Park Sung Hyun, South Korea
SILVER Lee Sung Jin, South Korea
BRONZE Alison Williamson, Great Britain

Women's team
GOLD South Korea
SILVER China
BRONZE Taiwan

BADMINTON

Men's singles
GOLD Taufik Hidayat, Indonesia
SILVER Shon Seung Mo, South Korea
BRONZE Soni Dwi Kuncoro, Indonesia

Men's doubles
GOLD Ha Tae Kwon and Kim Dong Moon, South Korea
SILVER Lee Dong Soo and Yoo Yong Sung, South Korea
BRONZE Eng Hian and Flandy Limpele, Indonesia

Women's singles
GOLD Zhang Ning, China
SILVER Mia Audina, Netherlands
BRONZE Zhou Mi, China

Women's doubles
GOLD Yang Wei and Zhang Jiewen, China
SILVER Gao Ling and Huang Sui, China
BRONZE Lee Kyung Won and Ra Kyung Min, South Korea

Mixed doubles
GOLD Zhang Jun and Gao Ling, China
SILVER Nathan Robertson and Gail Emms, Great Britain
BRONZE Jens Eriksen and Mette Schjoldager, Denmark

BASEBALL

GOLD Cuba
SILVER Australia
BRONZE Japan

BASKETBALL

Men
GOLD Argentina
SILVER Italy
BRONZE United States

Women
GOLD United States
SILVER Australia
BRONZE Russia

BEACH VOLLEYBALL

Men
GOLD Emanuel Rego and Ricardo Alex Santos, Brazil
SILVER Javier Bosma and Pablo Herrera, Spain
BRONZE Patrick Heuscher and Stefan Kobel, Switzerland

Women
GOLD Misty May and Kerri Walsh, United States
SILVER Shelda Bede and Adriana Behar, Brazil
BRONZE Holly McPeak and Elaine Youngs, United States

Beach volleyball players Shelda Bede and Adriana Behar, of Brazil (front row), and Misty May, Kerri Walsh, Holly McPeak, and Elaine Youngs, of the United States

BOXING

Light flyweight 106 lbs. (48 kg)
GOLD Yan Bhartelemy Varela, Cuba
SILVER Atagun Yalcinkaya, Turkey
BRONZE Zou Shimming, China, and
Sergey Kazakov, Russia

Flyweight 112 lbs. (51kg)
GOLD Yuriorkis Gamboa Toledano, Cuba
SILVER Jerome Thomas, France
BRONZE Fuad Aslanov, Azerbaijan, and
Rustamhodza Rahimov, Germany

Bantamweight 119 lbs. (54 kg)
GOLD Guillermo Rigondeaux Ortiz, Cuba
SILVER Worapoj Petchkoom, Thailand
BRONZE Aghasi Mammadov, Azerbaijan, and
Bahodirjon Sooltonov, Uzbekistan

Featherweight 126 lbs. (57kg)
GOLD Alexei Tichtchenko, Russia
SILVER Kim Song Guk, North Korea
BRONZE Vitali Tajbert, Germany, and Jo Seok Hwan,
South Korea

Lightweight 132 lbs. (60 kg)
GOLD Mario Cesar Kindelan Mesa, Cuba
SILVER Amir Khan, Great Britain
BRONZE Serik Yeleuov, Kazakhstan, and
Murat Khrachev, Russia

Light Welterweight 141 lbs. (64kg)
GOLD Manus Boonjumnong, Thailand
SILVER Yudel Johnson Cedeno, Cuba
BRONZE Boris Georgiev, Bulgaria, and
Ionut Gheorghe, Romania

Welterweight 152 lbs. (69kg)
GOLD Bakhtiyar Artayev, Kazakhstan
SILVER Lorenzo Aragon Armenteros, Cuba
BRONZE Oleg Saitov, Russia, and Kim Jung Joo,
South Korea

Middle Weight 165 lbs. (75kg)
GOLD Gaydarbek Gaydarbekov, Russia
SILVER Gennadiy Golovkin, Kazakhstan
BRONZE Suriya Prasathinphimai, Thailand, and
Andre Dirrell, United States

Light Heavyweight 179 lbs. (81 kg)
GOLD Andre Ward, United States
SILVER Magomed Aripgadjiev, Belarus
BRONZE Ahmed Ismail, Egypt, and
Utkirbek Haydarov, Uzbekistan

Heavyweight 201 lbs. (91 kg)
GOLD Odlanier Solis Fonte, Cuba
SILVER Viktar Zuyev, Belarus
BRONZE Mohamed Elsayed, Egypt, and
Naser Al Shami, Syria

**Super Heavyweight Over 201 lbs.
(Over 91 kg)**
GOLD Alexander Povetkin, Russia
SILVER Mohamed Aly, Egypt
BRONZE Michel Lopez Nunez, Cuba, and
Roberto Cammarelle, Italy

CANOE-KAYAK

MEN'S
SLALOM RACING
Canoe singles
GOLD Tony Estanguet, France
SILVER Michal Martikan, Slovakia
BRONZE Stefan Pfannmoeller, Germany

Canoe doubles
GOLD Pavol Hochschorner and Peter Hochschorner,
Slovakia
SILVER Marcus Becker and Stefan Henze, Germany
BRONZE Jaroslav Volf and Ondrej Stepanek, Czech Republic

Kayak singles
GOLD Benoit Peschier, France
SILVER Campbell Walsh, Great Britain
BRONZE Fabien Lefevre, France

MEN'S
FLATWATER
500-meter kayak singles
GOLD Adam van Koeverden, Canada
SILVER Nathan Baggaley, Australia
BRONZE Ian Wynne, Great Britain

500-meter canoe singles
GOLD Andreas Dittmer, Germany
SILVER David Cal, Spain
BRONZE Maxim Opalev, Russia

500-meter kayak doubles
GOLD Ronald Rauhe and Tim Wieskoetter, Germany
SILVER Clint Robinson and Nathan Baggaley, Australia
BRONZE Raman Piatrushenka and Vadzim Makhneu, Belarus

500-meter canoe doubles
GOLD Meng Guanliang and Yang Wenjun, China
SILVER Ibrahim Rojas Blanco and Ledis Frank Balceiro
Pajon, Cuba
BRONZE Alexander Kostoglod and Alexander Kovalev,
Russia

1,000-meter kayak singles
GOLD Eirik Veaas Larsen, Norway
SILVER Ben Fouhy, New Zealand
BRONZE Adam van Koeverden, Canada

1,000-meter canoe singles
GOLD David Cal, Spain
SILVER Andreas Dittmer, Germany
BRONZE Attila Vajda, Hungary

1,000-meter kayak doubles
GOLD Markus Oscarsson and Henrik Nilsson, Sweden
SILVER Antonio Rossi and Beniamino Bonomi, Italy
BRONZE Eirik Veraas Larsen and Nils Olav Fjeldheim,
Norway

1,000-meter canoe doubles
GOLD Christian Gille and Tomasz Wylenzek, Germany
SILVER Alexander Kostoglod and Alexander Kovalev,
Russia
BRONZE Gyorgy Kozmann and Gyorgy Kolonics, Hungary

1,000-meter kayak fours
GOLD Hungary
SILVER Germany
BRONZE Slovakia

* World record
** Olympic record

CANOE-KAYAK, CONTINUED

WOMEN'S
SLALOM RACING
Kayak singles
GOLD   Elena Kaliska, Slovakia
SILVER Rebecca Giddens, United States
BRONZE Helen Reeves, Great Britain

WOMEN'S
FLATWATER
500-meter kayak singles
GOLD   Natasa Janics, Hungary
SILVER Josefa Idem, Italy
BRONZE Caroline Brunet, Canada

500-meter kayak doubles
GOLD   Katalin Kovacs and Natasa Janics, Hungary
SILVER Birgit Fischer and Carolin Leonhardt, Germany
BRONZE Aneta Pastuszka and Beata Sokolowska Kulesza, Poland

500-meter kayak fours
GOLD   Germany
SILVER Hungary
BRONZE Ukraine

CYCLING

MEN
ROAD
Men's road race
GOLD   Paolo Bettini, Italy
SILVER Sergio Paulinho, Portugal
BRONZE Axel Merckx, Belgium

Men's individual time trial
GOLD   Tyler Hamilton, United States
SILVER Viatcheslav Ekimov, Russia
BRONZE Bobby Julich, United States

TRACK
Madison sprint
GOLD   Graeme Brown and Stuart O'Grady, Australia
SILVER Franco Marvulli and Bruno Risi, Switzerland
BRONZE Rob Hayles and Bradley Wiggins, Great Britain

Keirin sprint
GOLD   Ryan Bayley, Australia
SILVER Jose Escuredo, Spain
BRONZE Shane Kelly, Australia

Men sprint
GOLD   Ryan Bayley, Australia
SILVER Theo Bos, Netherlands
BRONZE Rene Wolff, Germany

Team sprint
GOLD   Germany
SILVER Japan
BRONZE France

4000-meter individual pursuit
GOLD   Bradley Wiggins, Great Britain **
SILVER Brad McGee, Australia
BRONZE Sergi Escobar, Spain

Team pursuit
GOLD   Australia*
SILVER Great Britain
BRONZE Spain

1-kilometer time trial
GOLD   Chris Hoy, Great Britain**
SILVER Arnaud Tournant, France
BRONZE Stefan Nimke, Germany

Points race
GOLD   Mikhail Ignatyev, Russia
SILVER Joan Llaneras, Spain
BRONZE Guido Fulst, Germany

MOUNTAIN BIKE
Mountain bike
GOLD   Julien Absalon, France
SILVER Jose Antonio Hermida, Spain
BRONZE Bart Brentjens, Netherlands

WOMEN
ROAD
Women's road race
GOLD   Sara Carrigan, Australia
SILVER Judith Arndt, Germany
BRONZE Olga Slyusareva, Russia

Women's individual time trial
GOLD   Leontien Zijlaard-van Moorsel, Netherlands
SILVER Deirdre Demet-Barry, United States
BRONZE Karin Thuerig, Switzerland

TRACK
500-meter time trial
GOLD   Anna Meares, Australia*
SILVER Jiang Yonghua, China
BRONZE Natallia Tsylinskaya, Belarus

Sprint
GOLD   Lori-Ann Muenzer, Canada
SILVER Tamilla Abassova, Russia
BRONZE Anna Meares, Australia

Individual pursuit
GOLD   Sarah Ulmer, New Zealand*
SILVER Kate Mactier, Australia
BRONZE Leontien Zijlaard-van Moorsel, Netherlands

Points race
GOLD   Olga Slyusareva, Russia
SILVER Belem Guerrero Mendez, Mexico
BRONZE Erin Mirabella, United States

MOUNTAIN BIKE
Mountain bike
GOLD   Gunn-Rita Dahle, Norway
SILVER Marie-Helene Premont, Canada
BRONZE Sabine Spitz, Germany

DIVING

Men's 3-meter springboard
GOLD   Peng Bo, China
SILVER Alexandre Despatie, Canada
BRONZE Dmitri Sautin, Russia

Men's 10-meter platform
GOLD   Hu Jia, China
SILVER Mathew Helm, Australia
BRONZE Tian Liang, China

Men's synchronized 3-meter springboard
GOLD   Nikolaos Siranidis and Thomas Bimis, Greece
SILVER Andreas Wels and Tobias Schellenberg, Germany
BRONZE Robert Newbery and Steven Barnett, Australia

* World record
** Olympic record

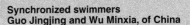
**Synchronized swimmers
Guo Jingjing and Wu Minxia, of China**

**Men's synchronized
10-meter platform**
GOLD	Tian Liang and Yang Jinghui, China
SILVER	Peter Waterfield and Leon Taylor, Great Britain
BRONZE	Mathew Helm and Robert Newbery, Australia

**Women's
3-meter springboard**
GOLD	Guo Jingjing, China
SILVER	Wu Minxia, China
BRONZE	Yulia Pakhalina, Russia

Women's 10-meter platform
GOLD	Chantelle Newbery, Australia
SILVER	Lao Lishi, China
BRONZE	Loudy Tourky, Australia

**Women's synchronized
3-meter springboard**
GOLD	Wu Minxia and Guo Jingjing, China
SILVER	Vera Ilyina and Yulia Pakhalina, Russia
BRONZE	Irina Lashko and Chantelle Newbery, Australia

**Women's synchronized
10-meter platform**
GOLD	Lao Lishi and Li Ting, China
SILVER	Natalia Goncharova and Yulia Koltunova, Russia
BRONZE	Blythe Hartley and Emilie Heymans, Canada

FENCING

INDIVIDUAL EVENTS
Men's epee
GOLD	Marcel Fischer, Switzerland
SILVER	Wang Lei, China
BRONZE	Pavel Kolobkov, Russia

Men's foil
GOLD	Brice Guyart, France
SILVER	Salvatore Sanzo, Italy
BRONZE	Andrea Cassara, Italy

Men's sabre
GOLD	Aldo Montano, Italy
SILVER	Zsolt Nemcsik, Hungary
BRONZE	Vladislav Tretiak, Ukraine

Women's epee
GOLD	Timea Nagy, Hungary
SILVER	Laura Flessel-Colovic, France
BRONZE	Maureen Nisima, France

Women's foil
GOLD	Valentina Vezzali, Italy
SILVER	Giovanna Trillini, Italy
BRONZE	Sylwia Gruchala, Poland

Women's sabre
GOLD	Mariel Zagunis, United States
SILVER	Tan Xue, China
BRONZE	Sada Jacobson, United States

TEAM EVENTS
Men's epee
GOLD	France
SILVER	Hungary
BRONZE	Germany

Men's foil
GOLD	Italy
SILVER	China
BRONZE	Russia

Men's sabre
GOLD	France
SILVER	Italy
BRONZE	Russia

Women's epee
GOLD	Russia
SILVER	Germany
BRONZE	France

EQUESTRIAN

INDIVIDUAL EVENTS
Jumping
GOLD	Cian O'Connor, Ireland
SILVER	Rodrigo Pessoa, Brazil
BRONZE	Chris Kappler, United States

Dressage
GOLD	Anky van Grunsven, Netherlands
SILVER	Ulla Salzgeber, Germany
BRONZE	Beatriz Ferrer Salat, Spain

Eventing
GOLD	Leslie Law, Great Britain
SILVER	Kim Severson, United States
BRONZE	Philippa Funnell, Great Britain

TEAM EVENTS
Jumping
GOLD	Germany
SILVER	United States
BRONZE	Sweden

Dressage
GOLD	Germany
SILVER	Spain
BRONZE	United States

Eventing
GOLD	France
SILVER	Great Britain
BRONZE	United States

FIELD HOCKEY

Men
GOLD	Australia
SILVER	Netherlands
BRONZE	Germany

Women
GOLD	Germany
SILVER	Netherlands
BRONZE	Argentina

GYMNASTICS

MEN
Team
GOLD	Japan
SILVER	United States
BRONZE	Romania

All-around
GOLD	Paul Hamm, United States
SILVER	Kim Dae Eun, South Korea
BRONZE	Yang Tae Young, South Korea

Floor exercise
GOLD	Kyle Shewfelt, Canada
SILVER	Marian Dragulescu, Romania
BRONZE	Jordan Jovtchev, Bulgaria

Pommel horse
GOLD	Teng Haibin, China
SILVER	Marius Daniel Urzica, Romania
BRONZE	Takehiro Kashima, Japan

Rings
GOLD	Dimosthenis Tampakos, Greece
SILVER	Jordan Jovtchev, Bulgaria
BRONZE	Yuri Chechi, Italy

Vault
GOLD	Gervasio Deferr, Spain
SILVER	Evgeni Sapronenko, Latvia
BRONZE	Marian Dragulescu, Romania

Parallel bars
GOLD	Valeri Goncharov, Ukraine
SILVER	Hiroyuki Tomita, Japan
BRONZE	Li Xiaopeng, China

Horizontal bar
GOLD	Igor Cassina, Italy
SILVER	Paul Hamm, United States
BRONZE	Isao Yoneda, Japan

Trampoline
GOLD	Yuri Nikitin, Ukraine
SILVER	Alexander Moskalenko, Russia
BRONZE	Henrik Stehlik, Germany

WOMEN
Team
GOLD	Romania
SILVER	United States
BRONZE	Russia

All-around
GOLD	Carly Patterson, United States
SILVER	Svetlana Khorkina, Russia
BRONZE	Zhang Nan, China

Vault
GOLD	Monica Rosu, Romania
SILVER	Annia Hatch, United States
BRONZE	Anna Pavlova, Russia

Uneven parallel bars
GOLD	Emilie Lepennec, France
SILVER	Terin Humphrey, United States
BRONZE	Courtney Kupets, United States

Balance beam
GOLD	Catalina Ponor, Romania
SILVER	Carly Patterson, United States
BRONZE	Alexandra Georgiana Eremia, Romania

Floor exercise
GOLD	Catalina Ponor, Romania
SILVER	Nicoleta Daniela Sofronie, Romania
BRONZE	Patricia Moreno, Spain

Trampoline
GOLD	Anna Dogonadze, Germany
SILVER	Karen Cockburn, Canada
BRONZE	Huang Shanshan, China

JUDO

MEN
Extra lightweight 132 lbs. (60 kg)
GOLD	Tadahiro Nomura, Japan
SILVER	Nestor Khergiani, Georgia
BRONZE	Tsagaanbaatar Khashbaatar, Mongolia, and Choi Min Ho, South Korea

Half-lightweight 146 lbs. (66 kg)
GOLD	Masato Uchishiba, Japan
SILVER	Jozef Krnac, Slovakia
BRONZE	Georgi Georgiev, Bulgaria, and Yordanis Arencibia Verdecia, Cuba

Lightweight 161 lbs. (73 kg)
GOLD	Lee Won Hee, South Korea
SILVER	Vitaliy Makarov, Russia
BRONZE	Leandro Guilheiro, Brazil, and James Pedro, United States

Half-middleweight 179 lbs. (81 kg)
GOLD	Ilias Iliadis, Greece
SILVER	Roman Gontyuk, Ukraine
BRONZE	Flavio Canto, Brazil, and Dmitri Nossov, Russia

Middleweight 198 lbs. (90 kg)
GOLD	Zurab Zviadauri, Georgia
SILVER	Hiroshi Izumi, Japan
BRONZE	Mark Huizinga, Netherlands, and Khasanbi Taov, Russia

Half-heavyweight 220 lbs. (100 kg)
GOLD	Ihar Makarau, Belarus
SILVER	Jang Sung Ho, South Korea
BRONZE	Michael Jurack, Germany, and Ariel Zeevi, Israel

Heavyweight over 220 lbs. (100 kg)
GOLD	Keiji Suzuki, Japan
SILVER	Tamerlan Tmenov, Russia
BRONZE	Indrek Pertelson, Estonia, and Dennis van Der Geest, Netherlands

MODERN PENTATHLON

MEN
GOLD	Andrey Moiseev, Russia
SILVER	Andrejus Zadneprovskis, Lithuania
BRONZE	Libor Capalini, Czech Republic

WOMEN
GOLD	Zsuzsanna Voros, Hungary
SILVER	Jelena Rublevska, Latvia
BRONZE	Georgina Harland, Great Britain

Gymnast Paul Hamm, of the United States

RHYTHMIC GYMNASTICS

INDIVIDUAL
GOLD	Alina Kabaeva, Russia
SILVER	Irina Tchachina, Russia
BRONZE	Anna Bessonova, Ukraine

TEAM
GOLD	Russia
SILVER	Italy
BRONZE	Bulgaria

WOMEN

Extra lightweight 106 lbs. (48 kg)
- GOLD   Ryoko Tani, Japan
- SILVER   Frederique Jossinet, France
- BRONZE   Feng Gao, China, and Julia Matijass, Germany

Half-lightweight 115 lbs. (52 kg)
- GOLD   Xian Dongmei, China
- SILVER   Yuki Yokosawa, Japan
- BRONZE   Ilse Heylen, Belgium, and Amarilys Savon, Cuba

Lightweight 126 lbs. (57 kg)
- GOLD   Yvonne Boenisch, Germany
- SILVER   Kye Sun Hui, North Korea
- BRONZE   Yurieleidys Lupetey Cobas, Cuba, and Deborah Gravenstijn, Netherlands

Half-middleweight 139 lbs. (63 kg)
- GOLD   Ayumi Tanimoto, Japan
- SILVER   Claudia Heill, Austria
- BRONZE   Driulys Gonzalez Morales, Cuba, and Urska Zolnir, Slovenia

Middleweight 154 lbs. (70 kg)
- GOLD   Masae Ueno, Japan
- SILVER   Edith Bosch, Netherlands
- BRONZE   Qin Dongya, China, and Annett Boehm, Germany

Half-heavyweight 172 lbs. (78 kg)
- GOLD   Noriko Anno, Japan
- SILVER   Liu Xia, China
- BRONZE   Yurisel Laborde, Cuba, and Lucia Morico, Italy

Heavyweight over 172 lbs. (78 kg)
- GOLD   Maki Tsukada, Japan
- SILVER   Dayma Beltran Guisado, Cuba
- BRONZE   Sun Fuming, China, and Tea Donguzashvili, Russia

SAILING

OPEN

49er dinghy sailing
- GOLD   Iker Martinez and Xavier Fernandez, Spain
- SILVER   Rodion Luka and George Leonchuk, Ukraine
- BRONZE   Chris Draper and Simon Hiscocks, Great Britain

Laser
- GOLD   Robert Scheidt, Brazil
- SILVER   Andreas Geritzer, Austria
- BRONZE   Vasilij Zbogar, Slovenia

Tornado
- GOLD   Roman Hagara and Hans Peter Steinacher, Austria
- SILVER   John Lovell and Charlie Ogeltree, United States
- BRONZE   Santiago Lange and Carlos Espinola, Argentina

MEN

Finn
- GOLD   Ben Ainslie, Great Britain
- SILVER   Rafael Trujillo, Spain
- BRONZE   Mateusz Kusznierewicz, Poland

Mistral (boards)
- GOLD   Gal Fridman, Israel
- SILVER   Nikolaos, Kaklamanakis, Greece
- BRONZE   Nick Dempsey, Great Britain

470
- GOLD   Paul Foerster and Kevin Burnham, United States
- SILVER   Nick Rogers and Joe Glanfield, Great Britain
- BRONZE   Kazuto Seki and Kenjiro Todoroki, Japan

ROWING

MEN

Single sculls
- GOLD   Olaf Tufte, Norway
- SILVER   Jueri Jaanson, Estonia
- BRONZE   Ivo Yanakiev, Bulgaria

Double sculls
- GOLD   Sebastien Vieilledent and Adrien Hardy, France
- SILVER   Luka Spik and Iztok Cop, Slovenia
- BRONZE   Rossano Galtarossa and Alessio Sartori, Italy

Lightweight double sculls
- GOLD   Tomasz Kucharski and Robert Sycz, Poland
- SILVER   Frederic Dufour and Pascal Touron, France
- BRONZE   Vasileios Polymeros and Nikolaos Skiathitis, Greece

Quadruple sculls
- GOLD   Russia
- SILVER   Czech Republic
- BRONZE   Ukraine

Pairs
- GOLD   Drew Ginn and James Tomkins, Australia
- SILVER   Sinisa Skelin and Niksa Skelin, Croatia
- BRONZE   Donovan Cech and Ramon di Clemente, South Africa

Fours
- GOLD   Great Britain
- SILVER   Canada
- BRONZE   Italy

Lightweight fours
- GOLD   Denmark
- SILVER   Australia
- BRONZE   Italy

Eights
- GOLD   United States
- SILVER   Netherlands
- BRONZE   Australia

WOMEN

Single sculls
- GOLD   Katrin Rutschow-Stomporowski, Germany
- SILVER   Ekaterina Karsten-Khodotovitch, Belarus
- BRONZE   Rumyana Neykova, Bulgaria

Double sculls
- GOLD   Georgina Evers-Swindell and Caroline Evers-Swindell, New Zealand
- SILVER   Peggy Waleska and Britta Oppelt, Germany
- BRONZE   Sarah Winckless and Elise Laverick, Great Britain

Lightweight double sculls
- GOLD   Constanta Burcica and Angela Alupei, Romania
- SILVER   Daniela Reimer and Claudia Blasberg, Germany
- BRONZE   Kirsten van Der Kolk and Marit van Eupen, Netherlands

Quadruple sculls
- GOLD   Germany
- SILVER   Great Britain
- BRONZE   Australia

Pairs
- GOLD   Georgeta Andrunache-Damian and Viorica Susanu, Romania
- SILVER   Katherine Grainger and Cath Bishop, Great Britain
- BRONZE   Yuliya Bichyk and Natallia Helakh, Belarus

Eights
- GOLD   Romania
- SILVER   United States
- BRONZE   Netherlands

* World record
** Olympic record

SAILING, CONTINUED

Star
GOLD	Torben Grael and Marcelo Ferreira, Brazil
SILVER	Ross Macdonald and Mike Wolfs, Canada
BRONZE	Xavier Rohart and Pascal Rambeau, France

WOMEN
Europe
GOLD	Siren Sundby, Norway
SILVER	Lenka Smidova, Czech Republic
BRONZE	Signe Livbjerg, Denmark

Mistral (boards)
GOLD	Faustine Merret, France
SILVER	Yin Jian, China
BRONZE	Alessandra Sensini, Italy

470
GOLD	Sofia Bekatorou and Aimilia Tsoulfa, Greece
SILVER	Natalia Via Dufresne and Sandra Azon, Spain
BRONZE	Therese Torgersson and Vendela Zachrisson, Sweden

Yngling
GOLD	Great Britain
SILVER	Ukraine
BRONZE	Denmark

SOCCER

MEN
GOLD	Argentina
SILVER	Paraguay
BRONZE	Italy

Women
GOLD	United States
SILVER	Brazil
BRONZE	Germany

SOFTBALL

GOLD	United States
SILVER	Australia
BRONZE	Japan

SHOOTING

RIFLE

Men's 10-meter air
GOLD	Zhu Qinan, China*
SILVER	Li Jie, China
BRONZE	Jozef Gonci, Slovakia

Men's 50-meter prone
GOLD	Matthew Emmons, United States
SILVER	Christian Lusch, Germany
BRONZE	Sergei Martynov, Belarus

Men's 50-meter 3 position
GOLD	Jia Zhanbo, China
SILVER	Michael Anti, United States
BRONZE	Christian Planer, Austria

Men's 10-meter running target
GOLD	Manfred Kurzer, Germany
SILVER	Alexander Blinov, Russia
BRONZE	Dimitri Lykin, Russia

Women's 10-meter air
GOLD	Li Du, China**
SILVER	Lioubov Galkina, Russia
BRONZE	Katerina Kurkova, Czech Republic

Women's 50-meter 3 position
GOLD	Lioubov Galkina, Russia**
SILVER	Valentina Turisini, Italy
BRONZE	Wang Chengyi, China

PISTOL

Men's 10-meter air
GOLD	Wang Yifu, China**
SILVER	Mikhail Nestruev, Russia
BRONZE	Vladimir Isakov, Russia

Men's 50-meter
GOLD	Mikhail Nestruev, Russia
SILVER	Jin Jong Oh, South Korea
BRONZE	Kim Jong Su, North Korea

Men's 25-meter rapid fire
GOLD	Ralf Schumann, Germany
SILVER	Sergei Poliakov, Russia
BRONZE	Sergei Alifirenko, Russia

Women's 10-meter air
GOLD	Olena Kostevych, Ukraine
SILVER	Jasna Sekaric, Serbia and Montenegro
BRONZE	Maria Grozdeva, Bulgaria

Women's 25-meter
GOLD	Maria Grozdeva, Bulgaria**
SILVER	Lenka Hykova, Czech Republic
BRONZE	Irada Ashumova, Azerbaijan

SHOTGUN

Men's trap
GOLD	Alexei Alipov, Russia
SILVER	Giovanni Pellielo, Italy
BRONZE	Adam Vella, Australia

Men's double trap
GOLD	Ahmed Almaktoum, United Arab Emirates
SILVER	Rajyavardhan Singh Rathore, India
BRONZE	Wang Zheng, China

Men's skeet
GOLD	Andrea Benelli, Italy
SILVER	Marko Kemppainen, Finland
BRONZE	Juan Miguel Rodriguez, Cuba

Women's trap
GOLD	Suzanne Balogh, Australia
SILVER	Maria Quintanal, Spain
BRONZE	Lee Bo Na, South Korea

Women's double trap
GOLD	Kimberly Rhode, United States
SILVER	Lee Bo Na, South Korea
BRONZE	Gao E, China

Women's skeet
GOLD	Diana Igaly, Hungary
SILVER	Wei Ning, China
BRONZE	Zemfira Meftakhetdinova, Azerbaijan

Pitcher Jennie Finch, of the United States

* World record
** Olympic record

SWIMMING

MEN

Men's 50-meter freestyle
GOLD	Gary Hall, United States	:21.93
SILVER	Duje Draganja, Crotia	
BRONZE	Roland Mark Schoeman, South Africa	

Men's 100-meter freestyle
GOLD	Pieter van den Hoogenband, Netherlands	:48.17
SILVER	Roland Mark Schoeman, South Africa	
BRONZE	Ian Thorpe, Australia	

Men's 200-meter freestyle
GOLD	Ian Thorpe, Australia	1:44.71**
SILVER	Pieter van den Hoogenband, Netherlands	
BRONZE	Michael Phelps, United States	

Men's 400-meter freestyle
GOLD	Ian Thorpe, Australia	3:43.10
SILVER	Grant Hackett, Australia	
BRONZE	Klete Keller, United States	

Men's 1,500-meter freestyle
GOLD	Grant Hackett, Australia	14:43.40**
SILVER	Larsen Jensen, United States	
BRONZE	David Davies, Great Britain	

Men's 100-meter backstroke
GOLD	Aaron Peirsol, United States	:53.45*
SILVER	Markus Rogan, Austria	
BRONZE	Tomomi Morita, Japan	

Men's 200-meter backstroke
GOLD	Aaron Peirsol, United States	1:54.95**
SILVER	Markus Rogan, Austria	
BRONZE	Razvan Florea, Romania	

Men's 100-meter breaststroke
GOLD	Kosuke Kitajima, Japan	1:00.08
SILVER	Brendan Hansen, United States	
BRONZE	Hugues Duboscq, France	

Men's 200-meter breaststroke
GOLD	Kosuke Kitajima, Japan	2:09.44**
SILVER	Daniel Gyurta, Hungary	
BRONZE	Brendan Hansen, United States	

Men's 100-meter butterfly
GOLD	Michael Phelps, United States	:51.25**
SILVER	Ian Crocker, United States	
BRONZE	Andriy Serdinov, Ukraine	

Men's 200-meter butterfly
GOLD	Michael Phelps, United States	1:54.04**
SILVER	Takashi Yamamoto, Japan	
BRONZE	Stephen Parry, Great Britain	

Men's 200-meter individual medley
GOLD	Michael Phelps, United States	1:57.14**
SILVER	Ryan Lochte, United States	
BRONZE	George Bovell, Trinidad and Tobago	

Men's 400-meter individual medley
GOLD	Michael Phelps, United States	4:08.26*
SILVER	Erik Vendt, United States	
BRONZE	Laszlo Cseh, Hunary	

Men's 4x100-meter freestyle relay
GOLD	South Africa	3:13.17*
SILVER	Netherlands	
BRONZE	United States	

Men's 4x200-meter freestyle relay
GOLD	United States	7:07.33
SILVER	Australia	
BRONZE	Italy	

Men's 4x100-meter medley relay
GOLD	United States	3:30.68*
SILVER	Germany	
BRONZE	Japan	

WOMEN

50-meter freestyle
GOLD	Inge de Bruijn, Netherlands	:24.58
SILVER	Malia Metella, France	
BRONZE	Lisbeth Lenton, Australia	

100-meter freestyle
GOLD	Jodie Henry, Australia	:53.84
SILVER	Inge de Bruijn, Netherlands	
BRONZE	Natalie Coughlin, United States	

200-meter freestyle
GOLD	Camelia Potec, Romania	1:58.03
SILVER	Federica Pellegrini, Italy	
BRONZE	Solenne Figues, France	

400-meter freestyle
GOLD	Laure Manaudou, France	4:05.34
SILVER	Otylia Jedrzejczak, Poland	
BRONZE	Kaitlin Sandeno, United States	

800-meter freestyle
GOLD	Ai Shibata, Japan	8:24.54
SILVER	Laure Manaudou, France	
BRONZE	Diana Munz, United States	

100-meter backstroke
GOLD	Natalie Coughlin, United States	:59.68**
SILVER	Kirsty Coventry, Zimbabwe	
BRONZE	Laure Manaudou, France	

200-meter backstroke
GOLD	Kirsty Coventry, Zimbabwe	2:09.19
SILVER	Stanislava Komarova, Russia	
BRONZE	Reiko Nakamura, Japan, and Antje Buschschulte, Germany	

100-meter breaststroke
GOLD	Luo Xuejuan, China	1:06.64**
SILVER	Brooke Hanson, Australia	
BRONZE	Leisel Jones, Australia	

200-meter breaststroke
GOLD	Amanda Beard, United States	2:23.37**
SILVER	Leisel Jones, Australia	
BRONZE	Anne Poleska, Germany	

100-meter butterfly
GOLD	Petria Thomas, Australia	:57.72
SILVER	Otylia Jedrzejczak, Poland	
BRONZE	Inge de Bruijn, Netherlands	

200-meter butterfly
GOLD	Otylia Jedrzejczak, Poland	2:06.05
SILVER	Petria Thomas, Australia	
BRONZE	Yuko Nakanishi, Japan	

200-meter individual medley
GOLD	Yana Klochkova, Ukraine	2:11.14
SILVER	Amanda Beard, United States	
BRONZE	Kirsty Coventry, Zimbabwe	

400-meter individual medley
GOLD	Yana Klochkova, Ukraine	4:34.83
SILVER	Kaitlin Sandeno, United States	
BRONZE	Georgina Bardach, Argentina	

4x100-meter freestyle relay
GOLD	Australia	3:35.94*
SILVER	United States	
BRONZE	Netherlands	

4x200-meter freestyle relay
GOLD	United States	7:53.42*
SILVER	China	
BRONZE	Germany	

4x100-meter medley relay
GOLD	Australia	3:57.32*
SILVER	United States	
BRONZE	Germany	

SYNCHRONIZED SWIMMING

TEAM
GOLD   Russia
SILVER   Japan
BRONZE   United States

DUET
GOLD   Anastasia Davydova and Anastasia Ermakova, Russia
SILVER   Miya Tachibana and Miho Takeda, Japan
BRONZE   Alison Bartosik and Anna Kozlova, United States

TABLE TENNIS

Men's singles
GOLD   Ryu Seung Min, South Korea
SILVER   Wang Hao, China
BRONZE   Wang Liqin, China

Men's doubles
GOLD   Chen Qi and Ma Lin, China
SILVER   Lai Chak Ko and Ching Li, Hong Kong
BRONZE   Michael Maze and Finn Tugwell, Denmark

Women's singles
GOLD   Zhang Yining, China
SILVER   Kim Hyang Mi, North Korea
BRONZE   Kim Kyung Ah, South Korea

Women's doubles
GOLD   Wang Nan and Zhang Yining, China
SILVER   Lee Eun Sil and Suk Eun Mi, South Korea
BRONZE   Guo Yue and Niu Jianfeng, China

TEAM HANDBALL

MEN
GOLD   Croatia
SILVER   Germany
BRONZE   Russia

WOMEN
GOLD   Denmark
SILVER   South Korea
BRONZE   Ukraine

TENNIS

Men's singles
GOLD   Nicolas Massu, Chile
SILVER   Mardy Fish, United States
BRONZE   Fernando Gonzalez, Chile

Men's doubles
GOLD   Fernando Gonzalez and Nicolas Massu, Chile
SILVER   Nicolas Kiefer and Rainer Schuettler, Germany
BRONZE   Mario Ancic and Ivan Ljubicic, Croatia

Women's singles
GOLD   Justine Henin-Hardenne, Belgium
SILVER   Amelie Mauresmo, France
BRONZE   Alicia Molik, Australia

Women's doubles
GOLD   Li Ting and Sun Tian Tian, China
SILVER   Conchita Martinez and Virginia Ruano Pascual, Spain
BRONZE   Paola Suarez and Patricia Tarabini, Argentina

Runner Meseret Defar, of Ethiopia

TAEKWONDO

MEN'S
Under 128 lbs. (58 kg)
GOLD   Mu Yen Chu, Taiwan
SILVER   Oscar Francisco Salazar Blanco, Mexico
BRONZE   Tamer Bayoumi, Egypt

Under 150 lbs. (68 kg)
GOLD   Hadi Saei Bonehkohal, Iran
SILVER   Chih Hsiung Huang, Taiwan
BRONZE   Song Myeong Seob, South Korea

Under 176 lbs. (80 kg)
GOLD   Steven Lopez, United States
SILVER   Bahri Tanrikulu, Turkey
BRONZE   Yossef Karami, Iran

Over 176 lbs. (80 kg)
GOLD   Moon Dae Sung, South Korea
SILVER   Alexandros Nikolaidis, Greece
BRONZE   Pascal Gentil, France

WOMEN'S
Under 108 lbs. (49 kg)
GOLD   Shih Hsin Chen, Taiwan
SILVER   Yanelis Yuliet Labrada Diaz, Cuba
BRONZE   Yaowapa Boorapolchai, Thailand

Under 126 lbs. (57 kg)
GOLD   Jang Ji Won, South Korea
SILVER   Nia Abdallah, United States
BRONZE   Iridia Salazar Blanco, Mexico

Under 148 lbs. (67 kg)
GOLD   Luo Wei, China
SILVER   Elisavet Mystakidou, Greece
BRONZE   Hwang Kyung Sun, South Korea

Over 148 lbs. (67 kg)
GOLD   Chen Zhong, China
SILVER   Myriam Baverel, France
BRONZE   Adriana Carmona, Venezuela

* World Record
** Olympic Record

TRACK AND FIELD

MEN

100 meters
GOLD	Justin Gatlin, United States	:9.85
SILVER	Francis Obikwelu, Portugal	
BRONZE	Maurice Greene, United States	

200 meters
GOLD	Shawn Crawford, United States	:19.79
SILVER	Bernard Williams, United States	
BRONZE	Justin Gatlin, United States	

400 meters
GOLD	Jeremy Wariner, United States	:44.00
SILVER	Otis Harris, Jr., United States	
BRONZE	Derrick Brew, United States	

800 meters
GOLD	Yuriy Borzakovskiy, Russia	1:44.45
SILVER	Mbulaeni Tongai Mulaudzi, South Africa	
BRONZE	Wilson Kipketer, Denmark	

1,500 meters
GOLD	Hicham El Guerrouj, Morocco	3:34.18
SILVER	Bernard Lagat, Kenya	
BRONZE	Rui Silva, Portugal	

5,000 meters
GOLD	Hicham El Guerrouj, Morocco	13:14.39
SILVER	Kenenisa Bekele, Ethiopia	
BRONZE	Eliud Kipchoge, Kenya	

10,000 meters
GOLD	Kenenisa Bekele, Ethiopia	27:05.10**
SILVER	Sileshi Sihine, Ethiopia	
BRONZE	Zersenay Tadesse, Eritrea	

Marathon
GOLD	Stefano Baldini, Italy	2:10:55
SILVER	Mebrahtom Keflezighi, United States	
BRONZE	Vanderlei Lima, Brazil	

110-meter hurdles
GOLD	Liu Xiang, China	:12.91**
SILVER	Terrence Trammell, United States	
BRONZE	Anier Garcia, Cuba	

400-meter hurdles
GOLD	Felix Sanchez, Dominican Republic	:47.63
SILVER	Danny McFarlane, Jamaica	
Bronze	Naman Keita, France	

3000-meter steeplechase
GOLD	Ezekiel Kemboi, Kenya	8:05.81
SILVER	Brimin Kipruto, Kenya	
BRONZE	Paul Kipsiele Koech, Kenya	

20-kilometer walk
GOLD	Ivano Brugnetti, Italy	1:19:40
SILVER	Francisco Javier Fernandez, Spain	
BRONZE	Nathan Deakes, Australia	

50-kilometer walk
GOLD	Robert Korzeniowski, Poland	3:38:46
SILVER	Denis Nizhegorodov, Russia	
BRONZE	Aleksey Voyevodin, Russia	

4x100-meter relay
GOLD	Great Britain	:38.07
SILVER	United States	
BRONZE	Nigeria	

4x400-meter relay
GOLD	United States	2:55.91
SILVER	Australia	
BRONZE	Nigeria	

High jump
GOLD	Stefan Holm, Sweden	7 ft. 9 in. (2.36 m)
SILVER	Matthew Hemingway, United States	
BRONZE	Jaroslav Baba, Czech Republic	

Pole vault
GOLD	Timothy Mack, United States	19 ft. 6 ¼ in. (5.95 m)**
SILVER	Toby Stevenson, United States	
BRONZE	Giuseppe Gibilisco, Italy	

Long jump
GOLD	Dwight Phillips, United States	28 ft. 2 in. (8.59 m)
SILVER	John Moffitt, United States	
BRONZE	Joan Lino Martinez, Spain	

Triple jump
GOLD	Christian Olsson, Sweden	58 ft. 4 ½ in. (17.79 m)
SILVER	Marian Oprea, Romania	
BRONZE	Danila Burkenya, Russia	

Shot-put
GOLD	Yuriy Bilonog, Ukraine	69 ft. 5 in. (21.16 m)
SILVER	Adam Nelson, United States	
BRONZE	Joachim Olsen, Denmark	

Discus
GOLD	Virgilijus Alekna, Lithuania	229 ft. 3 ½ in. (69.89 m)**
SILVER	Zoltan Kovago, Hungary	
BRONZE	Aleksander Tammert, Estonia	

Hammer
GOLD	Koji Murofushi, Japan	272 ft. (82.91 m)
SILVER	Ivan Tikhon, Belarus	
BRONZE	Esref Apak, Turkey	

Javelin
GOLD	Andreas Thorkildsen, Norway	283 ft. 9 ½ in. (86.50 m)
SILVER	Vadims Vasilevskis, Latvia	
BRONZE	Sergey Makarov, Russia	

Decathlon
GOLD	Roman Sebrle, Czech Republic	8,893 pts.**
SILVER	Bryan Clay, United States	
BRONZE	Dmitriy Karpov, Kazakhstan	

WOMEN

100 meters
GOLD	Yuliya Nesterenko, Belarus	:10.93
SILVER	Lauryn Williams, United States	
BRONZE	Veronica Campbell, Jamaica	

200 meters
GOLD	Veronica Campbell, Jamaica	:22.05
SILVER	Allyson Felix, United States	
BRONZE	Debbie Ferguson, Bahamas	

400 meters
GOLD	Tonique Williams-Darling, Bahamas	:49.41
SILVER	Ana Guevara, Mexico	
BRONZE	Natalya Antyukh, Russia	

800 meters
GOLD	Kelly Holmes, Great Britain	1:56.38
SILVER	Hasna Benhassi, Morocco	
BRONZE	Jolanda Ceplak, Slovenia	

1,500 meters
GOLD	Kelly Holmes, Great Britain	3:57.90
SILVER	Tatyana Tomashova, Russia	
BRONZE	Maria Cioncan, Romania	

5,000 meters
GOLD	Meseret Defar, Ethiopia	14:45.65
SILVER	Isabella Ochichi, Kenya	
BRONZE	Tirunesh Dibaba, Ethiopia	

TRACK AND FIELD, CONTINUED

10,000 meters
GOLD	Xing Huina, China	30:24.36
SILVER	Ejigayehu Dibaba, Ethiopia	
BRONZE	Derartu Tulu, Ethiopia	

Marathon
GOLD	Mizuki Noguchi, Japan	2:26:20
SILVER	Catherine Ndereba, Kenya	
BRONZE	Deena Kastor, United States	

Women 100-meter hurdles
GOLD	Joanna Hayes, United States	:12.37
SILVER	Olena Krasovska, Ukraine	
BRONZE	Melissa Morrison, United States	

Women 400-meter hurdles
GOLD	Fani Halkia, Greece	:52.82
SILVER	Ionela Tirlea-Manolache, Romania	
BRONZE	Tetiana Tereshchuk-Antipova, Ukraine	

20-kilometer walk
GOLD	Athanasia Tsoumeleka, Greece	1:29.12
SILVER	Olimpiada Ivanova, Russia	
BRONZE	Jane Saville, Australia	

4x100-meter relay
GOLD	Jamaica	:41.73
SILVER	Russia	
BRONZE	France	

4x400-meter relay
GOLD	United States	3:19.01
SILVER	Russia	
BRONZE	Jamaica	

High jump
GOLD	Yelena Slesarenko, Russia	6 ft. 9 in. (2.06 m)**
SILVER	Hestrie Cloete, South Africa	
BRONZE	Viktoriya Styopina, Ukraine	

Pole vault
GOLD	Yelena Isinbayeva, Russia	16 ft. 1-1/4 in. (4.91 m)*
SILVER	Svetlana Feofanova, Russia	
BRONZE	Anna Rogowska, Poland	

Long jump
GOLD	Tatyana Lebedeva, Russia	23 ft. 2-1/4 in. (7.07 m)
SILVER	Irina Simagina, Russia	
BRONZE	Tatyana Kotova, Russia	

Triple jump
GOLD	Francoise Mbango Etone, Cameroon	50 ft. 2-1/4 in. (15.30 m)
SILVER	Hrysopiyi Devetzi, Greece	
BRONZE	Tatyana Lebedeva, Russia	

Shot-put
GOLD	Yumileidi Cumba, Cuba	64 ft. 3-1/4 in. (19.59 m)
SILVER	Nadine Kleinert, Germany	
BRONZE	Svetlana Krivelyova, Russia	

Discus
GOLD	Natalya Sadova, Russia	219 ft. 10-1/2 in. (67.02 m)
SILVER	Anastasia Kelesidou, Greece	
BRONZE	Iryna Yatchenko, Belarus	

Hammer
GOLD	Olga Kuzenkova, Russia	246 ft. 1-1/2 in. (75.02 m)
SILVER	Yipsi Moreno, Cuba	
BRONZE	Yunaika Crawford, Cuba	

Javelin
GOLD	Osleidys Menendez, Cuba	234 ft. 8 in. (71.53 m)**
SILVER	Steffi Nerius, Germany	
BRONZE	Mirela Manjani, Greece	

Heptathlon
GOLD	Carolina Kluft, Sweden	6,952 pts.
SILVER	Austra Skujyte, Lithuania	
BRONZE	Kelly Sotherton, Great Britain	

TRIATHLON

Men
GOLD	Hamish Carter, New Zealand	
SILVER	Bevan Docherty New Zealand	
BRONZE	Sven Riederer, Switzerland	

Women
GOLD	Kate Allen, Austria	
SILVER	Loretta Harrop, Australia	
BRONZE	Susan Williams, United States	

VOLLEYBALL

Men		**Women**	
GOLD	Brazil	GOLD	China
SILVER	Italy	SILVER	Russia
BRONZE	Russia	BRONZE	Cuba

WATER POLO

Men's		**Women's**	
GOLD	Hungary	GOLD	Italy
SILVER	Serbia-Montenegro	SILVER	Greece
BRONZE	Russia	BRONZE	United States

WEIGHTLIFTING

MEN

123 lbs. (56 kg)
GOLD	Halil Mutlu, Turkey	650 lbs. (295.0 kg)
SILVER	Wu Meijin, China	
BRONZE	Sedat Artuc, Turkey	

137 lbs. (62 kg)
GOLD	Shi Zhiyong, China	717 lbs. (325.0 kg)
SILVER	Le Maosheng, China	
BRONZE	Israel Jose Rubio Rivero, Venezuela	

152 lbs. (69 kg)
GOLD	Zhang Guozheng, China	766 lbs. (347.5 kg)
SILVER	Lee Bae Young, South Korea	
BRONZE	Nikolay Pechalov, Croatia	

170 lbs. (77 kg)
GOLD	Taner Sagir, Turkey**	827 lbs. (375 kg)
SILVER	Sergey Filimonov, Kazakhstan	
BRONZE	Oleg Perepetchenov, Russia	

187 lbs. (85 kg)
GOLD	George Asanidze, Georgia	843 lbs. (382.5 kg)
SILVER	Andrei Rybakou, Belarus	
BRONZE	Pyrros Dimas, Greece	

207 lbs. (94 kg)
GOLD	Milen Dobrev, Buglaria	898 lbs. (407.5 kg)
SILVER	Khadjimourad Akkaev, Russia	
BRONZE	Alexey Petrov, Russia	

231 lbs. (105 kg)
GOLD	Dmitry Berestov, Russia	937 lbs. (425 kg)
SILVER	Igor Razoronov, Ukraine	
BRONZE	Gleb Pisarevskiy, Russia	

Over 231 lbs. (Over 105 kg)
GOLD	Hossein Reza Zadeh, Iran	1,042 lbs. (472.5 kg)
SILVER	Viktors Scerbatihs, Latvia	
BRONZE	Velichko Cholakov, Bulgaria	

* World record
** Olympic record

Weightlifter Hossein Reza Zadeh, of Iran

WRESTLING

MEN'S FREESTYLE

121 lbs. (55 kg)
GOLD   Mavlet Batirov, Russia
SILVER   Stephen Abas, United States
BRONZE   Chikara Tanabe, Japan

132 lbs. (60 kg)
GOLD   Yandro Miguel Quintana Rivalta, Cuba
SILVER   Masuod Mostafa Jokar, Iran
BRONZE   Kenji Inoue, Japan

146 lbs. (66 kg)
GOLD   Elbrus Tedeyev, Ukraine
SILVER   Jamill Kelly, United States
BRONZE   Makhach Murtazaliev, Russia

163 lbs. (74 kg)
GOLD   Buvaysa Saytiev, Russia
SILVER   Gennadiy Laliyev, Kazakhstan
BRONZE   Ivan Fundora Zaldivar, Cuba

185 lbs. (84 kg)
GOLD   Cael Sanderson, United States
SILVER   Moon Eui Jae, South Korea
BRONZE   Sazhid Sazhidov, Russia

212 lbs. (96 kg)
GOLD   Khadjimourat Gatsalov, Russia
SILVER   Magomed Ibragimov, Uzbekistan
BRONZE   Alireza Heidari, Iran

265 lbs. (120 kg)
GOLD   Artur Taymazov, Uzbekistan
SILVER   Alireza Rezaei, Iran
BRONZE   Aydin Polatci, Turkey

MEN'S GRECO-ROMAN

121 lbs. (55 kg)
GOLD   Istvan Majoros, Hungary
SILVER   Gueidar Mamedaliev, Russia
BRONZE   Artiom Kiouregkian, Greece

132 lbs. (60 kg)
GOLD   Jung Ji Hyun, South Korea
SILVER   Roberto Monzon Gonzalez, Cuba
BRONZE   Armen Nazarian, Bulgaria

146 lbs. (66 kg)
GOLD   Farid Mansurov, Azerbaijan
SILVER   Seref Eroglu, Turkey
BRONZE   Mkkhitar Manukyan, Kazakhstan

163 lbs. (74 kg)
GOLD   Alexandr Dokturishivili, Uzbekistan
SILVER   Marko Yli-Hannuksela, Finland
BRONZE   Varteres Samourgachev, Russia

185 lbs. (84 kg)
GOLD   Alexei Michine, Russia
SILVER   Ara Abrahamian, Sweden
BRONZE   Viachaslau Makaranka, Belarus

212 lbs. (96 kg)
GOLD   Karam Ibrahim, Egypt
SILVER   Ramaz Nozadze, Georgia
BRONZE   Mehmet Ozal, Turkey

265 lbs. (120 kg)
GOLD   Khasan Baroev, Russia
SILVER   Georgiy Tsurtsumia, Kazakhstan
BRONZE   Rulon Gardner, United States

WOMEN'S FREESTYLE

106 lbs. (48 kg)
GOLD   Irini Merleni, Ukraine
SILVER   Chiharu Icho, Japan
BRONZE   Patricia Miranda, United States

121 lbs. (55 kg)
GOLD   Saori Yoshida, Japan
SILVER   Tonya Verbeek, Canada
BRONZE   Anna Gomis, France

139 lbs. (63 kg)
GOLD   Kaori Icho, Japan
SILVER   Sara McMann, United States
BRONZE   Lise Legrand, France

159 lbs. (72 kg)
GOLD   Wang Xu, China
SILVER   Gouzel Maniourova, Russia
BRONZE   Kyoto Hamaguchi, Japan

WOMEN

106 lbs. (48 kg)
GOLD   Nurcan Taylan, Turkey   463 lbs. (210.0 kg)*
SILVER   Zhuo Li, China
BRONZE   Aree Wiratthaworn, Thailand

117 lbs. (53 kg)
GOLD   Udomporn Polsak, Thailand   491 lbs. (222.5 kg)
SILVER   Lisa Raema Rumbewas, Indonesia
BRONZE   Mabel Mosquera, Colombia

128 lbs. (58 kg)
GOLD   Chen Yanqing, China   524 lbs. (237.5 kg)**
SILVER   Ri Song Hui, North Korea
BRONZE   Wandee Kameaim, Thailand

139 lbs. (63 kg)
GOLD   Nataliya Skakun, Ukraine   535 lbs. (242.5 kg)
SILVER   Hanna Batsiushka, Belarus
BRONZE   Tatsiana Stukalava, Belarus

152 lbs. (69 kg)
GOLD   Liu Chunhong, China   606 lbs. (275.0 kg)*
SILVER   Eszter Krutzler, Hungary
BRONZE   Zarema Kasaeva, Russia

165 lbs. (75 kg)
GOLD   Pawina Thongsuk, Thailand   601 lbs. (272.5 kg)
SILVER   Natalia Zabolotnaia, Russia*
BRONZE   Valentina Popova, Russia

Over 165 lbs. (Over 75 kg)
GOLD   Tang Gonghong, China   672 lbs. (305.0 kg)*
SILVER   Jang Mi Ran, South Korea
BRONZE   Agata Wrobel, Poland

Pacific Islands.

The 35th Pacific Islands Forum convened in Apia, Samoa, on Aug. 5, 2004. The Forum was comprised of 14 independent Island nations plus Australia and New Zealand. New Caledonia, French Polynesia, and East Timor attended as official observers. Australia's Prime Minister John Howard made it clear that his nation intended to take a more active role in Island affairs. Australia is the largest single aid donor to Pacific nations.

Solomon Islands. Australia's activism in the region was exemplified by its leadership of the Regional Assistance Mission to the Solomon Islands (RAMSI). RAMSI was designed to restore order to a nation that had been wracked by violence between groups from the islands of Guadalcanal and Malaita, which led to a *coup* (overthrow) in June 2000. RAMSI's first year of successful operation was completed in July 2004. More than 4,000 offenders had been arrested, more than 3,000 weapons were confiscated, and the economy was on the rebound in 2004. The peacekeeping force stationed on the Solomons, which included troops from Fiji, New Zealand, Papua New Guinea, and Tonga, began to withdraw at the end of 2004. About 300 troops will remain in 2005, to lead a reformation of the Royal Solomon Islands Police.

Fiji. An era ended when Ratu Sir Kamisese Mara died on April 18, 2004, at the age of 83. Ratu Mara led Fiji to independence from the United Kingdom in 1970 and remained the dominant political personality in the region for the next three decades.

Mara's later years were clouded by a series of attempted coups, the first of which took place in 1987. The uprisings were designed to maintain the political power of native Fijians against the perceived threat of Indo-Fijians, who were originally brought to the islands from India as indentured laborers.

Palau. Koror, Palau's largest city, hosted the ninth Festival of the Pacific Arts, which was held for 10 days at the end of July.

About 6,000 people attended the festival, including delegates from 34 countries and territories. Arts on display ranged from traditional, such as tattooing with shell and bone tools, to modern, such as cinematography. The festival is held every four years.

Papua New Guinea. The foreign ministers of Papua New Guinea and Australia completed an agreement in August in which Australia will provide Papua New Guinea with $900 million (Australian) over a five-year period to help restore social order. The arrangement includes the deployment of 210 Australian police officers, the first of whom arrived in August. They received training in language and local cultures before being assigned to various parts of the country.

Kiribati, a tiny nation with a population of about 88,000 people, fielded a team of three in the Athens Olympics in September. Only one athlete, a weightlifter, qualified officially, but two runners received wild cards from the International Olympic Committee, allowing them to compete.

Federated States of Micronesia. On April 9, Typhoon Sudal struck Yap State with winds of more than 100 miles (160 kilometers) per hour. Ninety percent of all buildings were damaged or destroyed, and power and water were lost on most of the island. Sadal was the worst storm in Yapese history. By September, only 50 percent of government infrastructure had been restored, and schools had just begun to reopen.

Tonga. Royal Tongan Airlines (RTA) ceased operations in May. In April, the government of Brunei had impounded one of RTA's planes, stranding

A Fijian warrior stands guard as mourners pay their last respects to the late former President Ratu Sir Kamisese Mara on April 29, 2004. Ratu Mara was a major force in Fijian politics from 1970 until his death on April 18.

FACTS IN BRIEF ON PACIFIC ISLAND COUNTRIES

Country	Population	Government	Monetary unit*	Foreign trade (million U.S.$) Exports[†]	Imports[†]
Fiji	881,000	President Josefa Iloilo; Prime Minister Laisenia Qarase	dollar (1.73 = $1)	609	835
Kiribati	88,000	President Anote Tong	Australian dollar (1.38 = $1)	35	83
Marshall Islands	54,000	President Kessai Note	U.S. dollar	9	54
Micronesia, Federated States of	135,000	President Joseph J. Urusemal	U.S. dollar	22	149
Nauru	13,000	President Ludwig Scotty	Australian dollar (1.38 = $1)	18	31
New Zealand	3,890,000	Governor General Dame Silvia Cartwright; Prime Minister Helen Clark	dollar (1.48 = $1)	15,860	16,060
Palau	21,000	President Tommy Remengesau, Jr.	U.S. dollar	18	99
Papua New Guinea	5,606,000	Governor General Sir Paulius Matane; Prime Minister Sir Michael Somare	kina (3.05 = $1)	1,938	967
Samoa	176,000	Head of State Malietoa Tanumafili II; Prime Minister Tuila'epa Sailele Malielegaoi	tala (2.69 = $1)	14	113
Solomon Islands	509,000	Governor General Nathaniel Waena; Prime Minister Sir Allan Kemakeza	dollar (7.27 = $1)	90	100
Tonga	100,000	King Taufa'ahau Tupou IV; Prime Minister Lavaka ata Ulukalala	pa'anga (1.98 = $1)	27	86
Tuvalu	11,000	Governor General Faimalaga Luka; Prime Minister Maatia Toafa	Australian dollar (1.38 = $1)	1	17
Vanuatu	211,000	President Kalkot Matas Kelekele; Prime Minister Serge Vohor	vatu (113.30 = $1)	79	138

*Exchange rates as of Oct. 1, 2004, or latest available data.
[†]Latest available data.

some 500 passengers. Tonga had chartered the plane from Royal Brunei Airlines, and reports indicated that economic mismanagement had left the country unable to pay its bills. RTA had been headed by Prime Minister Lavaka Ata Ulukalala, one of the king of Tonga's sons. Seven of the nine elected commoner members of parliament called for the prince's resignation from the Cabinet. Commoner objections to the business activities of the royal family continued to increase through 2004.

Vanuatu. In August, a team of archaeologists from the Australian National University and the Vanuatu National Museum uncovered 13 headless skeletons, found with pottery that dated back to 1200 B.C. The pottery is of the Lapita type, widespread in the Pacific Islands east of the Solomons. Few human remains had been previously discovered in Lapita sites. The find was especially significant because "Lapita people" are regarded as the ancestors of all Polynesians.　　■ Eugene Ogan

See also **Australia; New Zealand.**

Painting. See Art.

Pakistan. The government of Pakistan disclosed in 2004 that a scientist with Pakistan's nuclear weapons program had secretly sold the technology for making such weapons to Iran, Libya, and North Korea. The announcement of this evasion of international efforts to restrict nuclear weapons ownership produced worldwide concern.

Nuclear admission. Western intelligence services in late 2003 detected a nuclear weapons program in Libya and intercepted Pakistan-type supplies headed to Libya. On Feb. 4, 2004, the founder of Pakistan's nuclear weapons program, Abdul Qadeer Khan, publicly admitted that he had shared the nation's nuclear secrets with other countries.

Khan, who was respected for having armed Pakistan with nuclear weapons, was pardoned by Pakistani President Pervez Musharraf. The investigation was officially closed, though Khan remained under surveillance and 10 of his scientists were detained. International affairs experts noted that Khan's nuclear program, created in 1975, a year after India tested a nuclear device, was directed by Pakistan's armed forces. The military, which had run the country most of the time the technology was being peddled abroad, had supplied planes and other aid for Khan's foreign contacts. The military had gotten help from North Korea in making guided missiles, possibly in return for bomb-building help.

Critics said Musharraf, a general who had remained head of the armed forces since seizing power in 1999, wanted to sweep the subject under the rug. Relatives of detained scientists said Musharraf's main concern was keeping the military from being tainted by making Khan the scapegoat.

War on terror. The United States, which needed Pakistan's help in fighting terrorism, officially accepted the story that Khan alone was to blame. On June 16, 2004, U.S. President George W. Bush named Pakistan "a major non-NATO ally," making it eligible for priority delivery of defense materials. The designation angered India, which accused Pakistan of carrying out acts of terrorism against India.

Al-Qa'ida terrorists and remnants of Taliban extremists from Afghanistan operated out of areas of Pakistan bordering Afghanistan during 2004. Pakistani army and police pursuit of these groups failed to eliminate their sanctuaries. Despite publicly supporting U.S. efforts to reduce terrorism and arresting major terrorism leaders, Musharraf did little to restrict Pakistan's own Islamic extremists who backed al-Qai'da and the Taliban. According to terrorism experts, extremists had backed the Army's long hold on power in Pakistan.

Religious violence. Violence flared throughout 2004 between Pakistan's Sunni Muslim majority and Shiah Muslim minority, which had fought off and on for at least 20 years. On March 2, more than 50 people were killed in an attack on a Shiah procession in Quetta. In September, a member of the outlawed Sunni militant group Lashkar-e-Jhangvi confessed to carrying out this and several other attacks on Shiites. Thirty-one Shiites died in a suicide bombing of a mosque on October 1. Six days later, a car bomb killed 41 Sunnis in Multan.

Governmental shakeups. Prime Minister Zafarullah Jamali, under pressure from Musharraf, resigned on June 26. Finance Minister Shaukat Aziz replaced him. Extremists tried to kill Aziz on July 30 but failed. Aziz, a veteran international banker, was sworn in as prime minister in August. He remained finance minister.

On April 19, Musharraf tightened his control of the government by establishing a National Security Council, which he claimed was consultative. However, critics viewed the 13-member body as an attempt to enhance the already entrenched political power of the armed forces.

While Musharraf was abroad on November 30, the acting president, Senate chairman Mohammed Mian Soomro, signed into law new legislation that allowed Musharraf to remain both president of Pakistan and head of the army. In 2003, Musharraf had said he would relinquish his post as army chief by the end of 2004, stating that becoming a civilian president would be a step toward returning Pakistan to democracy.   ■ Henry S. Bradsher

See also **Afghanistan; Asia; Disasters; India; Islam; Terrorism.**

Paleontology. The mass extinction episode that took place approximately 440 million years ago may have been caused by a blast of radiation from a nearby exploding star. So proposed a team of astronomers led by Adrian Melott of the University of Kansas in Lawrence in January 2004.

Within less than 1 million years at the end of the Ordovician Period (505 million to 440 million years ago), two-thirds of all marine species became extinct. Many previous ideas about this extinction had attributed its cause to a harsh but short-lived *ice age,* a period when vast areas of Earth are covered in ice sheets. These ideas were based on geological evidence that glaciers had once covered what is today northern Africa, a region that scientists believe was close to the South Pole during the Late Ordovician Period.

Melott and his colleagues suggested that a beam of gamma radiation from an exploding star called a supernova might have started a chain reaction that greatly altered Earth's atmosphere, triggering both the mass extinction and the ice age. According to this idea, the gamma radiation caused nitrogen molecules in the upper atmosphere to break apart, creating a brown "smog" dominated by nitrous oxides and other gases. Then, during chemical reactions, these gases destroyed much of Earth's protective *ozone layer,* a layer of the atmosphere that shields the planet's

In August, paleontologist Gregory Erickson of Florida State University discusses his team's findings about the growth rate of Sue, the *Tyrannosaurus rex* at The Field Museum in Chicago. Based on an analysis of Sue's fossilized bones, Erickson concluded that the huge dinosaur reached its adult size by age 18 and likely died by age 28.

surface from the ultraviolet (UV) rays of the sun. Sea life close to the ocean surface would have been harmed the most by the UV rays.

The astronomers noted that fossil researchers had previously observed that organisms living in shallow waters were the hardest hit by the extinction. The astronomers further argued that the brownish atmosphere they proposed would have produced an "icehouse" effect, chilling Earth enough to allow snow and ice to build up into glaciers. Other scientists agreed that the new proposal was intriguing, but they added that further research would be required to verify it.

Predation in ancient seas. Ancient fossil evidence of attempted predation by *carnivores* (meat-eating animals) was reported in September by paleontologists Tomasz Baumiller of the University of Michigan in Ann Arbor and Forest Gahn of the Smithsonian Institution in Washington, D.C. According to the scientists, fossil crinoids, or sea lilies, provide evidence of having been chewed on.

The scientists said they observed signs of *regeneration,* the regrowing of body parts that had been removed, in collections of well-preserved fossil crinoids. Such regrown parts are typically shorter and stubbier than normal parts. Baumiller and Gahn found evidence of regenerated arms, the featherlike feeding structures of crinoids, in a number of fossils. They surmised that, as with modern crinoids, the arms had been damaged by predators that nibbled on them. The scientists reported that fossil crinoids with regen-

erated arms can be seen in samples as old as the Ordovician Period, but they suddenly became more common during the Devonian Period (410 million to 360 million years ago).

The evidence supported an earlier proposal by paleontologists Philip Signor, formerly of the University of California at Davis, and Carlton Brett of the University of Cincinnati in Ohio. Both argued that predacious fish, which likely fed on crinoids, increased abruptly in the Devonian.

Long-necked reptile. A September report described a bizarre reptile that lived in southeastern China 240 million years ago, during the Triassic Period (248 million to 213 million years ago). Paleontologist Chun Li of the Chinese Academy of Sciences in Beijing and several colleagues described the remains of *Dinocephalosaurus orientalis,* a long-necked animal from Guizhou Province. The scientists said the reptile, which belonged to an extinct group called protorosaurs, had a neck 5.5 feet (1.7 meter) long—nearly double the length of the rest of its body (minus the tail). The neck was composed of 25 vertebrae equipped with flexible projections of bone, which likely anchored powerful throat muscles.

Li's team reported that *Dinocephalosaurus* apparently lived near the shorelines of shallow seas. The scientists said the reptile might have used its long neck to sneak its head close to swimming fish in murky waters. It then would have ambushed the fish by flexing its strong throat muscles to suck them into its mouth.

Dinosaurs slept like birds. A 135-million-year-old fossil provides a rare glimpse into dinosaur behavior during the Cretaceous Period (145 million to 65 million years ago), as well as insights into the evolution of birds. Paleontologists Xing Xu of the Chinese Academy of Sciences and Mark Norell of the American Museum of Natural History in New York City in October 2004 described a small carnivorous dinosaur from Liaoning, China. The species, named *Mei long,* was apparently buried in its sleep by a mudflow or debris flow.

The specimen was preserved with its forelimbs folded next to its body in a manner similar to the wing posture of resting birds. Furthermore, its neck was curved to one side, with the head nestled between the left elbow and body, a posture identical to that used by sleeping birds. The similarities in posture between the sleeping dinosaur and modern resting birds supported the idea that dinosaurs may have been the ancestors of birds, argued Xu and Norell. ■ Carlton E. Brett

Panama. On Sept. 1, 2004, Martin Torrijos Espino, of the New Homeland Alliance, was sworn to a five-year term as Panama's president. Torrijos was the son of General Omar Torrijos Herrera, who ruled Panama from 1968 to 1981. The general, who was widely revered by Panamanians, negotiated the 1977 treaty with the United States that ceded control of the Panama Canal to Panama in 1999.

President Torrijos, a graduate of Texas A&M University in College Station, embraced his father's legacy as a champion of the poor. The new president faced what he called Panama's "most important decision" of the 21st century—how to refurbish and widen the 90-year-old Panama Canal to accommodate the large, modern vessels used in world trade.

The planned renovation generated a great deal of controversy in 2004. Subsistence farmers whose lands would be flooded by a wider canal demanded that the construction plans take their needs into account. Many of these farmers were impoverished. ■ Nathan A. Haverstock
See also **Latin America.**

Papua New Guinea. See **Asia; Pacific Islands.**

Paraguay. See **Latin America.**

Pennsylvania. See **Philadelphia; State government.**

PEOPLE IN THE NEWS

in 2004 included those listed below, who were all from the United States unless otherwise indicated.

Abbas, Mahmoud (1935-), also known as Abu Mazen, was appointed chairman of the Executive Committee of the Palestine Liberation Organization (PLO), the political body that represents the Palestinian people, on Nov. 11, 2004. Abbas succeeded Yasir Arafat, who died on November 11. Since 1996, Abbas had served as secretary-general of the PLO Executive Committee, which directs day-to-day operations.

Although Abbas had little popular support among Palestinians, he was highly regarded in the international community for his moderate stance and peacemaking efforts. He opposed the 1987 *intifada* (the armed Palestinian uprising against Israel) and the second intifada, which began in 2000.

Abbas was born in Zefat in what is now northern Israel. During the war that followed the establishment of the nation of Israel in 1948, Abbas fled to Syria with his family. He became involved with the Palestinian independence movement in the 1950's. In the late 1950's, Abbas and Arafat helped found Fatah, a militant Palestinian group that is now part of the PLO.

In 1958, Abbas earned a bachelor's degree in law from the University of Damascus in Syria. In 1980, he became head of the PLO's national and international relations department. He earned a doctorate in history from the Institute of Oriental Studies in Moscow in 1982. In 1995, Abbas returned to live in Palestine for the first time since leaving for exile.

In March 2003, Arafat, acting under foreign pressure to make democratic reforms to his government, selected Abbas as prime minister of the Palestinian Authority (PA). The PA exercises limited governmental control over parts of the West Bank and Gaza Strip. However, Abbas quit in September 2004, after criticizing Arafat, Israel, and the United States for undermining his efforts.
See also **Israel; Middle East.**

Allawi, Ayad (1945-), an Iraqi physician and businessman who had long opposed former Iraqi President Saddam Hussein, was sworn in as prime minister of Iraq's interim government on June 28, 2004. Allawi spent more than 30 years in exile from Iraq, during which he helped establish the Iraqi National Accord (INA), a group dedicated to organizing Iraqi and international opposition to Hussein.

Allawi was born in 1945 to a prominent mer-

Ayad Allawi

chant family adhering to the Shiah branch of Islam. Although Shiah Muslims constitute a majority in Iraq, Sunni Muslims dominated the government under Hussein.

In 1961, Allawi joined the nationalist Baath Party, which seized control of Iraq in 1963. By 1971, however, Allawi had become critical of the government and left the country. He and his family settled in the United Kingdom, where he completed his medical education.

Allawi suffered severe wounds in a 1978 assassination attempt, believed to have been staged by Hussein's agents. In 1991, he helped found the INA with backing from the United States Central Intelligence Agency and the British intelligence service. A 1996 attempt by the INA to overthrow Hussein ended in failure.

Allawi returned to Iraq after the U.S.-led invasion in 2003 and was appointed to the Governing Council. In May 2004, the council chose him as interim prime minister.

See also **Iraq: A Special Report.**

Al-Sistani, Grand Ayatollah Ali (1930-),
the senior religious leader among Iraq's Shiah Muslims, took an increasingly prominent role in that country's political affairs in 2004. A moderate, al-Sistani repeatedly urged Iraqi Shiites not to offer military resistance to the United States-led coalition occupying Iraq. In August, he also negotiated an end to three weeks of fighting between U.S.-led coalition forces and Shiite militia members, who had

barricaded themselves in an important Shiah shrine in An Najaf.

At the same time, al-Sistani called for the establishment of an Islamic republic in Iraq. He also strongly opposed U.S. plans to allow appointed, rather than democratically elected, officials to select the members of Iraq's interim government.

Ali al-Husseini al-Sistani was born on Aug. 4, 1930, in Masshad, Iran, to a family of religious scholars. He began studying the Qur'an, the sacred book of Islam, at age 5. In 1952, he moved to An Najaf, where he studied with some of the most important Shiah religious leaders of the time, including Imam Abul Qassim al-Khoei. Al-Sistani was named a grand ayatollah after al-Khoei's death in 1992. Al-Sistani took little part in political activities during the rule of Iraqi President Saddam Hussein.

See also **Iraq: A Special Report.**

Angelopoulos-Daskalaki, Gianna
(1955-), a Greek socialite known for her forceful manner, successfully led the effort to construct the sports venues and other facilities needed for the 2004 Summer Olympic Games in Athens. She was the first woman to head a successful bid campaign and the first to lead an Olympic organizing committee.

Angelopoulos-Daskalaki had served as president of the Athens 2004 Olympic Games Bid Committee, which won the right to stage the 2004 Games in Greece, home of both the ancient Games and the first modern Games. Initially, she was to head the organizing committee as well. She stepped away from the job because of disputes among members. In May 2004, however, she accepted the position of executive director of the organizing committee, after the president of the International Olympic Committee strongly criticized the lack of preparation for the games by Athenian authorities.

Gianna Angelopoulos-Daskalaki

Angelopoulos-Daskalaki was born on Dec. 12, 1955, in Iraklion on the Greek island of Crete. After earning a law degree in 1983, she worked as a lawyer in Athens. She won election to the

Elouise Cobell

Cobell, Elouise

(1945-   ), a community activist and elder of the Blackfeet Nation, in 2004 continued her legal efforts to force the United States government to reform its system of managing American Indian-owned lands and repay landowners and their heirs what may amount to billions of dollars in lost or stolen funds. On October 2, a federal judge in Washington, D.C., ruled, as part of a 1996 class-action lawsuit known as the Cobell case, that the government must give Indian landowners a "full and accurate accounting, appraisal, and other relevant information" before selling land managed by the Indian Trust. The Trust, created in 1887, manages revenues from the sale of oil, timber, and other natural resources on land issued to Native Americans after some reservations were divided.

Elouise Cobell was born on Nov. 5, 1945. She grew up in a large family on a ranch on the Blackfeet reservation in Montana. After completing high school, she graduated in 1964 from Great Falls (Montana) Commercial College, where she studied accounting. She attended Montana State University in Bozeman but left in 1968 to care for her terminally ill mother.

In 1976, officials of the Blackfeet Nation offered Cobell the job of treasurer. In 1987, she helped establish the Blackfeet National Bank, the first Indian-owned bank in the United States.

Cobell spent many years unsuccessfully trying to persuade the U.S. government to reconcile the Indian Trust accounts. Finally in 1996, she and the Colorado-based Native American Rights Fund filed a lawsuit on behalf of some 300,000 Native Americans, the largest lawsuit ever brought against the U.S. government by any group.

In 1997, Cobell won a "genius award" from the John D. and Catherine T. MacArthur Foundation. A rancher and businesswoman, she also heads the Blackfeet Reservation Development Fund, Inc.

See also **Indian, American.**

Athens Municipal Council in 1986 and to the Greek parliament in 1989. In 1990, she married and resigned her seat in parliament to work in the family shipping business.

See also **Greece; Olympics: A Special Report.**

Bonds, Barry (1964-   ), on Sept. 17, 2004, became only the third major league baseball player in history—after Henry Aaron and Babe Ruth—to hit 700 or more career home runs. Also in 2004, Bonds led the National League in batting with a .362 average, broke Rickey Henderson's record of 2,190 walks in a career, and set a major league record of 232 walks in a season.

Bonds ranks as one of the best all-around players in baseball. A power hitter, he holds the major league record for home runs in a season with 73. He is also the only player in major league history to hit more than 400 home runs and steal more than 400 bases in his career. In addition, Bonds was an outstanding defensive outfielder and has won the Gold Glove Award several times for his defensive skill.

Bonds was named the National League's Most Valuable Player (MVP) six times—in 1990, 1992, 1993, 2001, 2002, and 2003. He became the first major league player to be named MVP more than three times.

Barry Lamar Bonds was born in Riverside, California, on July 24, 1964. His father, Bobby Bonds, was also a star outfielder in the major leagues. The Pittsburgh Pirates selected Barry Bonds in the first round of the 1985 free agent draft. He played in the minor leagues in 1985 and part of 1986 before moving up to the Pirates. Bonds signed with the San Francisco Giants as a free agent after the 1992 season.

See also **Baseball.**

Edwards, John (1953-   ), a United States senator from North Carolina, ran unsuccessfully for vice president on the Democratic Party ticket in the 2004 U.S. presidential election. Originally aiming to become the Democrats' presidential

candidate, Edwards dropped out of the race in March, after it became clear that he could not overtake Democratic front-runner John Kerry.

Edwards offered limited experience in government, having served only one term in the Senate. However, many Democrats applauded Kerry's selection of Edwards as his running mate because of Edwards's enthusiastic and appealing personality and his Southern and working-class roots. After the election, however, political observers noted that Edwards had failed to help Kerry win any Southern states.

John Reid Edwards was born on June 10, 1953, in Seneca, South Carolina, and grew up in Robbins, North Carolina. He earned a bachelor's degree from North Carolina State University in 1974 and a law degree in 1977 from the University of North Carolina at Chapel Hill. In 1993, after working for several law firms, Edwards and a partner established their own firm, specializing in personal injury cases. Edwards quickly gained a reputation for winning large settlements for injured people suing huge corporations. In 1998, Edwards won election to the U.S. Senate in his first attempt to gain public office.

See also **Elections; People in the news** (John Kerry).

Manmohan Singh (left) and Sonia Gandhi

Gandhi, Sonia (1946-   ), the leader of India's National Congress Party, declined on May 18, 2004, to accept the post of prime minister despite the victory of a Congress-led alliance in parliamentary elections. (In a parliamentary system, the leader of the winning party usually becomes the prime minister.) Gandhi, who was born in Italy, encountered fierce opposition from Hindu nationalists opposed to the idea of a foreign-born prime minister.

Gandhi was born Sonia Maino near Turin, Italy,

on Dec. 9, 1946. She joined India's most prominent political family in 1968 with her marriage to Rajiv Gandhi, the son of Indira Gandhi, India's first woman prime minister, and grandson of Jawaharlal Nehru, India's first prime minister.

Gandhi had little involvement in politics during her husband's lifetime. Rajiv Gandhi, who served as prime minister from 1984 to 1989, was assassinated in 1991. Sonia Gandhi joined the Congress Party—her husband's party—in 1997 at the urging of party leaders and became its president in 1998. She was elected to Parliament in 1999.

See also **India; People in the news** (Manmohan Singh).

Hamm, Paul (1982-   ), at the 2004 Summer Olympic Games in Athens, became the first American gymnast to win a gold medal in the Men's Individual All-Around category. He captured the gold on August 18 with near-perfect performances on the parallel bars and horizontal bar after dropping to 12th place because of a fall during the vault event. Hamm also won a silver medal in the Men's Horizontal Bar.

Hamm's victory in the All-Around competition was overshadowed by a dispute over a scoring error by the judges. On August 20, the South Korean Olympic Committee and South Korean gymnast Yang Tae Young filed a protest with the International Gymnastics Federation (FIG), claiming that the judges had mistakenly given Yang's routine a lower start value (degree of difficulty) than it deserved. As a result, Yang finished .049 of a point behind Hamm in the closest Men's All-Around contest in Olympic history. If the routine had been scored correctly, the complaint said, Yang would have won.

FIG agreed that the judges had scored Yang's routine unfairly but refused to change the results. At a meeting held on August 22, officials from the United States and Korean Olympic committees met to consider awarding gold medals to both Hamm and Yang. However, the U.S. committee withdrew the offer after FIG's president proclaimed Yang the winner and asked Hamm to give up his medal.

The South Koreans appealed FIG's decision to the Court of Arbitration for Sport in Lausanne, Switzerland. On October 21, the court ruled that regulations governing gymnastic competitions require any challenge to a judge's decision to be made during the event. The South Koreans, the court said, waited too long to file their protest.

Paul Hamm was born on Sept. 24, 1982, in Washburn, Wisconsin. He took up gymnastics in 1989. Hamm and his twin brother, Morgan, also a gymnast, competed in the 2000 Summer Games. In 2003, Paul Hamm became the first U.S. male to win a World All-Around championship.

See also **Olympics: A Special Report.**

Kerry, John (1943-   ), the Democratic candidate for president of the United States in 2004, lost to his Republican opponent, President George W. Bush, on November 2. During the tightly contested race, Kerry, a U.S. senator from Massachusetts, stressed jobs, health care, education, and other domestic issues. He also accused President Bush of mismanaging the war in Iraq.

John Forbes Kerry was born on Dec. 11, 1943, in Denver, Colorado, to a mother from a socially connected New England shipping family and a father in the diplomatic corp. He earned a bachelor's degree from Yale University in New Haven, Connecticut, in 1966. After graduation, Kerry enlisted in the U.S. Navy, serving until 1970. During the five months he spent in combat in Vietnam, he was wounded in battle and received three Purple Heart citations and the Silver Star and Bronze Star medals. After completing two military tours, Kerry helped found the Vietnam Veterans of America. He also expressed his opposition to the Vietnam War (1957-1975) by serving as a prominent spokesman for Vietnam Veterans Against the War.

In 1972, Kerry unsuccessfully ran for a seat in the U.S. House of Representatives from Massachusetts. He then enrolled at Boston College, graduating in 1976 with master's and law degrees. He practiced law until 1982, when he was elected lieutenant governor of Massachusetts. In 1984, Kerry won election to the U.S. Senate. He was reelected in 1990, 1996, and 2002.

As a senator, Kerry worked to support small businesses, protect the environment, and reform campaign-finance practices, while exposing a number of financial and government scandals. He also chaired a special Senate committee investigating the fate of U.S. soldiers declared missing in action during the Vietnam War.

Kerry officially declared his candidacy for the presidential nomination in 2003. After trailing several of his Democratic opponents for the remainder of the year, he came from behind to win the Iowa caucuses and the New Hampshire primary in January 2004. By mid-March, he had won enough caucuses and primary elections to assure his nomination. In July, at the Democratic Party's national convention in Boston, he formally became the party's presidential nominee.

See also **Democratic Party; Elections; and People in the news** (John Edwards).

Wangari Maathai

Maathai (mah DHEYE), **Wangari** (wan GAH ree) (1940-   ), a Kenyan environmentalist and political activist, became in October 2004 the first African woman to win the Nobel Peace Prize. Maathai is best known for founding the Green Belt Movement, a grass-roots conservation organization that promotes reforestation.

Maathai was born on April 1, 1940, in Nyeri, Kenya. She earned a degree in biology from Mount St. Scholastica College in Atchison, Kansas, in 1964 and a master's degree from the University of Pittsburgh in Pennsylvania in 1966. The doctorate in biological sciences Maathai received from the University of Nairobi in 1971 was the first doctoral degree awarded to a woman in East and Central Africa. In 1976, she became chair of Nairobi's Department of Veterinary Anatomy. In 2000, Wangari became a leader in the effort to win the cancellation of debts owed by poor African countries to richer nations. She was elected to Kenya's parliament in 2002, becoming assistant minister for Environment, Natural Resources, and Wildlife.

See also **Africa; Nobel prizes.**

Martin, Paul (1938-   ), in June 2004 led Canada's Liberal Party to a narrow victory in the first national election held since Martin became prime minister in December 2003. The Liberals' success capped Martin's 15-year effort to win the top post in his party and Canada's government.

Paul Edgar Philippe Martin was born on Aug. 28, 1938, in Windsor, Ontario, which his Liberal father represented in Parliament. After recovering from polio at age 8, Paul moved with his family to Ottawa, Canada's capital.

Martin graduated from St. Michael's College at the University of Toronto in 1962 with a degree in philosophy and history. He earned a law degree

from the university in 1964. In 1966, he moved to Montreal to work for Power Corporation of Canada, a large management company.

In 1967, however, Martin took a leave of absence from his job to help his father in his ultimately unsuccessful campaign for the leadership of the Liberal Party. Martin considered running for the seat that his father later exchanged for an appointment to Canada's Senate. However, he returned to business on his father's advice.

Martin quickly rose through the ranks at Power Corporation, becoming president of a subsidiary, Canada Steamship Lines (CSL), in 1973. In 1981, Martin and a partner bought CSL.

In 1987, Martin entered politics, winning a seat in Parliament from Montreal in 1988. In 1990, he made his first bid for the leadership of the Liberal Party, challenging, among others, Jean Chretien, who won the post. Martin and Chretien, who served as prime minister from 1993 to 2003, quickly became fierce rivals.

In 1993, Chretien offered Martin the post of minister of finance, a position that traditionally offered little opportunity for advancement. However, Martin won approval for eliminating a huge national deficit by significantly reducing federal spending and for introducing tax cuts. In June 2002, Chretien fired Martin from the Cabinet after Martin launched a leadership campaign against him. On Nov. 14, 2003, the Liberals chose Martin to head their party.

See also **Canada, Prime Minister of.**

Moore, Michael (1954-), a prizewinning filmmaker and writer known for his controversial documentary films, won both praise and scorn for his 2004 documentary *Fahrenheit 9/11*. The film, which became the most viewed documentary in motion-picture history, attacks the administration of U.S. President George W. Bush for its response to the terrorist attacks of Sept. 11, 2001, and its handling of the Iraq War. In 2004, the film received the Cannes International Film Festival's highest award, the Palme d'Or. Like his other films, *Fahrenheit 9/11* presented a satirical portrait of what Moore regarded as incompetence and wrong-headedness among U.S. leaders. The film, also like his other works, was strongly criticized for being one-sided and manipulative.

Moore was born on April 23, 1954, in Davison, Michigan. He gained attention as a filmmaker with *Roger & Me* (1989), a documentary about the closing of General Motors (GM) plants in Flint, Michigan. The film follows Moore's futile attempts to interview GM Chairman Roger B. Smith.

Moore won the 2003 Academy Award for best feature documentary for *Bowling for Columbine* (2002), an exploration of gun violence in the United States. His other films include *Canadian Bacon* (1995) and *The Big One* (1997). He is the author of *Downsize This!* (1996) and *Dude, Where's My Country?* (2003).

See also **Motion pictures.**

Norodom Sihamoni (1953-), a choreographer, cinematographer, and former ballet dancer, was crowned king of Cambodia on Oct. 29, 2004. He succeeded his father, King Norodom Sihanouk, who abdicated because of ill health after more than 60 years on the throne. Although Cambodia's king has limited political power, the position traditionally commands great popular esteem. In a written statement released before Sihamoni's coronation, the prince said he worried about fulfilling his duties because "I lack experience."

Sihamoni was born on May 14, 1953, in Phnom Penh, Cambodia's capital. He attended high school in Prague, in what was then Czechoslovakia, and graduated from the Prague Conservatory in 1971 and from the city's Academy of Music and Performing Arts in 1975. He then spent a year studying at the National Academy of Cinematography in Pyongyang, North Korea.

During the brutal rule of the Khmer Rouge Communist movement, from 1975 to 1979, Sihamoni and his parents lived under house arrest in

King Norodom Sihamoni

Phnom Penh. In 1981, Sihamoni moved to France to work as a ballet teacher. In Paris, he directed the ballet troupe Deva, which he founded, from 1984 to 1988. In 1988, he became film director and artistic director of Khemara Pictures. Sihamoni served as Cambodia's ambassador to the United Nations Educational, Scientific, and Cultural Organization in Paris from 1993 to 2004.

See also **Cambodia**.

Obama, Barack

(1961-   ), a Democratic state senator and university teacher, won election to the United States Senate from Illinois in November 2004 by the largest margin in that state's history. Obama, who collected 70 percent of the vote, became the first male African American Democrat ever elected to the Senate. In July, Obama won nationwide acclaim when he delivered an impassioned keynote address to the Democratic National Convention.

Barack Obama was born on Aug. 4, 1961, in Honolulu, Hawaii, to a white American mother and black Kenyan father. He earned a bachelor's degree in political science from Columbia University in New York City in 1983. He then worked for a community development organization in Chicago. In 1991, he received a law degree from Harvard Law School in Cambridge, Massachusetts, having been the first black president of the prestigious Harvard Law Review.

In 1992, Obama directed a voter registration campaign in Chicago. The next year, he joined a law firm, specializing in civil rights and employment cases. He also became a senior lecturer at the University of Chicago Law School. In 1996, Obama won election to the Illinois Senate. He was re-elected in 1998 and 2002. Obama is the author of *Dreams from My Father: A Story of Race and Inheritance* (1995), a memoir.

See also **Democratic Party; Elections; State government**.

Penn, Sean

(1960-   ), an actor widely praised for his strong and sensitive performances, won an Academy Award for best actor on Feb. 28, 2004, for his portrayal in *Mystic River* (2003) of a man seeking revenge for his daughter's mur-

Sean Penn and Charlize Theron

der. Penn previoiusly had been nominated for his performances as a prisoner awaiting execution in *Dead Man Walking* (1995) and as a mentally disabled man fighting for the custody of his daughter in *I Am Sam* (2001). In the 1980's, Penn was known for his controversial, sometimes violent, personal life.

Sean Penn was born on Aug. 17, 1960, in Burbank, California, to actress Eileen Ryan and director Leo Penn. Penn made his professional acting debut in 1979 with an appearance in the television series "Barnaby Jones" and his motion-picture debut in *Taps* (1981). His other films include *Fast Times at Ridgemont High* (1982), *Bad Boys* (1983), *The Falcon and the Snowman* (1985), *Carlito's Way* (1990), *The Thin Red Line* (1998), *The Weight of Water* (2002), and *21 Grams* (2003).

In the 1990's, Penn turned to film directing and screenwriting. He wrote and directed *The Indian Runner* (1991) and *The Crossing Guard* (1995) and directed *The Game* (1997) and *The Pledge* (2001).

See also **Motion pictures People in the news** (Charlize Theron).

Phelps, Michael

(1985-   ), one of the fastest and most versatile swimmers in history, tied the all-time record for individual Olympic medals by winning eight medals at the 2004 Summer Games in Athens. Phelps's total of six gold medals and two bronze medals tied the record set by Russian gymnast Aleksandr Michael Dityatin at the 1980 Summer Games.

At the 2004 Games, Phelps set a world record by winning the 400-meter individual medley and Olympic records by winning the 100-meter and the 200-meter butterfly and the 200-meter individual medley. Phelps also won gold medals as part of the United States 800-meter freestyle relay and 400-meter medley relay teams. Phelps won his bronze medals swimming in the 200-meter freestyle and in the 400-meter freestyle relay.

At the World Swimming Championships in Barcelona, Spain, in 2003, Phelps became the first swimmer to set five individual world records in a single meet. He also became the first man to break two individual records in one day.

Phelps was born on June 30, 1985, in Baltimore. He competed in the 2000 Summer Olympic Games at the age of 15, the youngest male swimmer on the U.S. Olympic team in 68 years. Phelps set his first world record, in the 200-meter butterfly, in 2001.

See also **Olympics; Swimming.**

Singh, Manmohan (1932-   ), became prime minister of India on May 22, 2004, after the National Congress Party in national elections won the most seats in the Lok Sabha, the more powerful of India's two houses of Parliament. Singh, a high-ranking member of the party, was named prime minister after party leader Sonia Gandhi refused the post. A member of the Sikh faith, Singh is the first non-Hindu to serve as prime minister of India.

Singh was born on Sept. 26, 1932, in Gah, in what is now the Pakistani province of Punjab. He was educated at Panjab University in Chandigarh, India, and at Cambridge and Oxford universities in England. In 1957, he returned to Panjab to teach economics. While teaching, he also earned a doctorate in economics from Oxford in 1962. In 1969, he became a professor at the Delhi School of Economics in India.

Beginning in 1971, Singh served in a variety of civil service positions involving economics, finance, and trade. He also held posts with international development organizations. In 1991, Singh won election to the Rajya Sabha, the less powerful house of Parliament. In 1999, he ran unsuccessfully for a seat in the Lok Sabha.

See also **India; People in the news** (Sonia Gandhi).

Theron, Charlize (1975-   ), a South African actress, won the Academy Award for best actress on Feb. 28, 2004, for her fictionalized portrayal of serial murderer Aileen Wuornos in *Monster* (2003). Theron radically altered her appearance to portray Wuornos, who confessed to the murders of six men and was executed in Florida in 2002. Theron's performance in *Monster* also netted her Golden Globe and National Society of Film Critics awards for best actress.

Theron was born on Aug. 7, 1975, in Benoni, South Africa, and grew up on her parents' farm nearby. In 1991, she won a modeling contest; moved to Milan, Italy; and began working as a model in Europe. Theron then moved to New York City, where she studied dance with the Joffrey Ballet. However, an injured knee soon ended her hopes of a ballet career.

In 1994, Theron moved to Los Angeles and quickly attracted the attention of a movie agent. She made her uncredited film debut in *Children of the Corn III* (1995). After several minor roles, she won a major part as a neglected, troubled wife in *The Devil's Advocate* (1997). In 1999, she won her first starring role in *Mighty Joe Young* (1998). Her other films include *The Cider House Rules* (1999), *Sweet November* (2001), *The Italian Job* (2003), and *Head in the Clouds* (2004).

See also **Motion pictures; People in the news** (Sean Penn).

Thorpe, Ian (1982-   ), an Australian swimmer, strengthened his reputation as one of the world's dominant freestyle swimmers during the 2004 Summer Olympic Games in Athens. Thorpe won gold medals in the 200-meter freestyle and 400-meter freestyle. He also set an Olympic record in the 200-meter race. In addition, he won a silver medal as a member of the Australian 800-meter freestyle relay team and a bronze medal in the 100-meter freestyle.

Ian Thorpe was born on Oct. 13, 1982, in Sydney. He began swimming at the age of 8. In 1998, at age 15, Thorpe became the youngest male world swimming champion in history by winning the 400-meter freestyle at the world swimming championships in Perth, Australia.

At the 2000 Summer Olympics in Sydney, Thorpe won a gold medal in the 400-meter freestyle and two others as a member of Australia's 400-meter and 800-meter freestyle relay teams. He set, or helped set, new world records in all three events.

See also **Olympics: A Special Report.**

Michael Phelps (left) and Ian Thorpe

Walters, Barbara (1931-   ), one of the most successful journalists in the history of American television, announced in September 2004 that she was leaving "20/20," the weekly news program she had hosted or cohosted for 25 years. The first woman to anchor a network evening newscast, Walters became known for her popular interviews of celebrities.

Barbara Ann Walters was born on Sept. 25, 1931, in Boston. She graduated from Sarah Lawrence College in Bronxville, New York, in 1953 and became a TV newswriter and producer in New York City. In 1961, she joined the staff of the NBC daily TV program "Today" as a writer, becoming a regular on-air member of the show in 1964. In 1974, she was promoted to cohost.

In 1976, Walters became coanchor of the "ABC Evening News" and telecast her first "Barbara Walters Special" interview program. In 1979, she joined "20/20." Since 1997, Walters also has worked as coexecutive producer and cohost of the ABC daytime news and entertainment program "The View." She planned to continue her interview specials and her appearances on "The View."

See also **Television**.

Zapatero, Jose Luiz Rodriguez

(1960-   ), the leader of Spain's Socialist Workers' Party, was sworn in as prime minister on March 18, 2004, after the Socialists won an upset victory in national elections. The elections occurred three days after bombs—allegedly planted by Islamic terrorists—exploded on commuter trains in Madrid, the capital, killing at least 200 people. Zapatero benefited from the widespread belief that the government's deeply unpopular decision to join the United States-led coalition in Iraq had left the country vulnerable to terrorist attack. In late June, Zapatero fulfilled a campaign pledge to remove Spanish troops from Iraq.

Zapatero was born in Valladolid, in northern Spain, on Aug. 4, 1960. He joined the Socialist party in 1979 while a teen-ager. After training as a lawyer, Zapatero in 1986 won a seat in parliament at age 26.

In 2000, Zapatero became the party's general secretary after the Socialists lost their second consecutive election to the conservative Popular Party (PP). As Socialist leader, he attempted to widen the party's appeal by adopting more moderate political positions. In 2003, however, Zapatero came under criticism for the Socialists' lackluster success in regional elections. Before the Madrid bombings, the PP had a comfortable lead over the Socialists in national polls, despite Zapatero's strong criticism of the PP's Iraq policy.

See also **Spain**.

■ Barbara A. Mayes

Peru. The government of Peru found itself mired in scandal in 2004. In July, President Alejandro Toledo invited auditors to examine his personal bank accounts after his former top adviser, Cesar Almeyda, accused the president of accepting a $5-million bribe. The money allegedly came from a Colombian brewing company in return for Toledo's efforts in helping the company acquire a Peruvian competitor. In the wake of the allegation, President Toledo's party lost control of the Peruvian Congress, and there was widespread speculation that the president might be forced out of office.

Job losses. Contributing to Toledo's problems was a continuing loss of jobs in Peru. Upon taking office in 2001, President Toledo had pledged that his administration would create 1 million new jobs. Instead, a net loss of 40,000 jobs occurred in 2003. The employment picture remained bleak in 2004 despite an upswing in Peru's exports, which were expected to reach a record value of $10 billion.

Foreign-owned mining operations produced half of Peru's export revenue. Mining revenue grew at an annual rate of 10 percent, but this growth did not translate into new jobs—largely because of increased efficiency in operations.

Anger at corruption. The alleged misuse of tax revenues from mining, which amounted to some $300 million annually, fueled public anger. In April, poverty-stricken Aymara Indians living in Peru's southeastern mining region, in and around the town of Ilave, lynched the local mayor, Fernando Cirilo Robles. The Indians had accused Robles and a number of councilmen, who were badly beaten, of corruption. The Indians had also blamed Robles for failing to keep his promises to pave a highway and build a market.

Spy chief corruption trials. The ongoing trials of former intelligence chief Vladimiro Montesinos in 2004 revealed massive corruption in the previous administration. Montesinos, who had been the right-hand man of former President Alberto Fujimori throughout the 1990's, fled to Venezuela in 2000 to escape charges of money laundering, drugs and arms smuggling, and other crimes. Venezuelan authorities apprehended him in 2001 and returned him to Peru. In 2004, he and more than 1,300 codefendants faced a lengthy series of trials.

Documents brought to light during the trials showed that the spy chief had paid bribes totaling more than $3 million a month to police officials, judges, opposition political leaders, and the owners of Peru's major television stations. The bribes were designed to maintain political support for President Fujimori. Fujimori fled to Japan in 2000 to escape charges of corruption and authorizing death squads.

Peruvians were both fascinated and appalled by the details of the proceedings. Court records showed, for example, that Montesinos paid television stations sizable sums of money for doing specific jobs. One television station received $50,000 for firing two reporters critical of the government. Dozens of opposition politicians were paid monthly bribes, ranging from $10,000 to $50,000 each. Many judges received one-time payoffs of $2,500 to $55,000.

Exiled former leaders. Exiled former President Fujimori successfully fought extradition from Japan in 2004. He also mounted an aggressive effort to rehabilitate himself with Peru's voters by recording hour-long radio programs, which were carried on dozens of Peruvian stations every Saturday morning. Fujimori's supporters, hoping for a comeback by their former leader, paid to air the programs.

Some public opinion polls in 2004 showed that Fujimori led, or placed second, in a crowded field of potential candidates for the 2006 presidential election. Fujimori's closest competitor was his predecessor, former President Alan Garcia, who was also the target of corruption charges and was living in exile outside the country.

■ Nathan A. Haverstock

See also **Latin America.**

Petroleum and gas. See Energy supply.

Philadelphia. Federal prosecutors issued a 150-page indictment in June 2004 against 12 people who had served in Philadelphia government or conducted business with the city. The indictment, part of a widespread corruption probe, was based on months of wiretaps by the Federal Bureau of Investigation (FBI). One of the main charges in the indictment stated that Ronald White, an attorney who had performed legal work for Philadelphia, gave former city treasurer Corey Kemp "corrupt payments" so that White could control business contracts with the city.

White, who was charged with conspiracy, fraud, and extortion, was among the top fundraisers for Mayor John F. Street. Kemp had been treasurer during Street's first term in office, from 2000 to 2004. Street, who was inaugurated for a second term on January 5, was not charged in the indictment, and he claimed publicly that he had done nothing wrong. However, the indictment alleged that the mayor instructed his staff to award city business to White or to firms that White backed if the firms appeared to be qualified.

The FBI investigation continued after the June indictment, and other charges were filed as federal authorities pieced together more information. In October—as part of the probe—a federal court found four people guilty of stealing more than $224,000 from an adult education program in Philadelphia.

After White died in November of complications related to cancer, prosecutors said they would continue to use wiretapped conversations of White against other defendants in the case.

NAACP convention. Approximately 7,000 visitors came to Philadelphia in July to attend the 95th annual convention of the National Association for the Advancement of Colored People (NAACP), one of the most influential organizations representing the interests of African Americans. The convention honored United States District Judge Robert L. Carter, who had been on the legal team that successfully argued the landmark case of *Brown v. Board of Education of Topeka* (Kansas). In the 1954 case, the U.S. Supreme Court ruled that schools could not segregate pupils on the basis of race.

Democratic presidential candidate Senator John F. Kerry, of Massachusetts, told the conventioneers he was campaigning "to end the division between the fortunate America and the forgotten America." President George W. Bush declined an invitation to speak at the convention for the fourth year in a row. The president criticized NAACP officials, noting that they had made disparaging remarks against him over the years. President Bush said he would seek the support of the group's members "in other ways."

Tourism climbs. The NAACP convention, as well as a major advertising campaign to market the city to tourists, led to Philadelphia's best summer tourism season in five years in 2004. Studies by the Greater Philadelphia Tourism Marketing Corp. showed that through much of the summer, hotel rooms were occupied at a 10-percent higher rate than in 2003. Independence National Historical Park—home of the Liberty Bell, Independence Hall, and other historic attractions—had more than a 25-percent increase in visitors, compared with 2003.

New baseball stadium. The Cincinnati Reds defeated the Philadelphia Phillies, 4-1, in the Phillies' first game at their new baseball stadium on April 12, 2004. Citizens Bank Park seats 43,500 fans in a "retro" ballpark setting, with architecture that gives the stadium the appearance of ballparks that were built in the early 1900's. The ballpark has a facade of red bricks and a natural grass playing field, in addition to a huge neon version of the Liberty Bell that rings for every Phillies' home run.

The baseball team spent more than $170 million for the stadium. The city of Philadelphia and state of Pennsylvania paid for the remainder of the ballpark, which cost more than $450 million.

■ Howard S. Shapiro

See also **Baseball; City; Elections.**

Philippines.

Gloria Macapagal-Arroyo won a six-year presidential term in elections held on May 10, 2004. She had been elected vice president in 1998 and assumed the presidency in 2001, when Joseph Estrada was forced out of the office by public and military opposition amid corruption charges.

Campaigns and the election. Macapagal-Arroyo campaigned in 2004 on the basis of her three-year effort to reduce corruption and improve the nation's economy. Since the Philippines' constitution limits presidents to only one elected term, she had the unusual advantage of being an incumbent who could claim credit for recent public works and other projects.

Her main opponent was Fernando Poe, Jr., a popular movie star. A high school dropout with no political experience, Poe was encouraged to run by Estrada, a former movie star whose trial for graft moved slowly through 2004. Many Filipinos saw Poe as a surrogate for Estrada. Poe's campaign featured public appearances by movie stars and other entertainers rather than policy ideas, which he refused to debate. He hoped to appeal to people who had become distrustful of mainstream politicians. At least 115 people died during the campaigns in assassinations, bombings, and other acts of violence.

When the preliminary election results showed that Macapagal-Arroyo had won, Poe insisted there had been vote rigging and other illegal activities. Finally, on June 20, a congressional committee certified that Macapagal-Arroyo had won by more than 1 million votes. The Philippines Supreme Court rejected a challenge on June 22, and Congress, in an all-night session, declared her the winner on June 24. Macapagal-Arroyo was sworn in for a new term on June 30. Poe died of natural causes on December 14.

Macapagal-Arroyo promised in her inaugural address to crack down on widespread tax evasion and to "stop extortion masquerading as tax collection." A former professor with a doctorate in economics, she called for a sweeping tax overhaul in a state of the nation speech on July 26. The president urged Congress to pass eight new tax bills in order to reduce public debt, which had ballooned to more than $60 billion since 1992.

The Philippine Congress had a record, however, of letting personal politics overwhelm national business and had failed to enact much legislation in recent years. Macapagal-Arroyo campaigned for a change from the Philippines' American-style presidential system of government to a more responsive British-style parliamentary system with a prime minister who directs legislative business. However, this controversial idea of constitutional change was not taken up immediately by the Congress.

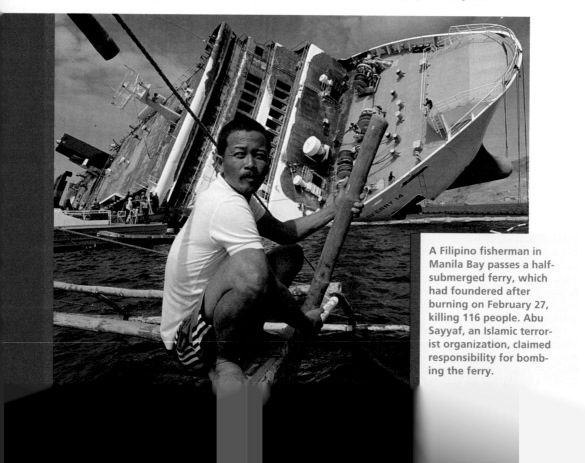

A Filipino fisherman in Manila Bay passes a half-submerged ferry, which had foundered after burning on February 27, killing 116 people. Abu Sayyaf, an Islamic terrorist organization, claimed responsibility for bombing the ferry.

Financial crisis. Macapagal-Arroyo hoped to attract investment that would create 6 million jobs in the next 6 years. With the country's unemployment rate at more than 10 percent in 2004, some 8 million Filipinos were forced to seek work abroad. Trying to rally congressional support for her tax package, the president warned on August 23 that the Philippines faced a financial crisis. To remedy the situation, she proposed increased taxes and fees on consumer goods.

Hostage. The Philippines sent a 51-member security team to Iraq in August and September of 2003 to support the U.S.-led occupation. In July 2004, Islamic militants kidnapped a Filipino truck driver working in Iraq for a Saudi Arabian company with a U.S. military contract. The kidnappers said that unless the Filipino team was withdrawn they would execute the man, who had eight children in the Philippines. The Philippine security team had been scheduled to return home in August, but Macapagal-Arroyo withdrew the force in late July over objections by the United States and Australia. The man was released on July 20, after team members had begun leaving.

President Macapagal-Arroyo's decision was criticized as contradicting her tough policy on terrorism in the Philippines. During her first three years in office, she had repeatedly ordered soldiers and police to confront and arrest terrorists.

Terrorism. A bombing aboard a ferry that sailed from Manila on February 27 left 116 people dead. Abu Sayyaf, an Islamic separatist group responsible for much of the terrorist activity in the Philippines, claimed responsibility for the attack. Although government officials initially denied Abu Sayyaf's claims, Macapagal-Arroyo stated in October that the group had bombed the ferry.

In March, government officials seized six Abu Sayyaf members who had planned to bomb shopping centers, trains, and other targets in or near Manila. The officials said the terrorists had trained with Jemaah Islamiyah, a Southeast Asian branch of the Middle East-based al-Qa'ida terrorist organization. The suspects reportedly were seized on the basis of information provided by the United States.

On April 8, soldiers killed a top Abu Sayyaf commander and five colleagues in a firefight on Basilan island. Two days later, 53 inmates of a Basilan prison, including Abu Sayyaf militants, escaped despite warnings by the army of an escape plan. Twenty-five of the escapees were recaptured, and nine others were killed.

Severe storms battered the Philippines in late November and early December. The ensuing flash floods and mudslides left more than 1,000 people dead and hundreds of thousands of others homeless.   ■ Henry S. Bradsher

See also **Asia; Disasters; Terrorism.**

Physics. On April 20, 2004, a Delta rocket blasted off from Vandenberg Air Force Base near Lompoc, California, lifting the Gravity Probe B (GP-B) satellite into orbit. The satellite was designed to carry out tests of one of the major cornerstones of modern physics—the general theory of relativity.

The general theory of relativity, developed by German-born scientist Albert Einstein in the early 1900's, states that planets and all other massive objects cause bends and warps in *space-time.* Space-time is a combination of the three dimensions of space (length, width, and height) with the dimension of time. Physicists describe space-time as a type of fabric that extends throughout the universe. A planet or star causes space-time to bend around it—just as a bowling ball on a rubber sheet causes the sheet to bend. Such bends, according to the theory, are the cause of gravity. For example, a moon orbits a planet because it is caught in the curvature of space-time around the planet—just as a marble rolls around the curvature of the rubber sheet surrounding the bowling ball.

Although the general theory of relativity has been well accepted by physicists for decades, GP-B was expected to produce the most precise measurements yet of how much massive objects warp space-time. Physicist Leonard Schiff of Stanford University in Stanford, California, first proposed such a project in 1960. Stanford physicist C. W. Francis Everitt was the principal investigator on the GP-B project.

The core of GP-B consisted of four extremely sensitive *gyroscopes,* spinning devices in which the axis of spin normally keeps pointing in the same direction. The gyroscopes on GP-B were virtually perfect spheres of quartz, spinning at 10,000 revolutions per minute. Special sensors in the satellite were to monitor the direction in which the spin axis of each gyroscope pointed—to an accuracy of 0.0005 of an *arcsecond.* An arcsecond is a unit equivalent to $\frac{1}{1,296,000}$ of the distance around a circle.

According to the general theory of relativity, Earth's gravity should cause the spin axis of a gyroscope to gradually shift as the gyroscope orbits the planet. This shift would be partly caused by the warping of space-time around the planet—an effect known as geodetic precession. The shift would also be caused by an effect called frame dragging, in which a heavy rotating object, such as Earth, drags and twists the fabric of space-time as the object rotates. GP-B was to make many precise measurements of both of these effects over a period of more than a year.

A rough measurement of the frame-dragging effect, obtained by observing how it distorts satellite orbits, was reported in October 2004 by physicists led by Erricos Pavlis of the National Aeronautics and Space Administration's Goddard Space Flight Center in Greenbelt, Maryland. The results provided support for Einstein's theory.

Phonograph physics. In May, physicists described how the same technology used in high-energy particle physics experiments could be applied to the restoration of scratchy old recordings on phonograph records and wax cylinders. Vitaliy Fadeyev and Carl Haber of the Lawrence Berkeley National Laboratory in Berkeley, California, made use of a new optical system designed for inspecting tracks made by subatomic particles in devices called particle detectors.

The physicists reprogrammed the optical system to map the swirling grooves that produce the sounds in old recordings. They then electronically processed the resulting images to remove the scratches and other flaws. Finally, they converted the patterns of the cleaned-up grooves into digital signals, the language of 0's and 1's used by computers. The digital signals produced scratch-free sounds.

The physicists conducted the research on behalf of the Library of Congress in Washington, D.C. The application of this technology was expected to result in greater public access to the many historic recordings of music and speeches owned by the library.   ■ Robert H. March

Poetry. Ted Kooser, who was named Poet Laureate of the United States in August 2004, assumed his duties on October 7 at a reading of his work at the Library of Congress in Washington, D.C. Kooser was born in Ames, Iowa. Upon the announcement of Kooser's appointment, James H. Billington, the librarian of Congress, said, "His verse reaches beyond his native region to touch on universal themes in accessible ways." The position of poet laureate allows writers to work on their own poetry; it includes a salary of $35,000 and an obligation to deliver and organize readings. Kooser is the author of 10 collections of poetry, including *Delights & Shadows* (2004) and *Sure Signs* (1980), for which he won the Society of Midland Authors Prize.

Kooser's poetry is often engaged with domestic events and memories. In "A Happy Birthday" from *Delights & Shadows,* he writes, "This evening, I sat by an open window/ and read till the light was gone and the book/ was no more than a part of the darkness./ I could easily have switched on a lamp,/ but I wanted to ride this day down into night,/ to sit alone and smooth the unreadable page/ with the pale gray ghost of my hand."

Pulitzer Prize. In April 2004, the Pulitzer Prize for poetry went to Franz Wright for his collection *Walking to Martha's Vineyard.* Wright was born in Vienna in 1953 and grew up in the United States.

His poems have often been described as prayer-like. He also exhibits a strong, even argumentative independence in matters of spiritual development, while displaying a sense of humor. The author relies upon his own sense of beauty and wonder and upon the ability of his reader to perceive it on his or her own terms.

National Book Award. Jean Valentine won the 2004 National Book Award for poetry for her collection *Door in the Mountain: New and Collected Poems.* In her poem "Annunciation," she writes, "I saw my soul become flesh breaking open/ the linseed oil breaking over the paper/ running down pouring/ no one to catch it my life breaking open/ no one to contain it my/ pelvis thinning out into God." Other nominees for the National Book Award included Donald Justice for his *Collected Poems,* William Heven for *Shoah Train,* Cole Swensen for *Goest,* and Carl Phillips for *The Rest of Love.*

Poetry Slam. The 2004 National Poetry Slam was held in St. Louis on August 4 to August 7. Teams and poets from more than 70 U.S. cities converged to compete in "slam," poetry mixed with performance that is also a competition. Individuals and teams are scored on content and delivery. The winning team was from Hollywood, California. Sonya Renee, representing Washington, D.C., and Baltimore, was the winning solo performer. Renee directs peer education at a non-profit organization promoting HIV prevention.

Deaths. Two prominent poets—both living in the San Francisco area—died in 2004. British-born poet Thom Gunn died on April 25 at the age of 74. Gunn was born on Aug. 29, 1929. He moved to San Francisco in 1954, where he was considered a maverick. The 1960's counterculture is reflected in many of his volumes, though unlike some other countercultural writers, Gunn maintained a rigor and form in his poetry. In *The Passages of Joy* (1982), Gunn wrote what might be considered a lament for his own passing in the poem "Elegy": "They keep leaving me/ and they don't/ tell me they don't/ warn me that this is/ the last time I'll be seeing them/ as they drop away. . . ."

Czeslaw Milosz, a Polish Nobel Laureate, died on Aug. 14, 2004 at the age of 93. Milosz was born on June 30, 1911, in Lithuania of Polish parents. His experiences during World War II (1939-1945) and Poland's subsequent transfer to the Soviet sphere of influence shaped much of his work. He immigrated to the United States in 1960, and his first volume of poetry was translated into English in 1973. He considered himself an exile not only from his homeland, but from many of the political and artistic movements to which he was tied. By the end of his life he was hailed by Poland, as well as the world, as a literary giant.   ■ Brian Bouldrey

See also **Pulitzer Prizes.**

Poland officially became a member of the European Union (EU) on May 1, 2004. On May 2, Leszek Miller stepped down as Poland's prime minister. President Aleksander Kwasniewski tapped Marek Belka of Miller's Democratic Left Alliance (SLD) to form a new government. Belka assembled a new governing coalition in the Polish parliament on June 23.

EU parliamentary elections. In EU-wide elections in mid-June, Poland elected its 54 representatives to the European Parliament (EP). The EP, part of the EU governmental structure, is a 700-plus-member advisory body, which meets in Strasbourg, France.

In the election, Poland's chief opposition party, Civic Platform, won nearly a quarter of the vote. Two avowedly anti-EU parties together took another quarter of the vote, while the ruling SLD garnered about 10 percent. Turnout for the election in Poland was less than 20 percent.

Economy. In 2004, Poland's economy grew at one of the fastest rates in Europe. In the first half of the year, growth in the gross domestic product (GDP)—the value of all goods and services produced in a year—topped 6 percent. Inflation accelerated in response to entry into the EU, economists noted. Unemployment hovered above 19 percent, the highest of any EU member country.

EU economists singled out Poland's debt-to-GDP ratio of 5.6 percent as a cause for particular concern in 2004. The ratio compares a country's longterm debt—represented by cumulative borrowing to meet government expenses—with its GDP. Responding to EU concerns, the Belka government proposed austerity measures, including reduction of annual increases in pension and disability payments. The parliament passed some of Belka's measures, changing or rejecting others.

Foreign policy. Polish leaders restated their support for the United States-led coalition in Iraq in the aftermath of terrorist bombings of commuter trains in Madrid, Spain, on March 11. According to political analysts, the attack triggered the defeat of pro-U.S. Prime Minister Jose Maria Aznar in Spanish parliamentary elections on March 14 and led to subsequent withdrawal of Spanish troops from Iraq.

In 2003, Poland contributed 2,500 troops to the U.S.-led coalition in Iraq. The Polish force remained at full strength throughout 2004. In October, Polish officials indicated that Poland would withdraw its troops from Iraq by the end of 2005, though no specific timetable was given. According to opinion surveys in 2004, 70 percent of Poles opposed the deployment of Polish troops in Iraq.   ■ Sharon L. Wolchik

See also **Europe; Iraq: A Special Report.**

Pollution. See Environmental Pollution.

Popular music. The music industry showed signs of a rebound during the first six months of 2004, according to the Recording Industry Association of America (RIAA). The RIAA is a Washington, D.C.-based trade organization that represents the recording industry in the United States. Shipments of all full-length compact discs (CD's) to retail outlets increased by 10.2 percent through June 2004, compared with the first six months in 2003. The sales of CD's had steadily declined since mid-2000. Many people in the music industry had blamed the decline on the illegal exchange of copyrighted music downloaded from the Internet.

The practice, sometimes called "music piracy," continued to be of concern to the recording industry in 2004 despite growth in the licensed digital download of music. The RIAA reported that the producers of top 50 albums shipped 16.7 percent fewer units in the first six months of 2004, compared with 2003; and the producers of the top 100 albums, which are most heavily pirated, shipped 19.7 percent fewer units.

Forcing early releases. The release date of one of the most highly anticipated albums of 2004, Eminem's *Encore,* was pushed up by one week in November after it was illegally made available in its entirety on the Internet. Piracy concerns prompted a similar release date shift for Snoop Dogg's *R&G (Rhythm and Gangsta): The Masterpiece,* also released in November.

Top sellers. Usher released *Confessions* in April. The rhythm-and-blues singer's album contained the autobiographical title song and the hit single "Yeah." It became one of 2004's best-selling albums. *Confessions* earned more than $1 million in its first week of release and sold 6.5 million copies by October, according to Nielsen SoundScan, a White Plains, New York, company that tracks the sales of music and music video products throughout the United States and Canada.

Jazz singer Norah Jones's second album, *Feels Like Home,* released in February, also earned more than $1 million in its first week. The year 2004 was the first since 2000 in which more than one album had sales surpassing the $1-million mark.

Country music enjoyed a resurgence in 2004 that recalled the genre's mainstream popularity of the early 1990's. Country album sales for the first six months of 2004 increased approximately 14 percent, compared with the same period in 2003, according to Nielsen SoundScan.

Gretchen Wilson, whose album, *Here for the Party,* contained the rowdy anthem, "Redneck Woman," was among a new generation of artists who topped the charts in 2004. The single was a celebration of the "everywoman." Big & Rich, a duo whose music combines country and elements of hip-hop, released their debut album, *Horse of a Different Color,* to critical and fan praise.

"Crying Time" for Ray Charles

Ray Charles, one of popular music's most influential figures, died on June 10, 2004, at age 73. Charles's musical style was influenced by several musical genres, including gospel, rhythm and blues, and jazz. He borrowed various elements from these styles to create what ultimately came to be called soul music. During his six-decade career, he received 12 Grammy Awards and a Recording Academy Lifetime Achievement Award, was inducted into the Rock and Roll Hall of Fame, and was a 1986 Kennedy Center Honors recipient. At that ceremony, Charles was described as "one of the most respected singers of his generation. . . . who broke down barriers between secular and sacred styles."

Ray Charles Robinson was born on Sept. 23, 1930, in Albany, Georgia, a town about 180 miles (290 kilometers) south of Atlanta. Hardship and poverty marked Charles's early life. His father abandoned the family when Charles was still an infant, and his mother soon relocated the family to Greenville, Florida. When he was 5 years old, Charles witnessed his younger brother, George, accidentally drown in a washtub. A few months later, an unknown ailment began to affect Ray's eyesight. By age 7 he was blind.

From 1937 to 1945, Charles attended the St. Augustine (Florida) School for the Deaf and Blind, where he learned to write music in Braille while honing his seemingly innate skills on the piano, clarinet, alto saxophone, trumpet, and organ. Following the death of his mother in 1945, the 15-year-old Charles traveled to Jacksonville, Florida, to find work as a musician. In the late 1940's, Charles formed various jazz groups and began touring. By the early 1950's, he dropped "Robinson" from his name to avoid confusion with Sugar Ray Robinson, a popular professional boxer of the era.

Charles's unique sound—which integrated gospel shouts with his deep, smooth voice—led to a recording contract with New York City-based Atlantic Records in 1953. In 1959, he jumped to ABC-Paramount Records in New York City. His albums merged musical categories into his own blend, melding big band, blues, country, gospel, jazz, and rock-and-roll into soul.

Charles's blues- and gospel-inspired songs were successful on rhythm-and-blues charts during the 1950's. One of his hits, "I Got a Woman" (1955), is widely considered the first song to be labeled "soul." He scored one of his first number-one hits with "What'd I Say" (1959) and continued to gain fame with "Georgia on My Mind" (1960), "Hit the Road Jack" (1961), and "Crying Time" (1966), which all became standards. Many fans consider his rendition of "America the Beautiful"—performed for President Ronald Reagan at a 1985 inaugural ball—as the most stirring ever recorded.

After playing more than 10,000 concerts during his career, Charles's health began to decline in 2003, forcing him to cancel a tour. He underwent hip replacement surgery later that year. Charles had planned to resume the cancelled tour in 2004 before he was diagnosed with the liver disease that led to his death. More than 1,200 people attended his funeral.

In his 1978 autobiography *Brother Ray,* Charles described the impact music had on his life. "I was born with music inside me," he wrote. "That's the only explanation I know of. . . ." For his fans, it was the only explanation necessary.

■ Tim Frystak

Several established artists released best-selling albums and greatest hits packages. They included Tim McGraw's *Live Like You Were Dyin'*; Alan Jackson's *What I Do;* George Strait's *50 Number Ones;* Brooks & Dunn's *Greatest Hits Collection, Volume II;* and Shania Twain's *Greatest Hits.* Jimmy Buffett's album *License to Chill,* which featured duets with such country stars as Jackson, Strait, Kenny Chesney, and Toby Keith, became the first album in his 30-year career to reach number one on the charts.

Chesney had the best-selling country album of 2004, according to Nielsen SoundScan. *When the Sun Goes Down* sold 2.7 million copies by October.

Loretta Lynn collaborated with Jack White of the rock group, the White Stripes on her critically acclaimed April release, *Van Lear Rose.* White also produced the album by the country music legend. Lynn wrote or cowrote all the songs on the album for the first time since the 1960's.

Punk rock opera. Green Day released *American Idiot* in September. Called a "punk rock opera," *American Idiot* explored conformity and narrow-mindedness in suburban American life through such alienated characters as Jesus of Suburbia and St. Jimmy, "the needle in the vein of the establishment." *American Idiot* was one of the most critically acclaimed albums in the band's career.

SMiLE. Beach Boys cofounder Brian Wilson released *SMiLE* to critical acclaim in September. Wilson had abandoned the *SMiLE* project in 1967, and music critics and fans had regarded it as one of rock music's legendary lost albums. Wilson originally conceived the ambitious album as "a teen-age symphony to God," but Wilson's band mates and record company considered some of the challenging music and enigmatic lyrics to be too great a departure from the Beach Boys' hit songs about surfing and summer fun. The project did yield songs that would become Beach Boys classics, including "Heroes and Villains" and "Surf's Up."

Publicized dispute. Rhythm-and-blues singer R. Kelly and rapper Jay-Z released *Unfinished Business* in October 2004. The collaboration debuted at number one on the album charts and was followed with a concert tour. However, Jay-Z kicked Kelly off the "Best of Both Worlds" tour in November after several highly publicized incidents. In October, during a concert in St. Louis, Missouri, Kelly left the

GRAMMY AWARD WINNERS IN 2004

Record of the Year, *Clocks,* Coldplay

Album of the Year, *Speakerboxxx/The Love Below,* OutKast

Song of the Year, "Dance With My Father," Richard Marx and Luther Vandross

New Artist, Evanescence

Pop Vocal Performance, Female, "Beautiful," Christina Aguilera

Pop Vocal Performance, Male, "Cry Me A River," Justin Timberlake

Pop Performance by a Duo or Group, "Underneath It All," No Doubt

Traditional Pop Vocal Album, *A Wonderful World,* Tony Bennett and k.d. lang

Rock Vocal Performance, Female, "Trouble," Pink

Rock Vocal Performance, Male, "Gravedigger," Dave Matthews

Rock Performance by a Duo or Group with Vocal, "Disorder In The House," Warren Zevon and Bruce Springsteen

Hard Rock Performance, "Bring Me To Life," Evanescence featuring Paul McCoy

Metal Performance, "St. Anger," Metallica

Rock Song, "Seven Nation Army," Jack White

Rock Album, *One By One,* Foo Fighters

Alternative Music Album, *Elephant,* The White Stripes

Rhythm-and-Blues Vocal Performance, Female, "Dangerously In Love 2," Beyonce

Rhythm-and-Blues Vocal Performance, Male, "Dance With My Father," Luther Vandross

Rhythm-and-Blues Performance by a Duo or Group with Vocal, "The Closer I Get To You," Luther Vandross and Beyonce

Rhythm-and-Blues Song, "Crazy In Love," Shawn Carter, Rich Harrison, Beyonce Knowles, and Eugene Record

Rhythm-and-Blues Album, *Dance With My Father,* Luther Vandross

Contemporary Rhythm-and-Blues Album, *Dangerously In Love,* Beyonce

Rap Solo Performance, Female "Work It," Missy Elliott

Rap Solo Performance, Male "Lose Yourself," Eminem

Rap Performance by a Duo or Group, "Shake Ya Tailfeather," Nelly, P. Diddy, and Murphy Lee

Rap Album, *Speakerboxxx/The Love Below,* OutKast

Rap Song, "Lose Yourself," J. Bass, M. Mathers, L. Resto

Contemporary Jazz Album, *34th N Lex,* Randy Brecker

Jazz Vocal Album, *A Little Moonlight,* Dianne Reeves

Jazz Instrumental, Solo, "Matrix," Chick Corea

Jazz Instrumental Album, Individual or Group, *Alegria,* Wayne Shorter

Large Jazz Ensemble Album, *Wide Angles,* Michael Brecker Quindectet

Country Album, *Livin', Lovin', Losin'—Songs of the Louvin Brothers,* Various Artists

Country Song, "It's Five O'Clock Somewhere," Jim "Moose" Brown and Don Rollins

Country Vocal Performance, Female, "Keep On The Sunny Side," June Carter Cash

Country Vocal Performance, Male, "Next Big Thing," Vince Gill

Country Performance by a Duo or Group with Vocal, "A Simple Life," Ricky Skaggs and Kentucky Thunder

Country Vocal Collaboration, "How's The World Treating You," James Taylor and Alison Krauss

Country Instrumental Performance, "Cluck Old Hen," Alison Krauss and Union Station

stage to argue with technicians over "technical problems." He cut short his performance, left the arena, and drove to a local fast-food restaurant where he served customers at the drive-through window. Kelly stopped another concert in New York City when he claimed to see two audience members with guns. He also alleged that a member of Jay-Z's entourage attacked him with pepper spray. On November 1, Kelly filed a $75-million breach-of-contract lawsuit against Jay-Z in New York State Supreme Court in New York City.

Bob Dylan published his autobiography, *Chronicles, Volume One,* in October. Considered a 20th-century icon, the folksinger and songwriter had guarded his privacy throughout his career. *Chronicles, Volume One* was not a standard autobiography. It was the first in a proposed series of personal histories. Dylan wrote about several pivotal events in his career, including his arrival in Greenwich Village in New York City, where he began his career; being labeled a spokesperson for his generation; his retreat from celebrity; and the production of two of his lesser-known releases, *New Morning* (1970) and *Oh Mercy* (1989).

Festival seating ban lifted. The city council in Cincinnati, Ohio, voted in August 2004 to lift its ban on festival, or unreserved, seating for rock concerts. The ban was imposed in 1979 after 11 people were crushed to death during a Who concert. The ban was temporarily lifted in 2002 for a Bruce Springsteen concert. Concert promoters and city officials lobbied to permanently eliminate the ban to lure major musical acts that bypassed Cincinnati because of the restrictions on festival seating. To ease concern about concertgoers' safety, Cincinnati adopted national standards for controlling festival seating.

Vote for Change tour. A partisan group of musicians who sought to defeat U.S. President George W. Bush in the November 2004 election embarked on a concert tour in October. More than 20 bands and performers, including the Dixie Chicks, Pearl Jam, Bonnie Raitt, R.E.M., Bruce Springsteen and the E Street Band, and James Taylor, staged concerts in 11 key battleground states. MoveOn PAC, a liberal political action committee that supported U.S. Senator John Kerry (D., Massachusetts), the Democratic presidential candidate, presented the tour. Several of the musicians involved in the tour experienced fan backlash, radio station boycotts, and media criticism.

Death. Johnny Ramone, cofounder of the punk rock band The Ramones, died on Sept. 15, 2004. He was born John Cummings in 1948. The Ramones debuted in 1974 and were a major influence on other bands, including Green Day and Nirvana.   ■ Donald Liebenson

See also **People in the news** (John Edwards, John Kerry).

Population. The total world population hit 6.4 billion in 2004 and was expected to rise to 8.9 billion by 2050, according to the United Nations Population Fund (UNPF). The fund pointed out a link between rapid population growth, poverty and poor health, lack of education, and gender bias. The UNPF promotes programs that try to develop solutions to such problems.

On Sept. 15, 2004, the UNPF published a comprehensive review of 10 years of activities designed to balance the world's population growth with available resources; to improve the status of women; and to ensure access to reproductive health care. The activities were part of a 20-year plan of action adopted by 179 countries at the International Conference on Population and Development in Cairo, Egypt, in 1994. The review was entitled State of the World Population 2004. Researchers reported that they had found some progress in a majority of countries. However, they warned that other efforts, such as the fight against HIV/AIDS and maternal deaths, were less successful.

A key component of the plan of action involved reproductive health care, including family planning. A UN survey found that a majority of countries have integrated family planning and safe motherhood into national policies and health care systems. Reproductive health care includes modern contraception and greater emphasis on safe sex practices. However, access to reproductive health care is not universal. The UN reported that 200 million women in the world's poorest countries cannot afford contraception. The annual cost of providing contraception to women around the world in 2004 was $3.9 billion. Public health officials suggested that universal access to contraception would prevent millions of unplanned births; reduce unsafe abortions and pregnancy-related deaths; and lower infant mortality rates.

Family planning programs remained unavailable to an estimated 300 million couples worldwide in 2004. Without access to family planning, populations in the 50 poorest countries of the world are expected to triple by 2050.

Young people. In April 2004, the UN Department of Economic and Social Affairs reported that many of the world's estimated 1.1 billion people aged 15 to 24 remain seriously challenged by lack of education, poverty, unemployment, and the impact of conflict. The research was published in the World Youth Report 2003. The authors of the report noted that 9 of 10 young people live in developing countries. Nearly 7,000 young people worldwide become infected with HIV every day. While there is a trend toward later marriage, young people are becoming sexually active at earlier ages. Many lack full knowledge of disease risks and means of protection.   ■ J. Tuyet Nguyen

Portugal underwent widening political instability in 2004 that ended with the resignation of the Social Democratic government of Prime Minister Pedro Santana Lopes in December. Santana Lopes had been chosen by the Social Democratic Party to replace Jose Manuel Durao Barroso as party leader and prime minister. Durao Barroso, who had led a center-right coalition government since 2002, resigned in July 2004 to become president of the European Commission (EC), the executive agency for the 25-nation European Union (EU). Durao Barroso, whose Social Democratic Party had formed a government with the Popular Party, worked to reduce Portugal's large budget deficit and combat a serious recession.

Santana Lopes had little experience in national politics and failed to maintain the government's unity. He clashed with his own finance minister over the advisability of instituting tax cuts and, in November, demoted his closest adviser, Henrique Chaves, from deputy prime minister to sports minister, prompting Chaves to resign. On November 30, President Jorge Sampaio announced he would dissolve the government because of the infighting and call for new elections in 2005, more than a year ahead of schedule. In response, Santana Lopes announced on Dec. 11, 2004, that his government was resigning and would serve as a caretaker government until the elections.

Economy. Portugal emerged from a recession in 2004. EC economists forecast that the country's *gross domestic product* (GDP—the value of goods and services produced in a year) would grow by 1.3 percent in 2004, after having declined by 1.2 percent in 2003. In November 2004, Santana Lopes introduced a budget for 2005 that would cut income taxes and increase retirement benefits. The EC warned that Portugal's deficit risked rising sharply above 3 percent of GDP, the limit for EU countries that use the euro.

Child abuse trial. Seven people went on trial in November 2004 on charges of sexually abusing children at the state-run orphanage Casa Pia. The case shocked the Portuguese because investigations revealed that police and government officials had ignored allegations of abuse for years.

Soccer championship. Portugal hosted the European Championship, held every four years, in 2004. The three-week tournament, the biggest in soccer after the World Cup, drew tens of thousands of fans from across the continent. Portugal advanced to the final on July 4 but lost, 1-0, to Greece, which had never before won a game in an international tournament. ■ Tom Buerkle

See also **Europe; Soccer.**

President of the United States.
See **United States, President of the.**

Prince Edward Island. See Canadian Provinces.

Prisons. The United States Department of Justice reported in November 2004 that 1,470,045 prisoners were detained under federal or state authority as of Dec. 31, 2003, with 1,387,848 inmates in federal or state prisons and 73,343 federal or state prisoners held in municipal or county jails. Between December 2002 and December 2003, the federal prisoner population increased by 5.8 percent; the state prisoner population, by 1.6 percent.

The overall U.S. prison population in 2003, including local jails and military and juvenile facilities, totaled 2,212,475, representing a 2.6-percent increase over the total prison population in 2002. In 2003, 1 out of every 140 U.S. residents was incarcerated in prison or jail.

Women, juveniles, and minorities. During 2003, the number of females under the jurisdiction of federal and state prison authorities grew by 3.6 percent, compared with a 2-percent increase for males. As of Dec. 31, 2003, the state and federal female inmate population was 101,179.

The number of sentenced juveniles—individuals under the age of 18—held in adult federal or state facilities on December 31 was 2,800. That number represented a 42-percent decline from the 4,800 juvenile inmates reported in 1995.

In 2003, 44.1 percent of all state and federal inmates were black; 35 percent were white; 19 percent were Hispanics; and just under 2 percent were identified as "other." Among persons aged 25 to 29 in the general U.S. population, 9.3 percent of all black males were incarcerated; 2.6 percent of Hispanic males were incarcerated; and 1.1 percent of white males were incarcerated.

Probation and parole. According to the Department of Justice, the number of adults on *probation* (a period of supervision in the community following a conviction) or *parole* (a period of conditional supervised release following a prison term) reached a record high of more than 4.8 million by the end of 2003. This number represented 70 percent of all persons under federal, state, or local correctional supervision. About 49 percent of individuals on probation had been convicted of a felony.

Death row. As of Dec. 31, 2003, a total of 3,374 prison inmates were awaiting execution in federal and state prisons. Federal and state authorities executed 65 individuals in the United States in 2003. Over half of those executions occurred in the contiguous states of Texas (24 executions) and Oklahoma (14). Between Jan. 1, 2004, and November 17, 59 individuals were executed—all by state authorities—in the United States. ■ Brian Bouldrey

See also **Courts; Crime; State government.**

Prizes. See Nobel prizes; Pulitzer Prizes.

Protestantism. Protestant affiliation in the United States dropped to a bare majority in the early 2000's and will, if trends continue, cease to represent the majority of the U.S. population in the near future, revealed a survey released in July 2004. The survey, which tracked Protestant affiliations professed by Americans from 1993 to 2002, was conducted by the National Opinion Research Center of the University of Chicago. Protestant affiliation, gauged at 63 percent of the population in 1993, had dropped to 52 percent by 2002, the survey indicated.

Protestants appeared to be losing adherents not to other religions but to the growing "unchurched" category, which expanded from 9 percent of the U.S. population in 1993 to nearly 14 percent in 2002. Sociologists speculated that the loss of statistical dominance by Protestants—for the first time in U.S. history—could have profound effects on American culture.

Homosexuality. Protestant denominations in 2004 continued to debate the role of homosexuals in the church. A February ruling by the Massachusetts Supreme Court that same-sex marriage must be recognized in the state imparted new urgency to questions concerning the status of gays and lesbians in churches.

In March, a United Methodist Church special court acquitted the Rev. Karen Dammann of Ellensburg, Washington, of violating church law by living in a lesbian relationship while serving as a pastor. However, the quadrennial general conference, meeting in Pittsburgh in May, rejected changing the policy that homosexuality is "incompatible with Christian teaching," and the church's highest court admonished bishops not to appoint practicing homosexuals to the ministry.

On December 2, a jury of 13 Methodist ministers voted 12-to-1 to find the Reverend Irene Elizabeth Stroud, of the First United Methodist Church of Germantown, Pennsylvania, guilty of violating the ban on self-avowed practicing homosexuals being ordained. Reverend Stroud's ministerial credentials were removed, barring her from administering baptisms, marriages, or Holy Communion. On December 27, she announced plans to file an appeal.

Delegates of the Presbyterian Church (U.S.A.) in a July meeting of the church's legislative General Assembly in Richmond, Virginia, voted to retain a ban on the ordination of practicing lesbians and gays. In the Episcopal Church, controversy surrounding the November 2003 ordination of openly gay Bishop Gene Robinson of New Hampshire continued to reverberate. Some Episcopalians who oppose gay ordination formed support networks for their cause within the church, while in a few parishes, majorities voted to withdraw from the church altogether. In the Episcopal diocese of Los Angeles, Bishop J. Jon Bruno appointed assistant bishops to reassert church control over several breakaway churches.

Churches and politics. Protestants, like most Americans, focused on presidential politics in 2004. During the campaign, President George W. Bush, the Republican candidate, solicited support from conservative Protestant churches. In June, his campaign officials sent a memo, asking such churches to submit membership rosters. In response, an official with the Southern Baptist Convention, a conservative group often supportive of the Bush administration, criticized the Bush campaign's "intrusion on local congregations." Other religious leaders described the solicitation as inappropriate, while legal experts questioned whether complying with such a request could endanger churches' tax-exempt status.

Israel and Palestine. The Presbyterian Church voted in 2004 to study whether to divest itself of investments in firms involved in Israel's occupation of the West Bank and Gaza. A number of Jewish organizations in the United States subsequently lodged protests with the Presbyterian Church, while acknowledging that Jewish-Presbyterian relations traditionally have been positive and constructive. The B'nai B'rith, a Jewish advocacy group, considered severing relations with the denomination.   ■ Martin E. Marty

Public health and safety. The United States in 2004 experienced a shortage of injectable influenza vaccine for the second consecutive flu season. The shortage during the flu season that began in October 2004 created significant public anxiety and led to vaccine rationing. The shortfall also prompted increased calls for more government involvement in the manufacture and distribution of flu vaccines.

The shortage resulted when possible bacterial contamination led British officials to suspend the operating license of a vaccine-production facility in Liverpool owned by the Chiron Corporation of Emeryville, California. Chiron was one of only two manufacturers licensed by the Food and Drug Administration to produce injectable flu vaccine for the United States. The facility had been expected to ship about 48 million doses, approximately half the U.S. supply.

In response, the U.S. Centers for Disease Control and Prevention (CDC) in Atlanta, Georgia, urged physicians and health officials to restrict the vaccine to people at high risk of developing serious complications from the flu. Among these were adults age 65 or older, children ages 6 to 23 months, the chronically ill, residents of nursing homes, and health care workers responsible for direct patient care. Several states, including Illinois and New Mexico, bought vaccine from Europe.

High demand. The vaccine shortage during the 2003-2004 flu season resulted from unexpectedly high demand triggered by an usually early start to the season and what appeared to be a greater-than-normal death rate among children. The CDC reported receiving notice of 152 laboratory-confirmed flu-related deaths in children under age 18 between October 2003 and May 2004. Among this number were 96 children under age 5. The CDC had previously estimated that about 92 children under age 5 die from flu-related causes each year.

The U.S. government announced in April 2004 that for the first time it would stockpile flu vaccine for children under 18. In May, U.S. health officials recommended that all children ages 6 to 23 months routinely receive an annual flu shot. Officials based the new policy on studies showing that children under age 2 are significantly more likely than older children to require hospitalization for pneumonia and other flu-related complications. In September, health officials in Canada made similar recommendations for that nation's children.

West Nile virus. The number of victims of West Nile virus in the United States fell dramatically in 2004. By mid-November, 2,313 people had contracted the virus and 79 had died, according to the CDC. In 2003, the CDC reported, the virus infected 9,862 people and caused 264 deaths.

The geographic focus of the West Nile virus continued to move westward across the United States in 2004. Cases in California and Arizona skyrocketed from 2003 levels, rising from 3 to 737 and from 13 to 390, respectively, as of Nov. 16, 2004. Colorado, which led the nation with 2,947 cases and 63 deaths in 2003, reported 276 cases and 3 deaths. Rates in other 2003 hot spots, including Nebraska, North Dakota, South Dakota, and Texas, also fell dramatically in 2004.

Bird flu. Two people in British Columbia contracted avian influenza (bird flu) in February after being exposed to poultry infected with a mild strain of the flu virus. To halt the spread of the virus, Canadian health officials ordered the slaughter of about 80 percent of the province's poultry stock. In the United States, outbreaks of bird flu occurred in poultry only in Texas and several eastern states. In October, the World Health Organization (WHO) reported 32 confirmed human deaths from bird flu in 2004, all in Thailand or Vietnam.

SARS. A small outbreak of severe acute respiratory syndrome (SARS) in China in April killed one person and infected eight others. WHO concluded in July that the National Institute of Virology in Beijing was probably the source of the outbreak. In 2003, the highly contagious SARS virus killed at least 700 people and infected at least 8,000 others in a total of 30 countries.   ■ Barbara A. Mayes

See also **Agriculture; Asia; Canada; Medicine.**

Puerto Rico. The outcome of Puerto Rico's election for governor on Nov. 2, 2004, remained unknown for several weeks. A recount of the votes was mandated by the narrowness of the margin between the top two candidates—Anibal Acevedo Vila of the ruling Popular Democratic Party and former Governor Pedro Rossello of the New Progressive Party. The recount was followed by legal wrangling over 28,000 disputed ballots. After Puerto Rico's Supreme Court and a U.S. district judge an appellate court in Boston weighed in on the matter, Acevedo Vila was finally declared the winner in late December.

Acevedo—who supported maintaining, but reforming, Puerto Rico's status as a commonwealth of the United States—pledged to convene a constitutional assembly in 2005 to discuss Puerto Rico's relationship with the United States. Rossello had favored a referendum limited to just two choices—either statehood or independence.

Naval base closed. The United States closed down the Roosevelt Roads Naval Station in Puerto Rico in March 2004. The shutdown, which had been demanded by protestors since the 1990's, meant the loss of an estimated $300 million that the base had pumped annually into Puerto Rico's economy. In addition, well over 1,000 civilian jobs were eliminated. The base closing came at a time when unemployment in Puerto Rico was nearly 12 percent.

Puerto Rico's government made plans to develop the abandoned site in order to reap as many economic benefits from it as possible. Commonwealth officials hoped to reuse the base's airport, hospital, and port for civilian purposes. The government also planned to set aside much of the property for tourists as a nature preserve and a science and technology center.

Pharmaceuticals buoy economy. Multinational pharmaceutical companies continued in 2004 to help buoy the economy of Puerto Rico, where 16 of the top 20 most profitable drugs sold in the United States were produced. For example, Abbott Laboratories Inc., headquartered near Chicago, was constructing a $350-million pharmaceutical plant in Barceloneta. Abbott planned to distribute the plant's first product, a drug for rheumatoid arthritis, in 2007.

New coliseum. The Jose Miguel Agrelot Coliseum opened in September 2004 in San Juan, the capital. The new coliseum was a state-of-the-art venue for performers and athletes that seated as many as 18,500 spectators. It was designed to accommodate basketball and hockey games, as well as music and theatrical events. The Puerto Rican government owned the facility, which was the largest music or sports complex in the commonwealth.   ■ Nathan A. Haverstock

See also **Latin America.**

Pulitzer Prizes in journalism, letters, drama, and music were awarded on April 5, 2004, by Columbia University in New York City on the recommendation of the Pulitzer Prize Board.

Journalism. The staff of the *Los Angeles Times* won the prize for breaking news reporting for its coverage of wildfires that endangered southern California. The investigative reporting prize went to Michael D. Sallah, Mitch Weiss, and Joe Mahr of *The Blade* (Toledo, Ohio) for a series of articles on crimes committed during the Vietnam War (1957-1975) by a United States Army platoon. The *Los Angeles Times* staff also won the prize for national reporting for its examination of how Wal-Mart became the largest company in the world. *Los Angeles Times* writer Dan Neil was given the prize for criticism for his automobile reviews. William R. Stall of the *Los Angeles Times* won the prize for editorial writing for his examination of California's troubled state government.

Anthony Shadid of *The Washington Post* won the international reporting prize for his highly personal stories of the lives of Iraqis in a time of war. David Barstow and Lowell Bergman of *The New York Times* shared the public service prize for a series of articles exposing U.S. businesses that broke basic safety rules. *The Wall Street Journal* earned two Pulitzer Prizes in 2004, one awarded to Kevin Helliker and Thomas M. Burton for explanatory reporting, given for their examination of *aneurysms* (swelling in blood vessels). The other award, for beat reporting, was given to Daniel Golden for his stories on admission preferences at U.S. universities.

Miami Herald writer Leonard Pitts, Jr., won the commentary prize for his columns on divisive issues. Matt Davies of *The Journal News* (White Plains, New York) received the editorial cartooning prize for his drawings on a variety of topics. David Leeson and Cheryl Diaz Meyer of *The Dallas Morning News* shared the prize for breaking news photography for their photographs of the war in Iraq. Carolyn Cole of the *Los Angeles Times* took the prize for feature photography, awarded for her depictions of life in civil war-torn Liberia. Although there were four finalists, no award was given for feature writing in 2004.

Letters, drama, and music. Edward P. Jones won the fiction prize for his novel *The Known World*. The drama prize went to Doug Wright for his play *I Am My Own Wife*. Steven Hahn was awarded the history prize for his book *A Nation Under Our Feet*. William Taubman's *Krushchev: The Man and His Era* won the prize for biography. Franz Wright won the prize for poetry for his collection *Walking to Martha's Vineyard*. The general nonfiction prize was given to Anne Applebaum for *Gulag: A History*. Composer Paul Moravec received the music prize for *Tempest Fantasy*. ■ Brian Bouldrey

Quebec. See **Canadian provinces.**

Radio. Questions surrounding on-air indecency dominated the radio industry in the United States for much of 2004. Broadcasters, station owners, and the Federal Communications Commission (FCC) grappled with the issue of what type of behavior violated good taste and broadcasting standards. The FCC is responsible for the regulation of U.S. and foreign communication by radio, television, wire, satellite, and cable. The agency develops, implements, and enforces a wide variety of federal rules and standards.

The FCC tightened the enforcement of decency standards for all broadcasters after popular music singer Janet Jackson exposed a portion of her breast during the Super Bowl XXXVIII halftime show on CBS television in February 2004. The agency quickly came under pressure from members of the U.S. Congress to more vigorously regulate what was aired.

Radio and television personality Howard Stern, host of the syndicated program "The Howard Stern Show," found himself at the center of the controversy in April after the FCC fined Clear Channel Communications, a San Antonio, Texas-based broadcasting company, $475,000 for airing a Stern program containing 18 allegedly indecent remarks. The remarks had been made during one of his radio shows in 2003. After the fine was announced, Clear Channel executives dropped Stern's program from their six stations that broadcast the show.

Clear Channel officials said Stern violated the company's "Responsible Broadcasting Initiative," which had been unveiled in February 2004. The policy called for a "zero tolerance policy for indecent content" and required an immediate suspension of any radio personality who faced FCC fines. In June, Clear Channel agreed to pay the FCC $1.75 million to resolve a number of indecency claims against Stern and other broadcasters.

Satellite radio. On October 6, Stern announced that he would leave the New York City-based Infinity Broadcasting Corporation and move in 2006 to Sirius Satellite Radio, also headquartered in New York City. Satellite radio delivers radio programming via satellite on a monthly basis in much the same way as subscription satellite television services. Sirius officials estimated that the agreement with Stern would cost the company approximately $100 million annually, including production costs associated with the program and Stern's salary. The FCC licenses satellite broadcasters, but the agency does not regulate content.

On Oct. 4, 2004, another satellite radio provider, XM Satellite Radio, headquartered in Washington, D.C., debuted "The Bob Edwards Show." The program was a blend of news and interviews hosted by former National Public Radio (NPR) "Morning Edition" host Bob Edwards.

Alistair Cooke:
The Best of
Two Worlds

British-born journalist, radio broadcaster, and television personality Alistair Cooke died on March 29, 2004, in New York City, at age 95. For most of his career, Cooke was a foreign correspondent who reported on politics, history, popular culture, and customs in the United States. As the host of "Letter from America," the longest-running solo radio series in broadcast history, Cooke was considered a peerless interpreter of American life. Critics credited him with improving understanding between the United Kingdom and the United States. Cooke also hosted several popular and award-winning television series.

Cooke was born in Manchester, England, on Nov. 20, 1908, and given the name Alfred. While a student at Cambridge University, studying English literature, he legally changed his first name to Alistair.

Alistair Cooke came to the United States in the 1930's and attended both Yale and Harvard universities. Following graduation, Cooke returned to Britain, where he was hired as a film critic for the British Broadcasting Corporation (BBC). In 1935, the National Broadcasting Corporation (NBC) hired him as its London correspondent.

Cooke moved back to the United States in 1937 to work as a radio commentator for the BBC. He became a naturalized U.S. citizen in 1941. In 1946, the BBC invited Cooke to present a weekly broadcast on topical aspects of American life and culture. The 15-minute program, "Letter from America," was planned as a 13-week series. It lasted 58 years and was broadcast to more than 50 countries.

Critics regularly praised Cooke for his elegantly spoken and insightfully observed commentary. One of his most dramatic broadcasts was his personal account of being a few yards from presidential candidate Robert Kennedy when he was assassinated in 1968. Cooke missed only three of the series' nearly 3,000 broadcasts. In March 2004, just weeks before his death, BBC officials announced Cooke's decision to retire.

While audiences worldwide were familiar with Cooke's work as a radio commentator, U.S. television audiences were perhaps more familiar with his introduction of several programs to the American public. From 1952 to 1961, Cooke hosted the successful television series "Omnibus," which over nine years aired on the commercial television networks CBS, ABC, and NBC. "Omnibus" was known for its intellectual programming focusing on the arts, sciences, drama, and history. Many critics consider it the prototype for the development of programming on public television. From 1971 to 1992, Cooke hosted the Public Broadcasting System (PBS) program "Masterpiece Theatre." Cooke introduced a number of British miniseries, including "I, Claudius," "The Jewel in the Crown," and "Upstairs, Downstairs," to American audiences. He provided viewers with background information about the writers and historical context. In 1972, Cooke cowrote and hosted the 13-part BBC documentary series "America," which he called "a personal history of the United States."

Cooke also was a prolific author. His works included *Alistair Cooke's America* (1973); *Douglas Fairbanks: The Making of a Screen Actor* (1940); *The Vintage Mencken* (1955); and *The Americans* (1977). He also served on the editorial board of the *World Book Year Book* for nearly 20 years.

For many Americans, Cooke was the quintessential British gentleman. Many of his own countrymen, however, believed Cooke was an American. "I feel totally at home in both countries," he once said. In 1973, Queen Elizabeth II awarded Cooke an honorary knighthood, and in 1974 he addressed the U.S. Congress on its 200th anniversary—testaments to the esteem in which Cooke was held by his fellow countrymen in both nations.   ■ Donald Liebenson

John Thune (left), the Republican candidate for the U.S. Senate seat from South Dakota, and Senator Tom Daschle (D., South Dakota), debate during an appearance on the NBC program "Meet the Press" in September 2004. Thune, a former U.S. representative, defeated Daschle, Democratic leader in the U.S. Senate, in a major victory for Republicans on November 2.

Edwards, who joined NPR in 1974, was removed as host of the popular program "Morning Edition" in April 2004. His unexplained reassignment stirred controversy among fans of "Morning Edition " NPR's most popular program.

Air America Radio. New York City-based Air America Radio took to the airwaves on March 31, in an effort to balance what people perceived as a conservative tilt to mainstream talk radio in the United States. The on-air line-up included actress and comedienne Janeane Garofalo and comedian, actor, and author Al Franken.

Problems surfaced almost immediately for Air America as the liberal radio network struggled to get off the ground. Radio stations in Los Angeles and Chicago, the second and third-largest cities in the United States, stopped broadcasting Air America in mid-April following a dispute over payments for air time. Air America also struggled as several executives from the company, including the chief executive officer and one of the cofounders, resigned during the course of the year or assumed lesser responsibilities within the organization.　　　　■ Gregory Paeth

See also **Newspaper; State government; Telecommunications; Television.**

Railroad. See Transportation.

Religion. See Islam; Judaism; Protestantism; Roman Catholic Church.

Republican Party. The Republican Party (or GOP for Grand Old Party) celebrated major victories in the Nov. 2, 2004, election. The GOP increased its majority in the U.S. Senate and the House of Representatives. The GOP also retained control of the presidency as George W. Bush defeated his Democratic Party challenger, Senator John Kerry of Massachusetts.

Presidential election. President Bush won 286 electoral votes on November 2, while Kerry finished with 252 electoral votes. President Bush won 60.6 million votes, compared with 57.2 million votes for Kerry. An estimated 119.8 million people voted in the 2004 presidential election, the highest election turnout since 1968.

U.S. Senate races. The GOP expanded the party's control of the U.S. Senate in 2004, gaining four seats to give the party a 55-44 majority. (One member of the Senate, James M. Jeffords of Vermont, was an independent who usually voted with Democrats.) Republican candidates won Senate seats vacated by Democrats in Florida, Georgia, Louisiana, North Carolina, and South Carolina. Republican candidates also won heavily contested elections in Alaska, Kentucky, and Oklahoma.

The most dramatic victory took place in South Dakota, where former U.S. Representative John Thune, a Republican, defeated Senator Tom Daschle, the leader of the Senate Democrats.

In Kentucky, Republican Senator Jim Bunning narrowly defeated Democratic challenger Daniel Mongiardo. In Oklahoma, former U.S. Representative Tom Coburn, a Republican, upset U.S. Representative Brad Carson (D., Oklahoma). Senator Lisa Murkowsi (R., Alaska) defeated Tony Knowles, a Democrat and a former governor of the state.

In Louisiana, voters elected U.S. Representative David Vitter, a Republican, to succeed Senator John Breaux, a Democrat who did not seek re-election. In Georgia, U.S. Representative Johnny Isakson, a Republican, easily won the Senate seat vacated by Senator Zell Miller, a conservative Democrat. In Florida, voters elected Republican Mel Martinez to succeed Democratic Senator Bob Graham. Jim DeMint, a Republican, won the election to succeed veteran Senator Ernest F. Hollings (D., South Carolina). North Carolina voters elected Richard Burr, a Republican, to succeed Senator John Edwards, who ran as the Democratic Party's vice-presidential candidate.

Republican incumbents managing easy victories included senators Christopher S. Bond of Missouri; Sam Brownback of Kansas; Charles E. Grassley of Iowa; Judd Gregg of New Hampshire; John McCain III of Arizona; Richard C. Shelby of Alabama; and George V. Voinovich of Ohio.

House races. The GOP extended its control of the House of Representatives, picking up enough seats to gain a 232 to 202 majority over Democrats. One representative, Bernard Sanders of Vermont, an independent not affiliated with either party, was also re-elected.

A redistricting plan in Texas, heavily aided by U.S. Representative Tom Delay (R., Texas), the House majority leader, helped the state elect the largest Republican delegation in Congress. Twenty-one Republicans were elected in Texas races for the House during the 2004 election. Critics argued that the redistricting unfairly divided Democratic residents from several areas of the state, giving Republican residents the majority vote in the election.

Gubernatorial elections. Republicans won 5 of 11 races for governor in November. Voters re-elected North Dakota Governor John Hoeven and Vermont Governor Jim Douglas, both Republicans. Republican Mitch Daniels, who had served as budget director under President Bush, defeated Indiana Governor Joseph Kernan, a Democrat. Republican Matt Blunt, Missouri's secretary of state, defeated Democrat Claire McCaskill, Missouri's state auditor, in the race for governor. In Utah's gubernatorial contest, Republican Jon Hunstman, Jr., defeated Democrat Scott Matheson. New Hampshire Governor Craig Benson failed in his bid for re-election. Benson was defeated by businessman John Lynch, a Democrat. State Attorney General Christine Gregoire, a Democrat, defeated Dino Rossi, a Republican, by 130 votes in the race for governor of Washington state. A recount of 2.7 million ballots left Gregoire the winner on December 30, though an earlier recount had indicated Rossi had won.

Resignation. Connecticut Governor John G. Rowland, a Republican, resigned on June 21 under investigation for federal corruption and state ethics violations. Lieutenant Governor M. Jodi Rell, a Republican, was sworn in as governor on July 1. On December 23, Rowland pled guilty to a single federal corruption charge.

Political fundraising increased in 2004. The Republican National Committee, the National Republican Senatorial Committee, and the National Republican Congressional Committee raised a total of $554.7 million in contributions through mid-October, according to the Federal Election Commission. The Democratic National Committee, Democratic Senatorial Campaign Committee, and the Democratic Congressional Campaign Committee raised $451.8 million over the same period. ■ Geoffrey A. Campbell

See also **Cabinet, U.S.; Congress of the United States; Democratic Party; Elections; People in the news** (John Edwards; John Kerry; Barack Obama); **State government; United States, Government of the; United States, President of the.**

Roman Catholic Church. Pope John
Paul II, in his annual New Year's Day message, issued on Jan. 1, 2004, went beyond conventional expressions of good will to invoke a system of international law centered in the United Nations (UN). "The need is ever more felt for a new international order," John Paul stated. He went on to insist that the international order must be "capable of providing adequate solutions to today's problems, founded on the dignity of the human person, on an integral development of society, on solidarity between rich countries and poor countries, and on sharing of resources. . . ."

Throughout his long pontificate, John Paul II has consistently supported the United Nations. As pope, he heads Vatican City, a sovereign state and a member of the world organization.

Some observers of the papacy interpreted the pope's New Year's message as a rebuke to the administration of United States President George W. Bush. The United States, which led an allied force into Iraq in March 2003 without the concurrence of the UN Security Council, failed to bring peace to Iraq in 2004, as insurgents in that country continued a campaign of terror against U.S.-led forces and Iraqi civilians.

Sex abuse report. On February 24, the National Review Board for the Protection of Children and Young People issued a 145-page report on the "causes and context" of clergy sex abuse in the U.S. Roman Catholic Church. At the same time, John Jay College of Criminal Justice in New York City publicized results of its investigation into the scope of the sexual abuse scandal. The U.S. Catholic bishops had impaneled the National Review Board of 12 prominent lay Catholics in 2002 and commissioned the John Jay study in response to a growing national sex abuse scandal.

The John Jay report found that, between 1950 and 2002, 10,667 minors (children and youth under age 18) were allegedly sexually molested by 4,392 Catholic clerics in the United States. The figure represents more than 4 percent of the approximately 110,000 priests serving in the U.S. Roman Catholic Church during the period.

The National Review Board noted in its report that "the overwhelming majority of the clergy have led honorable lives of dedication to the church and her people." However, the report characterized as "distressing" and "inadequate" the response of many U.S. Catholic bishops to abusing clergy. The report also highlighted the failure of Catholic seminaries to weed out candidates unfit for the priesthood and to prepare candidates for a life of celibacy in the church.

As of early 2004, the U.S. Roman Catholic Church had paid out more than $500 million in settlements with alleged victims and litigation costs. Some estimates put the church's costs of the sex abuse scandal as high as $750 million.

Communion controversy. In the 2004 election year, some U.S. Catholic politicians found themselves caught up in a controversy regarding whether they should be able to receive communion during mass. The reception of communion is a sign of being a faithful member of the Catholic community. However, conservative Roman Catholic bishops denounced Catholic politicians who do not uphold church opposition to abortion, and some bishops instructed priests under their charge to deny communion to such politicians.

Some conservative Catholics focused attention on John Kerry, the Democratic nominee for president in 2004. Kerry is a practicing Roman Catholic who nonetheless supported freedom of choice—freedom to choose to have a legal abortion.

United States Catholic bishops, in their June 2004 meeting in Denver, Colorado, refrained from making a definitive pronouncement on the issue. Instead, they said that the decision to withhold communion rests with individual bishops.

■ Thomas C. Fox

See also **Eastern Orthodox Churches; Elections; People in the news** (John Kerry); **Protestantism.**

Pope John Paul II in August prays before the grotto at Lourdes, site of a reputed appearance by Mary, the mother of Jesus, before a peasant girl in 1858. The pope counted himself as one of the thousands of ailing Roman Catholics who annually make the pilgrimage to the shrine in the small French town in the Pyrenees foothills.

Romania. In November 2004 elections, Prime Minister Adrian Nastase's ruling Social Democrats won 132 of 332 seats in the parliament. In the presidential election, held simultaneously, Nastase and Traian Basescu, the mayor of Bucharest, the capital, were the top vote-getters. In a December 12 runoff, Basescu won. As a result, Basescu, a member of the opposition Justice and Truth Alliance, assumed the presidency, while the Social Democratic Party—with by far the largest number of seats in parliament—was forced to organize a governing coalition.

Romania's economy grew by 6.5 percent in the first half of 2004. Unemployment decreased to 6.5 percent in June, compared with 7.2 percent in 2003. Economists predicted that Romania's inflation rate for 2004 would average about 10 percent, compared with 14 percent in 2003.

In March 2004, Romania became a member of the North Atlantic Treaty Organization. During 2004, Romanian officials continued negotiations with the European Union (EU) for entry into the association of 25 European nations, tentatively scheduled for 2007. However, EU officials warned Romania's government that it must do more to tackle corruption to qualify for EU membership.
■ Sharon L. Wolchik

See also **Europe**.
Rowing. See **Sports**.

Russia. President Vladimir Putin strengthened his control over Russia in 2004, developing a system he called "managed democracy." Regional leaders, wealthy businessmen, and the mass media have all come under increasing executive influence in the five years since Putin took power. Yet Putin also faced serious challenges, most importantly the ongoing war with separatist Chechnya. The unresolved conflict sparked several terrorist attacks in Russia in 2004.

Economy. Rising world oil prices buoyed Russia's economy again in 2004, as it remained one of the world's leading producers of oil and natural gas. The economy grew by nearly 7 percent, and the state budget had an unexpected surplus of nearly $17 billion. These factors contributed to rising inflation. Observers expressed hope that Russia would spend its windfall on long-overdue economic restructuring projects.

Russian economic policy suffered two setbacks in 2004. Steps to tighten banking regulations triggered runs on several large banks starting in April, and confidence-building measures by the central bank of Russia did not bring the situation under control until July. In August, protests broke out as the State Duma (parliament) passed a bill eliminating Soviet-era benefits, such as free public transportation, free medication, and discounts on utilities for retirees and veterans. The government

Russian President Vladimir Putin walks through the Kremlin's St. George's Hall during his inauguration ceremony on May 7. Putin was elected to a second term as president on March 14.

had announced its intention to replace the benefits with cash payments, which inflation-wary Russians consider less desirable.

Presidential elections. Vladimir Putin won his second presidential election decisively on March 14 with 71 percent of the vote. His closest competitor, Communist Party candidate Nikolai Kharitonov, garnered less than 14 percent. Several opposition candidates threatened to drop out during the race, citing pressures to withdraw, biased media coverage, and Putin's refusal to take part in televised debates. While speculation abounded that Putin would use his overwhelming support in the Duma to remove the two-term constitutional limit on the presidency, Putin announced that he plans to step down when his second term ends in 2008.

The 2004 election gave Putin an opportunity to replace out-of-favor Cabinet members and restructure the government. He dismissed Prime Minister Mikhail Kasyanov on February 24, a long-anticipated move that ousted one of the few remaining members of former President Boris Yeltsin's team. Putin replaced Kasyanov with the relatively obscure Mikhail Fradkov, Russia's representative to the European Union. Analysts suggested that the appointment demonstrated Putin's desire for a loyal, nonthreatening prime minister. Putin carried out further changes on March 9, cutting the number of ministries from 30 to 17. Putin tapped Russia's UN ambassador Sergei Lavrov to head the foreign ministry, replacing Yeltsin-era appointee Igor Ivanov. Putin's decisions kept key economic posts in the hands of technocrats from his native St. Petersburg. His fellow veterans of the KGB (Soviet spy agency) retained the top military and security posts.

State-business relations. The Putin adminis-
tration continued its efforts to bring big business under greater state control in 2004, especially in the vital oil and gas sectors. The ongoing legal battle over Yukos, Russia's largest oil company, represented the central chapter in this saga.

Russian authorities arrested Yukos Chief Executive Officer Mikhail Khodorkovsky in 2003, charging him with fraud, tax evasion, forgery, and embezzlement. Two other men arrested in connection with Yukos—shareholder Platon Lebedev and former head security officer Alexei Pichugin—also remained in custody throughout 2004. Other top Yukos executives fled the country. The arrests and the subsequent government decision to freeze the Yukos stock of key shareholders plunged the company into turmoil and derailed a planned merger with Sibneft, another major Russian oil company.

Khodorkovsky made repeated but futile efforts to placate the government after his arrest. On March 29, he published an open letter in the Russian business daily *Vedomosti* in which he praised Putin, criticized the controversial privatization process through which he had acquired Yukos, and called for higher taxes on businesses. He also offered to relinquish his shares in Yukos to save the company. Ignoring these pleas, the govern-

Chechen militants hold children hostage in a school in Beslan, Russia, on September 1. The situation ended three days later with a firefight between terrorists and Russian police, which left more than 330 hostages dead, including more than 150 children.

ment began Khodorkovsky and Lebedev's joint trial for their allegedly fraudulent 1994 acquisition of shares in the Apatit fertilizer plant and subsequent embezzlement of the company's assets.

The government asserted that Yukos owes more than $20 billion in back taxes and took steps in 2004 to begin collecting that money. Most importantly, Yuganskneftegaz, Yukos's main production subsidiary, was auctioned off in December. A little-known company, Baikal Finance Group, won the auction, paying $9.4 billion for the troubled company. The sale price was well below investment bank Dresdner Kleinwort Wasserstein's earlier $18-billion valuation of the company's worth.

Experts suggested that the auction signaled the government's intention to break up Yukos because the sale of Yuganskneftegaz alone seemed unlikely to cover Yukos's outstanding tax bill. In addition, the government continued to charge more Yukos employees with serious crimes, including Yukos-Moskva chief operations officer Aleksei Kurtsin and Yukos lawyer Dmitri Gololobov in November.

Putin also consolidated state power over other oil and gas corporations. In mid-2004, he named two close aides to chair the boards of state-owned companies Transneft and Rosneft. In November, the Cabinet approved Rosneft's takeover by Gazprom. A newly created company, Gazpromneft, will unite Gazprom's oil-sector holdings. Not only do earnings from Gazprom represent a major source of government revenue, but Gazprom's sales to former Soviet states and to Western Europe provide Russia with international political and economic leverage.

Terrorism. Chechen separatists carried out several terrorist attacks in Russia in 2004, as a negotiated solution to the ongoing conflict in Chechnya remained elusive. The Russian government first battled separatist forces in the tiny North Caucasus republic from 1994 to 1996. After a period of de facto Chechen independence, Russian troops entered Chechnya again in 1999. The move came after an incursion into neighboring Dagestan by Chechen warlord Shamil Basaev and a series of apartment-block bombings in Moscow that were blamed on Chechen separatists. The number and intensity of terrorist attacks rooted in the Chechen conflict hit a new height in 2004. On February 6, a bomb blast ripped through a Moscow subway station, killing 39 people. An explosion during a May 9 Victory Day celebration in the Chechen capital, Groznyy, killed pro-Russia Chechen President Akhmad Kadyrov and at least six others. Kadyrov, the third Chechen president to meet a violent death, took office in October 2003 after elections that international observers had widely condemned as fraudulent.

Terrorists struck again in August and September 2004. Terrorism experts connected these attacks with the August 30 election of Kadyrov's replace-

ment, Alu Alkhanov. Political experts suggested that Alkhanov had been chosen by Putin to aid Chechen-Russian relations. Alkhanov won the presidential election with a reported 74 percent of the vote, and a number of observers believed that the election had been rigged. Suicide bombers brought down two domestic flights from Moscow on August 24, killing 89 people. On August 31, 10 people died in a suicide bombing outside a Moscow subway station.

On September 1, terrorists stormed a school in the southern Russian town of Beslan, taking about 1,200 people hostage. After a three-day standoff, an explosion within the school grounds triggered a firefight between the terrorists and Russian forces as well as further explosions that left more than 330 hostages dead, many of whom were children. Shamil Basaev claimed responsibility for the Beslan attack, as he previously had for many other terrorist incidents in Russia.

The Beslan siege had major repercussions for Russia and the Putin administration. Most notably, Putin announced a series of significant changes to the Russian political system that he claimed would strengthen the government's ability to fight terrorism. He advanced the idea of electing the entire Duma through party-list voting and abolishing direct election of regional governors. Both measures would further concentrate power in Russia in the president. By appointing the regional governors, Putin could ensure their personal loyalty. Duma elections restricted to party-list voting would likely increase the already dominant representation of the Putin-affiliated United Russia political party. While international observers lambasted these moves, Putin's proposals met little opposition within Russia. Putin signed the bill canceling gubernatorial elections on December 12. The party-list bill seemed assured of legislative approval in 2005.

Relations with the European Union. On April 27, 2004, Russia and the EU, after long negotiations, agreed to terms for extending their Partnership and Cooperation Agreement to the 10 new EU member countries, including 8 formerly Communist nations. On May 21, Russia and the EU concluded another agreement that promised EU support for Russia's bid to join the World Trade Organization, a UN affiliate, in exchange for Russian ratification of the Kyoto Protocol. Without Russia, the environmental treaty, which sets limits on the emission of greenhouse gases, could not pass the support threshold necessary for ratification. Putin signed the Kyoto Protocol on November 5. ■ Juliet Johnson

See also **Baltic states; Disasters; Environmental pollution; Europe; Moldova; Terrorism.**

Sailing. See Boating.

Saskatchewan. See Canadian Provinces.

Saudi Arabia. Terrorist attacks by Islamic militants increased dramatically in Saudi Arabia in 2004. In April, a suicide car bomber blew himself up at the national police headquarters in Riyadh, the capital, killing five other people. The incident was the first terrorist attack directed against Saudi security forces. A group calling itself al-Haramayn Brigades, which experts believed to be linked to the al-Qa'ida terrorist network, claimed responsibility for the attack. In May, militants attacked a compound in Khobar that housed foreign oil industry workers and their families. The militants killed 22 people and held dozens of others hostage before escaping.

In June, Islamic militants in Riyadh kidnapped and beheaded Paul Johnson, Jr., a United States engineer who worked for Lockheed Martin Corp., headquartered in Bethesda, Maryland. After the beheading, Saudi security forces killed a number of militants in a Riyadh safehouse. Among the slain militants was Abdulaziz al-Moqrin, who led the al-Qa'ida branch in Saudi Arabia and was believed to be responsible for Johnson's death.

Gunmen attacked the U.S. Consulate in the Red Sea port of Jidda on December 6 in the first attack against a U.S. diplomatic mission in Saudi Arabia. At least nine people were killed in a resulting gun battle involving the attackers, Saudi security forces, and U.S. Marines. A militant group affiliated with al-Qa'ida claimed responsibility for the attack.

Crackdown. The Saudi government adopted a number of new tactics to fight militants in 2004, including rounding up hundreds of terrorist suspects, enacting anti-terror financing laws, and moving against charities suspected of funding al-Qa'ida. The government also offered amnesty from the death penalty to terrorists who turned themselves in during a one-month period in June and July. Eighty people reportedly surrendered during this period.

Human rights. In March, Saudi authorities arrested a number of human rights activists. The trigger for the arrests was a letter sent by the activists to Crown Prince Abdullah, informing him of their intention to set up an independent human rights organization. The activists also sent several petitions to the government demanding various political reforms.

Elections. The Saudi government announced in September that the first municipal elections in decades would be held in 2005, beginning in February. International observers noted that pressure from the United States, as well as internal Saudi pressure, probably prompted the announcement. ■ Mary-Jane Deeb

See also **Middle East; Terrorism.**

School. See Education.

Senegal. See Africa.

Serbia and Montenegro. A politically powerful nationalist movement in Serbia and separatist movements within the union of Serbia and Montenegro continued to threaten stability in the new state in 2004. Serbia and Montenegro came into being in early 2003, replacing the former Yugoslavia. Each republic has its own institutions, united under a weak national government.

Elections in Serbia. Boris Tadic of the reformist Democratic Party (DS) defeated Tomislav Nikolic of the ultranationalist Serbian Radical Party (SRS) in the June 2004 runoff election for president of Serbia. In the December 2003 parliamentary elections, Nikolic's SRS, led by Vojislav Seselj, had won the largest share of seats—82 out of a total of 250. Seselj, under indictment for alleged war crimes, was in detention at the international War Crimes Tribunal in the Hague, Netherlands. The party of former Yugoslav President Vojislav Kostunica, the Democratic Party of Serbia (DSS), won 53 seats.

In February 2004, Kostunica formed a coalition government that included the 22 deputies elected by the Socialist Party of Serbia (SPS). That party was led by former Serbian president Slobodan Milosevic, who was on trial for various crimes at the war crimes tribunal in the Hague throughout 2003 and 2004. European leaders expressed concern over the participation of Milosevic allies and urged the new government to cooperate with the war crimes tribunal.

War crimes. Milosevic and Seselj were just two of many individuals from Serbia and the other successor states of the former Yugoslavia who had been indicted by the tribunal. Their alleged crimes were associated with wars that accompanied the breakup of the former Yugoslavia during the 1990's. Some of the most sought after alleged criminals—including Bosnian Serb leader Radovan Karadzic and Serbian General Ratco Mladic—remained at large in 2004. However, Kostunica announced in February that extradition of alleged war criminals under tribunal indictment was not a high priority for his new government. In March, Serbia's parliament approved giving salaries to alleged war criminals. The United States responded by suspending $26 million in aid to Serbia and Montenegro.

In December, President Tadic, visiting Sarajevo, capital of Bosnia-Herzegovina, apologized to Bosnians for war crimes "committed in the name of the Serb people." The statement was the first acknowledgment by a Serbian official of Serbian complicity in war crimes committed by Bosnian Serbs in Bosnia's 1992–1995 civil war.

Montenegrin independence movement. Officials of Montenegro in 2004 criticized the functioning of the joint state with Serbia and argued for Montenegrin independence. In July, leaders of Montenegro's ruling party proposed talks with Serbia to dissolve the state of Serbia and Montenegro by 2006. Serbian leaders and officials of the European Union (EU) rejected the proposal.

Kosovo. New ethnic violence threatened the uneasy peace enforced by NATO troops in Kosovo in 2004. In March, ethnic Albanian mobs attacked ethnic Serb villages, killing 28 people and leaving several thousand others homeless. The violence strained a five-year effort by the United Nations (UN) to develop a viable multiethnic community in the province, which is technically part of Serbia but virtually autonomous. Serbian leaders proposed a partition of Kosovo along ethnic lines. However, most Albanian Kosovar leaders and international officials opposed the plan.

Kosovo's two main Albanian ethnic parties won a majority of seats in October parliamentary elections, which were largely boycotted by ethnic Serbs. In December, a newly formed governing coalition elected Ramush Haradinaj, a former ethnic Albanian rebel commander, as prime minister. Officials in Serbia, where Haradinaj was under indictment for alleged war crimes against ethnic Serbs, called on UN officials to annul Haradinaj's election.   ■ Sharon L. Wolchik

See also **Bosnia-Herzegovina; Europe; United Nations.**

Sierra Leone. President Ahmad Tejan Kabbah dismantled Sierra Leone's national disarmament committee on Feb. 4, 2004, concluding a campaign to demobilize and rehabilitate an estimated 72,000 combatants who had fought in Sierra Leone's 1991–2001 civil war. International sponsors, who had donated millions of dollars to support rehabilitation of former fighters in vocational training, jobs, or schools, hailed Sierra Leone's disarmament campaign as a model for other nations recovering from civil conflict.

Sierra Leone's civil war came to an official end in January 2002 following a cease-fire signed in May 2001 between Kabbah's government and the country's main rebel group, the Revolutionary United Front (RUF). The country successfully staged nationwide elections in May 2002.

UN peacekeepers. An important factor in Sierra Leone's pacification had been deployment in 1999 of a United Nations (UN) peacekeeping force called UNAMSIL, which was scheduled to leave Sierra Leone in December 2004. However, on September 17 the UN Security Council voted to extend the mission to June 30, 2005.

War crimes. In mid-2004, Sierra Leone's Special Court in Freetown, the capital, began hearing cases against individuals charged with war crimes and human rights abuses allegedly committed during the nation's civil war. The first trial, beginning on June 4, involved three senior militia commanders who had been allies of the Kabbah government. On July 5, three RUF commanders went on trial in the court.

The Special Court was set up under the terms of a 2002 agreement between Sierra Leone and the UN. The court consists of five UN-appointed judges and three Sierra Leonan judges.

UN officials and human rights organizations welcomed the Special Court as a forum in which victims of Sierra Leone's brutal 10-year civil war could confront their tormentors and see justice done. Other groups, however, expressed doubts about the court's effectiveness as long as Liberia's former President Charles Taylor—widely blamed for arming the RUF—remains at large. Taylor fled Liberia for exile in Nigeria in 2003, after Sierra Leone's Special Court indicted him for war crimes.

In local council elections on May 22, 2004, All People's Congress (APC), the country's main opposition party, captured a majority of council seats in Freetown. Analysts interpreted the unexpected outcome—a setback for President Kabbah's Sierra Leone's People's Party (SLPP)—as an expression of voters' dissatisfaction with the ruling party's performance since the 2002 election. In that election, the SLPP's Kabbah won 70 percent of the presidential vote.   ■ Simon Baynham

See also **Africa.**

Singapore. Lee Hsien Loong was sworn in on Aug. 12, 2004, as the island state's third prime minister. He succeeded Goh Chok Tong, who had in 1990 succeeded Lee's father, Lee Kuan Yew, the founder of modern Singapore. The 80-year-old Lee Kuan Yew was designated "minister mentor" to his son in the new Cabinet.

Lee Hsien Loong, at 52 years old in 2004, had long been groomed for the premiership. Holding a master's degree in public administration, he became an army brigadier general before entering the government at the age of 32. In 2001, he became finance minister, a post he continued to hold as prime minister. In 2003, Goh noted that "Loong's public persona is that of a no-nonsense, uncompromising, and tough minister." Lee subsequently worked to soften his image.

As prime minister, he announced steps to make it easier and cheaper for couples to have children. The government had been worried that too few babies were leading to a fall in population. He also cut civil servants' work week to five days.

After slumping to just 1.1-percent growth in 2003, the economy surged in 2004. The Ministry of Trade and Industry forecast growth at between 8 and 9 percent, but cautioned that growth was likely to slow in 2005.   ■ Henry S. Bradsher

See also **Asia.**

Skating. See Hockey; Ice skating; Sports.

Anja Paerson of Sweden races past a gate during the World Cup giant slalom event in Are, Sweden, on Feb. 22, 2004. Paerson went on to win the giant slalom title, in addition to the overall and slalom titles.

Skiing. Austria's Hermann Maier made one of the greatest comebacks in all of sports in 2004, winning his fourth career overall title less than three years after an August 2001 motorcycle crash caused him to nearly lose his right leg.

Maier, nicknamed "the Herminator," also claimed the super-giant title in 2004, his first full season since the crash, which occurred in Radstadt, Austria. In an especially tight finish, Maier bested fellow countrymen Stephan Eberharter and Benjamin Raich at the World Cup finals on March 13, 2004, in Sestriere, Italy. Raich had been in position to win after the first run of the final giant slalom event, but officials canceled the second run of the competition because of dense fog, spoiling Raich's bid to take the overall title.

During the competition, Bode Miller, aiming to become the first American to win the overall crown since Phil Mahre did so in 1983, won his first World Cup title when he took the giant-slalom championship. Miller skied off the course during his first run, costing him a shot at the overall title and apparently putting his giant-slalom hopes in jeopardy. However, the second race was cancelled due to fog, wiping out a brilliant run by Finland's Kalle Palander.

Maier finished the season with 1,265 points,

42 points ahead of Eberharter, the downhill champion, and 126 ahead of Raich. Miller finished fourth with 1,134 points.

On May 11, 2004, Austrian skier Rainer Schoenfelder was warned by his country's skiing federation for testing positive during the season for the banned stimulant Etilephrine. The federation could have banned him from competition for two years.

In women's alpine skiing, Sweden's Anja Paerson won her first World Cup overall title on March 13, finishing ahead of Austrian Renate Goetschl. Paerson, who claimed the slalom and giant slalom crowns in early February in Zwiesel, Germany, locked up the overall title on March 13 in Sestriere, Italy. Goetschl, the only woman close to Paerson in the standings, finished 24th in the race and ended the year 217 points behind Paerson's total of 1,561. Earlier in the competition, Goetschl had wrapped up the downhill and super-G titles.

Cross-country. On March 7, Rene Sommerfeldt became the first German to win the men's World Cup cross-country overall title with his sixth-place finish in Lahti, Finland. Italy's Gabriela Paruzzi won the women's overall title.

Nordic combined. Finland's Hannu Manninen won the men's Nordic combined overall title on March 5 in Lahti, Finland. He had captured seven events during the season.

Ski jumping. Finland's Janne Ahonen captured the overall World Cup title with his eighth-place finish in the final event of the season on March 14 in Oslo, Norway.   ■ Michael Kates

See also **Sports.**

Slovakia. On May 1, 2004, Slovakia officially became a member of the European Union (EU). A month earlier, on April 2, Slovakia had formally gained admission to the North Atlantic Treaty Organization. The two milestones fulfilled Slovak government policy goals adopted in the 1990's.

The coalition government of Prime Minister Mikulas Dzurinda suffered several setbacks in 2004. In January, the governing coalition lost its parliamentary majority when former defense minister Ivan Simko withdrew and formed a new party. In the presidential election on April 3, the candidate sponsored by Dzurinda's Slovak Christian Democratic Union, Eduard Kukan, came in third, failing to qualify for a runoff election. In Slovakia, the role of president is mainly ceremonial but is considered symbolically important.

In the April 17 presidential runoff election, Ivan Gasparovic ran against Vladimir Meciar, a former prime minister. The two men had once been political allies, but Gasparovic later broke with Meciar. Election returns gave Gasparovic a decisive victory. Analysts noted that as prime minister, Meciar had earned a reputation of being authoritarian.

Riots. In February, riots in Roma (Gypsy) neighborhoods in several eastern Slovakian towns prompted the government in Bratislava, the capital, to deploy 2,000 troops in the disturbed region. The rioters were protesting sharp cuts in government welfare benefits, Roma leaders said. Roma communities in Slovakia are among the poorest in Europe. In some neighborhoods, unemployment in 2004 approached 100 percent. The Dzurinda government refused to rescind the cuts but promised to offer a jobs package of community work to the affected Roma communities.

Economy. Slovakia's gross domestic product (GDP)—the value of all goods and services produced in a country in a given year—grew by 5.4 percent in the second quarter of 2004, compared with 4.2 percent in 2003. However, inflation increased from 4.2 percent in late 2003 to 7.2 percent in August 2004. Unemployment declined in the first half of the year, registering just under 14 percent in June.

Slovakia's record with economic reforms led investment experts in 2004 to rank the country as one of the world's most attractive locations for foreign investment. Two foreign automobile manufacturers—Hyundai/KIA of South Korea and PSA Peugeot Citroen of France—announced plans in 2004 to open or expand production plants in Slovakia. According to industry experts, Slovakia was destined to become a center of auto-making in Europe.

■ Sharon Wolchik

See also **Europe.**

Roma (Gypsy) families gather in a village in eastern Slovakia on Feb. 25, 2004, to protest cuts in government unemployment payments. Roma demonstrations, some violent, spread across Slovakia in response to the benefit reductions, part of an austerity program undertaken by the Slovak government.

Greek national player Angelos Haristeas leads the team through a crowd of celebrating fans in Athens on July 5, 2004. The previous day, the Greek team had shocked the world by upsetting Portugal 1-0 to win the European Championship.

Soccer. In one of the biggest upsets in international soccer history, unheralded Greece shocked Portugal in the final of the 2004 European Championships in Lisbon, Portugal, in July. Also in July, Brazil won the Copa America, the South American championship.

The United States women's team had a memorable season, winning a record 21 consecutive games, along with the Olympic gold medal. Mia Hamm retired in 2004, ending one of the most successful careers in the history of women's soccer.

International soccer. Greece shocked the soccer world on July 4, defeating Portugal 1-0 on a 57th-minute goal by Angelos Haristeas to win the European Championship, held every four years. The 16-team finals were played in Portugal in June and July. Greece began the finals tournament as a 100-to-1 longshot. In the group stage, they defeated host country Portugal 2-1 and went on to qualify for the knockout stage. They continued to produce shocking results, defeating defending champion France 1-0 in the quarterfinals and the Czech Republic 1-0 in the semifinals. They overpowered highly favored Portugal in the final at Estadio da Luz before a crowd of 62,865.

On July 25, Brazil defeated Argentina 4-2 on penalties in a thrilling shoot-out to win the Copa America, the South American championship, in Lima, Peru. Twelve countries participated, includ-

ing two guest teams, Mexico and Costa Rica. Brazil and Argentina, the favorites, finished second in their respective groups, but both teams eventually made it to the final. In the championship game, held at the National Stadium, Kily Gonzalez gave Argentina the lead with a penalty kick in the 21st minute, but Brazil's Luisao tied the game by scoring on the stroke of halftime. Cesar Delgado appeared to score the winning goal for Argentina in the 87th minute, but Adriano led Brazil back from the brink of defeat, tying the game in the dying seconds. Brazil then scored on all four shoot-out attempts, while Argentina missed two.

Argentina won the men's Olympic soccer gold medal, defeating Paraguay 1-0 in the final at Karaiskaki Stadium in Athens, on August 28. Italy had defeated Iraq 1-0 the day before to take the bronze medal. The U.S. team failed to qualify for the Olympics.

In qualifying competitions for the 2006 World Cup finals, the final group for the Confederation of North Central American and Caribbean Association Football (CONCACAF) zone was determined in 2004, with Costa Rica, Guatemala, Panama, Mexico, Trinidad and Tobago, and the United States set to battle for the three World Cup spots during 2005. The U.S. team topped its group, finishing with a 1-1 tie against Jamaica at Columbus Crew Stadium on Nov. 17, 2004, to take its record unbeaten streak to 13 games.

As of December, Brazil topped the men's FIFA World Rankings with 843 points, ahead of France (792) and Argentina (785). The United States (726) was ranked 11th, the same as in 2003.

International club competitions. Liga Deportiva Alajuelense beat Deportivo Saprissa 5-1 on aggregate to win the first-ever all-Costa Rican CONCACAF Champion Cup final. LD Alajuelense had tied Saprissa 1-1 in their away leg on May 5, 2004, and won their home leg 4-0 on May 12.

F.C. Porto (Portugal) defeated Monaco 3-0 in the final of the European Champions League (European Cup) on May 26 before a crowd of 53,000 people in Gelsenkirchen, Germany.

The Colombian team Once Caldas defeated the favorites Boca Juniors (Argentina) on penalties on July 1 to win the two-legged final of the Copa Libertadores. The two teams had fought to a 0-0 draw in the first game, held in Colombia on June 23. In the second game, the two teams were tied 1-1 at the end of regulation. Boca Juniors, who had won both their quarterfinal and their semifinal matches on penalties, failed on all four shoot-out attempts, while Once Caldas scored twice to take the championship.

F.C. Porto defeated Once Caldas 8-7 in a penalty shoot-out after a 0-0 tie in the match for the World Club Cup, played between the club champions of Europe and South America, in Yokohama, Japan, on December 12.

Major League Soccer (MLS). D.C. United defeated the Kansas City Wizards 3-2 in the MLS Cup Championship match at the Home Depot Center in Carson, California, on November 14 before a crowd of 25,797 fans. The Wizards took an early lead when Jose Burciaga scored a goal in the sixth minute. However, D.C. scored three goals in seven minutes to take control by halftime. Alecko Eskandarian equalized in the 19th minute and put D.C. ahead four minutes later. An own goal by Alex Zotinca made it 3-1 in the 26th minute.

Kansas City fought its way back into the game when Josh Wolff converted a penalty kick in the 58th minute, given when D.C.'s Dema Kovalenko touched a goal-bound shot from Jimmy Conrad with his hand. After Kovalenko was sent off, D.C. held out for the remainder of the game short one man to win their fourth MLS Cup title.

During the regular season, Kansas City finished atop the final Western Conference standings, while D.C. United placed second in the Eastern Conference behind Columbus. D.C. started its post-season campaign with a 2-0 win on the road against the (New Jersey) Metrostars and clinched its place in the conference final by defeating the Metrostars 2-0 at home. The New England Revolution defeated the Columbus Crew 2-1 on aggregate in the other semifinal. In the Conference final, D.C. defeated the Revolution 4-3 on penalty kicks after a 3-3 tie.

In the Western Conference, Kansas overcame a 2-0 deficit on their away leg and defeated the San Jose Earthquakes 3-0 at home to reach the final. The Los Angeles Galaxy also had to overturn a first-leg deficit, defeating the Rapids 2-0 after losing 1-0 in Denver. Kansas City defeated the Galaxy 2-0 in the conference final.

In July, MLS officials announced plans to expand the league to 12 teams for the 2005 season. The two new teams are Club Deporto Chivas USA (Los Angeles) and Real Salt Lake (Salt Lake City, Utah). In November 2004, MLS officials also expanded team rosters from 24 to 28 players for the 2005 season.

Women's soccer. The United States women's team had a successful season in 2004, winning a record 21 consecutive games and also winning the Olympic gold medal by defeating Brazil 2-1 after extra time on August 26. Lindsay Tarpley struck first for the United States in the first half and Brazil's Pretinha leveled the match for Brazil in the second half. Abby Wambach of the United States headed in the winner in the 112th minute.

Mia Hamm, the world's best-known female player, retired on December 8. During her 17-year career, Hamm, known for her speed and power, was twice named FIFA Player of the Year. She also scored a record 158 goals and led the U.S. team to World Cup titles in 1991 and 1999 and Olympic gold medals in 1996 and 2004. American stars Joy Fawcett and Julie Foudy also retired on December 8.

With 2,165 points, the U.S. team was second in the FIFA World Rankings at the end of December, only 16 points behind Germany.

In the FIFA Under-19 Women's World Championship finals, Germany defeated China 2-0 in the final at the Rajamangala National Stadium, Bangkok, on November 27. The United States, which lost 3-1 to Germany in the semifinals, defeated Brazil 3-0 for third place.

Laws. Law changes that took effect on July 1 included the abolition of "golden" and "silver" goals—goals scored in extra time that decided the winner of the match—and the acceptance of approved artificial turf for the first time. Also, players who remove their shirts after scoring now receive a caution (yellow card).

Awards. Ronaldinho of Brazil and Barcelona (Spain) was named FIFA men's Player of the Year on December 20. In the women's voting, Birgit Prinz (Germany) was voted Player of the Year.

▪ Norman Barrett

See also **Olympics: A Special Report.**

Social Security. Social Security revenue surpluses would continue through 2018, but the revenue would be exhausted by 2042, announced officials with the Social Security Administration (SSA) on March 23, 2004. SSA officials made the same analysis in their 2003 report. The 2004 report disclosed that Social Security paid approximately $470 billion in benefits in 2003 and ended the year with $1.5 trillion in assets. John Snow, secretary of the United States Department of the Treasury and a member of the SSA Board of Trustees, urged the U.S. Congress to establish personal retirement savings accounts to supplement Social Security.

Fraud warning. The SSA's Office of Inspector General (OIG) on May 28 issued a warning about the growing incidence of fraud by people claiming to be agency employees. Individuals posing as SSA officials typically ask Social Security recipients for personal information, such as Social Security or bank account numbers. Acting Inspector General Patrick O'Carroll, Jr., said people should be extremely cautious in divulging personal information and should never provide a Social Security number or other personal information over the telephone unless they themselves initiated the contact or are confident of the person to whom they are speaking.

■ Geoffrey A. Campbell
See also **United States, Government of the.**

South Africa. President Thabo Mbeki's ruling African National Congress (ANC) won decisive victories in the national parliament and in the provincial legislatures in elections on April 14, 2004. At the national level, the ANC captured 279 of 400 seats in parliament, winning 69.8 percent of votes cast. The ANC had won 266 seats in 1999.

The mainly white Democratic Alliance came in second with 50 seats (12.4 percent of the vote), followed by the Inkatha Freedom Party (IFP) with 28 seats (7 percent). The New National Party, heir to the National Party, which had led South Africa's former system of racial segregation called *apartheid*, took only 7 seats (1.65 percent). Eight other parties divided the remaining seats.

The ANC won clear majorities in seven provincial legislatures. The party came in first in all nine of South Africa's provinces but failed to win clear majorities in KwaZulu-Natal or Western Cape.

On April 27, 2004, Mbeki was sworn in for a second five-year term as president. The president in South Africa is elected by parliament, and the ANC landslide ensured Mbeki's re-election.

Cabinet changes. At the beginning of his new term, President Mbeki dropped IFP minister Mangosuthu Buthelezi from the cabinet. Two IFP deputy ministers then resigned in protest, depriving the ANC-dominated government of IFP participation for the first time since 1994.

The IFP is the largest predominantly black opposition party in South Africa. Identified with the Zulu ethnic group based in KwaZulu-Natal province, the IFP fought bitterly and sometimes violently with the ANC in the waning years of the apartheid era. ANC leader Nelson Mandela, South Africa's first postapartheid president, brought Buthelezi into his Cabinet in 1994, securing IFP cooperation with the new, ANC-dominated government.

Political analysts speculated that Buthelezi's dismissal might provoke new clashes between IFP and ANC partisans. However, the ANC and IFP defused tension with a power-sharing deal in KwaZulu-Natal in May 2004. Although the ANC had outpolled the IFP in the province, traditionally an IFP stronghold, it had failed to win an outright majority. The deal involved giving the IFP three ministerial posts in the provincial government and electing an IFP member of parliament as deputy speaker.

Spy allegation debunked. On January 20, a special judicial panel ruled on allegations that Bulelani Ngcuka, South Africa's chief prosecutor, had worked as a spy for the apartheid-era white minority government. The judicial panel found that the allegations were "ill-conceived and entirely unsubstantiated."

In September 2003, two ANC officials claimed they had seen intelligence documents from the 1980's identifying Ngcuka as a spy for the minority white regime then in power. Ngcuka denied the allegation. The accusers were close allies of Deputy President Jacob Zuma, the target of an ongoing investigation by the chief prosecutor's office in a bribery case.

Land reform. On May 25, 2004, Land Affairs Minister Thoko Didiza said that a real estate boom hampered the Mbeki administration's agricultural redistribution policy. Under the program, 30 percent of white-owned farmland is to be transferred to blacks by 2014 on the basis of a "willing buyer, willing seller." However, Didiza warned that, as a last resort, the government could use legislation authorizing land expropriation signed into law in January 2004 by President Mbeki. The legislation, called the Restitution of Land Rights Amendment Act, specifies conditions under which the Minister of Land Affairs may expropriate land for restitution purposes without a court order or the farmer's agreement.

Didiza's comments raised fears among South Africa's white farmers of a Zimbabwe-style "land grab." Since 2000, Zimbabwe's government has massively redistributed white-owned farms to blacks, regardless of their farming skills or experience, with the result that the country is experiencing severe food shortages.

Pilot Mike Melvill celebrates atop SpaceShipOne, the first privately funded rocket plane to fly in space, after a successful flight on Sept. 29, 2004. SpaceShipOne flew again on October 4, fulfilling the conditions to win the $10-million Ansari X-prize. The competition was held to encourage the growth of a nongovernmental space industry.

Aristide exile. On May 31, 2004, President Mbeki personally welcomed ousted Haitian leader Jean-Bertrand Aristide into exile in South Africa. Aristide's arrival in South Africa ended an odyssey that had started on February 29 when the Haitian president, under siege by rebels in the Haitian capital, Port-au-Prince, was flown out of Haiti on a United States-supplied aircraft. Analysts suggested that Mbeki's warm welcome for Aristide was part of a strategy to reach out to the "African diaspora"—that is, to the descendants of Africans who have been dispersed to other parts of the world over the centuries.

Sports coup. On May 15, the Federation Internationale de Football Association (FIFA) announced that South Africa would host the 2010 World Cup tournament. No African nation has ever before hosted the premier world soccer event. FIFA executive committee members said that former South African President Nelson Mandela played a key role in the decision by persuasively arguing his country's case before them. Economists estimate that hosting the competition could create as many as 150,000 jobs in South Africa. ■ Simon Baynham

See also **Africa; Haiti: A Special Report; Soccer; Zimbabwe.**

South America. See Latin America.
South Carolina. See State government.
South Dakota. See State government.

Space exploration. In 2004, the two-man crews aboard the International Space Station (ISS) struggled to maintain the craft's systems and science experiments; return of the United States shuttles to space was delayed; and a probe carrying samples of the solar wind crashed into the Utah desert. But the year brought successes, as well. A private rocket ship was launched into space, and two U.S. rovers explored Mars. In addition, a number of spacecraft began returning remarkable data from their studies of Earth, a comet, and other planets.

A new vision for space exploration. On January 14, U.S. President George W. Bush directed the National Aeronautics and Space Administration (NASA) to begin planning for a permanent human presence on the moon by 2020 and for using a moon base to test equipment for a trip to Mars. According to the president's "vision for space exploration," the U.S. space shuttles would be retired by 2010 and replaced with a new Crew Exploration Vehicle. However, the feasibility of the program depended on the willingness of the U.S. Congress to allocate funds for the project.

The International Space Station. Throughout 2004, NASA worked to get its three remaining space shuttles flying by correcting defects that destroyed the shuttle Columbia in February 2003. Since the shuttle loss, Russian Soyuz manned vehicles and Progress cargo capsules have ferried new crews and supplies to the orbiting outpost. In 2003,

During 2004, several
United States spacecraft
probed the mysteries of
Mars and Saturn.

The Cassini spacecraft, which was launched in 1997
and began orbiting Saturn in June 2004, captured an
image of the planet and its rings (above) during its
approach in March. Cassini was to spend four years
orbiting Saturn, studying the planet's rings, moons,
clouds, and other features.

An image taken by NASA's rover Opportunity in 2004 (above) provides an unprecedented, detailed view of a large Martian impact crater named Endurance. Scientists believe the depth of the crater and its exposed walls may reveal important information about the planet's past geologic processes. An artist's rendering (right) depicts one of two identical U.S. rovers—Spirit and Opportunity—that landed on opposite sides of Mars in January 2004. Both probes found evidence that liquid water had once flowed on the red planet.

During one of its orbits in June, Cassini took the first detailed photograph of Saturn's moon Phoebe (left), revealing a dusty world pocked by craters. On the walls of some of the craters, scientists detected white streaks that they speculated may be remnants of water ice or another substance that could, under different circumstances, nurture life.

station crews had been reduced to two members—one American and one Russian—instead of the normal three, to conserve water and other supplies. Although the two-man crews performed some important experiments, they were forced to spend so much time maintaining and repairing the six-year-old facility that the scientific results were significantly reduced.

U.S. astronaut Michael Foale and Russian cosmonaut Alexander Kaleri, who had replaced the previous station crew in October 2003, conducted a spacewalk on Feb. 26, 2004. They installed experiments to measure the effects of space debris on the facility and to monitor the amount of solar radiation to which spacewalkers are exposed.

In April, Russian cosmonaut Gennady Padalka and U.S. astronaut Michael Fincke replaced Foale and Kaleri. Padalka and Fincke completed three spacewalks during their six-month stay on the ISS. On July 1, the crew repaired one of the ISS's four gyroscopes, which maintain the station's position in space. On August 3, Padalka and Fincke attached laser reflectors and antennas to the station to help guide a new cargo vessel, the Automated Transfer Vehicle (ATV) built by the European Space Agency (ESA), to the station. ATV's were to begin helping to resupply the station in 2005 or 2006. A third spacewalk on Sept. 3, 2004, added more antennas for the ATV docking and replaced some cooling equipment. Padalka and Fincke were replaced in October by U.S. astronaut Leroy Chiao and Russian cosmonaut Salizhan Sharipov.

In October, NASA officials announced that several hurricanes in August and September had damaged the space shuttles' Florida launch site. Plans to return the vehicles to flight were delayed from March or April 2005 to May or June.

Two Mars exploration rovers named Spirit and Opportunity delivered the most exciting news from space in 2004. The pair had been launched by NASA in mid-2003 and landed about two weeks apart on opposite sides of Mars in January 2004. Both rovers began searching for evidence that liquid water had once flowed on the planet's dry, frozen surface. Opportunity rolled into a small crater with exposed bedrock. Using such devices as the RAT (Rock Abrasion Tool), the rover found clear evidence that the spot had once been a shallow sea or bog filled with liquid water. By March, Spirit had found minerals that suggested water once flowed on that side of Mars as well.

Cassini/Huygens at Saturn. On June 30, the Cassini spacecraft, launched in 1997, shot through a gap in the rings of Saturn and began orbiting the gas giant. Less than one month later, the spacecraft had returned hundreds of images to its controllers, revealing the planet's rings, clouds, and other features in unprecedented detail. Nestled against Cassini's side was the Huygens probe, supplied by

the ESA. Cassini was to study Saturn and its moons from orbit, while Huygens was to parachute down to the smog-shrouded surface of Saturn's largest moon, Titan, in January 2005.

A piece of the sun. A parachute failure sent Genesis, a solar sample return mission, crashing to the desert floor in Utah on Sept. 8, 2004. Genesis had been launched into space in August 2001 and had spent 30 months parked at a point outside Earth's magnetic field. There, the spacecraft had collected atoms streaming from the sun in a flood of particles known as the solar wind. A helicopter was to have made a midair catch of the capsule containing the samples as it reentered Earth's atmosphere. Instead, the capsule's parachute failed to open, and the vehicle shattered on the desert floor. Scientists believed that enough particles could be recovered to produce meaningful information about the gas cloud from which the solar system formed more than 4 billion years ago.

Other probes. On Jan. 2, 2004, NASA's Stardust spacecraft, launched in 1999, flew by comet Wild 2, capturing images of its canyons, mesas, and craters. Stardust collected dust samples from Wild 2 that were to be returned to Earth in 2006.

On July 15, 2004, NASA launched the third of its Earth observation satellites. Aura, which was to study Earth's atmosphere, joined sister satellites Aqua, involved in global studies of the water cycle, and Terra, which collects data from the land.

On August 3, NASA's Messenger spacecraft began a 6½-year journey to Mercury, the planet closest to the sun. Messenger, the first spacecraft to reach Mercury since Mariner 10 flew by the planet in 1974 and 1975, was to orbit Mercury for one year, studying its structure, atmosphere, and magnetic field.

NASA also hoped that a robot could extend the life of the Hubble Space Telescope (HST). After 14 years in orbit, the HST needed new batteries and gyroscopes to continue working beyond the end of 2009. After President Bush announced his plans for going to the moon and to Mars, NASA said it would not be able to send another shuttle to the telescope. However, astronomers and educators argued that the HST is too valuable a tool to abandon. NASA began to explore the possibility of sending a robot to perform the necessary work.

Private rocket ship in space. Historically, government agencies such as NASA and the ESA have led the way in space exploration. However, in 2004, private business owners paid for the development of SpaceShipOne, a rocket designed to carry three people into space. SpaceShipOne completed its third flight on October 4, winning the $10-million Ansari X-prize. The X-prize competition was held to encourage the growth of a nongovernment space industry.

■ Frank Morring, Jr.

See also **Astronomy.**

Spain suffered the worst terrorist attack in its history in 2004. The resulting political uproar helped the opposition Socialist Party defeat the long-ruling Popular Party in national elections.

Ten bombs hidden in backpacks exploded on four commuter trains as they were heading for, or arriving at, Madrid's main train station during the morning rush hour on March 11. The blasts killed 191 people and injured about 1,800 others.

Political backlash. The attack occurred three days before a national election. The conservative government of Prime Minister Jose Maria Aznar first blamed the blasts on the Basque separatist group ETA, which has waged a terror campaign for more than three decades in an attempt to win independence for Spain's Basque region. (In December, ETA was responsible for explosions in several Spanish cities that injured about 20 people.) Public opinion turned against the government, however, as evidence emerged linking the attacks to Islamic militants. Many Spaniards blamed the government's support for the United States-led war in Iraq for making the country a target.

The Popular Party, which had governed Spain since 1996, suffered a dramatic defeat. The party won 148 seats in the 350-seat parliament, compared with 164 seats for the Socialists. On April 17, 2004, a Socialist government headed by Prime Minister Jose Luis Rodriguez Zapatero, a 43-year-old lawyer, was sworn into office. Zapatero had campaigned on a promise to withdraw Spain's 1,300 troops from Iraq, which he did in May. The move strained relations with the United States, but Zapatero worked to improve ties with France and Germany.

Terror arrests. On April 3, seven men suspected of involvement in the attacks blew themselves up as police surrounded their apartment near Madrid. Some of the men were believed to have connections with the al-Qa'ida terrorist group of Osama bin Laden. Police detained 20 others suspected of involvement. In October and November, police arrested 33 people on suspicion of plotting to blow up Spain's High Court.

Spain's economy grew slightly in 2004. The nation's *gross domestic product* (GDP—the value of all goods and services produced in a country in a year) rose 2.6 percent, from 2.5 in 2003. Unemployment fell from 11.3 percent in 2003 to 11.1 in 2004.

Bank merger. Banco Santander, Spain's largest bank, agreed to buy Britain's Abbey National Plc for $16.4 billion on July 26 in one of Europe's biggest cross-border banking mergers. The deal was completed in November.

Royal wedding. Crown Prince Felipe, the heir to the Spanish throne, married Letizia Ortiz Rocasolano, a former television anchorwoman, at Madrid's Almudena Cathedral on May 22.

■ Tom Buerkle

See also **Europe; Iraq: A Special Report; People in the news** (Jose Luis Rodriguez Zapatero); **Terrorism.**

Mourners fill the Almudena Cathedral in Madrid on March 24, 2004, for the state funeral of victims of terrorist bombings on March 11. Bombs on trains heading for, or arriving at, a Madrid station during the morning rush hour killed 191 people and injured more than 1,800 others. Evidence linked the attacks to Islamic militants.

Sports. American cyclist Lance Armstrong captured an unprecedented sixth consecutive Tour de France in 2004, a year filled with several outstanding individual sports performances and several surprising team champions. However, the ongoing investigation into the Bay Area Laboratory Co-Operative (BALCO) and its owner, Victor Conte, cast a cloud over a number of athletes in 2004 as several high-profile male and female athletes were either accused of or rumored to be using various performance-enhancing substances. Prosecutors allege Conte created a synthetic and initially undetectable steroid, tetrahydrogestrinone (THG), which became the focal point of an international investigation.

Fiji's Vijay Singh toppled Eldrick "Tiger" Woods from his position as the world's top-ranked golfer with a 3-shot victory over Woods at the Deutsche Bank Championship in Norton, Massachusetts, on September 6. Singh's victory ended one of the most spectacular runs in sports, as Woods had held the top spot since Aug. 8, 1999. Also in men's golf in 2004, the European team defeated the American squad 18½ to 9½, Europe's largest margin of victory since the biannual Ryder Cup began in 1927.

In women's tennis, Russians won Grand Slam titles for the first time, with three different women winning the last three Grand Slam events: the French Open, Wimbledon, and the U.S. Open. Russian women occupied nearly half of the top 10 spots in the women's rankings by late 2004. In men's tennis, Switzerland's Roger Federer became the first man since 1988 to win three Grand Slam events in the same year.

In professional team sports, the surprising Detroit Pistons captured the National Basketball Association (NBA) title; the Tampa Bay Lightning captured that franchise's first Stanley Cup in the National Hockey League (NHL); the New England Patriots took Super Bowl XXXVIII in the National Football League (NFL), the team's second title in three years.

In baseball, the Boston Red Sox in October overcame one of the more infamous "curses" in sports by winning the World Series for the first time since 1918. Boston became the first team in baseball history to come back from being three games down in the seven-game American League Championship Series when the Sox beat the New York Yankees to reach the World Series. During the Series, the Red Sox swept the St. Louis Cardinals in four games. The Sox had shaken the "curse of the Bambino," which according to legend struck the team when it traded slugger Babe Ruth to the Yankees in 1920.

Tour de France. Lance Armstrong, who less than a decade earlier had been given only a 50-percent chance of surviving testicular cancer, took his record sixth consecutive Tour de France title on July 25, 2004, in Paris with one of the most dominant performances of his career. As in his previous five victories, Armstrong won the 2,110-mile (3,376-kilometer), 20-stage race in the mountainous part of the course, capturing three stages in the Alps, including a time trial.

He finished 6 minutes, 19 seconds in front of Andreas Kloden of Germany. Armstrong captured five solo stages and one team trial, more than in any of his previous Tour victories. He won the opening time trial with the third-fastest time in history. With his victory, Armstrong surpassed five-time winners Eddy Merckx of Belgium, Bernard Hinault of France, and Miguel Indurain of Spain.

BALCO scandal. In February, a federal grand jury in San Francisco handed down indictments against four men connected to BALCO and performance enhancing substances: Victor Conte, founder and president of the nutritional supplement company; James J. Valente, BALCO vice president; Greg Anderson, personal trainer to San Francisco Giants baseball star Barry Bonds; and Remy Korchemny, a renowned track coach.

The indictment detailed a conspiracy to distribute illegal steroids and misbranded drugs to athletes. Conte, Anderson, and Valente also were indicted for money laundering and conspiracy to distribute human growth hormone, which some athletes use illegally to increase endurance.

Authorities claim Conte was the source of THG, which had been undetectable until an unnamed track-and-field coach in 2003 provided the U.S. Anti-Doping Agency the names of athletes supposedly using the drug, as well as a syringe with the steroid. Authorities used the THG in the syringe to devise a test to detect the drug.

Before the indictments were handed down, the grand jury heard testimony from a parade of sports figures, including Bonds and New York Yankees star Jason Giambi; Olympic track star Marion Jones; several NFL players; and boxer Shane Mosley. No athletes were indicted in 2004.

College reforms. The University of Colorado (Boulder) suspended its football coach, Gary Barnett, in February after allegations of sexual assaults by players and recruits and assertions that the school used sex, drugs, and alcohol to lure recruits. Barnett was reinstated in May after an independent commission determined that neither coaches nor administrators knowingly had lured recruits through illegal or unethical means. Nevertheless, the commission recommended making sweeping changes to the school's recruiting practices to prevent further problems, including additional supervision during recruit visits.

Between 1997 and 2004, nine women, including a former place-kicker for the team, accused players or recruits of sexual assault. Although the women did not file criminal charges, three of them filed federal lawsuits, which were still pending in late 2004.

In response to the allegations at Colorado and the publication of a newspaper diary of a University of Miami recruit that described recruiters plying him with lobster and steak dinners and luxurious travel, the National Collegiate Athletic Association (NCAA) moved to enact stronger regulations on Division I recruiting. On August 5, the Division I board of directors endorsed measures requiring recruits to fly on commercial airlines in coach class.

Schools also must provide the same vehicles for athletes to which other prospective students have access, provide "standard" meals and lodging, and offer no personalized inducements, such as custom jerseys.

Kobe Bryant case. In arguably the most sensational court case involving an athlete since O. J. Simpson's trial for murder in 1995, sexual assault charges against Los Angeles Lakers basketball star Kobe Bryant were dismissed on Sept. 1, 2004, after the woman who had accused him informed prosecutors that she would not testify.

The announcement came during jury selection,

but few legal observers had expected the trial to go forward after the accuser's attorneys in August filed a civil suit on her behalf in federal court. The woman and her attorneys were outraged at the court for allegedly committing mistakes that led to her identity and details of her sexual history being released on the Internet.

Bryant's defense team had won a major decision during pretrial motions that allowed some evidence of the accuser's sexual history to be admissible at trial. Bryant's team planned to introduce evidence that she had been sexually

American cyclist Lance Armstrong (center in yellow jersey) rides down the Champ-Elysees in Paris during the final stage of the Tour de France on July 25. Armstrong had already sealed his record sixth consecutive win in the 2,100-mile (3,376-kilometer) event with a strong performance in the mountains.

active hours after the alleged assault on June 30, 2003, but before she reported the alleged rape.

Mountain climbing. Pemba Dorji Sherpa of Nepal broke the record for fastest ascent of Mount Everest on May 21, 2004, with a climb of 8 hours and 10 minutes, more than 2 hours faster than the previous record set in 2003. Speed ascents of Everest continue to be improved upon because climbers are allowed to use ropes and ladders put in place by previous climbers.

Britton Keeshan, a 22-year-old college student from Greenwich, Connecticut, became the youngest person to climb the highest peaks on all seven continents when he finished his ascent of Mount Everest on May 24, 2004.

Olympic scandal. Salt Lake City businessman David Simmons and former U.S. Olympic official Alfredo LaMont, the only two people convicted in the Salt Lake City Olympic bribery scandal, received no jail time when they were sentenced in September 2004. LaMont had pleaded guilty to tax evasion and conspiracy to evade taxes; Simmons had pleaded guilty to tax fraud.

Awards. Michael Phelps swept amateur athletics awards in 2004, given for performances in 2003. Phelps, who won six medals, including four golds, and set five world records at the 2003 World Swimming Championships, received the Amateur Athletic Association's American-International Athlete Trophy in March 2004, beating out cyclist Lance Armstrong. In April, Phelps became the first male swimmer since Mark Spitz in 1971 to win the James E. Sullivan Award, which is presented by the Amateur Athletic Union to the best U.S. amateur athlete.

Equestrian. The 2003 World Cup Final dressage champion, Ulla Salzgeber of Germany, in February 2004 was barred from the sport for two months when her horse tested positive for a banned substance. She forfeited her 2003 gold medal, which was awarded to Debbie McDonald of the United States. In 2004, Bruno Broucqsault of France was the individual show jumping champion at the World Cup Final. Anky van Grunsven of the Netherlands was the dressage champion.

Luge. Germany dominated the World Championships held in Nagano, Japan, in February. David Moeller won the men's singles event, Silke Kraushaar won the women's singles title, and Patric Leitner and Alexander Resch won the men's doubles event. Germany captured the team title.

Marathon. Catherine Ndereba of Kenya won the Boston Marathon for the third time, capturing the race on April 19 in a time of 2 hours, 24 minutes, and 27 seconds.

Rodeo. Trevor Brazile won the All-Around World Champion Cowboy title in the National Finals Rodeo on December 12.

Rowing. The Dutch club Hollandia Roeiclub captured the Grand Challenge Cup on July 4 at the Henley Royal Regatta in Henley-on-the-Thames, England, beating a team from Harvard University in Cambridge, Massachusetts.

Sled-dog racing. Mitch Seavey of Seward, Alaska, won the Iditarod Trail Sled Dog Race on March 16, finishing the 1,100-mile (1,770-kilometer) trip from Anchorage to Nome, Alaska, in 9 days, 12 hours, 20 minutes, and 22 seconds.

Soap box derby. Hilary Pearson, 12, of Kansas City, Missouri, won the Masters Division of the 67th All-American Soap Box Derby in Akron, Ohio, on July 31.

Speed skating. American Chad Hedrick broke the men's world overall points record on February 8 at the World All-Around Championships in Hamar, Norway. His four-race total of 150,478 points in the two-day meet beat teammate Shani Davis's 150,726 points. Mark Tuitert of the Netherlands set the previous record of 151,691 points at the 2004 European Championships. Renate Groenewold became the first Dutch woman in 30 years to win the women's title, finishing with 162,573 points to beat Germany's Claudia Pechstein. Erben Wennemars of the Netherlands captured his first world championship at the long-track world championships in Nagano, Japan, in January. Marianne Timmer of the Netherlands won the women's overall title.

South Korea's men and women won the gold medals at the Short-Track World Team Championships in St. Petersburg, Russia, in March.

Triathlon. Britain's Simon Lessing and Australia's Michellie Jones set records in the Escape from Alcatraz Triathlon, a race held in San Francisco on June 6 that included a 1.5-mile (2.4-kilometer) swim; 18-mile (29-kilometer) bicycle ride; and an 8-mile (12.8-kilometer) run. Lessing posted a time of 1 hour, 54 minutes, and 41 seconds, while Jones finished in 2 hours, 8 minutes, and 54 seconds.

World road cycling. Oscar Freire of Spain won the Union Cycliste Internationale world road cycling championship, in Verona, Italy, in October.

Other champions:

Archery. World Field Championships: men's compound, Christopher White, United Kingdom; women's compound, Francoise Volle, France; men's recurve, Sebastian Rohrberg, Germany; women's recurve, Jessica Tomasi, Italy; men's barebow, Erik Jonsson, Sweden; women's barebow, Monika Jentges, Germany; men's team, United Kingdom; women's team, France.

Biathlon. France's Raphael Poiree won three gold medals, a silver, and a bronze; his wife, Liv Grete Poiree, won four gold medals at the world championships in February in Oberhof, Germany.

Bobsledding. German sledders dominated in 2004, with Christoph Langen taking the overall World Cup bobsled title and Andre Lange leading his four-man bobsled team to the World Cup title in Germany in February.

Curling. Men's world champion: Sweden. Women's world champion: Canada.

Lacrosse. Men's National Collegiate Athletic Association Division I champion: Syracuse University. Women's NCAA Division I champion: University of Virginia.

Modern pentathlon. World championship titles: men's individual, Andrejus Zadneprovskis of Lithuania; men's team, Russia. Women's individual, Zsuzsanna Voros, Hungary; women's team, Great Britain.

Motorcyle racing. FIM Grand Prix 500-cc champion: Valentino Rossi of Italy.

Skeleton. World champions: men, Duff Gibson, Canada; women, Diana Sartor, Germany.

Snowboarding. World Cup champion: Jasey Jay Anderson of Canada.   ■ Michael Kates

See also **Baseball; Basketball; Football; Golf; Hockey; Ice skating; Olympics: A Special Report; Soccer; Swimming; Tennis.**

Sri Lanka. A 9.0-magnitude earthquake off the Indonesian island of Sumatra generated massive tsunamis that hit Sri Lanka with terrific force on Dec. 26, 2004. Walls of water as high as 40 feet (14 meters) devastated a wide stretch of the eastern coastline, from Jaffna in the north to beaches in the south crowded with tourists. On December 31, government officials confirmed that at least 25,000 people on Sri Lanka were killed and up to 1 million others were left homeless.

New prime minister. Mahinda Rajapaksa became prime minister on April 6, following Sri Lanka's third general election in less than four years. He was named to the job by President Chandrika Kumaratunga, leader of the Sri Lanka Freedom Party. The party and its ally, the nationalistic Marxist Janatha Vimukthi Peramuna (JVP), controlled 105 of 225 parliament seats, after taking 45.6 percent of the vote. Rajapaksa succeeded Prime Minister Ranil Wickremesinghe, whose United National Party held 82 seats after taking only 38 percent of the vote in the general election.

Rajapaksa formed a coalition government that included four ministers from the JVP, a party that Kumaratunga in 1988 had accused of assassinating her husband. The JVP had been critical of peace talks with a separatist movement, the Liberation Tigers of Tamil Eelam (LTTE). The LTTE has been fighting since 1983 to create a separate nation for the 3.2 million ethnic Tamil Hindus in the predominately Sinhalese Buddhist island nation. An estimated 64,000 people have died in the struggle.

Kumaratunga charged Wickremesinghe with having been too soft in peace talks with the LTTE. Participants in the talks explored the possibility of a federal system that would give Tamils regional *autonomy* (self-government). The JVP opposed granting any concessions to the Tamil group. Rajapaksa's coalition also included a Tamil party opposed to the LTTE, which had assassinated a number of Tamil politicians deemed disloyal.

Rebel strife. In March 2004, Vinayagamoorthy Muralitharan, the LTTE commander, who is known as Colonel Karuna, broke from the main organization of Vellupillai Prabhakaran, who commanded an estimated 9,000 fighters in the northeast. Karuna, who commanded some 6,000 fighters in eastern Sri Lanka, charged that the LTTE was dominated by northerners and that leaders in the LTTE were planning to break cease-fire agreements.

Karuna's elder brother, Vinayakamoorthy Sivanesasurai, led a battle against Prabhakaran's forces in April in which dozens of rebels died on each side. LTTE leaders killed Sivanesasurai in September while Karuna was in hiding. Sri Lanka's army denied accusations by Prabhakaran of having helped Karuna.   ■ Henry S. Bradsher

See also **Asia.**

State government. The Republican Party continued to hold a majority of the 50 governorships in the United States following 11 gubernatorial contests on Nov. 2, 2004. Party control of the governor's office switched for contests, leaving Republicans in control of 28 states.

Republicans won governors' offices previously held by members of the Democratic Party in Indiana and Missouri. Democrats took over previously Republican gubernatorial seats in Montana and New Hampshire. Democrats held on to governors' offices in Delaware, North Carolina, Washington, and West Virginia. Republicans kept the top office in North Dakota, Vermont, and Utah.

Incumbent victories. Two incumbent Democratic governors won re-election on November 2. In Delaware, Governor Ruth Ann Minner fought back a challenge by Republican Bill Lee, a retired state superior court judge. North Carolina Governor Michael Easley defeated Republican state Senator Patrick J. Ballantine.

Voters returned two Republican incumbents to office. In North Dakota, Governor John Hoeven defeated Democrat Joseph Satrom. Vermont Governor Jim Douglas defeated challenger Democrat Peter Clavelle, the mayor of Burlington, Vermont.

New governors took office in Indiana and New Hampshire following the election. In Indiana, Mitch Daniels, a Republican and former official in the administration of President George W. Bush, defeated Governor Joe Kernan. Kernan had been lieutenant governor when Governor Frank O'Bannon died in 2003. In New Hampshire, businessman John Lynch, a Democrat, defeated Governor Craig Benson, a Republican, in November 2004.

Failed re-election bids. The governors of Missouri and Utah each failed to win nomination by their parties in primary elections in 2004.

In Missouri, Claire McCaskill, the state auditor, defeated Governor Bob Holden during a Democratic primary election in August. Holden had served one term in office. Missouri Secretary of State Matt Blunt, a Republican, went on to defeat McCaskill in the November 2 gubernatorial race.

In May, Utah Governor Olene S. Walker lost the Republican nomination to Jon Huntsman, Jr., a businessman and former U.S. ambassador. Walker had been the state's lieutenant governor and was sworn in as governor in 2003 when former Governor Mike Leavitt was named administrator of the U.S. Environmental Protection Agency. Huntsman defeated his Democratic challenger, Scott Matheson, in the November 2004 election.

Other gubernatorial races. In Montana, rancher Brian Schweitzer became the first Democrat to capture the governor's office since 1989, defeating Republican Secretary of State Bob Brown in November 2004. Montana Governor Judy Martz, a Republican, did not seek re-election.

In West Virginia, Secretary of State Joe Manchin III, a Democrat, easily defeated Republican Monty Warner, a real estate developer. Governor Bob Wise, a Democrat, announced in 2003 that he would not seek re-election after admitting to an extramarital relationship.

In Washington, Attorney General Christine Gregoire, a Democrat, defeated Republican Dino Rossi, a former state senator, in the Nov. 2, 2004, election to succeed Governor Gary Locke. Washington Secretary of State Sam Reed ordered a recount of the 2.7 million votes on November 17. A machine recount in November gave the election to Rossi by 42 votes; a subsequent hand count in December showed that Gregoire had won by 130 votes.

Resignations. New governors took office in 2004 upon the resignation of two incumbents. Lieutenant Governor M. Jodi Rell replaced Connecticut Governor John G. Rowland, a Republican, who resigned on June 21 under federal investigation for corruption. On December 23, Rowland pleaded guilty in Federal District Court to one federal charge of corruption for accepting $107,000 in gratuities and failing to pay taxes on the money.

New Jersey Governor James E. McGreevey, a Democrat, on August 12 announced his resignation after admitting to a homosexual relationship with a former aide. McGreevey left office on November 15. Richard J. Codey, a Democrat and president of the state senate, was sworn in as acting governor.

Stem cell research. Voters in California approved a ballot measure on November 2 setting aside $3 billion in state bonds for embryonic stem cell research. Embryonic stem cells taken from human embryos have the ability to develop into any of the different cell types that make up the tissues and organs of the body. Opponents consider the research wrong because they believe embryos have status as human beings. Advocates justify the research on potential medical benefits.

Same-sex unions continued to be an issue in 2004. Voters in 11 states in the November 2 elections endorsed constitutional amendments defining marriage as a union between a man and a woman. Voters in Arkansas, Georgia, Kentucky, Michigan, Mississippi, Montana, North Dakota, Ohio, Oklahoma, Oregon, and Utah adopted marriage amendments. Louisiana and Missouri voters passed similar measures in primary elections. The amendments were put on the ballot after Massachusetts officials married the first same-sex couple in May, after the Massachusetts Supreme Judicial Court removed the last roadblock to such unions in February. In November, the U.S. Supreme Court refused to hear a case challenging Massachusetts's legalization of such marriage.

State budgets. States faced less severe financial problems in 2004 than they had for several years. State legislatures turned to a variety of means to cut spending and balance budgets, according to the National Conference of State Legislatures (NCSL), a nonprofit organization headquartered in Denver, Colorado. States made cuts in health-care programs, prison programs, and education programs.

In 2004, 44 states increased taxes by a total of $2.8 billion, compared with $8.8 billion in 2003, the NCSL reported in July 2004. However, the NCSL report was completed before budgets were settled in six states, including California and New York.

State budget shortfalls have meant less funding for health and education, according to a report released in September by the Center on Budget and Policy Priorities, a nonprofit research group based in Washington, D.C. The Center reported that at least 34 states had cut eligibility for public health insurance, removing coverage for approximately 1.2 million people. At least 23 states also have reduced the number of parents eligible for child-care subsidies. In education, kindergarten through 12th grade per-pupil aid declined in 34 states between 2003 and 2004, the Center reported.

Disputes over budgets in 2004 sessions often fell along partisan lines. New York Governor George Pataki, a Republican, vetoed $1.8 billion from the budget in August, which was enacted

State	Resident population*	Governor†	Legislature† House (D)	(R)	Senate (D)	(R)	State tax revenue‡	Tax revenue per capita‡	Public school expenditure per pupil§
Alabama	4,500,752	Bob Riley (R)	63	42	25	10	$ 6,416,000,000	$ 1,430	$ 5,370
Alaska	648,818	Frank Murkowski (R)	14	26	8	12	1,069,000,000	1,650	9,820
Arizona	5,580,811	Janet Napolitano (D)	22	38	12	18	8,692,000,000	1,560	5,300
Arkansas	2,725,714	Mike Huckabee (R)	72	28	27	8	5,146,000,000	1,890	5,860
California	35,484,453	Arnold Schwarzenegger (R)	48	32	25	15	79,198,000,000	2,230	7,720
Colorado	4,550,688	Bill F. Owens (R)	33	32	18	17	6,636,000,000	1,460	7,810
Connecticut	3,483,372	M. Jodi Rell (R)	99	52	24	12	9,509,000,000	2,730	11,690
Delaware	817,491	Ruth Ann Minner (D)	15	26	13	8	2,126,000,000	2,600	10,780
Florida	17,019,068	Jeb Bush (R)	36	84	14	26	26,905,000,000	1,580	6,570
Georgia	8,684,715	Sonny Perdue (R)	86	94	22	33	13,412,000,000	1,540	8,700
Hawaii	1,257,608	Linda Lingle (R)	41	10	20	5	3,570,000,000	2,840	7,540
Idaho	1,366,332	Dirk Kempthorne (R)	13	57	7	28	2,344,000,000	1,720	6,370
Illinois	12,653,544	Rod Blagojevich (D)	65	53	#31	27	22,148,000,000	1,750	9,110
Indiana	6,195,643	Mitch Daniels (R)	48	52	17	33	11,216,000,000	1,810	8,570
Iowa	2,944,062	Tom Vilsack (D)	49	51	25	25	5,059,000,000	1,720	7,100
Kansas	2,723,507	Kathleen Sebelius (D)	42	83	10	30	5,008,000,000	1,840	7,980
Kentucky	4,117,827	Ernie Fletcher (R)	57	43	15	23	8,319,000,000	2,020	7,510
Louisiana	4,496,334	Kathleen Blanco (D)	#68	36	26	13	7,449,000,000	1,660	7,080
Maine	1,305,728	John Baldacci (D)	**76	73	18	17	2,697,000,000	2,070	9,730
Maryland	5,508,909	Robert Erlich (R)	98	43	33	14	10,980,000,000	1,990	8,100
Massachusetts	6,433,422	Mitt Romney (R)	#139	20	34	6	15,611,000,000	2,430	11,040
Michigan	10,079,985	Jennifer Granholm (D)	52	58	16	22	22,748,000,000	2,260	8,380
Minnesota	5,059,375	Tim Pawlenty (R)	66	68	#35	31	13,404,000,000	2,650	8,920
Mississippi	2,881,281	Haley Barbour (R)	††75	47	#27	24	4,947,000,000	1,720	6,090
Missouri	5,704,484	Matt Blunt (R)	66	97	11	23	8,627,000,000	1,510	6,950
Montana	917,621	Brian Schweitzer (D)	‡‡49	50	27	23	1,487,000,000	1,620	7,800
Nebraska	1,739,291	Mike Johanns (R)	unicameral (49 nonpartisan)				3,348,000,000	1,930	7,320
Nevada	2,241,154	Kenny Guinn (R)	26	16	9	12	4,129,000,000	1,840	6,230
New Hampshire	1,287,687	John Lynch (D)	148	252	8	16	1,959,000,000	1,520	8,630
New Jersey	8,638,396	Richard J. Codey (D)	47	33	22	18	19,936,000,000	2,310	11,490
New Mexico	1,874,614	Bill Richardson (D)	42	28	23	19	3,607,000,000	1,920	7,120
New York	19,190,115	George E. Pataki (R)	104	46	26	34	40,558,000,000	2,110	12,270
North Carolina	8,407,248	Mike Easley (D)	63	57	29	21	15,849,000,000	1,890	6,730
North Dakota	633,837	John Hoeven (R)	26	66	15	32	1,178,000,000	1,860	6,840
Ohio	11,435,798	Robert Taft (R)	40	59	11	22	20,652,000,000	1,810	9,230
Oklahoma	3,511,532	Brad Henry (D)	44	57	26	22	5,906,000,000	1,680	7,010
Oregon	3,559,596	Ted Kulongoski (D)	27	33	18	12	5,702,000,000	1,600	7,700
Pennsylvania	12,365,455	Ed Rendell (D)	93	110	20	30	23,187,000,000	1,880	8,590
Rhode Island	1,076,164	Don Carcieri (R)	59	16	33	5	2,257,000,000	2,100	10,260
South Carolina	4,147,152	Mark Sanford (R)	50	74	19	27	6,353,000,000	1,530	7,790
South Dakota	764,309	Mike Rounds (R)	19	51	10	25	1,010,000,000	1,320	7,300
Tennessee	5,841,748	Phil Bredesen (D)	53	46	16	17	8,812,000,000	1,510	6,210
Texas	22,118,509	Rick Perry (R)	63	87	12	19	29,099,000,000	1,320	7,330
Utah	2,351,467	Jon Huntsman, Jr. (R)	19	56	8	21	3,951,000,000	1,680	5,100
Vermont	619,107	James Douglas (R)	§§83	60	21	9	1,559,000,000	2,520	10,610
Virginia	7,386,330	Mark Warner (D)	††37	61	16	24	12,969,000,000	1,760	6,460
Washington	6,131,445	Christine Gregoire (D)	55	43	25	23	12,960,000,000	2,110	7,450
West Virginia	1,810,354	Joe Manchin III (D)	68	32	21	13	3,589,000,000	1,980	9,170
Wisconsin	5,472,299	Jim Doyle (D)	39	60	14	19	12,185,000,000	2,230	9,480
Wyoming	501,242	Dave Freudenthal (D)	14	46	7	23	1,217,000,000	2,430	10,210

*July 1, 2003, estimates. Source: U.S. Census Bureau.
†As of December 2004. Source: National Governors' Association; National Conference of State Legislatures; state government officials.
‡2003 figures. Source: U.S. Census Bureau.
§2003-2004 estimates for elementary and secondary students in fall enrollment Source: National Education Association.

#One independent.
**One Green Party, one independent.
††Two independents.
‡‡One Constitutional Party.
§§Six Progressive Party, one independent.

nearly five months past its April 1 deadline. Pataki criticized the Democratic state Assembly for not closing a $6.1-billion spending gap for 2005.

In California, Governor Arnold Schwarzenegger, a Republican, criticized Democratic legislators for not passing a budget. He later praised the bipartisan agreement on the $105-billion budget enacted in July 2004.

In Kentucky, the Democratic-controlled state House of Representatives and Republican-controlled Senate failed to pass a budget in 2004.

Health care. State legislatures in at least eight states defied the federal government in 2004 and moved to help their residents import less expensive prescription medicine from Canada. Legislatures in Connecticut, Hawaii, Illinois, Minnesota, New Hampshire, North Dakota, Vermont, and Wisconsin approved various programs or started Web sites to help residents buy imported drugs. A program launched in October 2004 by Illinois and joined by Missouri and Wisconsin allowed residents of those states to buy drugs imported from approved pharmacies in Canada, Ireland, and the United Kingdom.

■ Elaine Stuart McDonald

See also **Courts; Democratic Party; Election; Health care issues; Republican Party; Supreme Court of the United States; United States, Government of the.**

Stocks and bonds. A rally sparked by the conclusion of the 2004 United States presidential election enabled the U.S. stock market to close the year with a gain. Small-company stocks led the advance, continuing a trend that began in 2003.

The Standard and Poor's 500 (S&P 500) index increased 5 percent to 1,173.82 through November 2004. The S&P 500 is a set of large-company stocks used to measure the level of the U.S. stock market. By contrast, the S&P 600 index of 600 small-company stocks was up 19 percent, to 321.99, through November. The Dow Jones Industrial Average remained flat for most of 2004, ending November at 10,428.02. The Dow is a composite of the stock prices of 30 major companies.

Concern over higher interest rates, including a series of interest rate increases begun in June by the Federal Reserve (the Fed), the central bank of the United States, dampened enthusiasm for stocks. Higher interest rates represent competition for investors' dollars and impose a drag on corporate profits. Profit growth began to slow beginning in July, after several months of strong gains that began in mid-2003.

Oil and the dollar. Higher oil prices posed a threat to the U.S. economy and corporate profits in 2004. Oil reached a record high of more than

People gather after midnight on May 17, 2004, outside the City Hall in Cambridge, Massachusetts, as clerks begin issuing marriage licenses to same-sex couples. In 2004, Massachusetts became the first state to legalize same-sex marriages, triggering 11 states to define a marriage as a union between a man and a woman.

$55 a barrel in October, twice the cost of oil in March 2003, when U.S. armed forces invaded Iraq. Gasoline prices at gas stations held above $2 a gallon across much of the United States throughout most of 2004. Economists noted that higher fuel prices divert spending dollars from other purchases and have a negative effect on the U.S. economy. However, shares of energy-related companies were the top-performing sector in the U.S. stock market in 2004.

Ongoing tensions in the Middle East as well as economic expansion in the United States, China, and East Asia prompted the climb in oil prices. Higher oil prices also reflected the weakening value of the dollar in currency markets. The value of the dollar against major international currencies has declined since early 2002. The pace of the decline increased in late summer 2004, sending the dollar to record lows against the euro, Europe's main currency.

Bonds hold firm. Despite the Fed's effort to boost short-term interest rates, longer-term rates held steady in 2004. Job growth improved, but the lackluster pace of job creation averted fears of inflation. The yield on 10-year U.S. Treasury bonds, which reflect changes in prices to accommodate current market rates, averaged about 4.3 percent in 2004. The rate also is used to calculate many home mortgage rates. Financial analysts said that the low percentages resulted in a strong housing market.

Winners and losers. While energy stocks were the top-performing sector in 2004, several technology stocks contributed to the year's gain. Shares of Apple Computer Inc., of Cupertino, California, tripled in value through November, reflecting strong sales of Apple's iPod digital music recorder. Online auction service eBay Inc., of San Jose, California, reported increases of nearly 80 percent during the same period.

However, stocks of companies that make semiconductors slumped. Semiconductors are materials, such as computer chips made of silicon, that conduct electric current. Overly optimistic sales forecasts at the beginning of 2004 led to excess inventories in the summer. Intel Corp., a Santa Clara, California-based semiconductor manufacturer, saw its stocks decline by 25 percent through the end of November.

Basic materials stocks, especially steelmakers, scored large gains in 2004. The demand for steel, copper, and other materials boosted prices worldwide. For example, the value of stock in Nucor Corporation, a Charlotte, North Carolina, steel producer, climbed 80 percent through November.

Major pharmaceutical makers and insurance companies in the United States were among the big losers of 2004. The stock value of pharma-

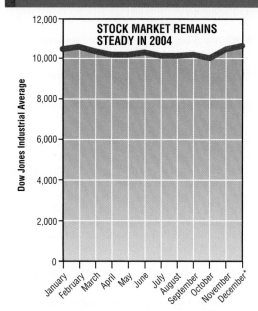

STOCK MARKET REMAINS STEADY IN 2004

Dow Jones Industrial Average

12,000 — 10,000 — 8,000 — 6,000 — 4,000 — 2,000 — 0

January, February, March, April, May, June, July, August, September, October, November, December*

Closing month averages for 2004
* December figure is as of the 13th.

The Dow Jones Industrial Average, a composite of the stock prices of 30 major companies, showed little fluctuation during 2004 but managed to stay above the 10,000 mark throughout the year.

ceutical manufacturer Merck & Co., headquartered in Whitehouse Station, New Jersey, lost nearly 40 percent through November. In September, the company withdrew Vioxx, its prescription arthritis and pain relief medication, from circulation after studies linked the product to heart attacks.

Shares of New York City-based Marsh & McLennan Companies, the largest insurance broker in the United States, fell 36 percent through November. New York State Attorney General Eliot Spitzer sued Marsh & McLennan in October for allegedly conducting illegal business practices.

International stock markets. Signs of ongoing economic recovery could be seen in several parts of the world, including Mexico, Europe, and Japan. The Mexico Bolsa Index was up 38 percent through November. The Dow Jones Stoxx 50 index of 50 major European companies rose 10 percent during the same period, while the Nikkei 225 index of 225 major Japanese companies reported a modest 2 percent increase. Asian stocks outside Japan fared better. The Hang Seng Index of 33 major companies traded on the Hong Kong Stock Exchange rose 12 percent. An S&P index of 200 top Australian stocks was up 19 percent.

■ Bill Barnhart

See also **Drugs; Economics.**

Sudan. The violent conflict in the western Sudanese region of Darfur worsened in 2004, drawing increasing international scrutiny. The conflict began in February 2003, when two local rebel groups—the Sudan Liberation Army and the Justice and Equality Movement—took up arms against government forces in the region. The rebels accused the government of decades of neglect and oppression. The government responded by arming ethnic militias, drawn primarily from nomadic tribes, to battle the rebels.

Throughout 2004, the government-supported Arab "Janjaweed" militia launched numerous attacks on the civilian population of Darfur. In August, the United Nations (UN) estimated that, over the previous 18 months, 30,000 to 50,000 people had been killed in the violence, and 200,000 others had fled to neighboring Chad. According to the UN, a total of 1.2 million people had been displaced in Darfur by August. These numbers increased as the year went on.

African Union. In April, the African Union (AU), an association of African nations cooperating on social, economic, and political issues, mediated a cease-fire agreement in Darfur. The AU deployed approximately 100 military observers to monitor the cease-fire. The limited deployment, however, failed to significantly stem the fighting.

International action. Under the threat of UN and European sanctions, Sudanese officials signed an agreement in July committing the government to improving the political, humanitarian, human rights, and security conditions in Darfur. In September, the UN Security Council passed a United States-backed resolution calling on the Sudanese government to rein in the Janjaweed and allow a larger AU monitoring force in Darfur.

The Sudanese government agreed in October to allow up to 3,500 AU troops and police into Darfur to help restore security. At AU-sponsored peace talks in Nigeria in November, government and rebel leaders agreed to further improve security in Darfur and allow humanitarian organizations to operate more freely. Despite these pledges from both sides, fighting raged in Darfur throughout the rest of 2004—even as another round of AU-sponsored negotiations was held in December.

Peace with southern rebels. On November 19, the Sudanese government and the Sudan People's Liberation Movement—a rebel group based in southern Sudan—vowed to end the 21-year-old civil war between government forces in the north and rebels in the south. They pledged to finalize a peace accord by the end of the year.

■ Mary-Jane Deeb

See also **Middle East; United Nations.**

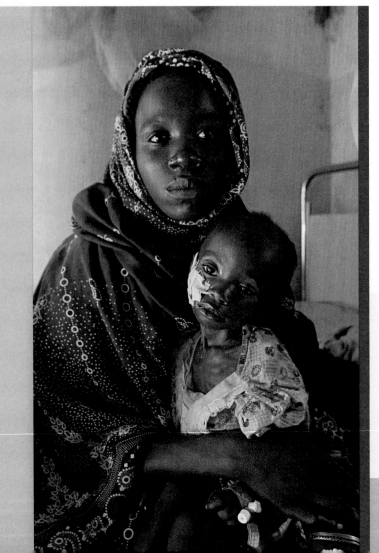

A Sudanese refugee cradles her sick child at a hospital in the embattled Darfur region of Sudan in June. In August, the United Nations estimated that as many as 50,000 people had been killed in fighting between government-backed militias and rebel groups in Darfur over the previous 18 months. More than 1 million others had been displaced by the conflict.

Supreme Court of the United States.

In 2004, the Supreme Court of the United States issued rulings on public college scholarships for ministry students, the application of the Americans with Disabilities Act, the inclusion of the phrase "under God" in the Pledge of Allegiance, and decisions in cases stemming from the war on terrorism.

Religion. By a 7-to-2 vote on February 23, the court ruled that state-funded college scholarships can be withheld from students preparing for the ministry, even if those scholarships are available to students studying nonreligious subjects. The case involved Washington state officials who refused to provide financial aid to a student studying for the ministry. The court ruled that the policy was not unconstitutional religious discrimination.

In June, the court disqualified a constitutional challenge to the phrase "one nation under God" in the Pledge of Allegiance that had been made by an *atheist* (a person who believes there is no God). By a 5-to-3 vote, the court dismissed the case in which the man objected to his daughter having to say the Pledge of Allegiance in her public school because of the reference to God. The court did not rule on the issue of whether the phrase violated the constitutional ban on the establishment of an official government religion. Instead, the court said that the man did not have legal standing to bring his suit because he did not have legal custody of his daughter.

Disability issues. By a 5-to-4 vote on May 17, the court ruled that under certain circumstances, states can be sued for damages for not making courthouses accessible to disabled persons. Individuals generally cannot sue states unless state officials agree to the litigation. However, the U.S. Congress can pass legislation that allows individuals to sue states in order to ensure the rights of citizens to the constitutional guarantee of equal protection and due process. In its decision, the court said that Congress properly used its power in the Americans with Disabilities Act to make sure that disabled persons are not denied the same access as able-bodied individuals to state courtrooms. The case before the Supreme Court involved six disabled Tennessee residents and centered on the inaccessibility of state courthouses to people with physical disabilities.

Rights of detainees. The Supreme Court issued a pair of rulings in June 2004 defining the scope of presidential authority in handling prisoners captured in connection with the war on terrorism and the attacks on the United States on Sept. 11, 2001.

In one case, decided on June 28, 2004, the court ruled 6 to 3 that foreign detainees have legal rights. The case involved several hundred men who were taken into U.S. custody during fighting in Afghanistan in fall 2001. The men had

been held at a U.S. naval base at Guantanamo Bay, Cuba, without being charged with crimes or given contact with lawyers or family members. The court declared that a U.S. military base in a foreign country is under U.S. control and is, therefore, under the jurisdiction of the U.S. court system. The decision meant that the detainees had the right to file claims in federal court or before a "neutral decision-maker" to contest their detention.

In a separate case, also handed down on June 28, 2004, the justices decided by an 8-to-1 vote that Yaser Esam Hamdi, an American-born man captured in Afghanistan in 2002 and designated an enemy *combatant* (fighter) was entitled by the Constitution's due process to challenge being imprisoned without criminal charges or access to a lawyer. In September 2004, officials with the U.S. Department of Justice announced that they had agreed to release Hamdi and deport him to Saudi Arabia, where he was required to renounce his U.S. citizenship.

Online protection. On June 29, 2004, the court ruled in a 5-to-4 vote that the 1998 Child Online Protection Act appeared to violate the Constitution's guarantee of free speech by blocking adults from seeing some online material that is legal for them to view, even though it may be inappropriate for children. The law makes it a crime to post sexually explicit Web content that is "harmful to minors" if it was being displayed for commercial purposes. The penalty for breaking the law included up to six months in prison and a maximum fine of $50,000. Web site operators could avoid penalties by requiring credit card numbers, identification codes, or other measures to check whether users are adults. The law was challenged in court and never took effect after a federal judge blocked its enforcement.

In its ruling, the Supreme Court said that the lower court was correct to block the law from taking effect because its scope was too broad. The federal government, however, could bring the case to trial again in a lower court.

Criminal law. On June 24, the court ruled that Washington state's sentencing guidelines violate the constitutional right to a jury trial by allowing judges to sometimes increase defendants' sentences based on facts that were not presented to a jury. By a vote of 5 to 4, the justices decided that juries, not judges acting alone, must consider each fact that could lengthen a prison term. Legal experts noted that the decision could affect thousands of prison sentences that have been handed out since the mid-1980's.

Open records. The Sierra Club, an environmental activist group headquartered in San Francisco, asked Justice Antonin Scalia in February 2004 to remove himself from participating in a case involving access to records from an energy task force that was headed by Vice President Dick Cheney. Attorneys representing the Sierra Club argued that Scalia's impartiality could be called into question because he had flown with the vice president to a Louisiana hunting trip in January 2004, a few weeks after the Supreme Court agreed to hear arguments in the case. Senator Patrick J. Leahy (D., Vermont) and Senator Joseph I. Lieberman (D., Connecticut) also questioned whether Scalia could remain fair and impartial.

On March 18, Scalia issued a 21-page memo explaining that he had not discussed the case with Vice President Cheney and did not believe it was necessary to step down. The court decided the case on June 24, voting 7 to 2 that Cheney could not immediately be forced to turn over records from the task force meetings. However, the court sent the case back to the U.S. Court of Appeals for the District of Columbia to reconsider whether the documents could remain secret.

Judicial ethics. Following the intense media scrutiny of Scalia's decision to hear the case, Chief Justice William Rehnquist appointed a six-member committee in May 2004 to study procedures for handling ethics complaints against federal judges. Under the Constitution, federal judges have lifetime tenure, but they can be impeached for misconduct. Judges on the U.S. district courts and courts of appeals follow a code of ethics that, among other things, gives guidelines for when they should disqualify themselves from cases. Supreme Court justices, however, determine for themselves when a conflict of interest requires them to step off particular cases. The committee, headed by Justice Stephen Breyer, was to look at the complaint process and issue a report sometime in 2006.

Blackmun papers. The Library of Congress made public an extensive collection of papers in March 2004 that former Justice Harry Blackmun had amassed during his 24 years on the court. Blackmun, who was nominated by President Richard Nixon in 1970, retired in 1994. Blackmun wrote numerous memos and notes about the court's activities and the justices' discussions of cases. He saved those along with journals, drafts of speeches, and letters.

Health concerns. Chief Justice William Rehnquist underwent throat surgery in October 2004 after physicians diagnosed thyroid cancer. In November, Rehnquist disclosed that he was undergoing radiation and chemotherapy.

■ Geoffrey A. Campbell

See also **Courts; Disability; Education; State government.**

Surgery. See Medicine.

Suriname. See Latin America.

Swaziland. See Africa.

Sweden enjoyed one of the strongest economic performances in Europe in 2004. The *gross domestic product* (GDP—the total output of goods and services produced in a country in a year) grew by 3.7 percent, up from 1.6 percent in 2003 and well above the 2.5 percent average for the 25 European Union nations. Strong gains in exports were the main factor behind the growth. Sweden's unemployment rate increased, however, to 6.3 percent from 5.6 percent in 2003, as sharp gains in productivity enabled companies to increase output without hiring more workers.

The Socialist government of Prime Minister Goran Persson introduced budget measures aimed at promoting the creation of new jobs. The budget, which was announced on Sept. 20, 2004, and was to take effect in January 2005, abolished inheritance and gift tax to enable family-owned enterprises to pass their businesses from one generation to the next; cut income taxes for low- and middle-income workers; and expanded government job programs by 20 percent.

Environmental taxes. The budget in 2004 also continued a shift in taxes designed to help the environment. Taxes were increased on gasoline, automobile registrations, and electricity by about $470 million. The increase was offset by a cut in income taxes of a similar amount. The change was part of a 10-year plan to shift a substantial portion of Sweden's tax burden onto fossil fuels and activities that cause pollution.

Lindh murder trial. A court in 2004 convicted a man for the murder in September 2003 of Foreign Minister Anna Lindh, one of Sweden's most popular politicians. Mijailo Mijailovic, a 25-year-old man who was arrested a few weeks after the murder, admitted stabbing Lindh in a Stockholm department store because of "voices in his head" rather than any political motive. On March 23, 2004, a Stockholm court sentenced him to life in prison, but an appeals court later ruled that Mijailovic was mentally ill and would be confined to a psychiatric facility. The country's Supreme Court reinstated the earlier decision on December 1.

Ericsson rebounds. The telecommunications equipment maker Ericsson, one of Sweden's largest companies, staged a strong recovery in 2004 after three years of heavy losses. The company posted earnings of $1.9 billion in the first nine months of 2004, compared with losses of $7 billion for the previous three years. The company agreed in January to cut the pay of its top managers by 10 percent after public criticism that it was raising executive salaries after having laid off half its work force over the past three years.

■ Tom Buerkle

See also **Europe.**

Swimmers jump into the Bosporus in Turkey on July 18, 2004, during the International Bosporus Swimming Competition. About 200 people competed in the event, which involved swimming across the strait that separates Europe and Asia.

Swimming. Americans Michael Phelps and Ed Moses dominated national swimming as well as some international competitions in 2004. Moses won every event in which he competed at three World Cup short-course meets in January. Phelps qualified in six individual Olympic events at the U.S. Olympic trials in Long Beach, California, in July.

World records tumbled at a furious pace at the U.S. Olympic trials. Phelps entered the meet hoping to sweep his six individual events, with the intention of swimming in five at the Olympic Games in Athens in August. He nearly met his goal at the trials, capturing four events. Phelps won the 400-meter individual medley (IM), the 200-meter freestyle, 200-meter butterfly, and 200-meter IM. He finished second in the 100-meter butterfly and the 200-meter backstroke. He topped his own world record in the 400-meter IM by more than a half-second with a winning swim of 4 minutes, 9.09 seconds. In the two events he lost, the winners posted world-record times. Aaron Peirsol topped his own world mark in the 200-meter backstroke with a time of 1 minute, 54.74 seconds. Ian Crocker shaved 0.22 second off his world record in the 100-meter butterfly with a time of 50.76 seconds.

Phelps opted not to enter the 200-meter backstroke at the Olympic Games in order to allow his teammate Peirsol to compete. Also, the event was slated to be held on the same night as two other semifinals. Phelps also earned slots on the 800-meter free-style and 400-meter freestyle relays, despite the fact that he had not officially qualified in the 100-meter freestyle at U.S. trials.

Brendan Hansen set two world records at the U.S. Olympic trials. On July 8, he broke the 100-meter breaststroke record with a time of 59.30 seconds. He went on to break the record in the 200-meter breaststroke on July 11, with a time of 2 minutes, 9.04 seconds.

Other world marks. Australian Libby Lenton set a women's world record in the 100-meter freestyle at the Australian Olympic trials in March with a time of 53.66 seconds. Australian Leisel Jones set a world record in Brisbane on July 10, finishing the 200-meter breaststroke in 2 minutes, 22.96 seconds.

Short course. Moses broke his own mark in the 200-meter breaststroke by 0.25 second, with a time of 2 minutes, 2.92 seconds at a World Cup meet in Berlin on January 17. Moses broke that record during a run of three meets, in Berlin, Stockholm, and Moscow, in which he won every event in which he competed. Moses, however, failed to qualify for the Olympics.

■ Michael Kates

See **Olympics: A Special Report.**

Switzerland. Swiss voters rejected proposals to relax the country's strict citizenship rules in 2004. The government had lobbied for the proposals, saying existing rules were preventing too many longtime residents from participating in politics. The right-wing Swiss People's Party campaigned against the proposals, saying Switzerland should protect its national identity from growing numbers of immigrants. About 1.5 million of the country's 7 million residents are foreigners and cannot vote even though some have lived in the country for decades.

One proposal would have made it easier for people who were born abroad but raised and educated in Switzerland to gain citizenship. Some 57 percent of voters opposed it in a referendum on September 26. A separate proposal to grant citizenship automatically to the grandchildren of immigrants was defeated as well, with 52 percent of voters opposing the idea.

Stem cell research. Voters approved a new law permitting scientific research on *stem cells* (cells that can develop into virtually any kind of human tissue) from human embryos. The law was backed by 66.4 percent of voters in a November 28 referendum. Switzerland's big pharmaceutical industry had campaigned in favor of the law, arguing that it could lead to treatments for degenerative illnesses such as Parkinson's disease.

Nigerian funds. The Justice Ministry agreed in August to return almost $500 million to Nigeria after determining that the money had been stolen by the country's former military leader Sani Abacha. Switzerland has faced increasing pressure to crack down on money laundering. The government froze more than $700 million in Swiss bank accounts in 1999 on suspicion of criminal links to Abacha, who ruled Nigeria from 1993 to 1998. It had previously returned $200 million to Nigeria.

EU agreement. Switzerland reached an agreement with the European Union (EU) aimed at deterring EU taxpayers from avoiding tax by putting money in Swiss banks. Under the agreement, reached on May 19, 2004, Switzerland will impose a withholding tax on savings accounts held by EU nationals in Swiss banks. In return, Swiss citizens will be allowed to enter most Western European EU countries without carrying passports.

World War II pardon. On March 3, 2004, the government pardoned a woman who smuggled Jewish refugees into Switzerland to escape Nazi persecution. Aimee Stitelmann was imprisoned for 15 days during World War II (1939-1945) for helping Jewish refugees flee France. She was the first person to benefit from a new law passed in 2004 offering pardons to those punished for violating Swiss neutrality in World War II. ■ Tom Buerkle

See also **Europe.**

Syria. President Bashar al-Assad of Syria made his first official visit to Turkey on Jan. 7, 2004, meeting with Turkish President Ahmet Necdet Sezer and Turkish Prime Minister Recep Erdogan. The leaders discussed Turkish help in restarting peace negotiations between Syria and Israel over disputed land in the Golan Heights, an area in the southwest corner of Syria. They also discussed the mutual problem that Syria and Turkey faced with Kurds, an ethnic group fighting for autonomy throughout much of southwest Asia.

Kurdish problem. In March, Arab tribesmen and Syrian security forces clashed with Kurds in several towns in northern Syria. More than 20 people were killed in the violence, and security forces arrested more than 1,000 Kurds. The fighting began in the town of Qamishli after Arab tribesmen accused the local Kurds of supporting pro-American Iraqi Kurdish leaders, who govern a largely autonomous part of Iraq. Kurdish resentment against the Syrian government grew during 2004, mostly because of a perceived discrimination against Kurds in institutions of higher education and the military.

International pressure. United States President George W. Bush signed an executive order in May implementing sanctions against Syria. The sanctions banned the export to Syria of all U.S.-made products except food and medicine. The order also froze Syrian assets in the United States.

These sanctions were meant to punish Syria for supporting the Islamic militant organization Hezbollah and Palestinian groups hostile to the peace process. The United States also alleged that Syria was an entry point for foreign fighters into Iraq and was seeking to develop chemical and biological weapons. Finally, the sanctions reflected international concern about the continued presence in Lebanon of Syrian troops, who had occupied the country since 1976.

Control over Lebanon grows. In September 2004, the United Nations Security Council passed a resolution calling for the withdrawal of all foreign forces from Lebanon—a direct reference to the Syrian occupation. The resolution was prompted by Syria's attempt to extend the term of the Syrian-controlled Lebanese President Emile Lahoud for three additional years. In defiance of the international community, Syria forced the rubber-stamp Lebanese parliament to extend President Lahoud's term. However, later in September, Syria began withdrawing troops from the Lebanese capital, Beirut.

Syrian control over Lebanon grew in October, when a new, pro-Syrian prime minister, Omar Karami, and Cabinet came to power in Lebanon. Karami replaced Rafiq Hariri, who was a political rival of President Lahoud. ■ Marius Deeb

See also **Iraq; Lebanon; Middle East.**

Taiwan. Chen Shui-bian was re-elected president of Taiwan on March 20, 2004, winning by 29,518 votes out of 13.25 million cast. He began a second term on May 20.

The election was held the day after Chen and his vice president, Annette Lu, were shot while riding in an open-top vehicle through Tainan, Chen's hometown. A bullet cut Chen across the abdomen, and Lu suffered a knee wound.

Chen's opponent, Lien Chan of the Kuomintang Party (KMT), suggested that Chen may have staged the assassination attempt in order to win sympathy votes. Foreign experts found no evidence that the shooting was staged, but no gun was found and neither attacker nor motive were identified. Chan claimed that the high number of invalid ballots was suspicious—though a liberal group had urged voters to spoil their ballots to show their disgust with Taiwanese politics. Chen ordered a recount of votes, which confirmed his election.

In his first term, Chen's Democratic Progressive Party (DPP) held a minority in the 225-seat legislature. This made it difficult for him to carry out a political program over KMT opposition. In elections on December 11, the DPP and its allies won only 101 seats in parliament. A KMT-led coalition won 114 seats to keep control of parliament.

The legislature voted on August 23 to cut its size to 113 seats in 2008. It also decided that future constitutional amendments would have to win three-quarters of legislative votes before being submitted to popular referendum, while denying the public a right to initiate amendments.

Relations with China continued to be tense in 2004. Both China and Taiwan consider the island state to be part of China, though it has been governed separately since the Communists took control of the mainland in 1949. Chen had talked in the past of declaring Taiwan's independence, but China had warned that it would invade the island if that happened.

On Feb. 28, 2004, more than 1 million people formed a human chain spanning the entire length of Taiwan to show opposition to China's military threats. After Chinese war games in July, Taiwan's defense minister warned that the island could be overrun by Chinese forces in little more than five days. The government sought legislative support for an $18-billion weapons purchase from the United States. At a show of Taiwan's air force on August 14, Chen stated that China's military buildup threatened Asian security.

On Taiwan's national day, October 10, Chen suggested a resumption of talks with China that had begun in Hong Kong in 1992 and led to a 1993 meeting in Singapore. However, the two sides differed on the terms agreed to in 1992, and China rejected the idea. ■ Henry S. Bradsher

See also **Asia; Building and construction; China.**

Tanzania. See Africa.

President Chen Shui-bian continues to campaign through Tainan, Taiwan, after being shot in the stomach (circled) on March 19. He was re-elected president of Taiwan on March 20.

Taxation. The Congress of the United States voted in September 2004 to approve a $145.9-billion extension of three tax cuts for individuals. Both the U.S. House of Representatives and the Senate passed the legislation on September 23. President George W. Bush signed the tax-cuts package on October 4.

Portions of the legislation extended a $1,000-per child tax credit through 2009. Another provision extended the elimination of the so-called "marriage penalty," anomalies in the tax structure that resulted in married couples paying higher taxes than single taxpayers.

Voter education programs. The Internal Revenue Service (IRS) on April 28, 2004, advised charities to use caution when conducting voter education programs or risk losing their tax-exempt status. Federal tax law prohibits charities, educational institutions, and religious organizations and churches from active involvement in any political campaign. The laws also prohibit such groups from endorsing candidates, making political campaign donations, political fund-raising, or engaging in an activity that is beneficial or detrimental to a candidate. IRS officials said that the groups may sponsor debates or voter education forums, but the activity may not show a preference toward a candidate.

E-filing soars. Statistics released by the IRS on May 10 showed that the number of taxpayers who filed their tax returns electronically increased to nearly 60 million people in 2004. The total marked a 15.4 percent increase from 2003. The IRS statistics also found that self-prepared tax returns that were e-filed by computer rose 21.7 percent. IRS officials expect at least half of all returns to be processed electronically in 2005.

Protecting taxpayer rights. In a report to Congress in July 2004, National Taxpayer Advocate Nina E. Olson revealed an aggressive agenda highlighting ways in which the IRS can protect taxpayer rights while enforcing U.S. tax laws. Olson said the IRS's Office of the Taxpayer Advocate would introduce reforms to make the agency more sensitive to taxpayer rights. Olson said that her office would prepare a Taxpayer Rights Impact Statement whenever the agency implements new rules or procedures. The statements will be designed to help the IRS incorporate awareness of taxpayer rights into its planning. Olson said her office would study IRS training programs for new employees and recommend how the programs can be improved to foster quality customer service and respect for taxpayer rights. ■ Geoffrey A. Campbell

See also **Congress of the United States, Economics; United States, Government of the.**

Telecommunications. Emerging from a slump unlike anything since the *Great Depression* (the severe economic downturn of the 1930's), the telecommunications industry in 2004 gave executives and shareholders reasons for optimism. However, industry experts emphasized that the industry was undergoing dramatic—perhaps radical—transformation in 2004, which would continue in the future. Local service phone companies, known as "Baby Bells," such as San Antonio-based SBC Communications Inc. and New York City-based Verizon Communications Inc., nevertheless began to spend money again for new equipment. They had held back since the 2001 collapse of "dot-com" companies revealed oversupply of network capacity.

Court ruling. In March 2004, a federal appeals court in Washington, D.C., ruled that Federal Communications Commission (FCC) regulations enacted to promote competition among phone service providers were invalid. The FCC is an independent federal agency that regulates communication by radio, television, wire, satellite, and cable. Officials with the U.S. Department of Justice announced in June that the ruling would not be appealed.

The invalidated FCC regulations mandated wholesale rates for use of Bell network components by Bell competitors. With these discounts, competitors were able to offer phone service for competitive rates. While the Baby Bells hailed the court's decision, competitors found the policy shift disastrous. The first casualty was New York City-based AT&T Corp., which announced in July that it would cease marketing phone service to consumers. Industry experts noted the irony in the retreat by the company that once was the monopoly known as "Ma Bell."

New voice technology. Even as AT&T pulled away from traditional phone service, it vigorously promoted a new technology—Voice over Internet Protocol (VoIP). The new technology uses broadband data lines to send voice calls over the Internet in much the same way electronic mail is transmitted. By converting voice calls to digital format and transmitting them in units called packets, VoIP technology reduces costs and enhances flexibility of call handling.

A pioneer in the technology, Vonage Holdings Corp. of Edison, New Jersey, attracted 300,000 customers for its VoIP service by 2004. By mid-2004, virtually every telecommunications company was developing a VoIP strategy, and industry experts said that the new technology could soon threaten the gains won by the Baby Bells in the March 2004 appeals court decision.

Wireless. With wired telecommunications mired in turmoil in 2004, wireless communication continued to thrive. Some industry experts had predicted that number portability, which enabled consumers to keep phone numbers when changing wireless

The Nokia 6630 mobile phone, marketed in June 2004, displays live video feed of a news program. The product, and similar offerings by other telecommunications companies, enables cell phone users to tap into some television shows.

Television. A provocative Super Bowl stunt early in 2004 led the United States government to crack down on programming perceived to be indecent. Reality shows continued to dominate prime time television, but by the fall, several new hits foreshadowed a resurgence of scripted shows. The finales of three popular series prompted industry observers to wonder whether *sitcoms* (situation comedies) were endangered. A contestant made game show history in 2004, and a veteran newsman apologized for a journalistic error before announcing his retirement.

Record fine. In September, the Federal Communications Commission (FCC) fined 20 CBS-owned television stations a record total of $550,000 for broadcasting singers Janet Jackson and Justin Timberlake's controversial performance at the Super Bowl XXXVIII half-time show in February. The FCC is responsible for the regulation of U.S. communications by radio, television, wire, satellite, and cable. The agency develops, implements, and enforces federal rules and standards.

Timberlake ended their live performance by ripping off a piece of Jackson's black leather top, exposing her breast. Timberlake apologized while Jackson repeatedly called the incident a "wardrobe malfunction." Approximately 90 million people saw the incident, and more than 500,000 people reportedly complained to the FCC.

In the wake of the half-time show, the FCC increased the enforcement of decency standards for broadcasters. The FCC, along with broadcasters and station owners, also debated "how far is too far" when it came to good taste and broadcasting standards.

The impact could still be felt several months later. In November, many ABC-affiliated stations, fearful of FCC sanctions similar to those imposed on the CBS stations, canceled a scheduled broadcast of the Academy Award-winning motion picture *Saving Private Ryan* (1998). ABC had broadcast the critically acclaimed film in 2001 and 2002, but because director Steven Spielberg forbid the R-rated film from being edited for content, station owners worried that the graphic language and violence might offend viewers. Stations in Atlanta, Georgia; Orlando, Florida; Lincoln, Nebraska; Phoenix, Arizona; and Tampa, Florida, were among those preempting the film.

"The Apprentice" was the top-rated reality series in the 2003-2004 television season and was a surprise hit for NBC following its premiere in January 2004. Eighteen contestants, divided into two teams, competed for a job with New York City real estate developer Donald Trump. Each week, the teams were given a sales or marketing task to complete. The losing team wound up in Trump's boardroom, where he and his two assistants, Carolyn Kepcher and George Ross, both executives

service, would wreak havoc in the industry when companies began offering the service in late 2003. As it turned out, the new service had little impact on most carriers. The major exception was AT&T Wireless, which lost customers and, in October 2004, was acquired by Cingular, a partnership of SBC and Atlanta-based BellSouth. The acquisition made Cingular the nation's number one wireless company.

Wireless carriers also began to build traction in the marketing of nonvoice services to cell phone customers in 2004. Picture-taking phones became so popular that some jurisdictions passed rules against using them in locker and rest rooms.

Wi-Fi (wireless fidelity), a wireless broadband technology that delivers high-speed Internet service, continued to expand its market in 2004, as Wi-Fi antennas sprouted in public places. Meanwhile, a new and improved wireless Internet service called Wi-Max appeared on the horizon. In 2004, the Institute of Electrical and Electronic Engineers (an international, nonprofit, technical professional association based in Cleveland, Ohio) unveiled standards for the new technology. While Wi-Fi service is effectively limited to a 300-foot (91-meter) range, Wi-Max promises to work well at distances of up to 30 miles (48 kilometers). With the promise of ultrafast connections that can support VoIP calls and supply data and video services, Wi-Max carried the potential of revolutionizing telecommunications in the near future. ■ Jon Van

George Ross (left), Donald Trump, and Carolyn Kepcher star in the NBC series, "The Apprentice." The show was the most highly rated reality television series in 2004 and spawned the popular catchphrase "You're fired."

within Trump's business organization, questioned team members about why they lost and who was most responsible. Trump dismissed one team member with the words, "You're fired," which became a popular culture catchphrase in 2004. Entrepreneur Bill Rancic was the first winner of the season. He was given the $250,000-a-year position of owners' representative for Trump's new hotel and residential complex in Chicago.

Year-round programming. Networks continued experimenting with premiering new series during the summer months instead of broadcasting reruns. However, the programming strategy backfired during the summer of 2004. Reruns of such established series as "CSI" and "Everybody Loves Raymond" were among the most highly rated programs of the summer, while ratings were lackluster for new series, such as the Fox programs "The Jury" and "The Casino," which were soon canceled.

Signing off. Three of television's most popular and honored series ended in 2004. The NBC sitcom "Frasier," which starred Kelsey Grammar as a radio psychiatrist with a hectic personal life, ended as the titled character finally found true love. The finale of

TOP-RATED U.S. TELEVISION SERIES

The following were among the most-watched television series for the 2003-2004 regular season, which ran from Sept. 22, 2003, to May 26, 2004.

1. "CSI" (CBS)
2. "American Idol" (Tuesday) (FOX)
3. "American Idol" (Wednesday) (FOX)
4. "Friends" (NBC)
5. "The Apprentice" (NBC)
6. "E.R." (NBC)
7. "Survivor: All-Stars" (CBS)
8. "Survivor: Pearl Islands" (CBS)
9. "CSI: Miami" (CBS)
10. "NFL Monday Night Football" (ABC)
11. "Everybody Loves Raymond" (CBS)
12. "Without a Trace" (CBS)
13. "Law and Order" (NBC)
14. "Will & Grace" (NBC)
15. (tie) "My Big Fat Obnoxious Fiance" (FOX)
    "Two and a Half Men" (CBS)
17. "60 Minutes" (CBS)
18. "Cold Case" (CBS)
19. "NFL Monday Showcase" (ABC)
20. "Law and Order: SVU" (NBC)

By permission of Nielsen Media Research, Inc.

the top-rated NBC sitcom "Friends" brought together two characters whose relationship had many ups and downs during the run of the series. HBO's "Sex and the City" also gave its central character, a columnist played by Sarah Jessica Parker, a happy, romantic ending.

Oprah Winfrey started her top-rated daytime talk show's 19th season in September with a "Wildest Dreams" theme and an unprecedented promotional stunt. Winfrey presented each person in her 276-member audience with a new Pontiac G6 sports sedan. Audience members were chosen because friends or family wrote about their need for a new car. Pontiac, part of Detroit-based General Motors Corporation, donated the vehicles, valued at approximately $28,400 each, as part of a promotion unveiling the new automobile. Pontiac paid such costs as state sales tax, though recipients were responsible for income tax on their cars.

"Saturday Night" live? For the first time since "Saturday Night Live" debuted in 1975, a musical performer was caught lip-syncing during a performance. In October 2004, singer Ashlee Simpson was about to perform her second song on the sketch comedy series. Although she was holding the microphone at her waist, Simpson's voice could be heard singing a song she had performed earlier in the show. She danced awkwardly before walking off the stage. Simpson first blamed her band and a computer mix-up for the error. She later explained she needed the prerecorded vocal track because she was suffering from acid reflux, a medical condition in which stomach acid flows back into the esophagus, causing inflammation.

Newsman apologizes. Dan Rather, a broadcast journalist for CBS television, apologized to viewers following the revelation that documents he used in a "60 Minutes" report in September about United States President George W. Bush's service in the Texas Air National Guard during the Vietnam War (1957-1975) were forgeries and could not be authenticated. Rather's statement concluded, "We should not have used them. That was a mistake, which we deeply regret."

On Nov. 23, 2004, Rather announced that he planned to step down as anchor and managing editor of the "CBS Evening News" in March 2005. Rather had hosted the news broadcast since 1981.

Tom Brokaw retired as anchorman of NBC's "Nightly News" on Dec. 1, 2004. Brokaw joined NBC in 1966 and began anchoring the newscast in 1982. Brian Williams succeeded Brokaw as "Nightly News" anchorman.

Game show winner. Ken Jennings, a software engineer from Salt Lake City, Utah, made history in 2004, when he won $2,520,700 during a 74-game winning streak on the syndicated game show "Jeopardy." Jennings's last "Jeopardy" appearance, taped in September, aired in November.

The fall season. Networks scheduled additional hours of reality television in 2004, but several new scripted series emerged as ratings successes. Ratings for "The Apprentice" and "The Bachelor" declined in fall 2004, and two shows similar to "The Apprentice"—"The Benefactor," featuring Mark Cuban, owner of the National Basketball Association's Dallas Mavericks, and "The Rebel Billionaire," starring British businessman Richard Branson—were poorly received by critics and viewers.

ABC, which had difficulty finding a ratings success in recent years, scored the new season's number-one series with "Desperate Housewives," starring Teri Hatcher and Felicity Huffman. The drama takes a darkly comedic look at a group of suburban housewives who reexamine their lives after a friend commits suicide. Another popular ABC series, "Lost," was plotted around survivors of a plane crash who must band together on a remote and mysterious island. The ensemble cast included Matthew Fox and Dominic Monaghan. CBS offered viewers "CSI: New York," starring Gary Sinise and Melina Kanakaredes. The crime drama quickly garnered high ratings.

■ Donald Liebenson

See also **People in the news** (Barbara Walters).

EMMY AWARD WINNERS IN 2004

COMEDY
Best Series: "Arrested Development"
Lead Actress: Sarah Jessica Parker, "Sex and the City"
Lead Actor: Kelsey Grammar, "Frasier"
Supporting Actress: Cynthia Nixon, "Sex and the City"
Supporting Actor: David Hyde Pierce, "Frasier"

DRAMA
Best Series: "The Sopranos"
Lead Actress: Allison Janney, "The West Wing"
Lead Actor: James Spader, "The Practice"
Supporting Actress: Drea de Matteo, "The Sopranos"
Supporting Actor: Michael Imperioli, "The Sopranos"

OTHER AWARDS
Miniseries: "Angels in America"

Reality/Competition Series: "The Amazing Race"

Variety, Music, or Comedy Series: "The Daily Show with Jon Stewart"

Made for Television Movie: "Something the Lord Made"

Lead Actress in a Miniseries or Movie: Meryl Streep, "Angels in America"

Lead Actor in a Miniseries or Movie: Al Pacino, "Angels in America"

Supporting Actress in a Miniseries or Movie: Mary-Louise Parker, "Angels in America"

Supporting Actor in a Miniseries or Movie: Jeffrey Wright, "Angels in America"

Jack Paar:
Talk show pioneer

Television talk show host Jack Paar died on Jan. 27, 2004, at age 85. As host of "The Tonight Show" from 1957 to 1962, Paar was known for bringing witty, intelligent, and provocative conversation to late night television.

Jack Harold Paar was born May 1, 1918, in Canton, Ohio. As a child, the future broadcaster had a stutter, which he claimed he cured by sticking buttons in his mouth and reading aloud. Paar joined the United States Army in 1942 and spent his tour of duty in a noncombat unit, entertaining the troops during World War II (1939-1945). Following his discharge, Paar went to Hollywood to pursue an acting career. Fame as a film star eluded him, though Paar found success on radio as the vacation replacement for comedian Jack Benny and for Don McNeill, host of "The Breakfast Club." After replacing newsman Walter Cronkite as host of the television series "CBS Morning Show," Paar hosted a number of his own TV programs—all game and variety shows. Although all were quickly canceled, NBC executives nevertheless selected Paar to replace Steve Allen as the host of "The Tonight Show." Paar's first broadcast, from New York City, was on July 29, 1957.

Many television critics credit Paar with pioneering the talk show format by intermingling guests from various fields. On "The Tonight Show," which NBC later renamed "The Jack Paar Show," guests on any given night might include a mix of athletes, entertainers, humorists, newspaper columnists, and politicians. Paar also brought a conversational style to his nightly monologue, helping to create a part of the talk show format that is now common. His ensemble of eccentric personalities and witty storytellers included pianist Oscar Levant, performer and writer Peter Ustinov, comedian Jonathan Winters, actress Peggy Cass, game show hostess Betty White, and French chanteuse Genevieve. Paar is credited with helping launch the careers of many entertainers, including Woody Allen, Carol Burnett, Bill Cosby, and Bob Newhart.

Paar was known for being unpredictable and temperamental. During one broadcast, he purposely mixed up the cue cards while Robert Goulet and Judy Garland tried to sing a duet. He also was notorious for conducting long-running, on-air feuds with critics and competitors. In 1960, he walked off in the middle of a show after network censors edited a joke from his monologue that involved a reference to a "water closet" —British slang for bathroom. "I am leaving 'The Tonight Show'," he told the stunned audience. "There must be a better way of making a living than this." He returned a few weeks later with the opening line, "As I was saying before I was interrupted."

Paar was an avid traveler and originated broadcasts from some of the world's trouble spots. He visited Cuba for a special report, "The Background of the Revolution," during which he hugged Cuban President Fidel Castro. He also was the first to originate a program from the Berlin Wall (a concrete barrier the Soviet Union constructed to prevent Germans from escaping Communist East Berlin for democratic West Berlin) less than a month after it was erected in 1961.

In March 1962, Paar retired from "The Jack Paar Show" but returned in September 1962 to host a prime-time talk show and variety series. In 1965, he again left television and in the late 1960's began producing prime-time travel documentaries. In 1975, he returned to late night television as one of several rotating hosts on "ABC's Wide World of Entertainment," which failed to gain an audience.

Upon Paar's death, Merv Griffin, another former talk show host, praised Paar for his contributions to television: "Jack invented the talk show format as we know it—the ability to sit down and make small talk big." ■ Donald Liebenson

Tennis. Russian women dominated women's tennis in 2004, as three Russian women won Grand Slam events. Venus and Serena Williams of the United States, who had dominated tennis in recent years, failed to win a major event. By late 2004, four of the top ten in women's tennis were Russians.

In men's tennis, Switzerland's Roger Federer became the first man since Sweden's Mats Wilander in 1988 to win three Grand Slam titles in one year, taking the Australian Open, Wimbledon, and the U.S. Open.

Australian Open. On Feb. 1, 2004, Federer, the world's top-ranked male player, routed unseeded Marat Safin in straight sets, winning 7-6 (3), 6-4, 6-2. Justine Henin-Hardenne defeated fellow Belgian Kim Clijsters 6-3, 4-6, 6-3 on January 31 for her third Grand Slam title.

Top-seeded Paola Suarez and Virginia Ruano Pascual won their first Australian Open women's doubles title; French duo Michael Llodra and Fabrice Santoro defended their men's doubles title; and Nenad Zimonjic and Elena Bovina won the mixed doubles championship.

French Open. On June 6, Argentina's Gaston Gaudio became the first man in 70 years to win the French Open after facing match point in the championship match. Gaudio, who was unseeded, defeated countryman Guillermo Coria 0-6, 3-6, 6-4, 6-1, 8-6.

Anastasia Myskina on June 5 became the first Russian woman to win a Grand Slam title, beating Elena Dementieva 6-1, 6-2.

Suarez and Ruano Pascual won the women's doubles title; Xavier Malisse and Olivier Rochus of Belgium won the men's doubles title; and Tatiana Golovin and Richard Gasquet of France won the mixed doubles title.

Wimbledon. Federer captured his second straight Wimbledon on July 4, with a rousing 4-6, 7-5, 7-6 (3), 6-4 victory over Andy Roddick. The match was the first Wimbledon final since 1982 to feature the top two seeds.

Maria Sharapova, 17, of Russia, stunned defending champion Serena Williams 6-1, 6-4 in the final on July 3, 2004, to become the first Russian to win a Wimbledon singles title. Sharapova also became the youngest player to win at Wimbledon since Martina Hingis won in 1997 at the age of 16. Sharapova moved to Florida with her family at the age of 7 to attend a tennis academy.

Karolina Sprem stunned third-seeded Venus Williams 7-6 (5), 7-6 (6) in the second round. It was the earliest exit for Venus since her first Wimbledon in 1997.

Australia's Todd Woodbridge earned a record ninth Wimbledon men's doubles title when he teamed with Jonas Bjorkman of Sweden for a 6-1, 6-4, 4-6, 6-4 win over Julian Knowle of Austria and Nenad Zimonjic of Serbia. Cara and Wayne Black of Zimbabwe won the mixed doubles title and Cara Black and Rennae Stubbs of Australia won the women's doubles title.

Martina Navratilova, 47, beat 24-year-old Catalina Castano of Colombia 6-0, 6-1 on June 21 to become the oldest woman since 1922 to win a match at Wimbledon. She lost in the second round and announced she would retire in 2004.

U.S. Open. For the first time since 1988, no Americans made it to the singles finals. Top-seeded Federer won his first U.S. Open on Sept. 12, 2004, crushing 2001 champion Lleyton Hewitt of Australia, 6-0, 7-6 (3), 6-0. Hewitt had not lost a set in the tournament until the final.

Svetlana Kuznetsova of Russia won the women's title, defeating French Open runner-up Dementieva 6-3, 7-5 on Sept. 11, 2004. Dementieva had ousted Jennifer Capriati in the semifinals while Kuznetsova beat Lindsay Davenport in the other semifinal.

Mark Knowles of the Bahamas and Daniel Nestor of Canada won the men's doubles title; Suarez and Ruano Pascual won the women's doubles title; and Bob Bryan of the United States and Vera Zvonareva of Russia won the mixed doubles crown.   ■ Michael Kates

See also **Sports.**

Terrorism. Terrorist attacks in 2004 killed more than 1,000 people and wounded many more in a wide arc of violence ranging from Europe to Southeast Asia. The figures on victims of terrorism did not include the ongoing struggles in Afghanistan and Iraq.

Europe. On March 11, 10 bombs exploded on four commuter trains in Madrid, Spain, killing 191 passengers and injuring more than 1,800 others. The discovery of a van with an Arabic language tape and several detonators led investigators to suspect involvement by al-Qa'ida, a terrorist organization that had threatened to punish Spain for sending troops to participate in the Iraq War.

Russia. Violent attacks on Russians by separatists fighting to free the republic of Chechnya from Russian control reached a new high in 2004. On February 6, a bomb exploded on a Moscow subway, killing 41 passengers and injuring more than 200 other people. On June 21, approximately 200 Chechen fighters attacked Russian government offices in the neighboring Russian republic of Ingushetia. Nearly 100 people died in the assault and the Russian counterattack. On August 24, two passenger jets exploded almost simultaneously in southern Russia. The explosions, believed to have been carried out by suicide bombers, killed all 90 people aboard. On

August 31, a female suicide bomber killed 10 people at a train station in Moscow.

The most violent terrorist attack in Russia in 2004 occurred on September 1, when 32 terrorists seized a public school in Beslan, a southern Russian town bordering Chechnya. The terrorists held more than 1,200 adults and children hostage. They demanded that the Russian government leave Chechnya or that Russian President Vladimir Putin remove himself from office. More than 339 people died when Russian police stormed the school on September 3. On September 17, Shamil Basaev, the leader of a militant Chechen group called the Shahid Brigade Riadus-Salahina, claimed responsibility for the attack.

Middle East. Two members of Hamas, a militant Palestinian organization, killed 16 people in Beersheba, Israel, on August 31. On October 7, in the Egyptian resort town of Taba, several car bomb explosions killed 32 tourists, mostly Israelis, and wounded more than 100 other people.

Saudi Arabia was the site of multiple acts of terrorism in 2004, with several attacks attributed to al-Qa'ida or affiliated organizations. Six people were killed and almost 150 others were wounded when a car bomb exploded outside police headquarters in Riyadh, the capital, on April 21. On May 1, four gunmen attacked a foreign oil company in Yanbu, killing six people and injuring 12 others. On May 29, four gunmen killed 22 people in raids on another foreign oil company in Khobar.

South Asia. Pakistan was the target of a number of terrorist attacks in 2004, most of which were related to the conflict between Sunni and Shiite Muslims. On March 2, militants used guns and grenades to attack a Shiah mosque in Quetta. More than 50 worshippers were killed. Fourteen more Shiites were killed and at least 200 people were injured following a suicide bomb attack on a mosque in Karachi on May 7.

A suicide bomb attack on a Shiah mosque in the eastern city of Sialkot on October 1 killed 31 people. On October 7, a car bomb ripped through a rally of 2,000 people marking the one-year anniversary of the death of a militant antigovernment leader, killing 41 people.

Southeast Asia. In Jakarta, Indonesia, on September 9, a driver detonated his vehicle with 440 pounds (200 kilograms) of explosives outside the Australian Embassy, killing 10 people and injuring more than 180 others. Before the blast, police received an e-mailed message demanding the release of Abu Bakar Bashir, a jailed cleric and leader of a militant group with suspected terrorist connections. ■ Richard E. Rubenstein

See also **Asia; Europe; India; Indonesia; Iraq: A Special Report; Middle East; Pakistan; Russia.**

Texas. See **Dallas; Houston; State government.**

Thailand. Violence flared in 2004 in southern Thailand, where some 6 million Muslims live in a predominantly Buddhist country. On January 4, four Buddhist soldiers were killed in an attack by unknown men who seized weapons and burned roughly 20 schools. Officials blamed a Muslim separatist movement that had fought Thai security forces in the area in the 1970's and 1980's.

On April 28, 2004, attackers hit 10 defense posts in the south. Security forces then killed more than 100 people identified as Muslim insurgents, including 32 people seeking refuge in a mosque. After critics claimed unarmed youths were shot down, Prime Minister Thaksin Shinawatra conceded that soldiers may have used excessive force.

Seven people were killed in the same area on October 25 as security forces put down a demonstration and arrested 1,300 people. The prisoners were jammed into trucks, where 78 of them died from suffocation. Nearby Islamic nations responded by labeling Thailand a "terrorist state."

Tsunamis triggered by a December 26 earthquake off Sumatra crashed into the western coast of southern Thailand, including the tourist resorts of Phuket and Phi Phi islands and Krabi and Phang Nga on the mainland. By December 31, at least 4,500 people, including many foreign visitors, were confirmed dead. ■ Henry S. Bradsher

See also **Asia.**

Theater. Politics in 2004 captured the imagination of the theater-going public, both in the United States and abroad, with several productions of new and classic plays on political themes. Coverage of the U.S. presidential campaign—which led up to the November 2004 re-election of President George W. Bush—dominated the U.S. media, and it came as little surprise that much of the year's theater also explored political issues. The threat of terrorism and continued fighting by U.S.-led forces in Iraq, which began in March 2003, were other pressing subjects in the United States and the United Kingdom, America's chief ally in the Iraq War.

Ancient Greek drama, often concerned with duplicity in politics and the hardships encountered during wartime, was an interesting choice for exploring subjects that resonated in 2004. At the National Theatre in London, director Katie Mitchell staged a production of Euripides's *Iphigenia at Aulis,* with Hattie Morahan as Iphigenia; Ben Daniels as her father, Agamemnon; and Kate Duchene as her mother, Clytemnestra. The play, which takes place at the outset of the Trojan War, portrays the sacrifice of Iphigenia by Agamemnon, who must kill his own daughter to appease the goddess Artemis and secure favorable winds for his fleet to sail to Troy. The National Theatre's updating of the play was set in the 1940's and featured big-band music, ballroom dancing, and other mod-

ern equivalents for ancient dramatic elements.

Other Greek dramas on the London stage in 2004 included Jonathan Kent's production of Euripides's *Hecuba* at the Donmar Warehouse and Martin Crimp's version of Sophocles's *Trachiniae,* titled *Cruel and Tender,* at the Young Vic Theatre. Clare Higgins received favorable notices for her portrayal of Hecuba, the Trojan queen who has been enslaved following the Trojan War with Greece. The play depicts the horrors of war and its aftermath, as Hecuba mourns the loss of her city, her husband, and her son Polydorus.

Cruel and Tender, directed by Luc Bondy, tells the story of Amelia (played by Kerry Fox), the wife of a general, who awaits her husband's return after a war. Set in present-day England, the play finds contemporary equivalents for Sophocles's plot. The general (played by Joe Dixon) destroys an African city that is rumored to harbor terrorists, while, back home, his wife moves among a room filled with modern exercise equipment. By the time the general returns, bloodied from the war, Amelia has killed herself.

The worldview conveyed by these Greek tragedies is bleak. As the theater critic Ben Brantley wrote in *The New York Times* on July 8, 2004, "Among [these plays'] incontrovertible principles are the beliefs that the human race was born to suffer and to inflict suffering; that empires rise only to fall; and that self-knowledge, if it ever arrives, comes too late." Other critics noted that suffering and the rise and fall of nations were subjects very much on the minds of the theater-going public in 2004, and attending plays that examined such subjects allowed viewers an opportunity for deeper consideration and catharsis.

Productions of Greek plays in the United States in 2004 included the National Theater of Greece's production at City Center in New York City of Aristophanes's *Lysistrata.* The comedy deals with women of ancient Greece withholding sexual favors from their husbands in an effort to stop a war. The Goodman Theatre in Chicago produced a modernization of Sophocles's *Electra.* Titled *Electricidad,* the ancient tragedy was relocated from ancient Greece to the American Southwest. Chicano gang members replaced the original cast of Greek royals.

Staging politics. Playwrights in 2004, like their ancient counterparts, were drawn to the political sphere for subject matter for the stage. A new play by Sam Shepard, titled *The God of Hell,* premiered in New York City on October 29, with a four-week limited run at the Actors Studio Drama School Theatre. The play—which featured performances by J. Smith-Cameron, Randy Quaid, and Tim Roth—centered on a Midwestern couple who are afraid of losing their farm to a government official.

Michael Frayn's most recent play, *Democracy,* premiered at the Brooks Atkinson Theater in New York City in November 2004. The play begins in 1969 and recounts the tensions of parliamentary politics under West German Chancellor Willy Brandt (played by James Naughton). Richard Thomas played Brandt's close personal assistant, Gunter Guillaume, who is also a double-agent for East Germany's Ministry of State Security. Directed by Frayn's longtime collaborator Michael Blakemore, the production received positive notices, despite its somewhat obscure subject.

Playwright David Hare, who has routinely included social and political commentary in his work, tackled political themes directly in his new play, *Stuff Happens.* The play deals with the beginnings of the Iraq War in 2003. Directed by Nicholas Hytner for the National Theatre in England, the production starred Alex Jennings as President Bush and Nicholas Farrell as British Prime Minister Tony Blair. Through broadly drawn characterizations, this political satire led audiences to reconsider the world of realpolitik and the actions of leaders.

If political ideas fueled theatrical productions in 2004, then politics itself, in the form of the Republican National Convention in New York City, had a negative effect on Broadway ticket sales. During the week ending September 5, sales for nearly 75 percent of all shows on Broadway suffered significant losses at the box office, some of the worst since the terrorist attacks on the World Trade Center in 2001. Sales for the long-running and hugely popular *The Lion King* dropped nearly $250,000 for the week ending Sept. 5, 2004, as people avoided the congestion in New York City created by the influx of conventioneers.

The Public picks a new head. The Public Theater in New York City announced in November that Oskar Eustis, formerly the artistic director at the Trinity Repertory Company in Providence, Rhode Island, would replace George C. Wolfe as the Public Theater's artistic director. As dramaturge and resident director of the Eureka Theatre Company in San Francisco, Eustis commissioned Tony Kushner's *Angels in America* and directed the play's world premiere at the Mark Taper Forum in Los Angeles. Playwright Kushner and Mike Nichols, director of the HBO version of *Angels in America,* were among Eustis's strongest champions for the position at the Public Theater.

Eustis will become only the fourth person to hold the position of artistic director at the Public Theater, after Wolfe, JoAnne Akalaitis, and founding director Joseph Papp. In addi-tion to plays staged in its building on Lafayette Street in the East Village, the Public Theater produces the free Shakespeare in Central Park performances each summer at the Delacorte Theater. Eustis joined the Public Theater at a time when many of its crushing financial difficulties had passed. By 2004, the theater showed an endowment of more than $17 million.

"Gem" on Broadway. A loss of funding endangered the New York City production of August Wilson's play *Gem of the Ocean.* Originally scheduled to open on November 11, the show needed an additional $1 million to cover its more than $2 million in production costs. Carole Shorenstein Hays, Jujamcyn Theaters, and the Araca Group took over for lead producer Benjamin Mordecai, and the show began previews on November 23. (Shorenstein, an increasingly powerful presence on Broadway, was the producer of the 2003 Tony Award-winning *Take Me Out.*) The play opened on Dec. 6, 2004, at the Walter Kerr Theater.

August Wilson's next play, *Radio Golf,* will premiere at the Yale Repertory Theatre in Hew Haven, Connecticut, in April 2005. The play completes Wilson's 10-play cycle on the African American experience in the 20th century.   ■ David Yezzi

Togo. See **Africa.**

TONY AWARD WINNERS IN 2004

Best Play, *I Am My Own Wife*
Best Musical, *Avenue Q*
Best Play Revival, *Henry IV*
Best Musical Revival, *Assassins*
Leading Actor in a Play, Jefferson Mays, *I Am My Own Wife*
Leading Actress in a Play, Phylicia Rashad, *A Raisin in the Sun*
Leading Actor in a Musical, Hugh Jackman, *The Boy from Oz*
Leading Actress in a Musical, Idina Menzel, *Wicked*
Featured Actor in a Play, Brian F. O'Byrne, *Frozen*
Featured Actress in a Play, Audra McDonald, *A Raisin in the Sun*
Featured Actor in a Musical, Michael Cerveris, *Assassins*
Featured Actress in a Musical, Anika Noni Rose, *Caroline, or Change*
Direction of a Play, Jack O'Brien, *Henry IV*
Direction of a Musical, Joe Mantello, *Assassins*
Book of a Musical, Jeff Whitty, *Avenue Q*
Original Musical Score, Robert Lopez and Jeff Marx, *Avenue Q*
Orchestration, Michael Starobin, *Assassins*
Scenic Design, Eugene Lee, *Wicked*
Costume Design, Susan Hilferty, *Wicked*
Lighting Design, Jules Fisher and Peggy Eisenhauer, *Assassins*
Choreography, Kathleen Marshall, *Wonderful Town*
Regional Theater, Cincinnati Playhouse in the Park
Lifetime Achievement, James M. Nederlander, theater owner

Toronto in 2004 endured municipal scandals and financial difficulties. However, 2004 also brought a resolution to a dispute over the Oak Ridges Moraine, the largest natural feature of the Greater Toronto region, and an announcement of plans for an addition to the Art Gallery of Ontario.

City budget. In the spring, Mayor David Miller faced a budget shortfall of $344 million in the city's $6.7 billion operating budget. (All amounts are in Canadian dollars.) The shortfall was the result of cutbacks by the federal and provincial governments, which share the costs for many municipally delivered services, such as housing, child care, and income support (welfare). Miller, a former city councilor and member of the left-wing New Democratic Party who scored an upset victory in the 2003 civic elections, faced the possibility of cutting services or imposing large tax increases.

Miller was saved by timely interventions from Canadian Prime Minister Paul Martin and Ontario Premier Dalton McGuinty. Both leaders had promised more assistance for cities during their election campaigns. The federal government allowed Toronto to keep $26 million in sales taxes, and the province provided $110 million in special aid.

The bailouts fell far short of the $5-billion share of provincial and federal gas taxes that Miller and other big city mayors had been seeking. However, in an October 2004 speech setting out his government's agenda for the coming year, Martin committed himself to sharing federal gas taxes with cities. That same month, McGuinty promised cities a 1-cent per liter share of the provincial gas tax in 2004, which was to increase to a 2-cent per liter share by 2006. The gas tax was expected to bring Toronto $91 million the first year it went into effect. Nevertheless, a quarrel broke out between McGuinty and Miller over whether the funds should be used for the Greater Toronto commuter transportation network or for Toronto's local transportation system.

Police scandal. In April 2004, a Royal Canadian Mounted Police investigation into police corruption led to charges against four Toronto police officers. By November, 15 officers had been charged, and Toronto faced the possibility of the largest police scandal in its history.

In June, the Toronto Police Services Board, made up of seven civilians appointed to oversee police conduct, denied a contract extension to Police Chief Julian Fantino. Fantino's five-year contract was to end in March 2005, and he had requested a two-year extension. The board's action grew out of long-running disputes between the police administration and the board. At the time of the contract review, only six members were sitting on the board. Board Chair Norm Gardner had been suspended in April 2004, while courts determined whether he had broken ethical guidelines in accepting 5,700 rounds of ammunition from police stores for personal use. In October, the board began the search for a new police chief.

Oak Ridges Moraine. In May, Ontario government officials resolved a dispute over development on the Oak Ridges Moraine, a 100-mile- (160-kilometer-) long ridge of sand and gravel left behind by ice age glaciers. The moraine absorbs rain and snowmelt and contains the headwaters of more than 60 rivers and streams. Environmentalists feared that spreading subdivisions, particularly in Richmond Hill, immediately north of Toronto, would damage the moraine's fragile ecosystem. The provincial settlement reduced the number of houses to be built on the Richmond Hill sector of the moraine from 6,600 to 5,700 and compensated developers who lost building rights. Most encouraging to environmentalists, the provincial settlement created a park of more than 1,000 acres (405 hectares).

Cultural venues. In January, the Art Gallery of Ontario unveiled plans for a $195-million addition designed by Toronto-born American architect Frank Gehry. The expanded art gallery was to join a striking $42.5-million addition to the Ontario College of Art and Design, designed by British architect Will Alsop, which opened in September.

■ David Lewis Stein

See also **Canada; Canadian provinces; City.**

Toys and games. Several major events affected the toy industry in the United States during 2004, including the possible sale of a major toy retailer, shipping delays at two U.S. ports, and the announcement of a retail merger.

In August, Toys "R" Us, Incorporated, of Wayne, New Jersey, the largest toy retail chain, announced that it was exploring the possible sale of its toy stores to concentrate on its baby products business. Toy retailers have lost sales to discount stores, where very low prices have attracted cost-conscious consumers. By 2004, more than 40 percent of all toy purchases in the United States were being made in discount stores.

During the fall, the busiest shipping season for toy manufacturers, the California ports of Los Angeles and Long Beach became backlogged with container ships waiting for cargo to be unloaded. The delays were the result of increased volume into and out of the ports, a rise of 10 to 13 percent over 2003. The two ports are the major points of entry for shipments of toys into the United States, about 80 percent of which are manufactured in Asia. As a result, there were spot shortages of some popular toys on store shelves during the holiday season.

In November 2004, two major retailers—Sears, Roebuck and Company of Hoffman Estates, Illinois, and Kmart Holding Corporation of Troy,

Nintendo Company of Japan launched its new, hand-held game system, Nintendo DS, on Nov. 21, 2004. Nintendo DS, the first of a new generation of portable gaming systems, includes dual 3-inch (76-millimeter) screens—one of which is touch-activated—and a wireless connection that allows gamers to play with other DS owners or to send instant text messages.

Michigan—announced a merger. Combined, these two companies would create the third-largest retailer in the United States, after Wal-Mart of Bentonville, Arkansas, and Atlanta, Georgia-based Home Depot, Inc. Over several holiday seasons in the early 2000's, toy retailer KB Toys Incorporated of Pittsfield, Massachusetts, had operated a "KB Toys at Sears" in many of the department store's retail locations.

I Love the 70's. Resurrecting the melody from the disco-era hit song "YMCA," the furry red creature known as Elmo, from the "Sesame Street" television series, introduced his own version of the song in 2004. Produced by Fisher-Price Brands of East Aurora, New York, the E-L-M-O toy was a big hit for the holiday season. With a squeeze of his hand, Elmo breaks out into his E-L-M-O theme song and raises his arms to form the letters—just as disco enthusiasts had done on the dance floor to "YMCA" by the singing group the Village People in the 1970's.

Robots rule. He can whistle, dance, and give a high-five—for six straight hours. He's Robosapien, the hottest robot toy for 2004, introduced by Wow Wee Limited of Hong Kong. Designed by a robotics physicist, Robosapien is a remote-controlled, 14-inch- (36 centimeter-) high robot with 67 programmable functions. The lifelike toy even apologizes when he "burps."

All aboard for the North Pole. Big-screen favorites in 2004 included *The Polar Express,* a motion picture based on the classic children's story of a young boy who tries to solve the mystery of Santa Claus during a hair-raising train ride to the North Pole. Lionel LLC of Chesterfield, Michigan, recreated the Polar Express train set, designing replicas of the story's Berkshire steam locomotive, tender, and passenger cars, with silhouettes in the windows of the coaches depicting scenes from the movie.

Toys for the ages. In November, three classic toys were inducted into the National Toy Hall of Fame: the G. I. Joe action figure, the rocking horse, and the Scrabble board game. The three playthings joined 28 others that have been inducted since the program debuted in 1998, among them Silly Putty, marbles, the View-Master viewer, the jigsaw puzzle, the Erector set, checkers, the Hula Hoop, and the teddy bear. The National Toy Hall of Fame recognizes toys that have achieved longevity and national significance in the world of play and imagination; foster learning or creativity; and are widely recognized, respected, and remembered. The National Toy Hall of Fame is part of the Strong Museum of Rochester, New York, which houses more than 70,000 toys and dolls, as well as objects of American culture dating back to the 1820's.

■ Diane P. Cardinale

Track and field. The emerging steroid scandal involving Bay Area Laboratory Co-Operative (BALCO), a California nutritional supplement company, affected track and field more than any other sport in 2004. Enforcement agencies within the sport took an aggressive stance against suspected users. They were so aggressive, in fact, that many high-profile athletes were banned from competing or otherwise punished for using performance-enhancing substances.

American sprinter Kelli White, who had her world titles in the 100 and 200 meters stripped in 2003 because of a positive test for the stimulant modafinil, accepted a two-year ban in 2004 from the United States Anti-Doping Agency (USADA) despite the lack of a positive drug test. White admitted to taking substances, including tetrahydrogestrinone (THG). The steroid was the subject of an international investigation because it could not be detected by tests until 2004.

British sprinter Dwain Chambers, the European 100-meter champion, was the first athlete to be punished for using THG. He was suspended for two years on February 24 and banned for life from the Olympic Games.

USADA officials in June moved to ban four American sprinters for life because of suspected use of THG: Tim Montgomery, world record holder in the 100 meters; Michelle Collins, 2003

world indoor champion in the 200 meters; Alvin Harrison, two-time gold medalist at the 2000 Olympics; and Chryste Gaines, a two-time Olympic relay medalist.

In August 2004, sprinter Torri Edwards, runner-up in the 100 meters at the U.S. Olympic trials, was banned from competition for two years after testing positive for the stimulant nikethamide at a meet in Martinique in April.

Other positive tests. Ukrainian shot-putter Vita Pavlysh was stripped of her world indoor title and banned from competition for life in June after her second positive test for steroids. Also in June, Russian sprinter Anastasiya Kapachinskaya was banned for two years after testing positive for a steroid at the indoor world championships in March. She also forfeited her world title in the indoor 200-meter event.

Jones under cloud. Marion Jones, one of the greatest all-time U.S. track and field stars, came under USADA investigation in 2004, but sanctions were not leveled. Jones was under suspicion primarily because the USADA had banned Tim Montgomery, the father of her child. Also, Jones's ex-husband, shot-putter C. J. Hunter, appeared before the grand jury investigating BALCO.

Golden moments. Triple-jumper Christian Olsson of Sweden and 400-meter runner Tonique

WORLD TRACK AND FIELD RECORDS ESTABLISHED IN 2004

Event	Holder	Country	Where set	Date	Record
MEN INDOOR					
5,000 meters	Kenenisa Bekele	Ethiopia	Birmingham, England	February 20	12:49.60
Triple jump	Christian Olsson	Sweden	Budapest, Hungary	March 7	17.83
WOMEN INDOOR					
Pole vault	Yelena Isinbayeva	Russia	Budapest, Hungary	March 6	4.86 m
5,000 meters	Berhane Adere	Ethiopia	Stuttgart, Germany	January 31	14:39.29
4x400-meter relay	Russia	Russia	Budapest, Hungary	March 7	3:23.88
MEN OUTDOOR					
5,000 meters	Kenenisa Bekele	Ethiopia	Hengelo, Netherlands	May 31	12:37.35
10,000 meters	Kenenisa Bekele	Ethiopia	Ostrava, Czech Rep.	June 8	26:20.31
3,000 meters	Saif Saaeed Shaheen	Qatar	Brussels	September 3	*7:53.63
110-meter hurdles	Xiang Liu	China	Athens	August 27	*12.91
25-kilometer race	Paul Kosgei	Kenya	Berlin	May 9	*1:12:45
WOMEN OUTDOOR					
5,000 meters	Elvan Abeylegesse	Turkey	Bergen, Norway	June 11	14:24.68
3,000 meters	Gulnara Samitova	Russia	Iraklion, Greece	July 4	9:01.59
Pole vault	Yelena Isinbayeva	Russia	Brussels	September 3	*4.92 m
Decathlon	Marie Collonville	France	Talence, France	September 26	*8,150 points

m = meters
* = not yet ratified.   Source: International Association of Athletics Federation (IAAF).

Williams-Darling of the Bahamas in September 2004 split the $1-million prize awarded to athletes who sweep their events in all six Golden League track meets.

Vaulting into record books. Svetlana Feofanova of Russia became the first woman to clear 16 feet (4.88 meters) in the pole vault on July 4 at Iraklion, Greece. On July 25, Yelena Isinbayeva of Russia cleared 16 feet, ¾ inch (4.90 meters) in Birmingham, England. Isinbayeva then broke her own mark two more times, jumping, 16 feet, 1½-inches (4.91 meters) at the Olympic Games in Athens, in August, and 16 feet, 1¾-inches (4.92 meters) in Brussels on September 3.

Other world records. Ethiopia's Kenenisa Bekele set the men's 5,000-meter world record on May 31 with a run of 12 minutes, 37.35 seconds at a meet in Hengelo, the Netherlands. Turkey's Elvan Abeylegesse set the women's mark in the 5,000 meters on June 11, 2004, at the Bislett Games in Bergen, Norway, finishing in 14 minutes, 24.68 seconds.

Russia's Olga Kotlyarova broke the indoor record in the 600 meters on February 1, in Moscow, finishing in 1 minute, 23.44 seconds.

Steeplechaser Saif Saaeed Shaheen of Qatar set a world mark in the 3,000-meter steeplechase on Sept. 3, 2004, in Brussels.　■ Michael Kates

See also **Olympics: A Special Report; Sports.**

Transportation. Rail transportation

became a target of terrorists in 2004. On the morning of March 11, bombs exploded on four commuter trains in Madrid, Spain. The bombs, hidden in backpacks, killed 191 people and injured hundreds of others. Most of the suspected bombers were Moroccan and were believed to have links to al-Qa'ida, the extremist Islamic network led by Osama bin Laden.

The events in Madrid heightened fears of similar attacks on subways or mainline railroads around the world. In the United States, the Transportation Security Administration (TSA), the federal agency responsible for protecting the nation's transportation systems, experimented in 2004 with ways to screen passengers and baggage on some long-distance Amtrak trains. Amtrak is the semipublic corporation that provides intercity passenger rail transportation in the United States. Security experts noted that securing a rail system with many stations is more difficult than securing airports.

Police in Boston conducted random searches of passengers on subway and commuter trains to tighten rail security during the national Democratic Party convention, which met in Boston between July 26 and 29. Civil libertarians raised concerns that the police searches violated the civil liberties of passengers.

Port security. On July 1, new federal regulations went into effect that required foreign ships visiting U.S. ports to meet specific security standards and give notice to authorities about crew and cargo four days before docking. Terrorism experts, however, continued to warn that terrorists could hide bombs in shipping containers, few of which were being inspected.

The Ghan. Australia achieved a long-awaited goal in early 2004, when passengers and goods were able to travel from the continent's southern coast to the northern coast on 1,851 miles (2,979 kilometers) of railroad track known as "the Ghan." The railroad route is named for Afghan camel drivers who helped open up Australia's desert interior "outback" and build the original Ghan connecting southern port Adelaide with outback station Alice Springs. In late 2003, construction crews completed the 882-mile (1,419-kilometer) northern extension of the Ghan, connecting Alice Springs with the northern coastal city of Darwin.

In January 2004, a freight train made the maiden voyage from Adelaide to Darwin. At the beginning of February, a passenger train carrying Australian dignitaries, celebrities, and others inaugurated passenger service on the route.

The Queen Mary 2 (QM2), the world's newest and largest passenger ocean liner, made its maiden voyage from Southampton, England, to New York City in April. During its New York sojourn, the QM2 berthed next to its predecessor, the Queen Elizabeth 2. When both ships departed simultaneously for the return trip to England, many older New Yorkers were reminded of the last time ships with these names set sail together from New York City—in 1940.

Freight train explosions. On Feb. 18, 2004, a runaway freight train carrying gasoline and fertilizer derailed at Neyshabur, Iran, and exploded. More than 300 people died in the wreck or from the effects of the explosion. On April 22 at Ryongchon, North Korea, problems with overhead electric cables led to the explosion of oil and chemicals in a passing train resulting in at least 160 deaths and considerable devastation of the surrounding area.

Great Lakes ferries. Two new high-speed ferry services came to the Great Lakes in June. One service is between Rochester, New York, and Toronto, Ontario, Canada, across Lake Ontario; the other travels between Milwaukee, Wisconsin, and Muskegon, Michigan, on Lake Michigan. At one time there were many long-distance ferry services on the Great Lakes, but the only such ferry line still in service by 2004 was the 50-year-old coal-fired S.S. Badger, which plied Lake Michigan between Manitowoc, Wisconsin, and Ludington, Michigan.

Minneapolis light rail. In June, Minneapolis, Minnesota, inaugurated the first leg of a light rail train commuter system, 50 years after the end of streetcar service in the city. With extensions completed in December, the rail system linked center-city neighborhoods, Minneapolis-St. Paul International Airport, and the Mall of America in suburban Bloomington, Minneapolis.

Train whistles. Municipalities across the United States installed improved railroad-crossing barriers and other safety devices in 2004 in anticipation of new federal regulations concerning the sounding of train whistles, expected in late 2004. However, the Federal Railroad Administration (FRA), the Department of Transportation agency that oversees railroad safety, postponed publication of the regulations and the deadline for compliance until early 2005.

The new FRA rules were expected to permit "quiet zones"—areas near low-risk crossings in which train engineers would no longer be required to signal a train's approach by sounding a whistle or horn. Communities could declare such quiet zones if they installed mandated safety devices. ■ Ian Savage

See also **Australia; Disasters; Spain; Terrorism.**

Trinidad and Tobago. See Latin America.

Tunisia. See Middle East.

Turkey. The European Union (EU) and Turkey reached agreement in December 2004 to begin negotiations in October 2005 that could lead to Turkey's eventual membership in the political and economic organization. However, the EU said that the talks would be contingent upon continued political and human-rights reforms in Turkey.

In September, Turkey's ruling Justice and Development Party (AKP) withdrew legislation in parliament that would have criminalized adultery. EU officials had warned that passing the measure would endanger Turkey's candidacy in the EU. The legislation was part of a larger effort to reform the Turkish penal code, including abolishing torture and expanding civil liberties. The EU supported this effort.

U.S. relations. Prime Minister Recep Tayyip Erdogan met with United States President George W. Bush at the White House in Washington, D.C., in January. Experts in international affairs interpreted the meeting as a gesture of reconciliation, following Turkey's refusal in 2003 to allow U.S. troops to launch military operations against Iraq from Turkish soil.

In June 2004, Prime Minister Erdogan joined a summit of the Group of Eight, an informal organization of major industrialized nations, on Sea Island, off the coast of Georgia. Later that month,

President Bush visited with Erdogan in the Turkish capital, Ankara, amid public demonstrations against the U.S.-led war in Iraq. President Bush also visited Istanbul for a meeting of the North Atlantic Treaty Organization to discuss the Iraq War.

Islamic schools. Turkey's parliament adopted a controversial education bill in May that had been introduced by the AKP. The bill permitted graduates from Islamic schools to obtain university degrees in any field—not just in divinity studies. Previously, Islamic school graduates were unable to hold public office because they could not obtain the required degrees. Opposition parties feared that the legislation would allow Islamic fundamentalists to infiltrate all levels of the government bureaucracy.

Mesut Yilmaz. Turkish lawmakers voted in July to require former Prime Minister Mesut Yilmaz and former Economy Minister Gunes Taner to stand trial on charges of corruption in a 1998 banking scandal. Yilmaz was accused of rigging the privatization of the state-owned Turkbank in favor of the eventual winner. A few days later, however, Turkey's constitutional court rejected the parliamentary decision, ruling that the vote was procedurally flawed. ■ Mary-Jane Deeb

See also **Iraq: A Special Report; United States, President of the.**

Turkmenistan. See Asia.

Uganda. Rebels of the Lord's Resistance Army (LRA) attacked a refugee camp in northern Uganda on Feb. 21, 2004, killing at least 230 people. According to eyewitnesses, the rebels shot up the camp with automatic weapons, then set fire to thatched huts in which terrified residents were hiding. The LRA is a cult that espouses "Christian rule" but, in fact, carries out a campaign of terror against civilians, especially children. Human rights groups estimate that as many as 20,000 children have been abducted by LRA fighters since the 1980's and forced to serve as soldiers or slaves.

In a summer 2004 offensive, Ugandan government troops killed or captured scores of LRA fighters. In September, Defense Minister Amama Mbabazi claimed that government forces were on the verge of victory over the LRA.

In September 2004, Ugandan Justice Minister Janat Mukwaya unveiled a plan to re-establish multiparty politics and remove the constitutional two-term limit on the presidency. Since 1995, President Museveni's National Resistance Movement (NRM) has dominated political activity in a "no-party" system that survived several court challenges. Opposition leaders charged that the government's proposal was merely an excuse to enable President Museveni to run for a third term in 2006. ■ Simon Baynham

See also **Africa; Sudan.**

Viktor Yushchenko signals his victory in Ukraine's highly contested presidential election re-match on December 26. Yushchenko took 52.3 percent of the vote, compared with Prime Minister Viktor Yanukovych's 43.9 percent. Nevertheless, Yanukovych refused to concede.

Commission (CEC) declared Yanukovich the official winner, sparking reports of massive electoral fraud. The Organization for Security and Cooperation in Europe, the Council of Europe, the European Parliament, and the North Atlantic Treaty Organization all condemned the balloting.

The widespread condemnation followed several contentious months of electoral politics during which Yushchenko, a former prime minister and central bank governor, developed a mysterious disfiguring illness. On November 22, as unofficial CEC results began leaning towards Yanukovich, thousands of Yushchenko supporters crowded into central Kiev, the capital, to protest. Their numbers swelled to an estimated 200,000 as the Ukrainian Supreme Court agreed to examine the allegations of fraud and the Ukrainian parliament passed a nonbinding resolution declaring the results invalid.

Under this intense pressure, Yanukovich and outgoing president Leonid Kuchma entered into European-mediated negotiations with Yushchenko and discussed the possibility of holding a new election. The standoff heightened tensions between Russia and the West, as Russian president Vladimir Putin ridiculed the idea of a new poll. Putin had strongly supported Yanukovich, who called for closer ties between Ukraine and Russia. On December 3, the Supreme Court annulled the November election and ruled that a new election must be held by December 26.

Poison. In mid-December, blood test results revealed that Yushchenko's illness had been caused by dioxin poisoning. Dioxins are highly toxic chemicals produced by many industrial processes. The amount in Yushchenko's bloodstream was more than 6,000 times the normal level. Scientists said it was the second highest level ever recorded in a human being. ■ Juliet Johnson

See also **Europe; Russia.**

Ukraine. A disputed presidential election plunged Ukraine's political future into uncertainty in 2004. In a repeat poll on December 26, challenger Viktor Yushchenko defeated Prime Minister Viktor Yanukovich for the presidency, taking more than 52 percent of the vote to Yanukovich's 43 percent. Yushchenko's victory, however, had been anything but easy.

November election. In an election held on October 21, Yushchenko took 39.87 percent of the vote, and Yanukovich garnered 39.32 percent. A runoff was held on November 21. Exit polls indicated that Yushchenko had solidly beaten Yanukovich and taken a majority of the vote. However, the Ukrainian Central Electoral

Unemployment. See Economics; Labor.
United Arab Emirates. See Middle East.

UNITED KINGDOM

Tony Blair's Labour Party government continued in 2004 to be shaped by the events of the Iraq War of 2003 and its aftermath. The government, first elected in 1997 and re-elected in 2001, supported the United States-led invasion and sent troops to Iraq despite the fact that the Labour Party and the British people were seriously divided over the issue. Blair had made a case for the war in terms of the security risk that Iraqi President Saddam Hussein's regime posed and its failure to comply with United Nations (UN) resolutions. Two major government inquiries about the role played by the United Kingdom (U.K.) in the build-up to war reported their findings during 2004. Despite heavy losses in local elections and in elections for the European Parliament, the Labour government remained narrowly ahead in most opinion polls throughout the year.

The Hutton inquiry. Blair's government had been rocked in 2003 by the suicide of David Kelly, a weapons expert at the Ministry of Defence. Kelly was the source for a controversial radio broadcast in May 2003 by Andrew Gilligan of the British Broadcasting Corporation (BBC). (The BBC is a public broadcaster financed by a license fee that all television owners in Britain pay.)

The broadcast claimed that the government knowingly had exaggerated evidence that Iraq possessed *weapons of mass destruction* (biological, chemical, or nuclear weapons) in a document published in September 2002 that was used to make the case for war. Gilligan alleged that the government had included the claim that Hussein had the capability to deploy weapons of mass destruction within 45 minutes, knowing it to be false. Kelly came under pressure before a government committee in which he admitted talking to Gilligan. Shortly afterwards, he took his own life.

The government appointed Lord Hutton, a *law lord* (member of Britain's highest court of appeal) to investigate Kelly's death and Gilligan's allegations. Lord Hutton held hearings in

A red telephone box—one of about 75,000 owned by British Telecom (BT) across the United Kingdom—is a familiar sight in front of London's Westminster Abbey. BT announced in 2004 that, because of the increase in mobile phone use, 10,000 of the iconic red boxes would be scrapped by 2005.

2003 and presented his report on Jan. 28, 2004. The purpose of the inquiry was not to examine the quality of the intelligence but to learn whether it had been altered by the government.

Lord Hutton maintained that the government had not knowingly changed the content of the document, and he criticized the BBC for allowing Gilligan to broadcast unfounded allegations and for failing to properly investigate the matter afterwards. He also found that the government had acted appropriately in its dealings with Kelly after the scientist had informed the Ministry of Defence that he had been Gilligan's informant. Lord Hutton confirmed that Kelly had committed suicide, rejecting allegations that he had been murdered.

Gavyn Davies, chairman of the BBC board of governors, immediately resigned, followed by BBC Director General Greg Dyke and Andrew Gilligan. The acting chairman of the BBC, Lord Ryder, issued an unreserved apology to the government. In a speech before the House of Commons on February 4, Blair claimed that the report had vindicated his government. Nevertheless, there was widespread criticism in the press of Lord Hutton's failure to criticize the government in any way and for the narrow scope of his inquiry.

The Butler report. Embarrassment about the failure to uncover weapons of mass destruction in Iraq forced Blair to convene an inquiry in February led by Lord Butler (the former Cabinet secretary) into the apparent failure of the intelligence services. When the Butler inquiry reported in July, it established that there were serious weaknesses in the intelligence that had been employed by the government when it went to war. Although the inquiry found that the government had not knowingly made false statements, the panel felt that the "seriously flawed" intelligence was used to the "outer limits" that the evidence supported. Blair took responsibility for the failings of the intelligence and admitted that "it seems increasingly clear that Saddam did not have stockpiles of chemical or biological weapons."

Iraq. The British government maintained its support for the U.S. presence in Iraq throughout 2004. Fresh controversy over the war emerged in February, when the Crown Prosecution Service abandoned its case against former civil servant Katharine Gun. Gun had leaked an e-mail from the U.S. National Security Agency to British intelli-

gence asking for assistance in placing wiretaps among UN Security Council members before the Iraq War. The following day, Clare Short, who had resigned as international development secretary in Blair's government in protest of its handling of the reconstruction of Iraq in 2003, claimed that British intelligence had taped the conversations of UN Secretary-General Kofi Annan. Some members of the government rejected these allegations. Blair maintained that a government should not comment on allegations about its intelligence services, though he did call Short's remarks "irresponsible."

In May 2004, *The Daily Mirror* newspaper, which opposed the Iraq War, published photographs of British soldiers allegedly mistreating Iraqi prisoners in Al Basrah. The photographs were published shortly after the release of photographs of U.S. soldiers abusing and humiliating Iraqi prisoners at the Abu Ghraib prison. However, the photographs of the British soldiers soon were proven to have been falsified. The editor of *The Daily Mirror,* Piers Morgan, resigned.

Later in 2004, Blair refused to be influenced by an extremist Islamic group that kidnapped Kenneth Bigley, a British engineer in Iraq. The group

A new office building, the Swiss Re Tower, adds its distinctive, aerodynamic shape to the London skyline. The 40-story tower, located in London's financial district, houses the new London headquarters of Zurich, Switzerland-based financial giant Swiss Re. Designed by British architect Lord Norman Foster, the building, which Londoners immediately dubbed "the Gherkin," was officially opened in April 2004.

demanded the release of women prisoners in U.K. and U.S. custody. Bigley was beheaded in October after being filmed making an appeal for Blair to act. The prime minister expressed his "utter revulsion" at the killing.

Also in October, the government agreed to allow the British Black Watch regiment to move from its base at Al Basrah in southern Iraq to assist U.S. marines in the north. Blair insisted the decision was not intended to help U.S. President George W. Bush in the forthcoming presidential elections but would ensure that the January 2005 elections in Iraq would take place as scheduled.

Budget. The Chancellor of the Exchequer, Gordon Brown, introduced his budget on March 17, 2004. He forecast that the economy would grow by 3 to 3.5 percent in 2004. Critics questioned whether Brown would be able to afford the enormous increases in public spending he had planned, especially as the public sector deficit was forecast to swell to £37.5 billion ($71.6 billion) during the year. The government increased its borrowing in 2004, and economists speculated that Brown might have to increase taxation to meet his spending commitments.

Conservative leader Michael Howard attacked the Chancellor's pledges, claiming that Brown's was "a credit card budget from a credit card chancellor." Brown increased spending on health and education and pledged to reduce government waste by cutting or relocating as many as 50,000 civil service jobs. Brown claimed that the economy was enjoying the longest period of sustained growth in 200 years and was closer to full employment than it had been for a generation.

European Union constitution. After resisting calls for a referendum on the new European Union (EU) constitutional treaty, Blair reversed his position on April 20 and announced that a referendum would be held. The treaty defined powers in the new Europe by consolidating all existing treaties that had accumulated since its foundation. Blair was criticized for the move as a capitulation to Eurosceptics. Public opinion in Britain had become steadily more critical of the EU since 1975, when a majority of Britons voted in a referendum to remain part of the EU.

Blair insisted that the constitution would not change Britain's relations with Europe; that Europe would not become a federal superstate; and that Britain would retain control of its own domestic and foreign policy matters. A veto by any EU member country would prevent the treaty from becoming law. Blair signed the treaty in Rome on Oct. 29, 2004 (subject to the referendum poll, which was to take place in 2006).

Security breaches. In March 2004, two activists from the international environmental organization Greenpeace were arrested after they

HOUSE OF COMMONS

Queen Elizabeth II opened the 2004-2005 session of Parliament on Nov. 23, 2004. As of December 14, the House of Commons was made up of the following:

407	Labour Party
163	Conservative Party
55	Liberal Democrats
7	Democratic Unionist
5	Scottish National Party
5	Ulster Unionist
4	Plaid Cymru
4	Sinn Fein
3	Social Democratic and Labour Party
1	Independent
1	Respect

In addition, the unaffiliated speaker and 3 deputies attend sessions but do not vote.

THE CABINET OF THE UNITED KINGDOM*

Tony Blair—prime minister; first lord of the treasury; minister for the civil service

John Prescott—deputy prime minister; first secretary of state

Gordon Brown—chancellor of the exchequer

Alan Milburn—chancellor of the duchy of Lancaster

Peter Hain—leader of the House of Commons, lord privy seal, and secretary of state for Wales

Lord Falconer of Thoroton—secretary of state for constitutional affairs

Jack Straw—secretary of state for foreign and Commonwealth affairs

Charles Clarke—secretary of state for the home department

Margaret Beckett—secretary of state for environment, food, and rural affairs

Hilary Benn—secretary of state for international development

Alan Johnson—secretary of state for work and pensions

Alistair Darling—secretary of state for transport and Scotland

John Reid—secretary of state for health

Paul Murphy—secretary of state for Northern Ireland

Geoff Hoon—secretary of state for defense

Paul Boateng—chief secretary to the treasury

Baroness Amos—leader of the House of Lords, lord president of the council

Patricia Hewitt—secretary of state for trade and industry

Ruth Kelly—secretary of state for education and skills

Tessa Jowell—secretary of state for culture, media, and sport

Hilary Armstrong—parliamentary secretary to the treasury, chief whip of the House of Commons

Ian McCartney—minister without portfolio, chairman of the Labour Party

*As of Dec. 16, 2004.

climbed Big Ben (the clock tower that forms part of the Houses of Parliament) as part of an anti-Iraq War demonstration. In May, two members of the activist group Fathers 4 Justice, which campaigns for equal rights for divorced fathers, threw condoms filled with purple dye at the prime minister from the House of Commons public gallery. One hit Blair's shoulder, and the House was evacuated amidst concerns that Parliament might be vulnerable to a terrorist attack. In September, another member of Fathers 4 Justice scaled the walls of Buckingham Palace dressed as Batman to draw attention to the rights of divorced fathers.

Also in September, supporters of the Countryside Alliance, a group that campaigned particularly against the government's attempt to ban fox hunting, gained access to the floor of the House of Commons itself during a demonstration. Among the protestors was Otis Ferry, son of rock star Bryan Ferry. The protestors were arrested. Fox hunting with dogs was banned in England and Wales on November 18, when the House of Commons forced the Hunting Bill through the House of Lords by invoking a rarely used law. The ban was to go into effect on Feb. 18, 2005.

Local and European elections. The Conservatives made significant gains in the June 2004 local elections, while Labour came in behind Charles Kennedy's Liberal Democrats—the first time that a governing party had come third in a local election. Michael Howard's Conservatives gained 37 percent of the vote, while the Liberal Democrats took 27 percent and Labour 26 percent. (The rest of the vote was distributed among smaller parties.) Labour's poor showing was blamed on the public's unhappiness with the Iraq War.

However, in the election for mayor of London, the Labour candidate, Ken Livingstone, was reelected. Livingstone had governed as an independent since his election in 2000 (having previously been a Labour MP), but he was readmitted to the Labour Party in January 2004. He had been thrown out of the party in 2000 after a dispute over the procedure for selecting the mayoral candidate.

In the simultaneous elections for the European Parliament, both of the main parties lost ground. The United Kingdom Independence Party (UKIP), which favored the withdrawal of the U.K. from the EU, obtained 16 percent of the vote. The rise of the UKIP threatened to take votes away from the Conservative party, which had established itself as a largely Eurosceptic party in recent years.

By-elections. In July 2004, two traditionally safe Labour constituencies held by-elections. The Liberal Democrats won in Leicester South, while Labour barely managed to hold Birmingham Hodge Hill. The desertion of Labour by Muslim voters following the Iraq War was blamed for the result.

Also in July, Blair nominated a controversial former minister, Peter Mandelson (who had twice been forced to resign from the Cabinet following accusations of corruption), as the sole U.K. representative on the European Commission of the EU. In a by-election for Mandelson's seat representing the constituency of Hartlepool in September, Labour won, with a heavily reduced majority, over the Liberal Democrats.

Identity cards. Home Secretary David Blunkett announced plans in April 2004 for a bill to introduce identity cards in Britain for the first time since World War II (1939-1945). The government was heavily divided over the issue, mainly because of the high cost of introducing the program. The proposal involved the creation of a national identity register by 2008. The system was to be voluntary initially, with compulsory cards being issued by 2014. Blunkett's proposal was motivated partly by concerns about terrorism but also by the problem of identity theft. The project was likely to use fingerprints or a *biometric* form of identification (such as iris scanning). The government's research on public opinion showed that most people in the U.K. supported the introduction of the cards but resisted having to pay for them.

Home Secretary David Blunkett was forced to resign on Dec. 15, 2004, following allegations that he had used his position to speed the visa application of the Filipino nanny of his former lover, Kimberly Quinn, through immigration. Blunkett claimed that he had done nothing wrong. However, though he retained the esteem of Tony Blair, Blunkett had lost the support of a number of his Cabinet colleagues and found his position untenable. He was replaced by Education Secretary Charles Clarke, who in turn was replaced by Ruth Kelly who joined the Cabinet.

Tuition fees. The government barely managed to get its controversial new proposals for funding higher education through Parliament in January 2004. The bill introduced tuition fees to be paid by students to fund the growth of universities, a move that essentially tripled the nominal tuition payments in place since 1998. Students were to begin paying as much as $5,500 per year, starting in 2006. Many MP's complained that the fees and the fear of debt would deter poorer students from attending universities even though payment of the fees would not begin until after the student graduated.

Princess Diana. In January 2004, a formal inquest was opened into the deaths of Princess Diana, her partner Dodi Fayed, and their driver Henri Paul in a car crash in 1997 in Paris. The coroner announced that he had asked Scotland Yard to assist in investigating allegations that the Princess had been murdered. The inquest was immediately adjourned to examine evidence assembled by French authorities, who had conducted the first inquest into the deaths.

■ Rohan McWilliam
See also **Europe; Iraq: A Special Report.**

United Kingdom, Prime Minister of.

In 2004, Tony Blair marked his tenth year as leader of the Labour Party and his seventh as prime minister of the United Kingdom. His close relationship with United States President George W. Bush remained controversial, especially as many Labour Party members opposed the U.S.-led war in Iraq.

Blair came under increasing pressure to apologize for committing British troops to the Iraq War after it became clear that no *weapons of mass destruction* (biological, chemical, or nuclear weapons) had been found in Iraq. Blair acknowledged failings in intelligence but said he continued to believe that it was right to remove Saddam Hussein from power, especially because of Hussein's failure to comply with United Nations resolutions. However, the prime minister's reputation for trustworthiness appeared to have been damaged in the eyes of many voters in the aftermath of the war.

In October, Blair revealed that he intended to run for a third term as prime minister. Also in October, Blair, who had had minor heart problems in 2003, had an operation to correct an irregular heart beat. The prime minister insisted he would be able to maintain his workload. He promised further reform of the public services and the welfare state if he won a third term in office.

■ Rohan McWilliam
See also **Iraq: A Special Report; United Kingdom.**

United Nations. The United Nations (UN)

General Assembly opened its 59th session on Sept. 14, 2004, with Jean Ping, the foreign minister of Gabon, as president. UN Secretary General Kofi Annan opened the session, urging political leaders to base their decisions on the rule of law, which he felt was being ignored worldwide. In opening remarks, many of the organization's 191 members called for reforms to make the UN more effective.

United States President George W. Bush delivered an address to the assembly on Sept. 21, 2004, defending his policies in the war on terrorism and the conflicts in Iraq and Afghanistan. President Bush asked the UN to remain firm in fighting for democracy and freedom around the world.

Iraq. In 2004, U.S.-led coalition forces deployed in Iraq since March 2003 continued to fight insurgents on several fronts. On June 8, 2004, the UN Security Council unanimously adopted Resolution 1546 to support a democratic and unified Iraq. The resolution set the mandate for a UN Mission, which was to play a "leading role" in helping the interim government adopt democratic processes and achieve national reconciliation. The resolution transformed the U.S.-led forces in Iraq into a multinational force with a UN mandate.

On June 28, an interim Iraqi government was established in Baghdad. On July 12, Annan appointed Ashraf Jehangir Qazi, a Pakistani diplomat, as special envoy to Iraq. Qazi replaced Sergio Vieira de Mello, who was killed in a suicide bomb attack on UN headquarters in Baghdad in 2003; 21 other UN staffers also died in the attack. Qazi led a small team to Baghdad in August 2004, restoring a UN presence in the country. Nevertheless, Annan in September said the UN could not deploy a larger staff because he feared that UN personnel would become "targets of violence" in Iraq.

The UN's $64-billion oil-for-food program in Iraq became the target of several investigations in 2004. The program, which was to ease sanctions imposed on Iraq after the Persian Gulf War of 1991, allowed Iraq to sell oil and use the proceeds to purchase food, medicine, and other goods for its people. In February 2004, allegations arose that the Hussein government may have pocketed $10 billion from the program and that several UN administrators may themselves have profited from it. In April, Annan appointed former U.S. Federal Reserve Chairman Paul Volcker to investigate the matter. Several U.S. congressional investigations began as well.

Middle East. The UN Security Council attempted during 2004 to resolve the conflict between Israel and the Palestinian people in the West Bank and Gaza Strip. On March 25, the United States vetoed a UN Security Council resolution that condemned Israel for the murder of Sheikh Ahmed Yassin, the leader of the Islamic group Hamas, which carried out frequent attacks against Israel. On October 5, the United States vetoed another resolution that demanded that Israel withdraw its military operations from the northern Gaza Strip. The UN reported that Israeli military operations between September 29 and October 5 had resulted in the deaths of 82 Palestinians. Five Israelis, including two girls, died during the same period. The Israelis launched the operations after the girls were killed by a rocket fired by Hamas.

The General Assembly also discussed Israel's construction of a wall along its borders to keep Palestinians out. On July 21, the assembly voted in favor of a resolution demanding that Israel stop the construction of the wall and compensate the Palestinians for damages caused by the wall.

Africa. Members of the UN Security Council witnessed in Nairobi, Kenya, on November 19 the signing of an accord between Sudan's Islamic national government and rebels seeking a greater share of power and wealth for the largely Christian and animist people of the south. The agreement, which specified that peace talks would be completed by December 31, was to end a 21-year civil war.

The accords, however, failed to end a conflict between Arab militias and African rebels that began in 2003 in the Darfur region of western Sudan. By September 2004, the conflict had resulted in the deaths of at least 50,000 black Africans and had displaced more than 1 million others. The UN Security Council on July 30 had adopted a resolution to impose an arms embargo on the Arab militias and demand that the Sudanese government carry out commitments to end the carnage. In October, Annan appointed a commission to investigate whether genocide had occurred in the area.

Peacekeeping. In 2004, UN peacekeeping missions were deployed in several countries with regional conflicts, including Ethiopia, Liberia, Cote d'Ivoire, the Democratic Republic of Congo, Burundi, and Haiti. Secretary General Annan reported in October that 30,000 uniformed personnel would be needed in addition to the 50,000 already serving in UN missions to keep up with the surge of demands for such missions in 2004.

Security Council. On October 15, the UN General Assembly elected five new members for the 15-nation Security Council—Argentina, Denmark, Greece, Japan, and Tanzania. Those nations were to begin a two-year term in January 2005, joining the council's permanent members—China, France, Russia, the United Kingdom, and the United States—and five members elected in 2003—Algeria, Benin, Brazil, the Philippines, and Romania.

■ J. Tuyet Nguyen

See also **Haiti: A Special Report; Iraq: A Special Report; Middle East; Sudan.**

United States, Government of the.

The threat of terrorism continued to dominate the government of the United States in 2004, a year that was marked by a flurry of commission reports, analyses, and proposals. The U.S. government also continued fielding soldiers in Iraq and Afghanistan.

Intelligence reform. On July 22, a bipartisan commission investigating the terrorist attacks on the United States issued a report warning that the U.S. government in 2004 needed to overhaul its intelligence agencies. The commission recommended that the current position of Central Intelligence Agency (CIA) director be replaced with a national intelligence director. The director would oversee and control the budget of the 15 intelligence agencies that function within the federal government. The U.S. House of Representatives and the Senate in December 2004 approved legislation that enacted most of the commission's recommendations, including creating the national intelligence director position.

According to the commission's report, the United States was safer than it had been prior to the 2001 attacks because of military actions taken against the al-Qa'ida terrorist network and improvements made to homeland security. However, the risk of future terrorist attacks against the United States still existed. "An attack of even greater magnitude is now possible and even probable. We do not have the luxury of time," said Commission Chairman Thomas H. Kean.

New CIA director. The commission's findings had a ripple effect throughout the federal government even before they became public. George Tenet resigned as CIA director in June 2004 in part because of criticism he anticipated over the agency's intelligence failures prior to the 2001 terrorist attacks. In August 2004, President George W. Bush nominated U.S. Representative Porter J. Goss (R., Florida) to replace Tenet. The Senate on September 22 voted 77 to 17 to confirm Goss, despite criticism from some Senate Democrats who claimed that he was too closely tied to the Republican Party to remain neutral as CIA director.

War in Iraq. The Senate Intelligence Committee issued a report on July 9 blasting the intelligence used to justify the war in Iraq, which was launched in March 2003. The panel found that although U.S. intelligence agencies had concluded that Iraq possessed chemical and biological weapons, the agencies themselves had been unable to substantiate the claims. The report stated that "in the end, what the president and the Congress used to send the country to war was information provided by the intelligence community, and that information was flawed." No chemical, biological, or nuclear weapons were found in Iraq.

Human rights. The United States received harsh criticism following revelations in April 2004 that U.S. soldiers had allegedly physi-cally and psychologically abused Iraqi prisoners of war at Abu Ghraib prison near Baghdad. President Bush appeared on Arab television in May and expressed regret about the prisoner abuse. On May 7, Donald Rumsfeld, secretary of the U.S. Department of Defense, also accepted blame for the abuse and offered an apology to Iraqis abused by the U.S. soldiers. A U.S. Army report released in August faulted senior military personnel for failing to adequately supervise the situation at the prison and allowing the abuse to take place. In December, the release of U.S. Army documents revealed that the military had investigated several allegations of threatened executions, physical abuse, and the shooting of detainees at prison camps in Iraq, Afghanistan, and Guantanamo Bay, Cuba, dating to 2001.

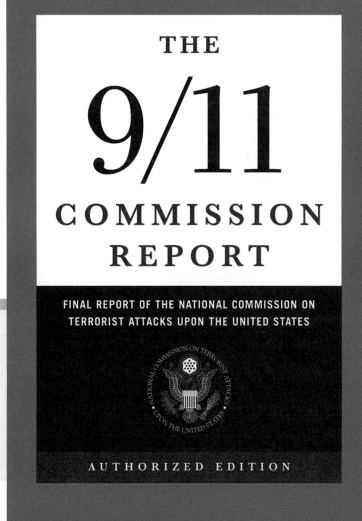

A final report by a bipartisan commission on the Sept. 11, 2001, terrorist attacks on the United States, known as *The 9/11 Commission Report*, concluded that the United States was still a target for future terrorist attacks. The report was a bestseller in 2004.

THE

9/11

COMMISSION

REPORT

FINAL REPORT OF THE NATIONAL COMMISSION ON TERRORIST ATTACKS UPON THE UNITED STATES

AUTHORIZED EDITION

Rights of detainees. The Supreme Court of the United States on June 28, 2004, issued two significant rulings outlining the scope of presidential authority in handling prisoners captured in connection with the U.S.-led war on terrorism.

The justices ruled 6 to 3 that foreign detainees who were taken into U.S. custody during fighting in Afghanistan had the right to file claims in federal court or before a "neutral decision-maker" to contest their detention. The men were among several hundred prisoners held for more than two years at a naval base at Guantanamo Bay, Cuba. They had been taken into U.S. custody during fighting in Afghanistan in 2001. None of the detainees had been charged with crimes or allowed contact with lawyers or family members.

In a separate case, decided by an 8-to-1 vote, the justices ruled that Yaser Esam Hamdi, a U.S. citizen of Arab descent captured in Afghanistan in 2002 and designated an enemy combatant, was entitled to a "meaningful opportunity" to challenge being imprisoned without criminal charges or access to an attorney. In September 2004, U.S. Department of Justice officials announced that they had agreed to release Hamdi and deport him to Saudi Arabia. Hamdi was required to renounce his U.S. citizenship.

Troop reassignments. The Bush administration on June 7 announced a plan to withdraw some 12,500 troops from South Korea as part of a broader effort to reposition soldiers around the world. One-third of the 37,000 troops stationed in South Korea are to be deployed to Iraq and elsewhere.

Sexual predators. Immigration officials on July 8 announced that more than 3,200 people had been arrested since mid-2003 as part of a federal program to safeguard children from sexual predators. Border and Transportation Security and Immigration and Customs Enforcement officials announced that 3,247 arrests had been made across the United States, with an additional 500 arrests made outside the country based on information from the U.S. government. The federal government program, called Operation Predator, coordinates investigative and intelligence resources to protect children from *pedophiles* (adults who are sexually attracted to children) in countries outside the United States, human traffickers, international sex tourists, and Internet pornographers.

Welfare caseloads decline. Tommy G. Thompson, secretary of the U.S. Department of Health and Human Services (HHS), on Aug. 23, 2004, announced that caseloads in the primary welfare program declined during 2003. Thompson said that the number of people participating in the Temporary Assistance for Needy Families (TANF) program fell 3 percent in 2003, and the number of families in the program fell by 1.8 percent; 2003 was the seventh consecutive year that the number of caseloads had declined, according to HHS officials. HHS reported that nearly 149,000 fewer people were using TANF benefits at the end of 2003 than at the end of 2002. At the end of 2003, 4,864,905 people and 2,008,233 families were receiving TANF benefits, compared with 5,013,728 people and 2,044,734 families at the end of 2002.

No-spam registry rejected. The Federal Trade Commission (FTC) on June 15, 2004, rejected a proposal to establish a national do-not-spam registry to stop unwanted e-mails. The FTC is an independent U.S. government agency that works to protect consumers from unfair or misleading practices. The do-not-spam registry was to be similar to the national do-not-call registry of consumers weary of telephone sales calls. FTC Chairman Timothy Muris said a do-not-spam registry would be unenforceable.

Greenhouse gases. In a major shift in policy, the Bush administration on August 25 reported to Congress that emissions of carbon dioxide and other heat-trapping gases are the only logical explanation for global warming. The Bush administration previously had maintained that scientific uncertainties about the effects of greenhouse gases made it unnecessary to impose binding restrictions on their release. In addition to global warming, the report revealed that studies indicated that carbon dioxide promotes the growth of weeds while inhibiting the growth of crops, which could have implications for the agricultural industry.

The Bush administration announced new regulations on May 10 designed to reduce emissions from diesel-powered vehicles. Under the new rules, refineries would be required to produce cleaner-burning diesel fuel, while engine makers would be required to reduce emissions by approximately 90 percent.

Snowmobile ban overturned. In October, a federal judge in Wyoming struck down a ban on snowmobiles in Yellowstone and Grand Teton national parks. The snowmobile ban had been instituted in 2001 because of concern for the health of the parks' wildlife, which suffered stress from the noise. Park rangers also expressed health concerns after being exposed to emissions from the vehicles. Rangers at entrances to Yellowstone Park in the past had felt it necessary to wear gas masks because of the buildup of fumes from idling snowmobiles. However, U.S. District Judge Clarence Brimmer ruled on Oct. 14, 2004, that the ban was imposed with inadequate input from the public and the states of Montana and Wyoming.

SELECTED AGENCIES AND BUREAUS OF THE U.S. GOVERNMENT*

Executive Office of the President
President, George W. Bush
 Vice President, Richard B. Cheney
 White House Chief of Staff, Andrew H. Card, Jr.
 Presidential Press Secretary, Scott McClellan
 Assistant to the President for Domestic Policy,
  Margaret Spellings
 Assistant to the President for National Security Affairs,
  Condoleezza Rice
 Director, Office of Science and Technology Policy,
  John H. Marburger III
 Council of Economic Advisers—Nicholas Gregory Mankiw,
  Chairperson
 Office of Management and Budget—
  Josh B. Bolten, Director
 Office of National Drug Control Policy—
  John P. Walters, Director
 U.S. Trade Representative, Robert B. Zoellick

Department of Agriculture
Secretary of Agriculture, Ann M. Veneman†

Department of Commerce
Secretary of Commerce, Donald L. Evans†
 Bureau of Economic Analysis—J. Steven Landefeld, Director
 Bureau of the Census—Charles Louis Kincannon, Director

Department of Defense
Secretary of Defense, Donald H. Rumsfeld
 Secretary of the Air Force, James G. Roche
 Acting Secretary of the Army, Les Brownlee
 Secretary of the Navy, Gordon R. England
 Joint Chiefs of Staff—
  General Richard B. Myers, Chairperson
  General John P. Jumper, Chief of Staff, Air Force
  General Peter J. Schoomaker, Chief of Staff, Army
  Admiral Vern Clark, Chief of Naval Operations
  General Michael W. Hagee, Commandant, Marine Corps

Department of Education
Secretary of Education, Roderick R. Paige†

Department of Energy
Secretary of Energy, Spencer Abraham†

Department of Health and Human Services
Secretary of Health and Human Services,
 Tommy G. Thompson**
 Office of Public Health and Science—Cristina Beato,
  Acting Assistant Secretary
 Centers for Disease Control and Prevention—
  Julie Louise Gerberding, Director
 Food and Drug Administration—Lester M. Crawford, Acting
  Commissioner
 National Institutes of Health—Elias A. Zerhouni, Director
 Surgeon General of the United States, Richard H. Carmona

Department of Homeland Security
Secretary of Homeland Security, Thomas J. Ridge†
 Bureau of Citizenship and Immigration Services—
  Eduardo Aguirre, Jr., Director
 U.S. Coast Guard—Admiral Thomas H. Collins, Commandant
 U.S. Secret Service—W. Ralph Basham, Director
 Federal Emergency Management Agency—Michael D. Brown,
  Undersecretary

Department of Housing and Urban Development
Secretary of Housing and Urban Development,
 Alphonso R. Jackson

Department of the Interior
Secretary of the Interior, Gale A. Norton

Department of Justice
Attorney General, John Ashcroft†
 Federal Bureau of Prisons—Harley G. Lappin, Director
 Drug Enforcement Administration—
  Karen P. Tandy, Administrator
 Federal Bureau of Investigation—
  Robert S. Mueller III, Director
 Acting Solicitor General, Paul D. Clement

Department of Labor
Secretary of Labor, Elaine L. Chao

Department of State
Secretary of State, Colin L. Powell†
 U.S. Ambassador to the United Nations, John C. Danforth†

Department of Transportation
Secretary of Transportation, Norman Y. Mineta
 Federal Aviation Administration—
  Marion C. Blakey, Administrator

Department of the Treasury
Secretary of the Treasury, John W. Snow
 Internal Revenue Service—Mark W. Everson, Commissioner
 Treasurer of the United States, Vacant
 Office of Thrift Supervision—James E. Gilleran, Director

Department of Veterans Affairs
Secretary of Veterans Affairs, Anthony J. Principi**

Supreme Court of the United States
Chief Justice of the United States, William H. Rehnquist
 Associate Justices—
  John Paul Stevens   David H. Souter
  Sandra Day O'Connor   Clarence Thomas
  Antonin Scalia   Ruth Bader Ginsburg
  Anthony M. Kennedy   Stephen G. Breyer

Congressional officials
President of the Senate pro tempore, Ted Stevens
 Senate Majority Leader, William H. Frist
 Senate Minority Leader, Tom Daschle
 Speaker of the House, J. Dennis Hastert
 House Majority Leader, Thomas DeLay
 House Minority Leader, Nancy Pelosi
 Congressional Budget Office—Douglas Holtz-Eakin, Director
 Government Accountability Office—David M. Walker, Comptroller
  General of the United States
 Library of Congress—James H. Billington, Librarian of Congress

Independent agencies
Central Intelligence Agency—Porter J. Goss, Director
Commission on Civil Rights—Mary Frances Berry, Chairperson
Commission of Fine Arts—David M. Childs, Chairperson
Consumer Product Safety Commission—
 Harold D. Stratton, Jr., Chairperson
Corporation for National and Community Service—
 Stephen Goldsmith, Chairperson
Environmental Protection Agency—Michael O. Leavitt, Administrator
Equal Employment Opportunity Commission—
 Cari M. Dominguez, Chairperson
Federal Communications Commission—Michael K. Powell, Chairperson
Federal Deposit Insurance Corporation—
 Donald E. Powell, Chairperson
Federal Election Commission—Bradley A. Smith, Chairperson
Federal Reserve System Board of Governors—
 Alan Greenspan, Chairperson
Federal Trade Commission—Deborah Platt Majoras, Chairperson
General Services Administration—Stephen A. Perry, Administrator
National Aeronautics and Space Administration—Sean O'Keefe**,
 Administrator
National Endowment for the Arts—Dana Gioia, Chairperson
National Endowment for the Humanities—Bruce Cole, Chairperson
National Labor Relations Board—Robert J. Battista, Chairperson
National Railroad Passenger Corporation (Amtrak)—
 David Gunn, President and CEO
National Science Foundation—Arden L. Bement, Jr., Acting Director
National Transportation Safety Board—
 Ellen Engleman Conners, Chairperson
Nuclear Regulatory Commission—Nils J. Diaz, Chairperson
Peace Corps—Gaddi H. Vasquez, Director
Securities and Exchange Commission—
 William H. Donaldson, Chairperson
Selective Service System—Jack Martin, Acting Director
Small Business Administration—Hector V. Barreto, Jr., Administrator
Smithsonian Institution—Lawrence M. Small, Secretary
Social Security Administration—Jo Anne Barnhart, Commissioner
U.S. Postal Service—John E. Potter, Postmaster General

*As of Dec. 31, 2004.   †Announced resignation in November 2004.
**Announced resignation in December 2004

Correctional population. Justice Department officials reported in July that the number of U.S. citizens in the criminal justice system increased by 130,700 people in 2003 to approximately 6.9 million people. The total includes people who are in jail, prison, or on probation or parole and accounted for approximately 3.2 percent of the entire adult population of the United States. Analysts attributed the rise to more stringent sentencing laws passed in the 1990's, which eventually resulted in more people being sent to prison with longer sentences.

Federal deficit. The U.S. Department of the Treasury announced on Oct. 14, 2004, that the federal deficit had soared to a record $413 billion. However, the figure was lower than many analysts had predicted. The Bush administration in February had forecast a $521 billion deficit.

John Danforth, the U.S. ambassador to the United Nations, announced his resignation in December. Danforth had served as ambassador since July. Danforth said he wanted to spend more time with his family.

New money. The U.S. Department of the Treasury introduced a redesigned $50 bill in April as part of an ongoing effort to make counterfeiting more difficult. The redesigned currency, which went into circulation in the fall, features a red and blue background and embedded threads that glow when exposed to ultraviolet light. The bill is printed with special ink, portions of which change from green to a copper color.

The U.S. Mint unveiled new designs for the nickel. The new five-cent piece, scheduled to go into circulation in 2005, features a larger image of President Thomas Jefferson. One version of the nickel features an American buffalo, while a second version celebrates the 200 anniversary of the Meriwether Lewis and William Clark Expedition, which concluded in 1805.

■ Geoffrey A. Campbell

See also **Armed forces; Congress of the United States; Democratic Party; Elections; People in the news** (John Edwards; John Kerry; Barack Obama); **Republican Party; State government; United States, President of the.**

FEDERAL SPENDING
United States budget for fiscal 2004*

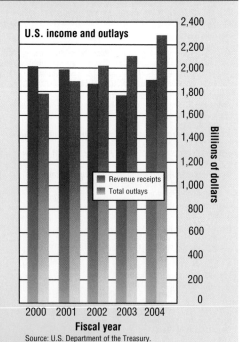

Billions of dollars	
National defense	455.5
International affairs	26.4
General science, space, technology	23.7
Energy	–0.3
Natural resources and environment	28.7
Agriculture	17.3
Commerce and housing credit	5.2
Transportation	64.6
Community and regional development	14.6
Education, training, employment, and social services	87.8
Health	239.8
Social security	495.6
Medicare	269.4
Income security	334.7
Veterans' benefits and services	59.8
Administration of justice	44.9
General government	22.7
Interest	160.5
Undistributed offsetting receipts	–58.5
Total budget outlays	**2,292.4**

*Oct. 1, 2003, to Sept. 30, 2004.
  Source: U.S. Department of the Treasury.

U.S. income and outlays

Revenue receipts
Total outlays

Fiscal year
Source: U.S. Department of the Treasury.

President George W. Bush speaks at Galatasaray University in Istanbul, in June 2004, at the conclusion of a five-day visit to Europe and Turkey. The president urged Muslim nations to embrace democracy.

United States, President of the.

President George W. Bush was re-elected on Nov. 2, 2004, the first Republican president to win a second term since Ronald Reagan in 1984. President Bush won 31 states to capture 286 electoral votes in the 2004 election. He received 60.6 million votes, or 51 percent of the popular vote. His challenger, U.S. Senator John Kerry (D., Massachusetts), won 19 states and the District of Columbia, taking 48 percent of the popular vote with 57.2 million votes.

Bipartisan commission. President Bush and Vice President Dick Cheney on April 29 met with members of a federal commission studying the terrorist attacks on the United States on Sept. 11, 2001. The president and vice president met for more than three hours with the 10-member bipartisan National Commission on Terrorist Attacks Upon the United States. The focus of the session was on the Bush administration's efforts to combat terrorism. However, President Bush would not provide details about what specific topics were discussed.

Intelligence panel. President Bush established a bipartisan commission on Feb. 6, 2004, to examine the quality of information utilized by the administration to justify the Iraq War. Critics had charged that certain information—such as former Iraqi President Saddam Hussein's efforts to obtain *weapons of mass destruction* (biological, chemical, or nuclear weapons)—was faulty and deliberately manipulated to make war with Iraq appear to be the only reasonable course of action.

President Bush named Charles Robb, a former Democratic senator and governor from Virginia, and Laurence Silberman, a Republican U.S. appeals court judge, as chairmen of the commission. The president gave the panel until March 2005 to submit a report.

Tax cuts. President Bush signed legislation on Oct. 4, 2004, approving a $145.9-billion extension of three tax cuts for individuals. Both the U.S. House of Representatives and the Senate approved the tax-cuts package in September.

Former presidents. Bill Clinton underwent successful quadruple coronary bypass surgery on September 6 after complaining of chest pains and shortness of breath.

Ronald Reagan died on June 5 at age 93. He had revealed in 1994 that he was suffering from Alzheimer's disease.

■ Geoffrey A. Campbell

See also **Congress of the United States; Elections; Iraq: A Special Report; News bytes; Republican Party; Taxation; United States, Government of the; United States, President of the: A Special Report.**

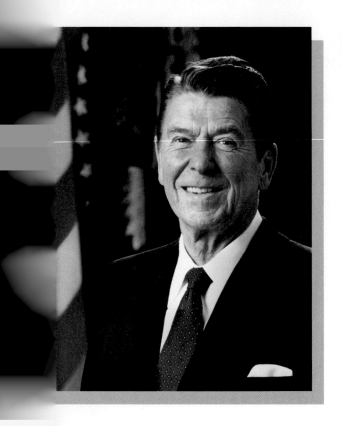

Ronald Reagan
(1911-2004)

The former United States president stirred feelings of patriotism in America and helped initiate change throughout the world.

By Alfred J. Smuskiewicz

Former United States President Ronald Reagan died on June 5, 2004, after coping with the effects of Alzheimer's disease for several years. At age 93, Reagan lived longer than any other president in U.S. history. During the week-long televised funeral proceedings, world leaders and U.S. citizens alike remembered the two-term president for reviving feelings of patriotism and confidence in the United States. He was also remembered for hastening the end of the *Cold War* (a period of intense rivalry between the United States and the Soviet Union following World War II [1939-1945]). In addition, commentators noted that Reagan had broadened the appeal of the Republican Party to include many traditional Democratic voters, including blue-collar workers and Southerners.

Ronald Wilson Reagan was born in Tampico, Illinois, a small town about 100 miles (160 kilometers) west of Chicago, on Feb. 6, 1911. He was the second son of John Edward Reagan, an often unemployed shoe salesman, and Nelle Wilson Reagan, a homemaker. The Reagans moved from town to town in western Illinois as John searched for work before the family finally settled in Dixon. There, young Ronald attended high school and worked summers as a lifeguard on the Rock River, which runs through Dixon.

After graduating from Eureka College in Eureka, Illinois, in 1932, where he studied sociology and economics, Reagan headed west to Iowa. His gift as a public speaker and his vivid imagination helped him land jobs at radio stations in Davenport and later Des Moines, where he recreated lively play-by-play accounts of sporting events from sketchy information that he received over a tickertape machine about the contests. A tickertape machine converted and printed data, usually stock prices or news, that was conveyed long distances over a telegraph wire. During a trip to California in 1937 to report on the Chicago Cubs baseball team's spring training, Reagan took a screen test for a motion picture studio. Studio executives liked what they saw and signed Reagan to an acting contract.

His days in Hollywood

The contract marked the beginning of a long career in front of the camera. From 1937 to 1964, Reagan made more than 50 feature-length films, mostly as a contract player for Warner Brothers studios. He usually portrayed wholesome, likable characters. One of his most acclaimed performances was as legendary college football player George "the Gipper" Gipp in *Knute Rockne—All American* (1940). In the film, the dying Gipp tells his coach Rockne to ". . . win just one for the Gipper." This phrase would later serve as a rallying campaign slogan for Reagan the politician. Reagan also received critical praise for his role in *Kings Row* (1942), playing a young man whose legs are amputated. Most film critics consider *Kings Row* Reagan's best work in Hollywood.

In 1940, Reagan married fellow Warner Brothers star Jane Wyman, with whom he acted in several films. The couple had a daughter, Maureen Elizabeth, and adopted a son, Michael Edward. The marriage ended in divorce in 1948. In 1952, Reagan married actress Nancy Davis, who subsequently gave up her acting career. They had a daughter, Patricia Ann, and a son, Ronald Prescott.

Reagan served as president of the Screen Actors Guild, the major union representing film performers, from 1947 to 1952 and again from 1959 to 1960. As union president, Reagan tried to block what he—and many other people at the time—saw as attempts by Communists to infiltrate the motion picture industry. The anti-Communist theme of this battle would have a profound influence on Reagan's political career.

Reagan's political viewpoints generally reflected the policies of the Democratic Party during the future politician's Hollywood period. Reagan strongly supported President Franklin Delano Roosevelt (1933-1945), and the actor campaigned for President Harry Truman (1945-1953) in 1948. However, as his Hollywood career began to wane and he developed a greater interest in world and national events, Reagan's allegiance gradually shifted from the Democratic Party to the Republican Party. Reagan later attributed this shift to his growing concerns about the spread of Communism and what he saw as excessive taxes and government regulation.

Reagan got a chance to articulate his beliefs while host of the weekly television series "The General Electric Theater," from 1954 to 1962. Part of this job involved touring the country as the public relations representative of the television show's corporate sponsor, General Electric, a leading manufacturer of electrical products headquartered in Fairfield, Connecticut. Reagan traveled from town to town delivering speeches about the importance of free enterprise and the dangers of big government.

Ann Sheridan, Ronald Reagan, and Robert Cummings (left to right) in a scene from *Kings Row* (1942). Most critics consider the film to be the best of Reagan's acting career.

The political spotlight

Reagan gained a nationwide audience for his political vision in 1964, when he delivered an impassioned half-hour television address on behalf of Republican presidential candidate Barry M. Goldwater. Reagan told his television audience, "This is the issue of this election . . . whether we believe in our capacity for self-government or whether we abandon the American Revolution and confess that a little intellectual elite in a far-distant capital can plan our lives for us better than we can plan them ourselves." Although President Lyndon B. Johnson (1963-1969) crushed Goldwater in the election, many historians credit Reagan's speech with igniting the modern conservative movement in the United States.

The speech also firmly positioned the Hollywood actor in the national political spotlight, and supporters of Reagan's ideas urged him to run for governor of California. When Reagan announced his candidacy for the 1966 gubernatorial race, the incumbent Democratic governor, Edmund G. (Pat) Brown, dismissed Reagan as "only a B-movie actor." Reagan, who defeated Brown in a landslide, was re-elected in 1970 and served until 1975. As governor, Reagan instituted reforms in California's social welfare system and slowed the growth of state spending. He also won the backing of national Republican leaders who were looking for a presidential candidate to carry the conservative banner into the White House. However, Reagan was unsuccessful in his bid to become the Republican Party's nominee for president in 1976. President Gerald R. Ford won the nomination but lost the election to Democratic challenger Jimmy Carter.

By the 1970's, many Americans began to lose confidence in the United States and its institutions, including the government, in the wake of losing the Vietnam War (1957-1975); the Watergate scandal that led to President Richard M. Nixon's resignation in 1974; and a stagnant U.S. economy. Historians suggest that this lack of confidence continued through the presidency of Jimmy Carter (1977-1981). During the Carter administration, the rate of inflation soared to 15 percent; the Soviet Union invaded Afghanistan; and Iranian militants seized 52 U.S. diplomats at the U.S. Embassy in Tehran, the capital of Iran, and held them hostage for more than a year. Carter himself spoke to the country about a national "malaise" and a "crisis of confidence." Some academics called for revising the U.S. Constitution to change the nature of the presidency, which, in their view, had become too big a job for any one man.

The author:
Alfred J. Smuskiewicz is a free-lance writer.

President of the United States

Reagan captured the Republican nomination for president in 1980 and mounted a vigorous challenge to Carter in the general election. Reagan borrowed a phrase from colonial leader John Winthrop, Puritan governor of the Massachusetts Bay Colony in the 1600's, when he spoke of the United States as a "shining city upon a hill." He maintained that the nation's best days lay ahead. Reagan's optimism was contagious. "Reagan Democrats"—Americans who normally would have voted Democratic—took a chance with the former actor and California governor. Reagan soundly defeated Carter, carrying 44 states and winning 489 electoral votes.

The optimistic tone of Reagan's presidency was set on the day he was inaugurated, Jan. 20, 1981, when the Iranian militants finally released their American hostages. His cheery confidence even survived an attempt on his life on March 30, 1981, when he was shot in Washington, D.C. He showed wit and sense of humor throughout the ordeal, quipping to his surgeons, "I hope you're all Republicans."

Reagan's positive attitude won him public support, as well as crucial backing in the U.S. Congress, as he worked to institute his controversial policies to roll back the size of the federal government and build up the strength of the U.S. military. During his first administration, Congress passed the largest income tax cut in U.S. history and scaled back the extent of social welfare and other federal programs. Various federal regulations on private enterprise were also reduced. The Reagan administration instituted the largest increase in defense spending in U.S. history and pursued aggressive policies to counter the interests of the Soviet Union, including lending military support to anti-Communist forces in Central America and moral support to the anti-Communist "Solidarity" workers movement in Poland. Reagan also started the Strategic Defense Initiative (SDI), which the press dubbed "Star Wars," a high-technology research program to develop a space-based defensive system against incoming missiles.

Many critics assailed Reagan's early economic policies as harmful to minority groups and low-income families. Part of his economic plan combined tax cuts with reductions in welfare and unemployment programs while increasing defense spending. The media dubbed the economic policy "Reaganomics." However, the U.S. Congress approved the majority of his economic plan in 1981.

A serious recession in 1981 and 1982 derailed Reagan's hopes for a rapid economic turnaround. But soon after, a national economic expansion began that continued into the early 1990's. Still, Reagan's policies led to ballooning budget deficits that affected the nation for several years.

President Reagan and First Lady Nancy Reagan greet well-wishers upon the president's return to the White House after he recovered from the 1981 attempt on his life.

Some critics of Reagan focused on his military buildup, which they believed was dangerous to world peace. However, Reagan defended it, saying ". . . our aim is to protect the peace by ensuring that no adversaries ever conclude they could best us in a war . . . ."

Reagan won re-election in a landslide in 1984, based largely on the strength of the economic recovery, defeating former Vice President Walter F. Mondale. Reagan carried 49 states and won 525 electoral votes—the most electoral votes ever won by a presidential candidate.

Changing the world

Foreign policy dominated Reagan's second term. In 1985, Mikhail Gorbachev became the leader of the Soviet Union, promising to institute many reforms in the Soviet economic and political systems. Gorbachev also showed a new willingness to negotiate for arms reductions with the United States. In 1987, Reagan and Gorbachev signed the Intermediate Range Nuclear Forces Treaty, which represented the first actual reduction in nuclear arms.

Also in 1987, Reagan issued a bold call to Gorbachev while visiting the Berlin Wall, a concrete barrier erected in 1961 to prevent Germans from escaping Communist East Berlin for democratic West Berlin. Reagan declared, "There is one sign the Soviets can make that would be unmistakable, that would advance dramatically the cause of freedom and peace . . . Mr. Gorbachev, tear down this wall!"

Although few academics at the time believed the Berlin Wall would fall any time soon, the wall did come down in 1989 in a wave of democracy that swept across Eastern Europe. By 1991, the Soviet Union itself had collapsed. Its Communist Party fell from power after 74 years, and the Soviet empire dissolved into several independent republics. How much credit Reagan deserves for this historic end to the Cold War will likely be debated for decades. Yet many historians likely may side with the assessment of presidential historian and author Michael Beschloss: "Reagan's defense buildup and SDI . . . pressed Gorbachev, while his economy was collapsing, to make arms deals and improve relations with the West, which contributed to the unraveling of his empire."

Despite Reagan's successes, he faced a crisis during his second term that almost undid his presidency. In 1987, a joint congressional committee investigated the Reagan administration for the sale of weapons to Iran to help win the freedom of American hostages held by Islamic

In a historic speech at the Brandenburg Gate in Berlin in 1987, President Reagan challenged Mikhail Gorbachev, leader of the Soviet Union, to tear down the Berlin Wall. Many historians view the speech as a turning point in the Cold War.

terrorists. The profits of this sale were diverted to fund contra rebels fighting the Communist government of Nicaragua. The arrangement was made despite the fact that the U.S. Congress had passed a law forbidding aid to the contras. Although Reagan claimed he knew nothing about the secret diversion of funds, the "Iran-contra affair" eroded his credibility. Nevertheless, Reagan left office in January 1989 with a 63-percent public approval rating.

President George W. Bush speaks at former President Ronald Reagan's funeral at the National Cathedral in Washington, D.C., on June 11, 2004.

Alzheimer's disease

In November 1994, the former president disclosed in a hand-written note addressed to the American people that he had been diagnosed with Alzheimer's disease, a degenerative brain disorder that causes a loss of memory and a failure of other mental abilities. The illness also gradually weakens the patient's physical condition.

When President Reagan died after his long illness, there was an outpouring of affection and admiration—from politicians of both major parties and from regular Americans—that had not been seen for a fallen American leader since the funeral of the assassinated President John F. Kennedy in 1963. Tens of thousands of Americans filed past Reagan's casket in separate memorials in California and in Washington, D.C., some waiting in line for several hours.

Historians agree that Reagan's legacy—like the legacy of all presidents—will long be a subject of discussion. Reagan himself said that the economic recovery and the recovery of American morale were his two greatest accomplishments. Many people will undoubtedly remember Reagan for his optimistic nature. In his letter disclosing his illness, Reagan wrote, "When the Lord calls me home, whenever that may be, I will leave with the greatest love for this country of ours and eternal optimism for its future."

Uzbekistan. Terrorist attacks in the capital, Tashkent, and in Bukhara in March and April 2004 left at least 47 people dead. On July 30, suicide bombings at the United States and Israeli embassies and the chief prosecutor's office in Tashkent killed seven others. By November, more than 100 people had been jailed in connection with the attacks. Authorities blamed the violence on Islamic extremist groups linked to al-Qa'ida. Political analysts observed that Uzbekistan's decision to host U.S. troops supporting operations in Afghanistan, and the Uzbek government's repression of Muslim clerics and activists, may have incited the attacks.

Human rights organizations continued in 2004 to accuse the Uzbek government of human rights violations. In April, the London-based European Bank for Reconstruction and Development cut off loans to Uzbekistan, and in July the U.S. State Department refused to certify the country for further military and economic aid. On November 1, as many as 10,000 Uzbeks staged a rare demonstration in the city of Kokand to protest new government restrictions on trading in Uzbek markets.

Uzbekistan held elections for the 120 seats in the Oliy Majlis, the lower legislative house, on December 26. Opposition parties were blocked from participation.   ■ Juliet Johnson

See also **Asia; Disasters; Iraq: A Special Report.**

Vanuatu. See Pacific Islands.

Venezuela. President Hugo Chavez Frias survived a serious challenge to his presidency on Aug. 15, 2004—winning a recall referendum by a margin of 59 percent to 41 percent. International election monitors vouched for the fairness of the vote, in which a record 8.5 million Venezuelans participated. Nonetheless, some of the president's opponents cried fraud.

The results meant that President Chavez would complete the remaining two years of his term and continue his populist "Bolivarian revolution," named for Simon Bolivar, the Venezuelan-born hero of South America's wars of independence in the early 1800's. Since Chavez's election in 1998, he had sought to overhaul Venezuela's corruption-ridden government and impose social reforms to redistribute wealth.

Oil profits. President Chavez's 2004 campaign to stay in office benefited from high global oil prices, which were around $40 a barrel at the time of the referendum. The oil revenues of Petroleos de Venezuela S.A., whose leadership Chavez had purged to bring it under his administration's control, were expected to exceed $7 billion in 2004, according to LatinSource, a network of economists based in New York City.

The Venezuelan government announced in July that $2 billion of the oil profits would be invested in a special development fund to finance public projects, including a hydroelectric dam and new state airline. Another $1.7 billion was earmarked for social programs to improve the living conditions of Venezuela's low income residents.

Business anxiety. The diversion of oil earnings into welfare programs caused great anxiety among the membership of Fedecamaras, Venezuela's largest business association. However, Chavez reached out to his opponents in the business world after the referendum, saying, "I call on private businessmen to work together with us to build the new economy, transforming the capitalistic economic model into a social, humanist, and equality economy."

Foreign investment needed. The importance of a strong collaboration between government and private interests was highlighted by the plans of Petroleos de Venezuela to nearly double production by 2009. The company's proposals to develop new oil and natural gas fields and refineries required an estimated $36 billion in fresh investment. Petroleos de Venezuela hoped to obtain much of this capital from foreign companies.   ■ Nathan A. Haverstock

See also **Latin America.**

Vermont. See State government.

Vice President of the United States. See United States, Government of the.

Vietnam. The ruling Communist Party in August 2004 began probing into allegations of corruption in government ministries. Several ministers were forced to resign in late 2004 after being accused of corruption. On October 25, Prime Minister Phan Van Khai announced the creation of an anticorruption agency, which was expected to investigate government operations in major Vietnamese cities and produce a report by early 2005.

Rapid economic growth in recent years led Vietnam to seek membership in the World Trade Organization (WTO), an international organization that promotes trade in goods and services among nations. Officials from Vietnam met with representatives of WTO member nations in 2004. Vietnam's booming garment industry was hampered by U.S. tariffs. WTO membership would free it of these quotas.

Demonstrations on Easter, April 18, by ethnic minorities of the Christian faith in Vietnam's central highlands resulted in dozens of people being injured. The demonstrators protested religious repression in the predominantly Buddhist nation and the confiscation of their land to benefit Vietnamese migrants into the highlands. Similar disturbances occurred in 2001.   ■ Henry S. Bradsher

See also **Asia.**

Virginia. See State government.

Vital statistics. See Census; Population.

The National World War II Memorial, with the Lincoln Memorial in the background, opens on April 29, 2004, with thousands of veterans in attendance. The memorial pays tribute to the millions of U.S. men and women who served during World War II (1939-1945).

Washington, D.C. Clifford B. Janey became the District of Columbia's fifth superintendent of schools in a decade on Sept. 15, 2004. He took the chief post at the school system, which has about 65,000 students, after a committee, which included Washington Mayor Anthony A. Williams, conducted a search for a new superintendent during the summer.

Janey had been a vice president at Scholastic Inc., an educational publishing company based in New York City. He also had served as superintendent of schools in Rochester, New York. In Washington, D.C., Janey took over a public school system at which standardized test scores were among the nation's lowest. The district did not have a coordinated curriculum, and Janey said he would work on a curriculum plan and a method of assessing student performance under systemwide standards. He was hired at an annual salary of $250,000.

The National World War II Memorial, honoring the millions of Americans who served in the United States armed forces during World War II (1939-1945), opened to the public on April 29. It is located between the Lincoln Memorial and the Washington Monument.

The $172-million memorial, designed by the Austrian-born American architect Friedrich St. Florian, is the first national monument to acknowledge the participation of all who served during the war as well as those who helped the war effort at home. The neoclassical memorial is centered around a sunken pool surrounded by a granite plaza. The plaza features two large arches, representing the two theaters of war (Europe and northern Africa, and Asia and the Pacific), and 56 piers, representing the 56 U.S. states and territories at the time of the war.

New museum. The Smithsonian Institution opened a new museum, the National Museum of the American Indian, on September 21. The curving structure was built at a cost of over $200 million on the last available piece of land on the National Mall, the parkway between the Capitol and the Washington Monument. Visitors from more than 400 tribes attended opening ceremonies.

Baseball to return to Washington. Baseball fans in the nation's capital experienced shifting hopes in 2004. Mayor Williams announced on September 29 that the Montreal Expos would move to Washington in time for the 2005 Major League season. However, Williams said on Dec. 15, 2004, that the deal was "close to dying" after initial cost estimates ballooned. Finally, on December 21, the city council approved a compromise reached by Williams, the council, and baseball officials that will allow for private financing for a new baseball stadium. However, if private financing is not found, the deal will not fall through. The city will split the cost of any overruns with Major League Baseball.

The new stadium is to be located in the southeast part of the city, near the Anacostia River. Plans call for the team, renamed the Washington Nationals, to play for three years at Robert F. Kennedy (RFK) Memorial Stadium, also in Washington, until the new stadium is completed. District of Columbia officials took bids for $13 million in renovations to RFK Stadium, in order to make it fit for Major League Baseball. Private funding for the stadium, local roads and infrastructure, and refurbishment of RFK Stadium is expected to reach $435 million.

Budget approved. Congress approved an $8.3-billion budget for the District of Columbia on Oct. 6, 2004. The budget provides the money to run both the district and the city of Washington. The 2005 budget increases by almost $9 million funds that helps the city's college students pay their tuition, provided they go to public colleges and universities that participate in the program. The increase brings the program's funding to about $26 million.   ■ Howard S. Shapiro

See also **Architecture; Indian, American.**

Washington. See **State government.**

Water. See **Environmental pollution.**

Weather. The year 2004 brought one of the coolest summers on record to the interior United States, as well as record numbers of hurricanes, typhoons, and other tropical cyclones around the world.

The year began with cold and snowy weather across the Pacific Northwest. A winter storm on January 6 and 7 brought an unaccustomed accumulation of snow and freezing rain to western Oregon and Washington state. Frigid air spread over the Northeast at midmonth. In Boston, the temperature fell to -7 °F (-21 °C) on January 16, the city's coldest day since 1980. A southward dip of the jet stream led to the Northeast having its 11th coldest January since 1895, with Massachusetts experiencing its coldest January on record.

Persistent chill and several snowfalls led to a deep covering of snow across the Northern Plains. Glasgow, Montana, had its greatest snow on record with 29 inches (74 centimeters) on Feb. 11, 2004. Winds of 70 miles (113 kilometers) per hour created 20-foot (6-meter) drifts in North Dakota, interrupting rail service in the Northern Plains.

Spring tornadoes. On March 4, two dozen tornadoes cut across Texas, Oklahoma, and Arkansas. The nation's first tornado-related fatalities occurred on April 20 when a twister packing winds over 150 miles (241 kilometers) per hour tore through North Utica, Illinois, killing eight people.

More than 500 tornadoes touched down in the United States in May, making it the second most prolific month for tornadoes on record.

Record heat and rain. March 2004 was one of the hottest on record in the West. More than 1,000 daily record highs were set, while at least a dozen cities observed their highest March temperature on record, including Las Vegas, Nevada (92 °F [33 °C]), and Seattle, Washington (78 °F [26 °C]). Frequent rains left conditions unusually wet in the Midwest and the Ohio Valley in May. Cities with record May rain totals included Detroit (8.46 inches [21.5 centimeters]) and Lexington, Kentucky (10.91 inches [27.7 centimeters]). In parts of the interior West and Plains, May was very dry.

Summer chill. The summer was one of the coolest on record in the Plains, Midwest, and Ohio Valley. Unseasonably cool air poured south from Canada in late June, causing more than 70 records to fall. Kansas City, Missouri, set three daily record lows in four days with 55 °F (13 °C), 53 °F (12 °C), and 52 °F (11 °C), on June 23, 25, and 26, respectively. Another cool air mass poured into the central states in late July, setting monthly records for daytime chill. On July 25, temperatures were the lowest on record for the month of July in St. Louis, Missouri (66 °F, 19 °C) and Lubbock, Texas (64 °F, 18 °C). The summer chill persisted into late summer, with Minnesota recording its coldest August since record keeping began in 1895.

Alaskan record highs and wildfires. Unprecedented heat hit Alaska in summer 2004. The cities of Fairbanks, Juneau, Anchorage, Nome, and Valdez each had their hottest summers of record. The state-wide average temperature was the warmest on record in every month from May through August. By the end of the summer, Juneau had 12 days with a temperature of 80 °F (27 °C) or higher, shattering the old record of 7 days set in 1951. The heat set the stage for Alaska's worst fire season. More than 6 million acres (2.4 hectares) of land had burned through August 2004, breaking the old record of 5 million acres (2.0 hectares) set in 1957. Wildfires in the contiguous states had burned just 1.2 million acres (0.5 hectares) through late September 2004, about 1 million acres (0.4 hectares) less than average.

Hurricanes, typhoons, and other tropical cyclones set records and led to widespread loss of life and property across the globe in 2004. Born in the tropical oceans, hurricanes, typhoons, and cyclones are essentially the same weather system but with different names in different parts of the world.

A hurricane developed in late March in the South Atlantic Ocean, where such storms are rare. The storm made landfall a day later in southern Brazil with estimated winds of 80 miles (129 kilometers) per hour. The hurricane was the first in the South Atlantic basin since satellite images of

Hurricane Ivan rolls toward the Gulf of Mexico in a satellite image (above) captured September 13. Ivan came ashore at Gulf Shores, Alabama, on September 16, slammed into Florida, and then caused extensive flooding to the East Coast.

A resident of Vero Beach, on Florida's eastern coast, paddles down a street as Hurricane Frances makes landfall on September 5 with winds of 105 miles (169 kilometers) per hour. Remnants of the storm flooded areas from Georgia to New York state.

Four highly destructive hurricanes—Charley, Frances, Ivan, and Jeanne—slammed into Florida in 2004.

A volunteer checks the damage to Peace River Church of Christ in Punta Gorda, Florida, on August 22. Hurricane Charley made landfall in the area, just north of Fort Myers, on August 13, with winds of 145 miles (233 kilometers) per hour. By late 2004, insurance claims of $14 billion had made Charley second only to Hurricane Andrew in 1992 as the most costly act of nature in the United States.

the region first began to be taken in 1966.

Ten typhoons swept across Japan in 2004, the highest number since record keeping began in 1951. Japanese airlines estimated total losses of typhoon-related flight disruptions in 2004 at more than $45 million.

In the Atlantic, an unnamed tropical disturbance stalled near the island of Hispaniola from May 18 to May 25 bringing torrential rain. Rainfall amounts of 20 inches (51 centimeters) near the border of Haiti and the Dominican Republic led to catastrophic flooding that was blamed for some 3,300 deaths.

Hurricane Charley. During August, eight tropical storms and hurricanes formed over the Atlantic Ocean, more than in any August on record. Hurricane Charley was the most intense. The storm became a hurricane on August 11 in the western Caribbean before turning north across western Cuba. Charley slammed into Florida just north of Fort Myers on August 13 with central winds estimated at 145 miles (233 kilometers) per hour. As it weakened, the storm tore across the peninsula, emerging near Daytona Beach eight hours later. Thirty-two deaths were blamed on the storm, and more than 2 million people lost power. Insurance claims of $14 billion made Hurricane Charley second only to Hurricane Andrew in 1992 as the most costly act of nature in the United States.

Hurricane Frances. In September 2004, three more hurricanes went on a rampage from the western Atlantic to the eastern United States. Hurricane Frances passed over the Turks and Caicos Islands with winds of 140 miles (225 kilometers) per hour on September 1. The storm crossed the central Bahamas and then weakened before hitting the Florida coast north of Palm Beach on September 5 with winds of 105 miles (169 kilometers) per hour. Remnants of the storm moved north, flooding areas from Georgia to New York state.

Hurricane Ivan intensified rapidly on September 5, becoming the most powerful hurricane on record so far south in the North Atlantic Ocean. Two days later, the storm devastated Grenada, damaging more than 90 percent of all buildings. Ivan went on to lash Jamaica with wind and flooding rain and then ravaged Grand Cayman Island before turning north. Waves up to 50 feet (15 meters) were recorded when the storm reached the central Gulf of Mexico. Ivan came ashore at Gulf Shores, Alabama, on September 16 with central winds of 130 miles (209 kilometers) per hour. The storm then slammed Florida and brought extensive flooding as it moved to the East Coast.

Hurricane Jeanne swiped Puerto Rico on September 15, cutting electrical power for most of the island's 4 million residents. The storm then triggered a second flooding disaster in Haiti, when excessive rain left more than 2,000 people dead.

On September 26, Jeanne made landfall in Florida at nearly the same spot as Hurricane Frances with winds of 120 miles (195 kilometers) per hour.

After the hurricanes. Flooding from the remnants of Hurricane Jeanne contributed to the wettest September on record in the Southeast United States. In addition, several of the hurricanes generated tornadoes. In August, the U.S. Department of Commerce Storm Prediction Center counted 173 tornadoes, breaking the 1979 record of 126. In September 2004, the center reported 247 twisters, surpassing the 1967 record of 139.

All told, insurance analysts estimated the damages from the four hurricanes that struck the United States in 2004 at $42 billion. Losses from the hurricane season of 1992—previously the most costly on record—totaled $20.3 billion.

In the West. A series of Pacific storms crossed the West Coast in October 2004, causing California to have one of its earliest starts to its rainy season. Both San Diego and Los Angeles had their wettest Octobers on record with 3.78 and 4.98 inches (9.6 and 12.6 centimeters) of rain measured, respectively. Across the Southwest, October was the wettest since record keeping began in 1895.

■ Fred Gadomski and Todd Miner

See also **Disasters; Haiti: A Special Report; Japan.**

Weightlifting. See Sports.

Welfare.
The number of people receiving benefits under the Temporary Assistance for Needy Families (TANF) program declined for the seventh consecutive year, Tommy G. Thompson, secretary of the U.S. Department of Health and Human Services (HHS), said in August 2004. TANF is a welfare program that provides cash assistance and helps with child care for low-income workers and the unemployed. Thompson said that enrollment in the program fell 3 percent in 2003, and the number of families in the program fell 1.8 percent. In December 2003, 4,864,905 individuals and 2,008,233 families received TANF benefits.

Children and working parents. The HHS's Administration for Children and Families released a report on March 5, 2004, showing that increases in adult employment as a result of welfare reform had either neutral or positive effects on the lives of school-age children. The HHS report analyzed studies in five states conducted between 1993 and 2000. HHS officials reviewed the studies for childrens' academic performance, social and emotional adjustment, and health and safety and concluded that having working parents did not adversely affect the children.

Child abuse and neglect. HHS officials on April 1, 2004, released a report revealing that approximately 896,000 children in the United States were the victims of abuse or neglect in

2002. Statistically, approximately 12.3 out of every 1,000 children suffered abuse or neglect, a slight decline from 2001 when 12.4 out of every 1,000 children had been victimized. The statistics were culled from information collected through the National Child Abuse and Neglect Data System.

According to HHS officials, child protective service agencies received approximately 2.6 million reports of possible abuse or neglect in 2002, of which 896,000 cases were substantiated. Approximately 1,400 children died of abuse or neglect in 2002, or 1.98 children for every 100,000 children in the U.S. population, HHS officials reported.

Food stamp program. Ann M. Veneman, secretary of the Department of Agriculture, announced changes in June 2004 to the Food Stamp Program, a U.S. government plan to help low-income households buy more and better food than they normally could afford. The program serves people receiving welfare aid and others with low incomes. The change involved replacing paper coupons, issued based on a household's income and size, with electronic benefit transfer (EBT) cards. Households use the EBT cards, which resemble credit cards, to make their food purchases. Funds are electronically transferred to the grocer from a special account established for each family. ■ Geoffrey A. Campbell

West Indies. The worst hurricane season since the 1950's caused death and destruction throughout the Caribbean in 2004. One of the worst-hit countries was Grenada, where Hurricane Ivan damaged or destroyed an estimated 90 percent of the island's businesses and residences in early September. In October, United States President George W. Bush requested that the U.S. Congress provide an additional $50 million for Caribbean relief, bringing the total pledged to the region to $113.3 million.

Dominican elections. On August 16, Leonel Fernandez Reyna, of the Dominican Liberation Party, was sworn to his second four-year term as president of the Dominican Republic. Fernandez, who had presided over a robust economy during his first term (1996–2000), faced daunting challenges. United States companies, which owned the country's power utilities, claimed they were owed $300 million in unpaid bills—most of it by the Dominican government. The companies shut off power several times in 2004.

The incoming Dominican administration blamed the country's financial woes on the previous administration, which had drained the treasury to bail out mostly wealthy depositors affected by scandal-ridden bank collapses. For example, the 2003 bailout of Banco Intercontinental, the Dominican Republic's second largest

bank, cost taxpayers an estimated $2.2 billion—the equivalent of nearly 70 percent of the annual national budget.

Natural gas boom. Trinidad and Tobago continued to experience a surge in economic activity in 2004. The country, which was the Western Hemisphere's leading supplier of liquefied natural gas, profited from sharply rising demand. The price of natural gas increased from $2 per thousand cubic feet in 1999 to $7 per thousand cubic feet in 2004.

Natural gas earnings spawned the construction of an array of chemical facilities in Trinidad and Tobago, including nine ammonia plants, an iron and steel complex, and two of the world's largest methanol plants. In October, the government proposed a budget aimed at channeling a sizeable portion of energy revenues into social programs. The budget also boosted retirement pensions by 10 percent. ■ Nathan A. Haverstock

See also **Haiti: A Special Report; Latin America.**

West Virginia. See State government.

Wisconsin. See State government.

Wyoming. See State government.

Yugoslavia. See Serbia and Montenegro.

Yukon Territory. See Canadian territories.

Zambia. See Africa.

Zimbabwe. The political and economic climate in Zimbabwe continued to deteriorate in 2004, as President Robert Mugabe's ruling Zimbabwe African National Union-Patriotic Front (ZANU-PF) prepared for parliamentary elections scheduled for March 2005. Mugabe's victory in the 2002 presidential polls and his party's win in the 2000 parliamentary elections had been widely condemned by international observers who alleged state-sponsored fraud and violence.

On Sept. 8, 2004, a state-run newspaper published a ZANU-PF-sponsored plan to have President Mugabe appoint every member of a commission that would oversee the upcoming election. In response, officials of the opposition Movement for Democratic Change (MDC) accused ZANU-PF of preparing to rig the 2005 vote.

Sanctions renewed. On Feb. 19, 2004, the European Union extended for one year "targeted" sanctions against Mugabe and other ZANU-PF leaders. The sanctions were originally introduced in 2002.

Food crisis. A June 2004 report by the Food and Agriculture Organization of the United Nations forecast that Zimbabwe's food shortfall in 2004 would be greater than in 2003, when donors provided emergency food aid to more than 40 percent of Zimbabwe's population. President Mugabe responded with a claim that the country's farmers would produce a bumper crop and that food aid would not be needed. However, a number of independent observers rejected that claim.

According to agriculture experts, the food shortages resulted from the eviction since 1999 of 4,000 white farmers from the country's most productive commercial farms. Mugabe critics alleged that most of the farms went to elite ZANU-PF officials rather than to landless farm workers to whom they had been promised.

Treason trial. On Oct. 16, 2004, MDC opposition leader Morgan Tsvangirai was acquitted of treason for allegedly planning to assassinate President Mugabe in 2002. Tsvangirai still faced a second treason charge for organizing a mass antigovernment strike in June 2003.

Mercenary trial. On Sept. 10, 2004, in Harare, the capital, Simon Mann, a former British special forces officer, was sentenced to seven years in prison at the conclusion of a trial that attracted international attention. According to prosecutors, Mann led a group of mercenaries who tried to buy arms in Zimbabwe for use in a plot to overthrow President Teodoro Mbasogo of Equatorial Guinea. Most of Mann's associates received lighter sentences.   ■ Simon Baynham

See also **Africa**.

Zoology. See Biology.

Zoos. Blockbuster exhibits—spectacular displays of animals in surroundings resembling elaborate movie sets—grew in popularity in 2004. Although it is not unusual for famous zoos in the United States to create such exhibits, lesser-known zoos were also getting into the act.

Big cats. "Range of the Jaguar" opened in March at the Jacksonville (Florida) Zoo. The exhibit housed four jaguars, though zoo officials said that eventually a dozen jaguars would live there.

Spanning 4.5 acres (1.8 hectares), the exhibit simulates forest habitat in Central and South America. Besides jaguars, the exhibit contains more than 100 kinds of animals native to the area. Looming over the jungle floor is the "Lost Temple," depicting ruins of an ancient Native American civilization through which the jaguars roam. Visitors can see vampire bats, anacondas, and bird-eating tarantulas.

Outside, in an area called "River's Edge," reside howler monkeys, giant anteaters, and capybaras, rodents as large as a pig. Visitors can enter an *aviary* (bird enclosure) called the "Emerald Forest" in which they are surrounded by free-flying birds, such as Inca doves and red-capped cardinals.

In July, "Asian Forest Sanctuary" opened at the Point Defiance Zoo & Aquarium in Tacoma, Washington. The exhibit covers 5 acres (2 hectares) and is set in a landscape with waterfalls, a pond, a stream, and a bamboo forest. Throughout the exhibit roam

Sumatran tigers, Malayan tapir, tragopan pheasants, and anoa, a kind of small buffalo.

African landscapes. The Henry Doorly Zoo in Omaha, Nebraska, opened "Hubbard Gorilla Valley" in April. The 3-acre (1.2-hectare) exhibit featured six gorillas in a tree-dotted, grassy "valley." An indoor area enables visitors to view gorillas, often only inches away, separated by a glass wall. During warm weather, the gorillas are outside. Visitors walk among the gorillas in the outside area via a glass-lined tunnel leading to two clear domes.

In June, the Denver (Colorado) Zoo opened "Predator Ridge," an exhibit based on the savannas of Kenya's Samburu National Reserve. Fifty animals from 14 African species—including African porcupines, spotted hyenas, and guinea fowl—inhabit the exhibit. The stars of the show are two lion *prides* (groups) and a pack of African wild dogs. Although separated from one another, the animals appear to roam the same landscape.

Birds were featured in exhibits opened by many zoos in 2004. "Eagle Canyon," with a rushing stream, pools, and waterfall debuted in May at the Oregon Zoo in Portland. Within the 20,800-square-foot (6,300-square-meter) exhibit, visitors walk through a forest of Douglas fir trees, where two bald eagles fly freely.

Parrots were in the limelight at the Queens Zoo in New York City and the Fort Worth (Texas) Zoo. In July, officials at the Queens Zoo opened an exhibit for thick-billed parrots, which are an endangered species. The exhibit takes visitors to the pine forests of Mexico's Sierra Madre Mountains, where many of the remaining birds live.

"Parrot Paradise" opened in June at the Fort Worth Zoo. People can mingle with more than 600 parrots from 6 *species* (kinds) within the large aviary. The birds are trained to swoop down to people and feed from their hands.

Shark news. The awe and fascination people hold for sharks provided the basis for an exhibit that opened in April at the Monterey Bay Aquarium in Monterey, California. "Sharks: Myth and Mystery" combines more than 20 species of sharks and rays in various displays, including a 20,000-gallon (75,700-liter) tropical reef exhibit and a 3,500-gallon (13,250-liter) tank for freshwater rays. The exhibit, scheduled to run through 2006, explored how cultures around the world view sharks.

Sharks made news at Monterey Bay in September 2004 when officials placed a young great white shark on exhibit, the only great white on exhibit in the United States. None of the species had ever been displayed for more than 16 days. Fishermen accidentally caught the 4-foot (1.2-meter) female shark in a fishing net off the coast of southern California in August. Zoo officials hoped to study the shark to learn more about shark behavior.

■ Edward Ricciuti

WORLD BOOK SUPPLEMENT

Eight new or revised articles are reprinted from the 2005 edition of *The World Book Encyclopedia.*

© Rudi Von Briel, PhotoEdit

A flower garden can beautify many different environments. City parks often include colorful flower gardens. This garden grows in a New York City neighborhood called the Lower East Side.

Gardening

Gardening is the growing and care of plants, usually as a hobby. People garden for many reasons. Most do so to provide flowers, vegetables, and other plant products for their own use. Other people garden to beautify their surroundings. Still others use gardening to reduce stress or even to help treat illness.

Gardening ranks as the most popular outdoor activity in much of the world. Many people who begin gardening as a hobby end up pursuing it in a more professional manner. They may decide to sell surplus plants or produce, or develop new varieties of plants. Many fully professional gardeners work for *botanical gardens,* which specialize in cultivating plants for artistic, educational, or scientific purposes. Others may work as *landscape architects,* designing and developing yards, gardens, parks, and other land areas. The profession of gardening belongs to a larger field called *horticulture.* Horticulture is a branch of agriculture specializing in fruits, vegetables, flowers, shrubs, and trees.

Traditionally, new gardeners learned from their parents or from experienced gardeners. Other gardening resources included books and magazines, garden supply companies, government agencies, and gardening programs on radio and television. All of these resources still exist, but computers and the Internet have enabled them to reach many more gardeners worldwide.

People divide gardens into two broad categories—outdoor gardens and indoor gardens. This article will describe both types and discuss how to plan, prepare, and care for them.

Shepherd Ogden, the contributor of this article, is a gardening consultant and the author of Step by Step Organic Flower Gardening *and* Step by Step Organic Vegetable Gardening.

Kinds of outdoor gardens

Outdoor gardens consist of two basic kinds: ornamental gardens and production gardens. Ornamental gardens exist purely to enhance the beauty of the landscape. Production gardens provide some sort of harvest for the gardener, including flowers, fruits, herbs, and vegetables. Some gardeners develop a combination of ornamental and production gardens.

Ornamental gardens. Growers of ornamental gardens may either place their plants in the open ground or in containers. More elaborate gardens, such as rock gardens or water gardens, may feature specially constructed environments for unusual plants. While most ornamental gardens feature flowers, some concentrate on displaying grasses, trees, or shrubs.

Flower gardens may be formal or informal. Some types, including cutting gardens, use elements of both. Formal flower gardens consist of relatively few types of plants, uniformly spaced in patterns as part of a clear design. Within the flower beds, all plants of a given type should grow to nearly the same height and width. These beds require significant effort to prepare and maintain the desired effect.

Informal flower gardens, sometimes called *cottage gardens,* have a natural, irregular shape. Such gardens prove much easier to develop and maintain than do formal gardens. Cottage gardens often include a wide variety of plants, either purposely arranged for a particular effect or chosen and planted randomly.

Wildflower gardens rank among the more popular informal gardens. They consist of plant species native to the area in which the garden is grown. Some wildflower gardens simply allow plants to spread on their own as they would in the wild.

Specialty gardens. Popular types of specialty gardens include rock gardens, water gardens, shade gardens, and water-conserving *Xeriscaped* gardens (pronounced *ZIHR uh skaypt).*

Rock gardens consist of plants grown among a natural or artificial outcropping of rocks. Gardeners cultivate the plants in crevices or pockets of soil or *scree* (gravelly areas) between the rocks. Such gardens create a good habitat for growing plants from high mountainous regions or other remote areas.

Water gardens re-create wetland habitats with plants native to those areas. They usually require a pool or pond with at least moderate water flow, and they may include ornamental fish or other animals. Both rock gardens and water gardens may demand much time and expense to build and maintain.

For shade gardens, people generally choose areas surrounded by mature trees or closely spaced buildings, which limit the amount of sunlight. Many attractive plants thrive in the shade, especially those with small flowers that do not show well in bright sun, or those with patterned or textured foliage. Many woodland wildflowers also grow well in shade gardens.

Gardeners developed a technique called *Xeriscaping* in the 1980's to help conserve water. This technique has become especially popular in drier regions. A Xeriscaped garden groups together wildflowers, grasses, and other plants that can easily adapt to their region's climate. It also uses water-saving irrigation techniques, *mulches* (coverings that help to prevent weeds from growing and keep the soil from losing moisture), and other procedures to conserve resources.

Container gardens. Gardeners without direct access to the land can grow plants in containers. Many city dwellers, for

Some popular garden vegetables

Vegetable	Earliest planting time	Space between plants	Weeks until harvest	Yield per 10-foot (3-meter) row
Beets	Early spring	1 in (2.5 cm)	8 to 9	5 lbs (2.3 kg)
Bush snap beans	Early spring	3 in (7.5 cm)	8	5 lbs (2.3 kg)
Carrots	Early spring	2 in (5 cm)	8 to 12	5 $\frac{1}{2}$ lbs (2.5 kg)
Leaf lettuce	Early spring	6 to 8 in (15 to 20 cm)	6 to 7	2 lbs (0.9 kg)
Onion sets	Spring	2 to 4 in (5 to 10 cm)	14	10 lbs (4.5 kg)
Radishes	Early spring	4 to 6 in (10 to 15 cm)	4 to 8	5 lbs (2.3 kg)
Spinach	Early spring	3 in (7.5 cm)	6	3 lbs (1.4 kg)
Swiss chard	Early spring	4 in (10 cm)	8	8 $\frac{1}{2}$ lbs (3.9 kg)
Tomato plants (staked)	Late spring	2 to 3 ft (61 to 91 cm)	8 to 12	8 lbs (3.6 kg) per plant

A vegetable garden plan

The garden plan below shows some popular high-yield vegetables in a small plot. It provides enough growing space for each plant. It also provides for *succession planting,* in which one crop is harvested and then followed by the planting of another.

WORLD BOOK illustrations by Jean Helmer

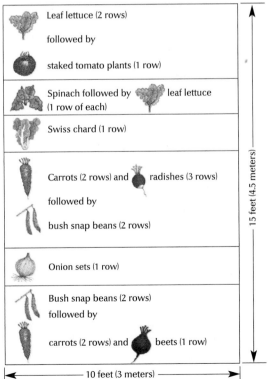

Leaf lettuce (2 rows)

followed by

staked tomato plants (1 row)

Spinach followed by leaf lettuce (1 row of each)

Swiss chard (1 row)

Carrots (2 rows) and radishes (3 rows)

followed by

bush snap beans (2 rows)

Onion sets (1 row)

Bush snap beans (2 rows)

followed by

carrots (2 rows) and beets (1 row)

15 feet (4.5 meters)

10 feet (3 meters)

example, grow container gardens on rooftops. Container gardens also provide a good choice for plants that do not grow well in the local soil or climate. Movable containers enable gardeners to place plants in the most desirable locations at different times of the day or growing season, thus extending the plants' lives. Especially popular container gardens consist of hanging baskets of ivy or other draping plants, used to beautify the exteriors of buildings.

Production gardens are grown chiefly for what people can harvest from them. They include cutting gardens, herb gardens, and kitchen gardens.

Cutting gardens, or *bouquet gardens,* produce flowers for floral arrangements. Such gardens usually contain many different plants of different ages, so the gardener always has plant material available.

Herb gardens provide herbs for cooking, medicine, and craftwork. Some herbs serve as ornamental plants as well. Herbs may also form part of a formal or informal flower garden, or gardeners may simply grow them in containers.

Kitchen gardens arguably rank as the oldest form of gardening. The practice of horticulture arose out of the need to produce food. Kitchen gardens range widely in style, with some having a highly ornamental appearance. Yet all exist primarily to produce plants for food.

Preparing an outdoor garden

The most popular outdoor gardens are informal flower gardens and kitchen gardens. A gardener can purchase everything necessary to start a garden from a nursery or garden supply company. Preparing a garden involves selecting a site, analyzing the soil, making a plan, and choosing the plants.

Choosing the site. In *temperate* regions, which have warm summers and cool or cold winters, gardeners often create flower gardens at the edges of lawns, preferring not to break up their lawn's grassy area. A good location will provide at least eight hours of sun a day. In hot, dry regions, flower garden sites should receive shade at midday. Kitchen gardens should lie near the house for convenient harvesting of crops. Gardeners usually place flower gardens and kitchen gardens on level or gently sloping ground. Steeply sloped ground should be *terraced* to keep soil from eroding. Terracing involves cutting level strips of land out of the slope.

To plan a garden for a shady lot, track where the patches of sun occur each day. Using stakes and string, outline the patches of sun at 8 a.m., at noon, and again at 4 p.m. Areas that receive sun at all three times will prove best for growing vegetables and any flowers described as needing "full sun." Areas that receive sun at two of the three periods will support plants that need "part sun" or "part shade." For areas that receive less sun, cultivate shade-loving plants.

Analyzing the soil. Good garden soil contains an ideal balance of mineral material, water, air, and *organic matter* (decaying plant and animal material). You should make certain that your garden site becomes neither too dry nor too wet. Drier soil usually proves better for gardening because it needs only irrigation. Areas where water collects after rain generally do not make good garden sites unless you create paths for excess water to drain away. To test if a site is too wet for a garden, dig a small hole about 1 foot (30 centimeters) deep, fill it with water, and see how long the hole takes to drain. If it takes more than a day, the soil in that spot will not suit most kinds of gardens.

Some popular garden flowers

Flowers that bloom in spring

Tall varieties	Light needs
Day lily*	Full sun and partial shade
Gladiolus*	Full sun
Iris	Full sun
Lupine	Full sun or partial shade
Peony	Full sun or partial shade

Medium varieties	
Aster*	Full sun
Columbine	Full sun or partial shade
Daffodil	Full sun or partial shade
Day lily*	Full sun and partial shade
Poppy*	Full sun
Tulip	Full sun or partial shade

Short varieties	
Amaryllis	Partial shade
Columbine	Full sun or partial shade
Crocus	Full sun or partial shade
Daisy*	Full sun or partial shade
Forget-me-not*	Partial shade
Hyacinth	Full sun
Iris	Full sun
Lily of the valley*	Partial shade
Pansy	Full sun or partial shade

*Blooms in all three seasons.

Flowers that bloom in summer

Tall varieties	Light needs
Clematis	Full sun or partial shade
Dahlia	Full sun
Foxglove	Full sun or partial shade
Hollyhock	Full sun
Phlox	Full sun or partial shade
Snapdragon	Full sun

Medium varieties	
Bachelor's-button	Full sun
Chrysanthemum	Full sun
Coleus	Full sun or partial shade
Coreopsis	Full sun
Phlox	Full sun or partial shade
Sage	Full sun or partial shade
Zinnia	Full sun

Short varieties	
Ageratum	Full sun
Carnation	Full sun
Lobelia	Full sun
Marigold	Full sun
Pansy	Full sun or partial shade
Petunia	Full sun or partial shade
Portulaca	Full sun
Wallflower	Partial shade

Flowers that bloom in fall

Tall varieties	Light needs
Aconite	Full sun or partial shade
Babies'-breath	Full sun
Chrysanthemum	Full sun
Clematis	Full sun or partial shade
Dahlia	Full sun
Hollyhock	Full sun
Larkspur	Full sun

Medium varieties	
Anemone	Partial shade
Canna	Full sun
Chrysanthemum	Full sun
Dahlia	Full sun
Daisy	Full sun
Lily	Partial shade

Short varieties	
Adonis	Full sun or partial shade
Allwood's pink	Full sun
Begonia	Partial shade
Carnation	Full sun
Cockscomb	Full sun
Crocus	Full sun or partial shade
Lily	Full sun
Petunia	Full sun or partial shade
Plumbago	Full sun or partial shade
Sage	Full sun or partial shade

How to plan a flower garden

A flower garden plan should take into account the height and blooming season of each plant. In the plan below, tall plants grow at the back of the garden and shorter ones in the front. Selecting flowers that bloom in different seasons creates a garden that will remain colorful most of the year.

WORLD BOOK illustration by Wendy Bramall, Wildlife Art Ltd.

Spring blooms   Summer blooms   Fall blooms

Hollyhock   Dahlia   Iris   Zinnia   Chrysanthemum   Day lily   Marigold   Pansy   Daisy

Adding organic matter can improve soil structure, thus correcting problems with soil moisture. Organic matter makes heavy clay soils drain better and helps dry, sandy soils hold moisture long enough for roots to absorb the water. During bed preparation, gardeners work into the soil such organic matter as finely chopped leaves, peat moss, or *spoiled hay* (hay that has become moldy or unfit for livestock feed). *Compost,* a mixture of decaying leaves and other plant material, is an especially good soil additive. Gardeners can make their own compost by layering garden wastes in a heap, with or without manure, and then allowing them to decay for several months.

Plants will not thrive without certain *nutrients,* chemical substances in the soil that are necessary for growth. The most important of these are nitrogen, phosphorus, and potassium. In the spring, if normally green plants have yellowish, purple, or bronze coloring at the leaf edges, the soil likely provides too little of one or more of these nutrients. Gardeners must then add fertilizer.

The amounts of *acid* and *alkali* chemicals in a soil also influence how well plants can grow there. Highly acidic or alkaline soils can harm many plants. An ideal gardening site should have neutral to slightly acidic soil. To make a soil less acidic, add lime. To make a soil less alkaline, add sulfur and organic matter at the same time.

You can determine the chemical makeup of your soil by asking other experienced gardeners or by using soil-testing kits. You can buy testing kits, with instructions on how to take a soil sample, at most garden centers. Such government agencies as county extension agents also provide kits. The test results returned to you will include a discussion of the acid and nutrient levels in your soil, and instructions for adding fertilizer if necessary.

Fertilizing. Gardeners use two basic types of fertilizers, synthetic fertilizers and natural fertilizers, such as animal manure. Synthetic fertilizers generally have higher levels of nitrogen, phosphorus, and potassium. But they release these nutrients quickly, and you must reapply them throughout the season. Be careful not to use too much highly concentrated artificial fertilizer because an overdose of nutrients can harm both soil and plants.

Natural fertilizers release nutrients over a much longer period, requiring less reapplication. Such fertilizers also provide organic matter that synthetic fertilizers do not. Compost provides some natural fertilizer in addition to improving the texture of the soil. Do not fertilize with fresh manure because it may contain disease-causing organisms.

Planning an informal flower garden. Many of the most beautiful informal flower gardens display subtle variation among the plants, both within the bed and over the course of the season. If possible, the beds should measure at least 4 feet (1.2 meters) across at the widest point. *Island beds,* surrounded by open space, should measure twice that width. Such lengths create enough space to achieve a progression from shorter plants to taller plants. For beds planted against a fence or wall, shorter plants should grow in front with taller ones behind. For island beds, shorter plants grow at the edges with taller ones in the center.

To create a pleasing design, always plant in clusters to avoid spacing the plants equally across the bed. Try also to achieve variation from side to side as well as from front to back. Finally, use gray-leaved or white-flowered plants to separate areas of colors that might clash visually if placed too close together.

Flower garden plants consist of (1) *annuals,* which live one year or less; (2) *biennials,* which live about two years; and (3) *perennials,* which live longer than two years. Annuals, such as marigolds and petunias, flower for an extended period. Biennials, such as hollyhocks and foxgloves, spend their first year growing and bloom for up to a month in their second season. Many flowers belong to the perennial group, including daffodils, lilies, and roses. Many perennials also do not bloom until their second year. But under good conditions, they will rebloom for a few weeks each season for many years.

Planting flowers that bloom in different seasons makes it possible for a garden to remain at least partly in bloom for most or all of the year. By planting a mixture of annuals, biennials, and perennials, the gardener need only replant certain parts of the garden each year.

Planning a kitchen garden. Kitchen gardens generally have a rectangular shape that makes for more efficient care and maintenance. For big gardens, especially those greater than 5,000 square feet (465 square meters), plant in large rows. Most kitchen gardens, however, measure less than about 300 square feet (28 square meters). For these gardens, use a bed system of planting. In bed systems, permanent beds of plants are separated by paths covered with sod or a layer of straw, wood chips, or other mulch to prevent weeds.

To plan an efficient and attractive kitchen garden, first make a clear distinction between bed and path. You may enclose the beds with fencing or other material. Or you may cut clean lines in the sod to define the beds. Boxed, raised beds prove especially good if the soil drains poorly. Whenever possible, make your beds narrow and set the rows of plants across the beds, not along them. This arrangement will enable you to cultivate from the path without stepping into the beds.

Two fairly simple planting techniques will greatly increase the amount of food grown in the garden: *succession planting* and *interplanting.* Succession planting involves planting in the same spot different crops at different times of the year. For example, you could plant and harvest lettuce early in the growing year, and then tomatoes later on. Succession planting requires that you learn which plants grow best during which seasons, and how much time different crops will take to grow.

Interplanting involves planting certain crops together, usually in the same bed. Most interplanting uses two species that benefit when grown together. Two such crops are carrots and radishes. Carrots sprout slowly and need space to grow. You must laboriously remove some of the young carrots from the row so the remaining carrots will gain size. But if you sow radish seeds lightly in the same row as carrots, the radishes will sprout quickly, well before the carrots. When you harvest the radishes, you will thin the carrots at the same time because pulling the radishes will uproot a number of carrot seedlings. As a result, radish harvesting makes the subsequent carrot harvesting easier.

Many crops, including tomatoes and beans, come in both bush and vine varieties. By cultivating vines on supporting poles called *trellises,* you can grow larger plants and produce bigger yields. Trellised crops also have more resistance to certain diseases because they are exposed to more sunlight and better air circulation.

Some vegetables can grow directly from seed. These include such quick-growing crops as lettuce, beets, and squash. Others are best cultivated from seedlings, including such slower-growing crops as cabbages, tomatoes, and peppers. Onions and garlic grow from bulbs.

Cultivating an outdoor garden

To create an informal flower garden or kitchen garden, the basic equipment consists of a spade, garden fork, hoe, and rake; a wedge-shaped digging tool called a *trowel;* and watering equipment. You could also use a wheelbarrow or cart to move things.

Before preparing the soil, first remove any debris or stones. Then clear off any unwanted growing plants. If you have the time, lay black plastic covering over the area for two to four weeks to deprive the regrowing plants of light. This will weaken them and make soil preparation easier.

Preparing the soil. Use the spade to cut through the soil surface to define the edge of the planting bed. Then cut the area inside the bed into strips. Standing outside the bed, slip the spade under the edge of a strip, 1 to 2 inches (2.5 to 5 centimeters) down. Rock the spade on its handle to break the roots of the old plants from the soil beneath. Then roll up the strip or remove it in slabs. Repeat this process until the entire surface is clear.

At this point, make sure the soil is neither too wet nor too dry. Take a handful of soil and squeeze your hand into a fist. If, when you release your grip, the soil retains its shape but crumbles when you poke it with a finger, then it has an appropriate amount of moisture.

Use the garden fork to lift and loosen the top 8 to 12 inches (20 to 30 centimeters) of soil. Remove any unwanted root pieces or stones. Next add the fertilizer, compost, or other materials needed to enhance the soil. Use the back of the fork to break up and distribute these additional materials. Finally, rake the bed smooth.

Planting and transplanting. Methods of planting and transplanting remain essentially the same for both flower and vegetable gardens. For crops planted in rows, like carrots or beets, make a furrow with the trowel or hoe that is twice as deep as you want the seed to be. Then sprinkle the seed into the furrow. Use more seed than recommended to allow for seeds that may not come up. Then pull the soil back over the seed and pat it down so that the seed lies at the appropriate depth.

To plant onion, shallot, and garlic bulbs, push them into the ground until the pointed top lies slightly below the surface. With onions, use the entire bulb. With shallots and garlic, separate the sections, or *cloves,* and plant them individually. Each clove will then grow to become a full head of multiple cloves.

Flower bulbs and the roots of some perennials, such as peonies, must be planted at precisely the right depth to flower properly. Before measuring your plot, determine the ground level by placing a small board on the ground to even out any surface irregularities. Measure the depth from that board. For these and all other plantings, be sure to include a tag that indicates where each crop was planted and the date of planting.

Transplanting involves moving a young plant from a container to a place in the garden. When transplanting, dig a hole slightly larger than the root ball on the seedling. Then set the plant at the same depth that it lay in its pot and firm the soil around the plant's base. You may mix a handful of fertilizer with the soil. Water the soil around the base of the plant to settle the roots and help the plant adjust to its new environment. In dry weather, shelter the plant for that first day. A basket or box shelter will protect the plant from drying out and wilting.

Caring for the garden. Ongoing care of a garden consists primarily of feeding and watering your plants, keeping weeds out, and making sure that pests and diseases do not gain a foothold.

Water. Most plants need about 1 inch (2.5 centimeters) of water a week to grow well. To tell if an individual plant needs water, dig down with your hand and determine if the soil beneath the surface is wet. If you go more than 4 inches (10 centimeters) down without coming to moist soil, then you need to water. People most often water with sprinklers and *drip irrigation.*

Use sprinklers during the early morning in cool, humid weather and during the evening in hot, dry weather. By watering in the morning, you give the leaves a chance to dry off by evening. Leaf diseases often attack moist leaves at night. In dry weather, water evaporates before it has a chance to sink into the soil. Watering in the evening allows plants to absorb water overnight.

For drip irrigation, gardeners may set up a network of thin tubes supported by spikes that run alongside their plants' beds. Water flows through the tubes and slowly

Some helpful gardening hints

Many kinds of gardens require considerable preparation and attention to grow well. The five gardening hints illustrated here can help make planning, starting, and caring for a garden easier.

Erect a small fence to protect flower beds and borders from getting trampled.

Spread mulch over the soil to prevent weeds from growing and to keep the soil moist.

Pinch back the main stem to produce a bushier plant or a larger number of flowers.

Cut off the side buds to produce an exceptionally large flower on the main stem.

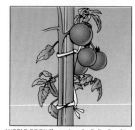

WORLD BOOK illustrations by Rolin Graphics

Tie the stem of a plant loosely when staking to protect the stem from injury.

drips from openings called *drip heads* or *emitters* that are spaced along the tubes. Drip irrigation wastes less water than sprinklers do. Some gardeners use soaker hoses that are perforated to allow water to trickle out along their length.

Weeds. Many weeds grow from seed. Try to pull such weeds before they flower. Other weeds, especially grasses, spread from underground roots. You must pull out the roots over and over. If possible, avoid chemical weed controls, which can harm the environment.

Pests. Such animals as deer, rabbits, voles, and woodchucks often present problems for home gardeners. Insects can also damage plants. Control such pests by keeping them away from plants or by making the plants less attractive to them. Fences and row covers exclude pests. Sprays of garlic or hot pepper juice on the plants will repel them. When using any spray, strictly follow the instructions on the label. If these methods fail, consider killing smaller pests as a last resort. Many pesticides kill pests either by infection or poisoning. See **Pest control.**

Disorders and diseases. Plant disorders occur because of improper growing conditions or poor weather. Diseases result from infection by another organism. At the first sign of deformity or discoloration, determine the problem quickly and seek a remedy. You may need to consult gardening books or local experts.

To prevent such problems from arising, choose varieties of plants resistant to the common disorders and diseases of your region. Seed packets and plant labels describe many such problems. Also make sure to irrigate properly so your plants do not stay continuously wet, which makes them susceptible to disease.

Mulching involves spreading a layer of chopped leaves, hay, straw, wood chips, or other organic material over the bare soil between plants. Such material will help regulate moisture and prevent weeds. In humid climates, gardeners must ensure that *slugs,* slow-moving types of snails that normally have no shell, do not hide in the mulch. Slugs can harm plants. Gardeners can detect slugs by noticing partially consumed leaves, or the shiny residue that slugs leave behind when they move.

Plant supports. Many plants need fences or other supports to look their best. They include such flowers as larkspurs, lilies, and peonies, and such vegetables as beans, peppers, and tomatoes. Providing supports also improves air circulation, which helps keep the leaves dry and helps prevent disease. You can buy trellises, wire cages, and other plant supports at garden centers or use bamboo poles and wire to make them.

Pruning. Many plants will be healthier if you prune them, but you must prune each type properly. For *dicots* (plants with two seed leaves), remove the top shoot. The plant will then branch out more vigorously, producing a larger number of small flowers and a fuller shape. Dicots include broccoli, tomatoes, and zinnias. *Monocots* (plants with one seed leaf) almost never need pruning. Monocots include corn, lilies, and onions. For information about pruning trees and shrubs, see **Pruning.**

Harvesting flower gardens usually involves removing the flowers from plants past their prime. This will enable the plants to produce more and extend the growing season. For bouquets, however, cut the flowers before they fully open, or they will not last long in the vase. Have a bucket of water with you and place the cut ends in water immediately.

© Judy Sedbrook

A Xeriscaped garden features wildflowers, grasses, and other plants that can tolerate dry conditions. Such gardens also use water-saving irrigation techniques and other procedures to conserve resources. Many people in drier regions plant such gardens.

Then let the flowers sit awhile in a cool, dark place before arranging them.

Gardeners should harvest most vegetables before they fully ripen. The major exceptions include winter squashes and pumpkins. These must ripen on the vine before harvesting, or they will not keep well.

Fall clean-up. In areas that do not have a year-round growing season, you must prepare your garden for winter. For hardy plants still in the ground, protect them with fluffy mulch or with such artificial covers as plastic sheeting. For less hardy plants, remove and discard them to prevent pests and diseases from attacking the plants. For some tender perennials and bulbs, lift them from the ground and store them indoors through the winter in pots or in a cool, dry storage area.

Kinds of indoor gardens

People grow most house plants for their ornamental form or foliage. House plants range in size from tiny ferns up to woody trees. Some homeowners construct greenhouses for large and expensive plant collections.

Terrariums consist of a collection of plants within a clear or faintly tinted container. A terrarium should have enough space to grow a collection of small plants from a particular environment. People often light their terrariums. They may even include small animals, such as snails, as part of the display. Well-designed terrariums look attractive and require little maintenance.

Preparing an indoor garden

Most indoor gardeners maintain house plants in a range of locations and containers. Houses with many windows can support a greater range of plants. The more light a house lets in, the greater the variety of plants it can support. Most homes can support certain rain forest plants, such as ferns or philodendrons, which need little light to survive. Most homes can also grow small plants on kitchen window sills and other areas. You can also provide additional artificial light. Just be sure to use lamps properly designed for plant growth.

Containers for house plants range widely in size and style. Clay pots designed for displaying small cactuses on window sills can measure as little as 3 inches (8 centime-

Some popular house plants

There are hundreds of kinds of house plants. They come in a wide variety of colors, shapes, and sizes. House plants differ in the type and amount of care they require. As a result, indoor gardeners should select them carefully. The illustrations here depict some of the most popular plants.

Wax begonia

Grows 6 to 14 in (15 to 36 cm) tall; blooms the year around; has orange, pink, red, white, or yellow flowers; requires medium to bright light and slightly dry soil.

Spider plant

Grows about 1 ft (30 cm) tall; has long, narrow, green leaves, often with a yellow or white stripe; usually planted in a hanging container; requires medium to bright light and moist soil.

Bunny ears cactus

Grows 3 to 4 ft (91 to 122 cm) tall; has green leaves with yellow markings; usually planted in a floor container; requires bright light and dry soil.

Corn plant

Grows 2 to 6 ft (61 to 183 cm) tall; has green leaves with yellow markings; usually planted in a floor container; requires medium light and moist soil.

Common coleus

Grows 2 to 3 ft (61 to 91 cm) tall; has green leaves with pink, red, or yellow markings; usually planted in a floor container; requires bright light and slightly moist soil.

Split-leaved philodendron

Grows over 2 ft (61 cm) tall; has dark green leaves; usually provided with a stake or trellis to which plant clings; requires medium light and slightly moist soil.

English ivy

Grows from 1 to over 2 ft (30 to 61 cm) tall; has green leaves with white markings; often planted in a hanging container or staked; requires bright light and moist soil.

Broad-leaved India rubber plant

Grows over 2 ft (61 cm) tall; has green leaves with brown or red markings; usually planted in a floor container; requires medium light and slightly moist soil.

African violet

Grows 4 to 6 in (10 to 15 cm) tall; blooms the year around; has blue, pink, purple, or white flowers; requires medium light and slightly moist soil.

ters) wide. Large floor pots reach 18 inches (46 centimeters) wide or wider. They may hold weeping figs 6 feet (1.8 meters) tall. Beautiful hanging baskets can feature spider plants by bay windows.

A good garden center or nursery can recommend plants based on your needs and space requirements. Consider bringing snapshots of the space in which you plan to grow plants. The plants will come potted with an appropriate soil mix and in a properly sized container.

Cultivating an indoor garden

Water. Watering requirements for house plants vary. Some plants prefer moist soil all the time, while others prefer the soil to dry out completely between waterings. Still others need watering only infrequently.

Plants that need the soil continuously moist include many rain forest plants. You may need to group these plants together near a small humidifier. Most homes are too dry for such plants, especially in winter. Having all the plants in one place makes watering easier.

Plants that need dry soil between waterings prefer relatively low humidity. On average, these plants should be watered only once a week. Apply enough water so that it runs out the bottom of the pot into the catch tray. The excess water will evaporate in a day or so.

Plants that need only infrequent watering include most cactus and other *succulents* (plants with fleshy leaves and

stems that store water). Water such plants only once every two weeks or so. The soil in their pots may have a large proportion of sand so that it does not hold water. Soil that stays too wet for too long can lead to root rot in these plants.

Fertilizer. Newly bought plants will likely have slow-release fertilizer mixed in with the potting soil. After the plants use up this fertilizer, in about three months, apply more fertilizer periodically.

Cleaning. Dust and other debris in the house will settle on plant leaves. Over time, such debris will inhibit the plants' ability to breathe through the *stomata* (pores) on the surface of their leaves. Take your small plants to the bathroom or kitchen sink for washing. For larger ones, wipe the leaves with a damp cloth or sponge. Such cleaning provides an opportunity to examine the leaves for insect pests. If you find pests, isolate that plant from the others until you have cured the infestation.

To keep plants looking good, remove dead or dying leaves, flowers, and branches regularly. Plants near windows often start to grow toward the light. Be sure to turn them periodically so that their growth remains balanced and they do not become lopsided.

Repotting should occur only rarely. Just because a plant looks too large for its container does not mean it needs repotting. Keeping plants in smaller pots constrains the roots and prevents the plants from growing too large. In some cases, however, a plant's roots may completely fill its con-

To repot a plant, hold the pot in one hand and place the other hand around the pot's edge. Turn the pot upside down and rap the bottom with your fist to dislodge the plant, *above left.* Then place the plant in a slightly larger pot, *above right.*

A traditional Japanese garden features sculpted plants set off by accents, such as rocks or the tall stone lantern shown. This garden grows at a Buddhist temple in Ohara, Japan, near Kyoto.

tainer, sticking up above the soil or out the drainage holes. At this point, consider repotting.

To repot a plant, spread some newspaper or cloth in an open space and hold the plant in one hand. Then place the palm of the other hand on the edge of the pot, so that your fingers surround the stem or stems. Turn the pot upside down, support it with the second hand, and rap on the bottom of the pot with your fist. This rapping should dislodge the plant from the pot. Some kinds of pots may require extra work to dislodge the plant. Plastic pots may require kneading, while ceramic pots may require that you rap the pot on its sides. Larger plants can prove especially difficult to extract, and you may need to break the old pot.

Once you extract the plant's root ball, knead it slightly to loosen it up. Then put the plant aside and prepare the new container, which should measure only slightly larger than the old one. Add enough potting soil so that the plant will lie at the same depth as before. Then place the plant in the pot and fill around it with more soil. Finally, firm the soil with your fingers.

For plants that like moist conditions, water them after repotting. Other types of plants, however, should not receive water at repotting time.

A traditional cottage garden features colorful flowers arranged in an informal, but carefully planned, way. The garden shown here grows at Sissinghurst Castle in the county of Kent, England. The English author V. Sackville-West and her husband, the diplomat and author Harold Nicolson, began developing the garden in the 1930's.

Obtaining new plants from cuttings. Plant owners can *propagate* plants—that is, obtain new plants from an old one—by taking cuttings, or *slips,* from the plant. Kept in proper conditions, the cuttings will form roots and grow into a new plant. This practice can even yield gift plants for others. Many books and Web sites provide information about how to grow plants from cuttings. See also **Plant** (Vegetative propagation).

History of gardening

People have planted gardens for thousands of years. Wallpaintings in ancient Egyptian tombs show gardens surrounding rectangular pools. The Hanging Gardens of Babylon, one of the Seven Wonders of the Ancient World, were built in what is now Iraq, probably from 605 to 562 B.C. Ancient writers described the hanging gardens as laid out on a brick terrace about 75 feet (23 meters) above the ground.

The Chinese developed their own garden styles over 3,000 years ago. These gardens often featured stylized, carefully placed plants surrounded by walls. Each plant had a symbolic meaning in Chinese culture. Eventually, the Japanese and other Asian cultures developed their own garden styles based on Chinese models.

The ancient Romans created formal, symmetrical gardens featuring fountains, hedges, sculptures, and *topiary* (sculpted plants). During the Middle Ages, from about the 400's through the 1400's, many expert gardeners were monks and nuns who kept large gardens at monasteries and convents. During the Renaissance, which started in the 1300's in Italy, gardeners began to re-create the formal gardens of ancient Greece and Rome. Such styles eventually spread from Italy to France and other countries.

In England, local gardeners developed a variety of informal cottage gardens. Such gardens spread to North America, Australia, and other parts of the world.

Since the 1800's, the development of new varieties of garden plants has grown dramatically. The availability of more and more kinds of plants, as well as more garden styles, has greatly increased the popularity of gardening as a hobby.　　Shepherd Ogden

© Filip Horvat, Saba

Baghdad is the capital and largest city of Iraq. Some parts of Baghdad feature wide boulevards and modern buildings, *shown here*. Other sections have narrow, dusty streets and colorful bazaars. Baghdad came under heavy bombardment during U.S.-led wars against Iraq in 1991 and 2003.

Iraq

Iraq, *ih RAHK* or *ih RAK,* is an Arab country at the head of the Persian Gulf in southwestern Asia. The country is bordered by Turkey, Iran, Kuwait, Saudi Arabia, Jordan, and Syria. Baghdad is Iraq's capital and largest city.

The world's first known civilization and other early cultures developed along the Tigris and Euphrates rivers in what is now Iraq. The ancient Greeks called part of Iraq and the surrounding region *Mesopotamia* (between rivers) because it lay between the Tigris and Euphrates rivers. For thousands of years, civilizations there have depended on controlling flooding from the two rivers and on using their waters for irrigation.

Iraq became part of the Arab Empire in the A.D. 600's and absorbed Arab Muslim culture. Today, about 75 percent of Iraq's people are Arabs. Iraq also has a large Kurdish population that has struggled on and off for self-government for many years.

Iraq's economy depends heavily on oil exports. From the 1950's through the 1970's, income produced by the oil industry improved living conditions for Iraq's people.

In the 1980's and the early 1990's, President Saddam Hussein and other leaders of the ruling Baath Party in-

Michel Le Gall, the contributor of this article, is Associate Professor of Middle Eastern History at St. Olaf College.

volved Iraq in two wars that had devastating effects on the country. Iraq fought a war with Iran from 1980 to 1988, when a cease-fire was declared. In 1990, Iraq invaded and occupied neighboring Kuwait. The United Nations (UN) condemned the invasion and imposed a trade embargo on Iraq. A coalition of 39 nations opposed the invasion and sent forces to the region. In early 1991, they defeated Iraq in the Persian Gulf War of 1991. The UN trade embargo continued after the war.

A military coalition made up mainly of United States forces overthrew Hussein's government in 2003, during

Facts in brief

Capital: Baghdad.
Official languages: Arabic and Kurdish.
Official name: State of Iraq.
Area: 169,235 mi² (438,317 km²). *Greatest distances*—north-south, 530 mi (853 km); east-west, 495 mi (797 km). *Coastline*—40 mi (64 km).
Elevation: *Highest*—about 11,840 ft (3,609 m) in Zagros Mountains. *Lowest*—sea level.
Population: *Estimated 2004 population*—25,576,000; density, 151 per mi² (58 per km²); distribution, 68 percent urban, 32 percent rural. *1997 census*—22,017,983.
Chief products: *Agriculture*—barley, dates, grapes, rice, tomatoes, and wheat. *Mining*—petroleum. *Manufacturing*—building materials, chemicals, flour, iron and steel, leather goods, petroleum refining, textiles.
Money: *Basic unit*—dinar. One thousand fils equal one dinar.

the Iraq War. Soon afterward, the UN lifted its trade embargo. Coalition forces remained in Iraq. A new Iraqi government is being established.

Government

National government. From 1968 to 2003, the ruling Baath Party controlled the government and eliminated or restricted all opposition. President Saddam Hussein governed Iraq as dictator from 1979 to 2003. In 2003, U.S.-led military forces overthrew Hussein, and a U.S.-led administration called the Coalition Provisional Authority (CPA) assumed control over Iraq. In June 2004, the CPA was dissolved, and power was handed over to an interim Iraqi government. At the same time, a temporary constitution went into effect. It calls for a 275-member transitional National Assembly to be elected by the people by the end of January 2005. The National Assembly will elect a Presidency Council consisting of a president and two deputy presidents. The Presidency Council will appoint a prime minister. The temporary constitution calls for the National Assembly to draft a permanent constitution and submit it to the people in a referendum in 2005.

Local government. Iraq has 18 provinces. Two Kurdish political groups control parts of northern Iraq.

Armed forces. In 2003, the CPA dissolved the Iraqi armed forces, and the U.S.-led coalition forces assumed responsibility for Iraq's security and defense. A new military, made up of Iraqis, is being formed.

People

Iraq has a high population growth rate, and so its population is expanding rapidly. About three-fourths of Iraq's people live in a fertile plain that extends from Baghdad south along the Tigris and Euphrates rivers. This area has many of Iraq's largest cities and towns.

Arabs make up about 75 percent of Iraq's population. About 20 percent of the people belong to Iraq's largest ethnic minority, the Kurds. Other ethnic groups in Iraq include Armenians, Assyrians, Turkomans, and Yazidis.

Language. Arabic is spoken throughout Iraq. Kurdish is spoken in Kurdish areas. Both are official languages.

City life. Most of Iraq's people live in cities. The number of people in urban areas has increased dramatically since the 1940's as a result of migration from rural areas. Many people have moved to the cities in search of work. Others fled rural villages and southern Iraqi cities that were damaged in the 1980's during Iraq's war with Iran. Overflowing urban populations have resulted in severe unemployment and housing shortages in some cities.

Wealthy city dwellers work in business and government. Many of them live in the suburbs. People at middle-income levels are office workers, craftworkers, and small business owners. Many of them reside in apartments in the cities. Many laborers and factory and oil workers commute to city jobs from nearby villages.

Clothing styles vary in Iraq's cities. Middle-class and wealthy people generally wear clothing similar to that worn by North Americans and Europeans. Most laborers prefer traditional clothes. For men, these garments include long cotton gowns and jackets. Traditional dress for women consists of a long, concealing gown and a scarf that covers much of the head.

Rural life. Many people who live in rural areas of Iraq are villagers who farm for a living. Herders form a small part of rural society. Bedouin *nomads* (wanderers) herd camels, goats, and sheep in western Iraq. Some Kurds graze livestock in northern Iraq.

Buildings in the rural areas of southern and central Iraq are made of dried mud and brick. In the north, villagers build stone houses.

Clothing in the countryside is traditional. Arab men wear gowns and checkered headdresses. Women dress in long black robes, and some veil their faces. Kurdish men wear shirts and baggy trousers with sashes. Kurdish women wear trousers but cover them with a dress.

Food and drink. Iraqis eat a varied diet that includes vegetables, rice, flat bread, meat, fish, and dates. Bread and rice are the main foods at many meals. Grilled lamb, chicken, and fish are popular. *Sanbusak,* a traditional Iraqi dish, consists of moon-shaped dough stuffed with cheese or meat. Popular beverages in Iraq include tea, coffee, and fruit juices.

Recreation. Iraqis enjoy a variety of sports and games, including soccer, horse racing, backgammon, and chess. Weddings and other family events are occasions for traditional folk dances and songs.

Religion. About 95 percent of Iraq's people are Muslims. Over half of Iraq's Muslims are Shiites (members of the Shiah branch of Islam). The other Muslims belong to the Sunni division. Most Arabs living southeast of Baghdad are Shiites. Central and southwestern Iraq is a mixture of Sunni and Shiite Arab populations. The Kurds are Sunnis. Christians and other groups make up about 5

Iraq's flag was originally adopted in 1963. The Arabic inscription on the white stripe means *God is great.*

The coat of arms, adopted in 1965, has an eagle resembling a sculpture in the castle of Saladin, an Arab warrior.

WORLD BOOK map

Iraq lies in southwestern Asia. It is bordered by Turkey, Iran, the Persian Gulf, Kuwait, Saudi Arabia, Jordan, and Syria.

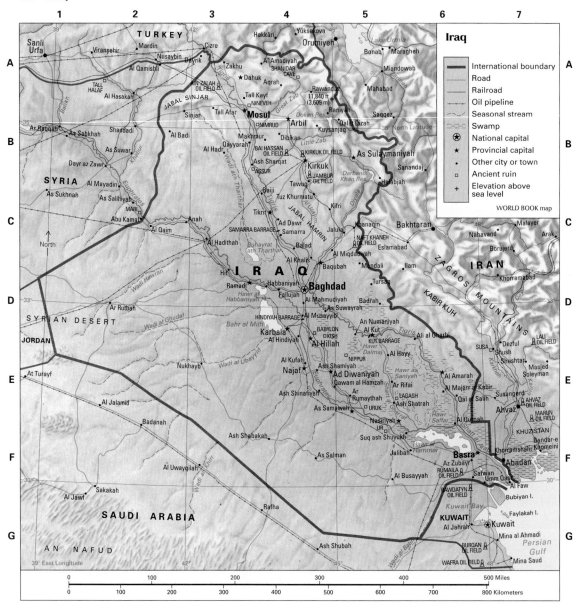

Map legend:

Iraq

- ▬▬ International boundary
- ─── Road
- ─┼─ Railroad
- ─·─ Oil pipeline
- Seasonal stream
- Swamp
- ⊛ National capital
- ★ Provincial capital
- • Other city or town
- □ Ancient ruin
- + Elevation above sea level

WORLD BOOK map

Iraq map index

Cities and towns

Abu al Khasib*	12,681	.F	7
Abu Ghurayb	10,554	.D	4
Ad Dawr		.C	4
Ad Diwani-yah	239,000	.E	5
Al Amarah	164,000	.E	6
Al Badi		.B	3
Al Busayyah		.F	6
Al Faw	27,000	.F	7
Al Hadithah	6,849	.C	3
Al Hadr		.B	3
Al Harithah	9,267	.F	6
Al Hayy	41,000	.E	5
Al Hillah	279,000	.D	4
Al Hindiyah	41,000	.D	4
Al Khalis	35,000	.C	4
Al Kufah	30,531	.E	4
Al Kut	141,000	.D	5
Al Mah-mudiyah	10,656	.D	4

Al Majarr al Kabir	8,971	.E	6
Al Miqda-diyah	31,000	.C	5
Al Musayyib	39,000	.D	4
Al Qaim		.C	2
Al Qasim	7,436	.E	5
Al Qurnah	4,988	.F	6
An Numa-niyah	29,000	.D	5
Anah	5,620	.C	3
Aqrah	8,671	.A	4
Arbil	479,000	.B	4
Ar Rifai	7,551	.E	5
Ar Ruma-ythah	10,433	.E	5
Ar Rutbah		.D	2
As Salman		.F	5
As Samawah	77,000	.E	5
As Sulay-maniyah	394,000	.B	5
Ash Shabakah		.F	4
Ash Shamiyah	32,000	.E	6

Ash Sharqat		.B	4
Ash Shatrah	46,000	.E	6
Ash Shinafiyah	6,476	.E	4
Az Zubayr	70,000	.D	4
Badrah		.D	5
Baghdad	5,908,000	.D	4
Baiji	7,042	.C	4
Balad	34,000	.C	4
Baqubah	165,000	.D	5
Basra	678,000	.D	6
Dahuk	42,000	.A	3
Fallujah	174,000	.D	4
Habbaniyah	48,000	.D	4
Halabjah	11,250	.B	5
Jalibah		.F	5
Jalula	31,000	.C	5
Karbala	237,000	.D	4
Khanaqin	58,000	.C	5
Kifri	8,267	.C	5
Kirkuk	404,000	.B	4
Kuysanjaq	10,379	.B	4
Mandali	10,951	.D	5
Mosul	748,000	.B	4

Najaf	423,000	.E	4
Nasiriyah	191,000	.F	5
Nukhayb		.E	3
Qawam al Hamzah	10,817	.E	5
Qayyarah		.B	3
Ramadi	174,000	.D	3
Rawanduz	5,411	.A	4
Safwan		.F	7
Samarra	78,000	.C	4
Sinjar	7,984	.B	3
Suq ash Shuyukh	41,000	.F	5
Tall Afar	104,000	.B	3
Tall Kayf	7,381	.A	4
Tawuq		.B	4
Tikrit	9,863	.C	4
Tursaq		.D	5
Tuz Khurmatu	35,000	.C	4
Umm Qasr		.F	7
Zakhu	36,000	.A	3

Physical features

Buhayrat ath Tharthar (lake)		.C	4
Euphrates River		.E	4
Great Zab River		.B	4
Hawr al Hab-baniyah (lake)		.D	4
Hawr al Hammar (lake)		.F	6
Hawr as Saniyah (lake)		.E	6
Hindiyah Barrage		.D	4
Kut Barrage		.E	5
Little Zab River		.B	4
Nineveh (ruins)		.B	4
Persian Gulf		.G	7
Samarra Barrage		.C	3
Shatt al Arab River		.F	6
Syrian Desert		.D	1
Tigris River		.C	4
Wadi al Ubayyid (river)		.E	3

*Does not appear on map; key shows general location.
Sources: 1991 estimates from the Center for International Research of the U.S. Census Bureau for largest cities; latest available census (1965) for other places.

© J. Pavlovsky, Corbis/Sygma

Shops in Baghdad offered many items before a United Nations embargo from 1990 to 2003 led to shortages.

© J. Pavlovsky, Corbis/Sygma

Craftsmen work on brass pots in Baghdad. Iraqi metalworkers produce beautiful trays, pitchers, and other objects.

percent of the Iraqi population. When the Baath Party ruled Iraq from 1968 to 2003, most of its high-ranking members were Arab Sunni Muslims. Many Shiites resented the Sunni monopoly on governmental power.

Education. Iraqi law requires all children from ages 6 through 12 to attend school. Some children continue their education in vocational or secondary schools. Iraq has universities in Arbil, Baghdad, Basra, Mosul, and Tikrit. A higher percentage of men than women attend colleges and universities. Over half of Iraq's adult population can read and write. For the country's literacy rate, see **Literacy** (table: Literacy rates for selected countries).

The land

Iraq has four main land regions: (1) the northern plain, (2) the southern plain, (3) the mountains, and (4) the desert.

The northern plain, a region of dry, rolling land, lies between the Tigris and Euphrates rivers north of the city of Samarra. The highest hills in the area rise about 1,000 feet (300 meters) above sea level. There are a small number of farming villages in the northern plain.

The southern plain begins near Samarra and extends southeast to the Persian Gulf. It includes the fertile delta between the Tigris and Euphrates rivers, where many people live. The Tigris and Euphrates meet at the town of Al Qurnah and form the Shatt al Arab river, which empties into the gulf. Some major oil fields lie between the Shatt al Arab and the border with Kuwait.

Complex dam and irrigation systems control the flow of water in the southern plain. The result has been increased agricultural productivity and more permanent human settlement, especially north of Al Kut. Much of the region south of Al Kut is swampland, due to frequent flooding and poor drainage. In 1993, the country began a program to dry up much of the swampland.

The mountains of northeast Iraq are part of a range that is called the Zagros in Iran and the Taurus in Turkey. The mountains rise to more than 10,000 feet (3,000 meters) near Iraq's borders with Iran and Turkey. Kurds live in the region's foothills and valleys. Valuable oil fields lie near the cities of Mosul and Kirkuk.

The desert covers southwestern and western Iraq. Most of this region of limestone hills and sand dunes is part of the Syrian Desert, which stretches into Syria, Jordan, and Saudi Arabia. Scattered throughout the desert are *wadis*—valleys that are dry most of the year but become rivers after a rain.

Climate

Iraq's climate ranges from moderate in the north to semitropical in the east and southeast. The west and southwest have a desert climate—warm or hot days and much cooler nights. Summer high temperatures average more than 100 °F (38 °C) throughout much of Iraq. Winter low temperatures may drop to around 35 °F (2 °C) in the desert and in the north.

In general, little rain falls in Iraq. Average annual precipitation ranges from 5 inches (13 centimeters) of rain in the desert to 15 inches (38 centimeters) of rain and snow in the northern mountains. Most of the precipitation falls between November and April.

Economy

The export of oil has played a vital role in Iraq's economy since the 1950's. However, Iraq has tried to become less dependent on oil exports by expanding the rest of its industrial sector. During the 1970's, Iraq's economy prospered. But the war with Iran in the 1980's, the Persian Gulf War of 1991, and the Iraq War, which began in 2003, greatly damaged the economy. Trade routes were disrupted, ports were closed, and factories were destroyed. In addition, the UN trade embargo imposed in August 1990 halted all oil exports from Iraq. The embargo was partially lifted in 1996 and fully lifted in 2003.

Industry includes mining, manufacturing, and construction. Oil is the chief mineral resource. Iraq was once the second-largest producer of oil in the Middle East. In the early 1980's, the oil industry accounted for about 60 percent of Iraq's gross domestic product (GDP). The GDP is the total value of all goods and services produced within a country in a year. But war damaged many oil reservoirs, pipelines, and refineries and interfered with the oil trade. Iraq's major oil fields are in

Dry grazing land covers much of the northern plain of Iraq. The northern plain lies between the Tigris and Euphrates rivers north of the city of Samarra.

© Superstock

southern Iraq near the Kuwait border, and west of Kirkuk in the north. Other natural resources mined in Iraq include phosphates, sulfur, and natural gas.

Oil refining and petrochemical production make up an important industry in Iraq, but wartime damage to refineries has hurt the industry. Several of Iraq's chemical and oil plants are located near the cities of Baiji, Basra, and Kirkuk. Other factories in Iraq process farm products or make such goods as cloth, soap, beverages, cement, iron, and steel.

Service industries provide jobs for many of the country's workers. Before the Iraq War, the government employed about 25 percent of the work force. Other major service industries include banking and real estate.

Agriculture. Iraq was importing about 70 percent of its food before the 1990 UN trade embargo. The government invested heavily in agriculture. But poor organization and a lack of labor and private investment have hampered growth. Major crops harvested in Iraq include barley, dates, grapes, rice, tomatoes, and wheat. Many farmers lease their land from the government.

Energy sources. Oil and natural gas are the main sources of energy in Iraq. War has interfered with the availability of electric power in the country.

International trade. Oil accounts for most of Iraq's exports. The UN trade embargo, which began in 1990, halted all oil exports from Iraq. In 1996, the embargo was eased when a UN "oil-for-food" program was implemented. Under this program, Iraq was allowed to export oil in exchange for food, medical supplies, and other nonmilitary goods. Iraq also exported oil illegally to nearby countries. In 2003, the UN trade embargo was lifted, allowing oil exports to fully resume.

Transportation and communication. A government-owned airline links Baghdad with other major cities in Iraq and the Middle East and in Europe. Roads and railways connect Iraq's largest cities to one another. The shipping facilities at Basra, once a major port, were damaged during Iraq's wars. As a result, use of the port has been limited. Many Iraqis rely on public transportation because they cannot afford automobiles. Over shorter distances in the cities, many people use bicycles. In the countryside, people often use buses, donkeys, and camels for transportation.

Under the Baath Party regime, the government controlled all print and broadcast media that originated in Iraq, except for the media in Kurdish-run areas of the north. After the Baath regime was overthrown in 2003, the U.S.-led Coalition Provisional Authority established radio and television stations in Iraq. In addition, more than 200 private newspapers and magazines and several private radio and TV stations emerged. Iraqis can also pick up radio and TV broadcasts from other countries. About 1 out of every 15 Iraqis owns a TV set. Many more people have radios.

History

Early days. The world's first known civilization developed in Sumer, now southeastern Iraq, about 3500 B.C. Sumer was part of Mesopotamia, an area that included most of present-day Iraq and parts of Syria and Turkey. Other ancient civilizations, including Assyria and Babylonia, flourished along the Tigris and Euphrates rivers between about 3500 and 539 B.C. See **Assyria; Babylonia; Mesopotamia; Sumer.**

In 539 B.C., the Persians conquered Mesopotamia. Greek and Macedonian armies under Alexander the Great took the area from the Persians in 331 B.C. Greek rule continued until the Parthians, from the Caspian Sea area, established control by 126 B.C. Except for brief periods of Roman rule, the Parthians controlled Mesopotamia until about A.D. 226. That year, the Persian Sassanid *dynasty* (family of rulers) seized Mesopotamia. The Sassanids ruled the region for about 400 years.

Arab rule. The birth of Islam in the A.D. 600's inspired Arab Muslims to conquer the Sassanids in 637. The Arabs brought the Arabic language and the new Islamic religion to Mesopotamia. The Abbasid dynasty came to power in 750, and soon founded Baghdad as the capital of the Arab Empire. Under the Abbasids, Arab civilization reached great heights. By 800, Baghdad had grown into a city of nearly a million people and was a world center of trade and culture.

In 1258, Mongols from central Asia invaded Mesopotamia and destroyed the Arab Empire. The Mongols neglected Mesopotamia, and the region deteriorated culturally and economically under their rule.

Ottoman control. The Ottoman Empire, which was

based in what is now Turkey, began to establish control over Mesopotamia in the early 1500's. The Ottomans battled with the Persians and local Arab leaders to maintain control over the region.

During the 1700's and 1800's, the Ottoman Empire declined in power and size in the face of new, strong nations that developed in Europe. The United Kingdom became involved in the Persian Gulf in the 1800's to protect its trade routes with India, which was then under British rule. By World War I (1914-1918), the United Kingdom had become interested in Mesopotamia's oil resources.

British rule. British troops took Mesopotamia from the Ottoman Empire during World War I. In 1920, the League of Nations, a forerunner to the United Nations, gave the United Kingdom a *mandate* (order to rule) over the area. The British set up a new government in Mesopotamia in 1921. They renamed the country Iraq and chose an Arab prince as King Faisal I.

During the 1920's, British advisers retained positions in the Iraqi government, and the British controlled Iraq's army, foreign policy, finances, and oil resources. Some Iraqis opposed British involvement, and a movement for independence developed.

Independence. Under pressure from Iraq's independence movement, the United Kingdom signed a treaty with Iraq in 1930. In the treaty, the United Kingdom promised military protection and eventual independence for Iraq. In return, Iraq promised the United Kingdom continued use of British air bases in Iraq. It also agreed to use foreign advisers from the United Kingdom only. The British mandate over Iraq ended in 1932, and Iraq became an independent nation.

In the 1930's, Iraq's politicians disagreed over the alliance with the United Kingdom. King Faisal worked to balance the interests of Iraq's political factions and to unify the country's ethnic and religious groups. Faisal died in 1933. His son Ghazi became king. Ghazi was a weak ruler, and tribal and ethnic rebellions broke out. In 1936, anti-British groups in the army took control of the government, though Ghazi officially was still king. Ghazi died in 1939. His 3-year-old son, Faisal II, became king, but the boy's uncle, Prince Abdul Ilah, ruled for him.

In 1940 and 1941, during World War II, Iraqi government leaders and army officers sought an alliance with the Axis powers—Germany, Italy, and Japan—in an attempt to end British influence in Iraq. The United Kingdom attempted to use Iraq as a military base under the provisions of the 1930 treaty, and an armed conflict broke out. The British defeated the Iraqi army in 1941, and the pro-Axis leaders left the country.

Iraq declared war on the Axis in 1943. Inflation and supply shortages brought on by World War II transformed Iraq's society and economy. A wide economic gap developed between the rich and poor. Many blamed the government for their economic situation.

Iraq helped found the Arab League, an association of Arab countries, in 1945. In 1948, Iraq joined other members of the league in a war against the newly created nation of Israel. The defeat of the Arabs touched off demonstrations in Iraq and other Arab countries.

The 1950's. In 1950 and 1952, the government of Iraq signed new agreements with foreign oil companies. The 1952 agreement gave Iraq 50 percent of the profits from oil drilled there. As a result of these agreements, Iraq's oil revenues rose dramatically. The government used some of this money to build hospitals, irrigation projects, roads, and schools. But the increased amount of money coming into Iraq also caused serious inflation.

Faisal II took full power in 1953 at the age of 18. In the 1950's, opposition to the monarchy grew steadily. Many Iraqis wanted a voice in government, and others felt that they had not benefited enough from Iraq's oil profits.

In addition, a large number of Iraqis opposed the government's ties to the West. In particular, they objected to the Baghdad Pact—a British-supported mutual defense agreement Iraq signed with Iran, Pakistan, and Turkey in 1955. Many Iraqis also felt that the ties with the West went against the political movement called *Pan-Arabism.* Advocates of Pan-Arabism believed that Arab countries should strive for political unity and be free of outside influence. In 1958, army officers overthrew the government and declared Iraq a republic. The rebels killed King Faisal and Prince Abdul Ilah.

The republic. The army officers set up a three-man Sovereignty Council consisting of a Shiite Arab, a Kurd, and a Sunni Arab. The council issued a temporary constitution giving the power to rule by decree with the council's approval. General Abdul Karim Kassem (also spelled Qasim), who led the revolution, became Iraq's premier. He reversed Iraq's pro-West policy and accepted both economic and military aid from Communist countries. Kassem set up land reform programs aimed at narrowing the gap between rich and poor. He also worked to develop industry in Iraq.

In 1961, Kurdish leaders asked Kassem to give the Kurds complete autonomy within Iraq and a share of the revenues from oil fields in northern Iraq. Kassem rejected the plan. In response, the Kurds revolted. A cease-fire was finally declared in 1964.

In 1963, army officers and members of the Baath Party assassinated Kassem. The Baath Party took control of the country and named Abdul Salam Arif president and Ahmed Hasan al-Bakr prime minister. Both were army officers. Later that year, Arif used the military to take over the government. Arif died in 1966, and his brother, Abdul Rahman Arif, became president. The Arifs followed socialist economic policies.

Al-Bakr overthrew Arif in 1968 and reestablished Baath control. The Baath Party quickly began to dominate all aspects of Iraqi politics. Party leaders wrote a new constitution in 1970 that institutionalized the party's control of the government. Al-Bakr supported further socialist economic reform and stronger ties with the Soviet Union. During al-Bakr's presidency, Saddam Hussein, who held important party and government posts, gained influence within the government.

In 1973, the Iraqi government completed a take-over of foreign oil companies in the country. After oil prices rose sharply later that year, Iraq made huge profits.

In 1970, al-Bakr signed an agreement with the Kurds ending eight years of on-and-off fighting. In the agreement, the government promised that beginning in 1974 the Kurds would have self-rule and several positions in the government. New fighting erupted in 1974, after the Kurds objected to revisions in the agreement. The revised agreement established limited autonomy for the Kurds in the Kurdish Autonomous Region in northern Iraq. Government forces largely defeated the Kurds by

March 1975. Al-Bakr resigned the presidency in 1979. Saddam Hussein succeeded him as president.

War with Iran. In September 1980, Iraq invaded Iran, and war broke out between the two countries. The war resulted in part from boundary disputes, from Iran's support for the rebellious Kurds, and from the efforts of Shiite leaders in Iran to incite rebellion in Iraq's Shiite population. In addition, Iraqi leaders believed Iran had become somewhat unstable as a result of its 1979 revolution. They felt Iran's weakened position offered Iraq an opportunity to increase its power in the region.

The war lasted eight years. An estimated 150,000 Iraqi soldiers died, and Iranian air attacks on major cities wounded and killed many of Iraq's civilians. The war also severely damaged Iraq's economy. Bombs damaged oil facilities in southern Iraq, and trade through the Persian Gulf was disrupted. Iraq and Iran finally agreed on a cease-fire in August 1988.

During the war with Iran, Iraq's Kurds supported Iran. In 1987 and 1988, the Iraqi government lashed out against the Kurds. The army released poison gas in Kurdish villages, killing thousands of people. There also were reports that the army destroyed several Kurdish towns and that the inhabitants fled to Turkey and Iran.

The Persian Gulf War of 1991. In August 1990, Iraqi forces invaded and occupied Kuwait. Hussein had accused Kuwait of violating oil production limits set by the Organization of the Petroleum Exporting Countries (OPEC), thus lowering the worldwide price of oil. Iraq and Kuwait had also disagreed over territory and over Iraq's multibillion-dollar debt to Kuwait. The UN called for Iraq to withdraw from Kuwait and passed a resolution stating that all nations should stop trading with Iraq, except for food and medical supplies under certain circumstances. A coalition of 39 countries, organized main-

Important dates in Iraq

3500 B.C. The world's first known civilization developed in Mesopotamia, now Iraq.

539 B.C. The Persians conquered Mesopotamia.

331 B.C. Alexander the Great seized Mesopotamia.

A.D. 227 The Sasanian dynasty of Persia conquered Mesopotamia.

637 Arab Muslims overthrew the Sasanians.

1258 The Mongols invaded Mesopotamia.

1500's The Ottoman Empire began to establish control over Mesopotamia.

1920 The League of Nations gave the United Kingdom a *mandate* (order to rule) over Mesopotamia.

1932 The British mandate ended, and Iraq became independent.

1958 Army officers overthrew the Iraqi government and declared the country a republic.

1968 The Baath Party took control of Iraq's government.

1973 The Iraqi government completed its take-over of foreign oil companies in Iraq.

1980 Iraq declared war on Iran.

1988 Iraq and Iran agreed to a cease-fire.

1990 Iraq invaded Kuwait.

1991 A coalition of 39 nations defeated Iraq in the Persian Gulf War of 1991.

2003 Forces led by the United States overthrew the Baath Party government of Saddam Hussein in the Iraq War.

ly by the UN and the United States, opposed the invasion and sent armed forces to the Persian Gulf region.

In November 1990, the UN Security Council approved the use of force to remove Iraqi troops from Kuwait if they did not leave by Jan. 15, 1991. Iraq refused to withdraw, and war broke out between the allied forces and Iraq early on January 17 Baghdad time (January 16 U.S. time). The United States and its allies bombed Iraqi military targets in Iraq and Kuwait. Iraq launched missiles against Saudi Arabia and Israel. On February 24 (February 23 U.S. time), allied land forces began moving into Iraq and Kuwait. They defeated the Iraqi army after 100 hours of fighting. On February 27 U.S. time (February 28 in the war area), U.S. President George H. W. Bush declared a halt to all allied military operations.

The Persian Gulf War of 1991 had a devastating effect on Iraq. Estimates of Iraqi soldiers killed in the war range from about 1,500 to as many as 100,000. A great number of civilians also died. Allied air raids destroyed roads, bridges, factories, and oil industry facilities and disrupted electric, telephone, and water service. Diseases spread through contaminated drinking water because water purification and sewage treatment facilities could not operate without electric power. Also, the trade embargo caused serious economic problems.

In March 1991, Kurdish and Shiite uprisings broke out. By April, Iraqi troops put down most of the rebellions. However, some fighting continued. Refugees flooded into Iran and Turkey. Allied forces transported supplies to the refugees and set up a safety zone in northern Iraq to protect the Kurds.

Iraq accepted the terms of a formal cease-fire agreement on April 6. On April 11, the UN Security Council officially declared an end to the war. In the cease-fire agreement, Iraq promised to pay Kuwait for war damages. Iraq also agreed to the destruction of all its biological and chemical weapons, its facilities for producing such weapons, and any facilities or materials it might have for producing nuclear weapons. After the formal cease-fire, the UN continued the embargo to pressure Iraq to carry out its agreements.

Iraq had also been staging air attacks against Shiites in southern Iraq who continued to oppose the Iraqi government. In August 1992, to protect the Shiites, the allies imposed a ban on Iraqi military and civilian aircraft over the region. The safety zone in the Kurdish region also included a flight ban. The areas where flights were banned came to be called "no-fly" zones.

The no-fly zone in southern Iraq did little to protect the Shiites living there. The Iraqi government sent troops and tanks against the Shiites, and dozens of villages were destroyed. In addition, in 1993, the government began to drain the swamplands where the Shiites lived. As a result, many Shiites who grew rice in these lands were deprived of a source of food. Thousands of Shiites fled to neighboring Iran.

In November 1994, Iraq formally recognized the independence of Kuwait and Kuwait's current boundaries. Also in 1994, fighting broke out between rival groups of Kurds in the safety zone in northern Iraq. In August 1996, the Iraqi government sent troops and tanks into the zone in support of one of the Kurdish groups. The United States opposed this action, and in September launched missiles against military targets in southern

Iraq. At the same time, the United States expanded the no-fly zone in southern Iraq.

In December 1996, the UN began an "oil-for-food" program that partially lifted the embargo on Iraq. This program allowed Iraq to export oil under strict UN supervision. Most money from the oil sales was to be used to buy food and medicine for the civilian population.

By 2002, Iraq still had not fulfilled the terms of the 1991 cease-fire agreement. On a number of occasions, Iraq had failed to cooperate with UN teams sent to inspect suspected weapons sites. In December 1998, the United States and the United Kingdom launched a series of air strikes against Iraq. United States and British officials said the attacks were aimed at limiting Iraq's ability to produce *weapons of mass destruction*—that is, biological, chemical, and nuclear weapons. Afterward, U.S. and British planes attacked targets in northern and southern Iraq many times to enforce the no-fly zones and to disable Iraq's air-defense systems. In 1998, Iraq began to refuse to allow UN weapons inspectors into the country. In 2002, under threat of military attack by the United States, Iraq began negotiating conditions for a return of the inspectors. In November of that year, Iraq allowed weapons inspectors to return to the country. During the inspections, the United States continued to accuse Iraq of violating the UN disarmament terms and maintained its threat of possible military action.

The Iraq War. On March 20, 2003 (March 19 in the United States), U.S.-led forces launched an air attack against Baghdad, marking the beginning of the Iraq War. United States officials claimed the military campaign was intended to overthrow Saddam Hussein and eliminate Iraq's weapons of mass destruction and its ability to produce them. British, Australian, Polish, and Danish forces participated in the war effort. The United States began the war without formal UN support. Although a number of countries, including Spain and Portugal, expressed support for the war effort, many others—notably France, Germany, Russia, and China—said the war was unjustified without clear UN backing.

After the initial strike on March 20, the U.S.-led coalition continued its campaign of heavy bombardment of Baghdad. Tens of thousands of coalition ground troops advanced through southern Iraq toward the city, sometimes meeting stiff resistance from Iraqi forces. Coalition air and ground attacks also occurred elsewhere in Iraq. The coalition troops reached Baghdad in early April, and on April 9, they took control of central Baghdad. United States officials declared that the Hussein government had been removed from power.

By mid-April, coalition forces held all of Iraq's major cities. The coalition, led by the United States, assumed administrative control of Iraq. Looting broke out in several Iraqi cities, and coalition troops attempted to establish order. Coalition troops also began searching for weapons of mass destruction. On May 1, the United States declared that major combat operations in Iraq had ended. See **Iraq War.**

Also in May, the UN Security Council voted to end the UN trade embargo against Iraq. In addition, the council recognized the U.S.-led administration, called the Coalition Provisional Authority (CPA), as the temporary governing authority in Iraq. In July, Hussein's sons Uday and Qusay, who had held high-ranking positions in their fa-

ther's regime, were killed in a firefight with U.S. troops. In December 2003, U.S. troops captured Saddam Hussein near his hometown of Tikrit.

In June 2004, the CPA was dissolved, and power was handed over to an interim Iraqi government. Iyad Allawi—a former Baath Party member who later became an opponent of Hussein and went into exile—became prime minister of this government. The U.S.-led coalition force remained in Iraq for security purposes. In August 2004, an interim national assembly was established.

After the end of major combat in May 2003, coalition troops and Iraqi police faced much resistance from both Sunni Muslim and Shiite Muslim militants in Iraq. A number of deadly guerrilla attacks and bombings were carried out against both military and nonmilitary targets, killing many thousands of people. Also, coalition inspectors continued to search for weapons of mass destruction in Iraq, but no such weapons were found.

Starting in mid-2004, coalition troops had frequent clashes with Sunni militants in central Iraq, especially in Fallujah, and with Shiite militants loyal to the radical Shiite cleric Moqtada Sadr. In mid-2004, the Sunni militants gained control of Fallujah and a few other cities in central Iraq.   Michel Le Gall

Related articles include:

Arab League	Iraq War	Persian Gulf War
Arabs	Kurds	of 1991
Assyria	Kuwait	Petroleum
Babylonia	Mesopotamia	Saudi Arabia
Basra	Middle East	Syrian Desert
Baghdad	Mosul	Tigris River
Euphrates River	Nineveh	United Nations
Faisal I	Organization of the	(The Persian Gulf
Hussein, Saddam	Petroleum Export-	War of 1991)
Iran	ing Countries	

Outline

I. Government
   A. National government   C. Armed forces
   B. Local government

II. People
   A. Language   D. Food and drink   F. Religion
   B. City life   E. Recreation   G. Education
   C. Rural life

III. The land
   A. The northern plain   C. The mountains
   B. The southern plain   D. The desert

IV. Climate

V. Economy
   A. Industry   E. International trade
   B. Service industries   F. Transportation and
   C. Agriculture   communication
   D. Energy sources

VI. History

Questions

How did Iraq gain its independence from the United Kingdom?
Where do most of Iraq's people live?
What is Iraq's most important mineral?
What are the country's chief agricultural products?
Which ancient civilization developed in what is now Iraq?
What effect did Mongolian rule have on Mesopotamia?
Why have many Iraqis moved to urban areas?
How has Iraq used its oil income?
How did the Persian Gulf War of 1991 affect Iraq's economy?
What is Iraq's most fertile region?

Additional resources

Foster, Leila M. *Iraq.* Children's Pr., 1998. Younger readers.
Tripp, Charles. *A History of Iraq.* Cambridge, 2000.
Yetiv, Steven A. *The Persian Gulf Crisis.* Greenwood, 1997.

Pyongyang is the capital and largest city of North Korea. It is also the country's cultural, economic, industrial, and military center. Here, a monument of the Communist Party stands among apartment buildings in a residential area of Pyongyang. The Communist Party controls the government of North Korea.

© Martin Sasse, laif/Aurora Photos

Korea, North, is one of two countries on the Korean Peninsula, which extends south from northeastern China in Asia. North Korea covers the northern half of the peninsula, and South Korea occupies the southern half.

North Korea's official name is the Democratic People's Republic of Korea. Pyongyang is its capital and largest city. North Korea has a Communist government, and its Communist Party holds political power.

People probably have lived on the Korean Peninsula for at least 30,000 years. Various Korean and foreign governments ruled the peninsula from ancient times to the 1900's. Korea was a colony of Japan from 1910 until World War II ended in 1945. After Japan's defeat in the war, Korea was divided. Communists gained control of the North in 1945. The separate governments of North and South Korea were formed in 1948.

In 1950, North Korean troops invaded South Korea. This action started the Korean War, which was part of the Cold War struggle between Communist and non-Communist nations. The Korean War ended in 1953. However neither side won a complete victory, and a permanent peace treaty has never been signed. See **Korean War.**

Mountains cover about 80 percent of North Korea. Plains stretch along the western and northeastern coasts of the country. Most of the North Korean people live on the coastal plains or in river valleys.

Until the early 1900's, the economy of what is now North Korea was based almost entirely on agriculture, and nearly all Koreans worked as farmers. Today, the economy of North Korea is dependent on heavy industry, and the government controls nearly all economic activity. North Korea's economy is far less developed than that of South Korea.

The contributors of this article are Bonnie Bongwan Cho Oh, Distinguished Professor of Korean Studies at Georgetown University; and John K. C. Oh, Banigan Professor of Politics Emeritus at the Catholic University of America.

Government

The North Korean Constitution says that political power belongs to the people. But the country's Communist Party, called the Korean Workers' Party, holds the real political power. The Constitution guarantees such rights as freedom of the press, religion, and speech. But the North Korean people have little freedom. The Communists maintain strict control over all aspects of life to ensure their dominance of the country.

National government. The chairman of the National Defense Commission, Kim Jong-il, is the head of state and North Korea's most powerful official. The Central People's Committee is the most powerful policymaking body. It varies in size but usually has about 20 members. These officials, who are all high-ranking members of the Communist Party, hold office on the committee because of their positions in the party.

North Korea's legislature, called the Supreme People's Assembly, has 687 members, elected by the people to five-year terms. The Constitution says the legislature is North Korea's highest government authority. But it actually has little power. The Communist Party selects all legislative candidates, who run without opposition in each of the 687 districts. The legislature meets only one or two weeks a year and functions according to the wishes of the Communist Party.

A body called the State Administrative Council is responsible for carrying out government policies. It is headed by a premier, who is appointed by the Supreme People's Assembly. Its other members consist of the heads of government ministries and commissions, who are appointed by the Central People's Committee.

Local government. North Korea has nine provinces. Four *Special Cities*—Kaesong, Najin Sonbong, Nampo, and Pyongyang—have the status of provinces. Smaller political units include cities, counties, towns, villages, and workers' settlements. The people of each unit elect a people's assembly that directs the local government.

Politics. The Communist Party, also called the Korean Workers' Party, is the ruling party of North Korea. Less than 15 percent of the people belong to the party. Even so, the party makes the country's laws, chooses all candidates for elections, and approves all people appointed to public office. Officially, North Korea has a number of other political parties. However, these parties may not oppose the policies of the Workers' Party.

Courts. The Central Court is North Korea's highest court. Its justices are chosen by the Communist Party and elected by the Supreme People's Assembly. Other courts include provincial courts and people's courts.

Armed forces. North Korea's military is one of the largest in the world. It consists of a 1 million-member army, an air force of about 85,000 members, and a navy of about 45,000. About 600,000 people serve in the army reserve, and about 65,000 in the naval reserve. About 4 million people are members of local militia forces. Militia members serve part-time.

The North Korean government drafts men 20 to 25 years old for military service. Members of the army must serve 5 to 12 years. The air force requires 3 to 4 years of service, and the navy requires 5 to 10 years. Women join the armed forces on a volunteer basis.

People

Ethnic Koreans make up almost the entire population of North Korea. A small minority of people are of Chinese descent.

Korean is the official language of North Korea. Many scholars classify it in the same language family as Japanese, but Korean is unlike any other language. About half of all Korean words come from Chinese. Korean has about six major *dialects* (local forms). Most Koreans understand all the dialects. The Korean alphabet, called *han'gul,* has 24 letters. It was developed by scholars at the court of King Sejong in the 1440's.

Way of life

Before the 1900's, the people of what is now North Korea lived in an agricultural society built on strong family ties. Most Koreans lived in small villages and worked on farms. In many families, several generations

---

Facts in brief about North Korea

Capital: Pyongyang.
Official language: Korean.
Official name: Choson-minjujuui-inmin-konghwaguk (Democratic People's Republic of Korea).
Area: 46,540 mi² (120,538 km²), including islands and excluding the 487-mi² (1,262-km²) demilitarized zone. *Greatest distances*—north-south, 370 mi (595 km); east-west, 320 mi (515 km). *Coastline*—665 mi (1,070 km).
Elevation: *Highest*—Paektu-san (Paektu Mountain), 9,003 ft (2,744 m) above sea level. *Lowest*—sea level.
Population: *Estimated 2004 population*—22,880,000; density, 492 per mi² (190 per km²); distribution, 59 percent urban, 41 percent rural. *1993 census*—21,213,378.
Chief products: *Agriculture*—barley, corn, millet, potatoes, rice, wheat. *Manufacturing*—cement, chemicals, iron and steel, machinery, metals, processed foods, textiles. *Mining*—coal, iron ore, magnesium, phosphates, salt, tungsten. *Fishing*—pollock, sardines, shellfish, squid.
Money: *Basic unit*—won. One hundred zeuns equal one won.

© Dermot Tatlow, Panos Pictures

North Korean soldiers march before a huge statue of former leader Kim Il-sung in Pyongyang. North Korea's military force is one of the largest in the world. Kim ruled North Korea from 1948, when the country was established, until his death in 1994.

Symbols of North Korea. The North's flag and coat of arms have a red star that represents Communism. Rice and an electric power plant on the coat of arms stand for the importance of agriculture and industry to the North.

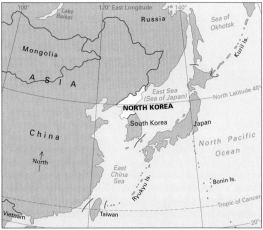

WORLD BOOK map

North Korea covers the northern part of the Korean Peninsula. China and Russia lie to the north. South Korea lies to the south.

North Korea map index

Provinces and Special Cities

Cities

*1987 official estimate.
Source: 1993 census, except
where indicated by *.

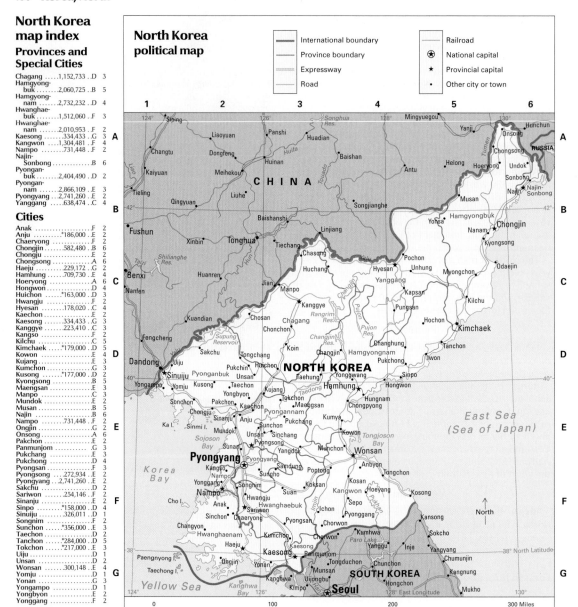

North Korea political map

WORLD BOOK map

lived together. The oldest male served as head of the family, and people were expected to obey their elders.

This way of life changed quickly after Japan seized control of the Korean Peninsula in 1910. The Japanese brought industry to Korean cities and took much farmland away from the farmers. They forcibly moved many young Koreans to the cities to work. The old way of life changed even more after Korea's division in the 1940's. In North Korea, the Communists took steps to establish an industrial society. Following Communist ideas, they also tried to weaken the importance of the family.

City life. Changes in North Korea since the 1950's have led to a rapid increase in the proportion of people living in cities. Most city dwellers in North Korea work in factories. The majority of them live in one- or two-room apartments built after Korea's division. Few city people besides high-ranking government officials have houses. Pyongyang is North Korea's most modern city, with skyscrapers, broad boulevards, cultural centers, and sports stadiums. However, it has few restaurants or places of entertainment. Few North Koreans own automobiles.

Rural life. After the division of Korea, the Communists in the North built many apartments on *collective farms* in rural areas. Most North Korean farmers work on such farms, which are operated cooperatively by a large group of farmers. Most farming is done with modern machinery. Virtually all homes have electric power.

Clothing. Most people in North Korea wear clothing

like that worn in other Asian countries, Europe, and the Americas. However, many people wear traditional clothing for holidays and special occasions. Traditional clothing for women consists of a long, full skirt and a tight-fitting jacket. For men, traditional clothing consists of loose-fitting trousers, shirts, and jackets.

Food and drink. Rice is the basic food of most North Koreans. Other common foods include barley; fish; such fruits as apples, peaches, pears, and melons; and such vegetables as beans, potatoes, and sweet potatoes. One of the most popular dishes other than rice is *kimchi,* a highly spiced mixture of cabbage, white radishes, and several other vegetables. Consumption of meat and dairy products is small but increasing.

Tea is a traditional drink in North Korea, but many people drink coffee. Adults drink *soju,* a distilled alcoholic beverage usually made from grain, as well as *ch'ongju,* known in the West as *sake* or rice wine. In the rural areas, a home-brewed drink known as *makkolli,* made from rice, has also been popular. Young adults frequently drink beer.

Recreation. Most forms of recreation and entertainment in North Korea are supported and controlled by the state. The government operates gymnasiums and promotes participation in organized sports programs. The cities have theaters for drama, opera, and motion pictures. Drama groups travel throughout the country to perform for workers in rural areas. North Koreans enjoy reading novels, short stories, and poems.

Religion. The North Korean Constitution guarantees religious freedom. But the government discourages religion because it conflicts with the teachings of Communism. Virtually no religious activities occur openly.

Traditionally, many Koreans have been followers of Confucianism, which is more a moral philosophy than a religion. It stresses the duties that people have toward one another. See **Confucianism.**

Education. Since the late 1940's, North Korea has made special efforts to improve its educational system. As a result, the number of North Koreans who can read and write increased from less than half of the adult population in the mid-1940's to almost all of the adults today. For the literacy rate of North Korea, see **Literacy** (table: Literacy rates for selected countries).

North Korea requires children to attend school for 11 years, including a year of preschool. The state pays all educational expenses. Students must work for the state during part of the summer.

Elementary school consists of grades 1 through 4, and senior middle school has grades 5 through 10. Students must have Communist Party approval to continue their education after senior middle school. Those who continue attend a two-year high school, a two-year vocational school, or a three- or four-year technical school that provides training in engineering and science. Students who finish high school or technical school may go to college immediately. Vocational school graduates must complete a year of special study before they enter college.

North Korea has one university—Kim Il-sung University in Pyongyang—and more than 200 specialized colleges. Each college offers training in one area, such as agriculture, engineering, or medicine. The government provides night schools for adults, training schools in factories, and courses for workers to take by mail.

The arts. Early Korean art developed under the influence of both Chinese art and the teachings of Buddhism and Confucianism. Popular themes included love of nature, respect for learning, and loyalty to the king. The most widely practiced art forms included music, poetry, pottery, sculpture, and painting.

In North Korea today, the government controls the work of artists. The government prohibits art that conflicts with Communist principles. It encourages artists to show support for the policies of the Communist Party.

The land

North Korea covers the northern part of the Korean Peninsula. A 487-square-mile (1,262-square-kilometer) *demilitarized* (neutral) zone separates North Korea from South Korea. North Korea shares most of its northern border with China. A small stretch of its northeastern border is shared with Russia. The East Sea, also called the Sea of Japan, lies east of North Korea and separates the country from Japan. The Korea Bay, part of the Yellow Sea, lies west of North Korea.

Rolling hills divide western North Korea into a series of broad, level plains. This region includes most of North Korea's farmland and its major industrial area, including Pyongyang. About half the North Korean people live in the western plains region.

Forested mountains cover almost all of central North Korea. These mountains are an important source of valuable minerals and forest products. North Korea's highest mountain, Paektu-san (Paektu Mountain), rises 9,003 feet (2,744 meters) on the border with China. North Korea's longest river, the Yalu, flows westward from this mountain along the border for 490 miles (789 kilometers) to the Yellow Sea. The Tumen (also spelled Tuman) River forms the border eastward from Paektu-san to the East Sea (Sea of Japan). Almost a fourth of North Korea's people live in the central mountain region.

The strip of land along North Korea's east coast consists of a series of narrow plains separated by low hills. The plains provide much farmland, and fishing also is

© Frilet, Sipa Press

Forested mountains cover almost all of the central region of North Korea. This rugged region is an important source of valuable minerals and forest products.

© Martin Sasse, laif/Aurora Photos

Bags of rice from South Korea are loaded onto a ship to be taken to North Korea. Since the mid-1990's, North Korea has had severe food shortages and has relied on international food aid.

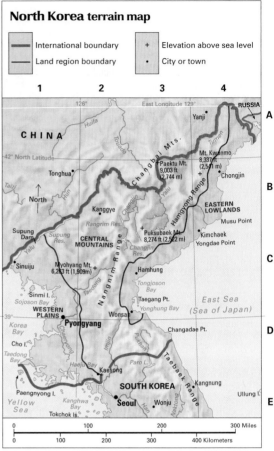

WORLD BOOK map

important in this region. The region also has some industrial areas. More than a fourth of North Korea's people live in the eastern lowland region.

Climate

Seasonal winds called *monsoons* affect North Korea's weather throughout the year. A monsoon blows in from the south and southeast during the summer, bringing hot, humid weather. A cold, dry monsoon blows in from the north and northwest during the winter, bringing cold weather.

July temperatures in North Korea average between 70 and 80 °F (21 and 27 °C). North Korea's massive mountains protect the east coast from the winter monsoon. As a result, the east coast generally has warmer winters than does the rest of the country. Average January temperatures are about –5 °F (–21 °C) in parts of the central mountains and about 18 °F (–9 °C) in Pyongyang.

Precipitation (rain, melted snow, and other forms of moisture) averages from 30 to 60 inches (76 to 150 centimeters) a year in most of North Korea. Heavy rainfall from June through August accounts for about half of the yearly precipitation. In most years, one or two typhoons hit the Korean Peninsula during July and August.

Economy

Before the Korean War (1950-1953), the economy of North Korea depended chiefly on agriculture, though there was some heavy industry. After the war, the country's economy grew rapidly. Industrial production, especially manufacturing, gained much importance.

In the 1970's, North Korea's economy began to decline. Rising debts, frequent droughts, mismanagement, and other factors have kept the country's economy from recovering. Today, North Korea's economy remains dependent on heavy industry. Its technology and economic production lag far behind that of South Korea.

North Korea releases little information about its economy, and so the statistics in this section are estimates. The value of goods and services produced each year in

Physical features

Chaeryong River	D 1	Puksubaek Mountain	C 3
Changadae Point	D 3	Rangrim Reservoir	C 2
Changjin Reservoir	C 3	Sinmi Island	D 1
Changjin River	B 2	Sojoson Bay	D 1
Cho Island	D 1	Supung Dam	C 1
Haeju Bay	E 2	Supung Reservoir	C 1
Hamgyong Range	B 3	Taedong Bay	D 1
Imjin River	D 2	Taedong River	C 2
Mount Kwanmo	B 4	Taegang Point	D 3
Musu Point	C 4	Tongjoson Bay	C 3
Myohyang Mountain	C 2	Tumen River	A 4
Nangnim Range	C 2	Yalu River	C 1
Paektu Mountain	B 3	Yongdae Point	C 4
Pukhan River	D 3	Yonghung Bay	D 3

North Korea totals an estimated $22 billion. This value is the country's *gross domestic product* (GDP). Industrial production probably accounts for the largest part of the GDP. Agriculture employs about 30 percent of North Korea's workers, manufacturing and mining about 30 percent, and service activities about 40 percent.

Service industries are economic activities that provide services rather than produce goods. Community, government, and personal services form North Korea's leading service industry group. This group includes such activities as education, health care, government, and the military. Trade, transportation, and communication are also important. The government owns nearly all service industries in North Korea.

Manufacturing and mining. North Korea's chief manufactured products are cement, chemicals, iron and steel, machinery, metals, processed foods, and textiles. The government owns nearly all North Korean factories, and it tightly controls all industry. North Korean mines yield coal, graphite, iron ore, lead, magnesium, phosphates, salt, silver, tungsten, and zinc.

Agriculture and fishing. The government controls all of North Korea's farms. Most farms are collective farms, known in North Korea as *cooperatives.* Workers on these farms receive a share of the products and some cash payment. They may also help manage the farms. A few farms, called *state farms,* are owned and managed completely by the government. The workers on state farms receive wages.

The western plains have most of North Korea's agriculture. Rice is by far the chief crop. Other major farm products include barley, corn, potatoes, and wheat.

North Korea's fishing industry centers on its eastern coast. The catch includes pollock, sardines, shellfish, and squid. Fishing cooperatives operate on both coasts.

International trade. North Korea's chief trading partners are China, Japan, and Russia. North Korea's leading exports are mined products, chiefly iron ore, lead, tungsten, and zinc. North Korea also exports cement, coal, machinery, rice, and textiles. Its major imports are grain, machinery, petroleum, and transportation equipment.

Energy sources. About three-quarters of North Korea's energy is produced by coal-burning plants. The rest of the country's energy comes from petroleum-burning plants and water power. North Korea mines all the coal it needs.

Transportation. Railroads carry most of North Korea's long-distance freight and passenger traffic. North Korea has greatly expanded its highway network since the mid-1960's. Buses operate in the cities and for short distances in rural areas. Almost all cars are government-owned and are intended for official business use. Many city people ride bicycles. North Korea operates an airline. The state runs the entire transportation system.

Communication. The government controls all broadcasting, publishing, and other communication in North Korea. It runs North Korea's radio and TV network and its broadcasting stations in the provinces. About five daily newspapers are published in North Korea.

History

This article discusses North Korean history from the mid-1940's to the present. For the history of the Korean Peninsula prior to 1948, see **Korea, History of.**

A divided peninsula. Korea was a colony of Japan from 1910 until 1945, when Japan was defeated in World War II. After Japan's defeat, United States troops occupied the southern half of Korea, and forces from the Soviet Union occupied the northern half. The United States and the Soviet Union tried to develop a plan for reuniting Korea. They failed, and the United States submitted the problem to the United Nations (UN) in 1947.

The UN wanted to supervise elections to choose one government for Korea. But the Soviet Union refused to allow UN representatives into the North. In the South, the Republic of Korea was formed on Aug. 15, 1948, under a government consisting of elected officials. In the North, the Communists announced the formation of the Democratic People's Republic of Korea on Sept. 9, 1948. Kim Il-sung became North Korea's leader. Both governments claimed to represent all of Korea.

In December 1948, the Soviet Union announced that

© Kyodo News

Garment workers assemble clothing at a factory in Pyongyang. Clothing and textiles are among North Korea's chief manufactured products. The government owns nearly all the factories.

all its troops had left North Korea. The United States withdrew its last troops from South Korea in mid-1949.

North Korean troops invaded the South in June 1950, and the Korean War began. The fighting continued until an armistice was signed in July 1953. Neither side won complete victory. The war involved not only the two Koreas, but also the most powerful Communist and non-Communist nations. The non-Communist nations fought under UN supervision. See **Korean War.**

Communism in North Korea. In 1946, when North Korea was still under Soviet occupation, the Communist government took over farmland from wealthy landowners and gave it to farmers living in poverty. The government also took control of most industries. Between 1953 and 1956, Kim Il-sung's government organized all farmland into collective farms. In 1954, it announced the first of a series of plans for economic development, all emphasizing heavy industry. North Korea also built up its military power. The government operated as a strict dictatorship. Kim remained in power until his death in 1994.

North-South relations. After the Korean War ended in 1953, the two sides remained hostile and suspicious of each other. In 1967, North Korean forces began making attacks in the *demilitarized* (neutral) zone between the North and the South and into South Korea. In 1968, about 30 North Korean troops raided Seoul in South Korea. They tried to assassinate South Korean President Park Chung Hee but failed.

In January 1968, North Korea seized the U.S. intelligence ship *Pueblo* in the East Sea (Sea of Japan). In 1969, North Korea shot down a U.S. Navy plane almost 100 miles (160 kilometers) off the North Korean coast.

In 1971, representatives of North and South Korea began formal reunification discussions for the first time since the Korean War. Tensions between the two re-

© Kurita Kaku, Gamma Presse

The demilitarized zone (DMZ) is a neutral strip of land that has separated North Korea from South Korea since the Korean War ended in 1953. The zone is $2\frac{1}{2}$ miles (4 kilometers) wide.

example, some North Korean and South Korean relatives have been allowed to visit one another, and a road has opened between the two countries.

In 2002, North Korea held talks with Japan, the United States, and other countries in efforts to establish friendlier relations. However, these efforts were thrown into disarray when North Korea revealed that it had a secret program to develop nuclear weapons. The program violated North Korea's 1994 agreement with the United States. In late 2002 and early 2003, North Korea expelled international atomic energy inspectors from the country and reactivated its nuclear facilities. Many experts believe North Korea already has one or more nuclear weapons.   Bonnie Bongwan Cho Oh and John K. C. Oh

Related articles include:

Army (The world's major armies)	Martial arts (Korean martial arts)
Chinese-Japanese wars	Panmunjom
Kim Il-sung	Pyongyang
Kim Jong-il	Russo-Japanese War
Korea, History of	Sculpture (Korea)
Korea, South	Tae kwon do
Korean War	Yalu River

Outline

I. Government
    A. National government
    B. Local government
    C. Politics
    D. Courts
    E. Armed forces
II. People
III. Way of life
    A. City life   E. Recreation
    B. Rural life   F. Religion
    C. Clothing   G. Education
    D. Food and drink   H. The arts
IV. The land
V. Climate
VI. Economy
    A. Service industries
    B. Manufacturing and mining
    C. Agriculture and fishing
    D. International trade
    E. Energy sources
    F. Transportation
    G. Communication
VII. History

Questions

When were North Korea and South Korea established?
What is the chief crop grown in North Korea?
Why did North Korea refuse to participate in the 1988 Summer Olympic Games?
What is the name of the strip of land that divides North and South Korea?
What is the difference between cooperatives and state farms?
How do monsoons affect the weather in North Korea?
What changes have taken place in North Korea's economy since the 1940's?
What was significant about the meeting between the leaders of North and South Korea in 2000?
What organization holds the real political power in North Korea?
Why do virtually no religious activities occur openly in North Korea?

Additional resources

Nanchu, and Hang, Xing. *In North Korea.* McFarland, 2003.
Salter, Christopher L. *North Korea.* Chelsea Hse., 2003.
Savada, Andrea M., ed. *North Korea: A Country Study.* 4th ed. 1994. Reprint. DIANE, 1995.
Yonhap News Agency staff. *North Korea Handbook.* M. E. Sharpe, 2003.

mained high, however. In 1983, a bomb blast killed 17 South Koreans, including four cabinet ministers, during an official South Korean presidential visit to Rangoon, Burma (now Yangon, Myanmar). A court in Burma found North Korean agents guilty of the bombing. In September and October 1988, South Korea hosted the Summer Olympics. North Korea refused to participate after its request to be named co-host was denied.

In 1991, the two governments agreed to accept each other's existence, and North and South Korea joined the UN as separate states. Also in 1991, talks resulted in several agreements, including a pact in which the two Koreas agreed not to use force against each other. As part of the pact, the two governments also agreed to increase trade and communication—which had been restricted—between them. Another accord prohibited North and South Korea from using or possessing nuclear weapons.

Recent developments. A crisis threatened to develop in 1994, when North Korea refused to allow international inspections of its nuclear sites. But North Korea signed a broad agreement with the United States promising to halt all nuclear weapons-related activities in return for energy assistance.

North Korea began experiencing severe food shortages in the mid-1990's. Floods and drought destroyed crops. Experts estimate that hundreds of thousands of North Koreans starved to death. Food aid from around the world began arriving in the late 1990's.

After Kim Il-sung died in 1994, a long struggle for power began. In 1998, North Korea's government proclaimed the deceased Kim Il-sung "eternal president." It then decreed that the head of the National Defense Commission would act as the country's highest living official. Kim Jong-il, Kim Il-sung's son, held this position and thus officially became North Korea's leader.

In 2000, Kim Jong-il met face-to-face in Pyongyang with South Korean President Kim Dae-jung to discuss relations. It was the first meeting between the leaders of North and South Korea since the peninsula was divided. As a result of this meeting, the two countries have made some additional moves toward improving relations. For

© Michael Setboun, Image Bank/Getty Images

Seoul is the capital and largest city of South Korea. It is also the center of the country's cultural, educational, commercial, and financial activities. Modern skyscrapers dominate the city's skyline. City Hall Plaza, *shown here,* is surrounded by office buildings, hotels, and crowded streets.

Korea, South, is one of two countries on the Korean Peninsula, which extends south from northeastern China in Asia. South Korea covers the southern half of the peninsula, and North Korea occupies the northern half.

South Korea's official name is the Republic of Korea. The country has a democratically elected government. Seoul is South Korea's capital and largest city.

People probably have lived on the Korean Peninsula for at least 30,000 years. Various Korean and foreign governments ruled the peninsula from ancient times to the 1900's. Korea was a colony of Japan from 1910 until World War II ended in 1945. After Japan's defeat in the war, Korea was divided. Communists gained control of the North in 1945. The separate governments of South and North Korea were formed in 1948.

In 1950, North Korean troops invaded South Korea. This action started the Korean War, which was part of the Cold War struggle between Communist and non-Communist nations. The Korean War ended in 1953. But neither side won a complete victory, and a permanent peace treaty has never been signed. See **Korean War.**

Facts in brief about South Korea

Capital: Seoul.
Official language: Korean.
Official name: Taehan-min'guk (Republic of Korea).
Area: 38,328 mi² (99,268 km²), including islands and excluding the 487-mi² (1,262-km²) demilitarized zone. *Greatest distances—*north-south, 300 mi (480 km); east-west, 185 mi (298 km). *Coastline—*819 mi (1,318 km).
Elevation: *Highest—*Halla-san (Halla Mountain), 6,398 ft (1,950 m) above sea level. *Lowest—*sea level.
Population: *Estimated 2004 population—*47,986,000; density, 1,252 per mi² (483 per km²); distribution, 79 percent urban, 21 percent rural. *2000 census—*45,985,289.
Chief products: *Agriculture—*apples, barley, cabbage, melons, onions, potatoes, rice, soybeans, sweet potatoes. *Manufacturing—*automobiles, chemicals, clothing, computer equipment, electric appliances, iron and steel, machinery, plywood, processed foods, rubber tires, ships, shoes, television sets, textiles. *Mining—*coal. *Fishing—*filefish, oysters, pollock.
Money: *Basic unit—*won. One hundred chon equal one won.

Plains stretch along the western and southern coasts of South Korea. Mountains cover most of the rest of the country. Most of the South Korean people live on the coastal plains or in river valleys.

Until the early 1900's, the economy of what is now South Korea was based almost entirely on agriculture, and nearly all Koreans were farmers. Today, industry is far more important than agriculture. Before the 1960's, South Korea was one of the world's poorest countries. However, the country has experienced huge economic growth since the 1960's. Today, South Korea has one of Asia's largest and wealthiest economies.

Government

According to its Constitution, South Korea is a republic. The Constitution calls for the election of national government leaders by the people. It guarantees such rights as freedom of the press and religion. But the government can limit freedom.

National government. The president of South Korea is the head of state and the country's most powerful official. The people elect the president to a five-year term. The president cannot be reelected. The president appoints a prime minister, who carries out the operations of the government. In addition, the president appoints 15 to 30 State Council members, who head government departments. South Korea's legislature, called the National Assembly, has 273 members. Voters elect the members of the National Assembly to four-year terms. South Koreans 20 years old or older may vote.

Local government. South Korea has nine provinces. The country also has seven cities that have the same status as provinces. Those cities are Inchon, Kwangju, Pusan, Seoul, Taegu, Taejon, and Ulsan. Each province is divided into two kinds of government units—cities and

---

The contributors of this article are Bonnie Bongwan Cho Oh, Distinguished Professor of Korean Studies at Georgetown University; and John K. C. Oh, Banigan Professor of Politics Emeritus at the Catholic University of America.

Symbols of South Korea. The South's flag and coat of arms feature a red and blue circle. This ancient Asian symbol represents the balance in the universe between opposites—such as night and day, and life and death.

WORLD BOOK map

South Korea occupies the southern part of the Korean Peninsula. North Korea occupies the northern part. The East Sea, also called the Sea of Japan, separates South Korea from Japan.

People

Ancestry. Ethnic Koreans make up almost the entire population of South Korea. A small minority of people are of Chinese descent.

Language. Korean is the official language of South Korea. Many scholars classify it in the same language family as Japanese, but Korean is unlike any other language. About half of all Korean words come from Chinese. Korean has about six major *dialects* (local forms). Most Koreans understand all the dialects.

The Korean alphabet, called *han'gul,* has 24 letters. It was developed by scholars at the court of King Sejong in the 1440's. South Koreans use some Chinese characters in addition to han'gul in their writing.

Way of life

Before the 1900's, the people of what is now South Korea lived in an agricultural society built on strong family ties. Most Koreans lived in small villages and worked on farms. In many families, several generations lived together. The oldest male served as head of the family, and people were expected to obey their elders.

This way of life changed quickly after Japan seized control of the Korean Peninsula in 1910. The Japanese brought industry to Korean cities and took much farmland away from the farmers. They forcibly moved many young Koreans to the cities to work. The old way of life changed even more after Korea's division into two countries in the 1940's. In South Korea, economic and political ties with Western nations brought South Koreans under the influence of Western culture.

City life. Changes in South Korea since the 1950's have led to a rapid increase in the proportion of city dwellers. South Koreans are attracted to cities because of the opportunities there. Factories and businesses provide jobs. The cities have colleges and universities, better health-care facilities, and a variety of entertainment.

counties. For many years, the president of South Korea appointed most local leaders. Since 1995, however, provincial governors, city mayors, and other city and county officials have been elected by the people.

Politics. Political parties in South Korea frequently change and reorganize. Today, important parties include the Democratic Labor Party, the Grand National Party, the Millennium Democratic Party, and the Uri Party.

Courts. The Supreme Court, which is South Korea's highest court, consists of a chief justice and up to 13 other justices. The president appoints the chief justice—and the other justices, who are recommended by the chief justice—with the approval of the National Assembly. All of the justices serve six-year terms. South Korea has a Constitutional Court that rules on such questions as the constitutionality of laws. Other courts include appeals courts, district courts, and a family court.

Armed forces. The South Korean army has about 520,000 members. South Korea also has a navy of about 60,000 and an air force of about 50,000. The government may draft men 17 to 33 years of age for 26 to 30 months of service. Women join the armed forces on a volunteer basis. About $3\frac{1}{2}$ million people are members of a civilian defense corps.

Korea National Tourist Office

Buddhism has had a strong influence on Korean culture. Today, many South Koreans, such as these monks, are Buddhists. Most South Koreans also participate in some Confucian practices.

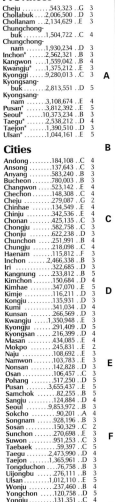

South Korea map index

Provinces

Cheju ....543,323 ..G 3
Chollabuk ...2,006,500 ..D 3
Chollanam ..2,134,629 ..E 3
Chungchong-
  buk ....1,504,722 ..C 4
Chungchong-
  nam ....1,930,234 ..D 3
Inchon* .....2,562,321 ..B 3
Kangwon ...1,559,042 ..B 4
Kwangju* ..1,375,212 ..E 3
Kyonggi ....9,280,013 ..C 3
Kyongsang-
  buk ....2,813,551 ..D 5
Kyongsang-
  nam ....3,108,674 ..E 4
Pusan* .....3,812,392 ..E 5
Seoul* ....10,373,234 ..B 3
Taegu* .....2,538,212 ..D 4
Taejon* ....1,390,510 ..D 3
Ulsan* ......1,044,161 ..E 5

Cities

Andong ....184,108 ..C 4
Ansong ....137,643 ..C 3
Anyang ....583,240 ..B 3
Bucheon ......780,003 ..B 3
Changwon ....523,142 ..E 4
Chechon ......148,308 ..C 4
Cheju ....279,087 ..G 2
Chinhae ......134,549 ..E 4
Chinju ....342,536 ..E 4
Chonan ....425,135 ..C 3
Chongju ......582,758 ..C 3
Chonju ....622,238 ..D 3
Chunchon ....251,991 ..B 4
Chungju ......218,098 ..C 4
Haenam ....115,812 ..F 3
Inchon ......2,466,338 ..B 3
Iri ....322,685 ..D 3
Kangnung ....233,812 ..B 5
Kimchon ......150,684 ..D 4
Kimhae ....347,070 ..E 5
Kimje ....116,211 ..D 3
Kongju ....135,931 ..D 3
Kumi ....341,034 ..D 4
Kumsan ....266,569 ..D 3
Kwangju ...1,350,948 ..E 3
Kyongju ......291,409 ..D 5
Kyongsan .....216,399 ..D 4
Masan ....434,085 ..E 4
Mokpo ....245,831 ..E 2
Naju ....108,692 ..E 3
Namwon ....103,783 ..E 3
Nonsan ....142,828 ..D 3
Osan ....106,457 ..C 3
Pohang ....517,250 ..D 5
Pusan ......3,655,437 ..E 5
Samchok ....82,255 ..B 5
Sangju ....124,884 ..D 4
Seoul ......9,853,972 ..B 3
Sokcho ....90,201 ..A 4
Songnam .....928,196 ..B 3
Sosan ....150,329 ..C 2
Sunchon ......270,698 ..E 3
Suwon ....951,253 ..C 3
Taebaek ....59,397 ..C 5
Taegu ......2,473,990 ..D 4
Taejon .....1,365,961 ..D 3
Tongduchon ...76,758 ..B 3
Uijongbu .....276,111 ..B 3
Ulsan ......1,012,110 ..E 5
Wonju ....237,460 ..B 4
Yongchon .....120,758 ..D 5
Yongju ....131,351 ..C 4
Yosu ....183,596 ..F 4

*Metropolitan area with province status.
Sources: 2000 census for provinces and largest cities; 2000 official estimates for other places.

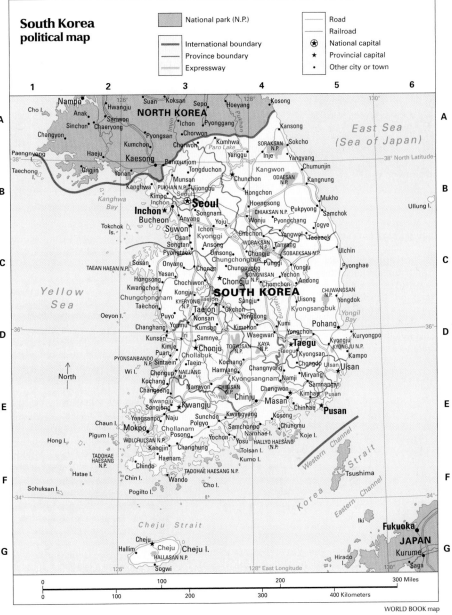

South Korea political map

National park (N.P.)
International boundary
Province boundary
Expressway
Road
Railroad
National capital
Provincial capital
Other city or town

WORLD BOOK map

Many high-rise apartment buildings and modern houses have been built in Seoul and other large South Korean cities. But it has been difficult to meet the rapidly rising need for housing, and many people must live in distant suburbs. The rise in population has also strained such public services as water, sewerage, and transportation. The crime rate in the cities has increased sharply. In addition, as South Koreans have become more prosperous, the number of automobiles has increased. Traffic jams are frequent, and major cities suffer from a severe pollution problem.

Rural life. Many South Koreans, including those in rural areas, live in houses made of bricks or concrete blocks, with roofs of cement tiles and slate. Many houses are two or three stories high, though such houses are

less common in rural areas than in the cities. Most houses have *ondol*—floors of thick stone slabs covered by oiled papers or mats. Traditionally, channels under the floors carried hot air from the kitchen or an indoor fireplace to heat the rooms. In many homes today, pipes carry heated water under the floors to provide heat. In the cities, many ondol are heated by electric coils. Almost all rural homes also have electric power.

The South Korean government maintains a campaign to improve roads, irrigation, and living conditions in rural areas. Most farmers have modern farm machinery.

Clothing. Most people in South Korea wear clothing like that worn in other Asian countries, Europe, and the Americas. However, many people wear traditional clothing for holidays and special occasions. Traditional cloth-

Traditional Korean music features several types of stringed instruments as well as drums, flutes, and gongs. These musicians are playing copies of instruments used hundreds of years ago.

Ministry of Culture and Information, Seoul, South Korea

ing for women consists of a long, full skirt and a tight-fitting jacket. For men, traditional clothing consists of loose-fitting trousers, shirts, and jackets.

Food and drink. Rice is the staple food of most South Korean diets. Other common foods include barley; fish; such fruits as apples, peaches, pears, and melons; and such vegetables as beans, potatoes, and sweet potatoes. A popular dish called *kimchi* consists of a highly spiced mixture of cabbage, white radishes, and several other vegetables. South Koreans consume small but increasing amounts of meat and dairy products.

Tea is South Korea's traditional beverage, but many people also drink coffee. Adults drink *soju,* a distilled alcoholic drink usually made from grain, as well as *ch'ongju,* known in the West as *sake* or rice wine. A home-brewed drink known as *makkolli,* made from rice, is popular in rural areas. Young adults often drink beer.

Recreation. South Koreans enjoy most sports common in the West, including baseball, boxing, golf, soccer, table tennis, tennis, and wrestling. They also enjoy such martial arts as *judo* and *tae kwon do*. Television and radio broadcasts of local and national athletic meets attract a wide audience. Each year, South Korea holds a national sports festival.

South Korean cities and towns have many theaters for motion pictures, plays, operas, and concerts. Orchestras perform classical and contemporary Western music. Television networks show dramas and comedies. South Koreans enjoy reading novels, short stories, and poems.

Religion. South Koreans have complete freedom of religion. Traditionally, many Koreans have been followers of Confucianism, which is more a moral philosophy than a religion. It stresses the duties that people have toward one another. Today, most South Koreans participate in at least some Confucian practices. For example, most families follow the Confucian practice of honoring their ancestors in special ceremonies. About 25 percent of South Koreans are Buddhists, about 20 percent are Protestants, and about 7 percent are Roman Catholics. Most of the rest of South Korea's people are not religiously active. See **Buddhism; Confucianism.**

Education. Since the late 1940's, South Korea has made special efforts to improve its educational system. As a result, the number of South Koreans who can read and write increased from less than half of the adult population in the mid-1940's to almost all of the adults today. For the literacy rate of South Korea, see **Literacy** (table:

Literacy rates for selected countries).

South Korean law requires that all children complete elementary school, which goes through grade 6. Public elementary schools in South Korea are free.

After completing elementary school, a South Korean student may go on to attend middle school (grades 7 through 9) and then high school (grades 10 through 12). Parents must pay tuition for public as well as private secondary schools. Nevertheless, the vast majority of children age 12 to 17 attend secondary school. Technical training, which prepares students for industrial jobs, begins in the middle schools and continues through all higher levels of education.

Qualified high school graduates may enter one of South Korea's more than 250 college-level schools. These schools provide training in a wide variety of subjects. More than 1 million students attend universities, colleges, and junior colleges in South Korea.

The arts. Early Korean art developed under the influence of both Chinese art and the teachings of Buddhism and Confucianism. Popular themes included love of nature, respect for learning, and loyalty to the king. The most widely practiced art forms included music, poetry, pottery, sculpture, and painting.

Today, South Korean artists work with traditional themes and with various Western art forms. Western art has influenced all South Korean art forms. This influence appears especially in the rapid development of Western forms of drama and of motion pictures since 1945.

The land

South Korea covers the southern part of the Korean Peninsula. A 487-square-mile (1,262-square-kilometer) *demilitarized* (neutral) zone separates South Korea from North Korea. The East Sea, also called the Sea of Japan, lies east of South Korea and separates the country from Japan. The Yellow Sea lies west of South Korea.

Forested mountains cover most of central and eastern South Korea, including much of the seacoast. River valleys, hillsides, and some land along the coast are used for farming. The coastal waters yield large amounts of fish. More than a fourth of the South Korean people live in the central and eastern mountains.

Plains separated by low hills cover the entire southern coast and almost the entire western coast. These regions are important centers for agriculture. Most of South Korea's important industrial centers, such as Pu-

Rice is by far the chief crop of South Korea. The country's major agricultural areas are a series of plains along the western and southern coasts. These rice fields lie near Kwangju, in the southern plains region. They are separated by low dirt walls called *dikes* or *levees,* which hold water in the fields.

© Craig J. Brown, Index Stock

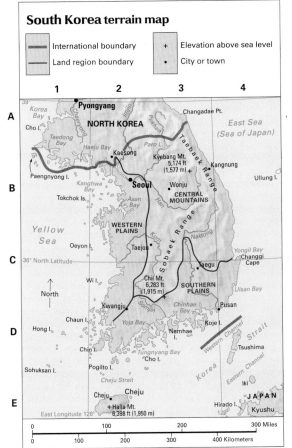

South Korea terrain map

▬▬ International boundary	+ Elevation above sea level
▬ Land region boundary	• City or town

0   100   200   300 Miles
0   100   200   300   400 Kilometers

WORLD BOOK map

Physical features

san and Seoul, are also in the south and west. About three-quarters of South Korea's people live in these southern and western plains regions.

The Naktong River, 325 miles (523 kilometers) long, is South Korea's longest river. It flows from the central mountains south to the Korea Strait. The Han River flows from the central mountains west to the Yellow Sea.

Most of South Korea's smaller islands are unpopulated. People live on the larger ones. Cheju Island, about 50 miles (80 kilometers) south of the peninsula, is the largest island. It covers about 700 square miles (1,800 square kilometers). Cheju has its own provincial government. Mainland provinces govern the other islands. South Korea's highest mountain, Halla-san (Halla Mountain), rises 6,398 feet (1,950 meters) on Cheju Island.

Climate

Seasonal winds called *monsoons* affect South Korea's weather throughout the year. A monsoon blows in from the south and southeast during the summer, bringing hot, humid weather. A cold, dry monsoon blows in from the north and northwest during the winter, bringing cold weather.

July temperatures in South Korea average between 70 and 80 °F (21 and 27 °C). South Korea's massive mountains protect the east coast from the winter monsoon. As a result, the east coast generally has warmer winters than does the rest of the country. Average January temperatures are about 35 °F (2 °C) in the southeast and about 23 °F (–5 °C) in Seoul.

Most of South Korea receives from 30 to 50 inches (76 to 130 centimeters) of precipitation (rain, melted snow, and other forms of moisture) yearly. Heavy rainfall from June through August accounts for about half of the yearly precipitation. In most years, one or two typhoons hit the Korean Peninsula during July and August.

Economy

Before the Korean War (1950-1953), South Korea's economy depended chiefly on agriculture, though there was some light industry. After the war, industrial production, especially manufacturing, gained much importance. In addition, such service activities as communication, government, trade, and transportation grew in importance.

Today, South Korea's economy is one of the largest in Asia, and its technology far exceeds that of North Korea.

A high-speed train, called Korea Train Express (KTX) operates between Pusan and Seoul. High-speed railroad service began in South Korea in 2004.

In the early 2000's, the value of goods and services produced each year in South Korea totaled about $475 billion. This value is the country's gross domestic product (GDP). Service industries account for about 55 percent of the GDP, and industrial production accounts for about 41 percent. Agriculture contributes about 4 percent. In the early 2000's, service activities employed about 61 percent of all South Korean workers, industrial activities about 28 percent, and agriculture about 11 percent.

Service industries are economic activities that provide services rather than produce goods. Such industries are especially important to the Seoul area.

Finance, insurance, real estate, and business services form South Korea's leading service industry group, in terms of the GDP. Government services and such community, social, and personal services as education and health care form the second-ranking group. This group employs about one-sixth of South Korea's people.

Wholesale and retail trade, hotels, and restaurants form the third-ranking group of service industries. This group, which benefits heavily from tourist activities, employs more than one-fourth of the country's workers. The fourth-ranking group, transportation and communication, is discussed later in this section.

Industrial activities. Almost all of South Korea's industry is privately owned. Manufacturing accounts for about 75 percent of the country's industrial production.

After the Korean War, South Korea developed heavy industry, and it now ranks as a major producer of chemicals, fertilizers, iron and steel, machinery, and ships. In the 1970's and 1980's, South Korea expanded its production of automobiles, computer equipment and parts, electric appliances, optical goods, telecommunications equipment, and television sets. Other manufactured products include paper, plywood, porcelain, and rubber tires. Food processing and the production of clothing and textiles are also important manufacturing activities.

South Korea's change from an agricultural economy to a modern industrial economy spurred a boom in construction. Factories, office and apartment buildings, highways, and water and sewerage systems have been built throughout the nation. Construction accounts for about 20 percent of industrial production, utilities account for about 7 percent, and mining accounts for less than 1 percent. Utilities include gas, electric, and water services. South Korea's leading mined products include *anthracite* (hard coal), gold, graphite, iron ore, lead,

limestone, tungsten, and zinc.

Agriculture and fishing. South Korea's $1\frac{1}{2}$ million farms average about $3\frac{1}{2}$ acres (1.4 hectares) in size. Almost all the farmland is privately owned. Rice is by far the country's chief crop. South Korean farms also produce apples, barley, cabbage, melons, onions, potatoes, soybeans, sweet potatoes, hogs, chickens, and cattle. The country's major agricultural areas lie along the western and southern coasts. A large orange crop is harvested on Cheju Island, off the southern coast.

South Korea is one of the world's leaders in the fishing industry. The catch includes filefish, oysters, pollock, squid, and tuna. Many farmers add to their income by fishing.

International trade. South Korea's chief trading partners are China, Japan, and the United States. South Korea's main exports include automobiles, clothing, electrical equipment, electronics, fish, ships, shoes, steel, and textiles. Its main imports include chemicals, crude oil and other industrial raw materials, and machinery.

Energy sources. Coal-, gas-, and petroleum-burning plants together provide about 55 percent of South Korea's electric power. Most of these plants use petroleum. South Korea imports all its petroleum. About 40 percent of South Korea's energy is generated by nuclear plants. A small percentage comes from water power.

Transportation. South Korea has an excellent government-owned railroad system and a highway network that includes expressways between the principal cities. However, traffic jams on the expressways occur frequently. South Korea has an average of about 1 automobile for every 5 people, and most urban households own a car. Buses and trains provide fast and frequent service. A high-speed railroad links Seoul and Pusan. Seoul has an extensive subway system. Many people in rural areas use bicycles for short trips.

Korean Air and Asiana Airlines, two privately owned airlines, provide international flights and service between major South Korean cities. Seoul, Pusan, and Inchon have international airports.

Communication. Private and government-owned radio and television networks broadcast throughout South Korea. About 60 daily newspapers are published in South Korea. The largest ones—*Choson Ilbo, Dong-A Ilbo, Hankook Ilbo,* and *Joong-ang Ilbo*—are all privately owned, published in Seoul, and sold throughout the country. There are two English-language dailies.

History

This article discusses South Korean history from the mid-1940's to the present. For the history of the Korean Peninsula prior to 1948, see **Korea, History of.**

A divided peninsula. Korea was a colony of Japan from 1910 until 1945, when Japan was defeated in World War II. After Japan's defeat, United States troops occupied the southern half of Korea, and forces of the Soviet Union occupied the northern half. The United States and the Soviet Union tried to develop a plan for reuniting Korea. They failed, and the United States submitted the problem to the United Nations (UN) in 1947.

The United Nations wanted to supervise elections to choose one government for Korea. But the Soviet Union refused to allow UN representatives into the North. In the South, in 1948, UN representatives supervised an election of representatives to a National Assembly. The Assembly drew up a constitution. In July 1948, the Assembly elected Syngman Rhee president of the Republic of Korea, which was formed on August 15. In northern Korea, the Communists announced formation of the Democratic People's Republic of Korea on September 9. Both governments claimed to represent all of Korea.

In December 1948, the Soviet Union announced that all its troops had left North Korea. The United States withdrew its last troops from South Korea in mid-1949.

North Korean troops invaded the South in June 1950, and the Korean War began. The fighting continued until an armistice was signed in July 1953. Neither side won complete victory. The war involved not only the two Koreas, but also the most powerful Communist and non-Communist nations. The non-Communist nations fought under UN supervision. See **Korean War.**

South Korea under Rhee. The division of Korea left the South with a weak economy. It had little industry and few electric power plants. The Korean War added to South Korea's economic problems. Fighting ruined farm crops and destroyed many factories. Hundreds of thousands of people were killed or wounded. South Korea had to rely heavily on aid from other countries.

Rhee's term was due to end in 1952. But members of the National Assembly had become increasingly critical of Rhee, and he feared the legislators would not reelect him. He pushed through the Assembly a constitutional amendment that turned over election of the president to the people. The voters reelected Rhee by a wide margin. In 1955, Rhee again had the Constitution amended to permit him to serve more than two terms. He was reelected to a third term in 1956. But an increasing number of South Koreans strongly opposed Rhee's undemocratic methods for keeping control of the government.

In March 1960, Rhee ran for a fourth term. He was unopposed because his opponent died one month before the election. Rhee and his party won. But in March and April, students led widespread demonstrations against the government. Rhee saw that he was rapidly losing political and military support, and he resigned in April.

Elections were held in July 1960, and a new government took office. But South Korea's economic difficulties continued, and the new government weakened as rival groups fought for political power. In May 1961, a group of military officers led by General Park Chung Hee overthrew the government. Park then became head of the new government. In 1963, Park called for elections to restore democratic government. He won the election for president, and his Democratic Republican Party gained a majority of the seats in the National Assembly.

South Korea under Park. South Korea's economy progressed rapidly under Park. His government concentrated on developing industries and increasing foreign trade. In 1967 and 1971, Park and his party won reelection by a large margin. In 1972, Park forced through a new constitution that gave him almost unlimited powers. It also provided that the president might serve an unlimited number of terms. Park was reelected by the country's electoral college—whose members had been chosen by his supporters—in a special election held that year. Park was reelected again in 1978. His party won the National Assembly elections in 1973 and 1978.

Park frequently used his power to suppress opposition to his government. Freedom of speech and of the press were limited, and many South Koreans who opposed Park were jailed. Many of Park's opponents denounced him as a dictator.

During the Korean War, United States troops had fought on the side of South Korea. After the war, thousands of U.S. troops were stationed in South Korea. In 1977—when about 38,000 troops remained—the United States government announced plans for a gradual withdrawal of all its troops. By mid-1979, about 10 percent of the troops had been withdrawn. But the United States government then said it would postpone further withdrawals until relations between North and South Korea improved. In 1981, U.S. President Ronald Reagan announced that no more U.S. troops would be withdrawn.

In October 1979, President Park was assassinated by Kim Jae Kyu, head of South Korea's Central Intelligence Agency (now called the Agency for National Security Planning). In December, Prime Minister Choi Kyu Hah was elected president by the electoral college.

The rise of Chun. Choi's government ended some of the restrictions on freedom of expression that Park had imposed. But the government delayed a promised constitutional revision that would allow the people to elect the president directly. Many South Koreans then staged demonstrations. In May 1980, military leaders declared martial law and reestablished the restrictions on freedom of expression. Choi remained president, but the military, led by Lieutenant General Chun Doo Hwan, dominated the government. After martial law was declared, violent clashes broke out between demonstrators and the military in the city of Kwangju. Hundreds of demonstrators were killed in what came to be known as the Kwangju Massacre.

In August 1980, Choi resigned, and the electoral college elected Chun president. In October, a new constitution was adopted. Martial law was repealed in January 1981. In February, Chun was again elected by the electoral college. The next month, Chun's Democratic Justice Party won a majority of seats in the National Assembly. Chun's government stabilized prices and increased exports, but scandals involving Chun's relatives lessened its popularity. Many students demonstrated against Chun and demanded a more democratic constitution.

A new constitution. In April 1987, demonstrations by citizens and students took place after Chun banned talks on constitutional reform until after the 1988 Summer

AP/Wide World

The leaders of South and North Korea met in 2000 for the first time since Korea was divided. North Korea's leader, Kim Jong-il, *left,* greeted South Korea's president, Kim Dae-jung, *right.*

Olympics in Seoul. In June, Chun designated Roh Tae Woo, his close associate and a former general, as the candidate for the Democratic Justice Party. Weeks of violent protests followed throughout the country. The protesters called for direct election of the president by the people rather than by the electoral college. At the end of June, Roh announced that he would support constitutional reform and direct election of the next president. The direct election was held in December, and Roh was elected president.

In October 1987, a new democratic constitution was adopted by a referendum of all the voters. It allows almost complete political freedom. Since its adoption, students have demonstrated in large numbers demanding correction of many social problems. Workers have staged frequent strikes for higher wages and better working conditions. The political and economic turmoil has slowed South Korea's economic growth.

North-South relations. After the Korean War ended in 1953, the two sides remained hostile and suspicious of each other. In 1967, North Korean forces began making attacks in the *demilitarized* (neutral) zone between the North and the South and into South Korea. In 1968, about 30 North Korean troops raided Seoul. They tried to assassinate President Park but failed.

In 1971, representatives of South and North Korea began formal reunification discussions for the first time since the Korean War. Tensions between the two remained high, however. In 1983, a bomb blast killed 17 South Koreans, including four cabinet ministers, during an official South Korean presidential visit to Rangoon, Burma (now Yangon, Myanmar). A court in Burma found North Korean agents guilty of the bombing. In September and October 1988, South Korea hosted the Summer Olympics. North Korea refused to participate after its request to be named co-host was denied.

In 1991, the two governments agreed to accept each other's existence, and North and South Korea joined the UN as separate states. Also in 1991, talks resulted in several agreements, including a pact in which the two Koreas agreed not to use force against each other. As part of the pact, the two governments also agreed to increase trade and communication—which had been restricted—between them. Another accord prohibited North and South Korea from using or possessing nuclear weapons.

Recent developments. In 1990, the Democratic Justice Party merged with two smaller parties to form the Democratic Liberal Party. Kim Young Sam, a Democratic Liberal, was elected president in 1992.

Kim Dae-jung, an advocate of democracy, was elected president in 1997. He was the first politician from an opposition party—a party that does not have a majority of seats in parliament—to hold South Korea's presidency.

Much of Asia experienced severe economic problems in the late 1990's. The value of South Korea's currency fell, and its stock market plunged. Businesses went bankrupt, and South Korea faced widespread unemployment. By 2000, the country largely recovered.

In 2000, Kim Dae-jung went to Pyongyang, North Korea, and met face-to-face with the North Korean leader, Kim Jong-il, to discuss relations. It was the first meeting between the leaders of South and North Korea since the peninsula was divided. As a result of this meeting, the two countries have made some additional moves toward improving relations. For example, some North Korean and South Korean relatives have been allowed to visit one another, and a road has been opened between the two countries. In 2002, however, North Korea admitted it was pursuing a nuclear weapons program, sparking an international crisis. As a result, tensions rose between North and South Korea.

In presidential elections in 2002, voters elected Roh Moo-hyun, the candidate from Kim Dae-jung's Millennium Democratic Party (MDP). Roh took office in 2003. In September of that year, Roh left the MDP. In March 2004, South Korea's National Assembly voted to impeach Roh, accusing him of election law violations and incompetence. In elections in April, the Uri Party, which supports Roh, won a majority in the National Assembly. In May, South Korea's Constitutional Court overturned Roh's impeachment, and he was reinstated as president.

Bonnie Bongwan Cho Oh and John K. C. Oh

Questions

When were South Korea and North Korea established?
What is the chief crop grown in South Korea?
How do monsoons affect the weather in South Korea?
What was the Kwangju Massacre?
What changes have taken place in South Korea's economy since the 1940's?
What was significant about the meeting between the leaders of South and North Korea in 2000?
What is the name of the strip of land that divides South and North Korea?
Who was Park Chung Hee?
What are South Korea's major manufacturing industries?

Additional resources

Lie, John. *Han Unbound: The Political Economy of South Korea.* Stanford, 1998.
Masse, Johanna. *South Korea.* Gareth Stevens, 2002. Younger readers.
Nahm, Andrew C., and Hoare, James. *Historical Dictionary of the Republic of Korea.* 2nd ed. Scarecrow, 2004.
Ryu, Je-Hun. *Reading the Korean Cultural Landscape.* Hollym, 2000.

Rock is the hard mineral substance that forms the solid part of Earth's crust. Mountains and canyons expose many different types of rock on their surfaces. Great cliffs of rock line the seashore in such places as Maine, California, and southern England. In many desert regions, rock formations rise above sandy plains. In most fairly flat areas, a layer of soil covers the underlying rock. Soil consists of tiny fragments of rock and grains of minerals mixed with decaying remains of plants and animals. Stones and pebbles are pieces of rock, and gravel consists of loose, rounded rock fragments.

Most rocks are *aggregates.* Aggregates contain crystals or grains of two or more minerals. Much granite, for example, contains grains of clear quartz, pinkish potassium feldspar, white plagioclase, and black biotite or hornblende. Some rocks have grains so small that they can be seen only under a microscope. A few kinds of rock consist almost entirely of only one mineral. *Quartzite,* for example, is composed of the mineral quartz, and *limestone* is made up of the mineral calcite.

People use rocks in many ways. Builders use granite, marble, and other rocks as construction materials. Cement is made from finely crushed and heated limestone. Sand and gravel or crushed stone mixed with wet cement makes strong, durable concrete, an artificial rock, for use in buildings, highways, and dams.

Such metals as aluminum, copper, iron, lead, tin, and zinc come from rocks called *ores.* Ores also supply radioactive metals, such as uranium, and nonmetallic minerals, such as borax, graphite, and trona. In Minnesota and western Australia, deposits of iron ore make up entire mountains. In tropical climates, *weathering* (the wearing away of rock) creates thick soils rich in the aluminum-bearing ore *bauxite.*

Some rocks hold valuable crystals. In Africa and Australia, workers mine diamonds from a rock called *kimberlite.* Beautiful green emeralds come from rocks in Colombia, India, Russia, and South Africa. Most blue aquamarine comes from Brazil and Madagascar. Emerald and aquamarine are gem forms of the mineral beryl.

Geologists study rocks to trace Earth's history. Petroleum geologists analyze the age, structure, and composition of rock layers to find petroleum deposits. *Paleontologists* study fossils found in rock to learn about living things that existed millions of years ago.

Many young people and adults collect rocks and minerals as a hobby. There are thousands of rock and mineral clubs throughout the world. These clubs hold regular meetings, sponsor study groups and museum exhibits, and organize field trips to collecting areas.

Geologists classify rock according to how it formed. The three classes of rock are: (1) *igneous* rock, (2) *sedimentary* rock, and (3) *metamorphic* rock.

Igneous rock

Igneous rock forms from *magma* (molten rock). Magma is extremely hot, with temperatures ranging from 1400 to 2300 °F (760 to 1300 °C). Most magma lies deep below Earth's surface. Sometimes, magma rises to the surface through *fissures* (deep cracks) in Earth's crust. Other times, magma travels up *conduits* (pipelike channels in the rock) and erupts at the surface, forming a volcano. Magma cools and hardens into igneous rock. Geologists divide igneous rock into two types: *extrusive* rock and *intrusive* rock.

Extrusive rock forms from magma that reaches Earth's surface. The magma emerges as streams of hot lava or as fine cinders and ash. Volcanoes are piles of lava, cinder, and ash that have accumulated over tens, hundreds, or even millions of years.

Magma hardens quickly when exposed to the cooler temperatures on the surface, leaving little time for minerals to *crystallize* (develop crystals). As a result, most extrusive rocks have small grains. In some cases, magma cools so quickly that it forms *obsidian,* a smooth, shiny volcanic glass with few crystals. Often, gas dissolved in the magma bubbles out as the magma cools. The gas bubbles leave cavities in the rock. Geologists call volcanic rock with many round or oval-shaped cavities *scoria.* Magmas rich in dissolved gases can form *pumice,* a rock filled with so many tiny cavities that it can float on water. Lava that hardens more slowly forms rocks composed entirely of crystals.

Dark-colored igneous rocks called *basalts* result from magmas that contain little dissolved gas and erupt rather slowly. Light-colored igneous rocks called *andesites* commonly come from magmas that contain much dissolved gas and erupt with explosive violence. Explosive eruptions produce rock fragments ranging from tiny particles of volcanic dust to lumps called *volcanic bombs* that measure 3 feet (1 meter) or more in diameter. Rocks called *volcanic breccias* consist of fragments of cooling magma that become welded together.

Intrusive rocks form from magma that does not rise all the way to Earth's surface. Instead, it pushes into older rock formations and hardens into structures called *intrusions.* Intrusions that cut across older rock layers are called *dikes. Sills* are intrusions that spread out between older rock layers, forming a parallel layer. Some sills, called *laccoliths,* push the rock layers above them into a domelike formation. Magma can melt older rocks and pass through them, creating huge intrusions called *batholiths* and smaller intrusions called *stocks.*

Beneath the surface, magma cools and hardens slowly. As a result, most intrusive rocks have crystal grains large enough to be seen with the unaided eye. Intrusive rocks include dark-colored *gabbros* and light-colored *diorites* and granites. In some places, the last pockets of slowly crystallizing magma are rich in rare elements and form giant crystal grains. These rocks, known as *pegmatites,* may contain beautiful crystals of tourmaline, beryl, spodumene, and other unusual minerals.

Sedimentary rock

Sedimentary rock forms from loose materials called *sediments.* Sediments can include plant and animal remains and fragments of older rocks. They accumulate in layers called *strata.* As more strata are deposited, the sediments harden into solid rock. Most sedimentary rock forms on the ocean floor, but some develops on land and in fresh water. Geologists classify sedimentary rocks by the type of sediments that formed them.

Clastic sediments are rock fragments that range in size from large boulders and stones, through pebbles and gravel, to grains of sand and particles of *silt* (fine dirt) and clay. Air, water, and frost create these sediments by weathering rock, breaking it into fragments.

Clastic sediments can be carried about and deposited by running water, wind, or glaciers. As the sediments accumulate, the weight of the upper strata compacts the sediments below, squeezing the water from them. These lower sediments turn to rock through a process called *lithification*. In lithification, natural chemical substances left behind by groundwater cement the grains together. Deposits of silt lithify to form the rock *siltstone*, and layers of clay lithify to form *shale*. Sandstones form from layers of sand. *Conglomerates* form where layers of water-worn boulders, stones, and pebbles become cemented together. *Sedimentary breccias* form from angular pieces of rock that have not been moved far and that have been rounded by flowing water.

Chemical sediments are minerals that dissolve in water. When the water evaporates, the minerals crystallize, leaving deposits of such minerals as *rock salt* (sodium chloride), *phosphate rock* (calcium phosphate), and *gypsum* (calcium sulfate). Many limestone

deposits formed from crystals of *calcite* (calcium carbonate), and most large iron ore deposits crystallized from iron oxide once dissolved in ancient oceans.

Organic sediments are the shells, skeletons, and other parts of once-living things. Shellfish take calcite from water and use it to build their shells. Corals use the same mineral to build coral reefs. Deposits of coral and shells can lithify to form *fossiliferous limestone*.

Rock can also form from the accumulation of skeletons of single-celled sea creatures, such as *foraminifera, diatoms,* and *radiolaria*. The calcite shells of foraminifera form chalky limestone, such as that which makes up the famous white cliffs of Dover, England. Diatom shells, made of the mineral silica, form *diatomite*. The silica skeletons of *radiolaria* form beds of a rock called *radiolarian chert* in the deep ocean.

Coal develops from accumulations of dead plant matter in tropical swamps. These deposits compact into a decayed plant material called *peat*. As the peat becomes buried, pressure and heat turn it into coal.

Metamorphic rock

Metamorphic rock forms when a rock's appearance—and, in most cases, its mineral composition—

Common rocks

Rocks are classified into three major groups. *Igneous rock* forms from hardened magma. Hardening of various plant, animal, and mineral materials results in *sedimentary rock. Metamorphic rock* generally forms when any kind of rock undergoes changes as a result of heat or pressure or both.

Igneous

A. W. Ambler, NAS/Photo Researchers
Basalt

Lee Boltin
Gabbro

WORLD BOOK photo
Granite

Lee Boltin
Obsidian

Sedimentary

L. S. Stepanowicz, Panographics
Bituminous coal

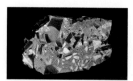
Lee Boltin
Breccia

L. S. Stepanowicz, Panographics
Flint

WORLD BOOK photo
Limestone

Metamorphic

L. S. Stepanowicz, Panographics
Amphibolite

Charles R. Belinky, Photo Researchers
Gneiss

L. S. Stepanowicz, Panographics
Pink marble

A. W. Ambler, NAS/Photo Researchers
Quartzite

changes. Geologists call this process of change *metamorphism.*

Metamorphism often takes place when heat and pressure increase as rock becomes more deeply buried. The intrusion of magma can heat nearby rock, causing *contact metamorphism.* The forces that create mountains not only produce heat and pressure but also deform the rocks. Metamorphism and deformation turn granite into *gneiss,* a metamorphic rock with wavy bands of feldspar, quartz, and mica crystals. Metamorphism can cause the calcite in limestone to recrystallize, forming marble. The grains in quartz-rich sandstone can grow together to form quartzite. Shales harden to form *slate,* a rock that splits into smooth slabs. At higher temperatures, shales and siltstones turn into *schists* that glisten with mica and other minerals, such as hornblende and chlorite. Some minerals, such as andalusite, kyanite, sillimanite, and staurolite, only form during metamorphism.

The rock cycle

Each type of rock develops from other types of rock. To help explain how rocks form, geologists sometimes refer to a series of transformations called the *rock cycle.* The rock cycle begins with igneous rock created by magma flowing to Earth's surface. Weathering alters the rock chemically and breaks it into particles. The particles accumulate and harden to form sedimentary rock. As the sedimentary rock becomes buried, heat and pressure transform it into metamorphic rock. With enough heating, metamorphic rocks melt into magma that can form igneous rock, completing the cycle.

Rock rarely proceeds through the entire rock cycle. The cycle may be halted, or steps can be skipped, repeated, or reversed. For example, some igneous rocks transform directly into metamorphic rock, and sedimentary rock can weather and then lithify to form other kinds of sedimentary rock.

Rocks as a hobby

You can find interesting rocks in many places near your home. Good "hunting grounds" include mines, quarries, building excavations, ocean cliffs and beaches, and the rocky sides of road cuts and riverbanks. Be careful when working near steep rock walls, roadways, deep holes, and other dangerous areas. Always obtain permission to visit private property.

Tools. You can start a collection by gathering loose rocks, but a few simple tools will help in obtaining good specimens. A rock hammer, the most important tool, has a square head and a pointed end for breaking specimens from the surrounding rock. A chisel helps loosen crystals. Some rock hunters use a magni-

Igneous rocks

Rock	Color	Structure
Basalt	Dark greenish-gray to black.	Dense, microscopic crystals, often form columns.
Gabbro	Greenish-gray to black.	Coarse crystals.
Granite	White to gray, pink to red.	Tightly arranged medium-to-coarse crystals.
Obsidian	Black, sometimes with brown streaks.	Glassy, no crystals, breaks with a shell-like fracture.
Peridotite	Greenish-gray.	Coarse crystals.
Pumice	Grayish-white.	Light, glassy, frothy, fine pores, floats on water.

Lee Boltin

Peridotite

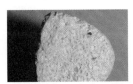

L. S. Stepanowicz, Panographics

Pumice

Sedimentary rocks

Rock	Color	Structure
Breccia	Gray to black, tan to red.	Angular pieces of rock, held together by natural cement.
Coal	Shiny to dull black.	Brittle, in seams or layers.
Flint	Dark gray, black, brown.	Hard, glassy, breaks with a sharp edge.
Limestone	White, gray, and buff to black and red.	Dense, forms thick beds and cliffs. May contain fossils.
Sandstone	White, gray, yellow, red.	Fine or coarse grains cemented together in beds.
Shale	Yellow, red, gray, green, black.	Dense, fine particles, soft, splits easily, smells like clay.

A. W. Ambler, NAS/Photo Researchers

Sandstone

A. W. Ambler, NAS/Photo Researchers

Shale

Metamorphic rocks

Rock	Color	Structure
Amphibolite	Light green to black.	Fine-to-coarse grains, hard, often sparkles.
Gneiss	Gray and pink to black and red.	Medium to coarse crystals arranged in bands.
Marble	Many colors, often mixed.	Medium to coarse crystals, may be banded.
Quartzite	White, gray, pink, buff.	Massive, hard, often glassy.
Schist	White, gray, red, green, black.	Flaky particles, finely banded, feels slippery, often sparkles with mica.
Slate	Black, red, green, purple.	Fine grains, dense, splits into thin, smooth slabs.

Lee Boltin

Schist

George Whitely, Photo Researchers

Slate

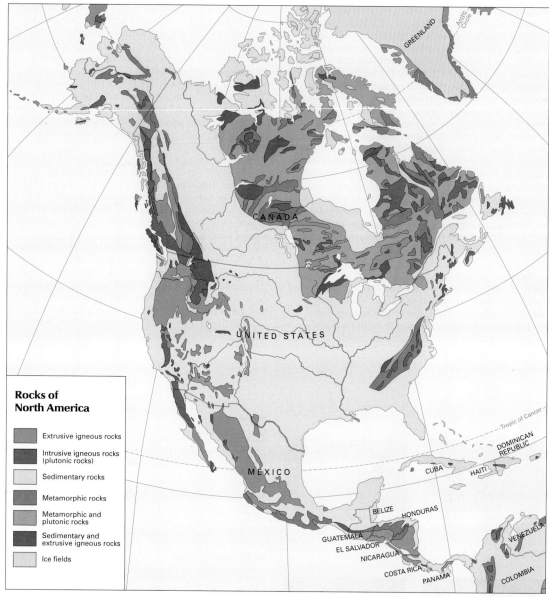

Rocks of North America

Extrusive igneous rocks

Intrusive igneous rocks (plutonic rocks)

Sedimentary rocks

Metamorphic rocks

Metamorphic and plutonic rocks

Sedimentary and extrusive igneous rocks

Ice fields

WORLD BOOK map

Interesting facts about rocks

Balanced Rock, in the Garden of the Gods near Colorado Springs, Colorado, is an enormous block of sandstone delicately balanced on a small base.

Bendable rock. Most rocks cannot be bent or squeezed out of shape. But thin slabs of itacolumite, a rare kind of sandstone found in India and North Carolina, can be bent by hand because of their crystalline structure.

Eight elements make up more than 98 percent of all the rocks in the world. These elements are found in about the following percentages: oxygen (46.5), silicon (27.6), aluminum (8.0), iron (5.0), calcium (3.6), sodium (2.8), potassium (2.6), and magnesium (2.0).

Floating rock. Pumice is a rock that floats on water. It was once volcanic lava filled with gases. When the gases escaped, they left millions of tiny holes that filled with air.

Rock of Gibraltar is a huge block of limestone near the southern tip of the mainland of Europe.

fying glass in choosing desirable specimens. Scratching a specimen across a piece of unglazed porcelain called a *streak plate* can help rock collectors recognize minerals. A pocketknife makes a handy tool for testing mineral hardness. You can buy all these tools inexpensively from a hardware store or mineral dealer and carry them in a small backpack. You can wrap specimens in newspaper or tissue paper to protect them.

As you collect, label each specimen with the location and date of collection and the kind of rock or mineral it may be. Later, you can transfer this information to a permanent record book or computer file.

Identifying rocks. You can identify a specimen by comparing it to pictures in a reference book or rock samples from a reference collection. A useful reference book for identifying rocks should feature good color photographs. You can purchase small reference collections of rocks and mineral specimens inexpensively from a rock or mineral dealer.

All minerals have special characteristics that can help you identify them. Experienced collectors also study the formations in which rocks are found.

Chemical composition may be determined by certain chemical tests for the mineral elements. For example, a simple chemical test for calcite in limestone is to pour a warm soft drink over the rock. The soft drink, a weak acid, fizzes vigorously on limestone.

Hardness is a measure of how easy it is to scratch a mineral. You can scratch soft minerals with your fingernail and harder minerals using a steel knife blade or pin. The hardest minerals resist scratching by all materials except diamond—the hardest mineral known.

Streak color is the color of the powder obtained by rubbing a mineral across a streak plate. The powder color often differs from the color of the mineral mass. For example, the mineral *pyrite* (ferrous sulfide) looks yellow in rocks. But its streak color is black.

Formations. You can often identify rocks by knowing where they are found and how they look. For example, you usually can recognize sedimentary rocks because they lie in *stratified* (layered) formations. Also, they often contain fossils, and many have markings, such as old mud cracks or ripple marks caused by waves.

Displaying rocks. The size of the rocks in your collection will depend on the available storage space. Some people collect *micromounts,* tiny samples that can be kept in small boxes and viewed under a low-power microscope. Other people prefer larger specimens of the size found in museum collections. Probably the best size for storage ranges from 2 by 3 inches (5 by 8 centimeters) to about 3 by 4 inches (8 by 10 centimeters). You can trim rocks to the desired size with a hammer, but be careful not to damage choice crystals. You can clean dirty specimens by washing them with soap and water and brushing them with a stiff brush. Specimens that contain rock salt cannot be washed, because the salt dissolves in water. You can brush or blow the dirt from most such specimens.

After cleaning your specimens, you can catalog them by painting a small white spot on each rock and writing a number on the spot with waterproof ink.

David R. Frazier

Rock hunters search for specimens near a stream. The man is using a rock hammer to chip a sample from a larger stone.

You can then refer to the corresponding number in your record book or computer file for information about the specimen.

A chest of drawers or a set of bookshelves makes an ideal storage unit. Place your rocks in shallow cardboard trays. You might keep small specimens and crystals in cardboard boxes or trays that have partitions. Small exhibits of choice specimens make attractive displays on mantels or shelves or in glass-front cases.

Rock collections. Many museums throughout the world exhibit excellent collections of rocks and minerals. Museums connected with local and regional geological surveys often have exhibits of fossils, minerals, and rocks found in the surrounding area.

Mark Cloos

Additional resources

Level I

Kittinger, Jo S. *A Look at Minerals.* Watts, 1998.
Staedter, Tracy. *Rocks and Minerals.* Reader's Digest, 1999.

Level II

Hurlbut, Cornelius S., and Sharp, W. E. *Dana's Minerals and How to Study Them.* Rev. ed. Wiley, 1997.
Vernon, Ron. Beneath *Our Feet: The Rocks of Planet Earth.* Cambridge, 2000.

A **Chinese Long March rocket** rises from its launch pad carrying an astronaut on the spacecraft Shenzhou 5. Most rockets use chemical reactions to expel gas, producing a force called *thrust.*

Rocket

Rocket is a type of engine that pushes itself forward or upward by producing thrust. Unlike a jet engine, which draws in outside air, a rocket engine uses only the substances carried within it. As a result, a rocket can operate in outer space, where there is almost no air. A rocket can produce more power for its size than any other kind of engine. For example, the main rocket engine of the space shuttle weighs only a fraction as much as a train engine, but it would take 39 train engines to produce the same amount of power. The word *rocket* can also mean a vehicle or object driven by a rocket engine.

Rockets come in a variety of sizes. Some rockets that shoot fireworks into the sky measure less than 2 feet (60 centimeters) long. Rockets 50 to 100 feet (15 to 30 meters) long serve as long-range missiles that can be used to bomb distant targets during wartime. Larger and more powerful rockets lift spacecraft, artificial satellites, and scientific probes into space. For example, the Saturn 5 rocket that carried astronauts to the moon stood about 363 feet (111 meters) tall.

Rocket engines generate thrust by expelling gas. Most rockets produce thrust by burning a mixture of fuel and an *oxidizer,* a substance that enables fuel to burn without drawing in outside air. This kind of rocket is called a *chemical rocket* because burning fuel is a chemical reaction. The fuel and oxidizer are called the *propellants.*

A chemical rocket can produce great power, but it burns propellants rapidly. As a result, it needs a large amount of propellants to work for even a short time. The Saturn 5 rocket burned more than 560,000 gallons (2,120,000 liters) of propellants during the first $2\frac{3}{4}$ minutes of flight. Chemical rocket engines become extremely hot as the propellants burn. The temperature in some engines reaches 6000 °F (3300 °C), much higher than the temperature at which steel melts.

Jet engines also burn fuel to generate thrust. Unlike rocket engines, however, jet engines work by drawing in oxygen from the surrounding air. For more information on jet engines, see **Jet propulsion.**

Researchers have also developed rockets that do not burn propellants. *Nuclear rockets* use heat generated by a nuclear fuel to produce thrust. In an *electric rocket,* electric energy produces thrust.

Military forces have used rockets in war for hundreds of years. In the 1200's, Chinese soldiers fired rockets against attacking armies. British troops used rockets to attack Fort McHenry in Maryland during the War of 1812 (1812-1815). After watching the battle, the American lawyer Francis Scott Key described "the rocket's red glare" in the song "The Star-Spangled Banner." During World War I (1914-1918), the French used rockets to shoot down enemy observation balloons. Germany attacked London with V-2 rockets during World War II (1939-1945). In the Persian Gulf War of 1991 and the Iraq War, which began in 2003, United States troops launched rocket-powered Patriot missiles to intercept and destroy Iraqi missiles.

Rockets are the only vehicles powerful enough to carry people and equipment into space. Since 1957, rockets have lifted hundreds of artificial satellites into orbit around Earth. These satellites take pictures of Earth's weather, gather information for scientific study, and transmit communications around the world. Rockets also carry scientific instruments far into space to explore and study other planets. Since 1961, rockets have launched spacecraft carrying astronauts and cosmonauts into orbit around Earth. In 1969, rockets carried astronauts to the first landing on the moon. In 1981, rockets lifted the first space shuttle into Earth orbit.

How rockets work

Rocket engines generate thrust by putting a gas under pressure. The pressure forces the gas out the end of the rocket. The gas escaping the rocket is called exhaust. As it escapes, the exhaust produces thrust according to

© Agence France Presse/Getty Images

The contributor of this article, Stephen D. Heister, is Professor of Aeronautics and Astronautics at Purdue University.

the laws of motion developed by the English scientist Isaac Newton. Newton's third law of motion states that for every action, there is an equal and opposite reaction. Thus, as the rocket pushes the exhaust backward, the exhaust pushes the rocket forward.

The amount of thrust produced by a rocket depends on the *momentum* of the exhaust—that is, the force with which it moves. The exhaust's momentum equals its *mass* (amount of matter) multiplied by the speed at which it exits the rocket. The more momentum the exhaust has, the more thrust the rocket produces. Engineers can therefore increase a rocket's thrust by increasing the mass of exhaust it produces. Alternately, they can increase the thrust by increasing the speed at which the exhaust leaves the rocket.

Parts of a rocket include the rocket engine and the equipment and cargo the rocket carries. The four major parts of a rocket are (1) the payload, (2) propellants, (3) the chamber, and (4) the nozzle.

The payload of a rocket includes the cargo, passengers, and equipment the rocket carries. The payload may consist of a spacecraft, scientific instruments, or even explosives. The space shuttle's payload, for example, is the shuttle orbiter and the mission astronauts and any satellites, scientific experiments, or supplies the orbiter carries. The payload of a missile may include explosives or other weapons. This kind of payload is called a *warhead.*

Propellants generally make up most of the weight of a rocket. For example, the fuel and oxidizer used by the space shuttle account for nearly 90 percent of its weight at liftoff. The shuttle needs such a large amount of propellant to overcome Earth's gravity and the resistance of the atmosphere.

The space shuttle and many other chemical rockets use liquid hydrogen as fuel. Hydrogen becomes a liquid only at extremely low temperatures, requiring powerful cooling systems. Kerosene, another liquid fuel, is easier to store because it remains liquid at room temperature.

Many rockets, including the space shuttle, use liquid oxygen, or *lox,* as their oxidizer. Like hydrogen, oxygen must be cooled to low temperatures to become a liquid. Other commonly used oxidizers include nitrogen tetroxide and hydrogen peroxide. These oxidizers remain liquid at room temperature and do not require cooling.

An electric or nuclear rocket uses a single propellant. These rockets store the propellant as a gas or liquid.

The chamber is the area of the rocket where propellants are put under pressure. Pressurizing the propellants enables the rocket to expel them at high speeds.

In a chemical rocket, the fuel and oxidizer combine and burn in an area called the *combustion chamber.* As they burn, the propellants expand rapidly, creating intense pressure.

Burning propellants create extreme heat and pressure in the combustion chamber. Temperatures in the chamber become hot enough to melt the steel, nickel, copper, and other materials used in its construction. Combustion chambers need insulation or cooling to survive the heat. The walls of the chamber must also be strong enough to withstand intense pressure. The pressure inside a rocket engine can exceed 3,000 pounds per square inch (200 kilograms per square centimeter), nearly 100 times the pressure in the tires of a car or truck.

In a nuclear rocket, the chamber is the area where nu-clear fuel heats the propellant, producing pressure. In an electric rocket, the chamber contains the electric devices used to force the propellant out of the nozzle.

The nozzle is the opening at the end of the chamber that allows the pressurized gases to escape. It converts the high pressure of the gases into thrust by forcing the exhaust through a narrow opening, which accelerates the exhaust to high speeds. The exhaust from the nozzle can travel more than 1 mile (1.6 kilometers) per second. Like the chamber, the nozzle requires cooling or insulation to withstand the heat of the exhaust.

Multistage rockets. Many chemical rockets work by burning propellants in a single combustion chamber. Engineers refer to these rockets as *single-stage rockets.* Missions that require long-distance travel, such as reaching Earth orbit, generally require *multiple-stage* or *multistage rockets.* A multistage rocket uses two or more sets of combustion chambers and propellant tanks. These sets, called *stages,* may be stacked end to end or attached side by side. When a stage runs out of propellant, the rocket discards it. Discarding the empty

How a multistage rocket works

A two-stage rocket consists of two units called *stages.* Each stage has its own propellant tanks and one or more engines. When the first stage runs out of propellant, it drops away. The second stage ignites, carrying the payload farther. Additional rockets called boosters can be attached to increase the rocket's power.

WORLD BOOK diagram by Oxford Designers and Illustrators

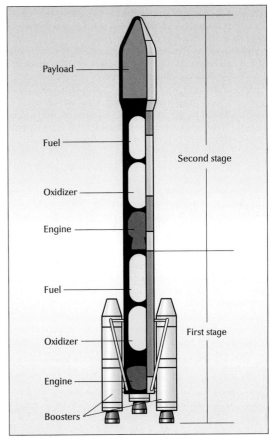

A Patriot missile takes off from its launcher in a blast of heat and smoke. Military rockets, such as the Patriot, use sophisticated guidance systems to reach distant targets. The Patriot can destroy enemy missiles in midair.

Raytheon Company

stage makes the rocket lighter, allowing the remaining stages to accelerate it more strongly. Engineers have designed and launched rockets with as many as five separate stages. The space shuttle uses two stages.

How rockets are used

People use rockets for high-speed, high-power transportation both within Earth's atmosphere and in space. Rockets are especially valuable for (1) military use, (2) atmospheric research, (3) launching probes and satellites, and (4) space travel.

Military use. Rockets used by the military vary in size from small rockets used on the battlefield to giant guided missiles that can fly across oceans. The *bazooka* is a small rocket launcher carried by soldiers for use against armored vehicles. A person using a bazooka has as much striking power as a small tank. Armies use larger rockets to fire explosives far behind enemy lines and to shoot down enemy aircraft. Fighter airplanes carry rocket-powered guided missiles to attack other planes and ground targets. Navy ships use guided missiles to attack other ships, land targets, and planes.

Powerful rockets propel a type of long-range guided missile called an *intercontinental ballistic missile* (ICBM). Such a missile can travel 3,400 miles (5,500 kilometers) or more to bomb an enemy target with nuclear explosives. An ICBM generally employs two or three separate stages to propel it during the early part of its flight. The ICBM coasts the rest of the way to its target.

Atmospheric research. Scientists use rockets to explore Earth's atmosphere. *Sounding rockets,* also called *meteorological rockets,* carry such equipment as barometers, cameras, and thermometers high into the atmosphere. These instruments collect information about the atmosphere and send it by radio to receiving equipment on the ground.

Rockets also provide the power for experimental research airplanes. Engineers use these planes in the development of spacecraft. By studying the flights of such planes as the rocket-powered X-1 and X-15, engineers learned how to control vehicles flying many times as fast as the speed of sound.

Launching probes and satellites. Rockets carry crewless spacecraft called *space probes* on long voyages to explore the solar system. Probes have explored the sun, the moon, and all the planets in our solar system except Pluto. They carry scientific instruments that gather information about the planets and transmit data back to Earth. Probes have landed on the surface of the moon, Venus, and Mars.

Rockets lift artificial satellites into orbit around Earth. Some orbiting satellites gather information for scientific research. Others relay telephone conversations and radio and television broadcasts across the oceans. Weather satellites track climate patterns and help scientists predict the weather. Navigation satellites, such as those that make up the Global Positioning System (GPS), enable receivers anywhere on Earth to determine their locations with great accuracy. The armed forces use satellites to observe enemy facilities and movements. They also use satellites to communicate, monitor weather, and watch for missile attacks. Not only are satellites launched by rockets, but many satellites use small rocket engines to maintain their proper orbits.

Rockets that launch satellites and probes are called *launch vehicles.* Most of these rockets have from two to four stages. The stages lift the satellite to its proper altitude and give it enough speed—about 17,000 miles (27,400 kilometers) per hour—to stay in orbit. A space probe's speed must reach about 25,000 miles (40,000 kilometers) per hour to escape Earth's gravity and continue on its voyage.

Engineers created the first launch vehicles by altering military rockets or sounding rockets to carry spacecraft. For example, they added stages to some of these rockets to increase their speed. Today, engineers sometimes attach smaller rockets to a launch vehicle. These rockets, called boosters, provide additional thrust to launch heavier spacecraft.

Space travel. Rockets launch spacecraft carrying astronauts that orbit Earth and travel into space. These rockets, like the ones used to launch probes and satellites, are called *launch vehicles.*

The Saturn 5 rocket, which carried astronauts to the moon, was the most powerful launch vehicle ever built by the United States. Before launch, it weighed more than 6 million pounds (2.7 million kilograms). It could send a spacecraft weighing more than 100,000 pounds (45,000 kilograms) to the moon. The Saturn 5 used 11 rocket engines to propel three stages.

Space shuttles are reusable rockets that can fly into space and return to Earth repeatedly. Engineers have also worked to develop *space tugs,* smaller rocket-powered vehicles that could tow satellites, boost space probes, and carry astronauts over short distances in orbit. For more information on rockets used in space travel, see **Space exploration.**

Other uses. People have fired rockets as distress signals from ships and airplanes and from the ground. Rockets also shoot rescue lines to ships in distress. Small rockets called JATO (jet-assisted take-off) units help heavily loaded airplanes take off. Rockets have long been used in fireworks displays.

Kinds of rocket engines

The vast majority of rockets are chemical rockets. The two most common types of chemical rockets are *solid-*

propellant rockets and *liquid-propellant rockets.* Engineers have tested a third type of chemical rocket, called a *hybrid rocket,* that combines liquid and solid propellants. Electric rockets have propelled space probes and maneuvered orbiting satellites. Researchers have designed experimental nuclear rockets.

Solid-propellant rockets burn a rubbery or plastic-like material called the *grain.* The grain consists of a fuel and an oxidizer in solid form. It is shaped like a cylinder with one or more channels or *ports* that run through it. The ports increase the surface area of the grain that the rocket burns. Unlike some liquid propellants, the fuel and oxidizer of a solid-propellant rocket do not burn upon contact with each other. Instead, an electric charge ignites a smaller grain. Hot exhaust gases from this grain ignite the main propellant surface.

International Launch Systems

An Atlas 5 rocket blasts off to lift an artificial satellite into orbit. The Atlas 5 and other powerful rockets that carry their cargo into space are called *launch vehicles.*

The temperature in the combustion chamber of a solid-propellant rocket ranges from 3000 to 6000 °F (1600 to 3300 °C). In most of these rockets, engineers build the chamber walls from high-strength steel or titanium to withstand the pressure and heat of combustion. They also may use composite materials consisting of high-strength fibers embedded in rubber or plastic. Composite chambers made from high-strength graphite fibers in a strong adhesive called *epoxy* weigh less than steel or titanium chambers, enabling the rocket to accelerate its payload more efficiently. Solid propellants burn at a rate of about 0.6 inch (1.5 centimeters) per second.

Solid propellants can remain effective after long storage and present little danger of combusting or exploding until ignited. Furthermore, they do not need the pumping and injecting equipment required by liquid propellants. On the other hand, rocket controllers cannot easily stop or restart the burning of solid propellant. This can make a solid-propellant rocket difficult to control. One method used to stop the burning of solid propellant involves blasting the entire nozzle section from the rocket. This method, however, prevents restarting.

Rocket designers often choose solid propellants for rockets that must be easy to store, transport, and launch. Military planners prefer solid-propellant rockets for many uses because they can be stored for a long time and fired with little preparation. Solid-propellant rockets power ICBM's, including the American Minuteman 2

and MX and the Russian RT-2. They also propel such smaller missiles as the American Hellfire, Patriot, Sparrow, and Sidewinder, and the French SSBS. Solid-propellant rockets often serve as sounding rockets and as boosters for launch vehicles and cruise missiles. They are also used in fireworks.

Liquid-propellant rockets burn a mixture of fuel and oxidizer in liquid form. These rockets carry the fuel and the oxidizer in separate tanks. A system of pipes and valves feeds the propellants into the combustion chamber. In larger engines, either the fuel or the oxidizer flows around the outside of the chamber before entering it. This flow cools the chamber and preheats the propellant for combustion.

A liquid-propellant rocket feeds the fuel and oxidizer into the combustion chamber using either pumps or high-pressure gas. The most common method uses pumps to force the fuel and oxidizer into the combustion chamber. Burning a small portion of the propellants provides the energy to drive the pumps. In the other method, high-pressure gas forces the fuel and oxidizer into the chamber. The gas may be nitrogen or some other gas stored under high pressure or may come from the burning of a small amount of propellants.

Some liquid propellants, called *hypergols,* ignite when the fuel and the oxidizer mix. But most liquid propellants require an ignition system. An electric spark may ignite the propellant, or the burning of a small amount of solid propellant in the combustion chamber may do so. Liquid propellants continue to burn as long as fuel and oxidizer flow into the combustion chamber.

Engineers use thin, high-strength steel or aluminum to construct most tanks that hold liquid propellants. They may also reinforce tanks with composite materials like those used in solid-propellant rocket chambers. Most combustion chambers in liquid-propellant rockets are made of steel or nickel.

Liquid propellants usually produce greater thrust than do equal amounts of solid propellants burned in the same amount of time. Controllers can easily adjust or stop burning in a liquid-propellant rocket by increasing or decreasing the flow of propellants into the chamber. Liquid propellants, however, are difficult to handle. If

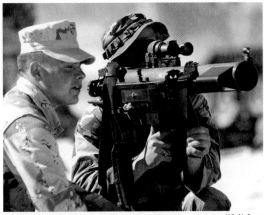

U.S. Air Force

A shoulder-fired rocket launcher, light enough for one person to carry, fires small, explosive rockets that can destroy tanks, other armored vehicles, and many types of buildings.

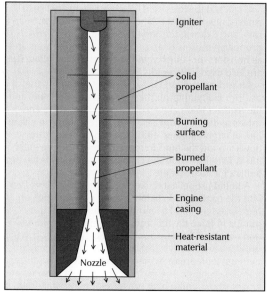

WORLD BOOK diagram by Precision Graphics

A solid-propellant rocket burns a solid material called the *grain*. Engineers design most grains with a hollow core. The propellant burns from the core outward. Unburned propellant shields the engine casing from the heat of combustion.

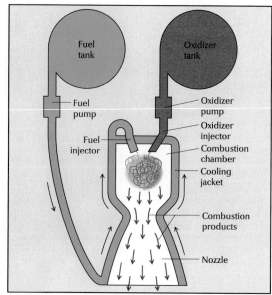

WORLD BOOK diagram by Precision Graphics

A liquid-propellant rocket carries fuel and an oxidizer in separate tanks. The fuel circulates through the engine's cooling jacket before entering the combustion chamber. This circulation preheats the fuel for combustion and helps cool the rocket.

the fuel and oxidizer blend without igniting, the resulting mixture often will explode easily. Liquid propellants also require complicated pumping machinery.

Scientists use liquid-propellant rockets for most space launch vehicles. Liquid-propellant rockets serve as the main engines of the space shuttle as well as Europe's Ariane rocket, Russia's Soyuz rocket, and China's Long March rocket.

Hybrid rockets combine some of the advantages of both solid-propellant and liquid-propellant rockets. A hybrid rocket uses a liquid oxidizer, such as liquid oxygen, and a solid-fuel grain made of plastic or rubber. The solid-fuel grain lines the inside of the combustion chamber. A pumping system sprays the oxidizer onto the surface of the grain, which is ignited by a smaller grain or torch.

Hybrid rockets are safer than solid-propellant rockets because the propellants are not premixed and so will not ignite accidentally. Also, unlike solid-propellant rockets, hybrid rockets can vary thrust or even stop combustion by adjusting the flow of oxidizer. Hybrid engines require only half the pumping gear of liquid-propellant rockets, making them simpler to build.

A key disadvantage of hybrid rockets is that their fuel burns slowly, limiting the amount of thrust they can produce. A hybrid rocket burns grain at a rate of about 0.04 inch (1 millimeter) per second. For a given amount of propellant, hybrid rockets typically produce more thrust than solid rockets and less than liquid engines. To generate more thrust, engineers must manufacture complex fuel grains with many separate ports through which oxidizer can flow. This exposes more grain to the oxidizer.

The safety of hybrid rockets has led engineers to develop them for use in human flight. The Scaled Composites company of Mojave, California, developed a hybrid rocket

called SpaceShipOne that launched from an airplane. On June 21, 2004, SpaceShipOne became the first privately funded craft to carry a person into space. It carried the American test pilot Michael Melvill more than 62 miles (100 kilometers) above Earth's surface during a brief flight.

Researchers have also used hybrid rockets to propel targets used in missile testing and to accelerate experimental motorcycles and cars attempting land speed records. In addition, they have worked to develop hybrid rockets to boost planetary probes, maneuver satellites in orbit, and power crew escape mechanisms for launch vehicles.

Electric rockets use electric energy to expel *ions* (electrically charged particles) from the nozzle. Solar panels or a nuclear reactor can provide the energy.

In one design, xenon gas passes through an electrified metal grid. The grid strips electrons from the xenon atoms, turning them into positively charged ions. A positively charged screen repels the ions, focusing them into a beam. The beam then enters a negatively charged device called an *accelerator*. The accelerator speeds up the ions and shoots them out through a nozzle.

The exhaust from such rockets travels extremely fast. However, the stream of xenon ions has a relatively low mass. As a result, an electric rocket cannot produce enough thrust to overcome Earth's gravity. Electric rockets used in space must therefore be launched by chemical rockets. Once in space, though, the low rate of mass flow becomes an advantage. It enables an electric rocket to operate for a long time without running out of propellant. The xenon rocket that powered the U.S. space probe Deep Space 1, launched in 1998, fired for a total of over 670 days using only 160 pounds (72 kilograms) of propellant. In addition, small electric rockets using xenon propellant have provided the thrust to keep communications satellites in position above Earth's surface.

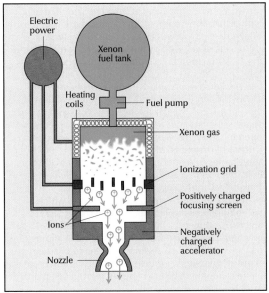

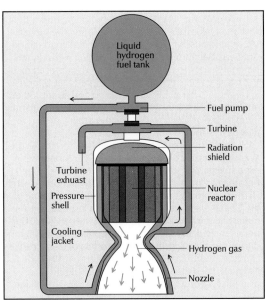

WORLD BOOK diagram by Precision Graphics

An ion rocket uses a metal *ionization grid* to change a gas into electrically charged particles called *ions*. A positively charged screen repels the ions, focusing them into a beam. A negatively charged accelerator shoots the ions out through the nozzle.

WORLD BOOK diagram by Precision Graphics

A nuclear rocket uses the heat from a nuclear reactor to change a liquid fuel into a gas. Most of the fuel flows through the reactor. Some of the fuel, heated by the nozzle of the rocket, flows through the turbine. The turbine drives the fuel pump.

Another type of electric rocket uses electromagnets rather than charged screens to accelerate xenon ions. This type of rocket powers the SMART-1 lunar probe, launched by the European Space Agency in 2003.

Nuclear rockets use the heat energy of a *nuclear reactor,* a device that releases energy by splitting atoms. Some proposed designs would use hydrogen as propellant. The rocket would store the hydrogen as a liquid. Heat from the reactor would boil the liquid, creating hydrogen gas. The gas would expand rapidly and push out from the nozzle.

The exhaust speed of a nuclear rocket might reach four times that of a chemical rocket. By expelling a large quantity of hydrogen, a nuclear rocket could therefore achieve high thrust. However, a nuclear rocket would require heavy shielding because a nuclear reactor uses radioactive materials. The shielding would weigh so much that the rocket could not be practically used to boost a launch vehicle. More practical applications would use small nuclear engines with low, continuous thrust to decrease flight times to Mars or other planets.

Nuclear rocket developers must also overcome public fears that accidents involving such devices could release harmful radioactive materials. Before nuclear rockets can be launched, engineers must convince the public that such devices are safe.

History

Historians believe the Chinese invented rockets, but they do not know exactly when. Historical accounts describe "arrows of flying fire"—believed to have been rockets—used by Chinese armies in A.D. 1232. By 1300, the use of rockets had spread throughout much of Asia and Europe. These first rockets burned a substance called *black powder*, which consisted of charcoal, salt-peter, and sulfur. For several hundred years, the use of rockets in fireworks displays outranked their military use in importance.

During the early 1800's, Colonel William Congreve of the British Army developed rockets that could carry explosives. Many of these rockets weighed about 32 pounds (15 kilograms) and could travel $1\frac{3}{4}$ miles (2.7 kilometers). British troops used Congreve rockets against the United States Army during the War of 1812. Austria, Russia, and several other countries also developed military rockets during the early 1800's.

The English inventor William Hale improved the accuracy of military rockets. He substituted three fins for the long wooden tail that had been used to guide the rocket. United States troops used Hale rockets in the Mexican War (1846-1848). During the American Civil War (1861-1865), both sides used rockets.

Rockets of the early 1900's. The Russian school teacher Konstantin E. Tsiolkovsky first stated the correct theory of rocket power. He described his theory in a scientific paper published in 1903. Tsiolkovsky also first presented the ideas of the multistage rocket and rockets using liquid oxygen and hydrogen propellants. In 1926, the American rocket pioneer Robert H. Goddard conducted the first successful launch of a liquid-propellant rocket. The rocket climbed 41 feet (13 meters) into the air at a speed of about 60 miles (97 kilometers) per hour and landed 184 feet (56 meters) away.

During the 1930's, rocket research advanced in Germany, the Soviet Union, and the United States. Hermann Oberth led a small group of German engineers and scientists that experimented with rockets. Leading Soviet rocket scientists included Fridrikh A. Tsander and Sergei P. Korolev. Goddard remained the most prominent rocket researcher in the United States.

During World War II, German engineers under the direction of Wernher von Braun developed the powerful V-2 guided missile. Germany bombarded London and Antwerp, Belgium, with hundreds of V-2's during the last months of the war. American forces captured many V-2 missiles and sent them to the United States for use in research. After the war, von Braun and about 150 other German scientists moved to the United States to continue their work with rockets. Some other German rocket experts went to the Soviet Union.

High-altitude rockets. For several years after World War II, U.S. scientists benefited greatly by conducting experiments with captured German V-2's. These V-2's became the first rockets used for high-altitude research.

The first high-altitude rockets designed and built in the United States included the WAC Corporal, the Aerobee, and the Viking. The 16-foot (4.9-meter) WAC Corporal reached altitudes of about 45 miles (72 kilometers) during test flights in 1945. Early models of the Aerobee climbed about 70 miles (110 kilometers). In 1949, the U.S. Navy launched the Viking, an improved liquid-propellant rocket based chiefly on the V-2. The Viking

From *Rocketry and Space Exploration* by Andrew G. Haley
© 1958 by Litton Education Publishing, Inc.

Chinese warriors fired rockets in battle during the A.D. 1200's. The use of rockets as weapons and fireworks spread from China throughout much of Asia and Europe during the next century.

measured more than 45 feet (14 meters) long, much longer than the Aerobee. But the first models of the Viking rose only about 50 miles (80 kilometers).

Rockets developed by the U.S. armed forces during the 1950's included the Jupiter and the Pershing. The Jupiter could travel about 1,600 miles (2,600 kilometers), and the Pershing about 450 miles (720 kilometers).

The U.S. Navy conducted the first successful launch of a Polaris underwater missile in 1960. United States space scientists later used many military rockets developed in the 1950's as the basis for launch vehicles.

Rocket-powered airplanes. On Oct. 14, 1947, Captain Charles E. Yeager of the U.S. Air Force made the first *supersonic* (faster than sound) flight. He flew a rocket-powered airplane called the X-1.

A rocket engine also powered the X-15, which set an unofficial airplane altitude record of 354,200 feet (107,960 meters) in 1963. In one flight, the X-15 reached a peak speed of 4,520 miles (7,274 kilometers) per hour—more than six times the speed of sound. A privately owned and developed rocket-powered plane called the EZ-Rocket began piloted test flights in 2001.

The space age began on Oct. 4, 1957, when the Soviet Union launched the first artificial satellite, Sputnik 1, aboard a two-stage rocket. On Jan. 31, 1958, the U.S. Army launched the first American satellite, Explorer 1, into orbit with a Juno I rocket.

On April 12, 1961, a Soviet rocket put a cosmonaut, Major Yuri A. Gagarin, into orbit around Earth for the first time. On May 5, 1961, a Redstone rocket launched Commander Alan B. Shepard, Jr., the first American to travel in space. On April 12, 1981, the United States launched the rocket-powered Columbia, the first space shuttle to orbit Earth. For more information on the history of rockets in space travel, see **Space exploration.**

Rocket research. In the early 2000's, engineers and scientists worked to develop lightweight rocket engines that used safer propellants. They also searched for more efficient propellants that did not require refrigeration. Engineers began designing and testing smaller rocket engines for use in smaller vehicles, such as tiny satellites that may weigh only a few pounds or kilograms when fully loaded.

Stephen D. Heister

© National Geographic Society courtesy Esther C. Goddard

Robert H. Goddard, *left,* a pioneer American rocket scientist, inspects a gasoline- and oxygen-powered rocket as his assistants look on. This rocket was built under Goddard's supervision in 1940.

AP/Wide World

The worst terrorist attack in United States history destroyed the towers of the World Trade Center in New York City on Sept. 11, 2001. Terrorists crashed hijacked planes into the buildings.

Terrorism is the use or threat of violence to create fear and alarm, usually to promote a movement or cause. Terrorists may set off bombs, murder and kidnap individuals, hijack airplanes, release harmful chemical and biological substances, or take other violent or threatening actions. Terrorists typically have political, religious, or other *ideological* goals—that is, goals having to do with beliefs and ideas. They hope to achieve their goals through violence and the creation of fear. Many terrorists represent revolutionary movements seeking a change in government or liberation from a governing power. Some hope to attract attention and support for particular political philosophies or religious beliefs. Others have unclear goals or simply oppose all forms of authority.

Individuals may commit terrorist acts, but terrorism is usually the work of organized networks or groups. Many groups operate within a single nation or region. Others have branches and operations in many countries. Because terrorists generally cannot match the strength of conventional military forces, they often rely on *guerrilla warfare*. Guerrilla warfare involves attacks by roving bands of fighters who torment the enemy with ambushes, bombings, sudden raids, and other hit-and-run tactics. The fighters blend in with ordinary citizens, strike suddenly, and try to avoid capture.

In addition to the death and destruction caused by the attacks, terrorists seek to create panic and fear throughout the general population. They may try to cripple the

---

Tom Mockaitis, the contributor of this article, is Professor of History at DePaul University.

economy by destroying bridges, dams, telephone networks, or other essential structures or services. Many terrorists hope that people who observe the attacks will lose their sense of security and their confidence in the existing government or political system.

All terrorist acts are crimes under international law. Many countries fight terrorism by gathering *intelligence* (information); by increasing security at airports, government buildings, and other likely targets; and by working together with international organizations and with other nations facing terrorist threats. Some countries train special military and law enforcement units to confront terrorist situations. Efforts to prevent terrorism are called *counterterrorism.*

Features of terrorism

Terrorist groups and individuals generally attack people who oppose their causes, or buildings and places that symbolize such opposition. Common victims of kidnappings and assassinations include business executives, diplomats, judges, police, and political leaders. Some terrorists attack churches, mosques, synagogues, and other places of worship. Others target airplanes, buses, trains, and nightclubs. Terrorists often choose targets certain to attract media coverage. Such targets include government buildings, national monuments and landmarks, and skyscrapers.

Terrorist methods. Terrorists seek to create instability and alarm through a number of methods. Traditional methods include bombings, assassinations, kidnappings, and hijackings. Newer threats include computer-based terrorism and *weapons of mass destruction*—that is, biological, chemical, and nuclear weapons.

Bombings make up about half of all terrorist acts. Bombs may be placed in automobiles, backpacks, garbage cans, suitcases, or elsewhere. Many bombings involve cars or trucks packed with explosives and parked next to a building or other target. Terrorists may also try to smuggle concealed bombs onto airplanes or into crowded sports arenas or concert halls. In some cases, a bomber may strap explosives to his or her own body and detonate them on a bus or in a crowded area. Such bombings are commonly called *suicide bombings,* because the terrorist takes his or her own life while conducting the attack.

Assassinations and kidnappings. Terrorists may seek to create alarm by assassinating government officials or other prominent individuals. Terrorists may also kidnap individuals and hold them hostage until certain demands are met. In some cases, terrorists target travelers from other countries in an attempt to discourage others from visiting.

Hijackings. Some terrorists *hijack,* or seize control of, airplanes, buses, or other vehicles. They typically use weapons or bomb threats to gain control. Once in control, hijackers may take passengers as hostages and threaten to kill the passengers if their demands are not met. In some cases, hijackers may threaten to blow up an airplane, or they may intentionally crash a plane into a target. Such hijackings are especially dangerous because planes loaded with fuel can become "flying bombs" capable of causing great destruction.

Biological attacks involve the intentional spreading of harmful bacteria, viruses, and *toxins* (poisons). The use of biological *agents* (substances) to inflict harm is sometimes called *germ warfare* or *bioterrorism.* Bioterrorists may seek to contaminate food or water supplies; to distribute toxins, such as ricin; or to spread dangerous diseases, such as anthrax or smallpox. They may put harmful bacteria in restaurant salad bars or send contaminated items through the mail. However, many biological weapons are difficult for terrorists to prepare and use effectively.

Chemical attacks involve the intentional release of toxic chemicals. Some chemical agents affect the central nervous system and can cause paralysis or death. Others can burn or damage the skin, eyes, nose, throat, or lungs. Dangerous chemical agents include mustard gas, a blistering agent that causes burns and blindness; hydrogen cyanide, a poisonous gas sometimes used to execute condemned criminals; and sarin, a deadly nerve gas. Terrorists may attempt to buy, steal, or manufacture chemical weapons and then disperse them in crowded areas. However, many chemical weapons are difficult for terrorists to prepare and use.

Nuclear attacks. Governments have long sought to keep nuclear materials out of the hands of terrorist organizations. As a result, no nuclear terrorist attack has yet occurred. However, counterterrorism experts have studied how terrorists might potentially use nuclear weapons or radioactive materials to conduct attacks.

Terrorist groups might seek to acquire nuclear devices from an underground weapons supplier or from a government that has such devices. Alternatively, terrorists might try to obtain radioactive materials—such as weapons-grade plutonium or uranium—and manufacture their own weapons. If terrorists are unable to acquire or build nuclear weapons, they might instead try to cause explosions at existing nuclear facilities. Terrorists might also bundle radioactive materials with conventional explosives to create *radiological dispersion devices.* Such devices—sometimes called "dirty bombs"—could give off invisible radiation capable of causing sickness or death. The radioactive contamination could keep people out of a vital area, such as a downtown business section, for months or even years.

Computer-based terrorism, also called *cyberterrorism,* involves the sabotage of computer information systems. Cyberterrorists may design and circulate *computer viruses,* which can disrupt computer operations and destroy data. Cyberterrorists may also seek to steal or alter sensitive or valuable information, or to attack systems that provide important services.

Other forms of terrorism. Terrorists may use any other form of violence or threats of violence to create fear and alarm. Some governments use terrorist methods—such as torture and murder—to intimidate their opposition and increase their power. The use of such methods by oppressive governments is called *state terrorism* or *state-conducted terrorism.* War crimes, genocide, and other international violations may also be considered acts of terror.

Terrorist organizations. Individuals may carry out terrorist acts—such as bombings or the distribution of computer viruses—without assistance from others. However, most terrorists are associated with specific movements or organized groups. Terrorist organizations vary greatly in terms of size and structure. Most groups are small and focus on activities within their own nation or region. Other groups, however, have international networks that carry out attacks throughout the world. One of the largest global terror groups is al-Qa'ida, which seeks to promote the goals of Islamic extremists.

Most terrorist organizations have a leader or group of leaders who develop strategies and direct operations. Active terrorists within the organization then carry out the plans. Many terrorist organizations consist of small groups called *cells.* Terrorist cells may receive specific instructions from leaders, or they may plan their own activities based on the organization's central goals. Terrorist groups generally take great efforts to hide the identities of group members, the locations of cells, and their channels of communication. Typically, only one member of each cell knows how to contact the larger organization. As a result, the larger group may remain safe even if a cell is discovered and destroyed. The secrecy and complexity of the cell structure makes it difficult for governments to gather information about terrorist groups.

Sources of funding for terrorist groups are usually carefully concealed. Some governments secretly support or sponsor terrorist groups by providing weapons, training, and money. Some terrorist groups raise money through criminal activities such as theft or the sale of illegal drugs. In some cases, a group posing as a social service organization may secretly direct donations, without the donors' knowledge, toward terrorist causes.

Fighting terrorism

Counterterrorism efforts involve numerous activities. Governments gather and evaluate information about suspected terrorists and terrorist groups. They identify potential terrorist threats and develop a wide variety of security measures and emergency procedures. Many governments refuse to negotiate with terrorists or with nations that support terrorists. National security services, such as the United States Department of Homeland Security and the United Kingdom's Security Service (MI5), lead advanced counterterrorism efforts. They receive assistance from intelligence services, such as Israel's Mossad, the United Kingdom's Secret Intelligence Service (MI6), and the U.S. Central Intelligence Agency (CIA). International organizations, such as the United Nations (UN) and Interpol, help nations work together for the prevention of terrorism.

Intelligence efforts. National governments, international organizations, police departments, and specialized intelligence services collect, share, and analyze information relating to terrorism. Such efforts can help prevent attacks by identifying terrorist suspects and by detecting terrorist plots while they are being planned.

Many intelligence and law enforcement agencies use *electronic surveillance* to monitor suspected terrorists and to intercept their communication. *Wiretapping* is the interception of telephone conversations by a listening device connected to a telephone wire or placed nearby. Other forms of surveillance include special aircraft and artificial satellites that can produce detailed images of suspected terrorist bases or camps.

Governments may work with agents from foreign countries or send undercover agents to obtain information from within a terrorist group. Governments may also receive valuable information by questioning de-

© Tokyo Shimbun, Corbis/Sygma

Chemical terrorism involves the intentional release of toxic chemicals. In 1995, members of a Japanese religious cult spread the nerve gas sarin in the Tokyo subway system, *shown here*.

tained terrorists and by searching areas where terrorists have lived or gathered.

In some cases, governments can examine financial records and trace the funding of terrorist organizations. They may order banks to *freeze* (make unusable) the assets of terrorists or of individuals or groups believed to be contributing to terrorist activity.

Security measures. Most governments work to protect, or "harden," potential terrorist targets, such as airports and airplanes, large public gatherings, and government buildings. Target-hardening efforts typically involve careful security systems and procedures and the work of trained security personnel.

Thorough security at airports and on airplanes can decrease the likelihood of hijackings and other attacks. People who travel on airplanes must pass through multiple airport checkpoints. Guards scan or search checked baggage and carry-on items, and they may *frisk* (search) passengers before letting them board the plane. Security measures on the airplane itself may include reinforced cockpit doors and armed air marshals.

Many structures, especially skyscrapers and government buildings, have physical barriers to keep car or truck bombs from getting near. Also, many buildings have metal detectors or other security checkpoints to search for dangerous items and to prevent unauthorized people from entering. Police officers may be assigned to guard bridges, tunnels, or monuments believed to be at risk. At some crowded events, cameras scan people's faces and attempt to match them with photos of suspected terrorists in a computer database.

The risk of cyberterrorism can be reduced by computer security measures, such as antivirus programs and electronic barriers called *firewalls*. As technology improves, new target-hardening methods will continue to emerge.

The protection of key sites is an essential part of counterterrorism. However, in many cases, target hardening may lead to *target displacement*—that is, it may cause terrorists to shift their plans to different sites that are not as well protected. No system of protection can fully safeguard every building, bridge, and tunnel. A site with relatively little protection is sometimes called a "soft" target.

Diplomatic, economic, and military pressure. Because of the global reach of terrorist activity, the cooperation of organizations and governments from various countries is an essential element of counterterrorism. The UN and other international bodies help promote this cooperation. Numerous treaties and international agreements have sought to address terrorist activity. For example, *extradition treaties* allow people linked to terrorism in one country to be arrested in a different country and deported for trial in the country where an attack took place. Such treaties make it difficult for terrorists to escape criminal charges.

The international community may isolate or punish nations that support terrorism. Governments may impose *economic sanctions* on nations that support terrorism. In other words, they may limit or end economic relations with the country until it changes its policies. If sanctions and diplomatic pressure fail, countries may launch military strikes against terrorist bases and camps or against countries that sponsor terrorism.

Counterterrorism and civil rights. A government's ability to fight terrorism depends largely on its ability to intercept communication to and from suspected terrorists, to search individuals for weapons and dangerous materials, and to investigate and detain suspects. However, many of these actions may conflict with the basic rights and freedoms associated with democracy. A major challenge facing governments today is the need to provide effective counterterrorism while still respecting individuals' privacy and civil rights. Government officials, legal scholars, and civil rights activists often disagree over how best to balance the two interests.

History of terrorism

The beginnings of terrorist violence closely followed the spread of early civilization. From ancient times to the present, individuals, rebel groups, and governments have used cruelty and force to eliminate enemies, to spread fear and panic, and to achieve political, religious, and other ideological goals.

Early terrorism. The empire builders of ancient times often maintained control over conquered peoples through brutality and fear. In 71 B.C., for instance, the Roman general Crassus crushed a revolt led by the gladiator Spartacus. Crassus then publicly crucified the captured rebels to warn others of the consequences of revolt. Some rebel groups used terrorist methods to resist their rulers. For instance, a Jewish group called the Sicarii waged violent campaigns against the Romans from about A.D. 6 to 73.

Starting in the 800's, Japanese *ninja*, members of a secret organization of peasant families, spread terror through sabotage, assassination, and kidnapping. Ninja were masters at various forms of armed and unarmed combat, including the use of disguises and poisons. In the 1100's, a secret society called *assassins* or *hashshashin* (hemp-eaters) carried out violent campaigns in Per-

AP/Wide World

Airport security procedures aim to prevent terrorist attacks involving airplanes. Trained security personnel check passengers and baggage for dangerous items and materials.

sia (now Iran) and Asia Minor (now part of Turkey). They smoked a drug called *hashish,* made from the hemp plant, and killed their enemies while under its influence. In the 1300's and 1400's, peasant uprisings in Europe produced widespread violence, much of which would now be considered terrorist in nature.

The beginnings of modern terrorism. The word *terrorism* first appeared during the French Revolution (1789-1799). Some of the revolutionaries who seized power adopted a policy of violence against people they considered enemies of the revolution. The revolutionary government executed around 40,000 people. Because of the number of executions and the fear that they produced, the period of rule by the revolutionaries became known as the Reign of Terror. By the early 1800's, terrorism had become a fixture of rebellion and conflict throughout the world.

In the 1930's, the dictators Adolf Hitler of Germany, Benito Mussolini of Italy, and Joseph Stalin of the Soviet Union used terrorist tactics to discourage opposition to

their governments. From 1973 to 1990, General Augusto Pinochet Ugarte controlled Chile as a military dictator. During his rule, more than 3,000 Chileans disappeared or were murdered, and many more were tortured. Many authoritarian governments continue to use state terrorism today to frighten and control the population.

Terrorist groups and movements have long used violence to pursue their goals. An American group, the Ku Klux Klan, has used terrorism to oppose the advancement of African Americans, Jews, and other minority groups since the late 1800's. In Northern Ireland, Roman Catholic extremists have used terrorism in efforts to end British rule and to unite Northern Ireland with the Republic of Ireland. At the same time, Protestant extremists have used similar methods to demand the continuation of British rule.

In Spain's Basque region, a group called Euskadi ta Askatasuna (Basque Homeland and Freedom), abbreviated ETA, has used violence to push for the creation of an independent Basque state. In Chechnya, rebel groups have used terrorism in an attempt to win independence from Russia. Chechen groups have taken hostages and conducted suicide bombings against Russian targets.

Before the independence of Israel in 1948, a Jewish group called Irgun Zvai Leumi (National Military Organization) used terror to speed the end of British rule in Palestine and create a Jewish homeland. Since 1960, Palestinian groups, including Hamas and Islamic Jihad of Palestine, have carried out campaigns of terrorism aimed at establishing an independent Palestinian state. Such groups have conducted numerous attacks—including a wave of suicide bombings in the early 2000's—against Israel. Israel has responded with military strikes that have taken civilian lives.

During the 1960's and 1970's, several terrorist groups sought the destruction of the political and economic systems in their home countries and the development of new systems. These groups included the Red Brigades in Italy, the Red Army Faction (also known as the Baader-Meinhof Gang) in West Germany, and the Weather Underground in the United States. Since the 1980's, Peru has faced attacks by leftist terrorist groups called Shin-

Granger Collection

The Reign of Terror was a period of the French Revolution (1789-1799) in which thousands of suspected opponents of the revolution were beheaded by guillotine. The word *terrorism* originated during the Reign of Terror.

The Ku Klux Klan, an American group, used terrorism to keep African Americans from voting and to deny other rights to African Americans, Jews, and other minority groups. This picture shows Klan members on horseback in Tulsa, Oklahoma, in 1923.

AP/Wide World

ing Path and the Tupac Amaru Revolutionary Movement.

Many terrorists have had religious motives rather than political ones. In 1995, members of a Japanese religious cult released the nerve gas sarin into the Tokyo subway system, killing 12 people and injuring thousands. In the United States and other countries, extremists opposed to abortion have bombed and burned down clinics and murdered doctors who performed abortions. People who strongly oppose abortion generally do so because of religious beliefs.

Some groups in the United States and other countries have used terrorism to promote animal rights and other causes relating to nature and the environment. Such groups—including the Earth Liberation Front and the Animal Liberation Front—have attacked lumber companies and laboratories that conduct research on animals. Terrorism for nature-related causes is often called *ecoterrorism.*

Individuals with unusual or unclear agendas have also committed acts of terror. From 1978 to 1995, an American known as the Unabomber sent bombs through the mail. Because he disliked modern industrial civilization, he targeted scientists and engineers in the computer industry and other high-technology fields. The Unabomber, identified as Theodore J. Kaczynski, was convicted in 1998. In 1995, two Americans, Timothy J. McVeigh and Terry L. Nichols, were convicted of bombing the Murrah Federal Building in Oklahoma City. They believed that actions of the U.S. government had deprived citizens of their freedom.

The changing face of terrorism. In the late 1900's, many terrorist groups began forming networks and operating on an increasingly global scale. Some of these groups, particularly in the Middle East, held a deep hatred for the United States and for Western countries in general. Concerns that terrorists might obtain weapons of mass destruction increased dramatically.

In 1993, a bomb exploded in the parking garage of the World Trade Center in New York City. A federal court convicted four men, including two Palestinians and an Egyptian cleric, of planning the bombing. In 1998, terrorists bombed U.S. embassies in Kenya and Tanzania. American officials linked the bombings to Osama bin Laden, a Saudi-born millionaire and Islamic extremist. Bin Laden's group, al-Qa'ida, has been suspected in numerous other attacks, including the bombing of the U.S. Navy warship *Cole* at a port in Yemen in 2000. Terrorists who claimed links to al-Qa'ida conducted a series of

train bombings in Madrid, Spain, in 2004.

The September 11 terrorist attacks. On Sept. 11, 2001, about 3,000 people died as a result of the worst terrorist attack in U.S. history. Qa'ida hijackers seized two commercial airplanes and deliberately crashed them into the two 110-story towers of the World Trade Center in New York City. Less than an hour later, another hijacked plane crashed into the Pentagon Building just outside Washington, D.C. Shortly after that, a fourth hijacked airplane crashed into a rural area in Somerset County, Pennsylvania.

In response to the September 11 attacks—commonly known as 9/11—U.S. President George W. Bush called for a worldwide campaign against international terrorist networks. He declared that he would target terrorist organizations and any governments that supported them. Bush's antiterrorism effort is commonly called the "war on terrorism" or the "war on terror."

At the time of the attacks, bin Laden and al-Qa'ida were being protected by the Taliban, a militant Islamic group that controlled the government of Afghanistan. Military strikes led by the United States caused the Taliban to fall from power in Afghanistan in December 2001. Numerous Qa'ida members and officers were captured or killed. However, bin Laden was not found.

Since the September 11 attacks, counterterrorism has become a top priority for governments throughout the world. In October 2001, the U.S. Congress passed the USA Patriot Act, which granted government authorities greater power to conduct searches, use wiretaps, and detain and question suspects. Other nations, including India and the United Kingdom, introduced similar antiterrorism measures. In 2002, Congress established the Department of Homeland Security, a new executive department devoted primarily to fighting terrorism.

The Iraq War. In March 2003, the United States led a military campaign against the Iraqi government of Saddam Hussein. The Bush administration claimed that Hussein supported terrorist organizations and could potentially supply such organizations with weapons of mass destruction. The invasion caused the fall of Hussein's government in early April.

In the following months, a number of terrorist attacks occurred throughout Iraq. United States officials suspected that the attacks were the work of Iraqi groups opposed to the U.S.-led invasion, of Hussein's supporters and allies, or of al-Qa'ida and other terrorist groups.

Tom Mockaitis

The world—the planet Earth—is home to a great variety of peoples and nations. The land masses in this photo of Earth taken from outer space include Africa, the Arabian Peninsula, and Antarctica.

World

World is the planet Earth viewed especially as the home of human beings and other living things. Earth is just one of countless heavenly bodies in the universe. However, it is the only one known to support life.

People have always adapted to and modified their cultural and physical environments. Some human beings live with low levels of technology. They hunt wild animals and gather native plant products for food. They make clothing from hides or furs and build shelters with such resources as branches and other natural materials. Others cultivate plants and animals for food. Those who farm usually settle in one place and produce enough food to feed many others, thus supporting the emergence of villages, towns, and cities whose occupants must learn to live together peaceably. The growth of urban centers makes necessary the development of new occupations and forms of government.

Over time, people have achieved advanced levels of technology and complex forms of social organization. They have built thriving cities, developed great civilizations, and discovered ways to control and modify some forces of nature.

David Clawson, the contributor for this article, is Professor of Geography at the University of New Orleans in Louisiana.

The world's surface consists of water and land. Air surrounds the surface and extends far above it. Water—chiefly the oceans—covers 71 percent of the world's surface. All living things must have water to live, just as they must have air. People also use water for industry, irrigation, power, and transportation. In addition, the lakes,

Interesting facts about the world

Area of the world's surface is about 196,900,000 square miles (510,000,000 square kilometers).

Population of the world in 2004 totaled about 6,350,500,000.

Largest continent is Asia, which covers about 17,028,000 square miles (44,103,000 square kilometers).

Smallest continent is Australia, excluding the Pacific Islands, which covers about 2,989,000 square miles (7,741,000 square kilometers).

Largest country is Russia, which covers 6,592,850 square miles (17,075,400 square kilometers).

Smallest country is Vatican City. It has an area of only $\frac{1}{6}$ square mile (0.4 square kilometer).

Most populous country is China, which had approximately 1,319,377,000 people in 2004.

Least populous country, Vatican City, had only about 1,000 citizens in 2004.

Highest point in the world, Mount Everest in Asia, rises 29,035 feet (8,850 meters) above sea level.

Lowest point on land is the shore of the Dead Sea in Asia. It lies 1,310 feet (399 meters) below sea level.

Deepest point in the world's oceans is Challenger Deep, 35,840 feet (10,924 meters) below the surface of the Pacific Ocean southwest of Guam in the Mariana Trench.

oceans, and rivers provide fish and other foods.

The oceans separate huge land masses called *continents.* Most of the world's countries lie on the continents. Others are on islands. Each country has its own political and economic systems. However, countries cooperate with one another in many ways. For example, they make trade agreements and sign treaties intended to reduce the likelihood of war.

The physical features of a country strongly influence where the people of that country live. People can most easily grow food on plains or in river valleys, where much of the soil is rich and deep. Mountainous regions generally are less suitable for crop farming because the soil is thin and easily washed away by rainfall. Many of the world's biggest cities began as trading centers on lakeshores, riverbanks, and seacoasts. Thus, the majority of people live on flat, fertile plains and in large cities that border major water transportation routes.

More than 6 billion people live in the world. They are distributed unevenly over the land. Many areas are heavily populated. Other areas have no people at all. The population is increasing far more rapidly in some countries than in others.

All human beings belong to the same species, *Homo sapiens,* which means they have a common ancestry. But many groups of people have lived apart for so long that they have developed physical variations.

In the past, scholars used physical variations to classify people into races. The members of one race were thought to resemble one another more than they resembled the members of other races. Today, most *anthropologists* (scientists who study human beings) reject the idea that human beings can be biologically classified into races. However, people in numerous societies continue to view themselves and others as members of various races. See **Races, Human.**

Physical differences among people have often been confused with cultural differences, such as differences in language or religion. Physical and cultural differences have been a basis of discrimination and prejudice. At times, these differences have served as an excuse for slavery, violence, and war.

This article provides an overview of the world as the home of human beings. It briefly describes the world's nations, people, and surface features. For information on the world as a planet, see **Earth.** For the story of human history and progress, see **World, History of the.**

Nations of the world

The world has 193 independent countries and more than 40 dependencies. An independent country controls its own affairs. Dependencies are controlled in some way by independent countries. In most cases, an independent country is responsible for the dependency's foreign relations and defense, and some of the dependency's local affairs. However, many dependencies have complete control of their local affairs. Almost all of the world's people live in independent countries. Only about 12 million people live in dependencies.

The world's largest nation in area is Russia. It covers 6,592,850 square miles (17,075,400 square kilometers). The next four largest nations, in descending order, are Canada, China, the United States, and Brazil—and each covers more than 3 million square miles (8 million square kilometers). Vatican City is the smallest independent country in the world, followed by Monaco, Nauru, Tuvalu, and San Marino. Each of these countries covers less than 25 square miles (65 square kilometers). Vatican City has an area of only $\frac{1}{6}$ square mile (0.4 square kilometer).

Throughout history, the political map of the world has changed repeatedly. The most important changes have resulted from major wars. During ancient times, such military leaders as Alexander the Great and Julius Caesar conquered many groups of people and established vast empires. Numerous empires rose and fell later in history, and boundaries changed again and again.

Beginning about 1500, many European nations established colonies in North America, South America, Asia, Africa, and Australia. Most national boundaries established by the ruling countries remained after the colonies gained their independence.

World War I (1914-1918) and World War II (1939-1945) resulted in many important changes on the world map. World War I led to the formation of a number of new nations in Europe, including Austria, Czechoslovakia, Hungary, and Yugoslavia. After World War II, several nations gained or lost territory. In addition, many new nations were established in Asia. In Africa, an independence movement swept the continent. More than 45 African colonies gained their independence in the middle and late 1900's. In 1991, the Soviet Union broke up into Russia and 14 other independent nations.

How nations are grouped. The nations of the world may be grouped in various ways. They may be grouped by region, such as the Middle East or Central America. People often call the countries of the Eastern Hemisphere the Old World and those of the Western Hemisphere the New World. In addition, countries are often identified by continent, such as African or Asian.

Economists generally divide the nations of the world into two groups—*developed countries* and *less developed countries.* Developed countries have a wide variety of industries and, in general, are wealthier than less developed countries. Less developed countries have few industries and have long depended on agriculture. Most of them are poor.

Developed nations include Australia, Canada, Japan, the United States, and most countries in western Europe. The majority of less developed countries are in Africa and Asia. Most industrial nations lie in the Northern Hemisphere.

Forms of government. Nearly all governments claim to be democracies. However, governments differ greatly in how closely they fulfill the democratic ideal of government by the people. In a democracy, the people elect representatives who make laws and govern the people according to those laws. Any qualified individual from among the people may run for office. The people's representatives may remove officials who behave improperly. Nations and governments can be classified as being more or less democratic, depending on the extent to which the people may take part in the process of government.

Democratic nations may be republics or constitutional monarchies. For example, the United States is a republic in which the president serves as head of state and head of government. The United Kingdom is a constitutional

Text continued on page 474.

Political map of the world

This map shows each continent in a different color. The names of continents and independent nations are printed in capital letters.

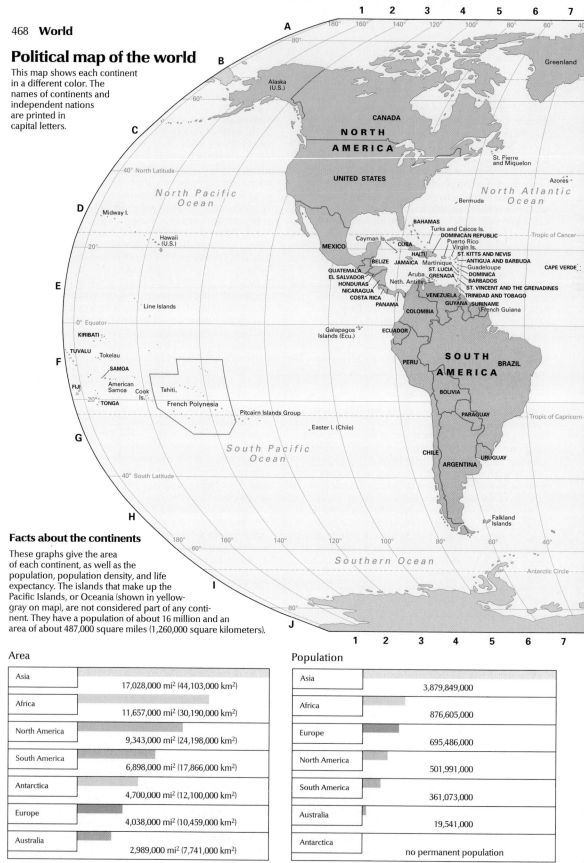

Facts about the continents

These graphs give the area of each continent, as well as the population, population density, and life expectancy. The islands that make up the Pacific Islands, or Oceania (shown in yellow-gray on map), are not considered part of any continent. They have a population of about 16 million and an area of about 487,000 square miles (1,260,000 square kilometers).

Area

Asia	17,028,000 mi² (44,103,000 km²)
Africa	11,657,000 mi² (30,190,000 km²)
North America	9,343,000 mi² (24,198,000 km²)
South America	6,898,000 mi² (17,866,000 km²)
Antarctica	4,700,000 mi² (12,100,000 km²)
Europe	4,038,000 mi² (10,459,000 km²)
Australia	2,989,000 mi² (7,741,000 km²)

Population

Asia	3,879,849,000
Africa	876,605,000
Europe	695,486,000
North America	501,991,000
South America	361,073,000
Australia	19,541,000
Antarctica	no permanent population

Sources: Area and population figures are 2004 estimates based on official government and United Nations sources. Life expectancy figures are Population Reference Bureau estimates for 2002.

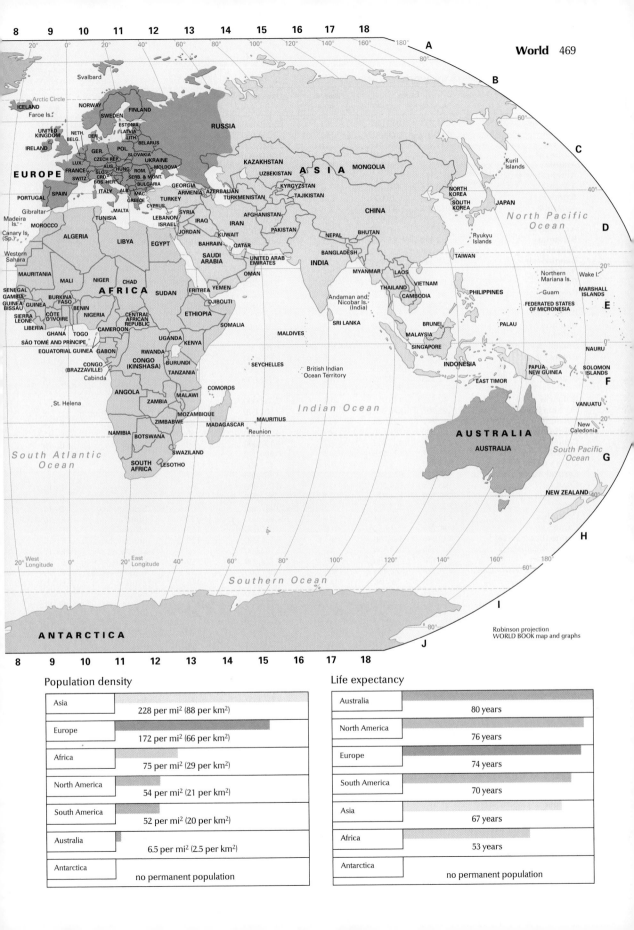

Population density

Asia	228 per mi² (88 per km²)
Europe	172 per mi² (66 per km²)
Africa	75 per mi² (29 per km²)
North America	54 per mi² (21 per km²)
South America	52 per mi² (20 per km²)
Australia	6.5 per mi² (2.5 per km²)
Antarctica	no permanent population

Life expectancy

Australia	80 years
North America	76 years
Europe	74 years
South America	70 years
Asia	67 years
Africa	53 years
Antarctica	no permanent population

Robinson projection
WORLD BOOK map and graphs

Independent countries of the world

Name	Area		Rank in area	Population[†]	Rank in population	Capital	Map key	
	In mi²	In km²						
Afghanistan	251,773	652,090	40	25,150,000	43	Kabul	D	11
Albania	11,100	28,748	140	3,214,000	130	Tiranë	C	11
Algeria	919,595	2,381,741	11	32,480,000	34	Algiers	D	10
Andorra‡	181	468	177	71,000	184	Andorra la Vella	C	10
Angola	481,354	1,246,700	22	14,777,000	62	Luanda	F	10
Antigua and Barbuda	171	442	180	78,000	182	St. John's	E	6
Argentina	1,073,518	2,780,400	8	37,533,000	32	Buenos Aires	G	6
Armenia	11,506	29,800	138	3,465,000	126	Yerevan	D	13
Australia	2,988,902	7,741,220	6	19,541,000	54	Canberra	G	16
Austria	32,378	83,859	112	8,041,000	90	Vienna	C	10
Azerbaijan	33,436	86,600	111	8,232,000	89	Baku	D	13
Bahamas	5,358	13,878	155	320,000	167	Nassau	D	6
Bahrain	268	694	174	673,000	156	Manama	D	12
Bangladesh	55,598	143,998	92	131,035,000	9	Dhaka	D	14
Barbados	166	430	181	271,000	170	Bridgetown	E	7
Belarus	80,155	207,600	83	9,885,000	81	Minsk	C	12
Belgium	11,787	30,528	136	10,286,000	77	Brussels	C	10
Belize	8,867	22,965	147	259,000	171	Belmopan	E	5
Benin	43,484	112,622	99	7,007,000	96	Porto-Novo	E	10
Bhutan	18,147	47,000	128	2,312,000	138	Thimphu	D	14
Bolivia	424,164	1,098,581	27	9,069,000	83	La Paz; Sucre	F	6
Bosnia-Herzegovina	19,767	51,197	124	4,160,000	118	Sarajevo	C	10
Botswana	224,607	581,730	45	1,575,000	144	Gaborone	G	11
Brazil	3,300,171	8,547,403	5	177,971,000	5	Brasília	F	7
Brunei	2,226	5,765	162	352,000	166	Bandar Seri Begawan	E	15
Bulgaria	42,823	110,912	102	7,742,000	91	Sofia	C	11
Burkina Faso	105,792	274,000	73	12,988,000	66	Ouagadougou	E	9
Burundi	10,747	27,834	142	7,154,000	93	Bujumbura	F	11
Cambodia	69,898	181,035	87	13,210,000	65	Phnom Penh	E	15
Cameroon	183,569	475,442	52	16,191,000	58	Yaoundé	E	10
Canada	3,849,674	9,970,610	2	30,806,000	37	Ottawa	C	4
Cape Verde	1,557	4,033	164	473,000	162	Praia	E	8
Central African Republic	240,535	622,984	42	3,967,000	121	Bangui	E	10
Chad	495,755	1,284,000	20	8,899,000	84	N'Djamena	E	10
Chile	292,135	756,626	37	15,942,000	60	Santiago	G	6
China	3,692,671	9,563,974	3	1,319,377,000	1	Beijing	D	14
Colombia	439,737	1,138,914	25	44,847,000	27	Bogotá	E	6
Comoros	719	1,862	168	631,000	158	Moroni	F	12
Congo (Brazzaville)	132,047	342,000	63	3,401,000	129	Brazzaville	F	10
Congo (Kinshasa)	905,355	2,344,858	12	58,103,000	22	Kinshasa	F	11
Costa Rica	19,730	51,100	125	4,129,000	119	San José	E	5
Côte d'Ivoire (Ivory Coast)	124,504	322,463	68	17,381,000	57	Yamoussoukro	E	9
Croatia	21,829	56,538	123	4,385,000	115	Zagreb	C	10
Cuba	42,804	110,861	103	11,334,000	70	Havana	D	5
Cyprus	3,572	9,251	161	773,000	154	Nicosia	D	11
Czech Republic	30,450	78,866	114	10,262,000	78	Prague	C	10
Denmark	16,639	43,094	130	5,375,000	107	Copenhagen	C	10
Djibouti	8,958	23,200	146	658,000	157	Djibouti	E	12
Dominica	290	751	170	72,000	183	Roseau	E	6
Dominican Republic	18,730	48,511	127	8,887,000	85	Santo Domingo	E	6
East Timor	5,743	14,874	154	828,000	153	Dili	F	16
Ecuador	109,484	283,561	72	13,549,000	63	Quito	F	6
Egypt	386,662	1,001,449	29	72,534,000	16	Cairo	D	11
El Salvador	8,124	21,041	149	6,748,000	97	San Salvador	E	5
Equatorial Guinea	10,831	28,051	141	511,000	160	Malabo	E	10
Eritrea	45,406	117,600	98	4,037,000	120	Asmara	E	12
Estonia	17,413	45,100	129	1,309,000	149	Tallinn	C	11
Ethiopia	426,373	1,104,300	26	69,195,000	18	Addis Ababa	E	11
Fiji	7,056	18,274	151	881,000	152	Suva	F	1
Finland	130,559	338,145	64	5,214,000	109	Helsinki	B	11
France	212,935	551,500	47	59,765,000	20	Paris	C	10
Gabon	103,347	267,668	75	1,357,000	146	Libreville	F	10
Gambia	4,361	11,295	157	1,432,000	145	Banjul	E	9
Georgia	26,911	69,700	118	5,151,000	111	Tbilisi	D	12
Germany	137,847	357,022	62	81,886,000	14	Berlin	C	10
Ghana	92,098	238,533	79	20,087,000	51	Accra	E	9
Greece	50,949	131,957	94	10,953,000	73	Athens	D	11
Grenada	133	344	183	102,000	178	St. George's	E	6
Guatemala	42,042	108,889	104	12,606,000	68	Guatemala City	E	5

See footnotes at end of table on page 472.

Independent countries of the world (continued)

Name	Area		Rank in area	Population[†]	Rank in population	Capital	Map key	
	In mi²	In km²						
Guinea	94,926	245,857	76	8,648,000	87	Conakry	E	9
Guinea-Bissau	13,948	36,125	133	1,319,000	147	Bissau	E	9
Guyana	83,000	214,969	82	767,000	155	Georgetown	E	7
Haiti	10,714	27,750	143	7,636,000	92	Port-au-Prince	E	6
Honduras	43,277	112,088	100	7,028,000	95	Tegucigalpa	E	5
Hungary	35,920	93,032	108	9,770,000	82	Budapest	C	10
Iceland	39,769	103,000	105	287,000	169	Reykjavík	B	9
India	1,269,219	3,287,263	7	1,075,516,000	2	New Delhi	D	13
Indonesia	735,358	1,904,569	15	213,483,000	4	Jakarta	F	16
Iran	636,372	1,648,195	17	74,293,000	15	Tehran	D	12
Iraq	169,235	438,317	57	25,576,000	41	Baghdad	D	12
Ireland	27,133	70,273	117	3,875,000	123	Dublin	C	9
Israel	8,130	21,056	148	6,543,000	98	Jerusalem	D	11
Italy	116,340	301,318	70	57,231,000	23	Rome	C	10
Jamaica	4,243	10,990	159	2,669,000	135	Kingston	E	6
Japan	145,881	377,829	61	127,638,000	10	Tokyo	D	16
Jordan	35,467	91,860	110	5,506,000	105	Amman	D	11
Kazakhstan	1,052,090	2,724,900	9	14,879,000	61	Astana	C	13
Kenya	224,081	580,367	46	31,524,000	36	Nairobi	E	11
Kiribati	280	726	172	88,000	180	Tarawa	F	1
Korea, North	46,540	120,538	96	22,880,000	48	Pyongyang	C	16
Korea, South	38,328	99,268	107	47,986,000	25	Seoul	D	16
Kuwait	6,880	17,818	152	2,118,000	140	Kuwait	D	12
Kyrgyzstan	76,834	199,000	84	5,153,000	110	Bishkek	C	15
Laos	91,429	236,800	81	5,782,000	101	Vientiane	E	15
Latvia	24,942	64,600	121	2,367,000	137	Riga	C	11
Lebanon	4,015	10,400	160	3,718,000	124	Beirut	D	11
Lesotho	11,720	30,355	137	2,297,000	139	Maseru	G	11
Liberia	43,000	111,369	101	3,415,000	128	Monrovia	E	9
Libya	679,362	1,759,540	16	5,771,000	102	Tripoli	D	10
Liechtenstein‡	62	160	188	34,000	187	Vaduz	C	10
Lithuania	25,174	65,200	120	3,661,000	125	Vilnius	C	11
Luxembourg	998	2,586	166	458,000	163	Luxembourg	C	10
Macedonia	9,928	25,713	145	2,059,000	141	Skopje	C	10
Madagascar	226,658	587,041	44	17,856,000	56	Antananarivo	F	12
Malawi	45,747	118,484	97	11,293,000	72	Lilongwe	F	11
Malaysia	127,320	329,758	66	23,786,000	45	Kuala Lumpur	E	15
Maldives	115	298	185	303,000	168	Male	E	13
Mali	478,841	1,240,192	23	12,731,000	67	Bamako	E	9
Malta	122	316	184	396,000	165	Valletta	D	10
Marshall Islands	70	181	187	54,000	185	Majuro	E	18
Mauritania	395,955	1,025,520	28	2,995,000	132	Nouakchott	D	9
Mauritius	788	2,040	167	1,199,000	150	Port Louis	G	12
Mexico	756,066	1,958,201	14	103,011,000	11	Mexico City	D	4
Micronesia, Federated States of	271	702	173	135,000	176	Palikir	E	17
Moldova	13,070	33,851	135	4,251,000	117	Chisinau	C	11
Monaco‡	0.58	1.49	192	33,000	188	Monaco	C	10
Mongolia	604,829	1,566,500	18	2,484,000	136	Ulaanbaatar	C	15
Morocco	172,414	446,550	56	32,063,000	35	Rabat	D	9
Mozambique	309,496	801,590	34	19,614,000	53	Maputo	F	11
Myanmar	261,228	676,578	39	50,003,000	24	Yangon	D	14
Namibia	318,261	824,292	33	1,844,000	143	Windhoek	G	11
Nauru	8	21	191	13,000	191	—	F	18
Nepal	56,827	147,181	91	25,257,000	42	Kathmandu	D	14
Netherlands	16,033	41,526	131	16,087,000	59	Amsterdam	C	10
New Zealand	104,454	270,534	74	3,890,000	122	Wellington	G	18
Nicaragua	50,193	130,000	95	5,617,000	103	Managua	E	5
Niger	489,191	1,267,000	21	12,493,000	69	Niamey	E	10
Nigeria	356,669	923,768	30	136,769,000	8	Abuja	E	10
Norway	149,151	386,299	60	4,536,000	114	Oslo	B	10
Oman	119,499	309,500	69	2,887,000	133	Muscat	E	12
Pakistan	307,374	796,095	35	156,164,000	6	Islamabad	D	13
Palau	177	459	178	21,000	190	Koror	E	16
Panama	29,157	75,517	115	3,005,000	131	Panama City	E	5
Papua New Guinea	178,704	462,840	53	5,606,000	104	Port Moresby	F	17
Paraguay	157,048	406,752	58	6,057,000	100	Asunción	G	7
Peru	496,225	1,285,216	19	27,344,000	38	Lima	F	6
Philippines	115,831	300,000	71	82,351,000	12	Manila	E	16
Poland	124,808	323,250	67	38,466,000	31	Warsaw	C	10
Portugal	35,514	91,982	109	10,068,000	79	Lisbon	D	9

See footnotes at end of table on page 472.

(Table continued on page 472.)

Independent countries of the world (continued)

Name	Area		Rank in area	Population[†]	Rank in population	Capital	Map key	
	In mi²	In km²						
Qatar	4,247	11,000	158	600,000	159	Doha	D	12
Romania	92,043	238,391	80	22,206,000	49	Bucharest	C	11
Russia	6,592,850	17,075,400	1	141,802,000	7	Moscow	C	13
Rwanda	10,169	26,338	144	8,272,000	88	Kigali	F	11
St. Kitts and Nevis‡	101	261	186	37,000	186	Basseterre	E	6
St. Lucia	208	539	176	163,000	174	Castries	E	6
St. Vincent and the Grenadines	150	388	182	116,000	177	Kingstown	E	6
Samoa	1,093	2,831	165	176,000	173	Apia	F	1
San Marino‡	24	61	189	28,000	189	San Marino	C	10
São Tomé and Príncipe	372	964	169	160,000	175	São Tomé	E	10
Saudi Arabia	830,000	2,149,690	13	22,998,000	46	Riyadh	D	12
Senegal	75,955	196,722	85	10,403,000	75	Dakar	E	9
Serbia and Montenegro§	39,449	102,173	106	10,489,000	74	Belgrade	C	10
Seychelles	176	455	179	84,000	181	Victoria	F	12
Sierra Leone	27,699	71,740	116	5,261,000	108	Freetown	E	9
Singapore	239	618	175	4,305,000	116	Singapore	E	15
Slovakia	18,924	49,012	126	5,416,000	106	Bratislava	C	11
Slovenia	7,821	20,256	150	1,978,000	142	Ljubljana	C	11
Solomon Islands	11,157	28,896	139	509,000	161	Honiara	F	18
Somalia	246,201	637,657	41	10,352,000	76	Mogadishu	E	12
South Africa	471,445	1,221,037	24	44,552,000	28	Cape Town; Pretoria; Bloemfontein	G	11
Spain	195,365	505,992	50	39,878,000	29	Madrid	C	9
Sri Lanka	25,332	65,610	119	19,646,000	52	Sri Jayewardenepura Kotte	E	14
Sudan	967,500	2,505,813	10	34,056,000	33	Khartoum	E	11
Suriname	63,037	163,265	90	424,000	164	Paramaribo	E	7
Swaziland	6,704	17,364	153	1,030,000	151	Mbabane	G	11
Sweden	173,732	449,964	54	8,796,000	86	Stockholm	B	10
Switzerland	15,940	41,284	132	7,153,000	94	Bern	C	10
Syria	71,498	185,180	86	17,905,000	55	Damascus	D	11
Taiwan#	13,892	35,980	134	22,912,000	47	Taipei	D	16
Tajikistan	54,865	142,100	93	6,298,000	99	Dushanbe	D	14
Tanzania	341,217	883,749	32	38,493,000	30	Dodoma	F	11
Thailand	198,115	513,115	49	63,418,000	19	Bangkok	E	15
Togo	21,925	56,785	122	5,007,000	113	Lomé	E	9
Tonga	289	748	171	100,000	179	Nuku'alofa	F	1
Trinidad and Tobago	1,981	5,130	163	1,317,000	148	Port-of-Spain	E	6
Tunisia	63,170	163,610	89	9,898,000	80	Tunis	D	10
Turkey	299,158	774,815	36	71,455,000	17	Ankara	D	11
Turkmenistan	188,456	488,100	51	5,103,000	112	Ashgabat	D	13
Tuvalu	10	26	190	11,000	192	Funafuti	F	1
Uganda	93,065	241,038	78	26,418,000	39	Kampala	E	11
Ukraine	233,090	603,700	43	47,730,000	26	Kiev	C	11
United Arab Emirates	32,278	83,600	113	2,790,000	134	Abu Dhabi	D	12
United Kingdom	93,784	242,900	77	59,107,000	21	London	C	9
United States	3,615,275	9,363,520	4	291,575,000	3	Washington, D.C.	C	4
Uruguay	67,574	175,016	88	3,431,000	127	Montevideo	G	7
Uzbekistan	172,742	447,400	55	26,293,000	40	Tashkent	D	14
Vanuatu	4,706	12,189	156	211,000	172	Port-Vila	F	18
Vatican City‡	0.17	0.44	193	1,000	193	—	C	10
Venezuela	352,144	912,050	31	23,950,000	44	Caracas	E	6
Vietnam	128,066	331,689	65	82,280,000	13	Hanoi	E	15
Yemen	203,850	527,968	48	21,524,000	50	Sanaa	E	12
Zambia	290,587	752,618	38	11,320,000	71	Lusaka	F	11
Zimbabwe	150,872	390,757	59	13,524,000	64	Harare	G	11

†Populations are 2004 estimates based on the latest figures from official government and United Nations sources.
‡Not on map; key shows general location.   §Formerly called Yugoslavia.   #Claimed by China.

Populated dependencies of the world*

Name	Area		Population[†]	Capital	Map key	
	In mi²	In km²				
American Samoa (United States)	77	199	77,000	Pago Pago	F	1
Anguilla (United Kingdom)‡	37	96	13,000	The Valley (unofficial)	E	6
Aruba (Netherlands)	75	193	115,000	Oranjestad	E	6
Azores (Portugal)	868	2,247	242,000	Ponta Delgada	D	8
Bermuda (United Kingdom)	20	53	65,000	Hamilton	D	6

See footnotes at end of table.

Populated dependencies of the world*

Name	Area		Population†	Capital	Map key	
	In mi²	In km²				
Cayman Islands (United Kingdom)	100	259	43,000	George Town	D	5
Channel Islands (United Kingdom)‡	76	197	144,000	St. Helier; St. Peter Port	C	9
Cook Islands (New Zealand)	93	240	21,000	Avarua	F	2
Easter Island (Chile)	47	122	3,000	—	G	5
Falkland Islands (United Kingdom)	4,699	12,170	2,000	Stanley	H	7
Faroe Islands (Denmark)	540	1,399	48,000	Tórshavn	B	9
French Guiana (France)	35,135	91,000	187,000	Cayenne	E	7
French Polynesia (France)	1,540	4,000	248,000	Papeete	F	2
Gaza Strip (§)‡	146	378	1,325,000	Gaza	D	11
Gibraltar (United Kingdom)	2.5	6.5	27,000	Gibraltar	D	9
Greenland (Denmark)	836,330	2,166,086	56,000	Nuuk	B	7
Guadeloupe (France)	658	1,704	442,000	Basse-Terre	E	6
Guam (United States)	209	541	165,000	Hagåtña	E	17
Madeira Islands (Portugal)	307	794	240,000	Funchal	D	9
Man, Isle of (United Kingdom)‡	221	572	78,000	Douglas	C	9
Martinique (France)	425	1,100	391,000	Fort-de-France	E	6
Mayotte (France)	144	373	186,000	Mamoudzou	F	12
Midway Island (United States)	2	5	400	—	D	1
Montserrat (United Kingdom)‡	39	102	5,000	—	E	6
Netherlands Antilles (Netherlands)	308	798	222,000	Willemstad	E	6
New Caledonia (France)	7,366	19,079	232,000	Nouméa	G	18
Niue Island (New Zealand)‡	100	260	2,000	—	F	1
Norfolk Island (Australia)‡	13	35	2,000	—	G	18
Northern Mariana Islands, Commonwealth of the (United States)	184	477	85,000	Saipan	E	17
Pitcairn Islands Group (United Kingdom)	17	44	50	—	G	3
Puerto Rico (United States)	3,515	9,103	3,944,000	San Juan	E	6
Reunion (France)	970	2,512	767,000	Saint-Denis	G	12
St. Helena Island Group (United Kingdom)	158	410	7,000	Jamestown	F	9
St.-Pierre and Miquelon (France)	93	242	7,000	St.-Pierre	C	7
Tokelau (New Zealand)	4	10	1,000	—	F	1
Turks and Caicos Islands (United Kingdom)	166	430	19,000	Grand Turk	D	6
Virgin Islands (United Kingdom)	59	153	26,000	Road Town	E	6
Virgin Islands (United States)	132	342	112,000	Charlotte Amalie	E	6
Wake Island (United States)	3	8	100	—	E	18
Wallis and Futuna Islands (France)‡	106	275	16,000	Mata-Utu	F	1
West Bank (#)‡	2,270	5,879	2,313,000	—	D	11
Western Sahara (**)	102,700	266,000	283,000	—	D	9

*The dependencies listed are controlled in some way by the country shown in parentheses.
†Populations are 2004 and earlier estimates based on the latest figures from official government and United Nations sources.
‡Not on map; key shows general location.

§Administered by the Palestinian Authority; Israel controls external security and foreign affairs.
#Part of the West Bank is administered by the Palestinian Authority with external security and foreign affairs controlled by Israel; other parts are occupied by Israel.
**Occupied by Morocco; claimed by Morocco and by the Polisario Front.

© Mario Tama, Getty Images

A United Nations (UN) General Assembly session brings together delegates from nearly all the world's nations. The UN works to settle disputes among countries, to maintain world peace, and to help people to better their way of life.

© Dimitar Dilkoff, AFP/Getty Images

Voting is a right of the citizens of many countries. People vote to choose their leaders and to decide public issues. This woman is casting a vote in a presidential election in Skopje, Macedonia.

monarchy. A king or queen serves as head of state, and a prime minister serves as head of government. Other countries with democratic governments include Australia, Canada, Japan, New Zealand, most countries of Europe, and many of the less developed countries of Africa, Asia, and Latin America.

Many countries that claim to be democracies actually have an *authoritarian* government. In such countries, relatively few people have power, and most citizens play a limited role in making decisions. Authoritarian governments may rule by persuasion, force, or both. Communist Party organizations control authoritarian governments in China and a few other nations. Dictators supported by military forces rule other countries. Saudi Arabia and several other Middle Eastern monarchies have authoritarian governments.

Economic systems. Every country has an economic system to determine how to use its resources. The three main economic systems today are (1) capitalism, (2) Communism, and (3) mixed economies.

Capitalism is based on *free enterprise*—that is, most of the resources needed for production are privately owned. Individuals and private firms determine what to produce and sell, and how to use their income. Capitalist economic systems exist in Australia, Canada, New Zealand, the United States, and many countries of Europe. The role of capitalism is expanding in many less developed countries as well.

Communism traditionally has been based on government ownership of most productive resources. The government also plays a large role in deciding what goods to produce and how to distribute income. Communism was once the main economic system in the Soviet Union and many nations of Eastern Europe. However, these nations began to decrease government control over their economies in the late 1980's and early 1990's. Today, only a few countries claim to run their economies on Communist principles. Even China and other countries that are often thought of as Communist have loosened government control over economic activities.

Mixed economies combine both private and government control. Under a mixed economy, the government may own such industries as banks, railroads, and steel. However, other industries are privately owned. The government does some economic planning, but it also allows much private choice. Denmark, Norway, Sweden, and some less developed countries have mixed economies.

Cooperation among nations. Every nation depends on other nations in some ways. The interdependence of the entire world and its peoples is called *globalism*. Nations trade with one another to earn money and to obtain manufactured goods or the natural resources that they lack. Nations with similar interests and political beliefs may pledge to support one another in case of war. Developed countries may provide less developed countries with financial aid and technical assistance. Such aid strengthens trade as well as defense ties.

Several international organizations promote cooperation among countries. The United Nations (UN) is the largest such organization. Nearly all independent countries are UN members. The UN works mainly to settle disputes among nations and to promote world peace. It also has programs to aid needy people and to improve health and education, particularly in less developed countries.

Many international organizations are designed to encourage economic progress among member nations. Such groups stimulate trade among members by eliminating tariffs and other trade barriers within the organization. These groups include the European Union, the North American Free Trade Association (NAFTA), and the Southern Common Market (Mercosur).

People of the world

Population. By the early 2000's, the world's population reached about $6\frac{1}{3}$ billion. The yearly rate of population growth is about 1.2 percent. At that rate, the world's population would double in about 60 years.

If all the world's people were distributed evenly over the land, about 110 people would live on every square mile of land (43 on every square kilometer). However, the world's people are not distributed evenly, and so the *population density* (the average number of people in a specific area) varies greatly. Some regions, including Antarctica and certain desert areas, have no permanent

Modern manufacturing systems are used to produce consumer goods in many parts of the world. This man uses a mechanical arm to assemble a minivan at an automobile factory in Tokyo.

© Junko Kimura, Getty Images

settlers at all, while the populations of many urban areas continue to grow rapidly (see **City** [table: The 100 largest urban centers in the world]).

The most densely populated regions of the world are in Europe and in southern and eastern Asia. North America has heavy concentrations of people in the northeastern and central regions and along the Pacific coast. Africa, Australia, and South America have densely populated areas near the coasts. The interiors of those continents are thinly settled.

Just as the population density varies from one part of the world to another, so does the rate of population growth. Less developed countries generally have higher average rates of increase than developed nations. Africa has a population growth rate of 2.3 percent yearly, the highest of all continents. South America has a 1.4 percent rate of increase, and Asia a 1.3 percent rate. North America's rate is 1.1 percent, and Australia's rate of increase is 1 percent. Europe's population is actually declining, losing 0.2 percent each year.

The world's largest countries in terms of population are China—which is the largest—and India. Each has

Where the people of the world live   This map shows how the world's population is distributed. About three-fourths of all people live in Asia and Europe. Regions with severe climates, such as desert areas, are thinly populated. The map also shows the location of some of the world's largest metropolitan areas.

WORLD BOOK map

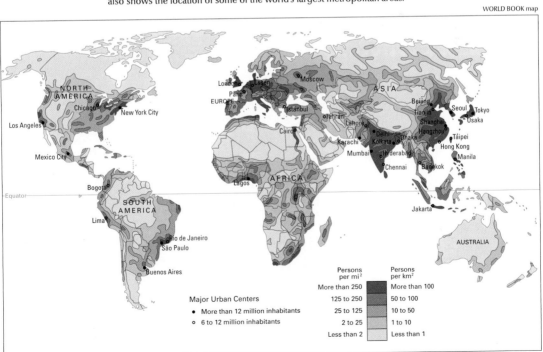

more than a billion people. The United States ranks as third largest, followed in descending order by Indonesia, Brazil, Pakistan, and Russia. Over half the world's total population lives in these seven nations. Vatican City has the smallest population of any of the world's nations. It has only about 1,000 people.

The growth and change of the world's population throughout history are described in the article **Population.** See also the articles on individual countries, states, and provinces for population details.

Languages. There are about 6,000 spoken languages in the world. But only about 10 of these are spoken by more than 100 million people. More people speak Mandarin Chinese than any other language. Arabic, Bengal, English, Hindi, Portuguese, Russian, and Spanish are among the other most-spoken languages.

Beginning in the late 1400's, Portugal and Spain, and then England and France, established colonies in various parts of the world. For this reason, Portuguese, Spanish, English, and French are now spoken in many nations outside their countries of origin. Portuguese became the main language of Angola, Brazil, and Mozambique. Spanish became the chief language throughout most countries of Latin America. English became the chief language in Australia, New Zealand, and the United States. It is also one of the main languages in Canada, India, and South Africa.

French, like English, is an important language of Canada. Most people in the province of Quebec speak French. French is also widely spoken in Algeria; Chad; Morocco; Senegal and some other countries in western Africa; and Vietnam.

For information about the development of the world's

languages, see **Language.** See also the articles on individual countries for the most widely used languages in those nations.

Religions. The peoples of the world practice thousands of religions. Christianity has about 2 billion members, more than any other religion. Islam has more than 1.1 billion members, and Hinduism has about 800 million. Other major religions or belief systems of the world include the Bahá'í Faith, Buddhism, Confucianism, Jainism, Judaism, Shinto, Sikhism, and Taoism.

Christianity originated in the Middle East. Today, Christianity is the major religion in Australia, Europe, and the Western Hemisphere, which includes North America and South America. Islam also began in the Middle East and is now the chief religion throughout most of that area. It is also the major faith in Afghanistan, northern Africa, Bangladesh, Indonesia, Malaysia, Pakistan, and some Asian countries of the former Soviet Union. Hinduism, Jainism, and Sikhism have most of their followers in India, where the religions originated. Buddhism, which also developed in India, is the major religion of Sri Lanka and the mainland of southeastern Asia. Buddhism also has many followers in such countries as Japan and South Korea. Shinto is the native religion of Japan. The Bahá'í Faith originated in what is now Iraq.

Confucianism and Taoism are native belief systems of China. China's Communist government tolerates the practice of religion, with certain restrictions. Chinese people living in Taiwan also practice Confucianism and Taoism. Judaism originated in the Middle East. Today, the largest number of Jews live in France, Israel, Russia, and the United States. Thousands of local traditional religions are practiced by ethnic groups in Africa, Asia,

Growth of the world's population

The world's population grew slowly before A.D. 1. It then almost doubled by the year 1000. In the 1700's and 1800's improvements in agriculture, transportation, and communication improved living conditions and reduced death rates. Improvements such as these helped the world's population increase rapidly since 1800. At its present rate of growth, the world's population will double in about 60 years. Most of this growth will occur in less developed regions.

World population growth, 2000 B.C to A.D. 2000

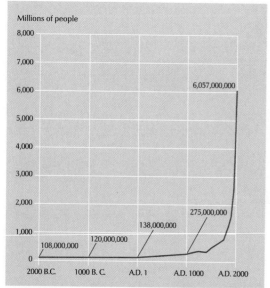

World population growth since 1800

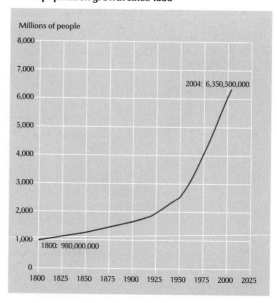

Source: WORLD BOOK estimates based on data from the United Nations.

Australia, North America, South America, and the Pacific Islands.

For a description of major religions, see **Religion** and the separate articles on the various faiths. See also the *Religion* section of the country and continent articles.

Problems among the world's people. Through the years, human beings have made great progress in providing for their basic needs. Modern methods of producing food, clothing, and shelter have helped many people live more comfortably. Education has become available to more and more people, and scientists have discovered cures for many diseases.

But serious challenges still face the world's people. Millions of people in less developed countries lack adequate food, clothing, shelter, medical care, and education. Many people in developed countries, especially in large cities, suffer from poverty, unemployment, and discrimination. Numerous nations face the growing problem of environmental pollution. In addition, ethnic, political, and religious differences continue to lead to conflicts among the peoples of the world.

Physical features of the world

The surface area of the world totals about 196,900,000 square miles (510,000,000 square kilometers). Water covers about 139,700,000 square miles (362,000,000 square kilometers), or 71 percent of the world's surface. Only 29 percent of the world's surface consists of land, which covers about 57,200,000 square miles (148,000,000 square kilometers).

The physical geography of a specific region includes the region's surface features and climate. It also includes the soil, mineral deposits, plant and animal life, and other natural resources. Physical geography thus helps determine a region's economy and its people's way of life.

This section describes the two major surface features of the world: (1) water and (2) land.

Water. Oceans, lakes, and rivers make up most of the water that covers the surface of the world. The water surface consists chiefly of three large oceans—the Pacific, the Atlantic, and the Indian.

The Pacific Ocean is the largest. It covers 66 million square miles (171 million square kilometers), or about a third of the world's surface. The Atlantic Ocean is about half as large as the Pacific Ocean, and the Indian Ocean is slightly smaller than the Atlantic. These three oceans meet the Southern Ocean at 60° south latitude. In the north, the Atlantic Ocean meets the Arctic Ocean near Greenland; and the Pacific Ocean meets the Arctic Ocean in the Bering Strait, between Russia and Alaska.

The world's largest lake is the Caspian Sea, a body of salt water that lies between Asia and Europe east of the Caucasus Mountains. The Caspian covers about 143,250 square miles (371,000 square kilometers). The world's largest body of fresh water is the Great Lakes in North America. These five lakes—Erie, Huron, Michigan, Ontario, and Superior—are interconnected, and so they can be referred to as one body of water. Together, they cover 94,230 square miles (244,060 square kilometers).

The longest river in the world is the Nile in Africa, which flows 4,160 miles (6,695 kilometers). The second longest river, the Amazon in South America, is 4,000 miles (6,437 kilometers) long. Although it is shorter than the Nile, the Amazon carries a much greater volume of water—about one-fifth of all the water that empties into the world's oceans.

All living things need water to stay alive. People obtain drinking water from rivers, freshwater lakes, and wells. We also require water to maintain our way of life. We use water in our homes for cleaning and cooking. The manufacture of almost all our products requires water. In dry regions, farmers draw water from

Text continued on page 480.

Physical map index

Physical map of the world

This map shows the world's chief physical features. Areas shown in shades of green generally have fertile soil and sufficient rainfall. Most of the world's people live in these areas.

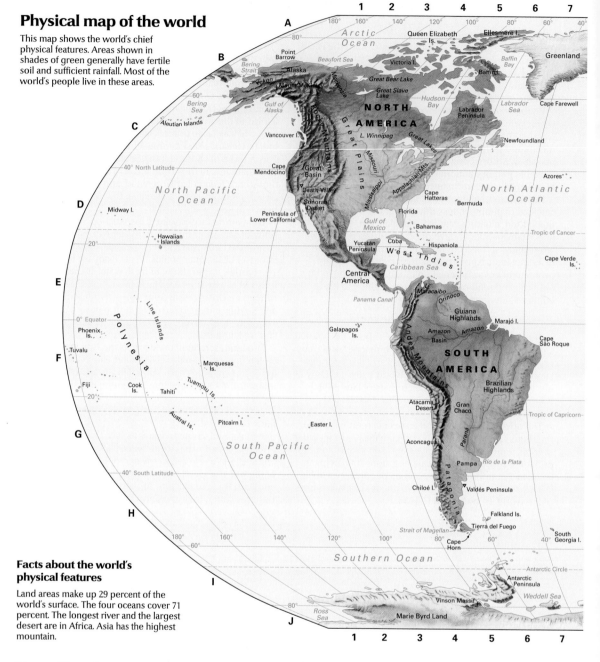

Facts about the world's physical features

Land areas make up 29 percent of the world's surface. The four oceans cover 71 percent. The longest river and the largest desert are in Africa. Asia has the highest mountain.

The world's surface

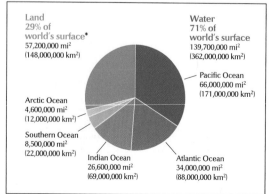

Land
29% of world's surface*
57,200,000 mi²
(148,000,000 km²)

Water
71% of world's surface
139,700,000 mi²
(362,000,000 km²)

Pacific Ocean
66,000,000 mi²
(171,000,000 km²)

Arctic Ocean
4,600,000 mi²
(12,000,000 km²)

Southern Ocean
8,500,000 mi²
(22,000,000 km²)

Indian Ocean
26,600,000 mi²
(69,000,000 km²)

Atlantic Ocean
34,000,000 mi²
(88,000,000 km²)

*Includes area of inland lakes.

Longest river on each continent

Africa	Nile	4,160 mi (6,695 km)
South America	Amazon	4,000 mi (6,437 km)
Asia	Yangtze	3,900 mi (6,275 km)
North America	Missouri	2,565 mi (4,130 km)
Europe	Volga	2,300 mi (3,700 km)
Australia	Murray	1,609 mi (2,589 km)
Antarctica	(no rivers)	

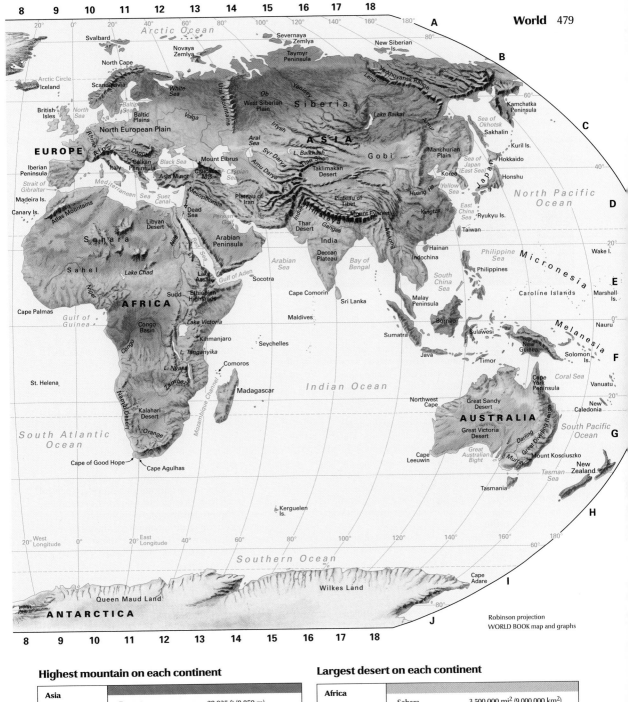

Robinson projection
WORLD BOOK map and graphs

Highest mountain on each continent

Continent	Mountain	Elevation
Asia	Everest	29,035 ft (8,850 m)
South America	Aconcagua	22,831 ft (6,959 m)
North America	McKinley	20,320 ft (6,194 m)
Africa	Kilimanjaro	19,340 ft (5,895 m)
Europe	Elbrus	18,510 ft (5,642 m)
Antarctica	Vinson Massif	16,067 ft (4,897 m)
Australia	Kosciuszko	7,310 ft (2,228 m)

Largest desert on each continent

Africa	Sahara	3,500,000 mi² (9,000,000 km²)
Asia	Gobi	500,000 mi² (1,300,000 km²)
Australia	Great Victoria	250,000 mi² (650,000 km²)
South America	Atacama	140,000 mi² (360,000 km²)
North America	Sonoran	120,000 mi² (310,000 km²)
Europe	(no deserts)	
Antarctica	(no deserts)	

Air pollution is a serious world problem. A major form of environmental pollution, it is a health hazard for people in many of the world's urban areas. This photograph shows Mexico City amid a haze of smog.

lakes, rivers, and wells to irrigate their crops. Lakes, oceans, and rivers supply us with fish and other foods.

Water is also a source of power. The force of falling water from dams, rivers, and waterfalls can be used to generate hydroelectric power. In such countries as Brazil and Norway, hydroelectric power stations supply nearly all the electric power used in industry and homes.

The waters of the world also serve as major transportation routes. Every day, thousands of cargo ships cross the oceans, sail along seacoasts, and travel on inland waters. A nation's location along a seacoast can have a powerful influence on its progress and prosperity. Japan, the United Kingdom, the United States, and some other leading trading nations have long coastlines. Many of the world's major cities border important water transportation routes.

Land. The land area of the world consists of seven continents and many thousands of islands. Asia is the largest continent, followed by Africa, North America, South America, Antarctica, Europe, and Australia. Geographers sometimes refer to Europe and Asia as one continent called Eurasia.

The world's land surface includes hills, mountains, plains, plateaus, and valleys. Relatively few people live in mountainous areas or on high plateaus. Most such regions are too cold, dry, or rugged for commercial crop farming and other economic activities. But some mountains and high, grassy plateaus serve as grazing lands for cattle, sheep, and other livestock.

Mountainous areas have certain limitations. Nevertheless, many of the largest cities in regions near the equator, such as parts of Africa, Asia, and Latin America, are in high mountain valleys. Because certain diseases thrive in tropical lowlands, these mountain valleys are healthier for human occupation than the nearby tropical lowlands are. For example, malaria and yellow fever are more common in tropical regions with a low altitude than in tropical regions with a high altitude.

The majority of the world's people live on plains or in hilly regions. Except for some tropical lowlands, most plains and hilly regions have fertile soils and enough

water for farming, manufacturing, and trade. Many areas less suitable for farming, particularly mountainous areas, have plentiful mineral resources. Some desert regions, especially in the Middle East, have large deposits of petroleum.

A region's natural resources influence its economic development. The Pampa, a grassy plain in central Argentina, has excellent pastureland for raising cattle and rich soil for growing wheat and other grains. Agricultural products make up Argentina's leading exports. The United Kingdom has relatively little farmland, but large deposits of coal and iron ore helped make the country an industrial power. Such countries as Canada, Russia, and the United States have various and abundant natural resources, which have greatly boosted their economies.

Threats to the environment. For hundreds of years, people have used the world's natural resources to make their lives more comfortable. However, these resources are not always used wisely. Many human practices threaten the environment.

Many water supplies have become polluted by sewage, industrial chemicals, and other wastes. The burning of fuel in motor vehicles, factories, and furnaces has caused severe air pollution in numerous cities. Many forest regions have been stripped of large areas of trees, resulting in soil erosion and the destruction of plant and animal life. Certain farming practices, including the use of chemical fertilizers and pesticides, have polluted the soil. Many farmers plant the same crop in a field year after year. This practice reduces the soil's fertility and increases the likelihood that plants will become diseased or infested with insects.

Since the mid-1900's, people have become increasingly aware of the need to protect and improve their natural environment. Local and national governments have passed laws to control the use of natural resources. But it takes many years to renew a water supply, grow a forest, or replace a layer of topsoil. People would need to practice wise resource management over extended periods to repair damage that has already occurred and to prevent future problems.

David L. Clawson

Index

How to use the index

This index covers the contents of the 2003, 2004, and 2005 editions.

Sutton, Josiah, **05:** 216
Suzuki, Ichiro, 05: 79
Swaziland, table, **05:** 41
Sweden, 05: *374,* **04:** *368-369;* **03:** *367;* table, **05:** 185
Swimming, 05: *375,* **04:** *370,* **03:** *368*
Switzerland, 05: *376,* **04:** *371,* **03:** *368;* table, **05:** 185
Syria, 05: 45, *376,* **04:** *371,* **03:** *369;* table, **05:** 276

Each index entry gives the edition year and the page number or page numbers—for example, **Suzuki, Ichiro.** This means that information on this person may be found on the page indicated in the 2005 edition.

T

Taba (Egypt), **05:** 384
Taiwan, 05: 56, *377,* **04:** *372,* **03:** *370;* motion pictures, **05:** 282; table, **05:** 59
Tajikistan, 03: *370;* table, **05:** 59
Tale of Despereaux, The (DiCamillo), **05:** 265
Taliban, 05: 322
Tamils, 05: 367
Tampa Bay Lightning, 05: 212-214
Tangle (Thomas), **05:** 115
Taniguchi, Yoshio, 05: 55
Tanzania, 05: 398; table, **05:** 41
Tarantino, Quentin, 05: 279
Taurasi, Diana, 05: 80 (il.)
Taxation, 05: *378,* 403, **04:** *372,* **03:** *370-371;* Austria, **05:** 68; Sweden, **05:** 374; Toronto, **05:** 387
Team New Zealand, 05: 87
Ted (airline), **05:** 72
Teen-agers. See Adolescents
Teen People (magazine), **05:** 268
Telecommunications, 05: *378-379,* **04:** *373-374,* **03:** *371-381;* Sweden, **05:** 374. See also **Computer; Internet**
Telescopes, Space, 04: *64-75*
Television, 05: *379-382,* **04:** *374-377,* **03:** *382-384*
Tempest Fantasy (Moravec), **05:** 114-115
Temporary Assistance for Needy Families, 05: 414
"10 Most Wanted Species" (list), **05:** 129
Tennessee, 05: 152; table, **05:** 369
Tennis, 05: *383,* **04:** *378-379,* **03:** *385-386*
Territorial Organization, Law on, 05: 266-267
Terrorism, 05: *383-384,* **04:** *379,* **03:** *386-387;* Asia, **05:** 56-57; aviation security, **05:** 72; Bangladesh, **05:** 74; Colombia, **05:** 116; court cases, **05:** 131, 373; food, **05:** 189; human rights abuses, **05:** 216-217; India, **05:** 221; Iraq, **05:** 228-231; Japan, **05:** 247; Pakistan, **05:** 57, 322, 384; Spain, **05:** 363; *WBE,* **05:** *461-465.* See also **Oklahoma City bombing; September 11 terrorist attacks**
Tetrahydrogestrinone (drug), **05:** 389
Texas, table, **05:** 369
Texas Medical Center, 05: 215
Thailand, 05: 56, *384,* **04:** *380,* **03:** *387;* motion pictures, **05:** 282; table, **05:** 59
Thaksin Shinawatra, 05: 296, 384
Thalia (magazine), **05:** 267
Theater, 05: *384-386,* **04:** *380-383,* **03:** *388-390;* Pulitzer Prize, **05:** 344
Thermohaline circulation, 05: 197
Theron, Charlize, 05: 281 (il.)
Thomas, Augusta Read, 05: 115
Thompson, Tommy G., 05: 414
3TC (drug), **05:** 45

A page number in italic type means that there is an article on this topic on the page or pages indicated. For example, there is an Update article on **Taiwan** on page 377 of the 2005 edition. The page numbers in roman type indicate additional references to this topic in other articles in the volumes covered.

The "see" and "see also" cross-references refer the reader to other entries in the index. For example, information on teen-agers will be found under the **Adolescents** heading, while additional information on telecommunications topics will be found under the **Computer** and **Internet** headings.

When there are many references to a topic, they are grouped alphabetically by clue words under the main topic. For example, the clue words under **Terrorism** group the references to that topic under numerous subtopics.

An entry followed by *WBE* refers to a new or revised *World Book Encyclopedia* article in the supplement section, as in **Terrorism.** This means that there is a *World Book Encyclopedia* article on pages 461 through 465 of the 2005 edition.

The indications (il.) or (ils.) mean that the reference on this page is to an illustration or illustrations only, as in **Theron, Charlize,** in the 2005 edition.

Acknowledgments

The publishers acknowledge the following sources for illustrations. Credits read from top to bottom, left to right, on their respective pages. An asterisk (*) denotes illustrations and photographs created exclusively for this edition. All maps, charts, and diagrams were prepared by the staff unless otherwise noted.

8 AP/Wide World
9 © Andy Lyons, Getty Images
10 © Gary Coronado, Palm Beach Post/Zuma Press
12 NASA/JPL/Cornell University
15 AP/Wide World
17 © Javier Soriano, AFP/Getty Images
18-21 © AFP/Getty Images
22 © Pauline Lubens, Getty Images
25 Kerry-Edwards 2004, Inc. from Sharon Farmer
26 © Andy Lyons, Getty Images
29 © Robert Galbraith, Reuters
31 AP/Wide World
32 © Mark Wilson, Getty Images
35 © Reuters/Corbis
38-46 AP/Wide World
48 Natalia Fedorova
50 © Mike Segar, Reuters
53 AP/Wide World
54 © Franco Origlia, Getty Images
57 AP/Wide World
60 NASA/ESA, S. Beckwith and HUDF Team
61 NASA/CXC/M. Weiss
62 © Bill Hearne, Newspix
68 © Johannes Simon, Getty Images
70 General Motors/Wieck Media Services; DaimlerChrysler
72 © Ian Hodgson, Reuters
74 AP/Wide World
78 © Stephen Dunn, Getty Images
80-81 AP/Wide World
84 © Topham Picturepoint/Image Works
86 © Martin Harvey, Corbis
89 © Steve Marcus, Reuters
91 © Jean-Bernard Vernier, AFP/Getty Images
99 AP/Wide World
101 Gehry International Architects
107 © David Klobucar, Chicago Tribune
108 © Jean-Marc Giboux; © E. Jason Wambsgans, Chicago Tribune
110 AP/Wide World
115 © Eric Mahoudeau
117 AP/Wide World
118 © PhotoDisc, Inc.
121 AP/Wide World
132 © Jewel Samad, AFP/Getty Images
136 © Michal Ruzicka, AFP/Getty Images
138 © Stephanie Berger
140 © AFP/Getty Images
141 NASA; © Corbis/Bettmann; © Jim Bourg, New York Times/Getty Images
142 © Corbis/Bettmann
143 © Getty Images
144 AP/Wide World; Getty Images
145 © Getty Images
146 © Getty Images; © Robert Patrick, Corbis
147 © Deborah Feingold, Getty Images; Kobal Collection
148 © Micheline Pelletier, Corbis; AP/Wide World; Getty Images
149 © Gary Hershorn, Reuters
151 AP/Wide World
152 © Arko Datta, Reuters; © Lana Slivar, Reuters
155 © Shah Marai, AFP/Getty Images
156 © Spencer Platt, Getty Images

158 AP/Wide World
162 © Corbis; © PhotoDisc, Inc.
164 © David Young-Wolff, PhotoEdit
166 © Corbis
169 © Bill Aron, PhotoEdit
170-174 AP/Wide World
176 Eric Draper, The White House
177 © Jim Bourg, Reuters/Corbis
180 © Dick Locher, Tribune Media Services
183 AP/Wide World
188 Dale DeBolt*
193 © Harry How, Getty Images
195 AP/Wide World
199 © Uwe Meinhold, AFP/Getty Images
200 © David Cannon, Getty Images
202 © Roberto Schmidt, AFP/Getty Images
203 © Lannis Waters, Palm Beach Post/Zuma Press
204 Granger Collection
205 © Michael Rougier, Time-Life Pictures/Getty Images
206 © Roberto Schmidt, AFP/Getty Images
207 © Thony Belizaire, AFP/Getty Images
208 © Martin Adler, Panos Pictures
211 © Daniel Morel, Reuters
213-220 AP/Wide World
222 AP/Wide World; Robert C. Lautman, Smithsonian Institution
223 AP/Wide World; © Alex Wong, Getty Images
224 © Paula Bronstein, Getty Images
229-231 AP/Wide World
232 © Wathiq Khuzaie, Getty Images
233 © Joe Raedle, Getty Images
234 AFP/Getty Images
235 © Karim Sahib, AFP/Getty Images
236 © Ceerwan Aziz, Reuters
237 © Lynsey Addario, Corbis
239 © Karim Sahib, AFP/Getty Images
243 © David Silverman, Getty Images
244-251 AP/Wide World
255 © Juan Barreto, AFP/Getty Images
260 AP/Wide World
265 Reprinted by permission of Mordicai Gerstein. The Man Who Walked Between the Towers. © 2003 by Mordicai Gerstein. Published by Roaring Brook Press. All rights reserved.
267 AP/Wide World
272 © Reuters
273 AP/Wide World
274 Getty Images
279 © Boris Horvat, AFP/Getty Images
280 © New Line Cinema from Everett Collection
281 © Warner Bros from Everett Collection; © Newmarket Releasing from Everett Collection
283 © Corbis/Bettmann
284 © Joe Traver, Gamma Presse; © PhotoDisc, Inc.
287 © Nick Elgar, Gamma Presse; © PhotoDisc, Inc.
289 © Lucasfilm Ltd. &TM. All rights reserved. Used under authorization; photograph George Riley, Museum of Science, Boston

290 © Lee Boltin, Bridgeman Art Library
291-293 AP/Wide World
295 © Jim Bourg, Reuters/Corbis
296-298 AP/Wide World
300 © Yuri Kadobnov, AFP/Getty Images; Ritz Collectibles; Eastman Kodak Company
301 Clinton Foundation; Pacific Cycle, Inc.
302 © Stephen Chernin, Getty Images; © Corbis
304 © Pius Utomi Ekpei, AFP/Getty Images
308 © Ian Waldie, Getty Images; © Creatas
311 AP/Wide World
312 © Odd Anderson, Getty Images
314 AP/Wide World
316 © Romeo Gacad, AFP/Getty Images
319-320 AP/Wide World
323 © Chuck Berman, Chicago Tribune
325 © Wathiq Khuzaie, Getty Images; © Guo Yong, Notimex/AFP
326 AP/Wide World
327 © Raveendran/AFP/Getty Images
328 AP/Wide World
329 © Jimin Lai, AFP/Getty Images
330 © Frank Micelotta, Getty Images
331 © Donald Miralle, Getty Images
334 © Romeo Ranoco, Reuters/Corbis
338-345 AP/Wide World
346 © Alex Wong, Getty Images
348 © Alessandro Bianchi, AFP/Getty Images
349 © Alexander Zemlianichenko, AFP/Getty Images
350 © Reuters/Corbis
354-355 AP/Wide World
356 © Milos Bicanski, Getty Images
359 © Robert Laberge, Getty Images
360-361 NASA/JPL/Cornell University; NASA/JPL/Space Science Institute
363-365 AP/Wide World
370 © Rick Friedman, Corbis
372 © Marcus Gyger, Reuters/Corbis
375-377 AP/Wide World
379 © Kalle Parkkinen, Lehtikuva/Reuters
380 Mark Burnett Productions
382 AFP/Getty Images
385 © Joan Marcus
388 Nintendo/Golin Harris
392 © Dimitar Dilkoff, AFP/Getty Images
393 AP/Wide World
394 © Julie Woodhouse, Alamy Images
399 National Archives and Records Administration
403 AP/Wide World
404 Ronald Reagan Library
406 © Underwood & Underwood/Corbis
407 © Ronald Reagan Library/Getty Images
408 © Wally McNamee, Corbis
409 © David Hume Kennerly, Getty Images
411 AP/Wide World
413 NOAA Imagery; © Gary Coronado, Palm Beach Post/Zuma Press; © Mario Tama, Getty Images